Lecture Notes in Computer Science 9291

Commenced Publication in 1973
Founding and Former Series Editors:
Gerhard Goos, Juris Hartmanis, and Jan van Leeuwen

Advanced Research in Computing and Software Science

Subline of Lecture Notes in Computer Science

More information about this series at http://www.springer.com/series/7407

Sandrine Blazy · Thomas Jensen (Eds.)

Static Analysis

22nd International Symposium, SAS 2015
Saint-Malo, France, September 9–11, 2015
Proceedings

Springer

Editors
Sandrine Blazy
Université Rennes 1
Rennes
France

Thomas Jensen
Inria
Rennes
France

ISSN 0302-9743 ISSN 1611-3349 (electronic)
Lecture Notes in Computer Science
ISBN 978-3-662-48287-2 ISBN 978-3-662-48288-9 (eBook)
DOI 10.1007/978-3-662-48288-9

Library of Congress Control Number: 2015946743

LNCS Sublibrary: SL1 – Theoretical Computer Science and General Issues

Springer Heidelberg New York Dordrecht London

Printed on acid-free paper

Springer-Verlag GmbH Berlin Heidelberg is part of Springer Science+Business Media
(www.springer.com)

Preface

Static Analysis is increasingly recognized as a fundamental tool for program verification, bug detection, compiler optimization, program understanding, and software maintenance. The series of Static Analysis Symposia has served as the primary venue for the presentation of theoretical, practical, and applicational advances in the area. Previous symposia were held in Munich, Seattle, Deauville, Venice, Perpignan, Los Angeles, Valencia, Kongens Lyngby, Seoul, London, Verona, San Diego, Madrid, Paris, Santa Barbara, Pisa, Aachen, Glasgow, and Namur. This volume contains the papers presented at SAS 2015, the 22nd International Static Analysis Symposium. The conference was held on September 9–11, 2015 in Saint-Malo, France.

The conference received 44 submissions, each of which was reviewed by at least three Program Committee members. The Program Committee decided to accept 18 papers, which appear in this volume. As in previous years, authors of SAS submissions were able to submit a virtual machine image with artifacts or evaluations presented in the paper. In accordance with this, 13 submissions came with an artifact. Artifacts were not formally evaluated but were used as an additional source of information during the evaluation of the submissions.

The Program Committee also invited three leading researchers to present invited talks: Josh Berdine (Microsoft Research, UK), Anders Møller (Aarhus University, Denmark), and Henny Sipma (Kestrel, USA).We thank these speakers for accepting the invitation and also for contributing articles to these proceedings.

SAS 2015 featured three associated workshops that were held the day before the conference: the SASB on static analysis and systems biology, TAPAS on tools for automatic program analysis, and Security, dedicated to static analysis and security of low-level code.

The work of the Program Committee and the editorial process were greatly facilitated by the EasyChair conference management system. We are grateful to Springer for publishing these proceedings, as they have done for all SAS meetings since 1993.

Many people contributed to the success of SAS 2015. The Program Committee worked hard at reviewing papers, holding extensive discussions during the on-line Program Committee meeting, and making final selections of accepted papers and invited speakers. Thanks are also due to the additional referees enlisted by Program Committee members. Finally, we would like to thank our sponsors: Inria, the University of Rennes 1, Facebook, Fondation Rennes 1, Région Bretagne, and Springer.

July 2015

Sandrine Blazy
Thomas Jensen

Organization

Program Committee

Elvira Albert	Complutense University of Madrid, Spain
Josh Berdine	Microsoft Research, UK
Sandrine Blazy	University of Rennes, France
Liqian Chen	National University of Defense Technology, China
Roberto Giacobazzi	University of Verona, Italy
Fritz Henglein	University of Copenhagen, Denmark
Thomas Jensen	Inria, France
Ranjit Jhala	UC San Diego, USA
Andy King	University of Kent, UK
Bjorn Lisper	University of Mälardalen, Sweden
Matt Might	University of Utah, USA
Antoine Mine	CNRS, France
Francesco Ranzato	University of Padova, Italy
Sukyong Ryu	KAIST, South Korea
Dave Sands	Chalmers University, Sweden
Axel Simon	Google Inc, USA
Arnaud Venet	Google Inc, USA
Dimitrios Vytiniotis	Microsoft Research, UK
Hongseok Yang	University of Oxford, UK

Additional Reviewers

Aldous, Peter
Babic, Domagoj
Bakhirkin, Alexey
Balakrishnan, Gogul
Ben-Amram, Amir
Bozzelli, Laura
Buiras, Pablo
Chawdhary, Aziem
Correas Fernández, Jesús
D'Silva, Vijay
Filinski, Andrzej
Genaim, Samir
Ghorbal, Khalil
Gilray, Thomas
Gomez-Zamalloa, Miguel
Griggio, Alberto
Gustavsson, Andreas
Hedin, Daniel
Heizmann, Matthias
Ivancic, Franjo
Ji, Tao
Jiang, Jiahong
Kincaid, Zachary
Knoop, Jens
Lhoták, Ondřej
Majumdar, Rupak
Martin-Martin, Enrique
Masud, Abu Naser
Midtgaard, Jan
Montenegro, Manuel
Nimkar, Kaustubh
Nori, Aditya
Podelski, Andreas
Robbins, Ed
Segura, Clara
Singh, Rishabh
Solar-Lezama, Armando
Spoto, Fausto
Urban, Caterina
Wu, Xueguang
Ying, Banghu
Zanardini, Damiano

Abstracts of Invited Talks

Static Analysis of x86 Executables Using Abstract Interpretation

Henny B. Sipma

Kestrel Technology, LLC, Palo Alto, CA 94304, USA
sipma@kestreltechnology.com

Analysis of executables is often a tedious and largely manual process that involves the application of a variety of static and dynamic analysis tools, such as IDA Pro and debuggers, to gain insight into the behavior of the executable. We are developing techniques for static binary analysis that aim to add some automation to this process and enable more precise analysis, in particular memory safety and information ow analysis.

The techniques are based on abstract interpretation, a mathematical theory for sound approximation of program behaviors [2]. Abstract interpretation is used to incrementally disassemble the executable and construct a higher-level representation in an iterative process of invariant generation and variable discovery. Invariants are generated in a variety of abstract domains, of which linear equalities [3] and Value Sets [1] have been found to be particularly useful in the generation of relationships required to resolve indirect memory accesses.

The techniques have been implemented in the CodeHawk x86 Binary Analyzer. Analysis results are saved in xml to enable integration with other static or dynamic analysis tools and are also accessible via a graphical user interface that shows call graph, control ow graphs, data propagation graphs, as well as stack layout diagrams, register contents, and annotated assembly code.

The analyzer is continuously being validated on a corpus of more than 600 executables and dll's, up to 8 MB in size, compiled from both C and C++, including several java native libraries with JNI callbacks.

Acknowledgements. This research was supported in part by IARPA contracts FA8650-10-C-7023 (subcontract P010056114) and FA8650-14-C-7425, and DHS contract FA8750-12-C-0277.

References

1. Balakrishnan, G., Reps, T.W.: WYSINWYX: what you see is not what you execute. ACM Trans. Program. Lang. Syst. **32**(6) (2010)
2. Cousot, P., Cousot, R.: Abstract interpretation: a unified lattice model for static analysis of programs by construction or approximation of fixpoints. In: Graham, R.M., Harrison, M.A., Sethi, R. (eds.) POPL, pp. 238–252. ACM (1977)
3. Karr, M.: Affine relationships among variables of a program. Acta Inf. **6**, 133–151 (1976)

Static Analysis for JavaScript

Anders Møller

Aarhus University, Denmark
amoeller@cs.au.dk

Abstract. JavaScript supports a powerful mix of object-oriented and functional programming, which provides flexibility for the programmers but also makes it difficult to reason about the behavior of the programs without actually running them. One of the main challenging for static program analysis tools is to handle the complex programming patterns that are found in widely used libraries, such as jQuery, without losing critical precision. Another challenge is the use of dynamic language features, such as 'eval'. This talk presents an overview of recent progress towards obtaining sound and effective static analysis techniques for JavaScript web applications.

The SLAYER Static Analyzer

Josh Berdine

Microsoft Research

SLAYER is a static analyzer intended to prove memory safety properties of low-level systems code. The code characteristic that has been most influential on the analyzer's design is manual memory deallocation, which enables a program to deallocate a live object, thereby creating a dangling pointer that may later be erroneously dereferenced. SLAYER attempts to prove that every memory access falls within the dynamic lifetime of the referenced object, and that every object is eventually deallocated. This precludes use of uninitialized pointers, use-after-free and double-free errors, as well as a form of memory leaks. In complement to several other analysis efforts, the focus for SLAYER has been on linked data structures, and array accesses are not checked to be within bounds.

The development of SLAYER has been guided by the specific instance of the memory safety with dangling pointers problem posed by Windows kernel drivers. A consequence of this application choice is that the analyzer need only scale to moderately sized code bases, on the order of tens of thousands of lines. This is a valuable application since the driver interface is trusted by the kernel, exposed to third-party developers, and only very informally documented. While the overall quality of driver code has improved significantly from that which motivated SLAM fifteen years ago, it remains that drivers are responsible for a majority of Windows crashes, and memory corruption due to unsafe code is a leading cause.

Perhaps as important as the code to be analyzed is the development process into which the analyzer is to be deployed. SLAYER is fully automatic: users are not expected to write code annotations, and the analyzer includes a specification of the interface between the kernel and driver. Another point of primary importance is what feedback from the analyzer is necessary to convince developers that code is faulty. For application to Windows drivers, this applied pressure toward full concrete executions. This influenced the design of SLAYER as a whole- program, flow- and calling-context-sensitive, interprocedural static analysis with partially relational procedure summaries.

Due to the unbounded nature of dynamically-allocated data structures, where their size depends on input data, abstraction is required to prove safety properties. SLAYER performs an abstract interpretation using a fragment of Separation Logic as an abstract representation of sets of program states. The widening operation abstracts anonymous objects of linked data structures using recursive predicates, generalizing from small to unbounded data structure instances. Soundness of the intraprocedural analysis follows from standard correct over-approximation results, while the interprocedural analysis also relies on soundness of Separation Logic's Frame rule.

Contents

Static Analysis of Non-interference in Expressive Low-Level Languages

Peter Aldous(✉) and Matthew Might

University of Utah, Salt Lake City, USA
{peteya,might}@cs.utah.edu

Abstract. Early work in implicit information flow detection applied only to flat, procedureless languages with structured control-flow (e.g., if statements, while loops). These techniques have yet to be adequately extended and generalized to expressive languages with interprocedural, exceptional and irregular control-flow behavior. We present an implicit information flow analysis suitable for languages with conditional jumps, dynamically dispatched methods, and exceptions. We implement this analysis for the Dalvik bytecode format, the substrate for Android. In order to capture information flows across interprocedural and exceptional boundaries, this analysis uses a projection of a small-step abstract interpreter's rich state graph instead of the control-flow graph typically used for such purposes in weaker linguistic settings. We present a proof of termination-insensitive non-interference. To our knowledge, it is the first analysis capable of proving non-trivial non-interference in a language with this combination of features.

1 Introduction

With increasing awareness of privacy concerns, there is a demand for verification that programs protect private information. Although many systems exist that purport to provide assurances about private data, most systems fail to address implicit information flows, especially in expressive low-level languages. Expressive low level languages, such as Dalvik bytecode, do not provide static guarantees about control-flow due to the presence of dynamic dispatch, exceptions and irregular local jumps.

To demonstrate that a program does not leak information, we prove *non-interference* [13]: any two executions of a *non-interfering* program that vary only in their "high-security" inputs (the values that should not leak) must exhibit the same observable behaviors; in other words, high-security values must never affect observable program behavior. Our analysis proves *termination-insensitive non-interference* [2,10,26].

For its foundation, our analysis uses a rich *static* taint analysis to track high-security values in a program: high-security values are marked as tainted and, as (small-step) abstract interpretation proceeds, any values affected by tainted values are also marked. (Taint analysis is a dynamic technique but an abstract interpretation of a concrete semantics enriched with taint-tracking makes it a static analysis.)

S. Blazy and T. Jensen (Eds.): SAS 2015, LNCS 9291, pp. 1–17, 2015.
DOI: 10.1007/978-3-662-48288-9_1

We enrich the taint analysis to track implicit flows and prove non-interference by executing the advice of Denning and Denning [7]. Their advice suggested that languages *without* statically bounded control-flow structures could precisely track implicit information flows with a static analysis that calculated the immediate postdominator (or immediate forward dominator) of every branch in the program's control-flow graph.[1] We show (and prove) that this old and simple principle fully (and formally) generalizes from flat, procedureless languages to rich, modern languages by constructing projections of abstract state graphs.

1.1 Contributions

This paper presents an analysis for a summarized version of Dalvik bytecode that preserves all essential features: conditional jumps, methods, and exceptional flow. This analysis is similar in spirit to the suggestion of Denning and Denning but uses an *execution point graph* instead of the program's control-flow graph. The execution point graph is formed by projecting the state graph that results from an small-step abstract interpreter [27]. Nodes in the execution point graph contain code points *and* contextual information such as the height of the stack to prevent subtle information leaks. Consider, for example, the function in Fig. 1.

There are two possible executions of `leak` when called when `top` is **`true`** (and when the captured value `printed` is initially set to **false**). In each case, `leak` immediately recurs, this time with `top` set to **false**. At this point, the topmost stack frame has `top` set to **false** and the other stack frame has `top` set to **`true`**. This leak exploits the difference between these stack frames by returning immediately (effectively setting `top` to **`true`**) in one case—and then proceeding to print the value of `top`.

```
static void leak(boolean top) {
  if (top) {
    leak(false);
  } else {
    if (sensitive) {
      return;
    }
  }
  if (!printed) {
    printed = true;
    System.out.println(top);
  }
}
```

Fig. 1. A leak after convergence

The execution point graph contains just enough information about the stack to prevent leakages of this variety. During small-step abstract interpretation, an implicit taint is added to any value that changes after control-flow has changed due to a high-security value. Convergence in the execution point graph indicates that control-flow has converged and, consequently, that no further information can be gleaned from it about high-security values. This calculation can be done lazily and is fully *a posteriori*; as such, it may be more efficient than performing one abstract interpretation to create the graph and another to perform taint analysis.

[1] A node P *postdominates* another node A in a directed graph if every walk from A to the exit node includes P.

An execution point graph whose nodes consist of a code point and the height of the stack is preferable to a more precise graph whose nodes contain full stacks; conflating more execution points means that, in some cases, convergence happens after fewer execution points. As a result, this less precise graph translates into more precise tracking of implicit flows.

Section 2 presents a language that summarizes the features of Dalvik bytecode, gives semantics for the language, and describes the abstraction of this dynamic analysis to a static analysis. Section 3 presents the proof of termination-insensitive non-interference. Further discussion and related work follow.

2 Language and Semantics

2.1 Syntax

The abstract syntax for our summarized bytecode language is given in Fig. 2.

In conjunction with this syntax, we need the following metafunctions:

- $\mathcal{M}$: MName $\rightarrow$ Method for method lookup
- $\mathcal{I}$: *CodePoint* $\rightarrow$ Stmt for statement lookup
- *next* : *CodePoint* $\rightharpoonup$ *CodePoint* gives the syntactic successor to the current code point
- $\mathcal{H}$: *CodePoint* $\rightharpoonup$ *CodePoint* gives the target of the first exception handler defined for a code point in the current function, if there is any.

$$
\begin{array}{rcl}
\mathit{prgm} \in \mathsf{Program} & = & \mathsf{ClassDef}^* \\
\mathit{classdef} \in \mathsf{ClassDef} & ::= & \texttt{Class}\ \mathit{className}\ \{\mathit{field}_1, \ldots, \mathit{field}_n, m_1, \ldots, m_m\} \\
m \in \mathsf{Method} & ::= & \texttt{Def}\ \mathit{mName}\ \{\mathit{handler}_1, \ldots, \mathit{handler}_n, \mathit{stmt}_1, \ldots, \mathit{stmt}_m\} \\
\mathit{handler} \in \mathsf{Handler} & ::= & \texttt{Catch(}\mathit{ln}, \mathit{ln}, \mathit{ln}\texttt{)} \\
\mathit{stmt} \in \mathsf{Stmt} & ::= & \mathit{ln}\ \texttt{Const(}r, c\texttt{)} \\
& | & \mathit{ln}\ \texttt{Move(}r, r\texttt{)} \\
& | & \mathit{ln}\ \texttt{Invoke(}\mathit{mName}, r_1, \ldots, r_n\texttt{)} \\
& | & \mathit{ln}\ \texttt{Return(}r\texttt{)} \\
& | & \mathit{ln}\ \texttt{IfEqz(}r, \mathit{ln}\texttt{)} \\
& | & \mathit{ln}\ \texttt{Add(}r, r, r\texttt{)} \\
& | & \mathit{ln}\ \texttt{NewInstance(}r, \mathit{className}\texttt{)} \\
& | & \mathit{ln}\ \texttt{Throw(}r\texttt{)} \\
& | & \mathit{ln}\ \texttt{IGet(}r, r, \mathit{field}\texttt{)} \\
& | & \mathit{ln}\ \texttt{IPut(}r, r, \mathit{field}\texttt{)} \\
r \in \mathsf{Register} & = & \{\texttt{result}, \texttt{exception}, 0, 1, \ldots\} \\
\mathit{ln} \in \mathsf{LineNumber} & & \text{is a set of line numbers} \\
\mathit{mName} \in \mathsf{MName} & & \text{is a set of method names} \\
\mathit{field} \in \mathsf{Field} & & \text{is a set of field names} \\
\mathit{cp} \in \mathit{CodePoint} & ::= & (\mathit{ln}, m)
\end{array}
$$

Fig. 2. Abstract syntax

- *init* : Method $\rightarrow$ *CodePoint* gives the first code point in a method.
- *jump* : *CodePoint* $\times$ `LineNumber` $\rightharpoonup$ *CodePoint* gives the code point in the same method as the given code point and at the line number specified.

2.2 State Space

A state ς contains six members, which are formally defined in Fig. 3:

1. A code point *cp*.
2. A frame pointer ϕ. All registers in the machine are frame-local. Frame addresses are represented as a pair consisting of a frame pointer and an index.
3. A store σ, which is a partial map from addresses to values.
4. A continuation κ.
5. A taint store *ts*, which is a map from addresses to taint values. It is updated in parallel with the store. Undefined addresses are mapped to the empty set.
6. A context taint set *ct*, which is a set of execution points where control-flow has diverged before reaching the current state.

2.3 Semantics

Our semantics require projection metafunctions. *height* : $Kont \rightarrow \mathbb{Z}$ calculates stack height and $p_\varsigma : \Sigma \rightarrow ExecPoint$ uses *height* to create execution points.

$$height\,(\kappa) = \begin{cases} 1 + height\,(\kappa') & \text{if } \kappa = \mathbf{retk}(cp, \phi, ct, \kappa') \\ 0 & \text{if } \kappa = \mathbf{halt} \end{cases}$$

$$\varsigma \in \Sigma ::= (cp, \phi, \sigma, \kappa, ts, ct) \mid \mathbf{errorstate} \mid \mathbf{endstate}$$
$$\phi \in FP \text{ is an infinite set of frame pointers}$$
$$\sigma \in Store = Addr \rightharpoonup Value$$
$$val \in Value = \mathsf{INT32} + ObjectAddress$$
$$\kappa \in Kont ::= \mathbf{retk}(cp, \phi, ct, \kappa) \mid \mathbf{halt}$$
$$ts \in TaintStore = Addr \rightharpoonup \mathcal{P}\,(TaintValue)$$
$$tv \in TaintValue = ExplicitTV + ImplicitTV$$
$$etv \in ExplicitTV = ExecPoint$$
$$itv \in ImplicitTV = ExecPoint \times ExecPoint$$
$$ct \in ContextTaint = \mathcal{P}\,(ExecPoint)$$
$$ep \in ExecPoint ::= \mathbf{ep}(cp, z) \mid \mathbf{errorsummary} \mid \mathbf{endsummary}$$
$$z \in \mathbb{Z} \text{ is the set of integers}$$
$$a \in Addr ::= sa \mid fa \mid oa \mid \mathtt{null}$$
$$sa \in StackAddress = FP \times \mathsf{Register}$$
$$fa \in FieldAddress = ObjectAddress \times \mathsf{Field}$$
$$oa \in ObjectAddress \text{ is an infinite set of addresses}$$

Fig. 3. Concrete state space

$$p_\varsigma(\varsigma) = \begin{cases} \mathbf{ep}(cp, z) & \text{if } \varsigma = (cp, \phi, \sigma, \kappa, ts, ct) \text{ and } z = \mathit{height}(\kappa) \\ \mathbf{endsummary} & \text{if } \varsigma = \mathbf{endstate} \\ \mathbf{errorsummary} & \text{if } \varsigma = \mathbf{errorstate} \end{cases}$$

The concrete semantics for our language are defined by the relation $(\rightarrow) \subseteq \Sigma \times \Sigma$. In its transition rules, we use the following shorthand: ep_ς is a state's execution point and itv_ς is the set of implicit taint values generated at a state. For a state ς with context taint set $\{ep_1, \ldots, ep_n\}$,

$$ep_\varsigma = p_\varsigma(\varsigma) \quad \text{and} \quad itv_\varsigma = \{(ep_1, ep_\varsigma), \ldots, (ep_n, ep_\varsigma)\}$$

The `Const` instruction writes a constant value to a register. Observe that implicit taints can be applied to a constant assignment.

$$\frac{\mathcal{I}(cp) = \texttt{Const}(r,\ \texttt{c})}{(cp, \phi, \sigma, \kappa, ts, ct) \rightarrow (\mathit{next}(cp), \phi, \sigma', \kappa, ts', ct)}, \text{ where}$$

$$\begin{aligned} sa &= (\phi, r) \\ \sigma' &= \sigma[sa \mapsto c] \\ ts' &= ts[sa \mapsto itv_\varsigma] \end{aligned}$$

The `Move` instruction simulates all of Dalvik bytecode's move instructions.

$$\frac{\mathcal{I}(cp) = \texttt{Move}(r_d,\ r_s)}{(cp, \phi, \sigma, \kappa, ts, ct) \rightarrow (\mathit{next}(cp), \phi, \sigma', \kappa, ts', ct)}, \text{ where}$$

$$\begin{aligned} sa_d &= (\phi, r_d) \\ sa_s &= (\phi, r_s) \\ \sigma' &= \sigma[sa_d \mapsto \sigma(sa_s)] \\ ts' &= ts[sa_d \mapsto ts(sa_s) \cup itv_\varsigma] \end{aligned}$$

The `Invoke` instruction simulates Dalvik's invoke instructions.

$$\frac{\mathcal{I}(cp) = \texttt{Invoke}(mName,\ \texttt{r}_1,\ \ldots,\ \texttt{r}_n)}{(cp, \phi, \sigma, \kappa, ts, ct) \rightarrow (cp', \phi', \sigma', \kappa', ts', ct')}, \text{ where}$$

$$\begin{aligned} cp' &= \mathit{init}(\mathcal{M}(mName)) \\ \kappa' &= \mathbf{retk}(cp, \phi, ct, \kappa) \\ \phi' &= \text{ is a fresh frame pointer address} \\ &\quad \text{for each } i \text{ from 1 to } n, \\ sa_{di} &= (\phi', i-1) \text{ and } sa_{si} = (\phi, r_i) \\ \sigma' &= \sigma[sa_{d1} \mapsto \sigma(sa_{s1}), \ldots, sa_{dn} \mapsto \sigma(sa_{sn})] \\ ts' &= ts[sa_{d1} \mapsto ts(sa_{s1}) \cup itv_\varsigma, \ldots, sa_{dn} \mapsto ts(sa_{sn}) \cup itv_\varsigma] \\ ct' &= \begin{cases} ct & \text{if } ts(sa_{s0}) = \emptyset \\ ct \cup \{ep_\varsigma\} & \text{if } ts(sa_{s0}) \neq \emptyset \end{cases} \end{aligned}$$

The **Return** instruction summarizes Dalvik's return instructions. The **Return** instruction introduces context taint if invocation occurred in a tainted context.

$$\frac{\mathcal{I}(cp) = \texttt{Return}(r) \quad \kappa = \mathbf{retk}(cp, \phi', ct_k, \kappa')}{(cp, \phi, \sigma, \kappa, ts, ct) \to (next(cp'), \phi', \sigma', \kappa', ts', ct')}, \text{ where}$$

$$sa_d = (\phi', \texttt{result})$$
$$sa_s = (\phi, r)$$
$$\sigma' = \sigma[sa_d \mapsto \sigma(sa_s)]$$
$$ts' = ts[sa_d \mapsto ts(sa_s) \cup itv_\varsigma]$$
$$ct' = \begin{cases} ct & \text{if } ct_k = \emptyset \\ ct \cup \{ep_\varsigma\} & \text{if } ct_k \neq \emptyset \end{cases}$$

$$\frac{\mathcal{I}(cp) = \texttt{Return}(r) \quad \kappa = \mathbf{halt}}{(cp, \phi, \sigma, \kappa, ts, ct) \to \mathbf{endstate}}$$

The `IfEqz` instruction jumps to the given target if its argument is 0:

$$\frac{\mathcal{I}(cp) = \texttt{IfEqz}(r,\ ln)}{(cp, \phi, \sigma, \kappa, ts, ct) \to (cp', \phi, \sigma, \kappa, ts, ct')}, \text{ where}$$

$$sa_s = (\phi, r)$$
$$cp' = \begin{cases} jump(cp, ln) & \text{if } \sigma(sa_s) = 0 \\ next(cp) & \text{if } \sigma(sa_s) \neq 0 \end{cases}$$
$$ct' = \begin{cases} ct & \text{if } ts(sa_s) = \emptyset \\ ct \cup \{ep_\varsigma\} & \text{if } ts(sa_s) \neq \emptyset \end{cases}$$

The `Add` instruction represents all arithmetic instructions. Since Java uses 32-bit two's complement integers, + represents 32-bit two's complement addition.

$$\frac{\mathcal{I}(cp) = \texttt{Add}(r_d,\ r_l,\ r_r)}{(cp, \phi, \sigma, \kappa, ts, ct) \to (next(cp), \phi, \sigma', \kappa, ts', ct)}, \text{ where}$$

$$sa_d = (\phi, r_d)$$
$$sa_l = (\phi, r_l)$$
$$sa_r = (\phi, r_r)$$
$$\sigma' = \sigma[sa_d \mapsto \sigma(sa_l) + \sigma(sa_r)]$$
$$ts' = ts[sa_d \mapsto ts(sa_l) \cup ts(sa_r) \cup itv_\varsigma]$$

Object instantiation is done with the `NewInstance` instruction:

$$\frac{\mathcal{I}(cp) = \texttt{NewInstance}(r,\ className)}{(cp, \phi, \sigma, \kappa, ts, ct) \to (next(cp), \phi, \sigma', \kappa, ts', ct)}, \text{ where}$$

oa is a fresh object address

$$sa = (\phi, r)$$
$$\sigma' = \sigma[sa \mapsto oa]$$
$$ts' = ts[sa \mapsto itv_\varsigma]$$

The remaining instructions use an additional metafunction:

$$\mathcal{T} : \mathit{CodePoint} \times \mathit{FP} \times \mathit{ContextTaint} \times \mathit{Kont} \rightharpoonup \mathit{CodePoint} \times \mathit{FP} \times \mathit{ContextTaint} \times \mathit{Kont}$$

$\mathcal{T}$ looks for an exception handler in the current function. If there is a handler, execution resumes there. If not, searches through the code points in the continuation stack. The accumulation of context taint simulates the accumulation that would happen through successive `Return` instructions. Formally:

$$\mathcal{T}(cp, \phi, ct, \kappa) = \begin{cases} (cp_h, \phi, ct, \kappa) & \text{if } \mathcal{H}(cp) = cp_h \\ \mathcal{T}(cp_k, \phi_k, ct, \kappa_k) & \text{if } cp \notin \mathit{dom}(\mathcal{H}) \text{ and } ct_k = \emptyset \\ & \text{and } \kappa = \mathbf{retk}(cp_k, \phi_k, ct_k, \kappa_k) \\ \mathcal{T}(cp_k, \phi_k, ct \cup itv_\varsigma, \kappa_k) & \text{if } cp \notin \mathit{dom}(\mathcal{H}) \text{ and } ct_k \neq \emptyset \\ & \text{and } \kappa = \mathbf{retk}(cp_k, \phi_k, ct_k, \kappa_k) \end{cases}$$

The `Throw` instruction requires two cases. One is for continued execution at the specified handler and one is for an error state when no handler can be found.

$$\frac{\mathcal{I}(cp) = \texttt{Throw}(r) \quad (cp, \phi, ct, \kappa) \in \mathit{dom}(\mathcal{T})}{(cp, \phi, \sigma, \kappa, ts, ct) \rightarrow (cp', \phi', \sigma', \kappa', ts', ct')}, \text{ where}$$

$$\begin{aligned} sa_s &= (\phi, r) \\ sa_d &= (\phi', \texttt{exception}) \\ (cp', \phi', ct', \kappa') &= \mathcal{T}(cp, \phi, ct, \kappa) \\ \sigma' &= \sigma[sa_d \mapsto \sigma(sa_s)] \\ ts' &= ts[sa_d \mapsto ts(sa_s) \cup itv_\varsigma] \end{aligned}$$

$$\frac{\mathcal{I}(cp) = \texttt{Throw}(r) \quad (cp, \phi, ct, \kappa) \notin \mathit{dom}(\mathcal{T})}{(cp, \phi, \sigma, \kappa, ts, ct) \rightarrow \mathbf{errorstate}}$$

The `IGet` instruction represents the family of instance accessor instructions in Dalvik bytecode. When the object address is null, it behaves like `Throw`.

$$\frac{\mathcal{I}(cp) = \texttt{IGet}(r_d,\ \texttt{r}_o,\ \mathit{field}) \quad oa \neq \texttt{null}}{(cp, \phi, \sigma, \kappa, ts, ct) \rightarrow (\mathit{next}(cp), \phi, \sigma', \kappa, ts', ct)}, \text{ where}$$

$$\begin{aligned} sa_d &= (\phi, r_d) \\ sa_o &= (\phi, r_o) \\ oa &= \sigma(sa_o) \\ fa &= (oa, \mathit{field}) \\ \sigma' &= \sigma[sa_d \mapsto \sigma(fa)] \\ ts' &= ts[sa_d \mapsto ts(oa) \cup ts(fa) \cup itv_\varsigma] \end{aligned}$$

The `IPut` instruction also represents a family of instructions; `IPut` stores values in objects. When the object address is null, `IPut` behaves like `Throw`.

$$\frac{\mathcal{I}\,(cp) = \texttt{IPut}\,(r_s,\ \texttt{r}_o,\ \mathit{field}) \quad oa \neq \texttt{null}}{(cp, \phi, \sigma, \kappa, ts, ct) \rightarrow (next\,(cp)\,, \phi, \sigma', \kappa, ts', ct)}, \text{ where}$$

$$sa_s = (\phi, r_s)$$
$$sa_o = (\phi, r_o)$$
$$oa = \sigma\,(sa_o)$$
$$fa = (oa, \mathit{field})$$
$$\sigma' = \sigma[fa \mapsto \sigma\,(sa_s)]$$
$$ts' = ts[fa \mapsto ts\,(sa_s) \cup itv_\varsigma]$$

2.4 Abstraction

A small-step analyzer as described by Van Horn and Might [27] overapproximates program behavior and suits our needs. Abstraction of taint stores and context taint sets is straightforward: they store execution points, which are code points and stack heights. Code points need no abstraction and the height of abstract stacks is suitable. Any abstraction of continuations (even that of PDCFA [8]) admits indeterminate stack heights; an abstract execution point with an indeterminate stack height cannot be a postdominator.

3 Non-interference

3.1 Influence

The influence of an execution point ep_0 is the set of execution points that lie along some path from ep_0 to its immediate postdominator ep_n (where ep_0 appears only at the end) in the execution point graph.

Given the set V of vertices in the execution point graph and the set E of edges in that same graph, we can define the set P of all paths from ep_0 to ep_n:

$$P = \{\langle ep_0, \ldots, ep_n\rangle \mid \forall i \in \{0, \ldots, n-1\}, (ep_i, ep_{i+1}) \in E \ \wedge ep_i \neq ep_n\}$$

With P defined, we can define the influence of ep_0 as:

$$\{ep \in V \mid \exists p = \langle ep_0, \ldots, ep_n\rangle \in P \ : \ ep \in p\} - \{ep_0, ep_n\}$$

3.2 Program Traces

A *program trace* π is a sequence $\langle \varsigma_1, \varsigma_2, \ldots, \varsigma_n\rangle$ of concrete states such that

$$\varsigma_1 \rightarrow \varsigma_2 \rightarrow \ldots \rightarrow \varsigma_n \text{ and } \varsigma_n \notin dom\,(\rightarrow)$$

3.3 Observable Behaviors

Which program behaviors are observable depends on the attack model and is a decision to be made by the user of this analysis. In this proof, we consider the general case: every program behavior is observable. A more realistic model would be that invocations of certain functions are observable, as well as top-level exceptions. Accordingly, we define $obs \subseteq \Sigma$ so that $obs = \Sigma$.

3.4 Valid Taints

The given semantics has no notion of taint removal; instead, some taints are *valid* and the others are disregarded. Explicit taints are always valid. Implicit taints are created when some assignment is made. An implicit taint is valid if and only if its assignment happens during the influence of its branch. Accordingly, we define the set of all valid taints:

$$valid = ExplicitTV \cup \{(ep_b, ep_a) \in ImplicitTV \mid ep_a \in influence\,(ep_b)\}$$

3.5 Labeled Behaviors

A state ς has a *labeled behavior* if and only if it reads values at one or more addresses with valid taint or if it occurs at a state with valid context taint. We define the function $inputs : \Sigma \to Addr^*$ and $labeled : \Sigma \to \mathcal{P}\,(TaintValue)$ so that *inputs* identifies the addresses read by ς's instruction and *labeled* identifies the valid taints at those addresses. The use of itv_ς reflects context taint. The formal definitions of *inputs* and *labeled* are given in Fig. 4.

3.6 Similar Stores

Two stores are *similar* with respect to two frame pointers, two continuations, and two taint stores if and only if they differ only at reachable addresses that are tainted in their respective taint stores. This definition requires some related definitions, which follow.

Two stores are similar with respect to two addresses and two taint stores iff:

$\mathcal{I}\,(cp) = \texttt{Const}(r,\ c)$	$\Rightarrow inputs\,(\varsigma) = \langle\rangle$
$\mathcal{I}\,(cp) = \texttt{Move}(r_d,\ r_s)$	$\Rightarrow inputs\,(\varsigma) = \langle(\phi, r_s)\rangle$
$\mathcal{I}\,(cp) = \texttt{Invoke}(mName,\ r_1,\ \ldots,\ r_n)$	$\Rightarrow inputs\,(\varsigma) = \langle(\phi, r_1), \ldots, (\phi, r_n)\rangle$
$\mathcal{I}\,(cp) = \texttt{Return}(r)$	$\Rightarrow inputs\,(\varsigma) = \langle(\phi, r)\rangle$
$\mathcal{I}\,(cp) = \texttt{IfEqz}(r,\ ln)$	$\Rightarrow inputs\,(\varsigma) = \langle(\phi, r)\rangle$
$\mathcal{I}\,(cp) = \texttt{Add}(r_d,\ r_l,\ r_r)$	$\Rightarrow inputs\,(\varsigma) = \langle(\phi, r_l), (\phi, r_r)\rangle$
$\mathcal{I}\,(cp) = \texttt{NewInstance}(r,\ className)$	$\Rightarrow inputs\,(\varsigma) = \langle\rangle$
$\mathcal{I}\,(cp) = \texttt{Throw}(r)$	$\Rightarrow inputs\,(\varsigma) = \langle(\phi, r)\rangle$
$\mathcal{I}\,(cp) = \texttt{IGet}(r_d,\ r_o,\ field)$	$\Rightarrow inputs\,(\varsigma) = \langle(\phi, r_o), \sigma\,((\phi, r_o)), \sigma\,(\sigma\,((\phi, r_o)), field)\rangle$
$\mathcal{I}\,(cp) = \texttt{IPut}(r_s,\ r_o,\ field)$	$\Rightarrow inputs\,(\varsigma) = \langle(\phi, r_s)\rangle$

$$labeled\,(\varsigma) = \{tv \in TaintValue \mid \exists\, a \in inputs\,(\varsigma) \cup \{itv_\varsigma\}\ :\ tv \in ts\,(a)\} \cap valid$$

Fig. 4. A definition of addresses read by instruction. $\varsigma = (cp, \phi, \sigma, \kappa, ts, ct)$

1. Both stores are undefined at their respective address, or
2. Either store is tainted at its respective address, or
3. The stores map their respective addresses to the same value, or
4. The stores map respective addresses to structurally identical objects.

Formally,

$$
\begin{aligned}
(\sigma_1, a_1, ts_1) &\approx_a (\sigma_2, a_2, ts_2) \\
&\Leftrightarrow \\
\left(a_1 \notin dom\left(\sigma_1\right) \wedge a_2 \notin dom\left(\sigma_2\right)\right) &\vee \qquad (1)\\
\left(\exists\, tv \in ts_1\left(a_1\right) \;:\; tv \in valid \;\vee\; \exists\, tv \in ts_2\left(a_2\right) \;:\; tv \in valid\right) &\vee \qquad (2)\\
\sigma_1\left(a_1\right) = \sigma_2\left(a_2\right) &\vee \qquad (3)\\
\left(\sigma_1\left(a_1\right) = oa_1 \;\wedge\; \sigma_2\left(a_2\right) = oa_2 \;\wedge\right. & \qquad (4)\\
\left.\forall\, field \in \mathsf{Field}, \left(\sigma_1, \left(oa_1, field\right), ts_1\right) \approx_a \left(\sigma_2, \left(oa_2, field\right), ts_2\right)\right) &
\end{aligned}
$$

With this definition, we can define similarity with respect to frame pointers. Two stores are similar with respect to two frame pointers and two taint stores if and only if they are similar with respect to every address containing the respective frame pointers.

Formally,

$$(\sigma_1, \phi_1, ts_1) \approx_\phi (\sigma_2, \phi_2, ts_2) \Leftrightarrow \forall r \in \mathsf{Register}, \left(\sigma_1, \left(\phi_1, r\right), ts_1\right) \approx_a \left(\sigma_2, \left(\phi_2, r\right), ts_2\right)$$

Two stores are similar with respect to two frame pointers, two continuations, and two taint stores iff:

1. The stores are similar with respect to the given pair of frame pointers, and
2. They are recursively similar with respect to the given continuations.

Formally,

$$
\begin{aligned}
(\sigma_1, \phi_1, \kappa_1, ts_1) &\approx_\sigma (\sigma_2, \phi_2, \kappa_2, ts_2) \\
&\Leftrightarrow \\
(\sigma_1, \phi_1, ts_1) \approx_\phi (\sigma_2, \phi_2, ts_2) &\wedge \qquad (1)\\
\left(\kappa_1 = \kappa_2 = \mathbf{halt}\right. &\vee \qquad (2)\\
\kappa_1 = \mathbf{retk}(cp_1, \phi_1', ct_1', \kappa_1') \;\wedge \kappa_2 = \mathbf{retk}(cp_2, \phi_2', ct_2', \kappa_2') &\wedge \\
\left.(\sigma_1, \phi_1', \kappa_1', ts_1) \approx_\sigma (\sigma_2, \phi_2', \kappa_2', ts_2)\right) &
\end{aligned}
$$

3.7 Similar States

Two states are *similar* if and only if their execution points are identical and their stores are similar with respect to their taint stores and frame pointers.

Formally, if $\varsigma_1 = (cp_1, \phi_1, \sigma_1, \kappa_1, ts_1, ct_1)$ and $\varsigma_2 = (cp_2, \phi_2, \sigma_2, \kappa_2, ts_2, ct_2)$, then $\varsigma_1 \approx_\varsigma \varsigma_2 \Leftrightarrow p_\varsigma(\varsigma_1) = p_\varsigma(\varsigma_2) \wedge (\sigma_1, \phi_1, ts_1) \approx_\sigma (\sigma_2, \phi_2, ts_2)$.

3.8 Similar Traces

Two traces $\pi = \langle \varsigma_1, \varsigma_2, \ldots, \varsigma_n \rangle$ and $\pi' = \langle \varsigma'_1, \varsigma'_2, \ldots, \varsigma'_m \rangle$ are *similar* if and only if their observable behaviors are identical except for those marked as tainted. We formulate the similarity of traces using a partial function $dual : \pi \rightharpoonup \pi'$. Similarity of traces is equivalent to the existence of a function *dual* such that:

1. *dual* is injective, and
2. *dual* maps each state in π to a similar state in π' if such a state exists, and
3. All states in π not paired by *dual* occur in a tainted context, and
4. All states in π' not paired by *dual* occur in a tainted context, and
5. The pairs of similar states occur in the same order in their respective traces.

Formally,

$$\pi \approx_\pi \pi' \Leftrightarrow \exists \; dual :$$

$$\forall \, i,j \in 1 \ldots n, \; i \neq j \Rightarrow dual\,(i) \neq dual\,(j) \land \tag{1}$$

$$\forall \, \varsigma_i \in dom\,(dual)\,, \; \varsigma_i \approx_\varsigma dual\,(\varsigma_i) \land \tag{2}$$

$$\forall \, \varsigma_i \notin dom\,(dual)\,, \; itv_\varsigma \in valid \land \tag{3}$$

$$\forall \, \varsigma'_j \notin range\,(dual)\,, \; itv_\varsigma \in valid \land \tag{4}$$

$$\forall \, i,j \in 1 \ldots n \; : \; dual\,(\varsigma_i) = \varsigma'_k \land dual\,(\varsigma_j) = \varsigma'_l, \tag{5}$$

$$i < j \Rightarrow k < l \quad \land \quad i = j \Rightarrow k = l \quad \land \quad i > j \Rightarrow k > l$$

3.9 Transitivity of Similarity

Lemma. If two states ς and ς' are similar and if their execution point's immediate postdominator in the execution point graph is ep_{pd}, the first successor of each state whose execution point is ep_{pd} is similar to the other successor.

Formally, if $\varsigma \approx_\varsigma \varsigma'$ and
$\varsigma \to \varsigma_1 \to \ldots \to \varsigma_n$ and $\varsigma' \to \varsigma'_1 \to \ldots \to \varsigma'_m$ and
$p_\varsigma(\varsigma) = p_\varsigma(\varsigma') = ep_0$ and $p_\varsigma(\varsigma_n) = p_\varsigma(\varsigma'_m) = ep_{pd}$ and
ep_{pd} is the immediate postdominator of ep_0, and
$\forall \, \varsigma_i \in \{\varsigma_1, \ldots, \varsigma_{n-1}\} \cup \{\varsigma'_1, \ldots, \varsigma'_{m-1}\}, \; p_\varsigma(\varsigma_i) \neq ep_{pd}$, then $\varsigma_n \approx_\varsigma \varsigma'_m$

Proof. Without loss of generality,

$$\varsigma = (cp, \phi, \sigma, \kappa, ts, ct) \text{ and } \varsigma' = (cp', \phi', \sigma', \kappa', ts', ct') \text{ and}$$
$$\varsigma_n = (cp_n, \phi_n, \sigma_n, \kappa_n, ts_n, ct_n) \text{ and } \varsigma'_m = (cp_m, \phi_m, \sigma_m, \kappa_m, ts_m, ct_m)$$

We refer to $\varsigma_1, \ldots, \varsigma_{n-1}$ and $\varsigma'_1, \ldots, \varsigma'_{m-1}$ as *intermediate states.*
It is given that $p_\varsigma(\varsigma_n) = p_\varsigma(\varsigma'_m)$. All that remains is to prove that

$$(\sigma_n, \phi_n, \kappa_n, ts_n) \approx_\sigma (\sigma_m, \phi_m, \kappa_m, ts_m)$$

We know by the definitions of influence and of *valid* and by induction on the instructions in the language that all changes to the store between ς and ς_n

and between ς' and ς'_m are marked as tainted. Crucially, this includes changes to heap values as well as to stack values. We state this in four cases, which cover all possible changes to the stores:

1. Addresses added to σ in some intermediate state,
2. Addresses added to σ' in some intermediate state,
3. Addresses changed in σ in some intermediate state,
4. Addresses changed in σ' in some intermediate state.

$$\forall a \in \mathit{Addr},$$
$$a \notin \mathit{dom}(\sigma) \wedge a \in \mathit{dom}(\sigma_n) \Rightarrow \mathit{ts}_n(a) \cap \mathit{valid} \neq \emptyset \tag{1}$$
$$a \notin \mathit{dom}(\sigma') \wedge a \in \mathit{dom}(\sigma_m) \Rightarrow \mathit{ts}_m(a) \cap \mathit{valid} \neq \emptyset \tag{2}$$
$$\sigma(a) \neq \sigma_n(a) \Rightarrow \mathit{ts}_n(a) \cap \mathit{valid} \neq \emptyset \tag{3}$$
$$\sigma'(a) \neq \sigma_m(a) \Rightarrow \mathit{ts}_m(a) \cap \mathit{valid} \neq \emptyset \tag{4}$$

The only changes that can occur to the continuation stack in any circumstance are removal of stack frames (`Return`, `Throw`, `IGet`, and `IPut` instructions) and the addition of new stack frames (`Invoke` instructions).

Since `Invoke` uses only fresh stack frames, all stack addresses with frames created in intermediate states (FP_f) are undefined in σ and σ':

$$\forall\, r \in \mathsf{Register}, \phi_f \in \mathit{FP}_f,\ (\phi_f, r) \notin \mathit{dom}(\sigma) \cup \mathit{dom}(\sigma')$$

This, together with our knowledge that all updates to heap values are tainted, proves that σ_n and σ_m are similar with respect to any pair of frame pointers if one of those is in FP_f:

$$\phi_n \in \mathit{FP}_f \vee \phi_m \in \mathit{FP}_f \Rightarrow (\sigma_n, \phi_n, \mathit{ts}_n) \approx_\phi (\sigma_m, \phi_m, \mathit{ts}_m)$$

We know from $p_\varsigma(\varsigma) = p_\varsigma(\varsigma')$ that the stack heights in ς and ς' are equal. We also know because of the restrictions of stack operations that ϕ_n is either ϕ, a fresh stack frame, or some stack frame from within κ. Similarly, we know that ϕ_m is either ϕ', a fresh stack frame, or some stack frame from within κ'. If ϕ_n is not fresh, we know the continuation stack below it is identical to some suffix of κ. Crucially, this means that no reordering of existing frame pointers is possible. The same relationship holds between ϕ_m and κ'. As such, ϕ_n and ϕ_m are either ϕ and ϕ', some pair from continuations at the same height from **halt**, or at least one of them is fresh. The same is true of each pair of frame pointers at identical height in κ_n and κ_m. In all of these cases, the two stores must be similar with respect to the frame pointers and their taint stores. Accordingly, we conclude:

$$(\sigma_n, \phi_n, \kappa_n, \mathit{ts}_n) \approx_\sigma (\sigma_m, \phi_m, \kappa_m, \mathit{ts}_m)$$

3.10 Global Transitivity of Similarity

Lemma. Any two finite program traces that begin with similar states are similar. Formally, if $\pi = \langle \varsigma_1, \ldots, \varsigma_n \rangle$ and $\pi' = \langle \varsigma_1', \ldots, \varsigma_m' \rangle$, then $\varsigma_1 \approx_\varsigma \varsigma_1' \Rightarrow \pi \approx_\pi \pi'$

Proof. By induction on transitivity of similarity.

3.11 Labeled Interference in Similar States

Lemma. Any two similar states exhibit the same behavior or at least one of them exhibits behavior that is labeled as insecure.

$$\varsigma_1 \approx_\varsigma \varsigma_2 \Rightarrow \mathit{labeled}\,(\varsigma_1) \neq \emptyset \vee \mathit{labeled}\,(\varsigma_2) \neq \emptyset \vee$$
$$\forall i \in \langle 1, \ldots n \rangle, (\sigma_1, a_i, ts_1) \approx_a (\sigma_2, a_i', ts_2)\,,\ \text{where}$$
$$\mathit{inputs}\,(\varsigma_1) = \langle a_1, \ldots, a_n \rangle \text{ and } \mathit{inputs}\,(\varsigma_2) = \langle a_1', \ldots, a_n' \rangle \text{ and}$$
$$\varsigma_1 = (cp_1, \phi_1, \sigma_1, \kappa_1, ts_1, ct_1) \text{ and } \varsigma_2 = (cp_2, \phi_2, \sigma_2, \kappa_2, ts_2, ct_2)$$

Proof. By the definition of similarity, the contents of both states' stores are identical at reachable, untainted addresses. Thus, one of the calls *labeled* must return an address or the calls to *inputs* must match.

3.12 Concrete Termination-Insensitive Labeled Interference

Any traces that begin with similar states exhibit the same observable behaviors except for those labeled as insecure.

Formally, if $\pi = \langle \varsigma_1, \varsigma_2, \ldots, \varsigma_n \rangle$ and $\pi' = \langle \varsigma_1', \varsigma_2', \ldots, \varsigma_m' \rangle$ and $\varsigma_1 \approx_\varsigma \varsigma_1'$, then

$$\forall\ \varsigma_i \in \pi,\ \varsigma_i \notin \mathit{obs}\ \vee\ \mathit{labeled}\,(\varsigma_i) \neq \emptyset\ \vee\ \exists\ \varsigma_j' \in \pi'\ :\ \varsigma_i \approx_\varsigma \varsigma_j'$$

Observe that because the choice of traces is arbitrary, π' is also examined.

Proof. By global transitivity of similarity, π and π' are similar. Every state in π or π', then, is similar to a state in the other trace or has a valid context taint. By the definition of *labeled*, states with valid context taints report those behaviors.

By the definition of similarity, similar states in similar traces occur in the same order.

3.13 Abstract Non-interference

Lemma. Abstract interpretation with the given semantics detects all possible variances in externally visible behaviors.

Proof. Since the abstract semantics are a sound overapproximation of the concrete semantics, they capture the behavior of all possible executions. Since concrete executions are proven to label all termination-insensitive interference, the absence of labels reported by abstract interpretation proves non-interference.

4 Discussion

Our analysis proves termination-insensitive non-interference, which allows divergence leaks; postdominance only considers paths that reach the exit node, so it excludes infinite paths. With termination analysis (a well understood technique), this analysis could prove non-interference without qualification. Side channel attacks, such as timing attacks, are beyond the scope of this paper.

It is possible that precision could be improved with less precise execution points. This would require a weaker definition of state similarity, such as similarity with respect to frame pointers but not to those in the continuation stacks.

Both the precision and complexity of this analysis depend on those of the abstract interpreter chosen. Imprecisions inherent to the choice of abstractions create false positives. For example, an abstract interpreter might simulate multiple branches executing when only one is possible—and, accordingly, would add unnecessary taint to values assigned during execution of those branches. Additionally, convergence admits some overtainting; different branches could assign identical values to a register. In this case, taint would be assigned unnecessarily. Accordingly, other improvements to precision may be possible.

5 Related Work

Sabelfeld and Myers [25] summarize the early work on information flows.

Denning [6] introduces the idea of taint values as lattices instead of booleans. Denning and Denning [7] describe a static analysis on a simple imperative language and discuss how it could be applied to a language with conditional jumps. They do not discuss how it could be applied to a language with procedures and exceptional flow. Volpano, et al. [29] validate the claims of Denning and Denning for languages with structured control-flow. Volpano and Smith [30] then extend it to handle loop termination leaks and some exceptional flow leaks.

Chang and Streiff [5] present a compiler-level tool that transforms untrusted C programs into C programs that enforce specified policies. Kim et al. [18] perform an abstract interpretation on Android programs. Arzt et al. [1] present FlowDroid, a static analyzer for Android applications. All of these papers limit their analyses to explicit information flows although the FlowDroid project does claim in a blog post to have support for implicit information flows.

Xu et al. [31] perform a source-to-source transformation on C programs to instrument them for taint tracking and track one class of implicit information flows. Kang et al. [17] perform a dynamic analysis called DTA++ that operates on Windows x86 binaries and tracks information flows. DTA++ explicitly allows for false negatives in order to minimize false positives. Liang and Might [20] present a Scheme-like core calculus for scripting languages like Python. Their core language is expressive enough to contain not only function calls but also call/cc as a primitive but do not detect implicit information flows.

Giacobazzi and Mastroeni [12] demonstrate an abstract interpreter on programs in a simple imperative language that lacks functions and exceptional control-flow—the kind of language that the technique suggested by Denning and Denning [7] addresses. Askarov, et al. [2] also noninterference in a Jif-like language with syntactic boundaries on its control-flow constructs and that lacks functions and exceptional control-flow. Liu and Milanova [21] perform a static analysis on Java programs that tracks implicit information flows. Their analysis does as Denning and Denning [7] suggested; it calculates postdominance to determine the extent of a conditional statement's effect on control-flow. However, they do not present a grammar, prove non-interference, or discuss exceptional control-flow. Pottier and Simonet [24] present a type system that guarantees noninterference in an ML-like language. Their technique relies on syntactic structures. Barthe and Rezk [3] perform an analysis on Java bytecode but assume a postdominance calculation, even for exceptional control-flow. They also assume type annotations for functions. Cousot and Radia [11] discuss non-interference but do not discuss interprocedural flows.

Cavallaro, et al. [4] dismiss the effectiveness of static techniques. They then discuss the shortcomings of dynamic analyses, particularly against intentionally malicious code. Moore, et al. [22] present a type system that, with runtime enforcement and a termination oracle, guarantees progress-sensitive noninterference (also called termination-sensitive noninterference). TaintDroid [9] is a dynamic extension to Android's runtime environment. Being a dynamic analysis, it does not purport to identify all possible program behaviors.

Venkatakrishnan, et al. [28] perform a static pre-pass that adds tracking instructions to inform a dynamic analysis. This analysis preserves termination-insensitive noninterference but ignores exceptional control-flow. Jia et al. [16] present a system that dynamically enforces annotations, including security labels and declassification. Myers [23] created JFlow, an extension to Java that allows programmers to annotate values and that uses a type system with both static and dynamic enforcement. It does not guarantee non-interference.

Liang, et al. [19] introduce *entry-point saturation* to properly model Android programs, which use several entry points instead of one. Entry-point saturation injects repeatedly into all entry points until encountering a fixed point and would allow the analysis in this paper to be applied to full Android programs. Van Horn and Might [27] demonstrated that abstract interpreters can be constructed automatically from concrete interpreters. Earl, et al. [8] demonstrated an abstract interpretation that operates in a pushdown automaton.

The official specifications for the bytecode language [14] and the dex file format [15] provide detailed information about Dalvik bytecode.

6 Conclusion

As we claimed, Denning and Denning's principle does generalize and extend to expressive low-level languages such as Dalvik bytecode. The key twist was to extend postdominance from control-flow graphs to interprocedural execution point graphs, and to extract these graphs as projections from small-step abstract interpretations over concrete semantics bearing taint-tracking machinery.

Acknowledgements. This article reports on work supported by the Defense Advanced Research Projects Agency under agreements no. AFRL FA8750-15-2-0092 and FA8750-12- 2-0106. The views expressed are those of the authors and do not reflect the official policy or position of the Department of Defense or the U.S. Government.

References

1. Arzt, S., Rasthofer, S., Fritz, C., Bodden, E., Bartel, A., Klein, J., Le Traon, Y., Octeau, D., McDaniel, P.: Flowdroid: precise context, flow, field, object-sensitive and lifecycle-aware taint analysis for android apps. In: Proceedings of the 35th ACM SIGPLAN Conference on Programming Language Design and Implementation, PLDI 2014, pp. 259–269. ACM, New York (2014)
2. Askarov, A., Hunt, S., Sabelfeld, A., Sands, D.: Termination-insensitive noninterference leaks more than just a bit. In: Jajodia, S., Lopez, J. (eds.) ESORICS 2008. LNCS, vol. 5283, pp. 333–348. Springer, Heidelberg (2008)
3. Barthe, G., Rezk, T.: Non-interference for a JVM-like language. In: Proceedings of the 2005 ACM SIGPLAN International Workshop on Types in Languages Design and Implementation, TLDI 2005, pp. 103–112. ACM, New York, January 2005
4. Cavallaro, L., Saxena, P., Sekar, R.: On the limits of information flow techniques for malware analysis and containment. In: Zamboni, D. (ed.) DIMVA 2008. LNCS, vol. 5137, pp. 143–163. Springer, Heidelberg (2008)
5. Chang, W., Streiff, B., Lin, C.: Efficient and extensible security enforcement using dynamic data flow analysis. In: Proceedings of the 15th ACM Conference on Computer and Communications Security, CCS 2008, pp. 39–50. ACM, New York (2008)
6. Denning, D.E.: A lattice model of secure information flow. Commun. ACM **19**(5), 236–243 (1976)
7. Denning, D.E., Denning, P.J.: Certification of programs for secure information flow. Commun. ACM **20**(7), 504–513 (1977)
8. Earl, C., Sergey, I., Might, M., Van Horn, D.: Introspective pushdown analysis of higher-order programs. In: Proceedings of the 17th ACM SIGPLAN International Conference on Functional Programming, ICFP 2012, pp. 177–188. ACM, New York (2012)
9. Enck, W., Gilbert, P., Chun, B.-G., Cox, L.P., Jung, J., McDaniel, P., Sheth, A.N.: Taintdroid: an information-flow tracking system for realtime privacy monitoring on smartphones, pp. 1–6 (2010)
10. Fenton, J.S.: Memoryless subsystems. Comput. J. **17**(2), 143–147 (1974)
11. Genaim, S., Spoto, F.: Information flow analysis for java bytecode. In: Cousot, R. (ed.) VMCAI 2005. LNCS, vol. 3385, pp. 346–362. Springer, Heidelberg (2005)
12. Giacobazzi, R., Mastroeni, I.: Abstract non-interference: parameterizing non-interference by abstract interpretation. In: Proceedings of the 31st ACM SIGPLAN-SIGACT Symposium on Principles of Programming Languages, POPL 2004, pp. 186–197. ACM, New York (2004)
13. Goguen, J.A., Meseguer, J.: Security policies and security models. In: 2012 IEEE Symposium on Security and Privacy, p. 11. IEEE Computer Society (1982)
14. Google. Bytecode for the Dalvik VM (2014). http://source.android.com/devices/tech/dalvik/dalvik-bytecode.html
15. Google. Dalvik executable format (2014). http://source.android.com/devices/tech/dalvik/dex-format.html

16. Jia, L., Aljuraidan, J., Fragkaki, E., Bauer, L., Stroucken, M., Fukushima, K., Kiyomoto, S., Miyake, Y.: Run-time enforcement of information-flow properties on android. In: Crampton, J., Jajodia, S., Mayes, K. (eds.) ESORICS 2013. LNCS, vol. 8134, pp. 775–792. Springer, Heidelberg (2013)
17. Kang, M.G., McCamant, S., Poosankam, P., Song, D.: DTA++: dynamic taint analysis with targeted control-flow propagation. In: Proceedings of the Network and Distributed System Security Symposium, NDSS 2011. The Internet Society, February 2011
18. Kim, J., Yoon, Y., Yi, K., Shin, J.: Scandal: static analyzer for detecting privacy leaks in android applications. In: Mobile Security Technologies (2012)
19. Liang, S., Keep, A.W., Might, M., Lyde, S., Gilray, T., Aldous, P., Van Horn, D.: Sound and precise malware analysis for android via pushdown reachability and entry-point saturation. In: Proceedings of the Third ACM Workshop on Security and Privacy in Smartphones & Mobile Devices, SPSM 2013, pp. 21–32. ACM, New York (2013)
20. Liang, S., Might, M.: Hash-flow taint analysis of higher-order programs. In: Proceedings of the 7th Workshop on Programming Languages and Analysis for Security, PLAS 2012, pp. 8:1–8:12. ACM, New York (2012)
21. Liu, Y., Milanova, A.: Static information flow analysis with handling of implicit flows and a study on effects of implicit flows vs explicit flows. In: 2010 14th European Conference on Software Maintenance and Reengineering (CSMR), pp. 146–155, March 2010
22. Moore, S., Askarov, A., Chong, S.: Precise enforcement of progress-sensitive security. In: Proceedings of the 2012 ACM Conference on Computer and Communications Security, CCS 2012, pp. 881–893. ACM, New York (2012)
23. Myers, A.C.: JFlow: practical mostly-static information flow control. In: Proceedings of the 26th ACM SIGPLAN-SIGACT Symposium on Principles of Programming Languages, POPL 1999, pp. 228–241. ACM, New York (1999)
24. Pottier, F., Simonet, V.: Information flow inference for ML. ACM Trans. Program. Lang. Syst. (TOPLAS) **25**(1), 117–158 (2003)
25. Sabelfeld, A., Myers, A.C.: Language-based information-flow security. IEEE J. Sel. Areas Commun. **21**(1), 5–19 (2006)
26. Sabelfeld, A., Sands, D.: A per model of secure information flow in sequential programs. In: Swierstra, S.D. (ed.) ESOP 1999. LNCS, vol. 1576, pp. 40–58. Springer, Heidelberg (1999)
27. Van Horn, D., Might, M.: Abstracting abstract machines. In: Proceedings of the 15th ACM SIGPLAN International Conference on Functional Programming, ICFP 2010, pp. 51–62. ACM, New York (2010)
28. Venkatakrishnan, V.N., Xu, W., DuVarney, D.C., Sekar, R.: Provably correct runtime enforcement of non-interference properties. In: Ning, P., Qing, S., Li, N. (eds.) ICICS 2006. LNCS, vol. 4307, pp. 332–351. Springer, Heidelberg (2006)
29. Volpano, D., Irvine, C., Smith, G.: A sound type system for secure flow analysis. J. Comput. Secur. **4**(2–3), 167–187 (1996)
30. Volpano, D., Smith, G.: Eliminating covert flows with minimum typings. In: Proceedings of the 10th Computer Security Foundations Workshop, pp. 156–168, June 1997
31. Xu, W., Bhatkar, S., Sekar, R.: Taint-enhanced policy enforcement: a practical approach to defeat a wide range of attacks. In: Proceedings of the 15th Conference on USENIX Security Symposium, USENIX-SS 2006, vol. 15, USENIX Association, Berkeley, CA, USA (2006)

Static Analysis with Set-Closure in Secrecy

Woosuk Lee(✉), Hyunsook Hong, Kwangkeun Yi, and Jung Hee Cheon

Seoul National University, Seoul, South Korea
{wslee,kwang}@ropas.snu.ac.kr,
{hongsuk07,jhcheon}@snu.ac.kr

Abstract. We report that the homomorphic encryption scheme can unleash the possibility of static analysis of encrypted programs. Static analysis in cipher-world is desirable in the static-analysis-as-a-service setting, because it allows the program owners to encrypt and upload their programs to the static analysis service while the service provider can still analyze the encrypted programs without decrypting them. Only the owner of the decryption key (the program owner) is able to decrypt the analysis result. As a concrete example, we describe how to perform a pointer analysis in secrecy. In our method, a somewhat homomorphic encryption scheme of depth $O(\log m)$ is able to evaluate a simple pointer analysis with $O(\log m)$ homomorphic matrix multiplications, for the number m of pointer variables when the maximal pointer level is bounded. We also demonstrate the viability of our method by implementing the pointer analysis in secrecy.

1 Introduction

In order for a *static-analysis-as-a-service* system [1] to be popular, we need to solve the users' copy-right concerns. Users are reluctant to upload their source to analysis server.

For more widespread use of such service, we explored a method of performing static analysis on encrypted programs. Figure 1 depicts the system.

Challenge. Our work is based on *homomorphic encryption* (HE). A HE scheme enables computation of arbitrary functions on encrypted data. In other words, a HE scheme provides the functions $f_\oplus$ and $f_\wedge$ that satisfy the following homomorphic properties for plaintexts $x, y \in \{0,1\}$ without any secrets:

$$\mathsf{Enc}(x \oplus y) = f_\oplus(\mathsf{Enc}(x), \mathsf{Enc}(y)), \qquad \mathsf{Enc}(x \wedge y) = f_\wedge(\mathsf{Enc}(x), \mathsf{Enc}(y))$$

A HE scheme was first shown in the work of Gentry [14]. Since then, although there have been many efforts to improve the efficiency [3,4,9,21], the cost is still too large for immediate applications into daily computations.

Due to the high complexity of HE operation, practical deployments of HE require *application-specific* techniques. Application-specific techniques are often demonstrated in other fields. Kim et al. [8] introduced an optimization technique to reduce the depth of an arithmetic circuit computing edit distance on

S. Blazy and T. Jensen (Eds.): SAS 2015, LNCS 9291, pp. 18–35, 2015.
DOI: 10.1007/978-3-662-48288-9_2

encrypted DNA sequences. In addition, methods of bubble sort and insertion sort on encrypted data have been proposed [6]. Also, private database query protocol using somewhat homomorphic encryption has been proposed [2].

Our Results. As a first step, we propose a pointer analysis in secrecy. As many analyses depends on the pointer information, we expect our work to have significant implications along the way to static analysis in secrecy.

We first describe a basic approach. We design an arithmetic circuit of the pointer analysis algorithm only using operations that a HE scheme supports. Program owner encrypts some numbers representing his program under the HE scheme. On the encrypted data, a server performs a series of corresponding homomorphic operations referring to the arithmetic circuit and outputs encrypted pointer analysis results. This basic approach is simple but very costly.

To decrease the cost of the basic approach, we apply two optimization techniques. One is to exploit the *ciphertext packing* technique not only for performance boost but also for decreasing the huge number of ciphertexts required for the basic scheme. The basic approach makes ciphertexts size grow by the square to the number of pointer variables in a program, which is far from practical. Ciphertext packing makes total ciphertexts size be linear to the number of variables. The other technique is *level-by-level analysis*. We analyze the pointers of the same level together from the highest to lowest. With this technique, the depth of the arithmetic circuit for the pointer analysis significantly decreases: from $O(m^2 \log m)$ to $O(n \log m)$ for the number m of pointer variables and the maximal pointer level n. By decreasing the depth, which is the most important in performance of HE schemes, the technique decreases both ciphertexts size and the cost of each homomorphic operation.

The improvement by the two optimizations is summarized in Table 1.

Table 1. The comparison between the basic and the improved scheme

	Multiplicative depth	# Ctxt
Basic	$O(m^2 \log m)$	$4m^2$
Improved	$O(n \log m)$	$(2n+2)m$

m : the number of pointer variables in the target program
n : the maximum level of pointer in the program, which does not exceed 5 in usual

Although our interest in this paper is limited to a pointer analysis, we expect other analyses in the same family will be performed in a similar manner to our method. Analyses in the family essentially compute a transitive closure of a graph subject to dynamic changes; new edges may be added during the analysis. Our method computes an encrypted transitive closure of a graph when both edge insertion queries and all the edges are encrypted. Thus, we expect only a few modifications to our method will make other similar analyses (*e.g.*, 0-CFA) be in secrecy.

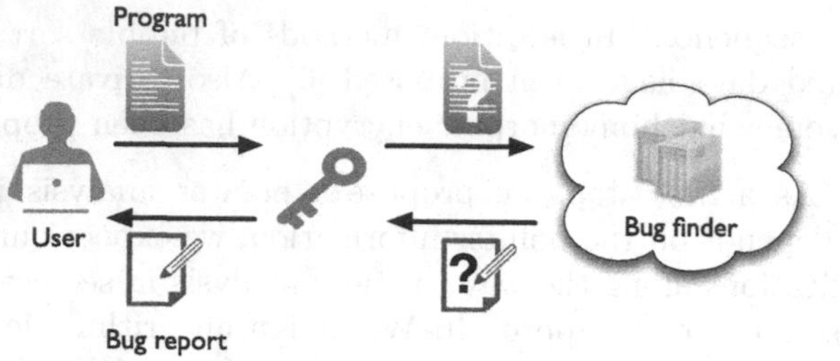

Fig. 1. Secure static analysis is performed in 3 steps: (1) target program encryption (2)analysis in secrecy, and (3) analysis result decryption

2 Background

In this section, we introduce the concept of homomorphic encryption, and describe the security model of our static analysis in secrecy.

2.1 Homomorphic Encryption

A homomorphic encryption (HE) scheme HE=(KG, Enc, Dec, Eval) is a quadruple of probabilistic polynomial-time algorithm as follows:

- $(\mathsf{pk}, \mathsf{evk}; \mathsf{sk}) \leftarrow \mathsf{HE.KG}(1^\lambda)$: The algorithm takes the security parameter λ as input and outputs a public encryption key pk, a public evaluation key evk, and a secret decryption key sk.
- $\bar{c} \leftarrow \mathsf{HE.Enc}_{\mathsf{pk}}(\mu, r)$: The algorithm takes the public key pk, a single bit message $\mu \in \{0, 1\}$,[1] and a randomizer r. It outputs a ciphertext $\bar{c}$. If we have no confusion, we omit the randomizer r.
- $\mu \leftarrow \mathsf{HE.Dec}_{\mathsf{sk}}(\bar{c})$: The algorithm takes the secret key sk and a ciphertext $\bar{c} = \mathsf{HE.Enc}_{\mathsf{pk}}(\mu)$ and outputs a message $\mu \in \{0, 1\}$
- $\bar{c}_f \leftarrow \mathsf{HE.Eval}_{\mathsf{evk}}(f; \bar{c}_1, \ldots, \bar{c}_l)$: The algorithm takes the evaluation key evk, a function $f : \{0, 1\}^l \rightarrow \{0, 1\}$ represented by an arithmetic circuit over $\mathbb{Z}_2 = \{0, 1\}$ with the addition and multiplication gates, and a set of l ciphertexts $\{\bar{c}_i = \mathsf{HE.Enc}(\mu_i)\}_{i=1}^{l}$, and outputs a ciphertext $\bar{c}_f = \mathsf{HE.Enc}(f(\mu_1, \cdots, \mu_l))$.

We say that a scheme HE=(KG, Enc, Dec, Eval) is *f-homomorphic* if for any set of inputs $(\mu_1, \cdots, \mu_l)$, and all sufficiently large λ, it holds that

$$\Pr\left[\mathsf{HE.Dec}_{\mathsf{sk}}\left(\mathsf{HE.Eval}_{\mathsf{evk}}(f; \bar{c}_1, \cdots, \bar{c}_l)\right) \neq f(\mu_1, \cdots, \mu_l)\right] = \mathrm{negl}(\lambda),$$

where negl is a negligible function, $(\mathsf{pk}, \mathsf{evk}; \mathsf{sk}) \leftarrow \mathsf{HE.KG}(1^\lambda)$, and $\bar{c}_i \leftarrow \mathsf{HE.Enc}_{\mathsf{pk}}(\mu_i)$.

If a HE scheme can evaluate all functions represented by arithmetic circuits over $\mathbb{Z}_2$ (equivalently, boolean circuits with AND and XOR gates[2]), the HE scheme is called *fully homomorphic*.

[1] For simplicity, we assume that the plaintext space is $\mathbb{Z}_2 = \{0, 1\}$, but extension to larger plaintext space is immediate.

[2] AND and XOR gates are sufficient to simulate all binary circuits.

To facilitate understanding of HE schemes, we introduce a simple symmetric version of the HE scheme [11] based on approximate common divisor problems [19]:

- $\mathsf{sk} \leftarrow \mathsf{KG}(1^\lambda)$: Choose an integer p and outputs the secret key $\mathsf{sk} = p$.
- $\bar{c} \leftarrow \mathsf{Enc}(\mu \in \{0,1\})$: Choose a random integer q and a random noise integer r with $|r| \ll |p|$. It outputs $\bar{c} = pq + 2r + \mu$.
- $\mu \leftarrow \mathsf{Dec}_{\mathsf{sk}}(\bar{c})$: Outputs $\mu = ((\bar{c} \bmod p) \bmod 2)$.
- $\bar{c}_{\mathsf{add}} \leftarrow \mathsf{Add}(\bar{c}_1, \bar{c}_2)$: Outputs $\bar{c}_{\mathsf{add}} = \bar{c}_1 + \bar{c}_2$.
- $\bar{c}_{\mathsf{mult}} \leftarrow \mathsf{Mult}(\bar{c}_1, \bar{c}_2)$: Outputs $\bar{c}_{\mathsf{mult}} = \bar{c}_1 \times \bar{c}_2$.

For ciphertexts $\bar{c}_1 \leftarrow \mathsf{Enc}(\mu_1)$ and $\bar{c}_2 \leftarrow \mathsf{Enc}(\mu_2)$, we know each $\bar{c}_i$ is of the form $\bar{c}_i = pq_i + 2r_i + \mu_i$ for some integer q_i and noise r_i. Hence $((\bar{c}_i \bmod p) \bmod 2) = \mu_i$, if $|2r_i + \mu_i| < p/2$. Then, the following equations hold:

$$\bar{c}_1 + \bar{c}_2 = p(q_1 + q_2) + \underbrace{2(r_1 + r_2) + \mu_1 + \mu_2}_{\text{noise}},$$

$$\bar{c}_1 \times \bar{c}_2 = p(pq_1q_2 + \cdots) + \underbrace{2(2r_1r_2 + r_1\mu_2 + r_2\mu_1) + \mu_1 \cdot \mu_2}_{\text{noise}}$$

Based on these properties,

$$\mathsf{Dec}_{\mathsf{sk}}(\bar{c}_1 + \bar{c}_2) = \mu_1 + \mu_2 \text{ and } \mathsf{Dec}_{\mathsf{sk}}(\bar{c}_1 \times \bar{c}_2) = \mu_1 \cdot \mu_2$$

if the absolute value of $2(2r_1r_2 + r_1\mu_2 + r_2\mu_1) + \mu_1\mu_2$ is less than $p/2$. The noise in the resulting ciphertext increases during homomorphic addition and multiplication (twice and quadratically as much noise as before respectively). If the noise becomes larger than $p/2$, the decryption result of the above scheme will be spoiled. As long as the noise is managed, the scheme is able to potentially evaluate all boolean circuits as the addition and multiplication in $\mathbb{Z}_2$ corresponds to the XOR and AND operations.

We consider somewhat homomorphic encryption (SWHE) schemes that adopt the modulus-switching [4,5,10,15] for the noise-management. The modulus-switching reduces the noise by scaling the factor of the modulus in the ciphertext space. SWHE schemes support a limited number of homomorphic operations on each ciphertext, as opposed to fully homomorphic encryption schemes [7,11,14,23] which are based on a different noise-management technique. But SWHE schemes are more efficient to support low-degree homomorphic computations.

In this paper, we will measure the efficiency of homomorphic evaluation by the *multiplicative depth* of an underlying circuit. The multiplicative depth is defined as the number of multiplication gates encountered along the longest path from input to output. When it comes to the depth of a circuit computing a function f, we discuss the circuit of the minimal depth among any circuits computing f. For example, if a somewhat homomorphic encryption scheme can evaluate circuits of depth L, we may maximally perform 2^L multiplications on the ciphertexts maintaining the correctness of the result. We do not consider the number of addition gates in counting the depth of a circuit because the noise increase by additions is negligible compared with the noise increase by multiplications. The multiplicative depth of a circuit is the most important factor in the performance of homomorphic evaluation of the circuit in the view of both the size of ciphertexts and the cost of per-gate homomorphic computation. Thus, minimizing the depth is the most important in performance.

2.2 The BGV-type Cryptosystem

Our underlying HE scheme is a variant of the Brakerski-Gentry-Vaikuntanathan (BGV)-type cryptosystem [4,15]. In this section, we only provide a brief review of the cryptosystem [4]. For more details, please refer to [4,15]. Let $\Phi(X)$ be an irreducible polynomial over $\mathbb{Z}$. The implementation of the scheme is based on the polynomial operations in ring $R = \mathbb{Z}[X]/(\Phi(X))$ which is the set of integer polynomials of degree less than $\deg(\Phi)$. Let $R_p := R/pR$ be the message space for a prime p and $R_q \times R_q$ be the ciphertext space for an integer q. Now, we describe the BGV cryptosystem as follows:

- $((a,b);\mathbf{s}) \leftarrow \mathsf{BGV.KG}(1^\lambda, \sigma, q)$: Choose a secret key $\mathbf{s}$ and a noise polynomial e from a discrete Gaussian distribution over R with standard deviation σ. Choose a random polynomial a from R_q and generate the public key $(a, b = a \cdot s + p \cdot e) \in R_q \times R_q$. Output the public key $\mathsf{pk} = (a,b)$ and the secret key $\mathsf{sk} = \mathbf{s}$.
- $\bar{\mathbf{c}} \leftarrow \mathsf{BGV.Enc}_{\mathsf{pk}}(\mu)$: To encrypt a message $\mu \in R_p$, choose a random polynomial v whose coefficients are in $\{0, \pm 1\}$ and two noise polynomials e_0, e_1. Output the ciphertext $\mathbf{c} = (c_0, c_1) = (bv + pe_0 + \mu, av + pe_1) \bmod (q, \Phi(X))$.
- $\mu \leftarrow \mathsf{BGV.Dec}_{\mathsf{sk}}(\bar{\mathbf{c}})$: Given a ciphertext $\bar{\mathbf{c}} = (c_0, c_1)$, it outputs $\mu = (((c_0 - c_1 \cdot \mathbf{s}) \bmod q) \bmod p)$.
- $\bar{\mathbf{c}}_{\mathsf{add}} \leftarrow \mathsf{BGV.Add}_{\mathsf{pk}}(\bar{\mathbf{c}}_1, \bar{\mathbf{c}}_2; \mathsf{evk})$: Given ciphertexts $\bar{\mathbf{c}}_1 = \mathsf{BGV.Enc}(\mu_1)$ and $\bar{\mathbf{c}}_2 = \mathsf{BGV.Enc}(\mu_2)$, it outputs the ciphertext $\bar{\mathbf{c}}_{\mathsf{add}} = \mathsf{BGV.Enc}(\mu_1 + \mu_2)$.
- $\bar{\mathbf{c}}_{\mathsf{mult}} \leftarrow \mathsf{BGV.Mult}_{\mathsf{pk}}(\bar{\mathbf{c}}_1, \bar{\mathbf{c}}_2; \mathsf{evk})$: Given ciphertexts $\bar{\mathbf{c}}_1 = \mathsf{BGV.Enc}(\mu_1)$ and $\bar{\mathbf{c}}_2 = \mathsf{BGV.Enc}(\mu_2)$, it outputs the ciphertext $\bar{\mathbf{c}}_{\mathsf{mult}} = \mathsf{BGV.Enc}(\mu_1 \cdot \mu_2)$.

2.3 Security Model

We assume that program owners and analyzer servers are semi-honest. In this model, the analyzer runs the protocol exactly as specified, but may try to learn as much as possible about the program information. However, in our method, since programs are encrypted under the BGV-type cryptosystem which is secure under the hardness of the ring learning with errors (RLWE) problem (see [4] for the details), analyzers cannot learn no more information than the program size.

3 A Basic Construction of a Pointer Analysis in Secrecy

In this section, we explain how to perform a pointer analysis in secrecy.

3.1 A Brief Review of a Pointer Analysis

We begin with a brief review of a pointer analysis. We consider flow- and context-insensitive pointer analyses. To simplify our presentation, we consider a tiny language consisting of primitive assignments involving just the operations * and &. A program P is a finite set of assignments A:

$$\mathtt{A} \rightarrow \mathtt{x} = \&\mathtt{y} \mid \mathtt{x} = \mathtt{y} \mid *\mathtt{x} = \mathtt{y} \mid \mathtt{x} = *\mathtt{y}$$

We present a pointer analysis algorithm with simple resolution rules in a similar manner to [18]. Given some program P, we construct resolution rules as specified in Table 2. In the first rule, the side condition "if x = &y in P" indicates that there is an instance of this rule for each occurrence of an assignment of the form x = &y in P. The side conditions in the other rules are similarly interpreted. Intuitively, an edge $\mathtt{x} \longrightarrow \&\mathtt{y}$ indicates that x can point to y. An edge $\mathtt{x} \longrightarrow \mathtt{y}$ indicates that for any variable v, if y may point to v then x may point to v. The pointer analysis is applying the resolution rules until reaching a fixpoint.

Table 2. Resolution rules for pointer analysis.

$$\frac{}{\mathtt{x} \longrightarrow \&\mathtt{y}} \text{ (if } \mathtt{x} = \&\mathtt{y} \text{ in } P) \quad \textsf{(New)} \qquad \frac{}{\mathtt{x} \longrightarrow \mathtt{y}} \text{ (if } \mathtt{x} = \mathtt{y} \text{ in } P) \quad \textsf{(Copy)}$$

$$\frac{\mathtt{x} \longrightarrow \&\mathtt{z}}{\mathtt{y} \longrightarrow \mathtt{z}} \text{ (if } \mathtt{y} = *\mathtt{x} \text{ in } P) \quad \textsf{(Load)} \qquad \frac{\mathtt{x} \longrightarrow \&\mathtt{z}}{\mathtt{z} \longrightarrow \mathtt{y}} \text{ (if } *\mathtt{x} = \mathtt{y} \text{ in } P) \quad \textsf{(Store)}$$

$$\frac{\mathtt{x} \longrightarrow \mathtt{z} \quad \mathtt{z} \longrightarrow \&\mathtt{y}}{\mathtt{x} \longrightarrow \&\mathtt{y}} \quad \textsf{(Trans)}$$

3.2 The Pointer Analysis in Secrecy

The analysis in secrecy will be performed in the following 3 steps. First, a program owner derives numbers that represent his program and encrypt them under a HE scheme. The encrypted numbers will be given to an analysis server. Next, the server performs homomorphic evaluation of an underlying arithmetic circuit representing the pointer analysis with the inputs from the program owner. Finally, the program owner obtains an encrypted analysis result and recovers a set of points-to relations by decryption.

Before beginning, we define some notations. We assume a program owner assigns a number to every variable using some numbering scheme. In the rest of the paper, we will denote a variable numbered i by $\mathtt{x_i}$. In addition, to express the arithmetic circuit of the pointer analysis algorithm, we define the notations $\delta_{i,j}$ and $\eta_{i,j}$ in $\mathbb{Z}$ for $i, j = 1, \cdots, m$ by

$$\delta_{i,j} \neq 0 \quad \text{iff} \quad \text{An edge } \mathtt{x_i} \longrightarrow \&\mathtt{x_j} \text{ is derived by the resolution rules.}$$
$$\eta_{i,j} \neq 0 \quad \text{iff} \quad \text{An edge } \mathtt{x_i} \longrightarrow \mathtt{x_j} \text{ is derived by the resolution rules.}$$

for variables $\mathtt{x_i}$ and $\mathtt{x_j}$, and the number m of pointer variables.

Inputs from Client. A client (program owner) derives the following numbers that represent his program P (here, m is the number of variables):

$$\{(\delta_{i,j}, \eta_{i,j}, u_{i,j}, v_{i,j}) \in \mathbb{Z} \times \mathbb{Z} \times \{0,1\} \times \{0,1\} \mid 1 \leq i,j \leq m\}$$

which are initially assigned as follows:

$$\delta_{i,j} \leftarrow \begin{cases} 1 & \text{if } \exists \texttt{x}_\texttt{i} = \&\texttt{x}_\texttt{j} \\ 0 & \text{otherwise} \end{cases} \qquad \eta_{i,j} \leftarrow \begin{cases} 1 & \text{if } \exists \texttt{x}_\texttt{i} = \texttt{x}_\texttt{j} \text{ or } i = j \\ 0 & \text{otherwise} \end{cases}$$

$$u_{i,j} \leftarrow \begin{cases} 1 & \text{if } \exists \texttt{x}_\texttt{j} = *\texttt{x}_\texttt{i} \\ 0 & \text{otherwise} \end{cases} \qquad v_{i,j} \leftarrow \begin{cases} 1 & \text{if } \exists *\texttt{x}_\texttt{j} = \texttt{x}_\texttt{i} \\ 0 & \text{otherwise} \end{cases}$$

In the assignment of $\delta_{i,j}$, the side condition $\exists \texttt{x}_\texttt{i} = \&\texttt{x}_\texttt{j}$ indicates that there is the assignment $\texttt{x}_\texttt{i} = \&\texttt{x}_\texttt{j}$ in the program P. The other side conditions are similarly interpreted.

The program owner encrypts the numbers using a HE scheme and provides them to the server. We denote the encryption of $\delta_{i,j}$, $\eta_{i,j}$, $u_{i,j}$, and $v_{i,j}$ by $\bar{\delta}_{i,j}$, $\bar{\eta}_{i,j}$, $\bar{u}_{i,j}$, and $\bar{v}_{i,j}$, respectively. Therefore, the program owner generates $4m^2$ ciphertexts where m is the number of pointer variables.

Server's Analysis. Provided the set of the ciphertexts from the program owner, the server homomorphically applies the resolution rules. With a slight abuse of notation, we will denote $+$ and $\cdot$ as homomorphic addition and multiplication respectively to simplify the presentation.

We begin with applying the Trans rule in Table 2. For $i, j = 1, \cdots, m$, the server updates $\bar{\delta}_{i,j}$ as follows:

$$\bar{\delta}_{i,j} \leftarrow \sum_{k=1}^{m} \bar{\eta}_{i,k} \cdot \bar{\delta}_{k,j}$$

If edges $\texttt{x}_\texttt{i} \longrightarrow \texttt{x}_\texttt{k}$ and $\texttt{x}_\texttt{k} \longrightarrow \&\texttt{x}_\texttt{j}$ are derived by the resolution rules for some variable $\texttt{x}_\texttt{k}$, then the edge $\texttt{x}_\texttt{i} \longrightarrow \&\texttt{x}_\texttt{j}$ will be derived by the Trans rule and the value $\delta_{i,j}$ will have a positive integer. If there is no variable $\texttt{x}_\texttt{k}$ that satisfies the conditions for all $k = 1, \cdots, m$, there will be no update on $\delta_{i,j}$ ($\because \eta_{i,i} = 1$).

Next, we describe applying the Load rule.

$$\bar{\eta}_{i,j} \leftarrow \bar{\eta}_{i,j} + \sum_{k=1}^{m} \bar{u}_{i,k} \cdot \bar{\delta}_{k,j}$$

If an edge $\texttt{x}_\texttt{k} \longrightarrow \&\texttt{x}_\texttt{j}$ is derived and the program P has a command $\texttt{x}_\texttt{i} := *\texttt{x}_\texttt{k}$ and for some integer k, then the edge $\texttt{x}_\texttt{i} \longrightarrow \texttt{x}_\texttt{j}$ will be derived and $\eta_{i,j}$ will have a positive value. If none of variables $\texttt{x}_\texttt{k}$ satisfies the conditions, there will be no update on $\eta_{i,j}$.

Finally, to apply the Store rule, the server performs the following operations:

$$\bar{\eta}_{i,j} \leftarrow \bar{\eta}_{i,j} + \sum_{k=1}^{m} \bar{v}_{j,k} \cdot \bar{\delta}_{k,i}$$

If an edge $\mathtt{x_k} \longrightarrow \&\mathtt{x_i}$ is derived and the program P has a command $*\mathtt{x_k} := \mathtt{x_j}$ for some variable $\mathtt{x_k}$, then an edge $\mathtt{x_i} \longrightarrow \mathtt{x_j}$ will be derived and $\eta_{i,j}$ will have a non-zero value.

Note that the server must repeat applying the rules as if in the worst case since the server cannot know whether a fixpoint is reached during the operations. The server may obtain a fixpoint by repeating the following two steps in turn m^2 times:

1. Applying the Trans rule m times
2. Applying the Load and Store rules

The reason for doing step 1 is that we may have a m-length path through edges as the longest one in the worst case. The reason for repeating the two steps m^2 times is that we may have a new edge by applying the Load and Store rules, and we may have at most m^2 edges at termination of the analysis.

We need $O(m^2 \log m)$ multiplicative depth in total. Because performing the step 1 entails m homomorphic multiplications on each $\bar{\delta}_{i,j}$, and repeating the two steps m^2 times performs about m^{m^2} homomorphic multiplications on each $\bar{\delta}_{i,j}$.

Output Determination. The client receives the updated $\{\bar{\delta}_{i,j} \mid 1 \leq i, j \leq m\}$ from the server and recovers a set of points-to relations as follows:

$$\{\mathtt{x_i} \longrightarrow \&\mathtt{x_j} \mid \mathsf{HE.Dec_{sk}}(\bar{\delta}_{i,j}) \neq 0 \text{ and } 1 \leq i, j \leq m\}$$

Why Do We Not Represent the Algorithm by a Boolean Circuit? One may wonder why we represent the pointer analysis algorithm by an arithmetic circuit rather than a Boolean circuit. As an example of applying the Trans rule, we might update $\delta_{i,j}$ by $\delta_{i,j} \leftarrow \bigvee_{1 \leq k \leq m} \eta_{i,k} \wedge \delta_{k,j}$. However, this representation causes more multiplicative depth than our current approach. The OR operation consists of the XOR and AND operations as follows: $x \vee y \stackrel{\mathsf{def}}{=} (x \wedge y) \oplus x \oplus y$. Note that the addition and multiplication in $\mathbb{Z}_2$ correspond to the XOR and AND operations, respectively. Since the OR operation requires a single multiplication over ciphertexts, this method requires m more multiplications than our current method to update $\delta_{i,j}$ once.

4 Improvement of the Pointer Analysis in Secrecy

In this section, we present three techniques to reduce the cost of the basic approach described in the Sect. 3.2. We begin with problems of the basic approach followed by our solutions.

4.1 Problems of the Basic Approach

The basic scheme has the following problems that make the scheme impractical.

- Huge # of homomorphic multiplications: The scheme described in the Sect. 3.2 can be implemented with a SWHE scheme of the depth $O(m^2 \log m)$. Homomorphic evaluation of a circuit over the hundreds depth is regarded unrealistic in usual. The depth of the arithmetic circuit described in the Sect. 3.2 exceeds 300 even if a program has only 10 variables.
- Huge # of ciphertexts: The basic approach requires $4m^2$ ciphertexts, where m is the number of pointer variables. When a program has 1000 variables, 4 million ciphertexts are necessary. For instance, the size of a single ciphertext in the BGV cryptosystem is about 2 MB when the depth is 20. In this case, the scheme requires 7.6 TB memory space for all the ciphertexts.
- Decryption error may happen: In our underlying HE scheme, the message space is the polynomial ring over modulus p. During the operations, $\delta_{i,j}$ and $\eta_{i,j}$ increase and may become p which is congruent to 0 modulo p. Since we are interested in whether each value is zero or not, incorrect results may be derived if the values become congruent to 0 modulo p by accident.

4.2 Overview of Improvement

For the number m of pointer variables and the maximal pointer level n, the followings are our solutions.

- **Level-by-level Analysis:** We analyze pointers of the same level together from the highest to lowest in order to decrease the depth of the arithmetic circuit described in the Sect. 3.2. To apply the technique, program owners are required to reveal an upper bound of the maximal pointer level. By this compromise, the depth of the arithmetic circuit significantly decreases: from $O(m^2 \log m)$ to $O(n \log m)$. We expect this information leak is not much compromise because the maximal pointer level is well known to be a small number in usual cases.
- **Ciphertext Packing:** We adopt ciphertext packing not only for performance boost but also for decreasing the huge number of ciphertexts required for the basic scheme. The technique makes total ciphertext sizes be linear to the number of variables.
- **Randomization of Ciphertexts:** We randomize ciphertexts to balance the probability of incorrect results and ciphertext size. We may obtain correct results with the probability of $(1 - \frac{1}{p-1})^{n(\lceil \log m \rceil + 3)}$.

The following table summarizes the improvement.

	Depth	# Ctxt
Basic	$O(m^2 \log m)$	$4m^2$
Improved	$O(n \log m)$	$(2n + 2)m$

4.3 Level-by-level Analysis

We significantly decrease the multiplicative depth by doing the analysis in a level by level manner in terms of *level of pointers*. The level of a pointer is the maximum level of possible indirect accesses from the pointer, *e.g.*, the pointer level of `p` in the definition "`int** p`" is 2. From this point, we denote the level of a pointer variable `x` by $\mathsf{ptl}(\mathtt{x})$.

We assume that type-casting a pointer value to a lower or higher-level pointer is absent in programs. For example, we do not consider a program that has type-casting from `void*` to `int**` because the pointer level increases from 1 to 2.

On the assumption, we analyze the pointers of the same level together from the highest to lowest. The correctness is guaranteed because lower-level pointers cannot affect pointer values of higher-level pointers during the analysis. For example, pointer values of x initialized by assignments of the form x = &y may change by assignments of the form x = y, x = *y, or *p = y (∵ p may point to x) during the analysis. The following table presents pointer levels of involved variables in the assignments that affects pointer values of x.

Assignment	Levels
x = y	$\mathsf{ptl}(\mathtt{x}) = \mathsf{ptl}(\mathtt{y})$
x = *y	$\mathsf{ptl}(\mathtt{y}) = \mathsf{ptl}(\mathtt{x}) + 1$
*p = y	$\mathsf{ptl}(\mathtt{p}) = \mathsf{ptl}(\mathtt{x}) + 1 \wedge \mathsf{ptl}(\mathtt{y}) = \mathsf{ptl}(\mathtt{x})$

Note that all the variables affect pointer values of x have higher or equal pointer level compared to x.

Now we describe the level-by-level analysis in secrecy similarly to the basic scheme. Before beginning, we define the notations $\delta_{i,j}^{(\ell)}$ and $\eta_{i,j}^{(\ell)}$ in $\mathbb{Z}$ for $i, j = 1, \cdots, m$ by

$$\delta_{i,j}^{(\ell)} \neq 0 \quad \text{iff} \quad \text{An edge } \mathtt{x_i} \longrightarrow \&\mathtt{x_j} \text{ is derived and } \mathsf{ptl}(\mathtt{x_i}) = \ell$$

$$\eta_{i,j}^{(\ell)} \neq 0 \quad \text{iff} \quad \text{An edge } \mathtt{x_i} \longrightarrow \mathtt{x_j} \text{ is derived and } \mathsf{ptl}(\mathtt{x_i}) = \ell.$$

Inputs from Client. For the level-by-level analysis, a program owner derives the following numbers that represent his program P (n is the maximal level of pointer in the program):

$$\{(\delta_{i,j}^{(\ell)}, \eta_{i,j}^{(\ell)}) \mid 1 \le i, j \le m, 1 \le \ell \le n\} \cup \{(u_{i,j}, v_{i,j}) \mid 1 \le i, j \le m\}$$

where $\delta_{i,j}^{(\ell)}$ and $\eta_{i,j}^{(\ell)}$ are defined as follows.

$$\delta_{i,j}^{(\ell)} = \begin{cases} 1 \text{ if } \exists \mathtt{x_i} = \&\mathtt{x_j}, \mathsf{ptl}(\mathtt{x_i}) = \ell \\ 0 \text{ o.w.} \end{cases} \qquad \eta_{i,j}^{(\ell)} = \begin{cases} 1 \text{ if } (\exists \mathtt{x_i} = \mathtt{x_j} \text{ or } i = j), \mathsf{ptl}(\mathtt{x_i}) = \ell \\ 0 \text{ o.w.} \end{cases}$$

The definitions of $u_{i,j}$ and $v_{i,j}$ are the same as in the Sect. 3.2. We denote the encryption of $\delta_{i,j}^{(\ell)}$ and $\eta_{i,j}^{(\ell)}$ by $\bar{\delta}_{i,j}^{(\ell)}$, $\bar{\eta}_{i,j}^{(\ell)}$, respectively.

Server's Analysis. Server's analysis begins with propagating pointer values of the maximal level n by applying the Trans rule as much as possible. In other words, for $i, j = 1, \cdots, m$, the server repeats the following update m times:

$$\bar{\delta}_{i,j}^{(n)} \leftarrow \sum_{k=1}^{m} \bar{\eta}_{i,k}^{(n)} \cdot \bar{\delta}_{k,j}^{(n)}$$

Next, from the level $n-1$ down to 1, the analysis at a level ℓ is carried out in the following steps:

1. applying the Load rule: $\bar{\eta}_{i,j}^{(\ell)} \leftarrow \bar{\eta}_{i,j}^{(\ell)} + \sum_{k=1}^{m} \bar{u}_{i,k} \cdot \bar{\delta}_{k,j}^{(\ell+1)}$
2. applying the Store rule: $\bar{\eta}_{i,j}^{(\ell)} \leftarrow \bar{\eta}_{i,j}^{(\ell)} + \sum_{k=1}^{m} \bar{v}_{j,k} \cdot \bar{\delta}_{k,i}^{(\ell+1)}$
3. applying the Trans rule: repeating the following update m times

$$\bar{\delta}_{i,j}^{(\ell)} \leftarrow \sum_{k=1}^{m} \bar{\eta}_{i,k}^{(\ell)} \cdot \bar{\delta}_{k,j}^{(\ell)}$$

Through steps 1 and 2, edges of the form $x_i \longrightarrow x_j$ are derived where either x_i or x_j is determined by pointer values of the immediate higher level $\ell + 1$. In step 3, pointer values of a current level ℓ are propagated as much as possible.

We need $O(n \log m)$ multiplicative depth in total because repeating the above 3 steps n times entails maximally m^n homomorphic multiplications on a single ciphertext.

Output Determination. The client receives the updated $\{\bar{\delta}_{i,j}^{(\ell)} \mid 1 \le i,j \le m, 1 \le \ell \le n\}$ from the server and recovers a set of points-to relations as follows:

$$\{\mathsf{x_i} \longrightarrow \&\mathsf{x_j} \mid \mathsf{HE.Dec_{sk}}(\bar{\delta}_{i,j}^{(\ell)}) \neq 0,\ 1 \le i,j \le m, \text{ and } 1 \le \ell \le n\}$$

4.4 Ciphertext Packing

Our use of ciphertext packing aims to decrease total ciphertext size by using fewer ciphertexts than the basic scheme. Thanks to ciphertext packing, a single ciphertext can hold multiple plaintexts rather than a single value. For given a vector of plaintexts $(\mu_1, \cdots, \mu_m)$, the BGV cryptosystem allows to obtain a ciphertext $\bar{\mathbf{c}} \leftarrow \mathsf{BGV.Enc}(\mu_1, \cdots, \mu_m)$.

Furthermore, as each ciphertext holds a vector of multiple plaintexts, homomorphic operations between such ciphertexts are performed component-wise. For given ciphetexts $\bar{\mathbf{c}}_1 = \mathsf{BGV.Enc}(\mu_{1,1}, \cdots, \mu_{1,m})$ and $\bar{\mathbf{c}}_2 = \mathsf{BGV.Enc}(\mu_{2,1}, \cdots, \mu_{2,m})$, the homomorphic addition and multiplication in the BGV scheme satisfy the following properties:

$$\mathsf{BGV.Add}(\bar{\mathbf{c}}_1, \bar{\mathbf{c}}_2) \text{ returns a ciphertext } \mathsf{BGV.Enc}(\mu_{1,1} + \mu_{2,1}, \cdots, \mu_{1,m} + \mu_{2,m})$$
$$\mathsf{BGV.Mult}(\bar{\mathbf{c}}_1, \bar{\mathbf{c}}_2) \text{ returns a ciphertext } \mathsf{BGV.Enc}(\mu_{1,1} \cdot \mu_{2,1}, \cdots, \mu_{1,m} \cdot \mu_{2,m})$$

The BGV scheme provides other homomorphic operations such as cyclic rotation. For example, we can perform cyclic rotation of vector by any amount on ciphertexts (*e.g.*, $\mathsf{BGV.Enc}(\mu_m, \mu_1, \cdots, \mu_{m-1})$ from $\mathsf{BGV.Enc}(\mu_1, \mu_2, \cdots, \mu_m)$). Using the homomorphic addition, multiplication, and other operations, we can perform the matrix addition, multiplication and transposition operations on encrypted matrices.

In this subsection, we describe ciphertext packing and the homomorphic matrix operations in more detail.

Principle of Ciphertext Packing. We begin with some notations. For an integer q, $\mathbb{Z}_q \stackrel{\text{def}}{=} [-q/2, q/2) \cap \mathbb{Z}$ and $x \bmod q$ denotes a number in $[-q/2, q/2) \cap \mathbb{Z}$ which is equivalent to x modulo q. Recall that the message space of the BGV cryptosystem is $R_p = \mathbb{Z}[X]/(p, \Phi(X))$ for a prime p and an irreducible polynomial $\Phi(X)$. We identify the polynomial ring R_p with $\{a_0 + a_1X + \cdots + a_{\deg \Phi - 1}X^{\deg \Phi - 1} \mid a_i \in \mathbb{Z}_p \text{ and } 0 \le i < \deg \Phi\}$.

In the basic approach, although the message space of the BGV scheme is the polynomial ring R_p, we have used only constant polynomials (*i.e.*, numbers) for plaintexts. Thus, if a vector of plaintexts is represented as a single non-constant polynomial, a single ciphertext can hold multiple plaintexts rather than a single value. Therefore we can save the total memory space by using fewer ciphertexts than the basic scheme. Suppose the factorization of $\Phi(X)$ modulo p is $\Phi(X) = \prod_{i=1}^{m} F_i(X) \bmod p$ where each F_i is an irreducible polynomial in $\mathbb{Z}_p[X]$. Then a polynomial $\mu(X) \in R_p$ can be viewed as a vector of m different small polynomials, $(\mu_1(X), \cdots, \mu_m(X))$ such that $\mu_i(X) = (\mu(X) \text{ modulo } F_i(X))$ for $i = 1, \cdots, m$.

From this observation, we can encrypt a vector $\boldsymbol{\mu} = (\mu_1, \cdots, \mu_m)$ of plaintexts in $\prod_{i=1}^{m} \mathbb{Z}_p$ into a single ciphertext by the following transitions:

$$\begin{array}{ccccccc} \mathbb{Z}_p \times \cdots \times \mathbb{Z}_p & \longrightarrow & \prod_{i=1}^{m} \mathbb{Z}_p[X]/(F_i(X)) & \longrightarrow & \mathbb{Z}_p[X]/(\Phi(X)) & \longrightarrow & R_q \\ (\mu_1, \cdots, \mu_m) & \overset{\mathsf{id}}{\longmapsto} & (\mu_1(X), \cdots, \mu_m(X)) & \overset{\text{CRT}}{\longmapsto} & \mu(X) & \overset{\mathsf{BGV.Enc}}{\longmapsto} & \bar{\mathbf{c}} \end{array}$$

First, we view a component μ_i in a vector $\boldsymbol{\mu} = (\mu_1, \cdots, \mu_m)$ as a contant polynomial $\mu_i \in \mathbb{Z}_p[X]/(F_i(X))$ for $i = 1, \cdots, m$. Then, we can compute the unique polynomial $\mu(X) \in R_p$ satisfying $\mu(X) = \mu_i \bmod (p, F_i(X))$ for $i = 1, \cdots, m$ by the Chinese Remainder Theorem (CRT) of polynomials. Finally, to encrypt a vector $\boldsymbol{\mu} = (\mu_1, \cdots, \mu_m)$ in $\prod_{i=1}^{m} \mathbb{Z}_p$, we encrypt the polynomial $\mu(X) \in R_p$ into a ciphertext $\bar{\mathbf{c}}$ which is denoted by $\mathsf{BGV.Enc}(\mu_1, \cdots, \mu_m)$. For more details to the ciphertext packing, we suggest that readers see the paper [22].

Homomorphic Matrix Operations. Applying the resolution rules in the level-by-level analysis in the Sect. 4.3 can be re-written in a matrix form as shown in Table 3. In Table 3, $\Delta_\ell = [\delta_{i,j}^{(\ell)}]$, $H_\ell = [\eta_{i,j}^{(\ell)}]$, $U = [u_{i,j}]$, and $V = [v_{i,j}]$ are $m \times m$ integer matrices. Let the i-th row of Δ_ℓ and H_ℓ be $\boldsymbol{\delta}_i^{(\ell)}$ and $\boldsymbol{\eta}_i^{(\ell)}$ respectively. And we denote the encryptions as $\bar{\boldsymbol{\delta}}_i^{(\ell)} = \mathsf{BGV.Enc}(\boldsymbol{\delta}_i^{(\ell)})$ and $\bar{\boldsymbol{\eta}}_i^{(\ell)} = \mathsf{BGV.Enc}(\boldsymbol{\eta}_i^{(\ell)})$.

Table 3. Circuit expression of the level-by-level analysis

Rule	Integer form	Matrix form
Trans	$\delta_{i,j}^{(\ell)} \leftarrow \sum_{k=1}^{m} \eta_{i,k}^{(\ell)} \cdot \delta_{k,j}^{(\ell)}$	$\Delta_\ell \leftarrow H_\ell \cdot \Delta_\ell$
Load	$\eta_{i,j}^{(\ell)} \leftarrow \eta_{i,j}^{(\ell)} + \sum_{k=1}^{m} u_{i,k} \cdot \delta_{k,j}^{(\ell+1)}$	$H_\ell \leftarrow H_\ell + U \cdot \Delta_{\ell+1}$
Store	$\eta_{i,j}^{(\ell)} \leftarrow \eta_{i,j}^{(\ell)} + \sum_{k=1}^{m} v_{j,k} \cdot \delta_{k,i}^{(\ell+1)}$	$H_\ell \leftarrow H_\ell + (V \cdot \Delta_{\ell+1})^T$

We follow the methods in [16] to perform multiplication between encrypted matrices. We use the Replicate homomorphic operation supported by the BGV scheme [16]. For a given ciphertext $\bar{\mathbf{c}} = \mathsf{BGV.Enc}(\mu_1, \cdots, \mu_m)$, the operation $\mathsf{Replicate}(\bar{\mathbf{c}}, i)$ generates a ciphertext $\mathsf{BGV.Enc}(\mu_i, \cdots, \mu_i)$ for $i = 1, \cdots, m$. Using the operation, we can generate an encryption of the i-th row of $(H_\ell \cdot \Delta_\ell)$ as follows:

$$\mathsf{BGV.Mult}\left(\mathsf{Replicate}(\bar{\boldsymbol{\eta}}_i^{(\ell)}, 1), \bar{\boldsymbol{\delta}}_1^{(\ell)}\right) + \cdots + \mathsf{BGV.Mult}\left(\mathsf{Replicate}(\bar{\boldsymbol{\eta}}_i^{(\ell)}, m), \bar{\boldsymbol{\delta}}_m^{(\ell)}\right).$$

Note that this method does not affect the asymptotic notation of the multiplicative depth since the operation Replicate entails only a single multiplication.

To compute a transpose of an encrypted matrix, we use the masking and cyclic rotation techniques described in [16]. Algorithms for the homomorphic operations on encrypted matrices are described in Fig. 3 in Appendix A.

4.5 Randomization of Ciphertexts

During the matrix multiplications, components of resulting matrices may become p by coincidence, which is congruent to 0 in $\mathbb{Z}_p$. In this case, incorrect results may happen. We randomize intermediate results to decrease the failure probability.

To multiply the matrices $H_\ell = [\eta_{i,j}^{(\ell)}]$ and $\Delta_\ell = [\delta_{i,j}^{(\ell)}]$, we choose non-zero random elements $\{r_{i,j}\}$ in $\mathbb{Z}_p$ for $i, j = 1, \cdots, m$ and compute $H'_\ell = [r_{i,j} \cdot \eta_{i,j}^{(\ell)}]$. Then, each component of a resulting matrix of the matrix multiplication $(H'_\ell \cdot \Delta_\ell)$ is almost uniformly distributed over $\mathbb{Z}_p$.

Thanks to the randomization, the probability for each component of $H' \cdot \Delta$ of being congruent to zero modulo p is in inverse proportion to p. We may obtain a correct component with the probability of $(1 - \frac{1}{p-1})$. Because we perform in total $n(\lceil \log m \rceil + 3) - 2$ matrix multiplications for the analysis, the probability for a component of being correct is greater than $(1 - \frac{1}{p-1})^{n(\lceil \log m \rceil + 3)}$. For example, in the case where $n = 2, m = 1000$ and $p = 503$, the success probability for a component is about 95 %.

Putting up altogether, we present the final protocol in Fig. 2 in Appendix A.

5 Experimental Result

In this section, we demonstrate the performance of the pointer analysis in secrecy. In our experiment, we use HElib library [16], an implementation of the BGV

Table 4. Experimental Result

Program	LOC	# Var	Enc	Propagation	Edge addition	Total	Depth
toy	10	9	26 s	28 m 49 s	5 m 58 s	35 m 13 s	37
buthead-1.0	46	17	1 m 26 s	5 h 41 m 36 s	56 m 19 s	6 h 39 m 21 s	43
wysihtml-0.13	202	32	2 m 59 s	18 h 11 m 50 s	2 h 59 m 38 s	21 h 14 m 27 s	49
cd-discid-1.1	259	41	3 m 49 s	32 h 22 m 33 s	5 h 22 m 35 s	37 h 48 m 57 s	49

Enc : time for program encryption, **Depth** : the depth required for the analysis
Propagation : time for homomorphic applications of the Trans rule
Edge addition : time for homomorphic applications of the Load and Store rules

cryptosystem. We test on 4 small C example programs including tiny linux packages. The experiment was done on a Linux 3.13 system running on 8 cores of Intel 3.2 GHz box with 24 GB of main memory. Our implementation runs in parallel on 8 cores using shared memory.

Table 4 shows the result. We set the security parameter 72 which is usually considered large enough. It means a ciphertext can be broken in a worst case time proportional to 2^{72}. In all the programs, the maximum pointer level is 2.

Why "Basic" Algorithm? Many optimization techniques to scale the pointer analysis to larger programs [12,13,17,18,20] cannot be applied into our setting without exposing much information of the program. Two key optimizations are the cycle elimination and the difference propagation. But neither method is applicable. The cycle elimination [12,17,18,20] aims to prevent redundant computation of transitive closure by collapsing each cycle's components into a single node. The method cannot be applied into our setting because cycles cannot be detected and collapsed as all the program information and intermediate analysis results are encrypted. The other technique, difference propagation [13,20], only propagates new reachability facts. Also, we cannot consider the technique because analysis server cannot determine which reachability fact is new as intermediate analysis results are encrypted.

6 Discussion

By combining language and cryptographic primitives, we confirm that the homomorphic encryption scheme can unleash the possibility of static analysis of encrypted programs. As a representative example, we show the feasibility of the pointer analysis in secrecy.

Although there is still a long way to go toward practical use, the experimental result is indicative of the viability of our idea. If the performance issue is properly handled in future, this idea can be used in many real-world cases. Besides depending on developments and advances in HE that are constantly being made, clients can help to improve the performance by encrypting only sensitive sub-parts of programs. The other parts are provided in plaintexts. In this case, analysis operations with the mixture of ciphertexts and plaintexts should be devised. This kind of operations are far cheaper than operations between ciphertexts because they lead to smaller noise increases.

A major future direction is adapting other kinds of static analysis operations(*e.g.*, arbitrary $\sqcup$, $\sqsubseteq$, and semantic operations) into HE schemes. For now, we expect other analyses similar to the pointer analysis (such as 0-CFA) will be performed in a similar manner.

Acknowledgment. The authors would like to thank the anonymous reviewers for their valuable comments. The first and third authors were supported by the Engineering Research Center of Excellence Program of Korea Ministry of Science, ICT & Future Planning(MSIP) / National Research Foundation of Korea(NRF) (Grant NRF-2008-0062609), and Samsung Electronics Software R&D Center (No. 0421–20140012). The second and last authors were supported by Samsung Electronics Software R&D Center (No. 0421–20140013).

A Algorithms

Figure 2 describes the protocol. Figure 3 describes the homomorphic matrix operations and necessary sub algorithms.

Main Protocol

Client Input: There are m pointer variables in the client's program with the maximal pointer level n. The sets $\left\{(\delta_{i,j}^{(\ell)}, \eta_{i,j}^{(\ell)}) \mid 1 \le i,j \le m, 1 \le \ell \le n\right\}$ and $\{(u_{i,j}, v_{i,j}) \mid 1 \le i,j \le m\}$ are initialized as described in Section 3.2 and 3.5. For a security parameter λ, the client generates the parameters $(\mathsf{pk}, \mathsf{evk}; \mathsf{sk}) \leftarrow \mathsf{BGV.KG}(1^\lambda)$ of the BGV scheme.

Sub-algorithms: In this protocol, we use the sub-algorithms in Fig. 3.

– **Program Encryption** (Client's work)
1. **for** $\ell = 1$ to n and **for** $i = 1$ to m **do**
2. $\quad\bar{\boldsymbol{\delta}}_i^{(\ell)} \leftarrow \mathsf{BGV.Enc}(\delta_{i,1}^{(\ell)}, \cdots, \delta_{i,m}^{(\ell)})$, $\bar{\boldsymbol{\eta}}_i^{(\ell)} \leftarrow \mathsf{BGV.Enc}(\eta_{i,1}^{(\ell)}, \cdots, \eta_{i,m}^{(\ell)})$
3. $\quad\bar{\boldsymbol{u}}_i \leftarrow \mathsf{BGV.Enc}(u_{i,1}, \cdots, u_{i,m})$, $\bar{\boldsymbol{v}}_i \leftarrow \mathsf{BGV.Enc}(v_{i,1}, \cdots, v_{i,m})$
4. **for** $\ell = 1$ to n **do**
5. $\quad\bar{\Delta}_\ell \leftarrow \left\langle \bar{\boldsymbol{\delta}}_1^{(\ell)} | \cdots | \bar{\boldsymbol{\delta}}_m^{(\ell)} \right\rangle^T$, $\bar{H}_\ell \leftarrow \left\langle \bar{\boldsymbol{\eta}}_1^{(\ell)} | \cdots | \bar{\boldsymbol{\eta}}_m^{(\ell)} \right\rangle^T$ // the i-th row of $\bar{\Delta}_\ell$ is $\bar{\boldsymbol{\delta}}_i^{(\ell)}$.
6. $\bar{U} \leftarrow \langle \bar{\mathbf{u}}_1 | \cdots | \bar{\mathbf{u}}_m \rangle^T$, $\bar{V} \leftarrow \langle \bar{\mathbf{v}}_1 | \cdots | \bar{\mathbf{v}}_m \rangle^T$ // the i-th row of $\bar{U}$ is $\bar{\mathbf{u}}_i$.
7. Client sends the sets $\left\{(\bar{\Delta}_\ell, \bar{H}_\ell) \mid 1 \le \ell \le n\right\}$ and $\left\{(\bar{U}, \bar{V})\right\}$ to server.

– **Analysis in Secrecy** (Server's work)
1. $\bar{\Delta}_n \leftarrow \mathsf{HE.MatMult}\left(\mathsf{HE.MatPower}(\bar{H}_n, m), \bar{\Delta}_n\right)$
2. **for** $\ell = n - 1$ to 1 **do**
3. $\quad\bar{A} \leftarrow \mathsf{HE.MatMult}(\bar{U}, \bar{\Delta}_{\ell+1})$, $\bar{B} \leftarrow \mathsf{HE.MatTrans}\left(\mathsf{HE.MatMult}(\bar{V}, \bar{\Delta}_{\ell+1})\right)$
4. $\quad\bar{H}_\ell \leftarrow \mathsf{HE.MatAdd}\left(\mathsf{HE.MatAdd}(\bar{H}_\ell, \bar{A}), \bar{B}\right)$ // apply Load and Store rules
5. $\quad\bar{\Delta}_\ell \leftarrow \mathsf{HE.MatMult}\left(\mathsf{HE.MatPower}(\bar{H}_\ell, m), \bar{\Delta}_\ell\right)$ // apply Trans rule
6. Server sends the ciphertext set $\left\{\bar{\boldsymbol{\delta}}_i^{(\ell)} \mid 1 \le \ell \le n \text{ and } 1 \le i \le m\right\}$ to client.

– **Output Determination** (Client's work)
1. **for** $i = 1$ to m and **for** $\ell = 1$ to n **do**
2. $\quad$Client computes $(\delta_{i,1}^{(\ell)}, \cdots, \delta_{i,m}^{(\ell)}) \leftarrow \mathsf{BGV.Dec}(\bar{\boldsymbol{\delta}}_i^{(\ell)})$.
3. Client determines the set $\left\{\mathtt{x_i} \longrightarrow \&\mathtt{x_j} \mid \delta_{i,j}^{(\ell)} \neq 0, 1 \le i,j \le m, 1 \le \ell \le n\right\}$.

Fig. 2. The pointer analysis in secrecy

// We assume that m is the same as the number of plaintext slots in the BGV scheme.
// A prime p is the modulus of message space in the BGV-type cryptosystem.
// We denote the encryption of the matrix $A = [a_{i,j}] \in \mathbb{Z}_p^{m \times m}$ by $\bar{A}$.
// The i-th row $\bar{\mathbf{a}}_i$ of $\bar{A}$ is the ciphertext $\mathsf{BGV.Enc}(a_{i,1}, \cdots, a_{i,m})$ for $i = 1, \cdots, m$.
// For ciphertexts $\bar{\mathbf{c}}_1, \cdots, \bar{\mathbf{c}}_m$, we denote the matrix whose rows are $\bar{\mathbf{c}}_i$ by $\langle \bar{\mathbf{c}}_1 | \cdots | \bar{\mathbf{c}}_m \rangle^T$

<u>HE.MatAdd</u>$(\bar{A}, \bar{B})$
// **Input** : $\bar{A}, \bar{B}$ are encryptions of $A = [a_{i,j}], B = [b_{i,j}]$.
// **Output** : $\overline{A+B}$ is an encryption of $A + B = [a_{i,j} + b_{i,j}]$.
for $i = 1$ to m **do** $\quad \bar{\mathbf{z}}_i \leftarrow \mathsf{BGV.Add}(\bar{\mathbf{a}}_i, \bar{\mathbf{b}}_j)$
return $\bar{Z} \leftarrow \langle \bar{\mathbf{z}}_1 | \bar{\mathbf{z}}_2 | \cdots | \bar{\mathbf{z}}_m \rangle^T$ // the i-th row of $\bar{Z}$ is $\bar{\mathbf{z}}_i$

<u>HE.MatMult</u>$(\bar{A}, \bar{B})$
// **Input** : $\bar{A}, \bar{B}$ are encryptions of $A = [a_{i,j}], B = [b_{i,j}]$.
// **Output** : $\overline{R_A \cdot B}$ is an encryption of $R_A \cdot B = [\sum_{k=1}^{m} r_{i,k} \cdot (a_{i,k} b_{k,j})]$,
// where $r_{i,j} \xleftarrow{\$} [-p/2, p/2) \cap \mathbb{Z}$ with $r_{i,j} \neq 0$.
$\bar{R} \leftarrow \mathsf{HE.MatRandomize}(\bar{A})$
for $i = 1$ to m **do** $\quad \bar{\mathbf{z}}_i \leftarrow \sum_{j=1}^{m} \mathsf{BGV.Mult}\,(\mathsf{HE.Replicate}(\bar{\mathbf{r}}_i, j), \bar{\mathbf{b}}_j)$ // ciphertext additions
return $\bar{Z} \leftarrow \langle \bar{\mathbf{z}}_1 | \bar{\mathbf{z}}_2 | \cdots | \bar{\mathbf{z}}_m \rangle^T$ // the i-th row of $\bar{Z}$ is $\bar{\mathbf{z}}_i$

<u>HE.MatPower</u>$(\bar{A}, k)$
// **Input** : $\bar{A}$ is an encryption of A.
// **Output** : $\overline{A^w}$ is an encryption of A^w, where $w = 2^{\lceil \log k \rceil}$.
$\bar{Z} \leftarrow \bar{A}$
for $i = 1$ to $\lceil \log k \rceil$ **do** $\quad \bar{Z} \leftarrow \mathsf{HE.MatrixMult}\,(\bar{Z}, \bar{Z})$
return $\bar{Z}$

<u>HE.MatTrans</u>$(\bar{A})$
// **Input** : $\bar{A}$ is an encryption of $A = [a_{i,j}]$.
// **Output** : $\overline{A^T}$ is an encryption of $A^T = [a_{j,i}]$.
for $i = 1$ to m **do**
  for $j = 1$ to m **do** $\quad \bar{\mathbf{z}}_{i,j} \leftarrow \mathsf{HE.Masking}(\bar{\mathbf{a}}_j, i)$
  $\bar{\mathbf{z}}_i \leftarrow \sum_{j=1}^{i-1} \mathsf{HE.Rotate}(\bar{\mathbf{z}}_{i,j}, j - i + m) + \sum_{j=i}^{m} \mathsf{HE.Rotate}(\bar{\mathbf{z}}_{i,j}, j - i)$ // ciphertext additions
return $\bar{Z} \leftarrow \langle \bar{\mathbf{z}}_1 | \bar{\mathbf{z}}_2 | \cdots | \bar{\mathbf{z}}_m \rangle^T$ // the i-th row of $\bar{Z}$ is $\bar{\mathbf{z}}_i$

<u>HE.MatRandomize</u>$(\bar{A})$
// **Input** : $\bar{A}$ is an encryption of $A = [a_{i,j}]$.
// **Output** : $\overline{R_A}$ is an encryption of $R_A = [r_{i,j} \cdot a_{i,j}]$, where $r_{i,j} \xleftarrow{\$} \mathbb{Z}_p$ with $r_{i,j} \neq 0$.
for $i = 1$ to m **do**
  Choose a vector $\mathbf{r}_i = (r_{i,1}, \cdots, r_{i,m}) \xleftarrow{\$} \mathbb{Z}_p^m$ with $r_{i,j} \neq 0 \bmod p$.
  $\bar{\mathbf{z}}_i \leftarrow \mathsf{BGV.multByConst}(\mathbf{r}_i, \bar{\mathbf{a}}_i)$
return $\bar{Z} \leftarrow \langle \bar{\mathbf{z}}_1 | \bar{\mathbf{z}}_2 | \cdots | \bar{\mathbf{z}}_m \rangle^T$ // the i-th row of $\bar{Z}$ is $\bar{\mathbf{z}}_i$

// The following algorithms are in the library HElib.
// Here, we only give preview of the algorithms.

<u>HE.Replicate</u>$(\bar{\mathbf{c}}, k)$
// The ciphertext $\bar{\mathbf{c}}$ is the encryption of $(\mu_1, \cdots, \mu_m)$
return the ciphertext $\mathsf{BGV.Enc}(\mu_k, \cdots, \mu_k)$

<u>HE.Masking</u>$(\bar{\mathbf{c}}, k)$
// The ciphertext $\bar{\mathbf{c}}$ is the encryption of $(\mu_1, \cdots, \mu_m)$
return the ciphertext $\mathsf{BGV.Enc}(0, \cdots, 0, \mu_k, 0 \cdots, 0)$ // μ_k is the k-th plaintext slot.

<u>HE.Rotate</u>$(\bar{\mathbf{c}}, k)$
// The ciphertext $\bar{\mathbf{c}}$ is the encryption of $(\mu_1, \cdots, \mu_m)$
// This operation is the right rotation as a linear array
return the ciphertext $\mathsf{BGV.Enc}(\mu_{m-k+2}, \cdots, \mu_m, \mu_1, \cdots, \mu_{m-k+1})$

<u>BGV.multByConst</u>$(\mathbf{r}, \bar{\mathbf{c}})$
// The operation of the multiply-by-constant induces "moderate" noise-growth,
// while a multiplication of ciphertexts induces "expensive" noise-growth.
// The constant vector $\mathbf{r} = (r_1, \cdots, r_m) \in \mathbb{Z}_p \times \cdots \times \mathbb{Z}_p$
// The ciphertext $\bar{\mathbf{c}}$ is the encryption of $(\mu_1, \cdots, \mu_m)$
return the ciphertext $\mathsf{BGV.Enc}(r_1\mu_1, \cdots, r_m\mu_m)$

Fig. 3. Pseudocode for the homomorphic matrix operations

References

1. Software clinic service. http://rosaec.snu.ac.kr/clinic
2. Boneh, D., Gentry, C., Halevi, S., Wang, F., Wu, D.J.: Private database queries using somewhat homomorphic encryption. In: Jacobson, M., Locasto, M., Mohassel, P., Safavi-Naini, R. (eds.) ACNS 2013. LNCS, vol. 7954, pp. 102–118. Springer, Heidelberg (2013)
3. Brakerski, Z.: Fully homomorphic encryption without modulus switching from classical gapSVP. In: Safavi-Naini, R., Canetti, R. (eds.) CRYPTO 2012. LNCS, vol. 7417, pp. 868–886. Springer, Heidelberg (2012)
4. Brakerski, Z., Gentry, C., Vaikuntanathan, V.: (Leveled) Fully homomorphic encryption without bootstrapping. In: ITCS (2012)
5. Brakerski, Z., Vaikuntanathan, V.: Efficient fully homomorphic encryption from (standard) LWE. In: FOCS (2011)
6. Chatterjee, A., Kaushal, M., Sengupta, I.: Accelerating sorting of fully homomorphic encrypted data. In: Paul, G., Vaudenay, S. (eds.) INDOCRYPT 2013. LNCS, vol. 8250, pp. 262–273. Springer, Heidelberg (2013)
7. Cheon, J.H., Coron, J.-S., Kim, J., Lee, M.S., Lepoint, T., Tibouchi, M., Yun, A.: Batch fully homomorphic encryption over the integers. In: Johansson, T., Nguyen, P.Q. (eds.) EUROCRYPT 2013. LNCS, vol. 7881, pp. 315–335. Springer, Heidelberg (2013)
8. Cheon, J.H., Kim, M., Lauter, K.: Homomorphic computation of edit distance. In: IACR Cryptology ePrint Archive, 2015:132. WAHC (2015) (to appear)
9. van Dijk, M., Gentry, C., Halevi, S., Vaikuntanathan, V.: Fully homomorphic encryption over the integers. In: Gilbert, H. (ed.) EUROCRYPT 2010. LNCS, vol. 6110, pp. 24–43. Springer, Heidelberg (2010)
10. Coron, J.-S., Naccache, D., Tibouchi, M.: Public key compression and modulus switching for fully homomorphic encryption over the integers. In: Pointcheval, D., Johansson, T. (eds.) EUROCRYPT 2012. LNCS, vol. 7237, pp. 446–464. Springer, Heidelberg (2012)
11. van Dijk, M., Gentry, C., Halevi, S., Vaikuntanathan, V.: Fully homomorphic encryption over the integers. In: Gilbert, H. (ed.) EUROCRYPT 2010. LNCS, vol. 6110, pp. 24–43. Springer, Heidelberg (2010)
12. Fähndrich, M., Foster, J.S., Su, Z., Aiken, A.: Partial online cycle elimination in inclusion constraint graphs. In: PLDI (1998)
13. Fecht, C., Seidl, H.: Propagating differences: an efficient new fixpoint algorithm for distributive constraint systems. Nord. J. Comput. **5**(4), 304–329 (1998)
14. Gentry, C.: A fully homomorphic encryption scheme. Ph.D. thesis, Stanford University (2009). http://crypto.stanford.edu/craig
15. Gentry, C., Halevi, S., Smart, N.P.: Homomorphic evaluation of the AES circuit. In: Safavi-Naini, R., Canetti, R. (eds.) CRYPTO 2012. LNCS, vol. 7417, pp. 850–867. Springer, Heidelberg (2012)
16. Halevi, S., Shoup, V.: Algorithms in HElib. In: Garay, J.A., Gennaro, R. (eds.) CRYPTO 2014, Part I. LNCS, vol. 8616, pp. 554–571. Springer, Heidelberg (2014). http://eprint.iacr.org/
17. Hardekopf, B., Lin, C.: The ant and the grasshopper: fast and accurate pointer analysis for millions of lines of code. In: PLDI (2007)
18. Heintze, N., Tardieu, O.: Ultra-fast aliasing analysis using CLA: a million lines of C code in a second. In: PLDI (2001)

19. Howgrave-Graham, N.: Approximate integer common divisors. In: Silverman, J.H. (ed.) CaLC 2001. LNCS, vol. 2146, pp. 51–66. Springer, Heidelberg (2001)
20. Pearce, D., Kelly, P., Hankin, C.: Online cycle detection and difference propagation for pointer analysis. In: SCAM (2003)
21. Smart, N., Vercauteren, F.: Fully homomorphic SIMD operations. Des. Codes Crypt. **71**(1), 57–81 (2014)
22. Smart, N.P., Vercauteren, F.: Fully homomorphic SIMD operations. In: IACR Cryptology ePrint Archive, 2011:133 (2011)
23. Smart, N.P., Vercauteren, F.: Fully homomorphic encryption with relatively small key and ciphertext sizes. In: Nguyen, P.Q., Pointcheval, D. (eds.) PKC 2010. LNCS, vol. 6056, pp. 420–443. Springer, Heidelberg (2010)

A Binary Decision Tree Abstract Domain Functor

Junjie Chen(✉) and Patrick Cousot

New York University, New York, USA
junjie@cs.nyu.edu

Abstract. We present an abstract domain functor whose elements are binary decision trees. It is parameterized by decision nodes which are a set of boolean tests appearing in the programs and by a numerical or symbolic abstract domain whose elements are the leaves. We first define the branch condition path abstraction which forms the decision nodes of the binary decision trees. It also provides a new prospective on partitioning the trace semantics of programs as well as separating properties in the leaves. We then discuss our binary decision tree abstract domain functor by giving algorithms for inclusion test, meet and join, transfer functions and extrapolation operators. We think the binary decision tree abstract domain functor may provide a flexible way of adjusting the cost/precision ratio in path-dependent static analysis.

1 Introduction

In past decades, abstract interpretation [5] has been widely and successfully applied to the static analysis and verification of programs. Abstract domains, one of the key concepts in abstract interpretation, aim at collecting information about the set of all possible values of the program variables. The biggest advantage of using abstract domains instead of logic predicates is that they are fully automatic and can easily scale up. Intervals [4], octagons [14] and polyhedra [6] are the most commonly used numerical abstract domains. These abstract domains are inferring a conjunction of linear constraints to maintain the information of all possible values of program variables and/or the possible relationships between them. The absence of disjunctions may cause rough approximations and produce much less precise results, gradually leading to false alarms or even worse to the complete failure to prove the desired program property.

Let us consider the following example which is modified from the one in [9]:

Work supported in part by NSF grant CNS-1446511.

S. Blazy and T. Jensen (Eds.): SAS 2015, LNCS 9291, pp. 36–53, 2015.
DOI: 10.1007/978-3-662-48288-9_3

Example 1. A motivating example.

```
x = 0; y = 0;
ˡwhile(y >= 0) {
    if (x <= 50) y++;
    else y--;
    x++;
}
```

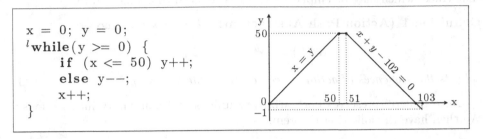

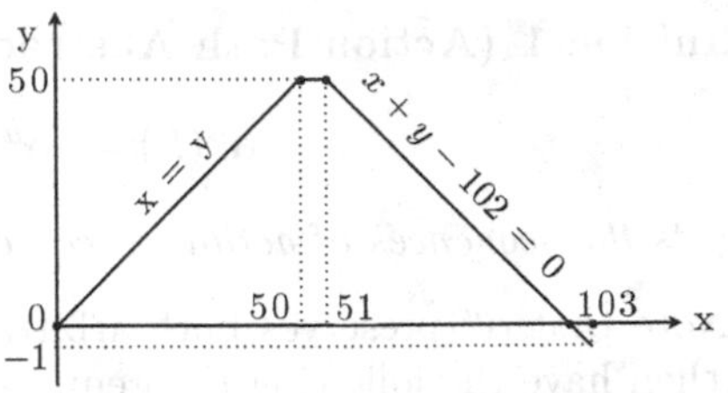

We know that the strongest invariant at program point ^{l} is $(0 <= \mathrm{x} <= 50 \wedge \mathrm{x} = \mathrm{y}) \vee (51 <= \mathrm{x} <= 103 \wedge x + y - 102 = 0)$. When we use the APRON numerical abstract domain library [12] to generate the invariant at program point ^{l}, we get $\mathrm{x} >= 0 \wedge \mathrm{y} >= -1$ with the box (interval) abstract domain and $\mathrm{y} >= -1 \wedge \mathrm{x} - \mathrm{y} >= 0 \wedge \mathrm{x} + 52\mathrm{y} >= 0$ with the polka (convex polyhedra) abstract domain. Both analyses are very imprecise compared to the strongest one. This is because the true and false branches of "if (x <= 50)" have different behaviors and those abstract domains do not consider them separately. □

Hence, we propose the binary decision tree abstract domain that takes those branches into consideration.

2 Action Path Semantics

We consider the following *abstract syntax* of commands which describes the abstract syntax trees (AST) representing the syntactic structure of source code:

$$\mathrm{C} \in \mathbb{C} ::= \mathrm{skip} \mid \mathrm{x} = \mathrm{E} \mid \mathrm{C}_1 ; \mathrm{C}_2 \mid \mathrm{if}\,(\mathrm{B})\;\{\mathrm{C}_1\}\;\mathrm{else}\;\{\mathrm{C}_2\} \mid \mathrm{while}\,(\mathrm{B})\;\{\mathrm{C}\}$$

The *trace semantics* $\mathcal{S}^t[\![\mathrm{C}]\!]$ of a command C describes all possible observations of executions of the command C. A *trace* π of length $|\pi| \triangleq n \geq 1$ is a pair $\pi = \langle \overline{\pi}, \underline{\pi} \rangle$ of a finite sequence $\overline{\pi} = \sigma_0\sigma_1...\sigma_{n-1}$ of states separated by a finite sequence $\underline{\pi} = \mathrm{A}_0\mathrm{A}_1...\mathrm{A}_{n-2}$ of actions. *States* record the current values of variables in the environment/memory as well as a label/control point specifying what remains to be executed while *actions* record which elementary indivisible elementary program steps are computed during the execution of commands. An action A $\in \mathbb{A}$ is either no operation "skip", an assignment "x = E" or a test which output is either true (tt) or false (ff). We use action "B" to record that the Boolean expression B evaluated to true (tt), while action "¬B" records that the Boolean expression B evaluated to false (ff).

The *action path abstraction* $\alpha^a(\mathcal{S})$ collects the set of action paths, that is sequences of actions performed along the traces of a trace semantics $\mathcal{S}$. Given a trace $\pi = \langle \bar{\pi}, \underline{\pi} \rangle$, $\alpha^a(\pi) \triangleq \underline{\pi}$ collects the sequence of actions $\underline{\pi}$ executed along that trace, which may be empty ε for traces reduced to a single state.

Definition 1 (Action Path Abstraction). *Given a set of traces $\mathcal{S}$,*

$$\alpha^a(\mathcal{S}) \triangleq \{\alpha^a(\pi) \mid \pi \in \mathcal{S}\}$$

collects the sequences of actions executed along the traces of $\mathcal{S}$. □

Note that α^a preserves both arbitrary unions and non-empty intersections. We then have the following theorem:

Theorem 1 (Homomorphic Abstraction). *Given a function $h : C \mapsto A$, let $\alpha_h(X) = \{h(x) \mid x \in X\}$ and $\gamma_h(Y) = \{x \mid h(x) \in Y\}$, then α_h and γ_h form a Galois connection:*

$$(\wp(C), \subseteq) \xleftarrow[\alpha_h]{\gamma_h} (\wp(A), \subseteq) \tag{1}$$

Proof. For all $X \in \wp(C)$ and $Y \in \wp(A)$,

$$
\begin{array}{lll}
& \alpha_h(X) \subseteq Y & \\
\Longleftrightarrow & \{h(x) \mid x \in X\} \subseteq Y & \{\text{definition of } \alpha_h\} \\
\Longleftrightarrow & \forall x \in X : h(x) \in Y & \{\text{definition of } \subseteq\} \\
\Longleftrightarrow & X \subseteq \{x \mid h(x) \in Y\} & \{\text{definition of } \subseteq\} \\
\Longleftrightarrow & X \subseteq \gamma_h(Y) & \{\text{definition of } \gamma_h\}
\end{array}
$$

□

Hence, by defining $\gamma^a(\mathcal{A}) \triangleq \{\pi \mid \alpha^a(\pi) \in \mathcal{A}\}$, we will have α^a and γ^a form the Galois connection by Theorem 1 where h is α^a.

A *control flow graph* (CFG) is a directed graph, in which nodes correspond to the actions in the program and the edges represent the possible flow of control. The CFG $\mathsf{G}[\![C]\!]$ of command C can be built by structural induction on the syntax of the command C:

$$\mathsf{G}[\![\text{skip}]\!] \triangleq \circ\!\!-\!\!\boxed{\text{skip}}\!\!-\!\!\circ \qquad \mathsf{G}[\![x := E]\!] \triangleq \circ\!\!-\!\!\boxed{x := E}\!\!-\!\!\circ$$

$$\mathsf{G}[\![C_1; C_2]\!] \triangleq \text{let } \mathsf{G}[\![C_1]\!] = \circ\!\!-\!\!\boxed{C_1}\!\!-\!\!\circ \text{ and } \mathsf{G}[\![C_2]\!] = \circ\!\!-\!\!\boxed{C_2}\!\!-\!\!\circ \text{ in}$$
$$\circ\!\!-\!\!\boxed{C_1}\!\!-\!\!\boxed{C_2}\!\!-\!\!\circ$$

$$\mathsf{G}[\![\text{if } (B) \{C_1\} \text{ else } \{C_2\}]\!] \triangleq \text{let } \mathsf{G}[\![C_1]\!] = \circ\!\!-\!\!\boxed{C_1}\!\!-\!\!\circ \text{ and } \mathsf{G}[\![C_2]\!] = \circ\!\!-\!\!\boxed{C_2}\!\!-\!\!\circ \text{ in}$$

$$\mathsf{G}[\![\text{while } (B) \{C\}]\!] \triangleq \text{let } \mathsf{G}[\![C]\!] = \circ\!\!-\!\!\boxed{C}\!\!-\!\!\circ \text{ in } \circ\!\!-\!\!\boxed{B}\!\!\overset{\text{tt}}{-}\!\!\boxed{C}$$

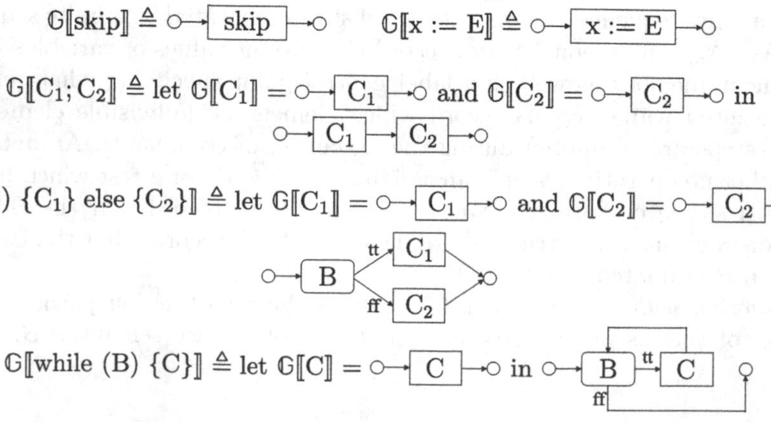

Then the *action path semantics* $\mathcal{G}^a[\![\mathbb{G}[\![C]\!]]\!]$ of CFG $\mathbb{G}[\![C]\!]$ of command C can be defined as:

$$\mathcal{G}^a[\![\circ\!\!\rightarrow\!\boxed{\text{skip}}\!\rightarrow\!\circ]\!] \triangleq \{\text{skip}\} \qquad \mathcal{G}^a[\![\circ\!\!\rightarrow\!\boxed{\text{x} := \text{E}}\!\rightarrow\!\circ]\!] \triangleq \{\text{x} = \text{E}\}$$

$$\mathcal{G}^a[\![\circ\!\!\rightarrow\!\boxed{\text{B}}\!\begin{smallmatrix}\text{tt}\!\boxed{C_1}\\ \text{ff}\!\boxed{C_2}\end{smallmatrix}\!\rightarrow\!\circ]\!] \triangleq \{\text{B}\} \cdot \mathcal{G}^a[\![\circ\!\!\rightarrow\!\boxed{C_1}\!\rightarrow\!\circ]\!] \cup \{\neg\text{B}\} \cdot \mathcal{G}^a[\![\circ\!\!\rightarrow\!\boxed{C_2}\!\rightarrow\!\circ]\!]$$

$$\mathcal{G}^a[\![\circ\!\!\rightarrow\!\boxed{C_1}\!\!\rightarrow\!\boxed{C_2}\!\rightarrow\!\circ]\!] \triangleq \mathcal{G}^a[\![\circ\!\!\rightarrow\!\boxed{C_1}\!\rightarrow\!\circ]\!] \cdot \mathcal{G}^a[\![\circ\!\!\rightarrow\!\boxed{C_2}\!\rightarrow\!\circ]\!]$$

$$\mathcal{F}^a[\![\circ\!\!\rightarrow\!\boxed{\text{B}}\!\!\xrightarrow{\text{tt}}\!\boxed{\text{C}}\!\!\rightarrow\!\circ]\!]X \triangleq \{\varepsilon\} \cup X \cdot \{\text{B}\} \cdot \mathcal{G}^a[\![\circ\!\!\rightarrow\!\boxed{\text{C}}\!\rightarrow\!\circ]\!]$$

$$\mathcal{G}^a[\![\circ\!\!\rightarrow\!\boxed{\text{B}}\!\!\xrightarrow{\text{tt}}\!\boxed{\text{C}}\!\!\rightarrow\!\circ]\!] \triangleq \text{lfp}^{\subseteq}\mathcal{F}^a[\![\circ\!\!\rightarrow\!\boxed{\text{B}}\!\!\xrightarrow{\text{tt}}\!\boxed{\text{C}}\!\!\rightarrow\!\circ]\!] \cdot \{\neg\text{B}\}$$

$$= (\{\text{B}\} \cdot \mathcal{G}^a[\![\circ\!\!\rightarrow\!\boxed{\text{C}}\!\rightarrow\!\circ]\!])^* \cdot \{\neg\text{B}\}$$

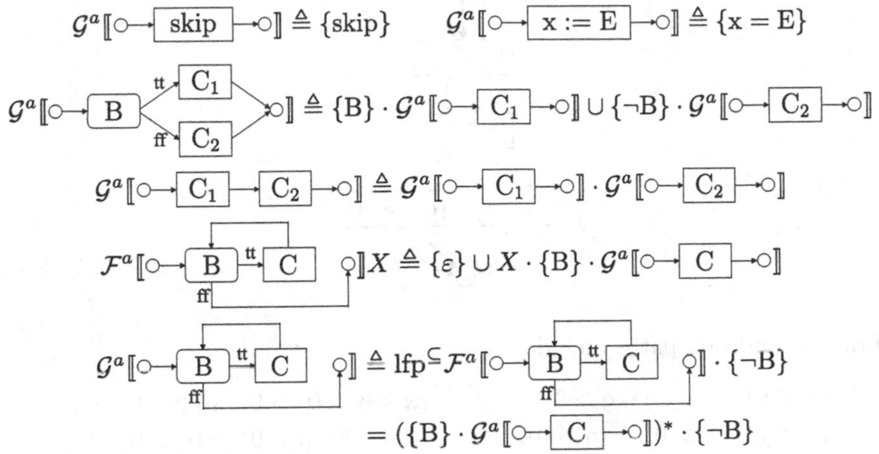

The following Theorem 2 states that the action path semantics of the control flow graph of a program is an over-approximation, hence a sound abstraction, of the action paths that would be collected directly from the trace semantics.

Theorem 2. $\alpha^a(\mathcal{S}^t[\![C]\!]) \subseteq \mathcal{G}^a[\![\mathbb{G}[\![C]\!]]\!]$.

Proof. The proof can be done by the structural induction on the syntax of the command C. More details can be found in the Appendix of [2]. □

3 Branch Condition Path Abstraction

We introduce branch condition graphs $\mathbb{G}^b[\![C]\!]$ of command C which can be viewed as further abstractions of the control flow graphs $\mathbb{G}[\![C]\!]$. We define the branch condition path semantics $\mathcal{G}^b[\![\mathbb{G}^b[\![C]\!]]\!]$ as an abstract interpretation α^b of the action path semantics $\mathcal{G}^a[\![\mathbb{G}[\![C]\!]]\!]$ of the control flow graph $\mathbb{G}[\![C]\!]$ of command C.

3.1 Branch Condition Graph

A *branch condition* is the test B occurring in a command "if (B) $\{C_1\}$ else $\{C_2\}$" while a *loop condition* is the test B occurring in a command "while (B) $\{C\}$". A *branch condition graph* (BCG) of a program is a directed acyclic graph, in which each node corresponds to a branch condition occurring in the program and has two outgoing edges representing its true and false branches. An edge from node A to node B means that the branch condition corresponding to node B occurs after the branch condition corresponding to node A in the program and there are no other branch conditions occurring between them. A trace from the entry point to the exit point of a BCG is called *branch condition path*. We use B to denote the true branch while ¬B denotes the false branch.

Example 2. Consider the following branch condition graph:

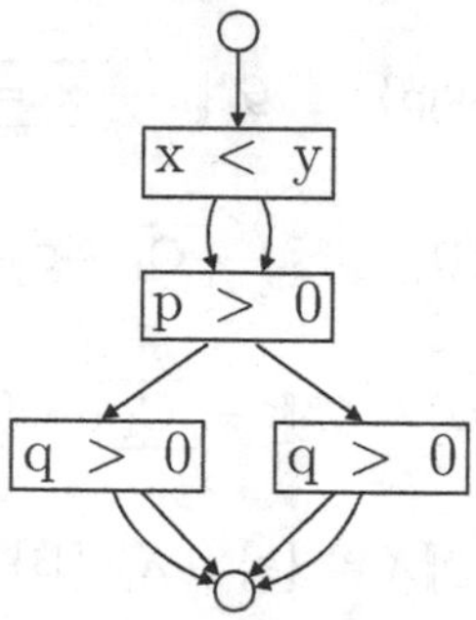

Its branch condition paths include:

$$(x < y) \cdot (p > 0) \cdot (q > 0), \qquad \neg(x < y) \cdot (p > 0) \cdot (q > 0),$$
$$(x < y) \cdot (p > 0) \cdot \neg(q > 0), \qquad \neg(x < y) \cdot (p > 0) \cdot \neg(q > 0),$$
$$(x < y) \cdot \neg(p > 0) \cdot (q > 0), \qquad \neg(x < y) \cdot \neg(p > 0) \cdot (q > 0),$$
$$(x < y) \cdot \neg(p > 0) \cdot \neg(q > 0), \qquad \neg(x < y) \cdot \neg(p > 0) \cdot \neg(q > 0).$$

□

The branch condition graph $\mathbb{G}^b[\![C]\!]$, like the CFG, can be defined by structural induction on the syntax of the command C:

$$\mathbb{G}^b[\![\text{skip}]\!] \triangleq \circ\!\!-\!\!\!-\!\!\!\circ \qquad \mathbb{G}^b[\![x := E]\!] \triangleq \circ\!\!-\!\!\!-\!\!\!\circ$$

$$\mathbb{G}^b[\![C_1; C_2]\!] \triangleq \text{let } \mathbb{G}^b[\![C_1]\!] = \circ\!\!-\!\!\boxed{C_1^b}\!\!-\!\!\circ \text{ and } \mathbb{G}^b[\![C_2]\!] = \circ\!\!-\!\!\boxed{C_2^b}\!\!-\!\!\circ \text{ in}$$
$$\circ\!\!-\!\!\boxed{C_1^b}\!\!-\!\!\boxed{C_2^b}\!\!-\!\!\circ$$

$$\mathbb{G}^b[\![\text{if } (B) \{C_1\} \text{ else } \{C_2\}]\!] \triangleq \text{let } \mathbb{G}^b[\![C_1]\!] = \circ\!\!-\!\!\boxed{C_1^b}\!\!-\!\!\circ \text{ and } \mathbb{G}^b[\![C_2]\!] = \circ\!\!-\!\!\boxed{C_2^b}\!\!-\!\!\circ$$

$$\text{in } \circ\!\!-\!\!\boxed{B} \overset{\text{tt}}{\underset{\text{ff}}{\diagdown}} \begin{matrix} \boxed{C_1^b} \\ \boxed{C_2^b} \end{matrix} \diagup\!\!\circ$$

$$\mathbb{G}^b[\![\text{while } (B) \{C\}]\!] \triangleq \text{let } \mathbb{G}^b[\![C]\!] = \circ\!\!-\!\!\boxed{C^b}\!\!-\!\!\circ \text{ in } \circ\!\!-\!\!\boxed{C^b}\!\!-\!\!\circ$$

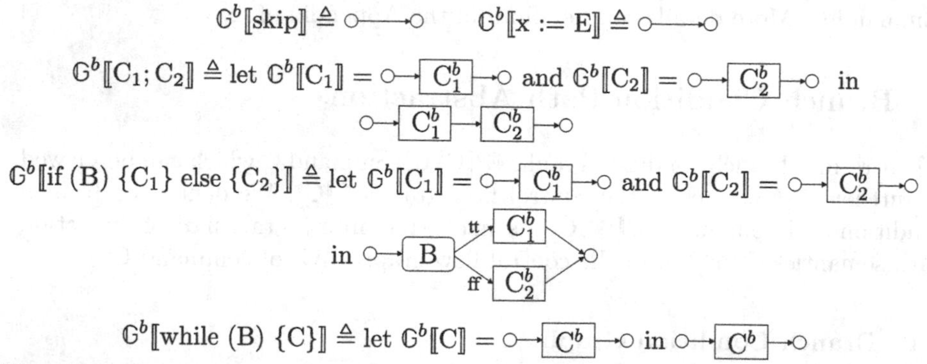

Note that the concatenation of $\circ\!\!-\!\!\!-\!\!\!\circ$ and $\circ\!\!-\!\!\!-\!\!\!\circ$ is still $\circ\!\!-\!\!\!-\!\!\!\circ$

3.2   Branch Condition Path Abstraction

We abstract finite action paths $A_1 \cdot A_2 \cdot \ldots \cdot A_n, n \geq 0$ by the finite branch condition path $A_1^b \cdot A_2^b \cdot \ldots \cdot A_m^b, m \leq n$ where $A_1^b = A_p, A_2^b = A_q, \ldots, A_m^b = A_r, 1 \leq p < q < \ldots < r \leq n$ are distinct branch conditions. The branch condition path is empty ε when there are no branch conditions occurred in the action path. We say that two branch conditions A_1^b, A_2^b are equal if and only if A_1^b and A_2^b occur at the same program point. Moreover, each branch condition in the branch condition

path must be the last occurrence in the action path being abstracted, that is, if A_i^b is a branch condition in the branch condition path $A_1^b \cdot A_2^b \cdot \ldots \cdot A_m^b$ abstracting the action path $A_1 \cdot A_2 \cdot \ldots \cdot A_n$ where $A_i^b = A_j$, then $\forall k : j < k \leq n, A_i^b \neq A_k$. Note that we only consider finite action paths hence safety properties.

Condition Path Abstraction. The condition path abstraction collects the set of finite sequences of conditions performed along the action path $\underline{\pi}$ and ignores any skip and assignment in $\underline{\pi}$. Given an action path $\underline{\pi}$, $\alpha^c(\underline{\pi})$ collects the sequence of conditions in the action path, which may be empty ε when there are no conditions occurred in the action path, by the following induction rules:

$$\alpha^c(\text{skip}) \triangleq \varepsilon \qquad \alpha^c(\text{B}) \triangleq \text{B}$$
$$\alpha^c(\text{x} = \text{E}) \triangleq \varepsilon \qquad \alpha^c(\neg\text{B}) \triangleq \neg\text{B}$$
$$\alpha^c(\underline{\pi}_1 \cdot \underline{\pi}_2) \triangleq \alpha^c(\underline{\pi}_1) \cdot \alpha^c(\underline{\pi}_2)$$

Note that $\varepsilon \cdot \underline{\pi_c} = \underline{\pi_c} \cdot \varepsilon = \underline{\pi_c}$. Let $\mathbb{A}^C$ be the set of conditions and $(\mathbb{A}^C)^*$ be the set of finite, possible empty, condition paths. Given a set of action paths $\mathcal{A}$, $\alpha^c(\mathcal{A})$ collects the sequences of conditions in the action paths $\mathcal{A}$:

$$\alpha^c \in \wp(\mathbb{A}^*) \mapsto \wp((\mathbb{A}^C)^*)$$
$$\alpha^c(\mathcal{A}) \triangleq \{\alpha^c(\underline{\pi}) \mid \underline{\pi} \in \mathcal{A}\}$$

It follows that α^c preserves arbitrary unions and non-empty intersections. By defining $\gamma^c(\mathcal{C}) \triangleq \{\underline{\pi} \mid \alpha^c(\underline{\pi}) \in \mathcal{C}\}$, we will have:

Corollary 1.

$$(\wp(\mathbb{A}^*), \subseteq) \underset{\alpha^c}{\overset{\gamma^c}{\leftrightarrows}} (\wp((\mathbb{A}^C)^*), \subseteq) \tag{2}$$

Proof. By Theorem 1 where h is α^c. □

Loop Condition Elimination. Given a finite condition path $\underline{\pi_c}$, $\alpha^d(\underline{\pi_c})$ collects the finite sequence of branch conditions (with duplications) by eliminating all loop conditions in $\underline{\pi_c}$. This sequence may be empty ε when there are no branch conditions occurred in $\underline{\pi_c}$. Let $\mathbb{A}^B$ be the set of branch conditions and $\mathbb{A}^L$ be the set of loop conditions, thus $\mathbb{A}^C \triangleq \mathbb{A}^B \cup \mathbb{A}^L$ and $\mathbb{A}^B \cap \mathbb{A}^L = \emptyset$. Note that we distinguish those conditions by the program points where they occur, not by themselves.

For all $\text{A}^b \in \mathbb{A}^B$ and $\text{A}^l \in \mathbb{A}^L$, we have

$$\alpha^d(\text{A}^b) \triangleq \text{A}^b \quad \text{and} \quad \alpha^d(\text{A}^l) \triangleq \varepsilon. \tag{3}$$

Then given two condition paths $\underline{\pi_{c_1}}$ and $\underline{\pi_{c_2}}$, we have

$$\alpha^d(\underline{\pi_{c_1}} \cdot \underline{\pi_{c_2}}) \triangleq \alpha^d(\underline{\pi_{c_1}}) \cdot \alpha^d(\underline{\pi_{c_2}}). \tag{4}$$

Note that $\varepsilon \cdot \underline{\pi_d} = \underline{\pi_d} \cdot \varepsilon = \underline{\pi_d}$. Let $(\mathbb{A}^B)^*$ be the set of finite, possible empty, sequences of branch conditions. Given a set of condition paths $\mathcal{C}$, $\alpha^d(\mathcal{C})$ collects the sequences of branch conditions (with duplications) from the condition paths $\mathcal{C}$:

$$\alpha^d \in \wp((\mathbb{A}^C)^*) \mapsto \wp((\mathbb{A}^B)^*)$$
$$\alpha^d(\mathcal{C}) \triangleq \{\alpha^d(\underline{\pi_c}) \mid \underline{\pi_c} \in \mathcal{C}\}$$

It's easy to see that α^d preserves both arbitrary unions and non-empty intersections. By defining $\gamma^d(\mathcal{D}) \triangleq \{\underline{\pi_c} \mid \alpha^d(\underline{\pi_c}) \in \mathcal{D}\}$, we will have:

Corollary 2.

$$(\wp((\mathbb{A}^C)^*), \subseteq) \underset{\alpha^d}{\overset{\gamma^d}{\leftrightarrows}} (\wp((\mathbb{A}^B)^*), \subseteq) \tag{5}$$

Proof. By Theorem 1 where h is α^d. □

Duplication Elimination. The branch condition paths are the sequences of branch conditions without duplications. In this part, we introduce the abstraction function that eliminates duplications in any sequence of branch conditions.

We first define two functions that are used in the abstraction function α^ℓ. Given a sequence *seq* and an element d of *seq*, $erase(seq, d)$ eliminates all elements in *seq* that is equal to d:

$$\begin{aligned} erase(d_1 d_2 d_3 ... d_n, d) \triangleq \text{ if } d_1 = d \text{ then } & erase(d_2 d_3 ... d_n, d) \\ \text{else } & d_1 \cdot erase(d_2 d_3 ... d_n, d) \end{aligned} \tag{6}$$

Note that $erase(seq, d)$ may return the empty sequence ε. Then $fold(seq)$ eliminates the duplications of each element in *seq* starting from the last element:

$$\begin{aligned} fold(d_1 d_2 ... d_n) \triangleq \text{ if } d_1 d_2 ... d_n = \varepsilon & \text{ then } \varepsilon \\ & \text{else } fold(erase(d_1 d_2 ... d_{n-1}, d_n)) \cdot d_n \end{aligned} \tag{7}$$

Hence, given a sequence of branch conditions $\underline{\pi_d}$, $\alpha^\ell(\underline{\pi_d}) = fold(\underline{\pi_d})$ eliminates duplications of each branch condition while keeping its last occurrence in $\underline{\pi_d}$. Let $\mathbb{D}$ be the set of sequences of branch conditions that have duplications. Given a set of sequences of branch conditions $\mathcal{D}$, $\alpha^\ell(\mathcal{D})$ collects branch condition paths (sequences of branch conditions without duplications):

$$\alpha^\ell \in \wp((\mathbb{A}^B)^*) \mapsto \wp((\mathbb{A}^B)^* \setminus \mathbb{D})$$
$$\alpha^\ell(\mathcal{D}) \triangleq \{\alpha^\ell(\underline{\pi_d}) \mid \underline{\pi_d} \in \mathcal{D}\}$$

Similarly, we have α^ℓ preserves both arbitrary unions and non-empty intersections. By defining $\gamma^\ell(\mathcal{B}) \triangleq \{\underline{\pi_d} \mid \alpha^\ell(\underline{\pi_d}) \in \mathcal{B}\}$, we will have:

Corollary 3.

$$(\wp((\mathbb{A}^B)^*), \subseteq) \underset{\alpha^\ell}{\overset{\gamma^\ell}{\leftrightarrows}} (\wp((\mathbb{A}^B)^* \setminus \mathbb{D}), \subseteq) \tag{8}$$

Proof. By Theorem 1 where h is α^ℓ. □

Branch Condition Path Abstraction. The branch condition path abstraction $\alpha^b[\![\mathcal{A}]\!]$ collects the branch condition paths, which is the set of sequences of branch conditions with no duplications along the action paths in $\mathcal{A}$. It can be defined by the composition of $\alpha^c, \alpha^d, \alpha^\ell$ defined in the previous sections as:

$$\alpha^b \in \wp(\mathbb{A}^*) \mapsto \wp((\mathbb{A}^B)^* \setminus \mathbb{D})$$
$$\alpha^b(\mathcal{A}) \triangleq \alpha^\ell \circ \alpha^d \circ \alpha^c(\mathcal{A})$$

Respectively, the concretization function $\gamma^b(\mathcal{B})$ can be defined by the composition of $\gamma^c, \gamma^d, \gamma^\ell$ as:

$$\gamma^b \in \wp((\mathbb{A}^B)^* \setminus \mathbb{D}) \mapsto \wp(\mathbb{A}^*)$$
$$\gamma^b(\mathcal{B}) \triangleq \gamma^c \circ \gamma^d \circ \gamma^\ell(\mathcal{B})$$

It follows that α^b and γ^b form a Galois connection:

$$(\wp(\mathbb{A}^*), \subseteq) \underset{\alpha^b}{\overset{\gamma^b}{\leftrightarrows}} (\wp((\mathbb{A}^B)^* \setminus \mathbb{D}), \subseteq) \tag{9}$$

Proof. The composition of Galois connections is still a Galois connection. □

Example 3. In Example 1, let $\mathcal{A}$ be all possible action path semantics of its CFG, then $\alpha^b(\mathcal{A}) = \{x \leq 50, \neg(x \leq 50)\}$.

4 Binary Decision Tree Abstract Domain Functor

We introduce the binary decision tree abstract domain functor to represent and manipulate invariants in the form of binary decision trees. The abstract property will be represented by the disjunction of leaves which are separated by the values of binary decisions, i.e., boolean tests, which will be organized in the decision nodes of the binary decision trees.

4.1 Definition

Given the trace semantics $\mathcal{S}^t[\![\mathrm{P}]\!]$ of a program P, $\alpha^b \circ \alpha^a(\mathcal{S}^t[\![\mathrm{P}]\!])$ abstracts $\mathcal{S}^t[\![\mathrm{P}]\!]$ into a finite set $\mathcal{B}$ of branch condition paths where $\mathcal{B} = \{\underline{\pi_{b_1}}, ..., \underline{\pi_{b_N}}\}$. Then for $\underline{\pi_{b_i}} \in \mathcal{B}$, we have $\gamma^a \circ \gamma^b(\underline{\pi_{b_i}}) \cap \mathcal{S}^t[\![\mathrm{P}]\!] \subseteq \mathcal{S}^t[\![\mathrm{P}]\!]$ and $\bigcup_{i \leq N}(\gamma^a \circ \gamma^b(\underline{\pi_{b_i}}) \cap \mathcal{S}^t[\![\mathrm{P}]\!]) = \mathcal{S}^t[\![\mathrm{P}]\!]$. Moreover, for all distinct pairs $(\underline{\pi_{b_1}}, \underline{\pi_{b_2}}) \in \mathcal{B} \times \mathcal{B}$, we have $(\gamma^a \circ \gamma^b(\underline{\pi_{b_1}}) \cap \mathcal{S}^t[\![\mathrm{P}]\!]) \cap (\gamma^a \circ \gamma^b(\underline{\pi_{b_2}}) \cap \mathcal{S}^t[\![\mathrm{P}]\!]) = \emptyset$. Each branch condition path $\underline{\pi_{b_i}}$ defines a subset of the trace semantics $\mathcal{S}^t[\![\mathrm{P}]\!]$ of a program P. If we can generate the invariants for each program point only using the information of one subset of the trace semantics, then for each program point, we will get a finite set of invariants. It follows that the disjunction of such set of invariants forms the invariant of that program point. Hence, we encapsulate the set of branch condition paths into the decision nodes of a binary decision tree where each top-down path (without leaf) of the binary decision tree represents a branch condition path, and store in each leaf nodes the invariant generated from the information of the subset of the trace semantics defined by the corresponding branch condition path.

We denote the binary decision tree in the parenthesized form

$$[\![\mathrm{B}_1 : [\![\mathrm{B}_2 : (\!| P_1 |\!), (\!| P_2 |\!)]\!], [\![\mathrm{B}_3 : (\!| P_3 |\!), (\!| P_4 |\!)]\!]]\!]$$

where $\mathrm{B}_1, \mathrm{B}_2, \mathrm{B}_3$ are decisions (branch conditions) and P_1, P_2, P_3, P_4 are invariants. It encodes the fact that either if B_1 and B_2 are both true then P_1 holds, or if B_1 is true and B_2 is false then P_2 holds, or if B_1 is false and B_3 is true then P_3 holds, or if B_1 and B_3 are both false then P_4 holds. The parenthesized representation of binary trees uses $(\!| \ldots |\!)$ for leaves and $[\![\mathrm{B} : t_l, t_r]\!]$ for the decision B and t_l (resp. t_r) represents its left subtree (resp. right subtree). In first order logic, the above binary decision tree would be be written as $(\mathrm{B}_1 \wedge \mathrm{B}_2 \wedge P_1) \vee (\mathrm{B}_1 \wedge \neg\mathrm{B}_2 \wedge P_2) \vee (\neg\mathrm{B}_1 \wedge \mathrm{B}_3 \wedge P_3) \vee (\neg\mathrm{B}_1 \wedge \neg\mathrm{B}_3 \wedge P_4)$ with an implicit universal quantification over free variables.

Let $D(\mathcal{B})$ denote the set of all branch conditions appearing in $\mathcal{B}$. Let $\beta =$ B or $\neg$B and $\mathcal{B}_{\backslash\beta}$ denote the removal of β and all branch conditions appearing before in each branch condition path in $\mathcal{B}$, then we define the binary decision tree as:

Definition 2. *A binary decision tree $t \in \mathbb{T}(\mathcal{B}, \mathbb{D}_\ell)$ over the set $\mathcal{B}$ of branch condition paths (with concretization $\gamma^a \circ \gamma^b$) and the leaf abstract domain $\mathbb{D}_\ell$ (with concretization γ_ℓ) is either $(\!| p |\!)$ with p is an element of $\mathbb{D}_\ell$ and $\mathcal{B}$ is empty or $[\![B : t_t, t_f]\!]$ where $B \in D(\mathcal{B})$ is the first element of all branch condition paths $\underline{\pi_b} \in \mathcal{B}$ and (t_t, t_f) are the left and right subtree of t represent its true and false branch such that $t_t, t_f \in \mathbb{T}(\mathcal{B}_{\backslash\beta}, \mathbb{D}_\ell)$.* □

Example 4. In Example 1, the binary decision tree at program point ^{l} will be $t = [\![\mathrm{x} \leq 50 : (\!| 0 \leq \mathrm{x} \leq 50 \wedge \mathrm{x} = \mathrm{y} |\!), (\!| 51 \leq \mathrm{x} \leq 103 \wedge \mathrm{x} + \mathrm{y} - 102 = 0 |\!)]\!]$.

Let ρ be the concrete environment assigning concrete values $\rho(x)$ to variables x and $[\![e]\!]\rho$ for the concrete value of the expression e in the concrete environment ρ, we can then define the concretization of the binary decision tree as

Definition 3. *The concretization of a binary decesion tree γ_t is either*

$$\gamma_t((\!| p |\!)) \triangleq \gamma_\ell(p)$$

when the binary decision tree is reduced to a leaf or

$$\gamma_t([\![B : t_t, t_f]\!]) \triangleq \{\rho \mid [\![B]\!]\rho = \mathit{true} \Longrightarrow \rho \in \gamma_t(t_t) \wedge [\![B]\!]\rho = \mathit{false} \Longrightarrow \rho \in \gamma_t(t_f)\}$$

when the binary decision tree is rooted at a decision node. □

Given $t_1, t_2 \in \mathbb{T}(\mathcal{B}, \mathbb{D}_\ell)$, we say that $t_1 \equiv_t t_2$ if and only if $\gamma_t(t_1) = \gamma_t(t_2)$. Let $\mathbb{T}(\mathcal{B}, \mathbb{D}_\ell)\backslash_{\equiv_t}$ be the quotient by the equivalence relation $\equiv_t$. The binary decision tree abstract domain functor is defined as:

Definition 4. *A binary decision tree abstract domain functor is a tuple*

$$\langle \mathbb{T}(\mathcal{B}, \mathbb{D}_\ell)\backslash_{\equiv_t}, \sqsubseteq_t, \bot_t, \top_t, \sqcup_t, \sqcap_t, \nabla_t, \Delta_t \rangle$$

on two parameters, a set $\mathcal{B}$ of branch condition paths and a leaf abstract domain $\mathbb{D}_\ell$ where ($\mathbb{T}$ is short for $\mathbb{T}(\mathcal{B}, \mathbb{D}_\ell)\backslash_{\equiv_t}$)

$$\begin{array}{rll}
P, Q, \ldots \in \mathbb{T} & \textit{abstract properties} & \\
\sqsubseteq_t \in \mathbb{T} \times \mathbb{T} \to \{\textit{false}, \textit{true}\} & \textit{abstract partial order} & \\
\bot_t, \top_t \in \mathbb{T} & \textit{infimum, supremum} & \\
 & (\forall P \in \mathbb{T} : \bot_t \sqsubseteq_t P \sqsubseteq_t \top_t) & (10) \\
\sqcup_t, \sqcap_t \in \mathbb{T} \times \mathbb{T} \to \mathbb{T} & \textit{abstract join, meet} & \\
\nabla_t, \Delta_t \in \mathbb{T} \times \mathbb{T} \to \mathbb{T} & \textit{abstract widening, narrowing} &
\end{array}$$

□

The set $\mathcal{B}$ of branch condition paths can be constructed from the CFG of the program. It can be done either in the pre-analysis or on the fly during the analysis. The static analyzer designer should allow to change the maximal length of branch condition paths in $\mathcal{B}$ so as to be able to adjust the cost/precision ratio of the analysis. The leaf abstract domain $\mathbb{D}_\ell$ for the leaves could be any numerical or symbolic abstract domains such as intervals, octagons and polyhedra, array domains, etc., or even the reduced product of two or more abstract domains. A list of available abstract domains that can be used at the leaves would be another option of the static analyzer designer. We can use any of these options to build a particular instance of the binary decision tree abstract functor. The advantage of this modular approach is that we can change those options to adjust the cost/precision ratio without having to change the structure of the analyzer.

4.2 Binary Operations

Inclusion and Equality. Given two binary decision tree $t_1, t_2 \in \mathbb{T}(\mathcal{B}, \mathbb{D}_\ell) \setminus \{\bot_t, \top_t\}$, we can check $t_1 \sqsubseteq_t t_2$ by comparing each pair (ℓ_1, ℓ_2) of leaves in (t_1, t_2) where ℓ_1 and ℓ_2 are defined by the same branch condition path $\underline{\pi_b} \in \mathcal{B}$. If each pair (ℓ_1, ℓ_2) satisfies $\ell_1 \sqsubseteq_\ell \ell_2$, we can conclude that $t_1 \sqsubseteq_t t_2$; otherwise, we have $t_1 \not\sqsubseteq_t t_2$.

```
include(t1, t2 : binary decision trees)
{
    if (t1 == (|l1|) && t2 == (|l2|)) then return t1 ⊑ℓ t2;

    let t1 = [[B: t1l, t1r]] and t2 = [[B: t2l, t2r]];
    return include(t1l, t2l) & include(t1r, t2r);
}
```

Example 5. We have $[\![x \leq 50 : (\!| x = 0 \wedge y = 0 |\!), (\!| \bot_\ell |\!)]\!] \sqsubseteq [\![x \leq 50 : (\!| 0 \leq x \leq 1 \wedge x = y |\!), (\!| \bot_\ell |\!)]\!]$ and $[\![x \leq 50 : (\!| x = 0 \wedge y = 0 |\!), (\!| \bot_\ell |\!)]\!] \not\sqsubseteq [\![x \leq 50 : (\!| x = 1 \wedge y = 1 |\!), (\!| \bot_\ell |\!)]\!]$.

The equality of t_1 and t_2 can be tested by the fact $t_1 =_t t_2 \triangleq t_1 \sqsubseteq_t t_2 \wedge t_2 \sqsubseteq_t t_1$. When the leaf abstract domain $\mathbb{D}_\ell$ has $=_\ell$, we can also check the equality for each pair (ℓ_1, ℓ_2) of leaves in (t_1, t_2) where ℓ_1 and ℓ_2 are defined by the same branch condition path $\underline{\pi_b} \in \mathcal{B}$.

Meet and Join. Given two binary decision tree $t_1, t_2 \in \mathbb{T}(\mathcal{B}, \mathbb{D}_\ell)$, the meet $t = t_1 \sqcap_t t_2$ can be computed using the meet $\sqcap_\ell$ in the leaf abstract domain $\mathbb{D}_\ell$. Let ℓ_1, ℓ_2 are leaves of t_1, t_2 respectively, where the same branch condition path $\underline{\pi_b} \in \mathcal{B}$ leads to ℓ_1 and ℓ_2, then $\ell = \ell_1 \sqcap_\ell \ell_2$ is the leaf of t led by the same branch condition path $\underline{\pi_b} \in \mathcal{B}$. After computing each leaf $\ell = \ell_1 \sqcap_\ell \ell_2$ in t, we then get $t = t_1 \sqcap_t t_2$.

```
meet(t1, t2 : binary decision trees)
{
    if (t1 == (|l1|) && t2 == (|l2|)) then return t1 ⊓ℓ t2;

    let t1 = [[B: t1l, t1r]] and t2 = [[B: t2l, t2r]];
    return [[B: meet(t1l, t2l), meet(t1r, t2r)]];
}
```

Similar to the meet, we can compute the join $t = t_1 \sqcup_t t_2$ using the join $\sqcup_\ell$ in the leaf abstract domain $\mathbb{D}_\ell$. But instead of computing the join $\ell_1 \sqcup_\ell \ell_2$ for each pair (ℓ_1, ℓ_2) of leaves in (t_1, t_2) where ℓ_1 and ℓ_2 are led by the same branch condition path $\underline{\pi_b} \in \mathcal{B}$, we also use the branch conditions in $\underline{\pi_b}$ as bound to prevent precision loss. Let $\underline{\pi_b} = \beta_1 \cdot \beta_2 \cdot ... \cdot \beta_n$ where $\beta_i = \mathrm{B}_i$ or $\neg \mathrm{B}_i, i = 1, ..., n$, we have $\ell = (\ell_1 \sqcup_\ell \ell_2) \sqcap_\ell \mathbb{D}_\ell(\beta_1) \sqcap_\ell \mathbb{D}_\ell(\beta_2) \sqcap_\ell ... \sqcap_\ell \mathbb{D}_\ell(\beta_n)$ ($\mathbb{D}_\ell(\beta)$ means the representation of β in $\mathbb{D}_\ell$, when α_ℓ exists in the leaf abstract domain $\mathbb{D}_\ell$, we can use $\alpha_\ell(\beta)$ instead).

```
join(t1, t2 : binary decision trees, bound = ⊤)
{
    if (t1 == (|l1|) && t2 == (|l2|)) then return (t1 ⊔ℓ t2) ⊓ℓ bound;

    let t1 = [[B: t1l, t1r]] and t2 = [[B: t2l, t2r]];
    return [[B: join(t1l, t2l, bound ⊓ℓ Dℓ(B)),
          join(t1r, t2r, bound ⊓ℓ Dℓ(¬B))]];
}
```

Example 6. Let $t_1 = [\![\mathrm{x} \leq 50 : (\!| \mathrm{x} = 0 \wedge \mathrm{y} = 0 |\!), (\!| \bot_\ell |\!)]\!], t_2 = [\![\mathrm{x} \leq 50 : (\!| \mathrm{x} = 1 \wedge \mathrm{y} = 1 |\!), (\!| \bot_\ell |\!)]\!], t_3 = [\![\mathrm{x} \leq 50 : (\!| 0 \leq \mathrm{x} \leq 1 \wedge \mathrm{x} = \mathrm{y} |\!), (\!| \bot_\ell |\!)]\!]$, we have $t_1 \sqcap_t t_2 = \bot_t, t_1 \sqcap_t t_3 = t_1$ and $t_1 \sqcup_t t_2 = t_3, t_2 \sqcap_t t_3 = t_3$.

4.3 Transfer Functions

We define transfer functions for both tests and assignments. The tests either occur in a loop head or occur in the branch. Hence, we define both loop test transfer function and branch test abstract function for the binary decision tree abstract domain.

Loop Test Transfer Function. The transfer function for the loop tests is simple. Given a binary decision tree $t \in \mathbb{T}(\mathcal{B}, \mathbb{D}_\ell)$ and a loop test B, we first define $t \sqcap_t \mathrm{B}$ as:

$$\begin{aligned}
\bot_t \sqcap_t \mathrm{B} &\triangleq \bot_t \\
\top_t \sqcap_t \mathrm{B} &\triangleq (\!| \mathrm{B} |\!) \\
t \sqcap_t \textit{false} &\triangleq \bot_t \\
t \sqcap_t \textit{true} &\triangleq t \\
(\!| p |\!) \sqcap_t \mathrm{B} &\triangleq (\!| p \sqcap_\ell \mathbb{D}_\ell(\mathrm{B}) |\!) \\
[\![\mathrm{B}' : t_l, t_r]\!] \sqcap_t \mathrm{B} &\triangleq [\![\mathrm{B}' : t_l \sqcap_t \mathbb{D}_\ell(\mathrm{B}' \cap \mathrm{B}), t_r \sqcap_t \mathbb{D}_\ell(\neg \mathrm{B}' \cap \mathrm{B})]\!]
\end{aligned}$$

Then the transfer function $f_L[\![\mathrm{B}]\!]t$ for the loop test B of the binary decision tree t can be defined as:

$$f_L[\![\mathrm{B}]\!]t \triangleq t \sqcap_t \mathrm{B}.$$

Example 7. Let t be the binary decision tree in Example 4, then $f_L[\![\mathrm{y} >= 0]\!]t = [\![\mathrm{x} \leq 50 : (\!| 0 \leq \mathrm{x} \leq 50 \wedge \mathrm{x} = \mathrm{y} |\!), (\!| 51 \leq \mathrm{x} \leq 102 \wedge \mathrm{x} + \mathrm{y} - 102 = 0 |\!)]\!]$.

Branch Test Transfer Function. The binary decision tree can be constructed in two different ways. On one hand, it can be generated immediately after the set $\mathcal{B}$ of branch condition paths has been generated in the pre-analysis. In this way, all leaves of the binary decision tree will be set to $\top_\ell$ for the first program point and $\bot_\ell$ for others ($\top_\ell, \bot_\ell \in \mathbb{D}_\ell$) at the beginning. On the other hand, both binary decision tree and $\mathcal{B}$ can be constructed on the fly during the static analysis. In this last case, we have $\mathcal{B} = \emptyset$ and the binary decision tree $t = (\!| \top_\ell |\!)$ for the first program point and $t = (\!| \bot_\ell |\!)$ for others at the beginning.

In the latter case, the branch test transfer function should first construct the new binary decision tree from the old one by splitting on the branch condition when it has been first met in the analysis. Given a binary decision condition $t \in \mathbb{T}(\mathcal{B}, \mathbb{D}_\ell)$ and a branch test B that's been first met, there are two situations. One situation is that the branch condition B is independent, that is, it does not occur inside any scope of a branch. In this situation, the new binary decision tree

t' can be constructed by replacing each leaf p in the binary tree t with a subtree $[\![\mathrm{B} : (\!| p \sqcap_\ell \mathbb{D}_\ell(\mathrm{B}) |\!), (\!| p \sqcap_\ell \mathbb{D}_\ell(\neg\mathrm{B}) |\!)]\!]$. We also have $\mathcal{B}' = \{\underline{\pi_b} \cdot \mathrm{B} \mid \underline{\pi_b} \in \mathcal{B}\} \cup \{\underline{\pi_b} \cdot \neg\mathrm{B} \mid \underline{\pi_b} \in \mathcal{B}\}$. The other situation is that the branch condition B is inside a scope of a branch. Let B' be the condition of the branch and there is no other branch scope between B and B', if B is inside the true branch of B', then the new binary decision tree t' can be constructed by replacing each left leaf p of B' in the binary tree t with a subtree $[\![\mathrm{B} : (\!| p \sqcap_\ell \mathbb{D}_\ell(\mathrm{B}) |\!), (\!| p \sqcap_\ell \mathbb{D}_\ell(\neg\mathrm{B}) |\!)]\!]$. We also have $\mathcal{B}' = \{\underline{\pi_b} \cdot \mathrm{B}' \cdot \mathrm{B} \mid \underline{\pi_b} \cdot \mathrm{B}' \in \mathcal{B}\} \cup \{\underline{\pi_b} \cdot \mathrm{B}' \cdot \neg\mathrm{B} \mid \underline{\pi_b} \cdot \mathrm{B}' \in \mathcal{B}\} \cup (\mathcal{B} \setminus \{\underline{\pi_b} \cdot \mathrm{B}' \mid \underline{\pi_b} \cdot \mathrm{B}' \in \mathcal{B}\})$. If B is inside the false branch of B', the right leaves of B' instead of left leaves should be replaced by the same subtrees and $\mathcal{B}' = \{\underline{\pi_b} \cdot \neg\mathrm{B}' \cdot \mathrm{B} \mid \underline{\pi_b} \cdot \neg\mathrm{B}' \in \mathcal{B}\} \cup \{\underline{\pi_b} \cdot \neg\mathrm{B}' \cdot \neg\mathrm{B} \mid \underline{\pi_b} \cdot \neg\mathrm{B}' \in \mathcal{B}\} \cup (\mathcal{B} \setminus \{\underline{\pi_b} \cdot \neg\mathrm{B}' \mid \underline{\pi_b} \cdot \neg\mathrm{B}' \in \mathcal{B}\})$.

Then in both ways, the branch test transfer function will do the same thing as loop test transfer function. Given the branch test B and the binary decision tree $t \in \mathbb{T}(\mathcal{B}, \mathbb{D}_\ell)$, we have:

$$f_B[\![\mathrm{B}]\!]t \triangleq t \sqcap_t \mathrm{B}.$$

Example 8. Let t be the binary decision tree in Example 4, then $f_B[\![\mathrm{x} <= 50]\!]t = [\![\mathrm{x} \leq 50 : (\!| 0 \leq \mathrm{x} \leq 50 \wedge \mathrm{x} = \mathrm{y} |\!), (\!| \bot_\ell |\!)]\!]$.

Assignment Transfer Function. Given a binary decision tree $t \in \mathbb{T}(\mathcal{B}, \mathbb{D}_\ell)$, the assignment x = E can be performed at each leaf in t by using the assignment transfer function of $\mathbb{D}_\ell$. E.g., let $t = [\![x \leq 50 : (\!| 0 \leq x \leq 50 |\!), (\!| \bot_\ell |\!)]\!]$ and given an assignment $x = x + 1$, after performing the assignment transfer function of Polyhedra abstract domain on each leaf of t, we will get $t' = [\![x \leq 50 : (\!| 1 \leq x \leq 51 |\!), (\!| \bot_\ell |\!)]\!]$. Generally, the branch condition paths in $\mathcal{B}$ are used as labels separating the abstract properties in disjunctions which are gathered in the leaves. But this is not always the case. For example, in the join operator, we use the branch conditions in $\mathcal{B}$ to reduce the result of the join. After performing the assignment transfer function of leaf abstract domain $\mathbb{D}_\ell$ on each leaf, we may also need to manipulate the leaves using the branch condition paths in $\mathcal{B}$. Let's check the above result t' after the assignment, it appears that some leaves in the new binary decision tree may not satisfy some branch conditions in the branch condition paths which are leading to them. For example, $1 \leq x \leq 51$ is not satisfying the branch condition $x \leq 50$. We know the violation part is actually satisfying the negation of those branch conditions. Hence we need to use the branch condition $x \leq 50$ to separate $1 \leq x \leq 51$ into $1 \leq x \leq 50 \vee x = 51$ and update the corresponding leaves. For example, we have $t'' = [\![x \leq 50 : (\!| 1 \leq x \leq 50 |\!), (\!| x = 51 |\!)]\!]$.

We call this procedure *reconstruction on leaves*. Given a binary decision tree t after an assignment, we define the procedure as follow:

1. Collecting all leave properties in t, let it be $\{p_1, p_2, ..., p_n\}$;
2. For each leaf in t, let $\underline{\pi_b} = \beta_1 \cdot \beta_2 \cdot ... \cdot \beta_n$ be the branch condition path leading to it. We then calculate $p_i' = p_i \sqcap_\ell (\mathbb{D}_\ell(\beta_1 \wedge \beta_2 \wedge ... \wedge \beta_n))$.

3. For each leaf in t, update it with $p'_1 \sqcup_\ell p'_2 \sqcup_\ell ... \sqcup_\ell p'_n$.

Correctness. Let $p = p_1 \vee p_2 \vee ... \vee p_n$ be the disjunction of all properties in leaves before reconstruction on leaves. For each leaf ℓ_i in t, we have $\ell_i = (p_1 \sqcap_\ell (\mathbb{D}_\ell(\beta_1^i \wedge \beta_2^i \wedge ... \wedge \beta_n^i))) \sqcup_\ell ... \sqcup_\ell (p_n \sqcap_\ell (\mathbb{D}_\ell(\beta_1^i \wedge \beta_2^i \wedge ... \wedge \beta_n^i))) = (p_1 \sqcup_\ell ... \sqcup_\ell p_n) \sqcap_\ell (\mathbb{D}_\ell(\beta_1^i \wedge \beta_2^i \wedge ... \wedge \beta_n^i))$ after reconstruction on leaves. We then have the disjunction of all properties in leaves after reconstruction on leaves is $p' = \ell_1 \vee ... \vee \ell_n = (p_1 \sqcup_\ell ... \sqcup_\ell p_n) \sqcap_\ell (\mathbb{D}_\ell(\beta_1^1 \wedge \beta_2^1 \wedge ... \wedge \beta_n^1)) \vee ... \vee (p_1 \sqcup_\ell ... \sqcup_\ell p_n) \sqcap_\ell (\mathbb{D}_\ell(\beta_1^n \wedge \beta_2^n \wedge ... \wedge \beta_n^n)) = (p_1 \sqcup_\ell ... \sqcup_\ell p_n) \sqcap_\ell ((\mathbb{D}_\ell(\beta_1^1 \wedge \beta_2^1 \wedge ... \wedge \beta_n^1)) \vee ... \vee (\mathbb{D}_\ell(\beta_1^n \wedge \beta_2^n \wedge ... \wedge \beta_n^n))) = (p_1 \sqcup_\ell ... \sqcup_\ell p_n) \sqcap_\ell \mathit{true} = p_1 \sqcup_\ell ... \sqcup_\ell p_n \equiv p$. This shows that the reconstruction on leaves procedure will not change the result of the assignment transfer function.

4.4 Extrapolation Operators

When the leaf abstract domain $\mathbb{D}_\ell$ has strictly increasing and/or strictly decreasing infinite chains, widening and/or narrowing operators are required in the binary decision tree abstract domain to accelerate the convergence of fixpoint iterates.

Widening. Given two binary decision tree $t_1, t_2 \in \mathbb{T}(\mathcal{B}, \mathbb{D}_\ell)$, the widening $t = t_1 \nabla_t t_2$ can be computed using the widening ∇_ℓ in the leaf abstract domain $\mathbb{D}_\ell$ similar to the join operator, that is, computing the widening $\ell_1 \nabla_\ell \ell_2$ for each pair (ℓ_1, ℓ_2) of leaves in (t_1, t_2) where ℓ_1 and ℓ_2 are led by the same branch condition path $\underline{\pi_b} \in \mathcal{B}$ while the branch conditions in $\underline{\pi_b}$ are also used as the threshold. Let $\underline{\pi_b} = \beta_1 \cdot \beta_2 \cdot ... \cdot \beta_n$ where $\beta_i = \mathrm{B}_i$ or $\neg\mathrm{B}_i, i = 1, ..., n$, we have each leaf $\ell = (\ell_1 \nabla_\ell \ell_2) \sqcap_\ell \mathbb{D}_\ell(\beta_1) \sqcap_\ell \mathbb{D}_\ell(\beta_2) \sqcap_\ell ... \sqcap_\ell \mathbb{D}_\ell(\beta_n)$.

```
widening(t1, t2 : binary decision trees, bound = ⊤)
{
    if (t1 == (|l1|) && t2 == (|l2|)) then return (t1 ∇ℓ t2) ⊓ℓ bound;

    let t1 = ⟦B: t1l, t1r⟧ and t2 = ⟦B: t2l, t2r⟧;
    return ⟦B: widening(t1l, t2l, bound ⊓ℓ Dℓ(B)),
        widening(t1r, t2r, bound ⊓ℓ Dℓ(¬B))⟧;
}
```

Narrowing. The narrowing operator in the binary decision tree abstract domain is very similar to its meet operator. Given two binary decision tree $t_1, t_2 \in \mathbb{T}(\mathcal{B}, \mathbb{D}_\ell)$, the narrowing $t = t_1 \Delta_t t_2$ can be computed using the narrowing Δ_ℓ in the leaf abstract domain $\mathbb{D}_\ell$. Let ℓ_1, ℓ_2 are leaves of t_1, t_2 respectively, where the same branch condition path $\underline{\pi_b} \in \mathcal{B}$ leads to ℓ_1 and ℓ_2, then $\ell = \ell_1 \Delta_\ell \ell_2$ is the leaf of t led by the same branch condition path $\underline{\pi_b} \in \mathcal{B}$. After computing each leaf $\ell = \ell_1 \Delta_\ell \ell_2$ in t, we then get $t = t_1 \Delta_t t_2$.

```
narrowing(t1, t2 : binary decision trees)
{
    if (t1 == (|l1|) && t2 == (|l2|)) then return t1 Δℓ t2;

    let t1 = [[B: t1l, t1r]] and t2 = [[B: t2l, t2r]];
    return [[B: narrowing(t1l, t2l), narrowing(t1r, t2r)]];
}
```

Example 9. Let $t_1 = [\![\mathrm{x} \leq 50 : (\!| \mathrm{x} = 0 \wedge \mathrm{y} = 0 |\!), (\!| \perp_\ell |\!)]\!]$ and $t_2 = [\![\mathrm{x} \leq 50 : (\!| \mathrm{x} = \mathrm{y} \wedge 0 \leq \mathrm{x} \leq 1 |\!), (\!| \perp_\ell |\!)]\!]$. It's easy to see that $t_1 \sqsubseteq t_2$. In polyhedra, we have $(\mathrm{x} = 0 \wedge \mathrm{y} = 0) \nabla_t (\mathrm{x} = \mathrm{y} \wedge 0 \leq \mathrm{x} \leq 1) = \mathrm{x} \geq 0 \wedge \mathrm{x} = \mathrm{y}$. Hence, we have $t_1 \nabla_t t_2 = [\![\mathrm{x} \leq 50 : (\!| 0 \leq \mathrm{x} \leq 50 \wedge \mathrm{x} = \mathrm{y} |\!), (\!| \perp_\ell |\!)]\!]$.

4.5 Other Operators

Although the number of branch conditions in a program is always finite, it may still be a very large number. A large number of branch conditions means a large binary decision tree, with a potentially exponential growth which is not acceptable in practice. Hence, we need limit the size (depth) of the binary decision trees.

One method is to eliminate decision nodes by merging their subtrees when the binary decision tree grows too deep. This can be done as follow:

1. Pick up a branch condition B. We can simply use the one in the root, or the nearest one to the leaves, or by random. We can also design a ranking function based on the information from the analysis for each branch condition to estimate how likely it is to be eliminated with minimal information loss. Then we always choose the most likely one.
2. Eliminate B (B or ¬B) from each branch condition path in $\mathcal{B}$.
3. For each subtree of the form $[\![B : t_t, t_f]\!]$, if t_t and t_f have identical decision nodes, replace it by $t_t \sqcup_t t_f$.
4. Otherwise, there are decision nodes existing only in t_t or t_f. For each of those decision nodes, (recursively) eliminate it by merging its subtrees. When no such decision node exists, we get t'_t and t'_f, and they must have identical decision nodes, so $[\![B : t_t, t_f]\!]$ can be replaced by $t'_t \sqcup_t t'_f$.

Another method is to generate a smaller $\mathcal{B}$ by abstracting the branch condition paths in $\mathcal{B}$ into shorter ones. We may partition the set of branch conditions by its appearance inside or outside loops and then only keep the ones appeared inside the loops in $\mathcal{B}$. We may also only keep the branch conditions which have some particular form, such as $ax \leqslant b$, etc.

The second method is different from the first one because it can be done in the pre-analysis or on the fly before splitting trees, thus no merging is needed during the analysis. This reduces the cost of the analysis, thus improves its efficiency. But because all the branch conditions being eliminated are not based on the information that is collected during the static analysis, the result may be less precise than the one generated from the first method. Moreover, eliminating branch conditions and merging their subtrees allow us to dynamically change the binary decision trees on the fly. This provides a more flexible way of adjusting the cost/precision ratio of the static analysis.

5 Example

Let us come back to Example 1. We choose the polyhedra abstract domain as the leaf abstract domain and we have $\mathcal{B} = \{x <= 50, \neg(x <= 50)\}$. Initially, we set $t = (\!|\, \bot_\ell \,|\!)$ in the program point ^{l}. After the assignment "x = 0; y = 0;", we have "$t = (\!|\, x = 0 \wedge y = 0 \,|\!)$". Let t_i be the abstract property at program point ^{l} after the i-th iteration, then $t_0 = (\!|\, x = 0 \wedge y = y \,|\!)$. In the first iteration, we have to construct the binary decision tree when first reaching the branch test "x <= 50". In this case, we have $t'_0 = [\![x \leq 50 : (\!|\, x = 0 \wedge y = 0 \,|\!), (\!|\, \bot_\ell \,|\!)]\!]$. At the end of the first iteration, we get $t''_0 = [\![x \leq 50 : (\!|\, x = 1 \wedge y = 1 \,|\!), (\!|\, \bot_\ell \,|\!)]\!]$. Then $t_1 = t_0 \cup_t t''_0 = [\![x \leq 50 : (\!|\, x = y \wedge 0 \leq x \leq 1 \,|\!), (\!|\, \bot_\ell \,|\!)]\!]$. Afterwards, we apply the widening and get $t'_1 = t_0 \triangledown t_1 = [\![x \leq 50 : (\!|\, 0 \leq x \leq 50 \wedge x = y \,|\!), (\!|\, \bot_\ell \,|\!)]\!]$. In the second iteration, the assignment "x++;" leads to reconstruction on leaves, hence we get $t''_1 = [\![x \leq 50 : (\!|\, 1 \leq x \leq 50 \wedge x = y \,|\!), (\!|\, x = 51 \wedge y = 51 \,|\!)]\!]$. Then $t_2 = t_1 \cup_t t''_1 = [\![x \leq 50 : (\!|\, 0 \leq x \leq 50 \wedge x = y \,|\!), (\!|\, x = 51 \wedge y = 51 \,|\!)]\!]$. After the third iteration, $t_3 = [\![x \leq 50 : (\!|\, 0 \leq x \leq 50 \wedge x = y \,|\!), (\!|\, x + y - 102 = 0 \wedge 51 \leq x \leq 52 \,|\!)]\!]$. We then apply the widening and get $t'_3 = t_2 \triangledown t_3 = [\![x \leq 50 : (\!|\, 0 \leq x \leq 50 \wedge x = y \,|\!), (\!|\, x + y - 102 = 0 \wedge x \geq 51 \,|\!)]\!]$. One more iteration yields $t_4 = [\![x \leq 50 : (\!|\, 0 \leq x \leq 50 \wedge x = y \,|\!), (\!|\, x + y - 102 = 0 \wedge 51 \leq x \leq 103 \,|\!)]\!]$. It follows that the program analysis converges. Hence t_4 is the invariant at program point ^{l}.

6 Related Work

A systematic characterization of the least bases for the disjunctive completion of abstract domains can be found in [8]. The trace partitioning using control flows was first introduced in [3]. A static analysis framework via trace partitioning was proposed by [11]. In this framework, the control flow is used to choose which disjunctions to keep but it lacks the merge of partitions, which may lead to exponential cost. In [13], a trace partitioning domain, where the partitioning of traces are based on the history of the control flow, has been proposed. The main difference between their partitionings and ours is we only use (part of) branch conditions while they are considering all conditions and other information.

Decision trees have been used for the disjunctive refinement of an abstract domain such as [10] for the interval abstract domain based on decision trees. A general segmented decision tree abstract domain, where disjunctions are determined by values of variables is introduced in [7]. Moreover, [16] proposed a general disjunctive refinement of an abstract domain based on decision trees extended with linear constraints for program termination. The difference between those works and ours is their partitionings are mainly based on the value of some variables while ours are directly based on the branch conditions.

There also exist several works on directly allowing disjunction in the domain, i.e., powerset domain [1]. In [15], the disjunctions are computed on an elaboration, which can be viewed as a multiply duplication, of the programs CFG structure. Moreover, our binary decision tree abstract domain functor can also be useful to scale traditional path-sensitive program analysis [17].

7 Conclusion

In this paper, we have introduced a series of abstractions which generates a set of branch condition paths. Those branch condition paths define a kind of trace partitioning on the concrete level (trace semantics of program). By using such information for trace partitioning, we proposed a binary decision tree abstract domain functor that allows finite disjunction of abstract properties generated by existing abstract domains[1]. We also discussed the implementation of our binary decision tree abstract domain functor by providing algorithms for inclusion test, meet and join, transfer functions and extrapolation operators. Although we bound the number of disjunctions only to the number of branch conditions in the program, the cost of our domain may still be excessive. Thus we also discussed how to limit the number of disjunctions. Our binary decision tree abstract domain functor may provide a flexible way of adjusting the cost/precision ratio for static analysis.

References

1. Bagnara, R., Hill, P.M., Zaffanella, E.: Widening operators for powerset domains. STTT **9**(3–4), 413–414 (2007)
2. Chen, J.: SMT-based and disjunctive relational abstract domains for static analysis. Ph.D. thesis, New York University (May 2015)
3. Cousot, P.: Semantic foundations of program analysis. In: Muchnick, S., Jones, N. (eds.) Program Flow Analysis: Theory and Applications, pp. 303–342. Prentice-Hall Inc., Englewood Cliffs (1981). Chapter. 10
4. Cousot, P., Cousot, R.: Static determination of dynamic properties of programs. In: Proceedings of the Second International Symposium on Programming, pp. 106–130. Dunod, Paris, France (1976)
5. Cousot, P., Cousot, R.: Abstract interpretation frameworks. J. Logic. Comput. **2**(4), 511–547 (1992)
6. Cousot, P., Halbwachs, N.: Automatic discovery of linear restraints among variables of a program. In: Conference Record of the Fifth Annual ACM SIGPLAN-SIGACT Symposium on Principles of Programming Languages, pp. 84–97. ACM Press, New York, NY, Tucson, Arizona (1978)

[1] Note that all examples in this paper are numerical, but this does not mean that our abstract domain functor is limited to numerical abstract domains. Symbolic abstract domains are also allowed.

7. Cousot, P., Cousot, R., Mauborgne, L.: A scalable segmented decision tree abstract domain. In: Manna, Z., Peled, D.A. (eds.) Time for Verification. LNCS, vol. 6200, pp. 72–95. Springer, Heidelberg (2010)
8. Giacobazzi, R., Ranzato, F.: Optimal domains for disjunctive abstract intepretation. Sci. Comput. Program. **32**(1–3), 177–210 (1998)
9. Gopan, D., Reps, T.: Guided static analysis. In: Riis Nielson, H., Filé, G. (eds.) SAS 2007. LNCS, vol. 4634, pp. 349–365. Springer, Heidelberg (2007)
10. Gurfinkel, A., Chaki, S.: Boxes: a symbolic abstract domain of boxes. In: Cousot, R., Martel, M. (eds.) SAS 2010. LNCS, vol. 6337, pp. 287–303. Springer, Heidelberg (2010)
11. Handjieva, M., Tzolovski, S.: Refining static analyses by trace-based partitioning using control flow. In: Levi, G. (ed.) SAS 1998. LNCS, vol. 1503, pp. 200–214. Springer, Heidelberg (1998)
12. Jeannet, B., Miné, A.: Apron: a library of numerical abstract domains for static analysis. In: Bouajjani, A., Maler, O. (eds.) CAV 2009. LNCS, vol. 5643, pp. 661–667. Springer, Heidelberg (2009)
13. Mauborgne, L., Rival, X.: Trace partitioning in abstract interpretation based static analyzers. In: Sagiv, M. (ed.) ESOP 2005. LNCS, vol. 3444, pp. 5–20. Springer, Heidelberg (2005)
14. Miné, A.: The octagon abstract domain. High. Ord. Symbolic Comput. (HOSC) **19**(1), 31–100 (2006). http://www.di.ens.fr/ mine/publi/article-mine-HOSC06.pdf
15. Sankaranarayanan, S., Ivančić, F., Shlyakhter, I., Gupta, A.: Static analysis in disjunctive numerical domains. In: Yi, K. (ed.) SAS 2006. LNCS, vol. 4134, pp. 3–17. Springer, Heidelberg (2006)
16. Urban, C., Miné, A.: A decision tree abstract domain for proving conditional termination. In: Müller-Olm, M., Seidl, H. (eds.) SAS 2014. LNCS, vol. 8723, pp. 302–318. Springer, Heidelberg (2014)
17. Winter, K., Zhang, C., Hayes, I.J., Keynes, N., Cifuentes, C., Li, L.: Path-sensitive data flow analysis simplified. In: Groves, L., Sun, J. (eds.) ICFEM 2013. LNCS, vol. 8144, pp. 415–430. Springer, Heidelberg (2013)

Precise Data Flow Analysis in the Presence of Correlated Method Calls

Marianna Rapoport[1](✉), Ondřej Lhoták[1], and Frank Tip[2]

[1] University of Waterloo, Waterloo, Ontario, Canada
{mrapoport,olhotak}@uwaterloo.ca
[2] Samsung Research America, San Jose, CA, USA
ftip@samsung.com

Abstract. When two methods are invoked on the same object, the dispatch behaviours of these method calls will be correlated. If two correlated method calls are polymorphic (i.e., they dispatch to different method definitions depending on the type of the receiver object), a program's interprocedural control-flow graph will contain infeasible paths. Existing algorithms for data-flow analysis are unable to ignore such infeasible paths, giving rise to loss of precision.

We show how infeasible paths due to correlated calls can be eliminated for *Interprocedural Finite Distributive Subset* (IFDS) problems, a large class of data-flow analysis problems with broad applications. Our approach is to transform an IFDS problem into an *Interprocedural Distributive Environment* (IDE) problem, in which edge functions filter out data flow along infeasible paths. A solution to this IDE problem can be mapped back to the solution space of the original IFDS problem. We formalize the approach, prove it correct, and report on an implementation in the WALA analysis framework.

1 Introduction

A control-flow graph (CFG) is an over-approximation of the possible flows of control in concrete executions of a program. It may contain *infeasible* paths that cannot occur at runtime. The precision of a data-flow analysis algorithm depends on its ability to detect and disregard such infeasible paths. The *Interprocedural Finite Distributive Subset* (IFDS) algorithm [16] is a general data-flow analysis algorithm that avoids infeasible interprocedural paths in which calls and returns to/from functions are not properly matched. The *Interprocedural Distributive Environment* (IDE) algorithm [18] has the same property, but supports a broader range of data-flow problems.

This paper presents an approach to data-flow analysis that avoids a type of infeasible path that arises in object-oriented programs when two or more methods are dynamically dispatched on the same receiver object. If the method

This research was supported by the Natural Sciences and Engineering Research Council of Canada and the Ontario Ministry of Research and Innovation.

S. Blazy and T. Jensen (Eds.): SAS 2015, LNCS 9291, pp. 54–71, 2015.
DOI: 10.1007/978-3-662-48288-9_4

calls are polymorphic (i.e., the method invoked depends on the run-time type of the receiver), then their dispatch behaviours are correlated, and some of the paths between them are infeasible. A recent paper [21] made this observation but did not present any concrete algorithm to take advantage of it.

Our approach transforms an IFDS problem into an IDE problem that precisely accounts for infeasible paths due to correlated calls. The results of this IDE problem can be mapped back to the data-flow domain of the original IFDS problem, but are more precise than the results of directly applying the IFDS algorithm to the original problem. We present a formalization of the transformation and prove its correctness: specifically, we prove it still soundly considers all paths that are feasible, and that it avoids flow along all paths that are infeasible due to correlated calls.

We implemented the correlated-calls transformation and the IDE algorithm in Scala, on top of the WALA framework for static analysis of JVM bytecode [5]. Our prototype implementation was tested extensively by using it to transform an IFDS-based taint analysis into a more precise IDE-based taint analysis, and applying the latter to small example programs with correlated calls. Our prototype along with all tests will be made available to the artifact evaluation committee.

The remainder of this paper is organized as follows. Section 2 presents a motivating example. Section 3 reviews the IFDS and IDE algorithms. Section 4 presents the correlated-calls transformation, states the correctness properties[1], and discusses our implementation. Related work is discussed in Sect. 5. Finally, Sect. 6 presents conclusions and directions for future work.

2 Motivation

We illustrate our approach using a small example that applies our technique to improve the precision of taint analysis. A taint analysis computes how string values may flow from "sources", which are typically statements that read untrusted input, to "sinks", which are typically security-sensitive operations such as calls to a database. In previous research [2,6], taint analysis algorithms have been formulated as IFDS problems.

Figure 1 shows a small Java program. The program declares a class A with a subclass B, where A defines methods foo() and bar() that are overridden in B. We assume that secret values are created by an unspecified function secret(), which is called in A.foo() on line 2. Any write to standard output is assumed to be a sink (e.g., the call to System.out.println() in B.bar()). Depending on the number of arguments passed to the program, the main() method of the example program creates either an A-object or a B-object. The program then calls foo() on this object on line 18, which is followed by a call to bar() on the same object.

We wish to answer the following question: Is it possible for the untrusted value that is read on line 2 to flow to the print statement? Consider the control-flow supergraph for the example program that is shown in Fig. 2. The nodes

[1] Detailed proofs of our lemmas and theorems can be found in the Technical Report [15].

```
1  class A {
2    String foo { return secret (); }
3    void bar(String s) {}
4  }
5  class B extends A {
6    String foo {
7      return "not␣secret";
8    }
9    void bar(String s) {
10     System.out. println (s);
11   }
12 }
13
14 class Main {
15   static void main(String[] args) {
16     A a = (args == null)
17           ? new A() : new B();
18     String v = a.foo();
19     a.bar(v);
20   }
21 }
```

Fig. 1. Example program containing correlated calls

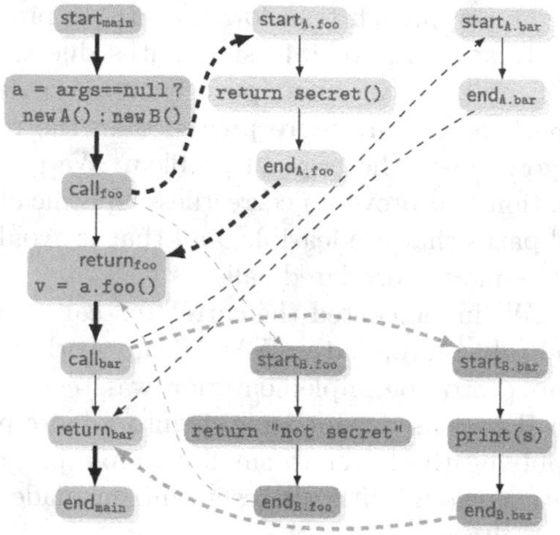

Fig. 2. Control flow supergraph for the example program of Fig. 1. Dashed lines depict interprocedural edges. An infeasible path is shown in bold.

in this graph correspond to statements, method entry points (start nodes) and method exit points (end nodes). For each method call, the graph contains a distinct call-node and a return-node. Edges in the graph reflect intraprocedural control flow, flow of control from a caller to a callee (edges from call-nodes to start-nodes), or flow of control from a callee back to a caller (edges from end-nodes to return-nodes).

In our example, the control flow within each method is straightforward and all interesting issues arise from interprocedural control flow. In particular, since a may point to either an A-object or a B-object, the call on line 18 may dispatch to either A.foo() or to B.foo(), as is reflected by edges from the node labeled call_{foo} to the nodes labeled $\text{start}_{\text{A.foo()}}$ and $\text{start}_{\text{B.foo()}}$ and by edges from the nodes labeled $\text{end}_{\text{A.foo}}$ and $\text{end}_{\text{B.foo}}$ to the node labeled $\text{return}_{\text{foo}}$. Similarly, there are edges from the node labeled call_{bar} to the nodes $\text{start}_{\text{A.bar()}}$ and $\text{start}_{\text{B.bar()}}$, and edges from the nodes labeled $\text{end}_{\text{A.bar}}$ and $\text{end}_{\text{B.bar}}$ to the node labeled $\text{return}_{\text{bar}}$.

An IFDS analysis propagates data-flow facts along the edges of a control flow supergraph such as the one in Fig. 2. The IFDS algorithm already avoids flow along infeasible paths from one call site, through a target method, and returning to a different call site of the target method. However, in this example, all methods are called in exactly one place, so IFDS is unable to eliminate data flow along any of the paths shown in the figure. As a result, IFDS-based taint analysis algorithms such as [2,6] would report that the secret value read on line 2 might flow to the print statement on line 10.

As we discussed previously, the calls to foo() and bar() may dispatch to the implementations in classes A and B, because the receiver variable a may be bound to objects of type A or B at run time. However, the methods foo() and bar() are invoked on *the same object*. Thus the behaviours of the method calls are *correlated*: if the call to foo() dispatches to A.foo(), then the call to bar() must dispatch to A.bar(), and analogously for B.foo() and B.bar(). Consequently, paths such as the one shown in bold in Fig. 2 where the calls dispatch to A.foo() and B.bar() are infeasible.

Our main contribution is an algorithm for transforming an IFDS problem into an IDE problem that expresses the feasibility of paths in light of correlated calls. The approach associates with each interprocedural CFG edge a function that records the types of variables that are used as the receiver of correlated method calls. Paths that are composed of edges in which the same receiver expression has different types are infeasible, and the propagation of data-flow facts along such paths is prevented. Applying our technique to an IFDS-based taint analysis would enable the resulting IDE-based taint analysis to determine that no secret value can flow from line 2 to the print statement on line 10.

While the discussion in this section has focused on the specific problem of taint analysis, our technique generally applies to *any* data-flow-analysis problem that can be expressed in the IFDS framework. This includes many common analysis tasks such as reaching definitions, constant propagation, slicing, typestate analysis, pointer analysis, and lightweight shape analysis.

2.1 Occurrences of Correlated Calls

How often do correlated calls occur in practice? To assess the benefit of the correlated-calls analysis, we counted the number of correlated calls that occur in programs of the Dacapo benchmarks [3], using the WALA framework [5]. Our goal was to obtain an upper bound on the number of redundant IFDS-result nodes that could be potentially removed by our analysis. The results are shown in the Technical Report [15].

In these programs, on average, 3 % of all call sites C are polymorphic call sites C_P. Out of these polymorphic call sites, a significant fraction (39 %) are correlated call sites $C^{\Subset}$. We also see that, on average, each correlated-call receiver is involved in approximately three correlated calls.

2.2 An Example from the Scala Collections Library

The Scala collections library contains the trait TraversableOnce that is shared by both collections and iterators over them. The toArray method of this trait creates an array and copies the contents of the collection or iterator into it:

```
val result = new Array[B](this.size)
this.copyToArray(result, 0)
```

When this refers to an iterator rather than a collection, the call to this.size extracts all elements of the iterator to count them. At the call to copyToArray, the iterator is already empty, so nothing is copied to the newly created array. One could design an IFDS analysis to detect this kind of bug.

However, the implementation of TraversableOnce.toArray is actually correct because the above code is guarded with a test: if (this.isTraversableAgain) ... When the isTraversableAgain method returns false, as it does for an iterator, the toArray method uses a different (less efficient) implementation. The bug report would therefore be a false positive. The isTraversableAgain method is easy to analyze: it returns the constant true in a collection and the constant false in an iterator. However, in order to eliminate the false positive bug report, an analysis would need to rule out infeasible paths using correlated calls. Specifically, the following path triggers the bug, but is infeasible: first, call isTraversableAgain on a collection, returning true, then call size and copyToArray on an iterator. Our correlated calls analysis could determine that this path is infeasible because it calls the collection version of isTraversableAgain but the iterator versions of size and copyToArray. The relevant code from TraversableOnce and other related traits is shown in the Technical Report [15].

3 Background

This section defines terminology and presents the IFDS and IDE algorithms.

3.1 Terminology and Notation

The *control-flow graph* of a procedure is a directed graph whose nodes are instructions, which contains an edge from n_1 to n_2 whenever n_2 may execute immediately after n_1. A CFG has a distinguished *start node* start_p and *end node* end_p. Following the presentation of Reps et al. [16,18], we follow every call instruction with a no-op instruction, so that every *call node* is immediately followed by a *return node* in the CFG. The *control-flow supergraph* of a program contains the CFGs of all of the procedures as subgraphs. In addition, for each call instruction c, the supergraph contains a *call-to-start* edge to the start node of every procedure that may be called from c, and an *end-to-return* edge from the end node of the procedure back to the call instruction.

A call site is *monomorphic* if it always calls the same procedure. In an object-oriented language, a call site $r.m(\ldots)$ can dynamically dispatch to multiple methods depending on the runtime type of the object pointed to by the receiver r. A call site that calls multiple procedures is called *polymorphic.* We define a function lookup to specify the dynamic dispatch: if s is the signature of m and t is the runtime type of the object pointed to by r, $\mathsf{lookup}(s, t)$ gives the procedure that will be invoked by the call $r.m(\ldots)$. We also define a function τ that may be viewed as the inverse of lookup: given a signature s and a specific invoked procedure f, $\tau(s, f)$ gives the set of all runtime types of r that cause $r.m(\ldots)$ to dispatch to f: $\tau(s, f) = \{t \mid \mathsf{lookup}(s, t) = f\}$.

A path in the control-flow supergraph is *valid* if it follows the usual stack-based calling discipline: every end-to-return edge on the path returns to the site of the most recent call that has not yet been matched by a return. The set of all valid paths from the program entry point to a node n is denoted $\mathsf{VP}(n)$.

A *lattice*[2] is a partially ordered set $(S, \sqsubseteq)$ in which every subset has a least upper bound, called *join* or $\sqcup$, and a greatest lower bound, called *meet* or $\sqcap$. A *meet semilattice* is a partially ordered set in which every subset only has a greatest lower bound. The symbols $\bot$ and $\top$ are used to denote the greatest lower bound of S and of the empty set, respectively.

We denote a map m as a set of pairs of keys and values, with each key appearing at most once. For a map m, $m(k)$ is the value paired with the key k. We denote by $m[x \to y]$ a map that maps x to y and every other key k to $m(k)$.

3.2 IFDS

The IFDS framework [16] is a precise and efficient algorithm for data-flow analysis that has been used to solve a variety of data-flow analysis problems [4,9,12,22]. The IFDS framework is an instance of the *functional approach* to data-flow analysis [19] because it constructs summaries of the effects of called procedures. The IFDS framework is applicable to *interprocedural* data-flow problems whose domain consists of *subsets* of a *finite* set D, and whose data-flow functions are *distributive*. A function f is distributive if $f(x_1 \sqcap x_2) = f(x_1) \sqcap f(x_2)$.

The IFDS algorithm is notable because it computes a meet-over-valid paths solution in polynomial time. Most other interprocedural analysis algorithms are either: (i) imprecise due to invalid paths, (ii) general but do not run in polynomial time [7,19], or (iii) handle a very specific set of problems [8].

The input to the IFDS algorithm is specified as $(G^*, D, F, M_F, \sqcap)$, where $G^* = (N^*, E^*)$ is the supergraph of the input program with nodes N^* and edges E^*, D is a finite set of *data-flow facts*, F is a set of distributive data-flow functions of type $2^D \to 2^D$, $M_F : E^* \to F$ assigns a data-flow function to each supergraph edge, and $\sqcap$ is the *meet operator* on the powerset 2^D, either union or intersection. In our presentation, the meet operator will always be union, but all of the results apply dually when the meet is intersection.

The output of the IFDS algorithm is, for each node n in the supergraph, the *meet-over-all-valid-paths* solution $\mathsf{MVP}_F(n) = \bigsqcap_{q \in \mathsf{VP}(n)} M_F(q)(\top)$, where M_F is extended from edges to paths by composition.

Overview of the IFDS Algorithm. The key idea behind the IFDS algorithm is that it is possible to represent any distributive function f from 2^D to 2^D by a *representation relation* $R_f \subseteq (D \cup \{0\}) \times (D \cup \{0\})$. The representation relation can be visualized as a bipartite graph with edges from one instance of $D \cup \{0\}$ to another instance of $D \cup \{0\}$. The IFDS algorithm uses such graphs to efficiently represent both the input data-flow functions and the summary functions that it computes for called procedures. Specifically, the representation relation R_f of a function f is defined as:

[2] The definitions that we give here are of *complete* lattices and semilattices. Since all of the (semi)lattices discussed in this paper are required to be complete, we omit the *complete* qualifier.

$$R_f = \{(\mathbf{0}, \mathbf{0})\} \cup \{(\mathbf{0}, d_j) \,|\, d_j \in f(\varnothing)\} \cup \{(d_i, d_j) \,|\, d_j \in f(\{d_i\}) \setminus f(\varnothing)\}.$$

Example 1. Given $D = \{u, v, w\}$ and $f(S) = S \setminus \{v\} \cup \{u\}$, the representation relation $R_f = \{(\mathbf{0}, \mathbf{0}), (\mathbf{0}, u), (w, w)\}$, which is depicted in Fig. 3.

The representation relation decomposes a flow function into functions (edges) that operate on each fact individually. This is possible due to distributivity: applying the flow function to a set of facts is equivalent to applying it on each fact individually and then taking the union of the results.

The meet of two functions can be computed as simply the union of their representation functions: $R_{f \sqcap f'} = R_f \cup R_{f'}$. The composition of two functions can be computed by combining their representation graphs, merging the range nodes of the first function with the corresponding domain nodes of the second function, and finding paths in the resulting graph.

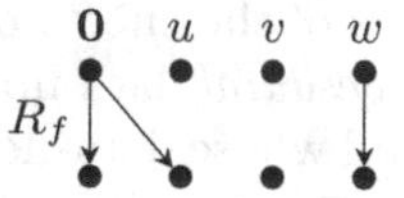

Fig. 3. $R_f = \{(\mathbf{0}, \mathbf{0}), (\mathbf{0}, u), (w, w)\}$

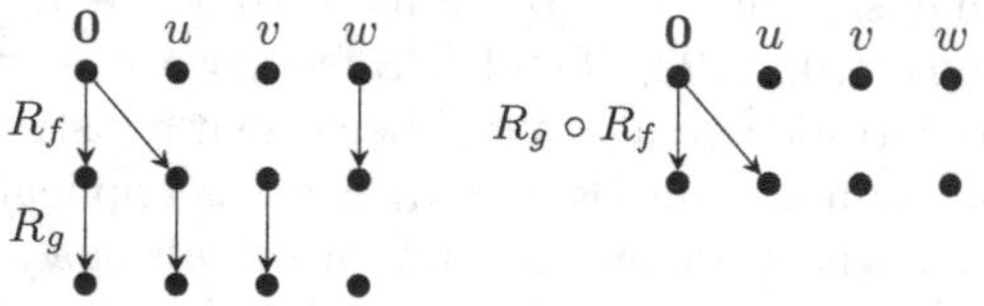

Fig. 4. $R_g \circ R_f$

Example 2. If $g(S) = S \setminus \{w\}$ and $f(S) = S \setminus \{v\} \cup \{u\}$, then $R_g \circ R_f = \{(\mathbf{0}, \mathbf{0}), (\mathbf{0}, u)\}$, as illustrated in Fig. 4.

Composition of two distributive functions f and f' corresponds to finding reachable nodes in a graph composed from their representation relations R_f and $R_{f'}$. Therefore, evaluating the composed data-flow function for a control flow path corresponds to finding reachable nodes in a graph composed from the representation relations of the data-flow functions for individual instructions.

It is this graph of representation relations that the IFDS algorithm operates on. In this graph, called the *exploded supergraph*, each node is a pair (n, d), where $n \in N^*$ is a node of the control-flow supergraph and d is an element of $D \cup \{\mathbf{0}\}$. For each edge $(n \to n') \in E^*$, the exploded supergraph contains a set of edges $(n, d_i) \to (n', d_j)$, which form the representation relation of the data-flow function $M_F(n \to n')$. The IFDS algorithm finds all exploded supergraph edges that are reachable by *realizable* paths in the exploded supergraph. A path is *realizable* if its projection to the (non-exploded) supergraph is a valid path (i.e., if it is of the form $(n_0, d_0) \to (n_1, d_1) \to \cdots \to (n_m, d_m)$ and where $n_0 \to n_1 \to \cdots \to n_m$ is a valid path).

Example 3. The exploded supergraph for Listing 1 is shown in Fig. 5. The labels on the edges will be explained in Sect. 3.3 We can see that there is a realizable path, highlighted in bold, from the start node of the exploded graph to the variable `s` at the node `print(s)` in the `B.bar` method. This means that `s` is considered secret at that node.

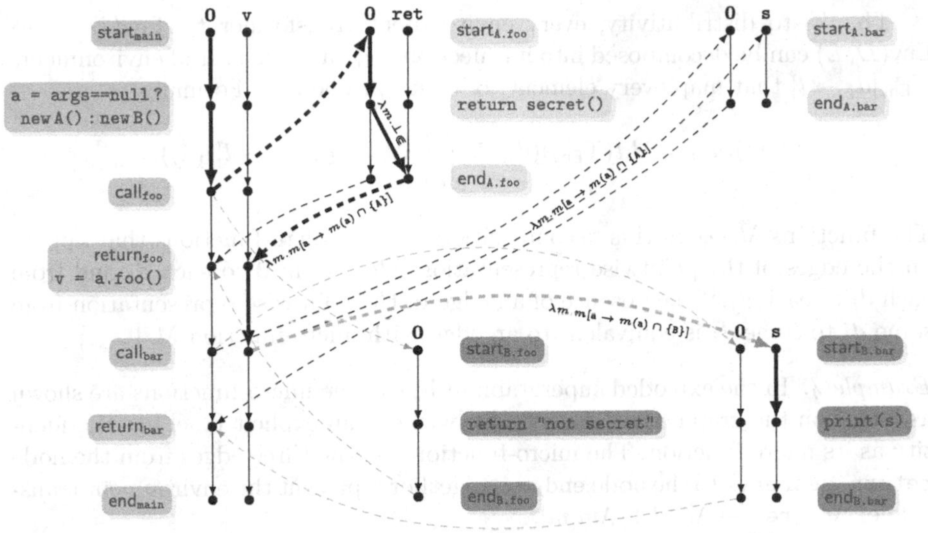

Fig. 5. An example program demonstrating correlated-call edge functions on the **0**-node path for Listing 1. All non-labeled edges are implicitly labeled with identity functions id. The variable `ret` denotes the return value of the `A.foo` method.

3.3 IDE

The IDE algorithm [18] extends IFDS to *interprocedural distributive environment* problems. An IDE problem is one whose data-flow lattice is the lattice $\mathsf{Env}(D, L)$ of maps from a finite set D to a meet semilattice L of finite height, ordered pointwise. Like IFDS, IDE requires the data-flow functions to be distributive.

The input to the IDE algorithm is $(G^*, D, L, M_{\mathsf{Env}})$ where G^* is a control-flow supergraph, D is a set of data-flow facts, L is a meet semilattice of finite height, and $M_{\mathsf{Env}} : E^* \rightarrow (\mathsf{Env}(D, L) \rightarrow \mathsf{Env}(D, L))$ assigns a data-flow function to each supergraph edge.

The output of the IDE algorithm is, for each node n in the supergraph, the *meet-over-all-valid-paths* solution $\mathsf{MVP}_{\mathsf{Env}}(n) = \bigsqcap_{q \in \mathsf{VP}(n)} M_{\mathsf{Env}}(q)(\top_{\mathsf{Env}})$, where $\top_{\mathsf{Env}} = \lambda d.\top$ is the top element of the lattice of environments, and M_{Env} is extended from edges to paths by composition.

Overview of the IDE Algorithm. Just as any distributive function from 2^D to 2^D can be represented with a representation relation, it is also possible to represent any distributive function from $\mathsf{Env}(D, L)$ to $\mathsf{Env}(D, L)$ with a *pointwise representation*. A pointwise representation is a bipartite graph with the same nodes[3] and edges as a representation relation, except that each edge is labelled with a *micro-function*, which is a function from L to L.

[3] The IDE literature uses the symbol Λ for the node that is denoted **0** in the IFDS literature. We use **0** throughout this paper for consistency.

Thanks to distributivity, every environment transformer $t : \mathsf{Env}(D, L) \rightarrow \mathsf{Env}(D, L)$ can be decomposed into its effect on $\top_{\mathsf{Env}}$ and on a set of environments $\top_{\mathsf{Env}}[d_i \rightarrow l]$ that map every element to $\top$ except one (d_i). Formally,

$$t(m)(d_j) = \lambda l.t(\top_{\mathsf{Env}})(d_j) \sqcap \prod_{d_i \in D} \lambda l.t(\top_{\mathsf{Env}}[d_i \rightarrow l])(d_j).$$

The functions $\lambda l. \cdots$ in this decomposition are the micro-functions that appear on the edges of the pointwise representation edges from **0** to each d_j and from each d_i to each d_j.[4] The absence of an edge in the pointwise representation from some d_i to some d_j is equivalent to an edge with micro-function $\lambda l.\top$.

Example 4. In the exploded supergraph in Fig. 5, the micro-functions are shown as labels on the graph edges. Every edge without an explicit label has the identity as its micro-function. The micro-functions on the three edges from the node `return secret()` to the node $\mathsf{end}_{\mathtt{A.foo}}$ together represent the environment transformer $\lambda e.e[\mathtt{ret} \rightarrow \lambda m.\bot \sqcap \lambda m.m]$.

To eliminate infeasible paths due to correlated calls, we encode the taint analysis using environments $e \in \mathsf{Env}(D, L)$, where D is the set of variables and L is a map from receiver variables to sets of possible types. The interpretation of such an environment e is that a given variable $v \in D$ may contain a secret value in an execution in which the runtime types of the objects pointed to by the receiver variables are in the sets specified by $e(v)$.

The meet of two environment transformers t_1, t_2 is computed as the union of the edges in their pointwise representations. When the same edge appears in the pointwise representations of both t_1 and t_2, the micro-function for that edge in $t_1 \sqcap t_2$ is the meet of the micro-functions for that same edge in t_1 and in t_2.

The composition of two environment transformers can be computed by combining their pointwise representation graphs in the same fashion as IFDS representation relations, and computing the composition of the micro-functions appearing along each path in the resulting graph.

The IDE algorithm operates on the same exploded supergraph as the IFDS algorithm (but its edges are labelled with micro-functions). For each pair (n, d) of node and fact, IDE computes a micro-function equal to the meet of the micro-functions of all the realizable paths from the program entry point to the pair.

In order to do this efficiently, the IDE algorithm requires a representation of micro-functions that is general enough to express the basic micro-functions of the data-flow functions for individual instructions, and that supports computing the meet and composition of micro-functions.

A practical implementation of the IDE algorithm requires the input data-flow functions to be provided in their pointwise representation as exploded supergraph edges labelled with micro-functions. Specifically, the input is generally provided as a function $\mathsf{EdgeFn} : (N^* \times D) \times (N^* \times D) \rightarrow F$, where F is the set of

[4] The IDE paper defines a more complicated but equivalent set of micro-functions that eliminate some duplication of computation.

representations of micro-functions from L to L. Given an exploded supergraph edge $e = (n, d) \to (n', d')$, $\mathsf{EdgeFn}((n, d), (n', d'))$ returns the micro-function that appears on the exploded supergraph edge e. In an implementation, it can be convenient to split the function EdgeFn into separate functions that handle the cases when $n \to n'$ is an intraprocedural edge, a call-to-return edge, a call-to-start edge, or an end-to-return edge.

4 Correlated Calls Analysis

4.1 Transformations from IFDS to IDE

Let $G^{\#}$ be the exploded supergraph of an arbitrary IFDS problem. A *transformation* $\mathcal{T} : (G^{\#}) \to (G^{\#}, L, \mathsf{EdgeFn})$ converts the IFDS problem into an IDE problem. We consider two IFDS-to-IDE transformations: an *equivalence transformation* $\mathcal{T}^{\equiv}$ (pronounced "t-equiv") and a *correlated-calls transformation* $\mathcal{T}_S^{\Subset}$ (pronounced "t-c-c") for a set of receivers S. Both transformations keep the exploded supergraph $G^{\#}$ the same, and only generate different edge functions. The solution of the IDE problem can be mapped back to an IFDS solution. If the equivalence transformation was used, then this solution is identical to the solution that would be computed by the IFDS algorithm for the original IFDS problem. If the correlated-calls transformation was used, then this solution is more precise because it excludes flow along infeasible paths due to correlated calls.

Equivalence Transformation. The lattice for the equivalence transformation $\mathcal{T}^{\equiv}$ is the two-point lattice $L^{\equiv} = \{\bot, \top\}$, where $\bot$ means "reachable", and $\top$ means "not reachable". The edge functions $\mathsf{EdgeFn}^{\equiv}$ are defined as

$$\mathsf{EdgeFn}^{\equiv} = \begin{cases} \lambda e\,.\,\lambda m\,.\,\bot & \text{if } e = (n_1, \mathbf{0}) \to (n_2, d_2), \text{ where } d_2 \neq \mathbf{0}; \\ \lambda e\,.\,\mathsf{id} & \text{otherwise.} \end{cases} \tag{1}$$

At a "diagonal" edge from a **0**-fact to a non-**0**-fact d, the micro function returns $\bot$ to make the fact d reachable. All other micro-functions are the identity function.

Correlated-Calls Transformation. In the correlated-calls transformation $\mathcal{T}_R^{\Subset}$, the lattice elements are maps from receivers to sets of types: $L^{\Subset} = \{m : R \to 2^T\}$, where R is the set of considered receivers and T is the set of all types. For each receiver r, the map gives an overapproximation of the possible runtime types of r. Sets of types are ordered by the superset relation, and this is lifted to maps from receivers to sets of types, so the bottom element $\bot_{\Subset}$ maps every receiver to the set of all types, and the top element $\top_{\Subset}$ maps every receiver to the empty set of types. During an actual execution, every receiver r points to an object of some runtime type. Therefore, a data-flow fact is unreachable along a given path if its corresponding lattice element maps any receiver to the empty set of types.

A micro-function $f \in L^{\Subset} \to L^{\Subset}$ defines how the map from receivers to types should be updated when an instruction is executed. The micro-function for most kinds of instructions is the identity. On a call to and return from a specific method m called on receiver r, the micro-function restricts the receiver-to-type map to map r only to types consistent with the polymorphic dispatch to method m. Finally, when an instruction assigns an object of unknown type to a receiver r, the corresponding micro-function updates the map to map r to the set of all types. This is made precise by the following definition:

Definition 1. *Given a previously fixed set $S \subseteq R$ of receivers, the micro-function $\varepsilon_S(e)$ of a supergraph edge e is defined as:*

$$\varepsilon_S(e) = \lambda m\,. \tag{2}$$
$$\begin{cases} m[r \to m(r) \cap \tau(s, f)], & \text{if } e \text{ is a call-start edge } r.c() \to \mathsf{start}_f \text{ that calls procedure } f \text{ with signature } s, \text{ and } r \in S; \\ m[r \to m(r) \cap \tau(s, f)]\,[v_1 \to \bot_T] \ldots [v_k \to \bot_T], & \text{if } e \text{ is an end-return edge } \mathsf{end}_f \to \mathsf{return}_{r.c()} \text{ from method } f \text{ with signature } s \text{ to the return node corresponding to the call } r.c(),\ v_1, \ldots, v_k \in S \text{ are the local variables in } f, \text{ and } r \in S; \\ m\,[r \to \bot_T]\,, & \text{if } e = n_1 \to n_2 \text{ and } n_1 \text{ contains an assignment to } r \in S; \\ m & \text{otherwise.} \end{cases}$$

In the above definition, the purpose of the set S is to limit the set of considered receivers. We will use S in Sect. 4.5.

We can now define EdgeFn, which assigns a micro-function to each edge in the exploded supergraph. Along a **0**-edge, the micro function is the identity. On a "diagonal" edge from **0** to a non-**0** fact that corresponds to some data-flow fact becoming reachable, $\varepsilon_S(e)$ is applied to $\bot_{\Subset}$ that maps every receiver to an object of every possible type. On all other edges, $\varepsilon_S(e)$ is applied to the existing map before the edge. The is formalized in the following definition.

Definition 2. *For each edge $e = (n_1, d_1) \to (n_2, d_2)$, $\mathsf{EdgeFn}_S^{\Subset}(e)$ is defined as follows:*

$$\mathsf{EdgeFn}_S^{\Subset}(e) = \begin{cases} \mathsf{id} & \text{if } d_1 = d_2 = \mathbf{0}, \\ \lambda m\,.\,\varepsilon_S(e)(\bot_{\Subset}) & \text{if } d_1 = \mathbf{0} \text{ and } d_2 \neq \mathbf{0}, \\ \lambda m\,.\,\varepsilon_S(e)(m) & \text{otherwise.} \end{cases} \tag{3}$$

Example 5. Consider the program from Fig. 1, whose exploded supergraph appeared in Fig. 5. Returning a secret value in method A.foo creates a "diagonal" edge from the **0**-fact to the method's return value r. The diagonal edge is labeled with $\lambda m\,.\,\bot_{\Subset}$, so every receiver is mapped to the set of all types $\bot_T$. On the end-return edge from A.foo to main, the set of types of a is restricted by the micro function $\lambda m\,.\,m[\mathsf{a} \to m(\mathsf{a}) \cap \{\mathsf{A}\}]$ corresponding to the assignment of the return value r to v. On the call-start edge from main to B.bar, the possible types of a are further restricted by the micro-function $\lambda m \,.\, m[\mathsf{a} \to m(\mathsf{a}) \cap \{\mathsf{B}\}]$ on the edge that passes the argument v to the parameter s. The composition of these micro functions results in the empty set as the possible types of a, indicating that this path is infeasible.

4.2 Converting IDE Results to IFDS Results

An IFDS solution $\mathcal{R}_{\text{IFDS}}$ has type $N^* \to 2^D$: it maps each program point n to a set of facts d that may be reached at n. An IDE solution $\mathcal{R}_{\text{IDE}}$ pairs each such fact d with a lattice element ℓ, so its type is $N^* \to (D \to L)$.

In the equivalence transformation lattice $L^{\equiv}$, $\bot$ means reachable and $\top$ means unreachable. Therefore, an IDE solution ρ computed using $\mathcal{T}^{\equiv}$ is converted to an IFDS solution as: $\mathcal{U}^{\equiv}(\rho) = \lambda n.\{d \mid \rho(n)(d) \neq \top\}$. In the correlated-calls transformation lattice $L^{\Subset}$, a map that maps any receiver to the empty set of possible types means that the corresponding data-flow path is infeasible. Therefore, an IDE solution ρ computed using $\mathcal{T}_S^{\Subset}$ is converted to an IFDS solution as

$$\mathcal{U}^{\Subset}(\rho) = \lambda n.\{d \mid \forall r \in S \,.\, \rho(n)(d)(r) \neq \top_T\}. \tag{4}$$

4.3 Implementation of Correlated Calls Micro-Functions

Conceptually, micro-functions are functions from L to L, where L is the IDE lattice, either $L^{\equiv}$ or $L^{\Subset}$ in our context. The IDE algorithm requires an efficient representation of micro-functions. The representation must support the basic micro-functions that we presented in Sect. 4.1, and it must support function application, comparison, and be closed under function composition and meet. We now propose such a representation for the correlated-calls micro-functions.

The representation of a micro-function is a map from receivers to pairs of sets of types $I(r)$ and $U(r)$, where $U(r)$ is required to be a subset of $I(r)$. We use the notation $\langle I, U\rangle$ to represent such a map, and $I(r)$ and $U(r)$ to look up the sets corresponding to a particular receiver r. The micro-function takes the existing set of possible types of the receiver r, intersects it with $I(r)$, then unions it with $U(r)$: $[\![\langle I, U\rangle]\!] = \lambda m \,.\, \lambda r \,.\, (m(r) \cap I(r)) \cup U(r)$.

All of the basic micro-functions defined in Definition 1 can be expressed in this representation. The following lemmas show how function comparison, composition, and meet can be implemented using basic set operations on I and U. The proofs of all of the lemmas and theorems are in the Technical Report [15].

Lemma 1. *For any pair of micro-function representations* $\langle I, U\rangle$, $\langle I', U'\rangle$,

$$\forall r \,.\, I(r) = I'(r) \wedge U(r) = U'(r) \iff [\![\langle I, U\rangle]\!] = [\![\langle I', U'\rangle]\!]. \tag{5}$$

Lemma 2. *For any pair of micro-function representations* $\langle I, U\rangle$, $\langle I', U'\rangle$,

$$[\![\langle I, U\rangle \circ \langle I', U'\rangle]\!] = [\![\langle I, U\rangle]\!] \circ [\![\langle I', U'\rangle]\!],$$

where the composition of two micro-function representations is defined as follows:

$$\langle I, U\rangle \circ \langle I', U'\rangle = \langle \lambda r\,.\,(I(r) \cap I'(r)) \cup U(r),\, \lambda r\,.\,(I(r) \cap U'(r)) \cup U(r)\rangle.$$

Lemma 3. *Let* $[\![\langle I, U\rangle]\!] \sqcap [\![\langle I', U'\rangle]\!] = \lambda m.\lambda r.[\![\langle I, U\rangle]\!](m)(r) \cup [\![\langle I', U'\rangle]\!](m)(r)$. *For any pair of micro-function representations* $\langle I, U\rangle$, $\langle I', U'\rangle$,

$$[\![\langle I, U\rangle \sqcap \langle I', U'\rangle]\!] = [\![\langle I, U\rangle]\!] \sqcap [\![\langle I', U'\rangle]\!], \tag{6}$$

where the meet of two micro-function representations is defined as follows:

$$\langle I, U\rangle \sqcap \langle I', U'\rangle = \langle \lambda r\,.\,I(r) \cup I'(r),\, \lambda r\,.\,U(r) \cup U'(r)\rangle\,.$$

4.4 Theoretical Results

The following lemma shows that our analysis is sound, i.e. that the resulting IDE problem still considers all data-flow paths that are actually feasible.

Lemma 4 (Soundness). *Let* P *be an IFDS problem and* $p = [\mathsf{start}_{main}, \ldots, n]$ *a concrete execution path, and let* $d \in D$. *If* $d \in M_F(p)(\varnothing)$, *then*

$$d \in \mathcal{U}^{\Subset}\left(\mathcal{R}_{IDE}(\mathcal{T}_R^{\Subset}(P))\right)(n)\,.$$

We also show that the result of an IDE problem obtained through a correlated-calls transformation is a subset of the original IFDS result.

Lemma 5 (Precision). *For an IFDS problem* P *and all* $n \in N^*$,

$$\mathcal{U}^{\Subset}\left(\mathcal{R}_{IDE}(\mathcal{T}_R^{\Subset}(P))\right)(n) \subseteq \mathcal{R}_{IFDS}(P)(n)\,. \tag{7}$$

4.5 Correlated-Call Receivers

We will now show that in a correlated-calls transformation, it is enough to consider only some of the receivers of set R.

Definition 3. *If* $r \in R$ *is the receiver of at least two polymorphic call sites, then we call* r *a correlated-call receiver, and we define* $R^{\Subset}$ *as the set of all such receivers.*

We will show that it is sufficient for the correlated-calls micro-functions to be defined only on correlated-call receivers. Specifically, a "reduced" correlated-calls transformation that considers only correlated-call receivers in the micro-functions yields the same solution as the full correlated-calls transformation (i.e. no precision is lost).

Lemma 6. *Let* P *be an IFDS problem. Then*

$$\mathcal{U}^{\Subset}\left(\mathcal{R}_{IDE}\left(\mathcal{T}_{R^{\Subset}}^{\Subset}(P)\right)\right) = \mathcal{U}^{\Subset}(\mathcal{R}_{IDE}\left(\mathcal{T}_R^{\Subset}(P)\right))\,. \tag{8}$$

4.6 Efficiency

Both the IFDS and IDE algorithms have been proven to run in $O(ED^3)$ time [16,18], where E is the number of edges in the (non-exploded) supergraph, and D is the size of the set of facts. The IDE algorithm may evaluate micro-functions up to $O(ED^3)$ times, so this running time must be multiplied by the cost of evaluating a micro-function. We show that the micro-functions in the correlated-calls IDE analysis can be evaluated in time $O(R^{\Subset}T)$, where $R^{\Subset}$ is the number of correlated-call receivers $R^{\Subset}$ and the T is the number of run-time types. Therefore, the overall worst-case cost of the correlated-calls IDE analysis is $O(ED^3R^{\Subset}T)$. In practice, $R^{\Subset}$ is much smaller than R, so Lemma 6 is significant for performance.

Specifically, the complexity proof for the IDE algorithm requires the implementation of the micro-functions to be *efficient* according to a list of specific criteria. Our micro-function implementation does satisfy the criteria:

Lemma 7. *The correlated-call representation of a micro function is efficient according to the IDE criteria [18] and the required operations on micro-functions can be computed in time* $O(R^{\Subset}T)$.

4.7 Implementation of the Correlated-Calls Analysis

We implemented the correlated-calls analysis in Scala [14]. Our implementation analyzes JVM bytecode compiled from input programs written in Java. We use WALA [5] to retrieve information about an input program, such as its control-flow supergraph and the set of receivers and their types. Since WALA does not contain an implementation of the IDE algorithm, we implemented it from scratch; we are working on contributing our infrastructure to WALA.

We tested our correlated-calls analysis using an IFDS taint-analysis as a client analysis. To this end, we converted the IFDS taint analysis into an IDE problem with an implementation of $\mathcal{T}^{\Subset}_{R^{\Subset}}$. We extensively tested the correlated-calls analysis to ensure that, in the absence of correlated calls, the analysis produces the same results as an IFDS-equivalent analysis, and that it produces more precise results in the presence of correlated calls as expected.

To evaluate the practicality of our approach, we applied two variants of the IFDS taint analysis to the SPEC JVM98 benchmarks: (i) an equivalent IDE taint analysis obtained using $\mathcal{T}^{\equiv}$, and (ii) an IDE taint analysis obtained using $\mathcal{T}^{\Subset}_{R^{\Subset}}$ that avoids imprecision due to correlated method calls.

The equivalence analysis is there for two reasons: (i) to explain how a correlated-calls-IDE problem can be derived from an IDE problem that has the same meaning as the original IFDS problem, and (ii) to provide a base line against which to compare the efficiency of the correlated-calls analysis. We compare the efficiency of the correlated-calls analysis against the equivalence-IDE analysis instead of the IFDS analysis because the time complexities of an IFDS and an equivalent IDE analysis are the same: an equivalent IDE analysis is just an IFDS analysis in which all edges are labeled with identity micro functions, and all operations on those functions are optimized to be constant-time.

The running times $t_{\Subset}$ of the correlated-calls and $t_{\equiv}$ equivalence analyses are shown in Table 1. In the table, N_r^* is the number of reachable nodes in the control-flow supergraph, and $N_r^\#$ the number of reachable nodes in the exploded supergraph.

Table 1. Running times of the analyses

Benchmark	N_r^*	$N_r^\#$	$t_{\equiv}$	$t_{\Subset}$
Compress	2,155	24,730	0:00:02	0:00:04
Db	2,285	22,938	0:00:06	0:00:12
Jack	17,602	284,625	0:06:06	0:11:31
Javac	40,430	510,810	0:46:06	1:45:57
Jess	14,448	316,418	0:10:19	0:13:33
Mpegaudio	11,959	224,886	0:01:57	0:00:54
Mtrt	3,597	88,267	0:00:34	0:00:33
Raytrace	3,597	88,267	0:00:38	0:00:37

The results suggest that the overhead of tracking correlated calls is acceptable. In particular, the correlated-calls analysis takes at most twice as long as the equivalence analysis. The absolute times range from a few seconds on the smaller SPEC programs to about two hours on `javac`.

Our implementation is a research prototype and many opportunities for optimization remain. For the specific combination of this IFDS client analysis and these benchmark programs, tracking correlated calls did not impact precision.

5 Related Work

The IFDS algorithm is an instance of the functional approach to data-flow analysis developed by Sharir and Pnueli [19]. IFDS has been used to encode a variety of data-flow problems such as typestate analysis [12,23] and shape analysis [9]. IFDS has been used [2,22] and extended [10] to solve taint-analysis problems.

Naeem and Lhoták [13] proposed several extensions of IFDS. In particular, they propose several techniques for improving the algorithm's efficiency, as well as a technique that improves expressiveness by extending applicability to a wider class of dataflow analysis problems. These extensions are orthogonal to, and could be combined with the approach presented in this paper. Our work differs from theirs by targeting analysis precision, not efficiency or expressiveness.

Bodden et al. [4] presents a framework for applying IFDS analyses to software product lines. Their approach enables the analysis of all possible products derived from a product line in a single analysis pass. Like our approach, their approach transforms IFDS problems to IDE problems. The micro-functions keep track of the possible program variations specified by the product line. Rodriguez and Lhoták evaluate a parallelized implementation of the IFDS algorithm using actors [17] that can take advantage of multiple processors.

The idea of using correlated calls to remove infeasible paths in data-flow analyses of object-oriented programs was introduced by Tip [21]. The possibility of using IDE to achieve this is mentioned, but not elaborated upon. Our work is the first to present and implement a concrete solution.

Recent work on correlation tracking for JavaScript [20] also eliminates infeasible paths. Instead of infeasible paths between dynamically dispatched method calls, their approach eliminates infeasible paths between reads and writes of different properties of an object. The approach differs from ours in that it targets points-to analysis rather than IFDS analyses, in that it targets infeasible paths due to different property names rather than different dynamically dispatched methods, and in that it employs context sensitivity to improve precision.

Our approach superficially resembles, but is orthogonal to, context sensitivity, including the CPA algorithm [1] and such variations as object sensitivity [11]. Context-sensitive points-to analysis is orthogonal to our work because it analyzes the flow of data (pointers), whereas we analyze control flow paths. Also, object-sensitive points-to analysis is flow-insensitive, while IFDS and IDE are flow-sensitive analyses. Note that our transformation only makes sense in a flow-sensitive setting since a flow-insensitive analysis already introduces many infeasible control flow paths.

It would be possible to simulate the effect of our correlated calls transformation in the following way inspired by context-sensitivity: we could re-analyze each method in a number of contexts. There would be a separate context for every possible assignment of concrete types to all of the pointers in the method that are used as receivers at a call site. The number of such contexts for each method would be $O(R^T)$, where R is the number of receiver pointers in the method and T is the number of possible concrete types that could be assigned to a receiver pointer. Our approach computes equally precise analysis results but avoids this exponential cost.

6 Conclusions

Previous algorithms for data-flow analysis are unable to avoid propagating data-flow facts along infeasible paths that arise in the presence of correlated polymorphic method calls. We present an approach for transforming an IFDS problem into an IDE problem in which path feasibility is encoded into functions associated with edges in an exploded control-flow supergraph. The solution to this IDE problem can be mapped back to the solution space of the original IFDS problem, and is more precise for some client programs because data flow along infeasible paths is prevented. We present a formalization of the transformation, prove its correctness, and briefly report on preliminary experiments with our prototype implementation. Full proof details are available in the Technical Report [15]. As future work, it is possible to adapt our approach to work on IDE problems. We would convert an initial IDE problem into a more complex IDE problem, such that the solution of the latter generates a more precise solution to former, by preventing data flow along infeasible paths.

References

1. Agesen, O.: Concrete Type Inference: Delivering Object-Oriented Applications. Ph.D. thesis, Stanford University (1995)
2. Arzt, S., Rasthofer, S., Fritz, C., Bodden, E., Bartel, A., Klein, J., Traon, Y.L., Octeau, D., McDaniel, P.: FlowDroid: precise context, flow, field, object-sensitive and lifecycle-aware taint analysis for Android apps. In: PLDI 2014, p. 29 (2014)
3. Blackburn, S.M., Garner, R., Hoffmann, C., Khan, A.M., McKinley, K.S., Bentzur, R., Diwan, A., Feinberg, D., Frampton, D., Guyer, S.Z., Hirzel, M., Hosking, A.L., Jump, M., Lee, H.B., Moss, J.E.B., Phansalkar, A., Stefanovic, D., VanDrunen, T., von Dincklage, D., Wiedermann, B.: The DaCapo benchmarks: Java benchmarking development and analysis. In: OOPSLA 2006, pp. 169–190 (2006)
4. Bodden, E., Tolêdo, T., Ribeiro, M., Brabrand, C., Borba, P., Mezini, M.: SPLLIFT - statically analyzing software product lines in minutes instead of years. In: Software Engineering 2014, pp. 81–82 (2014)
5. Fink, S., Dolby, J.: WALA – the TJ Watson libraries for analysis (2012). http://wala.sourceforge.net
6. Guarnieri, S., Pistoia, M., Tripp, O., Dolby, J., Teilhet, S., Berg, R.: Saving the world wide web from vulnerable JavaScript. In: ISSTA 2011, pp. 177–187 (2011)
7. Knoop, J., Steffen, B.: The interprocedural coincidence theorem. In: CC 1992, pp. 125–140 (1992)
8. Knoop, J., Steffen, B., Vollmer, J.: Parallelism for free: efficient and optimal bitvector analyses for parallel programs. ACM Trans. Program. Lang. Syst. **3**, 268–299 (1996)
9. Kreiker, J., Reps, T., Rinetzky, N., Sagiv, M., Wilhelm, R., Yahav, E.: Interprocedural shape analysis for effectively cutpoint-free programs. In: Voronkov, A., Weidenbach, C. (eds.) Programming Logics. LNCS, vol. 7797, pp. 414–445. Springer, Heidelberg (2013)
10. Lerch, J., Hermann, B., Bodden, E., Mezini, M.: FlowTwist: efficient context-sensitive inside-out taint analysis for large codebases. In: FSE 2014, pp. 98–108 (2014)
11. Milanova, A., Rountev, A., Ryder, B.G.: Parameterized object sensitivity for points-to analysis for Java. ACM Trans. Softw. Eng. Methodol. **14**(1), 1–41 (2005)
12. Naeem, N.A., Lhoták, O.: Typestate-like analysis of multiple interacting objects. In: OOPSLA 2008, pp. 347–366 (2008)
13. Naeem, N.A., Lhoták, O., Rodriguez, J.: Practical extensions to the IFDS algorithm. In: CC 2010, pp. 124–144 (2010)
14. Odersky, M.: Essentials of Scala. In: LMO 2009, p. 2 (2009)
15. Rapoport, M., Lhoták, O., Tip, F.: Precise data flow analysis in the presence of correlated method calls. Technical report CS-2015-07, University of Waterloo (2015)
16. Reps, T.W., Horwitz, S., Sagiv, S.: Precise interprocedural dataflow analysis via graph reachability. In: POPL 1995, pp. 49–61 (1995)
17. Rodriguez, J.D.: A concurrent IFDS dataflow analysis algorithm using actors. Master's thesis, University of Waterloo (2010)
18. Sagiv, S., Reps, T. W., and Horwitz, S.: Precise interprocedural dataflow analysis with applications to constant propagation. In: TAPSOFT 1995, pp. 651–665 (1995)
19. Sharir, M., Pnueli, A.: Two approaches to interprocedural data flow analysis. In: Program Flow Analysis: Theory and Applications, pp. 189–234 (1981)

20. Sridharan, M., Dolby, J., Chandra, S., Schäfer, M., Tip, F.: Correlation tracking for points-to analysis of JavaScript. In: Noble, J. (ed.) ECOOP 2012. LNCS, vol. 7313, pp. 435–458. Springer, Heidelberg (2012)
21. Tip, F.: Infeasible paths in object-oriented programs. Sci. Comput. Program. **97**, 91–97 (2015)
22. Tripp, O., Pistoia, M., Fink, S.J., Sridharan, M., Weisman, O.: TAJ: effective taint analysis of web applications. In: PLDI 2009, pp. 87–97 (2009)
23. Zhang, X., Mangal, R., Grigore, R., Naik, M., Yang, H.: On abstraction refinement for program analyses in Datalog. In: PLDI 2014, p. 27 (2014)

May-Happen-in-Parallel Analysis for Asynchronous Programs with Inter-Procedural Synchronization

Elvira Albert, Samir Genaim, and Pablo Gordillo(✉)

Complutense University of Madrid (UCM), Madrid, Spain
pabgordi@ucm.es

Abstract. A may-happen-in-parallel (MHP) analysis computes pairs of program points that may execute *in parallel* across different distributed components. This information has been proven to be essential to infer both safety properties (e.g., deadlock freedom) and liveness properties (e.g., termination and resource boundedness) of asynchronous programs. Existing MHP analyses take advantage of the synchronization points to learn that one task has finished and thus will not happen in parallel with other tasks that are still active. Our starting point is an existing MHP analysis developed for *intra-procedural* synchronization, i.e., it only allows synchronizing with tasks that have been spawned inside the current task. This paper leverages such MHP analysis to handle *inter-procedural* synchronization, i.e., a task spawned by one task can be awaited within a different task. This is challenging because task synchronization goes beyond the boundaries of methods, and thus the inference of MHP relations requires novel extensions to capture inter-procedural dependencies. The analysis has been implemented and it can be tried online.

1 Introduction

In order to improve program performance and responsiveness, many modern programming languages and libraries promote an asynchronous programming model, in which *asynchronous* tasks can execute concurrently with their caller tasks, and their callers can explicitly wait for their completion. Our analysis is formalized for an abstract model that includes procedures, asynchronous calls, and future variables for synchronization [7,8]. In this model, a method call m on some parameters $\overline{x}$, written as f=m($\overline{x}$) , spawns an asynchronous task. Here, f is a *future variable* which allows synchronizing with the termination of the task executing m. The instruction **await** f? allows checking whether m has finished, and blocks the execution of the current task if m is still running. As concurrently-executing tasks interleave their accesses to shared memory, asynchronous

This work was funded partially by the EU project FP7-ICT-610582 ENVISAGE: Engineering Virtualized Services (http://www.envisage-project.eu), by the Spanish MINECO project TIN2012-38137, and by the CM project S2013/ICE-3006.

S. Blazy and T. Jensen (Eds.): SAS 2015, LNCS 9291, pp. 72–89, 2015.
DOI: 10.1007/978-3-662-48288-9_5

programs are prone to concurrency-related errors [6]. Automatically proving safety and liveness properties still remains a challenging endeavor today.

MHP is an analysis of utmost importance to ensure both liveness and safety properties of concurrent programs. The analysis computes MHP *pairs*, which are pairs of program points whose execution might happen in parallel across different distributed components. In this fragment of code f=m(..);...; **await** f?; the execution of the instructions of the asynchronous task m may happen in parallel with the instructions between the asynchronous call and the **await**. However, due to the **await** instruction, the MHP analysis is able to ensure that they will not run in parallel with the instructions after the **await**. This piece of information is fundamental to prove more complex properties: in [9], MHP pairs are used to discard unfeasible deadlock cycles; in [4], the use of MHP pairs allows proving termination and inferring the resource consumption of loops with concurrent interleavings. As a simple example, consider a procedure g that contains as unique instruction y=-1, where y is a global variable. The following loop y=1; **while**(i>0){i=i-y;} might not terminate if g runs in parallel with it, since g can modify y to a negative value and the loop counter will keep on increasing. However, if we can guarantee that g will not run in parallel with this code, we can ensure termination and resource-boundedness for the loop.

This paper leverages an existing MHP analysis [3] developed for intra-procedural synchronization to the more general setting of inter-procedural synchronization. This is a fundamental extension because it allows synchronizing with the termination of a task outside the scope in which the task is spawned, as it is available in most concurrent languages. In the above example, if task g is awaited outside the boundary of the method that has spawned it, the analysis of [3] assumes that it may run in parallel with the loop and hence it fails to prove termination and resource boundedness. The enhancement to inter-procedural synchronization requires the following relevant extensions to the analysis:

1. *Must-Have-Finished Analysis* (MHF): the development of a novel MHF analysis which infers *inter-procedural dependencies* among the tasks. Such dependencies allow us to determine that, when a task finishes, those that are awaited for on it must have finished as well. The analysis is based on using Boolean logic to represent abstract states and simulate corresponding operations. The key contribution is the use of logical implication to delay the incorporation of procedure summaries until synchronization points are reached. This addresses a challenge in the analysis of asynchronous programs.
2. *Local MHP Phase*: the integration of the above MHF information in the local phase of the original MHP analysis in which methods are analyzed locally, i.e., without taking indirect calls into account. This will require the use of richer analysis information in order to consider the inter-procedural dependencies inferred in point 1 above.
3. *Global MHP phase*: the refinement of the global phase of the MHP analysis – where the information of the local MHP analysis in point 2 is composed– in order to eliminate spurious MHP pairs which appear when inter-procedural dependencies are not tracked. This will require to refine the way in which MHP pairs are computed.

We have implemented our approach in SACO [2], a static analyzer for concurrent objects which is able to infer the aforementioned liveness and safety properties. The system can be used online at http://costa.ls.fi.upm.es/saco/web, where the examples used in the paper are also available.

2 Language

Our analysis is formalized for an abstract model that includes procedures, asynchronous calls, and future variables [7,8]. It also includes conditional and loop constructs, however, conditions in these constructs are simply non-deterministic choices. Developing the analysis at such abstract level is convenient [11], since the actual computations are simply ignored in the analysis and what is actually tracked is the control flow that originates from asynchronously calling methods and synchronizing with their termination. Our implementation, however, is done for the full concurrent object-oriented language ABS [10] (see Sect. 6).

A program P is a set of methods that adhere to the following grammar:

$$M ::= m(\bar{x})\ \{s\}$$
$$s ::= \epsilon \mid b; s$$
$$b ::= \textbf{if}\ (*)\ \textbf{then}\ s_1\ \textbf{else}\ s_2 \mid \textbf{while}\ (*)\ \textbf{do}\ s \mid y = m(\bar{x}) \mid \textbf{await}\ x? \mid \textbf{skip}$$

Here all variables are future variables, which are used to synchronize with the termination of the called methods. Those future variables that are used in a method but are not in its parameters are the *local future variables* of the method (thus we do not need any special instruction for declaring them). In loops and conditions, the symbol $*$ stands for non-deterministic choice (*true* or *false*). The instruction $y = m(\bar{x})$ creates a new task which executes method m, and binds the future variable y with this new task so we can synchronize with its termination later. Inter-procedural synchronization is realized in the language by passing future variables as parameters, since the method that receives the future variable can await for the termination of the associated task (created outside its scope). For simplifying the presentation, we assume that *method parameters are not modified inside each method.* For a method m, we let P_m be the set of its parameters, L_m the set of its local variables, and $V_m = P_m \cup L_m$.

The instruction **await** x? blocks the execution of the current task until the task associated with x terminates. Instruction **skip** has no effect, it is simply used when abstracting from a richer language, e.g., ABS in our case, to abstract instructions such as assignments. Programs should include a method main from which the execution (and the analysis) starts. We assume that instructions are labeled with unique identifiers that we call program points. For **if** and **while** the identifier refers to the corresponding condition. We also assume that each method has an exit program point ℓ_m. We let $\texttt{ppoints}(m)$ and $\texttt{ppoints}(P)$ be the sets of program points of method m and program P, resp., I_ℓ be the instruction at program point ℓ, and $\texttt{pre}(\ell)$ be the set of program points preceding ℓ.

Next we define a formal (interleaving) operational semantics for our language. A task is of the form $tsk(tid, l, s)$ where tid is a unique identifier, l is a mapping

$$(\textsc{skip})\quad \frac{}{tsk(tid,l,\mathbf{skip};s) \rightsquigarrow tsk(tid,l,s)}$$

$$(\textsc{if})\quad \frac{b \equiv \mathbf{if}\ (*)\ \mathbf{then}\ s_1\ \mathbf{else}\ s_2,\ \text{set } s' \text{ non-deterministically to } s_1;s \text{ or } s_2;s}{tsk(tid,l,b;s) \rightsquigarrow tsk(tid,l,s')}$$

$$(\textsc{loop})\quad \frac{b \equiv \mathbf{while}\ (*)\ \mathbf{do}\ s_1,\ \text{set } s' \text{ non-deterministically to } s_1;b;s \text{ or } s}{tsk(tid,l,b;s) \rightsquigarrow tsk(tid,l,s')}$$

$$(\textsc{call})\quad \frac{\bar{z} \text{ are the formal parameters of } m,\ tid' \text{ is a fresh id, } l' = \{z_i \mapsto l(x_i)\}}{tsk(tid,l,y=m(\bar{x});s) \rightsquigarrow tsk(tid,l[y \mapsto tid'],s), tsk(tid',l',body(m))}$$

$$(\textsc{await})\quad \frac{l(x) = tid'}{tsk(tid,l,\mathbf{await}\ x?;s), tsk(tid',l',\epsilon) \rightsquigarrow tsk(tid,l,s), tsk(tid',l',\epsilon)}$$

Fig. 1. Derivation rules

from local variables and parameters to task identifiers, and s is a sequence of instructions. Local futures are initialized to the special value $\perp$ which is the default value for future variable (i.e., $\perp$ like **null** for reference variables in Java). A state S is a set of tasks that are executing in parallel. From a state S we can reach a state S' in one execution step, denoted $S \rightsquigarrow S'$, if S can be rewritten using one of the derivation rules of Fig. 1 as follows: if the conclusion of the rule is $A \rightsquigarrow B$ such that $A \subseteq S$ and the premise holds, then $S' = (S \setminus A) \cup B$. The meaning of the derivation rules is quite straightforward: (SKIP) advances the execution of the corresponding task to the next instruction; (IF) nondeterministically chooses between one of the branches; (LOOP) nondeterministically chooses between executing the loop body or advancing to the instruction after the loop; (CALL) creates a new task with a fresh identifier tid', initializes the formal parameters $\bar{z}$ of m to those of the actual parameters $\bar{x}$, sets future variable y in the calling task to tid', so one can synchronize with its termination later (other local futures of m are assumed to have the special value $\perp$); and (AWAIT) advances to the next instruction if the task associated to x has terminated already. Note that when a task terminates, it does not disappear from the state but rather its sequence of instructions remains empty.

An execution is a sequence of states $S_0 \rightsquigarrow S_1 \rightsquigarrow \cdots \rightsquigarrow S_n$, sometimes denoted as $S_0 \rightsquigarrow^* S_n$, where $S_0 = \{tsk(0,l,body(\mathsf{main}))\}$ is an initial state which includes a single task that corresponds to method main, and l is an empty mapping. At each step there might be several ways to move to the next state depending on the task selected, and thus executions are nondeterministic.

In what follows, given a task $tsk(tid,l,s)$, we let $pp(s)$ be the program point of the first instruction in s. When s is an empty sequence, $pp(s)$ refers to the exit program point of the corresponding method. Given a state S, we define its set of MHP pairs, i.e., the set of program points that execute in parallel in S, as $\mathcal{E}(S) = \{(pp(s_1), pp(s_2)) \mid tsk(tid_1,l_1,s_1), tsk(tid_2,l_2,s_2) \in S, tid_1 \neq tid_2\}$. The set of MHP pairs for a program P is then defined as the set of MHP pairs of all reachable states, namely $\mathcal{E}_P = \cup\{\mathcal{E}(S_n) \mid S_0 \rightsquigarrow^* S_n\}$.

Example 1. Figure 2 shows some examples in our language, where m_1, m_2 and m_3 are main methods. The following are some steps in a possible derivation for m_2:

$$\begin{array}{l}\mathbf{S_0} \equiv tsk(0,\emptyset,body(\mathsf{m}_2)) \rightsquigarrow^* \mathbf{S_1} \equiv tsk(0,[x \mapsto 1],\{16,\ldots\}),tsk(1,\emptyset,body(\mathsf{f})) \rightsquigarrow^* \\ \mathbf{S_2} \equiv tsk(0,[x \mapsto 1, z \mapsto 2],\{18,\ldots\}),tsk(1,\emptyset,body(\mathsf{f})),tsk(2,[w \mapsto 1],body(\mathsf{g})) \rightsquigarrow^* \\ \mathbf{S_3} \equiv tsk(0,[x \mapsto 1, z \mapsto 2],\{19,\ldots\}),tsk(1,\emptyset,\epsilon),tsk(2,[w \mapsto 1],body(\mathsf{g})) \rightsquigarrow^* \\ \mathbf{S_4} \equiv tsk(0,[x \mapsto 1, z \mapsto 2],\{20,\ldots\}),tsk(1,\emptyset,\epsilon),tsk(2,[w \mapsto 1],\epsilon) \rightsquigarrow \ldots\end{array}$$

In S_1 we execute until the asynchronous call to f which creates a new task identified as 1 and binds x to this new task. In S_2 we have executed the skip and the asynchronous invocation to g that adds in the new task the binding of the formal parameter w to the task identified as 1. In S_3 we proceed with the execution of the instructions in m_2 until reaching the **await** that blocks this task until g terminates. Also, in S_3 we have executed entirely f (denoted by ϵ). S_4 proceeds with the execution of g whose **await** can be executed since task 1 is at its exit point ϵ. We have the following MHP pairs in this fragment of the derivation, among many others: from S_1 we have (16,35) that captures that the first instruction of f executes in parallel with the instruction 16 of m2, from S_2 we have (18,35) and (18,38). The important point is that we have no pair (20,35) since when the **await** at L19 executes at S_4, it is guaranteed that f has finished. This is due to the inter-procedural dependency at L39 of g where the task f is awaited: variable x is passed as argument to g, which allows g to synchronize with the termination of f at L39 even if f was called in a different method.

3 An Informal Account of Our Method

In this section, we provide an overview of our method by explaining the analysis of m_2. Our goal is to infer precise MHP information that describes, among others, the following representative cases: (1) any program point of g cannot run in parallel with L20, because at L19 method m_2 awaits for g to terminate; (2) L35 cannot run in parallel with L20, since when waiting for the termination of g at L19 we know that f *must-have-finished* as well due to the *dependency* relation that arises when m_2 implicitly waits for the termination of f; and (3) L35 cannot run in parallel with L40, because f *must-have-finished* due to the synchronization on the local future variable w at L39 that refers to future variable x of m_2.

Let us first informally explain which MHP information the analysis of [3] is able to infer for m_2, and identify the reasons why it fails to infer some of the desired information. The analysis of [3] is carried out in two phases: (1) each method is *analyzed separately* to infer local MHP information; and (2) the local information is used to construct a global MHP graph from which MHP pairs are extracted by checking reachability conditions among the nodes.

The local analysis infers, for each program point, a *multiset* of MHP atoms where each atom describes a task that might be executing in parallel when reaching that program point, but only considering tasks that have been invoked directly in the analyzed method. An atom of the form $x{:}\tilde{m}$ indicates that there might be an *active* instance of m executing at any of its program points, and is

1 m₁() {	13 m₂() {	25 m₃() {	37 g(w) {	49 k(a,b) {
2 x=f();	14 **skip**;	26 z=f();	38 **skip**;	50 **skip**;
3 z=q();	15 **x=f()**;	27 **while** (∗)	39 **await** w?	51 **await** a?;
4 **skip**	16 **skip**;	28 x=q();	40 **skip**;	52 **skip**;
5 **if** (∗) **then**	17 z=g(x);	29 w=h(x,z);	41 }	53 **await** b?;
6 w=g(x);	18 **skip**;	30 **await** w?;		54 **skip**;
7 **skip**;	19 **await** z?;	31 **skip**;	43 h(a,b) {	55 }
8 **else**	20 **skip**;	32 }	44 **skip**;	56
9 w=k(x,z);	21 }	33	45 z=g(a);	57 q() {
10 **skip**;	22	34 f() {	46 **skip**;	58 **skip**;
11 **await** w?;	23	35 **skip**;	47 **await** z?;	59 }
12 }	24	36 }	48 }	60

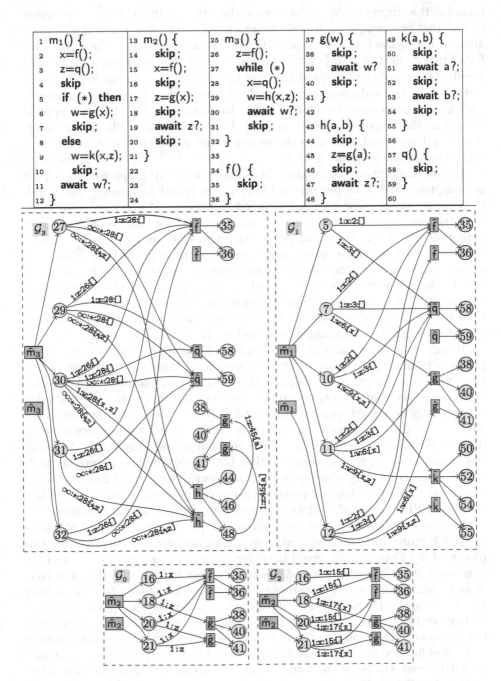

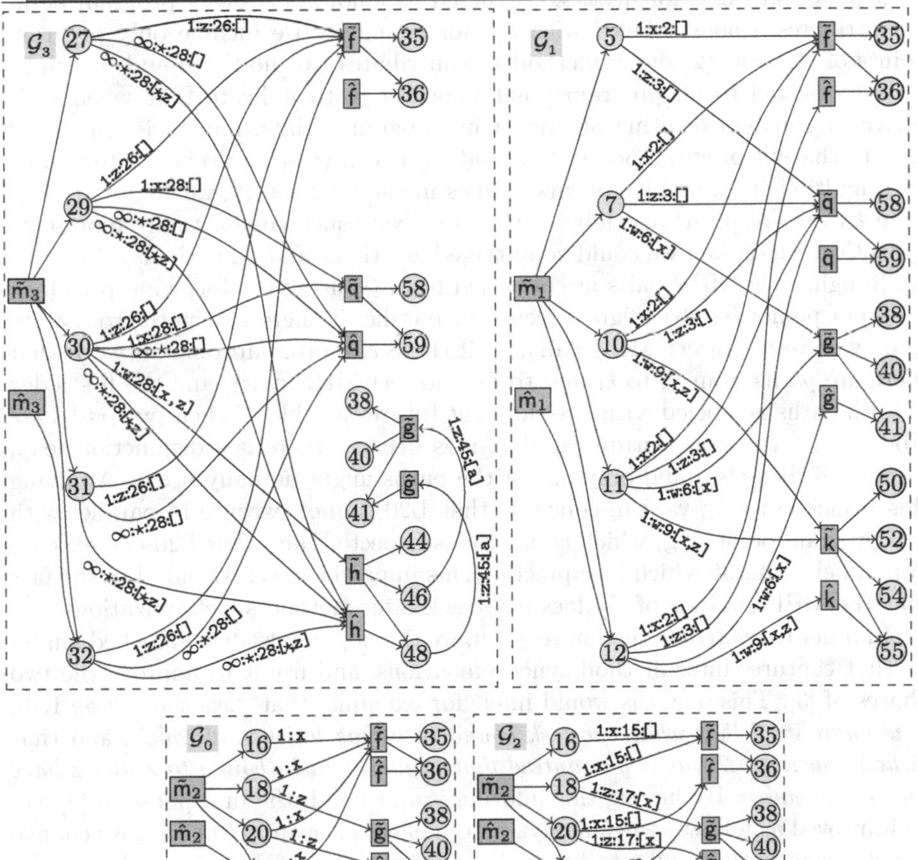

Fig. 2. (TOP) Examples for MHP analysis (m₁, m₂, m₃ are main methods). (BOTTOM) MHP graph $\mathcal{G}_i$ corresponds to analyzing m$_i$, and $\mathcal{G}_0$ to analyzing m₂ as in [3].

bound to the future variable x. An atom of the form $x{:}\hat{m}$ differs from the previous one in that m must be at its exit program point, i.e., has finished executing already. For method m_2, the local MHP analysis infers, among others, $\{\mathsf{x}{:}\tilde{\mathsf{f}}\}$ for L16, $\{\mathsf{x}{:}\tilde{\mathsf{f}}, \mathsf{z}{:}\tilde{\mathsf{g}}\}$ for L18, and $\{\mathsf{x}{:}\tilde{\mathsf{f}}, \mathsf{z}{:}\hat{\mathsf{g}}\}$ for L20 and L21, because g has been awaited locally. Observe that the sets of L20 and L21 include $\mathsf{x}{:}\tilde{\mathsf{f}}$ and not $\mathsf{x}{:}\hat{\mathsf{f}}$, although method f has finished already when reaching L20 and L21 (since g has finished). This information cannot be inferred by the local analysis of [3] since it is applied to each method separately, ignoring (*a*) indirect (non-local) calls and (*b*) inter-procedural synchronizations. In the sequel we let Ψ_ℓ be the result of the local MHP analysis for program point ℓ.

In the second phase, the analysis of [3] builds an MHP graph whose purpose is to capture MHP relations due to indirect calls (point (*a*) above). The graph $\mathcal{G}_0$ depicted in Fig. 2 for m_2 is constructed as follows: (1) every program point ℓ contributes a node labeled with ℓ – for simplicity we include only program points of interest; (2) every method m contributes two nodes $\tilde{m}$ and $\hat{m}$, where $\tilde{m}$ is connected to all program point nodes of m to indicate that when m is active, it can be executing at any of its program points, and $\hat{m}$ is connected only to the exit program point of m; and (3) if $x{:}\tilde{m}$ (resp. $x{:}\hat{m}$) is an atom of Ψ_ℓ with multiplicity i, i.e., it appears i times in the multiset Ψ_ℓ, we create an edge from ℓ to $\tilde{m}$ (resp. $\hat{m}$) and label it with $i{:}x$. Note such edge actually represents i identical edges, i.e., we could copy the edge i times and omit the label i.

Roughly, the MHP pairs are obtained from $\mathcal{G}_0$ using the following principle: program points (ℓ_1, ℓ_2) might execute in parallel if there is a path from ℓ_1 to ℓ_2 or vice versa (direct MHP pair); or if there is a program point ℓ_3 such that there are paths from ℓ_3 to ℓ_1 and to ℓ_2 (indirect MHP pair), and the first edge of both paths is labeled with two different future variables. When two paths are labeled with the same future variable, it is because there is a disjunction (e.g., from an if-then-else) and only one of the paths might actually occur. Applying this principle to $\mathcal{G}_0$, we can conclude that L20 cannot execute in parallel with any program point of g, which is precise as expected, and that L20 can execute in parallel with L35 which is imprecise. This imprecision is attributed to the fact that the MHP analysis of [3] does not track inter-method synchronizations.

In order to overcome the imprecision, we develop a must-have-finished analysis that captures inter-method synchronizations, and use it to improve the two phases of [3]. This analysis would infer, for example, that "*when reaching* L40, *it is guaranteed that whatever task bound to* w *has finished already*", and that "*when reaching* L20, *it is guaranteed that whatever tasks bound to* x *and* z *have finished already*". By having this information at hand, the first phase of [3] can be improved as follows: when analyzing the effect of **await** z? at L20, we change the status of both g and f to finished, because we know that any task bound z and x has finished already. In addition, we modify the MHP atoms as follows: an MHP atom will be of the form $y{:}\ell{:}\tilde{m}(\bar{x})$ or $y{:}\ell{:}\hat{m}(\bar{x})$, where the new information ℓ and $\bar{x}$ are the calling site and the parameters passed to m. The need for this extra information will become clear later in this section. In summary, the modified first phase will infer $\{\mathsf{x}{:}15{:}\tilde{\mathsf{f}}()\}$ for L16, $\{\mathsf{x}{:}15{:}\tilde{\mathsf{f}}(), \mathsf{z}{:}17{:}\tilde{\mathsf{g}}(\mathsf{x})\}$ for L18, and $\{\mathsf{x}{:}15{:}\hat{\mathsf{f}}(), \mathsf{z}{:}17{:}\hat{\mathsf{g}}(\mathsf{x})\}$ for L20 and L21.

In the second phase of the analysis: (i) the construction of the MHP graph is modified to use the new local MHP information; and (ii) the principle used to extract MHP pairs is modified to make use to the must-have-finished information. The new MHP graph constructed for m_2 is depicted in Fig. 2 as $\mathcal{G}_2$. Observe that the labels on the edges include the new information available in the MHP atoms. Importantly, the spurious MHP information that is inferred by [3] is not included in this graph: (1) in contrast to $\mathcal{G}_0$, $\mathcal{G}_2$ does not include edges from nodes 20 and 21 to $\tilde{\mathsf{f}}$, but to $\hat{\mathsf{f}}$. This implies that L35 cannot run in parallel with L20 or L21; (2) in $\mathcal{G}_2$, we still have paths from 18 to 35 and 40, which means, if the old principle for extracting MHP pairs is used, that L35 and L40 might happen in parallel. The main point is that, using the labels on the edges, we know that the first path uses a call to f that is bound to x, and that this same x is passed to g, using the parameter w, in the first edge of the second path. Now since the must-have-finished analysis tell us that at L40 any task bound w is finished already, we conclude that f must be at its exit program point when the execution reaches L40, and thus the MHP pair (35,40) is spurious because L35 is not an exit program point of f. This last point explains why the MHP atoms are designed to include the actual parameters of method calls.

4 Must-Have-Finished Analysis

In this section we present a novel inter-procedural Must-Have-Finished (MHF) analysis that can be used to compute, for each program point ℓ, a set of *finished future variables*, i.e., whenever ℓ is reached those variables are either not bound to any task (i.e., have the default value $\bot$) or their bound tasks are guaranteed to have terminated. We refer to such sets as MHF sets.

Example 2. The following are MHF sets for the program points of Fig. 2:

L2: {x,w,z}	L9 : {w}	L16: {z}	L26: {x,z,w}	L32: {x,w}	L41: {w}	L50: {}	L58: {}
L3: {z,w}	L10: {}	L17: {z}	L27: {x,w}	L35: {}	L44: {z}	L51: {}	L59: {}
L4: {w}	L11: {}	L18: {}	L28: {x,w}	L36: {}	L45: {z}	L52: {a}	
L5: {w}	L12: {x,w}	L19: {}	L29: {w}	L38: {}	L46: {}	L53: {a}	
L6: {w}	L14: {x,z}	L20: {x,z}	L30: {}	L39: {}	L47: {}	L54: {a,b}	
L7: {}	L15: {x,z}	L21: {x,z}	L31: {x,w}	L40: {w}	L48: {a,z}	L55: {a,b}	

Here, at program points that correspond to method entries, all local variables (but not the parameters) are finished since they point to no task. For g: at L38 and L39 no task is guaranteed to have finished, because the task bound to w might be still executing; at L40 and L41, since we passed through **await** w? already, it is guaranteed that w is finished. For k: at L50 and L51 no task is guaranteed to have finished; at L52 and L53 a is finished since we already passed through **await** a?; and at L54 and L55 both a and b are finished. For m_1: at L12 both w and x are finished. Note that w is finished because of **await** w? , and x is finished due to the implicit dependency between the termination of x and w.

4.1 Definition of MHF

By carefully examining the MHF sets of Example 2, we can see that an analysis that simply tracks MHF sets would be imprecise. For example, since the MHF set at L11 is empty, the only information we can deduce for L12 is that w is finished. To deduce that x is finished we must track the implicit dependency between w and x. Next we define a more general MHF property that captures such dependencies, and from which we can easily compute the MHF sets.

Definition 1. *Given a program point* $\ell \in \mathtt{ppoints}(P)$*, we let* $\mathcal{F}(\ell) = \{f(S_i, l) \mid S_0 \leadsto^* S_i, tsk(tid, l, s) \in S_i, pp(s) = \ell\}$ *where* $f(S, l) = \{x \mid x \in dom(l),\ l(x) = \bot \vee (l(x) = tid' \wedge tsk(tid', l', \epsilon) \in S)\}$*.*

Intuitively, $f(S, l)$ is the set of all future variables, from those defined in l, whose corresponding tasks are finished in S. The set $\mathcal{F}(\ell)$ considers all possible ways of reaching ℓ, and for each one it computes a corresponding set $f(S, l)$ of finished future variables. Thus, $\mathcal{F}(\ell)$ describes all possible sets of finished future variables when reaching ℓ. The set of *all* finished future variables at ℓ is then defined as $\mathtt{mhf}(\ell) = \cap\{F \mid F \in \mathcal{F}(\ell)\}$, i.e., the intersection of all sets in $\mathcal{F}(\ell)$.

Example 3. The values of $\mathcal{F}(\ell)$ for selected program points from Fig. 2 are:

L5 : {{w,x,z},{w,z},{w,x},{w}}	L31: {{w,x,z},{w,x}}	L46: {{a,z},{a},{}, {a,b,z},{a,b},{b}}
L11: {{w,x,z},{w,x},{x,z},{z},{x},{}}	L32: {{w,x,z},{w,x}}	L48: {{a,z},{a,b,z}}
L12: {{w,x,z},{w,x}}	L35: {{}}	L52: {{a},{a,b}}
L20: {{x,z}}	L38: {{w},{}}	L54: {{a,b}}
L27: {{w,x,z},{w,x}}	L40: {{w}}	L58: {{}}
L30: {{w,x,z},{w,x},{x,z},{x},{z},{}}		

In L5 different sets arise by considering all possible orderings in the execution of tasks f, q and m_1, but $\mathtt{mhf}(L5) = \{\mathsf{w}\}$. Note that for any $F \in \mathcal{F}(11)$, if $\mathsf{w} \in F$ then $\mathsf{x} \in F$, which means that if w is finished at L11, then x must have finished.

4.2 An Analysis to Infer MHF Sets

Our goal is to infer $\mathtt{mhf}(\ell)$, or a subset of it, for each $\ell \in \mathtt{ppoints}(P)$. Note that any set X that over-approximates $\mathcal{F}(\ell)$, i.e., $\mathcal{F}(\ell) \subseteq X$, can be used to compute a subset of $\mathtt{mhf}(\ell)$, because $\cap\{F \mid F \in X\} \subseteq \cap\{F \mid F \in \mathcal{F}(\ell)\}$. In the rest of this section we develop an analysis to over-approximate $\mathcal{F}(\ell)$. We will use Boolean formulas, whose models naturally represent MHF sets, and Boolean connectives to smoothly model the abstract execution of the different instructions.

An MHF state for the program points of a method m is a propositional formula $\Phi : V_m \mapsto \{true, false\}$ of the form $\vee_i \wedge_j c_{ij}$, where an atomic proposition c_{ij} is either x or $y \rightarrow x$ such that $x \in V_m \cup \{true, false\}$ and $y \in L_m$. Intuitively, an atomic proposition x states that x is finished, and $y \rightarrow x$ states that if y is finished then x is finished as well. Note that we do not allow the parameters of m to appear in the premise of an implication (we require $y \in L_m$). When Φ

is *false* or of the form $\vee_j \wedge_j x_{ij}$ where x_{ij} is a propositional variable, we call it monotone. Recall that $\sigma \subseteq V_m$ is a *model* of Φ, iff an assignment that maps variables from σ to *true* and other variables to *false* is a satisfying assignment for Φ. The set of all models of Φ is denoted $[\![\Phi]\!]$. The set of all MHF states for m, together with the formulas *true* and *false*, is denoted $\mathcal{A}_m$.

Example 4. Assume $V_m = \{x, y, z\}$. The Boolean formula $x \vee y$ states that either x or y or both are finished, and that z can be in any status. This information is precisely captured by the models $[\![x \vee y]\!] = \{\{x\},\{y\},\{x,y\},\{x,z\},\{y,z\},\{x,y,z\}\}$. The Boolean formula $z \wedge (x \rightarrow y)$ states that z is finished, and if x is finished then y is finished. This is reflected in $[\![z \wedge (x \rightarrow y)]\!] = \{\{z\}, \{z, y\}, \{z, x, y\}\}$ since z belongs to all models, and any model that includes x includes y as well. The formula *false* means that the corresponding program point is not reachable. The following MHF states correspond to some selected program points from Fig. 2:

Φ_5 : w	Φ_{12}: w $\wedge$ x	Φ_{27}: w $\wedge$ x	Φ_{31}: w $\wedge$ x	Φ_{35}: *true*	Φ_{40}: w	Φ_{48}: a $\wedge$ z	Φ_{54}: a $\wedge$ b
Φ_{11}: w$\rightarrow$x	Φ_{20}: x $\wedge$ z	Φ_{30}: w$\rightarrow$x	Φ_{32}: w $\wedge$ x	Φ_{38}: *true*	Φ_{46}: z$\rightarrow$a	Φ_{52}: a	Φ_{58}: *true*

Note that the models $[\![\Phi_\ell]\!]$ coincide with $\mathcal{F}(\ell)$ from Example 3.

Now, we proceed to explain how the execution of the different instructions can be modeled with Boolean formulas. Let us first define some auxiliary operations. Given a variable x and an MHF state $\Phi \in \mathcal{A}_m$, we let $\exists x.\Phi = \Phi[x \mapsto true] \vee \Phi[x \mapsto false]$, i.e., this operation eliminates variable x from (the domain of) Φ. Note that $\exists x.\Phi \in \mathcal{A}_m$ and that $[\![\Phi]\!] \models [\![\exists x.\Phi]\!]$. For a tuple of variables $\bar{x}$ we let $\exists \bar{x}.\Phi$ be $\exists x_1.\exists x_2.\dots.\exists x_n.\Phi$, i.e., eliminate all variables $\bar{x}$ from Φ. We also let $\bar{\exists} \bar{x}.\Phi$ stand for eliminating all variables but $\bar{x}$ from Φ. Note that if $\Phi \in \mathcal{A}_m$ is monotone, and $x \in L_m$, then $x \rightarrow \Phi$ is a formula in $\mathcal{A}_m$ as well.

Given a program point ℓ, an MHF state Φ_ℓ, and an instruction to execute I_ℓ, our aim is to compute a new MHF state, denoted $\mu(I_\ell)$, that represents the effect of executing I_ℓ within Φ_ℓ. If I_ℓ is **skip**, then clearly $\mu(I_\ell) \equiv \Phi_\ell$. If I_ℓ is an **await** x? instruction, then $\mu(I_\ell)$ is $x \wedge \Phi_\ell$, which restricts the MHF state of Φ_ℓ to those cases (i.e., models) in which x is finished. If I_ℓ is a call $y = m(\bar{x})$, where m is a method with parameters named $\bar{z}$, and, at the exit program point of m we know that the MHF state Φ_{ℓ_m} holds, then $\mu(I_\ell)$ is computed as follows:

- We compute an MHF state Φ_m that describes "what happens to tasks bound to $\bar{x}$ when m terminates". This is done by projecting Φ_{ℓ_m} onto the method parameters, and then renaming the formal parameters $\bar{z}$ to the actual parameters $\bar{x}$, i.e., $\Phi_m = (\bar{\exists} \bar{z}.\Phi_{\ell_m})[\bar{z}/\bar{x}]$, where $[\bar{z}/\bar{x}]$ denotes the renaming.
- Now assume that ξ is a new (future) variable to which m is bound. Then $\xi \rightarrow \Phi_m$ states that "when m terminates, Φ_m must hold". Note that it says nothing about $\bar{x}$ if m has not terminated yet. It is also important to note that Φ_m is monotone and thus $\xi \rightarrow \Phi_m$ is a valid MHF state.
- Next we add $\xi \rightarrow \Phi_m$ to Φ_ℓ, eliminate (old) y since the variable is rewritten, and rename ξ to (new) y. Note that we use ξ as a temporary variable just not to conflict with the old value of y.

The above reasoning is equivalent to $(\exists y.(\Phi_\ell \wedge (\xi \rightarrow (\bar{\exists} \bar{z}.\Phi_{\ell_m})[\bar{z}/\bar{x}]))[\xi/y]$, and is denoted by $\oplus(\Phi_\ell, y, \Phi_{\ell_m}, \bar{x}, \bar{z})$. Note that the use of logical implication $\rightarrow$, to abstractly simulate method calls, allows delaying the incorporation of the method summary Φ_m until corresponding synchronization point is reached.

Example 5. Let $\Phi_{11} = \mathsf{x} \rightarrow \mathsf{w}$ be the MHF state at L11. The effect of executing I_{11}, i.e., **await** w?, within Φ_{11} should eliminate all models that do not include w. This is done using $\mathsf{w} \wedge \Phi_{11}$ which results in $\Phi_{12} = \mathsf{w} \wedge \mathsf{x}$. Now let $\Phi_{29} = \mathsf{w}$ be the MHF state at L29. The effect of executing the instruction at L29, i.e., w=h(x,z), within Φ_{29} is defined as $\oplus(\Phi_{29}, \mathsf{w}, \Phi_{48}, \langle \mathsf{x}, \mathsf{z} \rangle, \langle \mathsf{a}, \mathsf{b} \rangle)$ and computed as follows: (1) we restrict $\Phi_{48} = \mathsf{a} \wedge \mathsf{z}$ to the method parameters $\langle \mathsf{a}, \mathsf{b} \rangle$, which results in a; (2) we rename the formal parameters $\langle \mathsf{a}, \mathsf{b} \rangle$ to the actual ones $\langle \mathsf{x}, \mathsf{z} \rangle$ which results in $\Phi_\mathsf{h} = \mathsf{x}$; (3) we compute $\exists \mathsf{w}.(\Phi_{29} \wedge (\xi \rightarrow \Phi_\mathsf{h}))$, which results in $\xi \rightarrow \mathsf{x}$; and finally (4) we rename ξ to w which results in $\Phi_{30} = \mathsf{w} \rightarrow \mathsf{x}$.

Next we describe how to generate a set of data-flow equations whose solutions associate to each $\ell \in \mathtt{ppoints}(P)$ an MHF state Φ_ℓ that over-approximates $\mathcal{F}(\ell)$, i.e., $\mathcal{F}(\ell) \subseteq [\![\Phi_\ell]\!]$. Each $\ell \in \mathtt{ppoints}(P)$ contributes one equation as follows:

- if ℓ is not a method entry, we generate $\Phi_\ell = \vee\{\mu(\ell') \mid \ell' \in \mathtt{pre}(\ell)\}$. This considers each program point ℓ' that immediately precedes ℓ, computes the effect $\mu(\ell')$ of executing $I_{\ell'}$ within $\Phi_{\ell'}$, and the takes their disjunction;
- if ℓ is an entry of method m, we generate $\Phi_\ell = \wedge\{x \mid x \in L_m\}$, i.e., all local variables point to finished tasks (since they are mapped to $\perp$ when entering a method), and we do not know anything about the parameters.

The set of all equations for a program P is denoted by $\mathcal{H}_P$.

Example 6. The following are the equations for the program points of m_3:

$\Phi_{27} = \oplus(\Phi_{26}, \mathsf{z}, \Phi_{36}, \langle\rangle, \langle\rangle) \vee \Phi_{31}$	$\Phi_{28} = \Phi_{27}$	$\Phi_{29} = \oplus(\Phi_{28}, \mathsf{x}, \Phi_{59}, \langle\rangle, \langle\rangle)$	$\Phi_{31} = \mathsf{w} \wedge \Phi_{30}$
$\Phi_{30} = \oplus(\Phi_{29}, \mathsf{w}, \Phi_{48}, \langle \mathsf{x}, \mathsf{z} \rangle, \langle \mathsf{a}, \mathsf{b} \rangle)$		$\Phi_{26} = \mathsf{w} \wedge \mathsf{x} \wedge \mathsf{z}$	$\Phi_{32} = \Phi_{27}$

Note the circular dependency of Φ_{27} and Φ_{31} which originates from the corresponding while loop. Recall that m_3 is a main method.

The next step is to solve $\mathcal{H}_P$, i.e., compute an MHF state Φ_ℓ, for each $\ell \in \mathtt{ppoints}(P)$, such that $\mathcal{H}_P$ is satisfiable. This can be done iteratively as follows. We start from an initial solution where $\Phi_\ell = \mathit{false}$ for each $\ell \in \mathtt{ppoints}(P)$. Then repeat the following until a fixed-point is reached: (1) substitute the current solution in the right hand side of the equations, and obtain new values for each Φ_ℓ; and (2) merge the new and old values of each Φ_ℓ using $\vee$. E.g., solving the equation of Example 6, among other equations that were omitted, results in a solution that includes, among others, the MHF states of Example 4. In what follows we assume that $\mathcal{H}_P$ has been solved, and let Φ_ℓ be the MHF state at ℓ in such solution.

Theorem 1. *For any program point* $\ell \in \mathtt{ppoints}(P)$*, we have* $\mathcal{F}(\ell) \subseteq [\![\Phi_\ell]\!]$.

In the rest of this article we let $\mathtt{mhf}_\alpha(\ell) = \{x \mid x \in V_m,\ \Phi_\ell \models x\}$, i.e., the set of finished future variables at ℓ that is induced by Φ_ℓ. Theorem 1 implies $\mathtt{mhf}_\alpha(\ell) \subseteq \mathtt{mhf}(\ell)$. Computing $\mathtt{mhf}_\alpha(\ell)$ using the MHF states of Example 4, among others that are omitted, results exactly in the MHF sets of Example 2.

5 MHP Analysis

In this section we present our MHP analysis, which is based on incorporating the MHF sets of Sect. 4 into the MHP analysis of [3]. In Sects. 5.1 and 5.2 we describe how we modify the two phases of the original analysis, and describe the gain of precision with respect to [3] in each phase.

5.1 Local MHP

The local MHP analysis (LMHP) considers each method m separately, and for each $\ell \in \mathtt{ppoints}(m)$ it infers an LMHP state that describes the tasks that might be executing when reaching ℓ (considering only tasks invoked in m). An LMHP state Ψ is a *multiset* of MHP atoms, where each atom represents a task and can be: (1) $y{:}\ell'{:}\tilde{m}(\bar{x})$, which represents an *active* task that might be at any of its program points, including the exit one, and is bound to future variable y. Moreover, this task is an instance of method m that was called at program point ℓ' (the *calling site*) with future parameters $\bar{x}$; or (2) $y{:}\ell'{:}\hat{m}(\bar{x})$, which differs from the previous one in that the task can only be at the exit program point, i.e., it is a *finished* task. In both cases, future variables y and $\bar{x}$ can be $\star$, which is a special symbol indicating that we have no information on the future variable.

Intuitively, the MHP atoms of Ψ represent (local) tasks that are executing in parallel. However, since a variable y cannot be bound to more than one task at the same time, atoms bound to the same variable represent mutually exclusive tasks, i.e., cannot be executing at the same time. The same holds for atoms that use *mutually exclusive calling sites* ℓ_1 and ℓ_2 (i.e., there is no path from ℓ_1 and ℓ_2 and vice versa). The use of multisets allows including the same atom several times to represent different instances of the same method. We let $(a, i) \in \Psi$ indicate that a appears i times in Ψ. Note that i can be ∞, which happens when the atom corresponds to a calling site inside a loop, this guarantees convergence of the analysis. Recall that the MHP atoms of [3] do not use the parameters $\bar{x}$ and the calling site ℓ', since they do not benefit from such extra information.

Example 7. The following are LMHP states for some program points from Fig. 2:

L5 : $\{x{:}2{:}\tilde{f}(),z{:}3{:}\tilde{q}()\}$
L7 : $\{x{:}2{:}\tilde{f}(),z{:}3{:}\tilde{q}(),w{:}6{:}\tilde{g}(x)\}$
L10: $\{x{:}2{:}\tilde{f}(),z{:}3{:}\tilde{q}(),w{:}9{:}\tilde{k}(x,z)\}$
L11: $\{x{:}2{:}\tilde{f}(),z{:}3{:}\tilde{q}(),w{:}6{:}\tilde{g}(x),w{:}9{:}\tilde{k}(x,z)\}$
L12: $\{x{:}2{:}\hat{f}(),z{:}3{:}\tilde{q}(),w{:}6{:}\hat{g}(x),w{:}9{:}\hat{k}(x,z)\}$
L16: $\{x{:}15{:}\tilde{f}()\}$
L18: $\{x{:}15{:}\tilde{f}(),z{:}17{:}\tilde{g}(x)\}$
L20: $\{x{:}15{:}\hat{f}(),z{:}17{:}\hat{g}(x)\}$
L21: $\{x{:}15{:}\hat{f}(),z{:}17{:}\hat{g}(x)\}$
L27: $\{z{:}26{:}\tilde{f}(),(\star{:}28{:}\hat{q}(),\infty),(\star{:}29{:}\hat{h}(\star,z),\infty)\}$
L29: L27 $\cup$ $\{x{:}28{:}\tilde{q}()\}$
L30: L29 $\cup$ $\{w{:}29{:}\tilde{h}(x,z)\}$
L31: $\{z{:}26{:}\tilde{f}(),(\star{:}28{:}\hat{q}(),\infty),(\star{:}29{:}\hat{h}(\star,z),\infty)\}$
L32: $\{z{:}26{:}\tilde{f}(),(\star{:}28{:}\hat{q}(),\infty),(\star{:}29{:}\hat{h}(\star,z),\infty)\}$
L44: $\{\}$
L46: $\{z{:}45{:}\tilde{g}(a)\}$
L48: $\{z{:}45{:}\hat{g}(a)\}$

Let us explain some of the above LMHP states. The state at L5 includes $x{:}2{:}\tilde{f}()$ and $z{:}3{:}\tilde{q}()$ for the active tasks invoked at L2 and L3. The state at L11 includes an atom for each task invoked in m1. Note that those of g and h are bound to the same future variable w, which means that only one of them might be executing at L11, depending on which branch of the **if** statement is taken. The state at L12 includes $z{:}3{:}\tilde{q}()$ since q might be active at L12 if we take the **then** branch of the **if** statement, and the other atoms correspond to tasks that are finished. The state at L27 includes $z{:}26{:}\tilde{f}()$ for the active task invoked at L26, and $\star{:}28{:}\hat{q}()$ and $\star{:}29{:}\hat{h}(\star,z)$ with ∞ multiplicity for the tasks created inside the loop. Note that the first parameter of h is $\star$ since x is rewritten at each iteration.

The LMHP states are inferred by a *data-flow analysis* which is defined as a solution of a set of LMHP constraints obtained by applying the following transfer function τ to the instructions. Given an LMHP state Ψ_ℓ, the effect of executing instruction I_ℓ within Ψ_ℓ, denoted by $\tau(I_\ell)$, is defined as follows:

- if I_ℓ is a call $y = m(\bar{x})$, then $\tau(I_\ell) = \Psi_\ell[y/\star] \cup \{y{:}\ell'{:}\tilde{m}(\bar{x})\}$, which replaces each occurrence of y by $\star$, since it is rewritten, and then adds a new atom $y{:}\ell{:}\tilde{m}(\bar{x})$ for the newly created task. E.g., the LMHP state of L30 in Example 7 is obtained from the one of L29 by adding $w{:}29{:}\tilde{h}(x,z)$ for the call at L29;
- if I_ℓ is **await** $y?$, and ℓ' is the program point after ℓ, then we mark all tasks that are bound to a finished future variable as finished, i.e., $\tau(I_\ell)$ is obtained by turning each $z{:}\ell''{:}\tilde{m}(\bar{x}) \in \Psi_\ell$ to $z{:}\ell''{:}\hat{m}(\bar{x})$ for each $z \in \mathtt{mhf}_\alpha(\ell')$. E.g., the LMHP state of L12 in Example 7 is obtained from the one of L11 by turning the status of g, k, and f to finished (since w and x are finished at L12);
- otherwise, $\tau(I_\ell) = \Psi_\ell$.

The main difference w.r.t. the analysis of [3] is the treatment of **await** $y?$: while we use an MHF set computed using the inter-procedural MHF analysis of Sect. 4, in [3] the MHF set $\{y\}$ is used, which is obtained syntactically from the instruction. Our LMHP analysis, as [3], is defined as a solution of a set of LMHP constraints. In what follows we assume that the results of the LMHP analysis are available, and we will refer to the LMHP state of program point ℓ as Ψ_ℓ.

5.2 Global MHP

The results of the LMHP analysis are used to construct an MHP graph, from which we can compute the desired set of MHP pairs. The construction is exactly as in [3] except that we carry the new information in the MHP atoms. However, the process of extracting the MHP pairs from such graphs will be modified.

In what follows, we use $y{:}\ell{:}\check{m}(\bar{x})$ to refer to an MHP atom without specifying if it corresponds to an active or finished task, i.e., the symbol $\check{m}$ can be matched to $\tilde{m}$ or $\hat{m}$. As in [3], the nodes of the MHP graph consist of two method nodes $\tilde{m}$ and $\hat{m}$ for each method m, and a program point node ℓ for each $\ell \in \texttt{ppoints}(P)$. Edges from $\tilde{m}$ to each $\ell \in \texttt{ppoints}(m)$ indicate that when m is active, it can be executing at any program point, including the exit, but only one. An edge from $\hat{m}$ to ℓ_m indicates that when m is finished it can be only at its exit program point. The out-going edges from a program point node ℓ reflect the atoms of the LMHP state Ψ_ℓ as follows: if $(y{:}\ell'{:}\check{m}(\bar{x}), i) \in \Psi_\ell$, then there is an edge from node ℓ to node $\check{m}$ and it is labeled with $i{:}y{:}\ell'{:}\bar{x}$. These edges simply indicate which tasks might be executing in parallel when reaching ℓ, exactly as Ψ_ℓ does.

Example 8. The MHP graphs $\mathcal{G}_1$, $\mathcal{G}_2$, and $\mathcal{G}_3$ in Fig. 2, correspond to methods $\mathsf{m_1}$, $\mathsf{m_2}$, and $\mathsf{m_3}$, each analyzed together with its reachable methods. For simplicity, the graphs include only some program points of interest. Note that the out-going edges of program point nodes coincide with the LMHP states of Example 7.

The procedure of [3] for extracting the MHP pairs from the MHP graph of a program P, denoted $\mathcal{G}_P$, is based on the following principle: (ℓ_1, ℓ_2) is an MHP pair induced by $\mathcal{G}_P$ iff (i) $\ell_1 \rightsquigarrow \ell_2 \in \mathcal{G}_P$ or $\ell_2 \rightsquigarrow \ell_1 \in \mathcal{G}_P$; or (ii) there is a program point node ℓ_3 and paths $\ell_3 \rightsquigarrow \ell_1 \in \mathcal{G}_P$ and $\ell_3 \rightsquigarrow \ell_2 \in \mathcal{G}_P$, such that the first edges of these paths are different and they do not correspond to mutually exclusive MHP atoms, i.e., they use different future variables and do not correspond to mutually exclusive calling sites (see Sect. 5.1). Edges with multiplicity $i > 1$ represent i different edges. The first (resp. second) case is called direct (resp. indirect) MHP, see Sect. 3.

Example 9. Let us explain some of the MHP pairs induced by $\mathcal{G}_1$ of Fig. 2. Since $11 \rightsquigarrow 35 \in \mathcal{G}_1$ and $11 \rightsquigarrow 58 \in \mathcal{G}_1$, we conclude that (11,58) and (11,35) are direct MHP pairs. Moreover, since these paths originate in the same node 11, and the first edges use different future variables, we conclude that (58,35) is an indirect MHP pair. Similarly, since $11 \rightsquigarrow 38 \in \mathcal{G}_1$ and $11 \rightsquigarrow 50 \in \mathcal{G}_1$ we conclude that (11,38) and (11,50) are direct MHP pairs. However, in this case (38,50) is not an (indirect) MHP pair because the first edges of these paths use the same future variable w. Indeed, the calls to g and k appear in different branches of an **if** statement. To see the improvement w.r.t. to [3] note that node 12 does not have an edge to $\tilde{\mathsf{f}}$, since our MHF analysis infers that x is finished at that L12. The analysis of [3] would have an edge to $\tilde{\mathsf{f}}$ instead of $\hat{\mathsf{f}}$, and thus it produces spurious pairs such as (12,35). Similar improvements occur also in $\mathcal{G}_2$ and $\mathcal{G}_3$.

Now consider nodes 35 and 40, and note that we have $11 \rightsquigarrow 35 \in \mathcal{G}_1$ and $11 \rightsquigarrow 40 \in \mathcal{G}_1$, and moreover these paths use different future variables. Thus, we conclude that (35,40) is an indirect MHP pair. However, carefully looking at the program we can see that this is a spurious pair, because x (to which task f is bound) is passed to method g, as parameter w, and w is guaranteed to finish when executing **await** w? at L39. A similar behavior occurs also in $\mathcal{G}_2$ and $\mathcal{G}_3$. For example, the paths $30 \rightsquigarrow 58 \in \mathcal{G}_3$ and $30 \rightsquigarrow 40 \in \mathcal{G}_3$ induce the indirect MHP pair (58,40), which is spurious since x is passed to h at L45, as parameter a, which in turn is passed to g at L45, as parameter w, and w is guaranteed to finish when executing **await** w? at L39.

The spurious pairs in the above example show that even if we used our improved LMHP analysis when constructing the MHP graph, using the procedure of [3] to extract MHP pairs might produce spurious pairs. Next, we address this imprecision by modifying the process of extracting the MHP pairs to have an extra condition to eliminate such spurious MHP pairs. This condition is based on identifying, for a given path $\check{m} \rightsquigarrow \ell \in \mathcal{G}_P$, which of the parameters of m are guaranteed to finish before reaching ℓ, and thus, any task that is passed to m in those parameters cannot execute in parallel with ℓ.

Definition 2. *Let p be a path $\check{m} \rightsquigarrow \ell \in \mathcal{G}_P$, $\bar{z}$ be the formal parameter of m, and I a set of parameter indices of method m. We say that I is* not alive *along p if (i) p has a single edge, and for some $i \in I$ the parameter z_i is in $\mathtt{mhf}_\alpha(\ell)$; or (ii) p is of the form $\check{m} \longrightarrow \ell_1 \overset{k:y:\ell':\bar{x}}{\longrightarrow} \check{m}_1 \rightsquigarrow \ell$, and for some $i \in I$ the parameter z_i is in $\mathtt{mhf}_\alpha(\ell_1)$ or $I' = \{j \mid i \in I, z_i = x_j\}$ is not alive along $\check{m}_1 \rightsquigarrow \ell$.*

Intuitively, I is not alive along p if some parameter z_i, with $i \in I$, is finished at some point in p. Thus, any task bound to z_i cannot execute in parallel with ℓ.

Example 10. Consider $p \equiv \tilde{g} \rightsquigarrow 40 \in \mathcal{G}_1$, and let $I = \{1\}$, then I is not alive along p since it is a path that consists of a single edge and $\mathsf{w} \in \mathtt{mhf}_\alpha(40)$. Now consider $\tilde{h} \rightsquigarrow 40 \in \mathcal{G}_3$, and let $I = \{1\}$, then I is not alive along p since $I' = \{1\}$ is not alive along $\tilde{g} \rightsquigarrow 40$.

The notion of "*not alive along a path*" can be used to eliminate spurious MHP pairs as follows. Consider two paths

$$p_1 \equiv \ell_3 \overset{i_1:y_1:\ell_1':\bar{w}}{\longrightarrow} \tilde{m}_1 \rightsquigarrow \ell_1 \in \mathcal{G}_P \text{ and } p_2 \equiv \ell_3 \overset{i_2:y_2:\ell_2':\bar{x}}{\longrightarrow} \check{m}_2 \rightsquigarrow \ell_2 \in \mathcal{G}_P$$

such that $y_1 \neq \star$, and the first node after $\tilde{m}_1$ does not correspond to the exit program point of m_1, i.e., m_1 might be executing and bound to y_1. Define

- $F = \{y_1\} \cup \{y \mid \Phi_{\ell_3} \models y \rightarrow y_1\}$, i.e., the set of future variables at ℓ_3 such that when any of them is finished, y_1 is finished as well; and
- $I = \{i \mid y \in F,\ x_i = y\}$, i.e., the indices of the parameters of m_2 to which we pass variables from F (in p_2).

We claim that if I is not alive along p_2, then the MHP pair (ℓ_1, ℓ_2) is spurious. This is because before reaching ℓ_2, some task from F is guaranteed to terminate, and hence the one bound to y_1, which contradicts the assumption that m_1 is not finished. In such case p_1 and p_2 are called mutually exclusive paths.

Example 11. We reconsider the spurious indirect MHP pairs of Example 9. Consider first (35,40), which originates from

$$p_1 \equiv 11 \overset{1:\mathsf{x}:2:[]}{\longrightarrow} \tilde{f} \leadsto 35 \in \mathcal{G}_1 \text{ and } p_2 \equiv 11 \overset{1:\mathsf{w}:6:[\mathsf{x}]}{\longrightarrow} \tilde{g} \leadsto 40.$$

We have $F = \{\mathsf{x}, \mathsf{w}\}$, $I = \{1\}$, and we have seen in Example 10 that I is not alive along $\tilde{g} \leadsto 40 \in \mathcal{G}_1$, thus p_1 and p_2 are mutually exclusive and we eliminate this pair. Similarly, consider (58,40) which originates from

$$p_1 \equiv 30 \overset{1:\mathsf{x}:28:[]}{\longrightarrow} \tilde{q} \leadsto 58 \in \mathcal{G}_3 \text{ and } p_2 \equiv 30 \overset{1:\mathsf{w}:29:[\mathsf{x},\mathsf{z}]}{\longrightarrow} \tilde{h} \leadsto 40.$$

Again $F = \{\mathsf{x}, \mathsf{w}\}$, $I = \{1\}$, and we have seen in Example 10 that I is not alive along $\tilde{h} \leadsto 40 \in \mathcal{G}_3$, thus p_1 and p_2 are mutually exclusive and we eliminate this pair.

Recall that $\mathcal{E}_P$ is the set of all concrete MHP pairs. Let $\tilde{\mathcal{E}}_P$ be the set of all MHP pairs obtained by applying the process of [3], modified to eliminate indirect pairs that correspond to mutually exclusive paths.

Theorem 2. $\mathcal{E}_P \subseteq \tilde{\mathcal{E}}_P$.

6 Conclusions, Implementation and Related Work

The main contribution of this work has been the enhancement of an MHP analysis that could only handle a restricted form of intra-procedural synchronization to the more general inter-procedural setting, as available in today's concurrent languages. Our analysis has a wide application scope on the inference of the main properties of concurrent programs, namely the new MHP relations are essential to infer (among others) the properties of the termination, resource usage and deadlock freedom of programs that use inter-procedural synchronization.

The analysis has been implemented in SACO [2], a *S*tatic *A*nalyzer for *C*oncurrent *O*bjects, which is able to infer deadlock, termination and resource boundedness of ABS programs [10] that follow the concurrent objects paradigm. Concurrent objects are based on the notion of concurrently running objects, similar to the actor-based and active-objects approaches [12,13]. These models take advantage of the concurrency implicit in the notion of object to provide programmers with high-level concurrency constructs that help in producing concurrent applications more modularly and in a less error-prone way. Concurrent objects communicate via *asynchronous* method calls and use **await** instructions to synchronize with the termination of the asynchronous tasks. Therefore, the abstract model used in Sect. 2 fully captures the MHP relations arising in ABS programs.

The implementation has been built on top of the original MHP analysis in SACO. The MHF analysis has been implemented and its output has been used within the local and global phases of the MHP analysis, which have been adapted to this new input as described in the technical sections. The remaining analyses in SACO did not require any modification and now they work for inter-procedural synchronization as well. Our method can be tried online at: http://costa.ls.fi.upm.es/saco/web by enabling the option `Inter-Procedural Synchronization` of the `MHP` analysis in the `Settings` section. One can then apply the MHP analysis by selecting it from the menu for the types of analyses and then clicking on `Apply`. All examples used in the paper are available in the folder `SAS15` adapted to the syntax of the ABS language. In the near future, we plan to apply our analysis to industrial case studies that are being developed in ABS but that are not ready for experimentation yet.

There is an increasing interest in asynchronous programming and in concurrent objects, and in the development of program analyses that reason on safety and liveness properties [6]. Existing MHP analyses for asynchronous programs [1,3,11] lose all information when future variables are used as parameters, as they do not handle inter-procedural synchronization. As a consequence, existing analysis for more advanced properties [4,9] that rely on the MHP relations do all lose the associated analysis information on such futures. In future work we plan to study the complexity of our analysis, which we conjuncture to be in the same complexity order as [3]. In addition, we plan to study the computational complexity of deciding MHP, for our abstract models, with and without inter-procedural synchronizations in a similar way to what has been done in [5] for the problem of state reachability.

References

1. Agarwal, S., Barik, R., Sarkar, V., Shyamasundar, R.K.: May-happen-in-parallel analysis of X10 programs. In: Yelick, K.A., Mellor-Crummey, J.M. (ed.), Proceedings of PPOPP 2007, pp. 183–193. ACM (2007)
2. Albert, E., Arenas, P., Flores-Montoya, A., Genaim, S., Gómez-Zamalloa, M., Martin-Martin, E., Puebla, G., Román-Díez, G.: SACO: static analyzer for concurrent objects. In: Ábrahám, E., Havelund, K. (eds.) TACAS 2014 (ETAPS). LNCS, vol. 8413, pp. 562–567. Springer, Heidelberg (2014)
3. Albert, E., Flores-Montoya, A.E., Genaim, S.: Analysis of may-happen-in-parallel in concurrent objects. In: Giese, H., Rosu, G. (eds.) FORTE 2012 and FMOODS 2012. LNCS, vol. 7273, pp. 35–51. Springer, Heidelberg (2012)
4. Albert, E., Flores-Montoya, A., Genaim, S., Martin-Martin, E.: Termination and cost analysis of loops with concurrent interleavings. In: Van Hung, D., Ogawa, M. (eds.) ATVA 2013. LNCS, vol. 8172, pp. 349–364. Springer, Heidelberg (2013)
5. Bouajjani, A., Emmi, M.: Analysis of recursively parallel programs. ACM Trans. Program. Lang. Syst. **35**(3), 10 (2013)
6. Bouajjani, A., Emmi, M., Enea, C., Hamza, J.: Tractable refinement checking for concurrent objects. In: Proceedings of POPL 2015, pp. 651–662. ACM (2015)
7. de Boer, F.S., Clarke, D., Johnsen, E.B.: A complete guide to the future. In: De Nicola, R. (ed.) ESOP 2007. LNCS, vol. 4421, pp. 316–330. Springer, Heidelberg (2007)
8. Flanagan, C., Felleisen, M.: The semantics of future and its use in program optimization. In: 22nd ACM SIGPLAN-SIGACT Symposium on Principles of Programming Languages (1995)

9. Flores-Montoya, A.E., Albert, E., Genaim, S.: May-happen-in-parallel based deadlock analysis for concurrent objects. In: Beyer, D., Boreale, M. (eds.) FORTE 2013 and FMOODS 2013. LNCS, vol. 7892, pp. 273–288. Springer, Heidelberg (2013)
10. Johnsen, E.B., Hähnle, R., Schäfer, J., Schlatte, R., Steffen, M.: ABS: a core language for abstract behavioral specification. In: Aichernig, B.K., de Boer, F.S., Bonsangue, M.M. (eds.) Formal Methods for Components and Objects. LNCS, vol. 6957, pp. 142–164. Springer, Heidelberg (2011)
11. Lee, J.K., Palsberg, J., Majumdar, R., Hong, H.: Efficient may happen in parallel analysis for async-finish parallelism. In: Miné, A., Schmidt, D. (eds.) SAS 2012. LNCS, vol. 7460, pp. 5–23. Springer, Heidelberg (2012)
12. Schäfer, J., Poetzsch-Heffter, A.: JCoBox: generalizing active objects to concurrent components. In: D'Hondt, T. (ed.) ECOOP 2010. LNCS, vol. 6183, pp. 275–299. Springer, Heidelberg (2010)
13. Srinivasan, S., Mycroft, A.: Kilim: isolation-typed actors for java. In: Vitek, J. (ed.) ECOOP 2008. LNCS, vol. 5142, pp. 104–128. Springer, Heidelberg (2008)

Shape Analysis for Unstructured Sharing

Huisong Li[1], Xavier Rival[1(✉)], and Bor-Yuh Evan Chang[2]

[1] INRIA, ENS, CNRS, PSL*, Paris, France
Xavier.rival@inria.fr
[2] University of Colorado, Boulder, CO, USA

Abstract. Shape analysis aims to infer precise structural properties of imperative memory states and has been applied heavily to verify safety properties on imperative code over pointer-based data structures. Recent advances in shape analysis based on separation logic has leveraged summarization predicates that describe unbounded heap regions like lists or trees using inductive definitions. Unfortunately, data structures with *unstructured sharing*, such as graphs, are challenging to describe and reason about in such frameworks. In particular, when the sharing is unstructured, it cannot be described inductively in a local manner. In this paper, we propose a global abstraction of sharing based on set-valued variables that when integrated with inductive definitions enables the specification and shape analysis of structures with unstructured sharing.

1 Introduction

Many recent advances in shape analysis have been made by building on separation logic [24] with inductive definitions. Such frameworks (e.g., [1,7,14]) leverage (1) separating conjunction $*$ to enable local reasoning and strong updates by combining properties holding over disjoint memory regions and (2) inductive definitions to summarize recursive structures of unbounded size. While this approach has been effective for many applications, a significant limitation has been its inability to effectively handle *unstructured sharing.*

We say that a data structure has *sharing* whenever a given cell in the data structure may be pointed to by several other cells. Singly-linked lists and trees are *unshared data structures*, while other important structures, such as directed-acyclic graphs (DAGs) and graphs in general, are *shared data structures.* Certain shared data structures have regular sharing patterns that can be described using a bounded number of constraints on each cell. For example, doubly-linked lists can be summarized using the following inductive definition:

$$\alpha \cdot \mathbf{dll}(\delta) ::= (\mathbf{emp} \wedge \alpha = 0) \vee (\alpha.\mathtt{prev} \mapsto \delta * \alpha.\mathtt{next} \mapsto \beta * \beta \cdot \mathbf{dll}(\alpha) \wedge \alpha \neq 0)$$

The research leading to these results has received funding from the European Research Council under the FP7 grant agreement 278673, Project MemCAD, and from the ARTEMIS Joint Undertaking no 269335 (see Article II.9 of the JU Grant Agreement) and the United States National Science Foundation under grant CCF-1055066.

S. Blazy and T. Jensen (Eds.): SAS 2015, LNCS 9291, pp. 90–108, 2015.
DOI: 10.1007/978-3-662-48288-9_6

This definition states that α is a doubly-linked list pointer if and only if it is either null (0) or a pointer to a list element; in the latter case, the `prev` field of α points to δ, and the tail β should be a doubly-linked list such that the `prev` field of its first element should point back to α itself. We say that doubly-linked lists have *structured sharing*—sharing occurs because each cell points back to its predecessor, but since each cell has *exactly one* predecessor (except for the first cell), it can be specified by the parameter δ. A skip list is another such example [7].

On the other hand, the case of structures with unstructured sharing, such as general graphs, is much more challenging since the number of predecessors of a node is unbounded and since the predecessors could be anywhere in the structure. To make the challenges more concrete, consider the representation of graphs shown in Fig. 1. Figure 1(a) shows a type definition for representing graphs as *adjacency lists*: a graph is a list of nodes, each node has a list of edges, and an edge is a pointer to its destination node. Figure 1(c) shows a representation of the graph of Fig. 1(b), where node i is described at address $\mathtt{n}_i$. To extend shape analysis techniques to this structure (and prove memory safety or functional

```
typedef struct node{              typedef struct edge{
    struct node * next;               struct node * dest;
    int id;                           struct edge * next;
    struct edge * edges;          } edge;
} node;
```

(a) Type definitions for a list of adjacency lists

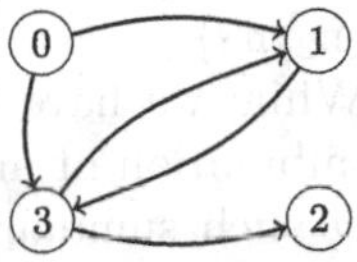

(b) A simple graph

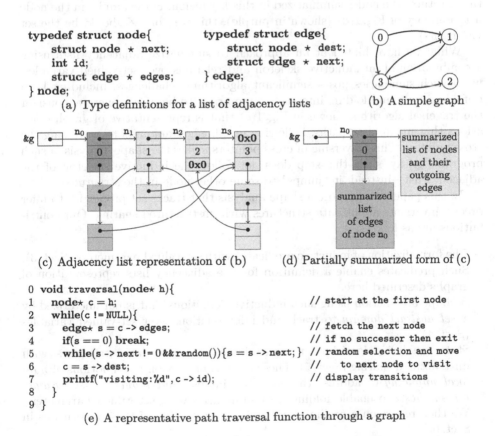

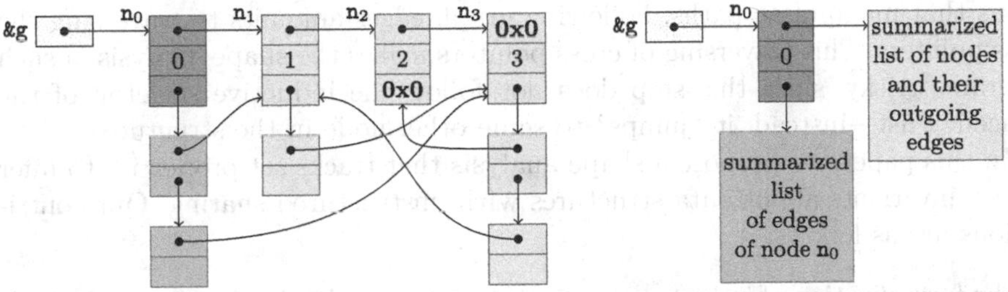

(c) Adjacency list representation of (b)

(d) Partially summarized form of (c)

```
void traversal(node* h){
  node* c = h;                                        // start at the first node
  while(c != NULL){
    edge* s = c -> edges;                             // fetch the next node
    if(s == 0) break;                                 // if no successor then exit
    while(s -> next != 0 && random()){s = s -> next; } // random selection and move
    c = s -> dest;                                    //    to next node to visit
    printf("visiting:%d", c -> id);                   // display transitions
  }
}
```

(e) A representative path traversal function through a graph

Fig. 1. Graph represented by adjacency lists and traversal function.

properties of algorithms manipulating it), we need an effective method to summarize instances of this structure and to manipulate such summaries. A natural approach to summarization is to exploit the list-of-lists inductive skeleton of adjacency lists, as hinted at in Fig. 1(d): at node $\mathtt{n_0}$, the list of its adjacent nodes is inductively summarized in the green region, while the adjacency list of the other nodes in the graph are summarized in the purple region. What is implicit in this informal diagram is that these summarized regions must, for precision, capture complex, unstructured, cross pointer relations (i.e., the curving lines in Fig. 1(c)).

To capture this unstructured sharing precisely, we observe that the correctness of the structure stems from the fact that each edge pointer points to an address in $\mathscr{E} = \{\mathtt{n_0}, \mathtt{n_1}, \mathtt{n_2}, \mathtt{n_3}\}$. Thus, the absence of dangling edges can be captured by adjoining a *set property* to a conventional list predicate. We need to capture that all edge pointers point to nodes belonging to the set $\mathscr{E}$ of valid nodes in the graph for each node's adjacency list. To give an inductive definition for the outer list of nodes, we need to ensure that this list of nodes is consistent with the set $\mathscr{E}$ of valid nodes, and thus we require a second set variable $\mathscr{F}$ that captures the nodes summarized in this list region. For example, in the node list summary of Fig. 1(d) (shown in purple), this variable $\mathscr{F}$ should be the set $\{\mathtt{n_1}, \mathtt{n_2}, \mathtt{n_3}\}$.

While we have hinted at an approach to summarize adjacency lists using a combination of an inductive skeleton and relations over set-valued variables, using such summaries poses significant algorithmic challenges, including both unfolding from and folding into such summaries. To be more concrete, consider the traversal algorithm shown in Fig. 1(e) that is representative of graph operations that manipulate paths. Following graph edges amounts to traversing the cross pointers. This traversing of cross pointers makes the shape analysis of such programs tricky, since this step does not follow the inductive skeleton of the adjacency list—instead, it "jumps" to some other node in the structure.

In this paper, we propose a shape analysis that tracks set properties to infer precise invariants about data structures with unstructured sharing. Our contributions are as follows:

- The formalization of inductive predicates with set-valued parameters (Sect. 3). Such predicates enable a definition for the adjacency lists representation of graphs described here.
- A shape abstraction using such inductive definitions that is parameterized by a *set abstract domain* to track and infer relations over set-valued variables (Sect. 4).
- Static analysis algorithms to infer invariants over data structures with unstructured sharing (Sect. 5). These algorithms rely on novel notions of *non-local unfolding* to address the issue of "jumps" and *inductive set parameter synthesis* to enable folding into summaries with set-valued parameters. We then report on a preliminary empirical evaluation of these algorithms in Sect. 6.

2 Overview

Graph Inductive Predicate. The first step towards an analysis to verify graph algorithms is to set up inductive predicates to summarize the structure of Fig. 1. Such predicates are based on generic inductive definitions, which describe a disjunction of cases, each of which consists of a *memory formula* (a separating conjunction $F_0 * \ldots * F_n$ of points-to predicates of the form $\alpha \cdot \mathtt{f} \mapsto \beta$ and inductive predicates of the form $\alpha \cdot \iota$, where ι is another inductive definition) and a *pure formula* (a conjunction of value properties, such as pointer equalities). The set of outgoing edges of a node consists of a list of records, thus the predicate to summarize such a region can be based on a classical list inductive definition, such as $\alpha \cdot \mathbf{list}$, as shown in the top of Fig. 2(a). This inductive definition states that α is either a null pointer (the list then spans over an empty region), or a non-null pointer to a record made of two fields but it does not further characterize the `dest` field.

However, this definition does not express that all instances of field `dest` contain a pointer to a node of the graph as the value β of that field is unconstrained. To resolve this issue, we simply need to add the constraint $\beta \in \mathscr{E}$, where $\mathscr{E}$ should denote the set of all node addresses in the graph. The abstract domain should also keep track of those predicates through folding and unfolding steps. Therefore, we obtain inductive definition **edges** shown in Fig. 2(a), which takes the additional parameter $\mathscr{E}$, and where the value predicate of the non-empty case has been strengthened with set predicate $\beta \in \mathscr{E}$.

Moreover, the inductive definition of a graph needs to capture two set properties: (1) the destination of all edges are in set $\mathscr{E}$ (as described by inductive definition **edges**) and (2) the set of nodes in the adjacency list should correspond *exactly* to $\mathscr{E}$. Thus, inductive definition **nodes** shown in Fig. 2(a) takes two set parameters: (1) $\mathscr{E}$ is constant over the whole induction and (2) $\mathscr{F}$ stands for the set of nodes described in the graph fragment described by an **nodes** instance. We note that the set predicates $\mathscr{F} = \emptyset$ (base case) and $\mathscr{F} = \mathscr{F}' \uplus \{\alpha\}$ (inductive case) guarantee that $\mathscr{F}$ is exactly the set of nodes described by predicate $\alpha \cdot \mathbf{nodes}(\mathscr{E}, \mathscr{F})$.

Abstraction of Memory States. Using these definitions, a complete graph with set of nodes $\mathscr{E}$ can be fully summarized by inductive predicate $\alpha \cdot \mathbf{nodes}(\mathscr{E}, \mathscr{E})$, where symbolic variable $\mathscr{E}$ denotes all the nodes of the concrete graph. Similarly, Fig. 2(b) displays a partially summarized abstraction, following the splitting of Fig. 1(d), where thin edges denote points-to predicates and bold edges stand for inductive predicates, annotated by inductive definition instances, with arguments denoting sets of concrete values. Colors are consistent with Fig. 1(d) to highlight the memory region each edge describes. Additional set predicates ($\mathscr{E} = \mathscr{F}' \uplus \{\alpha\} \ldots$) are represented in a *set abstract domain* [11]. This means, that a concrete state represented by this state should bind α to an address and $\mathscr{E}, \mathscr{F}'$ to sets of addresses satisfying the aforementioned property, in the same way as the numerical constraint $\alpha \neq 0$ specifies α should be bound to a non-null pointer value.

$$
\begin{aligned}
&\alpha \cdot \mathbf{list} ::= \\
&\quad (\mathbf{emp}, \alpha = 0) \\
&\quad \vee\, (\alpha \cdot \mathbf{dest} \mapsto \beta * \alpha \cdot \mathbf{next} \mapsto \gamma * \gamma \cdot \mathbf{list}, \alpha \neq 0) \\
&\alpha \cdot \mathbf{edges}(\mathscr{E}) ::= \\
&\quad (\mathbf{emp}, \alpha = 0 \wedge \mathbf{true}) \\
&\quad \vee\, (\alpha \cdot \mathbf{dest} \mapsto \beta * \alpha \cdot \mathbf{next} \mapsto \gamma \\
&\quad\quad * \gamma \cdot \mathbf{edges}(\mathscr{E}), \alpha \neq 0 \wedge \beta \in \mathscr{E}) \\
&\alpha \cdot \mathbf{nodes}(\mathscr{E}, \mathscr{F}) ::= \\
&\quad (\mathbf{emp}, \alpha = 0 \wedge \mathscr{F} = \emptyset) \\
&\quad \vee\, (\alpha \cdot \mathbf{next} \mapsto \beta * \alpha \cdot \mathbf{id} \mapsto \gamma * \alpha \cdot \mathbf{edges} \mapsto \delta \\
&\quad\quad * \beta \cdot \mathbf{nodes}(\mathscr{E}, \mathscr{F}') * \delta \cdot \mathbf{edges}(\mathscr{E}), \\
&\quad\quad \alpha \neq 0 \wedge \mathscr{F} = \mathscr{F}' \uplus \{\alpha\})
\end{aligned}
$$

(a) Inductive definitions

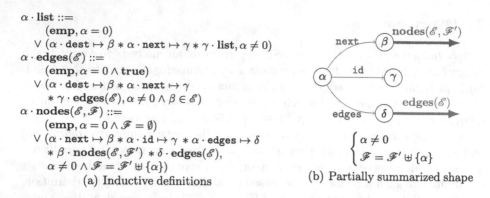

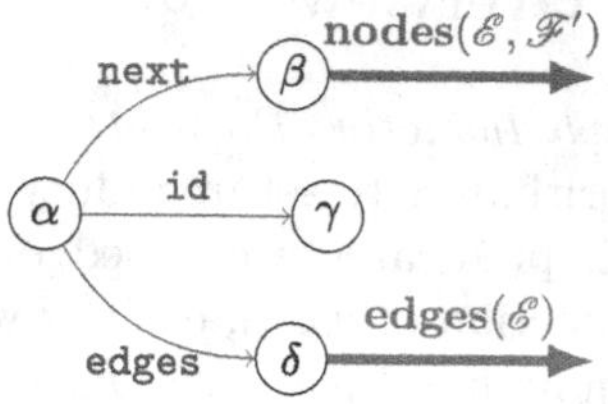

$$
\begin{cases} \alpha \neq 0 \\ \mathscr{F} = \mathscr{F}' \uplus \{\alpha\} \end{cases}
$$

(b) Partially summarized shape

Fig. 2. Summarizing graph data-structures using inductive predicates

Shape Analysis Extension. We now discuss automatic shape analysis algorithms to verify programs manipulating such graphs. Properties of interest include memory safety (absence of null or dangling pointer dereferences) and the preservation of structural invariants. As a benchmark property, we consider the verification of the memory safety of the random traversal algorithm of Fig. 1(e).

In particular, to establish no dangling pointer is dereferenced, the analysis should precisely track the fact that c should point to a valid node of the graph, or be the null pointer (which causes the program to exit) at all times. Figure 3 shows the main local abstract invariant involved in the verification of this property, described as shapes. For the sake of concision, only parts of the shapes that play a role in the analysis are shown, and we discuss mainly the novel parts of the analysis. We use the same conventions as in Fig. 2(b). The pre-condition shown at line 0 specifies that the function starts with a correct graph, with set of nodes $\mathscr{E}$. At line 1, cursor c is initialized to h. The analysis of the loop body requires the analysis to unfold [5] summaries to perform mutation over summarized regions, at lines 6 and 7, and to utilize a widening [5] operator for the convergence of the abstract iterates over both nested loops. The invariant at the head of the main loop, at line 3, shows a node list segment between nodes α and α' that denote the respective values of h and c. This segment describes a memory region encompassing a set of nodes of the graph together with their adjacency list. The segment predicate parameters are most interesting: the first specifies that all edges from nodes allocated in that region point to an address in $\mathscr{E}$ (global graph correctness property) whereas the second states that the set of the addresses of the nodes represented in that region is exactly $\mathscr{F}$. The side property $\mathscr{E} = \mathscr{F} \uplus \mathscr{F}'$ states that the splitting of the graph into the two summaries partitions its nodes.

The abstract state at line 7 is significantly more complex, and c does not immediately appear to point in the **nodes** inductive backbone anymore. Yet, the dereference of `c -> id` requires the materialization of an edge from that node, although no edge (points-to or summary) starts from node β. However, the analysis infers that $\beta \in \mathscr{E}$ (i.e., β is the address of an element of the graph adjacency list), and $\mathscr{E} = \mathscr{F} \uplus \{\alpha'\} \uplus \mathscr{F}''$. Thus, either $\beta \in \mathscr{F}$, or $\beta = \alpha'$,

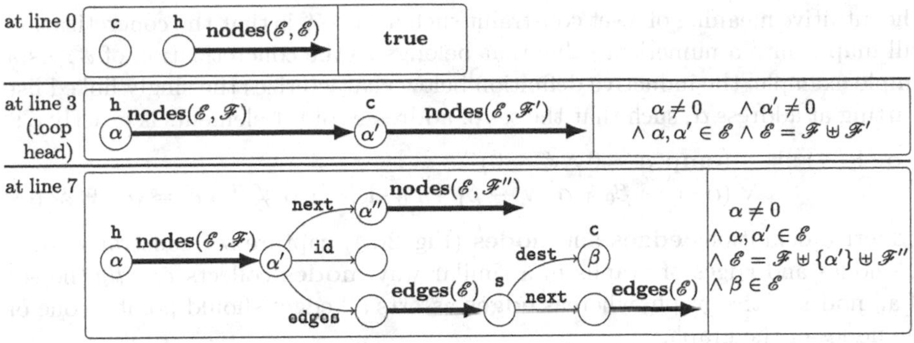

Fig. 3. Abstract pre-condition and local invariants

or $\beta \in \mathscr{F}''$. If $\beta \in \mathscr{F}$, then it is the address of a node in the segment from α to α', and it can be *materialized* as such, by splitting the segment (the case $\beta \in \mathscr{F}''$ is similar, and means that c points in the tail of the structure). This form of unfolding is much more complex than more conventional forms of inductive predicates unfolding [5] as it needs to utilize the set properties to localize β. To achieve this, the analysis needs to track all set predicates shown in Fig. 3, through unfolding, updates and widening steps.

3 Inductive Definitions with Set Predicates

The analysis presented in this paper is *parameterized* by a set of inductive definitions, which means the abstract domain is generic, and can deal with a wide family of data-structures. We extend the relational inductive definitions of [5] with set predicates. A concrete memory $m \in \mathbb{M} = \mathbb{V}_{\text{addr}} \longrightarrow \mathbb{V}$ maps addresses into values. Structure fields are considered numerical offsets, so that $a + \mathtt{f}$ denotes the address at base address a and offset $\mathtt{f}$. In the abstract level, symbolic variables $(\alpha, \beta, \ldots \in \mathbb{V}^\sharp)$ abstract numerical values. A *valuation* ν is a function that maps each numerical variable $\alpha \in \mathbb{V}^\sharp$ (resp., set variable $\mathscr{E} \in \mathbb{T}^\sharp$) to a numerical value $\nu(\alpha)$ (resp., set of numerical values $\nu(\mathscr{E})$). We write $\mathbb{V}\mathrm{al}$ for the set of valuations.

$$
\begin{array}{rcll}
r & ::= & (F_{\text{Heap}}, F_{\text{Pure}}) & \\
F_{\text{Heap}} & ::= & \mathbf{emp} & \\
 & | & \alpha \cdot \mathtt{f} \mapsto \beta & \\
 & | & \alpha \cdot \iota(\mathscr{E}_0, \ldots, \mathscr{E}_{n-1}) & \\
 & | & F_{\text{Heap}} * F_{\text{Heap}} & \\
F_{\text{Pure}} & ::= & \alpha = c & (c \in \mathbb{V}) \\
 & | & \alpha \neq c & (c \in \mathbb{V}) \\
 & | & \alpha \in \mathscr{E} & \\
 & | & \mathscr{E} = \{\alpha\} \uplus \mathscr{F} & \\
 & | & \mathscr{E} = \{\alpha\} \cup \mathscr{F} & \\
 & | & \ldots &
\end{array}
$$

Inductive Definitions. An *inductive definition* $\alpha \cdot \iota(\mathscr{E}_1, \ldots, \mathscr{E}_n) ::= r_0 \vee r_1 \vee \ldots \vee r_k$ takes a pointer parameter α and a list of set parameters $\mathscr{E}_1, \ldots, \mathscr{E}_n$ and defines a scheme to summarize heap regions that satisfy some inductive property, specified as a disjunction of *rules*, which comprise a *heap* part and a *pure* part, as described in the inset. The heap part is a separating conjunction of memory cells (predicates of the form $\alpha \cdot \mathtt{f} \mapsto \beta$) and recursive calls to inductive definitions. The pure part comprises not only numerical constraints, but also set constraints, over the symbolic variables exposed in the heap part, and the set parameters $\mathscr{E}_1, \ldots, \mathscr{E}_n$, as shown in F_{Pure}.

The intuitive meaning of a set constraint such as $\alpha \in \mathscr{E}$ is that the concretization will map α into a numerical value that belongs to the concretization of $\mathscr{E}$. As a simple example, the inductive definition below characterizes the singly linked list starting at address α, such that the set of addresses of list elements is exactly $\mathscr{E}$:

$$\begin{aligned} \alpha \cdot \mathbf{l}_{\mathrm{s}}(\mathscr{E}) ::= \quad & (\mathbf{emp}, \alpha = 0 \wedge \mathscr{E} = \emptyset) \\ & \vee (\alpha \cdot \mathbf{n} \mapsto \beta_0 * \alpha \cdot \mathbf{v} \mapsto \beta_1 * \beta_0 \cdot \mathbf{l}_{\mathrm{s}}(\mathscr{E}'), \alpha \neq 0 \wedge \mathscr{E} = \{\alpha\} \uplus \mathscr{E}') \end{aligned}$$

Inductive definitions **edges** and **nodes** (Fig. 2(a)) capture set constraints over the nodes and edges of graphs in a similar way: **nodes** collects *exactly* the set of all nodes of the graph, whereas **edges** asserts all edges should point to one of the nodes of the graph.

Properties of Set Parameters. Analysis algorithms (Sect. 5) need to infer instances of inductive definitions, including their set parameters. Computing set parameters accurately is a very hard task, as it depends on complex properties of the data-structures shapes and contents. Yet, properties of set parameters may make their computation simpler. We define the following set parameters *kinds*:

- **Constant Parameters.** In definition **edges** (Fig. 2(a)), the set parameter is propagated with no modification to the recursive call of the inductive definition. We call it a *constant parameter*, that is a parameter $\mathscr{E}$ of inductive definition ι such that any recursive call $\alpha' \cdot \iota(\mathscr{E}')$ in the definition of $\alpha \cdot \iota(\mathscr{E})$ is such that $\mathscr{E} = \mathscr{E}'$. We note that the first parameter ($\mathscr{E}$) of **nodes** also satisfies this property.
- **Head Parameters:** The second parameter of **nodes** is clearly not constant, but it satisfies another interesting property: it collects the set of head nodes in all recursive inductive calls, and can be computed exactly from the values of the same parameters in the recursive calls, since $\mathscr{F} = \emptyset$ in the empty rule and $\mathscr{F} = \{\alpha\} \uplus \mathscr{F}'$ in the second rule, where α is the address of the head of the structure and $\mathscr{F}'$ is the parameter of the tail. We call such a parameter a *head parameter*. This definition generalizes to non-linear structures (i.e., with several recursive calls, corresponding to distinct sub-structures). Parameter $\mathscr{E}$ of the $\mathbf{l}_{\mathrm{s}}$ definition also satisfies this property.

These set parameter kinds are computed by a very simple analysis of inductive definitions. In the following, we write $\iota \vdash \mathscr{E} : \mathbf{cst}$ (resp., $\iota \vdash \mathscr{E} : \mathbf{head}$) to denote that parameter $\mathscr{E}$ of inductive definition ι is constant (resp., head).

In this paper, we provide static analysis algorithms that are sound whatever the properties of the set parameters. However, precise folding and materialization will only be supported for *constant* and *head* parameters. Note that other kinds of set parameters may be proposed though, so as to recover precise static analyses even when the above properties are not satisfied.

4 Composite Memory Abstraction with Set Predicates

We now formalize our shape abstract domain $\mathbb{M}^\sharp$, that is parameterized by the inductive predicates of Sect. 3, and an abstract domain $\mathbb{S}^\sharp$ for constraints over value and set symbolic variables.

Abstract States. An *abstract state* is a pair (G, S) made of a *shape* $G \in \mathbb{G}^\sharp$ and an element $S \in \mathbb{S}^\sharp$. The syntax of shapes is shown in the inset: a shape is either empty, or a single points-to edge $\alpha \cdot \mathbf{f} \mapsto \beta$, or an inductive predicate $\alpha \cdot \iota(\vec{\mathscr{E}})$ (instantiating an inductive definition ι defined as in Sect. 3), or a segment $\alpha \cdot \iota(\vec{\mathscr{E}}) \mathrel{*\!\!=} \beta \cdot \iota(\vec{\mathscr{E}})$ describing an incomplete inductive structure, or a separating product of such predicates. Intuitively, a segment describes incomplete induction, with a missing sub-structure, hence a segment of an **list** structure effectively describes a conventional list segment (similarly, a tree segment would describe a "tree minus a subtree"). Inductive and segment predicates comprise a number of parameters that matches their definition (Sect. 3). Our analysis supports inductive predicates with any number of set parameters (although, in the rest of the paper, we sometimes write properties in the case of definitions using a single parameter, for the sake of readability).

$$
\begin{array}{rl}
G ::= & \mathbf{emp} \\
| & \alpha \cdot \mathbf{f} \mapsto \beta \\
| & \alpha \cdot \iota(\vec{\mathscr{E}}) \\
| & \alpha \cdot \iota(\vec{\mathscr{E}}) \mathrel{*\!\!=} \beta \cdot \iota(\vec{\mathscr{E}}) \\
| & G * G
\end{array}
$$

Concretization. We assume that elements of $\mathbb{S}^\sharp$ concretize into sets of valuations, satisfying both sets and value constraints, thus $\gamma_{\mathbb{S}} : \mathbb{S}^\sharp \longrightarrow \mathcal{P}(\mathbb{V}\mathrm{al})$. Similarly, the concretization of a shape is a set of memory states together with value and set valuations, thus $\gamma_{\mathbb{G}} : \mathbb{G}^\sharp \longrightarrow \mathcal{P}(\mathbb{M} \times \mathbb{V}\mathrm{al})$. Figure 4(a) displays the concretization rules for shapes. The first three rules describe the usual concretization for empty shapes, single points-to edges and separating conjunction [24]. The last rule defines the concretization for inductive and segment predicates using the standard notion of *syntactic unfolding*: the unfolding of an inductive or segment predicate selects a

$$
\frac{}{([], \nu) \in \gamma_{\mathbb{G}}(\mathbf{emp})}
\qquad
\frac{a = \nu(\alpha) + \mathbf{f} \qquad v = \nu(\beta)}{([a \mapsto v], \nu) \in \gamma_{\mathbb{G}}(\alpha \cdot \mathbf{f} \mapsto \beta)}
\qquad
\frac{\forall i,\ (m_i, \nu) \in \gamma_{\mathbb{G}}(G_i)}{(m_0 \uplus m_1, \nu) \in \gamma_{\mathbb{G}}(G_0 * G_1)}
$$

$$
\frac{G \rightsquigarrow_{\mathrm{U}} (F_{\mathbf{Heap}}, F_{\mathbf{Pure}}) \qquad (m, \nu) \in \gamma_{\mathbb{G}}(F_{\mathbf{Heap}}) \qquad \nu \vdash F_{\mathbf{Pure}}}{(m, \nu) \in \gamma_{\mathbb{G}}(G)}
$$

(a) Concretization rules

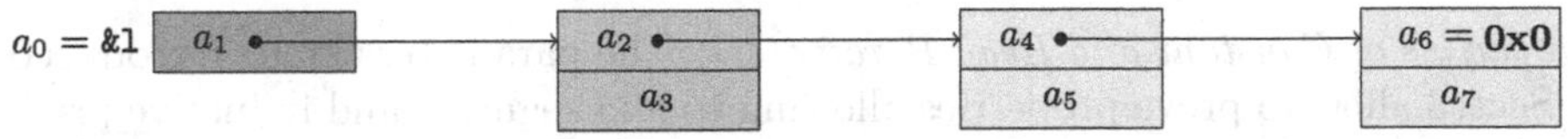

(b) An example concrete memory

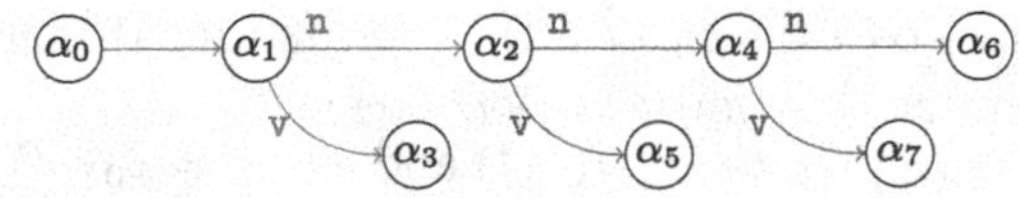

(c) Shape, no summarization

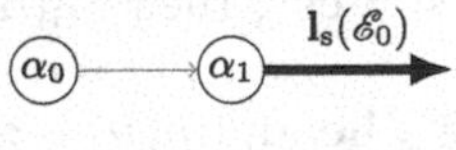

(d) Shape, summarization

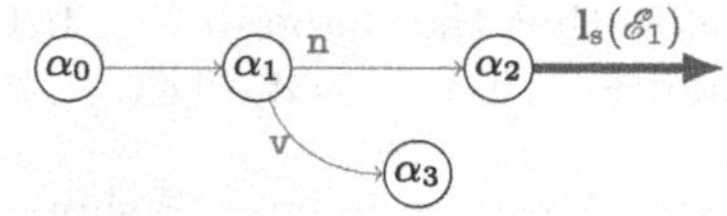

(e) Shape, partial summarization

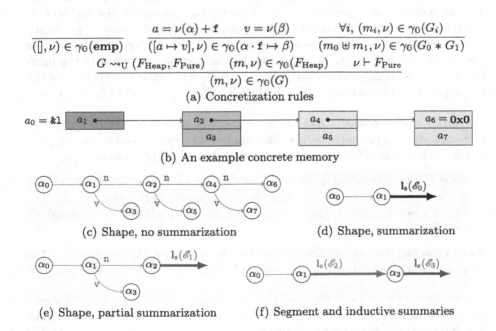

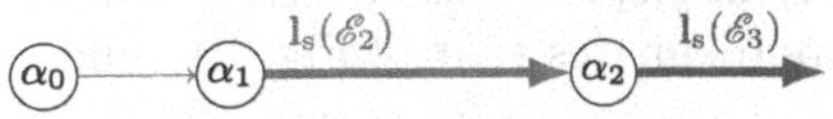

(f) Segment and inductive summaries

Fig. 4. Shapes and their concretizations

rule r in the corresponding inductive definition, and replaces the predicate with the heap part of r and constrains value and set valuations with the pure part of r. This construction is standard and is fully described in [7].

Examples. Fig. 4 shows a few abstractions of the concrete memory state m shown in Fig. 4(b), where `l` stores a pointer to a list of length 3, and where $a_0, a_1, \ldots, a_7$ denote numerical values/addresses. The shape of Fig. 4(c) abstracts this state without any summarization (it contains no inductive predicate). Its concretization into m results in $\forall i,\ \nu(\alpha_i) = a_i$ (in particular, $\nu(\alpha_6) = a_6 = \mathbf{0x0}$), and can be fully expressed using the points-to and separating product rules of Fig. 4(a). The shape of Fig. 4(d) summarizes the list completely into a single inductive predicate $\alpha_1 \cdot \mathbf{l}_s(\mathscr{E}_0)$. In this case, the concretization also needs to bind $\mathscr{E}_0$ to a set of concrete addresses: by the definition of $\mathbf{l}_s$ (Sect. 3), this boils down to $\nu(\mathscr{E}_0) = \{a_1, a_2, a_4\}$. Moreover, this concretization needs to trigger the unfolding rule (last rule in Fig. 4(a)) in order to produce the shape of Fig. 4(c). The shape of Fig. 4(e) summarizes only the last two elements of the list (in purple) while the first element (in red) is preserved in its unfolded form. Similarly to the previous case, the unfolding of this shape needs to trigger three times the unfolding rule in order to get the shape of Fig. 4(c) and to map $\mathscr{E}_1$ to $\nu(\mathscr{E}_1) = \{a_2, a_4\}$.

Finally, the shape of Fig. 4(f) summarizes two list elements with inductive predicate $\alpha_2 \cdot \mathbf{l}_s(\mathscr{E}_3)$ (in purple) and the rest of the list with a segment predicate (in red). This segment predicate should take a form $\alpha_1 \cdot \mathbf{l}_s(\mathscr{F}_1) \ast\!\!= \alpha_2 \cdot \mathbf{l}_s(\mathscr{F}_2)$, where $\mathscr{F}_1, \mathscr{F}_2$ describe two sets of addresses such that the set of addresses of the list elements summarized in the segment is exactly $\nu(\mathscr{F}_1) \setminus \nu(\mathscr{F}_2)$, by the definition of $\mathbf{l}_s$. The fact that only the difference of these two sets matters is actually a direct consequence of the fact that the parameter of $\mathbf{l}_s$ is *head* (Sect. 3). Therefore, when an inductive definition parameter is head, segment predicates are decorated with only one parameter. In the example of Fig. 4(f), the segment predicates writes down $\alpha_1 \cdot \mathbf{l}_s \ast\!\!=_{(\mathscr{E}_2)} \alpha_2 \cdot \mathbf{l}_s$; the graphical notation in the figure condenses this slightly, into a single $\mathbf{l}_s(\mathscr{E}_2)$ parameter. The concretization of this shape produces the memory of Fig. 4(b) with $\nu(\mathscr{E}_2) = \{a_1\}$ and $\nu(\mathscr{E}_3) = \{a_2, a_4\}$.

Properties of Constant and Head Parameters. The parameters kinds introduced in Sect. 3 allow to prove properties allowing to fold segment and inductive predicates, such as the following concretization inclusions/implications:

- if $\iota \vdash \mathscr{E} : \mathbf{cst}$, then $\gamma_{\mathbb{G}}(\alpha_0 \cdot \iota \ast\!\!=_{(\mathscr{E})} \alpha_1 \cdot \iota \ast \alpha_1 \cdot \iota(\mathscr{E})) \subseteq \gamma_{\mathbb{G}}(\alpha_0 \cdot \iota(\mathscr{E}))$, and $\gamma_{\mathbb{G}}(\alpha_0 \cdot \iota \ast\!\!=_{(\mathscr{E})} \alpha_1 \cdot \iota \ast \alpha_1 \cdot \iota \ast\!\!=_{(\mathscr{E})} \alpha_2 \cdot \iota) \subseteq \gamma_{\mathbb{G}}(\alpha_0 \cdot \iota \ast\!\!=_{(\mathscr{E})} \alpha_2 \cdot \iota)$;
- if $\iota \vdash \mathscr{E} : \mathbf{head}$, $(m, \nu) \in \gamma_{\mathbb{G}}(\alpha_0 \cdot \iota \ast\!\!=_{(\mathscr{E}_0)} \alpha_1 \cdot \iota \ast \alpha_1 \cdot \iota(\mathscr{E}_1))$ and $\nu \vdash \mathscr{E} = \mathscr{E}_0 \uplus \mathscr{E}_1$, then $(m, \nu) \in \gamma_{\mathbb{G}}(\alpha_0 \cdot \iota(\mathscr{E}))$.

As an example, the last of these rules allows to show that the shape in Fig. 4(d) over-approximates that of Fig. 4(f) under the condition that $\mathscr{E}_0 = \mathscr{E}_2 \uplus \mathscr{E}_3$.

Abstraction of Constraints Over Sets and Addresses. Abstract domain $\mathbb{S}^\sharp$ should provide an abstraction for constraints over set variables and symbolic variables. For instance, the constraints of the invariant of Fig. 3 corresponding to line

3 in the program of Fig. 1(e) collects value constraints $\alpha \neq 0$, $\alpha' \neq 0$ and set constraints $\alpha, \alpha' \in \mathscr{E}$, $\mathscr{E} = \mathscr{F} \uplus \mathscr{F}'$, thus abstract domain $\mathbb{S}^\sharp$ should be able to express these constraints. A suitable such abstract domain can be obtained as a reduced product [10] of the interval abstract domain [9], of a domain representing inequalities and of a set abstract domain (two set domains were used in the evaluation—see Sect. 6 for discussion). For more expressiveness, more powerful numerical/set abstract domains can be used instead.

Combined Abstract Domain. The concretization of an abstract memory state $M = (G, S) \in \mathbb{M}^\sharp$ is defined as the set of memory states for which a pair of valuations can be found, that satisfy all constraints from G and S:

$$\gamma_{\mathbb{M}}(G, S) = \{m \in \mathbb{M} \mid \exists \nu \in \gamma_{\mathbb{S}}(S),\ (m, \nu) \in \gamma_{\mathbb{G}}(G)\}$$

While this concretization looks similar to that of a reduced product [9], the composite abstract domain actually has the structure of a *cofibered abstract domain* [29], since the set of symbolic variables present in the S component are exactly the nodes in shape G, and the analysis should maintain this consistency at all times.

5 Static Analysis Algorithms

We now describe algorithms to infer invariants involving inductive predicates with set parameters. Extending [5], it inputs an abstract pre-condition, and performs a forward abstract interpretation to compute a *sound abstract post-condition* satisfied by any execution starting from the pre-condition. We emphasize the novel aspects of this analysis, namely non-local unfolding (in Sect. 5.1) and set parameters synthesis during folding (in Sect. 5.2). Our analysis assumes abstract domain $\mathbb{S}^\sharp$ provide *sound* abstract join $\sqcup_{\mathbb{S}}$, abstract inclusion test $\sqsubseteq_{\mathbb{S}}$, widening $\nabla_{\mathbb{S}}$, supremum $\top$ and *sound transfer functions*: $\mathfrak{guard}_{\mathbb{S}}$ inputs an abstract value S and a set constraint C, and returns an abstract value refined with C and $\mathfrak{prove}_{\mathbb{S}}$ inputs an abstract value S and a set constraint and returns **true** when it successfully establishes that S entails C.

5.1 Transfer Functions, Local and Non-local Unfolding

Given a concrete post-condition function $\mathbf{f} : \mathcal{P}(\mathbb{M}) \to \mathcal{P}(\mathbb{M})$, the corresponding *abstract transfer function* $\mathbf{f}^\sharp : \mathbb{M}^\sharp \to \mathbb{M}^\sharp$ should over-approximate the effect of $\mathbf{f}$, in the sense that $\mathbf{f} \circ \gamma_{\mathbb{M}} \subseteq \gamma_{\mathbb{M}} \circ \mathbf{f}^\sharp$. In this section, we consider the case of a pointer assignment and let f be $[\![\mathtt{l} := \mathtt{e}]\!]$ since condition tests, allocation, and deallocation follow similar principles. We assume pre-condition $M = (G, S)$. If l-value $\mathtt{l}$ evaluates to points-to edge $\alpha \cdot \mathtt{f} \mapsto \beta$ in M, r-value $\mathtt{e}$ evaluates to node β' in M and $G = \alpha \cdot \mathtt{f} \mapsto \beta * G'$, then the abstract assignment should simply replace the old edge with a new one and produce $[\![\mathtt{l} := \mathtt{e}]\!](M) = (\alpha \cdot \mathtt{f} \mapsto \beta' * G', S)$. The local reasoning principle [18,24] ensures the soundness of this mechanism.

As an example, Fig. 5(a) and (b) display the pre and post-condition of assignment `s = s -> next` in the program of Fig. 1(e), at line 5 (for the sake of clarity, shapes are simplified to the relevant memory regions). In pre-condition M (Fig. 5(a)), the modified memory cell corresponds to edge $\alpha_0 \mapsto \alpha_1$, and the r-value describes node α_2. Thus, abstract transfer function $[\![\texttt{s := s -> next}]\!]^\sharp$ simply returns the shape of Fig. 5(b).

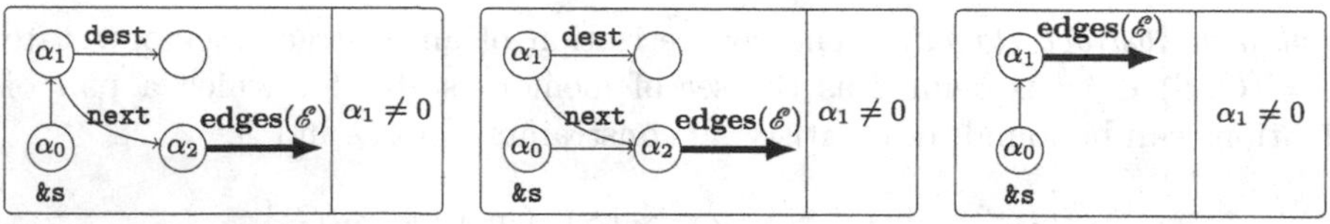

(a) "Pre"-shape M (b) "Post"-shape (c) Folded "pre"-shape M'

Fig. 5. Assignment and (local) unfolding

The Unfolding Transformation. However, the above scheme cannot work when the over-written memory cell or the memory read in the r-value is part of an inductive predicate. This case actually happens in the analysis of the program of Fig. 1(e), since the actual pre-condition is shown in Fig. 5(c) and does not allow to evaluate `s -> next` into a node. *Unfolding* [1,5,14] resolves this issue, by replacing the inductive predicate $\alpha_1 \cdot \mathbf{edges}(\mathscr{E})$ with its inductive definition and producing a disjunction of two cases (one per inductive rule).

Theorem 1 (Unfolding Soundness). *Given inductive definition* $\alpha \cdot \iota(\mathscr{E}) ::= \bigvee\{(F_{\text{Heap},i}, F_{\text{Pure},i}) \mid 1 \leq i \leq k\}$*:*

$$\gamma_{\mathbb{M}}(\alpha \cdot \iota(\mathscr{E}) * G, S) \subseteq \bigcup_{i=1}^{k} \gamma_{\mathbb{M}}(F_{\text{Heap},i} * G, \mathfrak{guard}_{\mathbb{S}}(F_{\text{Pure},i}, S))$$

In the example of Fig. 5, the inductive rule corresponding to the empty list of edges is ruled out, since M' contains constraint $\alpha_1 \neq 0$ in the $\mathbb{S}^\sharp$ component, thus unfolding produces M (Fig. 5(a)) as a single disjunct. Thus, when applied to M' abstract transfer function $[\![\texttt{s := s->next}]\!]^\sharp$ first invokes the unfolding procedure, and then proceeds as explained above. Theorem 1 ensures the soundness of the resulting abstract operations. We write $G \leadsto_{\mathrm{U}} (G_u, F_{\text{Pure}})$ when a predicate of G can be unfolded so as to produce G_u with side constraints F_{Pure}.

Non-local Unfolding. The unfolding case studied so far is quite straightforward as the node at which inductive predicate should be unfolded is well specified, by the transfer function (α_1 in Fig. 5). The analysis of an instruction reading `c->id` from the abstract state corresponding to line 7 appears in Fig. 3: in this state `c` points to β in the abstract level, but node β is neither the origin of a points-to predicate nor that of an inductive predicate that could be unfolded. Intuitively, β could be any node in the graph as shown by the set property $\beta \in \mathscr{F} \uplus \{\alpha'\} \uplus \mathscr{F}''$, thus we expect the abstract memory state to reflect this. This intuition is formalized as follows: the second parameter of **nodes** is a *head parameter* (Sect. 3), and the side predicates carry out the fact that $\beta \in \mathscr{F} \uplus \{\alpha'\} \uplus \mathscr{F}''$, where $\mathscr{F}$ and $\mathscr{F}''$ appear as a second parameter for both **nodes** predicates in the shape, which allows to localize β. This principle is a direct consequence of a property of head parameters:

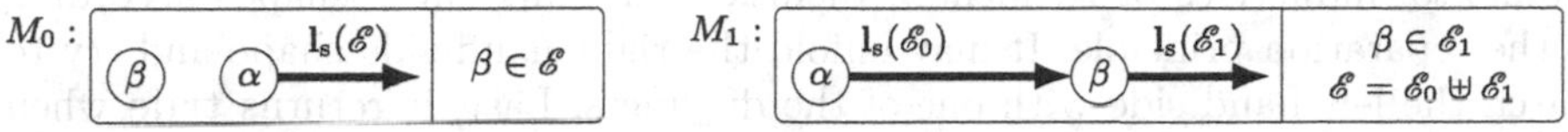

Fig. 6. Non-local unfolding

Theorem 2 (Non-local Unfolding Principle). *Let* ι *be a single parameter inductive, such that* $\alpha \cdot \iota(\mathscr{E}) \vdash \mathscr{E} : \textbf{head}$. *Let* $(m, \nu) \in \gamma_{\mathbb{G}}(\alpha \cdot \iota(\mathscr{E}))$ *such that* $\nu(\beta) \in \nu(\mathscr{E})$. *Given* $\mathscr{E}_0, \mathscr{E}_1$ *fresh set variables,* ν *can be extended into* ν'*, such that* $(m, \nu') \in \gamma_{\mathbb{G}}(\alpha \cdot \iota \ast\!=_{(\mathscr{E}_0)} \beta \cdot \iota \ast \beta \cdot \iota(\mathscr{E}_1))$, $\nu'(\mathscr{E}) = \nu'(\mathscr{E}_0) \uplus \nu'(\mathscr{E}_1)$ *and* $\nu'(\beta) \in \nu'(\mathscr{E}_1)$.

The proof follows directly from the definition of head parameters. Figure 6 illustrates this *non-local* unfolding principle. While Theorem 2 states the result for inductive definitions with a single set parameter, the result generalizes directly to the case of definitions with several parameters (only the parameter supporting non-local unfolding is then required to be a head parameter). It also generalizes to segments.

To conclude, the analysis of an assignment proceeds along the following steps:

1. it attempts to evaluate all l-values to edges and r-values to symbolic variables;
2. when step 1 fails as no points-to edge can be found at offset $\alpha \cdot \mathtt{f}$, it searches for a local unfolding at α, that is either a segment or an inductive predicate starting from α;
3. when no such local unfolding can be found, it searches for predicates of the form $\alpha \in \{\alpha_0, \ldots, \alpha_k\} \uplus \mathscr{E}_0 \uplus \ldots \uplus \mathscr{E}_l$, where $\mathscr{E}_0, \ldots, \mathscr{E}_l$ appear as head parameters; when it finds such a predicate, the analysis produces a disjunction of cases, where either $\alpha = \alpha_i$ (and it goes back to step 1), or where $\alpha \in \mathscr{E}_i$ and it performs non-local unfolding of the corresponding predicate (Theorem 1);
4. last, it performs the abstract operation on the unfolded disjuncts

Note that failure to fully materialize all required nodes would produce imprecise results; thus, in absence of information about parameters, the analysis may fail to produce a precise post-condition.

5.2 Folding of Inductive Summaries: Inclusion Test, Join and Widening

While transfer functions *unfold* inductive predicates, inclusion checking, join and widening operators need to discover valid set parameters so as to *fold* them back.

Inclusion Checking. The inclusion checking abstract operation $\sqsubseteq$ inputs two abstract memory states M_l, M_r and returns **true** if it successfully establishes that $\gamma_{\mathbb{M}}(M_l) \subseteq \gamma_{\mathbb{M}}(M_r)$ (it is conservative) using inclusion testing functions $\sqsubseteq_{\mathbf{G}}$, $\sqsubseteq_{\mathbf{S}}$. It attempts to construct a proof of inclusion, following a set of logical rules an excerpt of which is shown in Fig. 7(a). Some rules were already introduced in [5]. For instance, the bottom left rule states that any shape is included in itself; the inclusion checking algorithm actually applies it to single predicates (points-to, inductives or segments). Inclusion checking splits shapes according to the separation principle. It may unfold the right hand side shape and try to match the left hand side with one of the disjuncts. Last, it returns **true** when both the comparison of shapes and of side predicates return **true**.

$$\frac{S_l \vdash G_l \sqsubseteq_{\mathbf{G}} G_r}{S_l \vdash G_l * G \sqsubseteq_{\mathbf{G}} G_r * G} \qquad \frac{S_l \vdash G_l \sqsubseteq_{\mathbf{G}} G_u \qquad G_r \rightsquigarrow_{\mathrm{U}} (G_u, F_{\mathrm{Pure}}) \qquad \mathfrak{proves}_{\mathrm{S}}(S_l, F_{\mathrm{Pure}}) = \mathbf{true}}{S_l \vdash G_l \sqsubseteq_{\mathbf{G}} G_r}$$

$$\frac{\mathfrak{proves}_{\mathrm{S}}(S_l, \mathscr{E}_0 \subseteq \mathscr{E}) \qquad \mathscr{E}_1 \text{ fresh (denotes } \mathscr{E} \setminus \mathscr{E}_0) \qquad S_l \vdash G_l \sqsubseteq_{\mathbf{G}} \beta \cdot \iota(\mathscr{E}_1) \qquad \alpha \cdot \iota(\mathscr{E}) \vdash \mathscr{E} : \mathbf{head}}{S_l \vdash \alpha \cdot \iota *\!\!=_{(\mathscr{E}_0)} \beta \cdot \iota * G_l \sqsubseteq_{\mathbf{G}} \alpha \cdot \iota(\mathscr{E})}$$

$$\overline{S_l \vdash G \sqsubseteq_{\mathbf{G}} G} \qquad \frac{S_l \vdash G_l \sqsubseteq_{\mathbf{G}} \beta \cdot \iota(\mathscr{E}) \qquad \alpha \cdot \iota(\mathscr{E}) \vdash \mathscr{E} : \mathbf{cst}}{S_l \vdash \alpha \cdot \iota *\!\!=_{(\mathscr{E})} \beta \cdot \iota * G_l \sqsubseteq_{\mathbf{G}} \alpha \cdot \iota(\mathscr{E})} \qquad \frac{S_l \vdash G_l \sqsubseteq_{\mathbf{G}} G_r \qquad S_l \sqsubseteq_{\mathbf{S}} S_r}{\vdash (G_l, S_l) \sqsubseteq (G_r, S_r)}$$

(a) Logical rules for inclusion checking over shapes ($\sqsubseteq_{\mathbf{G}}$) and over memory states ($\sqsubseteq$)

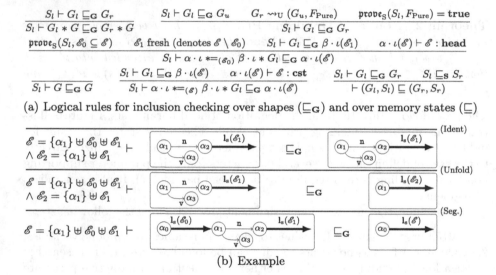

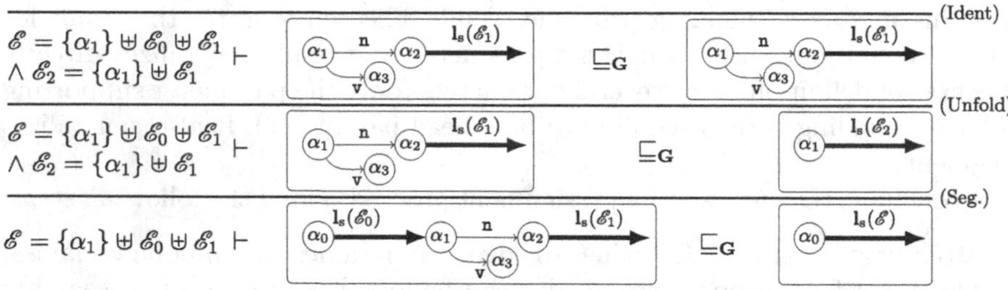

(b) Example

Fig. 7. Inclusion checking

However, the matching of segments and inductive predicates with set parameters requires some specific rules. Figure 7(a) shows two such rules, that apply when trying to compare a segment on the left and an inductive predicate on the right, that correspond to the same definition and the same origin:

- The bottom middle rule applies to the case of a *constant* set parameter and simply requires inductive and segment to share the same set parameter.
- The middle rule applies to the case of a *head* set parameter and enforces its additiveness by checking $\mathscr{E}_0 \subseteq \mathscr{E}$ and choosing fresh $\mathscr{E}_1$ so that $\mathscr{E} = \mathscr{E}_0 \uplus \mathscr{E}_1$, following the properties of head parameters shown in Sect. 4.

Similar rules apply to the comparison of segments in both sides. Soundness follows from the soundness of each rule:

Theorem 3 (Inclusion Checking Soundness). *If $S_l \vdash G_l \sqsubseteq_{\mathbf{G}} G_r$, $(m, \nu) \in \gamma_{\mathbb{G}}(G_l)$, and $\nu \in \gamma_{\mathbb{S}}(S_l)$, then $(m, \nu) \in \gamma_{\mathbb{G}}(G_r)$. Moreover, if $\vdash (G_l, S_l) \sqsubseteq (G_r, S_r)$, then $\gamma_{\mathbb{M}}(G_l, S_l) \subseteq \gamma_{\mathbb{M}}(G_r, S_r)$.*

Fig. 7(b) illustrates this algorithm on an example based on the $\mathbf{l_s}$ definition, which behaves similarly to **nodes** in its second parameter (it resembles inclusion tests ran in the analysis of the program of Fig. 1(e)). The inclusion proof search starts from the bottom shapes, where α_0 is the origin of a segment in the left, and of an inductive predicate in the right. Since $\mathbf{l_s}$ has a *head* parameter, the rule specific to this case applies, and the inclusion test "consumes" the segment, effectively removing it from the left argument, and adding a fresh $\mathscr{E}_2$ variable, such that $\mathscr{E} = \mathscr{E}_0 \uplus \mathscr{E}_2$ (thus, constraint $\mathscr{E}_2 = \{\alpha_1\} \uplus \mathscr{E}_1$ is added). Then, the algorithm derives inclusion holds after unfolding and matching three pairs of identical predicate.

Join and Widening. In the shape domain $\mathbb{G}^\sharp$, *join* and *widening* rely on the same algorithm. A basic version of this algorithm is formalized in [5], and we extend it here so as to handle set parameters. To over-approximate $M_l = (G_l, S_l)$ and $M_r = (G_r, S_r)$, the join algorithm starts from a configuration $[M_l \sqcup_{\mathbf{G}} M_r | \mathbf{emp}]$, and incrementally selects components of both inputs that can be over-approximated likewise, and moves their common over-approximation to the third (output) element. The two fundamental rules are shown in Fig. 8(a). The first rule states that, if both inputs contain a same region G, then these regions can be joined immediately (it is applied incrementally for points-to, inductive and segment predicates). The second rule states that, if a common over-approximation G_o for G_l, G_r can be found and checked with $\sqsubseteq_{\mathbf{G}}$, abstract join can rewrite these into G_o. This algorithm is a widening: it ensures termination of sequences of abstract iterates.

Novel rules are needed to *introduce* segments and inductive predicates. Let ι be an inductive definition with a single set parameter. Then, a segment predicate $\alpha \cdot \iota *\!\!=_{(\mathscr{E})} \beta \cdot \iota$ (where $\mathscr{E}$ is fresh) can be introduced when $G_l = \mathbf{emp}$, $S \vdash \alpha = \beta$, $S_r \vdash G_r \sqsubseteq_{\mathbf{G}} \alpha \cdot \iota *\!\!=_{(\mathscr{E})} \beta \cdot \iota$, and when:

- either $\mathscr{E}$ is *constant* ($\alpha \cdot \iota(\mathscr{E}) \vdash \mathscr{E} : \mathbf{cst}$);
- or $\mathscr{E}$ is a *head parameter* ($\alpha \cdot \iota(\mathscr{E}) \vdash \mathscr{E} : \mathbf{head}$), and $S_l' = \mathfrak{guard}_{\mathbb{S}}(S_l, \mathscr{E} = \emptyset)$;

The inclusion checking algorithm may then discover new constraints between fresh variable $\mathscr{E}$ and the other set variables, and enrich S_r accordingly. These constraints indirectly stem from the constant or head kind of the set parameters. Additional rules allow to introduce inductive predicates, and extend segment or inductive predicates in a similar way, as the above segment weakening. Soundness follows from step by step preservation of concretization (the convergence property of the shape join is proved in [5]):

Theorem 4 (Soundness of Join). *If $[(G_l, S_l) \sqcup_{\mathbf{G}} (G_r, S_r) | G_o] \rightsquigarrow_{\sqcup} [(G_l', S_l') \sqcup_{\mathbf{G}} (G_r', S_r') | G_o']$, then, $\forall i \in \{l, r\}$, $\gamma_{\mathbb{M}}(G_i * G_o, S_i) \subseteq \gamma_{\mathbb{M}}(G_i' * G_o', S_i')$.*

Therefore, if $[M_l \sqcup_{\mathbf{G}} M_r | \mathbf{emp}] \rightsquigarrow_{\sqcup}^{\star} [(\mathbf{emp}, S_l') \sqcup_{\mathbf{G}} (\mathbf{emp}, S_r') | G_o']$, then $(G_o', S_l' \sqcup_{\mathbf{S}} S_r')$ (resp., $(G_o', S_l' \triangledown_{\mathbf{S}} S_r')$) provides a sound join (resp., widening) for M_l, M_r.

$$\frac{\begin{array}{c}[(G_l * G, S_l) \sqcup_{\mathbf{G}} (G_r * G, S_r)|G_o] \rightsquigarrow_{\sqcup} [(G_l, S_l) \sqcup_{\mathbf{G}} (G_r, S_r)|G_o * G] \\ S'_l \text{ (resp., } S'_r\text{) extends } S_l \text{ (resp., } S_r\text{)} \qquad S'_l \vdash G'_l \sqsubseteq_{\mathbf{G}} G'_o \qquad S'_r \vdash G'_r \sqsubseteq_{\mathbf{G}} G'_o\end{array}}{[(G_l * G'_l, S_l) \sqcup_{\mathbf{G}} (G_r * G'_r, S_r)|G_o] \rightsquigarrow_{\sqcup} [(G_l, S'_l) \sqcup_{\mathbf{G}} (G_r, S'_r)|G_o * G'_o]}$$

(a) Computational rules

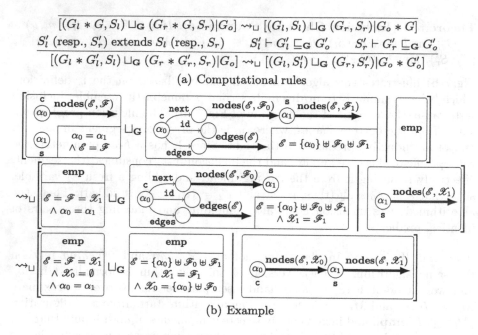

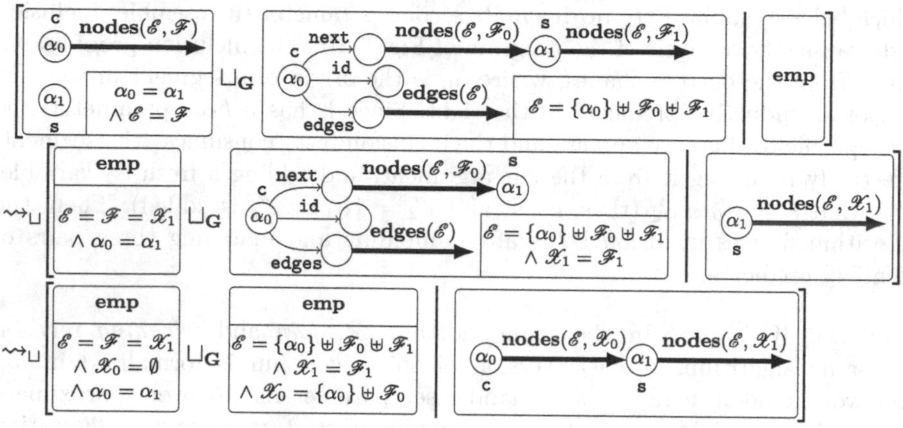

(b) Example

Fig. 8. Join and widening algorithms

Figure 8(b) shows a simplified instance of a join taken from the analysis of the program of Fig. 1(e). Initially, both inputs contain very similar **nodes** inductive predicates at α_0, thus the first step moves these predicates into the output component. The first parameter is constant, and is equal to $\mathscr{E}$ everywhere. The second parameter is a head parameter, so a new variable $\mathscr{X}_1$ is introduced, and S_l (resp., S_r) is enriched with constraint $\mathscr{X}_1 = \mathscr{F}$ (resp., $\mathscr{X}_1 = \mathscr{F}_1$). In the second step, a segment is introduced. Again, the constant parameter is equal to $\mathscr{E}$ everywhere. In the left, constraint $\mathscr{X}_0 = \emptyset$ is added. In the right, inclusion check discovers constraint $\mathscr{X}_0 = \{\alpha_0\} \uplus \mathscr{F}_0$. This configuration is final, and allows to compute the set constraints $\mathscr{E} = \mathscr{X}_0 \uplus \mathscr{X}_1$.

6 Empirical Evaluation

We implemented inductive definitions with set predicates into the MemCAD static analyzer [26,27] and integrated set constraints as part of the numerical domain [6], so as to assess (1) whether it achieves the verification of structure preservation in the presence of sharing, and (2) if the memory abstract domain efficiency is preserved. The analysis takes a set abstract domain as a parameter to represent set constraints. We have considered two set abstract domains:

- the first one is based on an encoding of set constraints into BDDs, and utilizes a BDD library [17], following an idea of [11] (this domain is called "BDD" in the results table);

- the second one relies on a compact representation of constraints of the form $\mathscr{E}_i = \{\alpha_0, \ldots, \alpha_n\} \uplus \mathscr{F}_0 \uplus \ldots \uplus \mathscr{F}_m$ as well set equalities, inclusion and membership constraints (this domain is called "LIN" in the results table, since the main set constraints expressed here are of "linear" form).

Both abstract domains were implemented in OCaml, and integrated into the MemCAD static analyzer.

Table 1. Analysis of a set of fundamental graph manipulation functions. Analysis times (in milliseconds) are measured on one core of an Intel Xeon at 3.20 GHz with 16 GB of RAM running Ubuntu 14.04.2 LTS (we show overall time including front-end and iterator shape domain and set domain), with "BDD" and "LIN" set domains. "Property" columns: inference of structural properties.

Description	LOCs	Nested loops	"BDD" time (ms)			"BDD"	"LIN" time (ms)			"LIN"
			Total	Shape	Set	Property	Total	Shape	Set	Property
Node: add	27	0	44	0.3	11	yes	28	0.3	0.2	yes
Edge: add	26	0	31	0.2	4	yes	27	0.2	0.1	yes
Edge: delete	22	0	45	0.4	16	yes	30	0.3	0.2	yes
Node list traversal	25	1	117	1.5	87	yes	28	0.5	0.3	yes
Edge list iteration + dest. read	34	1	332	2.7	293	yes	36	3.5	2.4	yes
Graph path: deterministic	31	2	360	2.7	323	yes	35	2.4	2	yes
Graph path: random	43	2	765	7.1	711	yes	41	4.1	3	yes

The analysis inputs inductive definition parameters, a C program, and a pre-condition, and computes and verifies abstract post-conditions. We ran the analysis on a basic graph library, chosen to assess specifically the handling of shared structures (addition or removal operations, structure traversals, and traversals following paths including the program of Fig. 1(e)). Results are shown in Table 1. In all cases, the analysis successfully establishes memory safety (absence of null/dangling pointer dereference), structural preservation for the graph modifying functions, and precise cursor localization for the traversal functions, with both set domains. Note that, in the case of path traversals, memory safety requires the analysis to localize the cursor as a valid graph node, at all times (the strongest set property, captured by the graph inductive definitions of Fig. 2). The analysis time spent in the shape domain is in line with those usually observed in the analyzer [26,27], yet the BDD-based set domain proves inefficient in this situation and accounts for most of the analysis time for two reasons: (1) it is far too expressive and keeps properties that are not relevant to the analysis and (2) set variables renaming (required after joins) necessitate full recomputation of BDDs. By contrast, the "LIN" set domain is tailored for the predicates required in the analysis, and produces very quick analysis run-times. In several cases, the time spent in the shape domain is even reduced compared to "BDD", due to shorter iteration sequences.

7 Related Work

A wide family of shape analysis techniques have been proposed so as to deal with inductive structures, often based on 3-valued logic [21,25] or on separation logic [1,2,4,5,14,23]. Such analyses often deal very well with list and tree like structures, but are often challenged with *unbounded* sharing. In this paper, we augmented a separation logic based analysis [5,7] with set predicates to account for unbounded sharing, both in summaries and in unfolded regions, and retain the parameterizability of this analysis. A shape analysis tracking properties of structure contents was presented in [28], although with a less general set abstraction interface, and without support for unfolding guided by set parameters. Another related approach was proposed in [8], that utilizes a set of data-structure specific analysis rules and encodes sharing information into instrumentalized variables in order to analyze programs manipulating trees and graphs. By contrast, our analysis does no such instrumentation and requires no built-in inductive definitions. Recently, a set of works [15,19,20,26] targeted *overlaid* structures, which feature some form of *structured* sharing, such as a tree overlaid on a list. Typically, these analyses combine several abstractions specific to the different layer. We believe that problem is orthogonal to ours, since we consider a form of sharing that is not structured, and need to achieve *non-local* materialization. Another line of work that is slightly related to ours are the hybrid analyses that aim at discovering relations between the structures and their contents [3,5,16]. Our set predicates actually fit in the domain product formalized in [5], and can also indirectly capture through sets relations between structures and their contents. Abstractions of set properties have recently been used in order to capture relations between sets of keys of dictionaries [12,13] or groups of array cells [22]. A noticeable result is that our analysis tracks very similar predicates, although for a radically different application.

8 Conclusion

In this paper, we have set up a shape analysis able to cope with unbounded sharing. This analysis combines separation logic based shape abstractions and a *set abstract domain*, that tracks pointer sharing properties. Reduction across domains is done lazily at non-local materialization and join. This abstraction was implemented into the MemCAD static analyzer and could cope with graphs described with adjacency lists. Future works will experiment with other set abstract domains and combine this abstraction with other memory abstractions [26,27].

Acknowledgments. We would like to thank Arlen Cox for suggestions about the implementation of the set domain, and François Bérenger for providing very helpful tool support. We also thank Tie Cheng, Antoine Toubhans and the anonymous referees for comments helping us improve this paper.

References

1. Berdine, J., Calcagno, C., Cook, B., Distefano, D., O'Hearn, P.W., Wies, T., Yang, H.: Shape analysis for composite data structures. In: Damm, W., Hermanns, H. (eds.) CAV 2007. LNCS, vol. 4590, pp. 178–192. Springer, Heidelberg (2007)
2. Berdine, J., Calcagno, C., O'Hearn, P.W.: Symbolic execution with separation logic. In: Yi, K. (ed.) APLAS 2005. LNCS, vol. 3780, pp. 52–68. Springer, Heidelberg (2005)
3. Bouajjani, A., Drăgoi, C., Enea, C., Sighireanu, M.: Abstract domains for automated reasoning about list-manipulating programs with infinite data. In: Kuncak, V., Rybalchenko, A. (eds.) VMCAI 2012. LNCS, vol. 7148, pp. 1–22. Springer, Heidelberg (2012)
4. Calcagno, C., Distefano, D., O'Hearn, P., Yang, H.: Compositional shape analysis by means of bi-abduction. In: Symposium on Principles of Programming Languages (POPL), pp. 289–300. ACM (2009)
5. Chang, B.-Y.E., Rival, X.: Relational inductive shape analysis. In: Symposium on Principles of Programming Languages (POPL), pp. 247–260. ACM (2008)
6. Chang, B.-Y.E., Rival, X.: Modular construction of shape-numeric analyzers. In: Festschrift for Dave Schmidt. ENTCS, pp. 161–185 (2013)
7. Chang, B.-Y.E., Rival, X., Necula, G.C.: Shape analysis with structural invariant checkers. In: Riis Nielson, H., Filé, G. (eds.) SAS 2007. LNCS, vol. 4634, pp. 384–401. Springer, Heidelberg (2007)
8. Cherini, R., Rearte, L., Blanco, J.: A shape analysis for non-linear data structures. In: Cousot, R., Martel, M. (eds.) SAS 2010. LNCS, vol. 6337, pp. 201–217. Springer, Heidelberg (2010)
9. Cousot, P., Cousot, R.: Abstract interpretation: a unified lattice model for static analysis of programs by construction or approximation of fixpoints. In: Symposium on Principles of Programming Languages (POPL) (1977)
10. Cousot, P., Cousot, R.: Systematic design of program analysis frameworks. In: Symposium on Principles of Programming Languages (POPL) (1979)
11. Cox, A.: Binary-Decision-Diagrams for Set Abstraction. ArXiv e-prints, March 2015
12. Cox, A., Chang, B.-Y.E., Rival, X.: Automatic analysis of open objects in dynamic language programs. In: Müller-Olm, M., Seidl, H. (eds.) SAS 2014. LNCS, vol. 8723, pp. 134–150. Springer, Heidelberg (2014)
13. Dillig, I., Dillig, T., Aiken, A.: Precise reasoning for programs using containers. In: Symposium on Principles of Programming Languages (POPL), pp. 187–200. ACM (2011)
14. Distefano, D., O'Hearn, P.W., Yang, H.: A local shape analysis based on separation logic. In: Hermanns, H., Palsberg, J. (eds.) TACAS 2006. LNCS, vol. 3920, pp. 287–302. Springer, Heidelberg (2006)
15. Drăgoi, C., Enea, C., Sighireanu, M.: Local shape analysis for overlaid data structures. In: Logozzo, F., Fähndrich, M. (eds.) SAS 2013. LNCS, vol. 7935, pp. 150–171. Springer, Heidelberg (2013)

16. Ferrara, P., Fuchs, R., Juhasz, U.: TVAL+ : TVLA and value analyses together. In: Eleftherakis, G., Hinchey, M., Holcombe, M. (eds.) SEFM 2012. LNCS, vol. 7504, pp. 63–77. Springer, Heidelberg (2012)
17. Filliatre, J.-C.: Bdd ocaml library. https://www.lri.fr/filliatr/ftp/ocaml/bdd/
18. Ishtiaq, S.S., O'Hearn, P.: BI as an assertion language for mutable data structures. In: Symposium on Principles of Programming Languages (POPL), pp. 14–26. ACM (2001)
19. Kreiker, J., Seidl, H., Vojdani, V.: Shape analysis of low-level C with overlapping structures. In: Barthe, G., Hermenegildo, M. (eds.) VMCAI 2010. LNCS, vol. 5944, pp. 214–230. Springer, Heidelberg (2010)
20. Lee, O., Yang, H., Petersen, R.: Program Analysis for Overlaid Data Structures. In: Gopalakrishnan, G., Qadeer, S. (eds.) CAV 2011. LNCS, vol. 6806, pp. 592–608. Springer, Heidelberg (2011)
21. Lev-Ami, T., Sagiv, M.: TVLA: a system for implementing static analyses. In: Palsberg, J. (ed.) SAS 2000. LNCS, vol. 1824, pp. 280–302. Springer, Heidelberg (2000)
22. Liu, J., Rival, X.: Abstraction of arrays based on non contiguous partitions. In: D'Souza, D., Lal, A., Larsen, K.G. (eds.) VMCAI 2015. LNCS, vol. 8931, pp. 282–299. Springer, Heidelberg (2015)
23. Nguyen, H.H., David, C., Qin, S.C., Chin, W.-N.: Automated verification of shape and size properties via separation logic. In: Cook, B., Podelski, A. (eds.) VMCAI 2007. LNCS, vol. 4349, pp. 251–266. Springer, Heidelberg (2007)
24. Reynolds, J.: Separation logic: a logic for shared mutable data structures. In: Symposium on Logics In Computer Science (LICS), pp. 55–74. IEEE (2002)
25. Sagiv, M., Reps, T., Wilhelm, R.: Parametric shape analysis via 3-valued logic. ACM Trans. Program. Lang. Syst. (TOPLAS) **24**(3), 217–298 (2002)
26. Toubhans, A., Chang, B.-Y.E., Rival, X.: Reduced Product Combination of Abstract Domains for Shapes. In: Giacobazzi, R., Berdine, J., Mastroeni, I. (eds.) VMCAI 2013. LNCS, vol. 7737, pp. 375–395. Springer, Heidelberg (2013)
27. Toubhans, A., Chang, B.-Y.E., Rival, X.: An abstract domain combinator for separately conjoining memory abstractions. In: Müller-Olm, M., Seidl, H. (eds.) SAS 2014. LNCS, vol. 8723, pp. 285–301. Springer, Heidelberg (2014)
28. Vafeiadis, V.: Shape-value abstraction for verifying linearizability. In: Jones, N.D., Müller-Olm, M. (eds.) VMCAI 2009. LNCS, vol. 5403, pp. 335–348. Springer, Heidelberg (2009)
29. Venet, A.: Abstract cofibered domains: application to the alias analysis of untyped programs. In: Cousot, R., Schmidt, D.A. (eds.) SAS 1996. LNCS, vol. 1145, pp. 366–382. Springer, Heidelberg (1996)

Synthesizing Heap Manipulations via Integer Linear Programming

Anshul Garg and Subhajit Roy(✉)

Department of Computer Science and Engineering,
Indian Institute of Technology Kanpur, Kanpur, India
garganshul6002@gmail.com, subhajit@iitk.ac.in

Abstract. Writing heap manipulating programs is hard. Even though the high-level algorithms may be simple, it is often tedious to express them using low-level operations. We present a new tool — SYNLIP — that uses expression of intent in the form of concrete examples drawn using box-and-arrow diagrams to synthesize heap-manipulations automatically. Instead of modeling the concrete examples in a monolithic manner, SYNLIP attempts to extract a set of *patterns of manipulation* that can be applied repeatedly to construct such programs. It, then, attempts to infer these *patterns* as linear transformations, leveraging the power of ILP solvers for program synthesis.

In contrast to many current tools, SYNLIP does not need a bound on the number of statements and the number of temporaries to be used in the desired program. Also, it is almost insensitive to the size of the concrete examples and, thus, tends to be scalable. SYNLIP was found to be quite fast; it takes less than 10 seconds for most of our benchmark tasks spanning data-structures like singly and doubly linked-lists, AVL trees and binary search trees.

1 Introduction

Writing heap manipulating programs is hard. Even though the high-level algorithms may be simple, it is often tedious to express them using low-level operations like putfield, getfield and pointer assignments. Consider the following task: split a singly linked-list L into two linked-lists L_1, L_2 such that:

- All nodes in L_1 have values less than or equal to a specified value stored in a variable y, while all nodes in L_2 have values larger than y;
- In the lists L_1 and L_2, the nodes must appear in the reverse order of the nodes in the input linked-list.

A high-level algorithm for the above task is not difficult to design: iterate through each node of L and insert a node in L_1 or L_2 (in the *reverse* order) depending on the value of y. Let us explain this high level algorithm using box and arrow diagrams: Fig. 1 illustrates our high-level algorithm on a concrete

The first author is now with Flipkart, India.

S. Blazy and T. Jensen (Eds.): SAS 2015, LNCS 9291, pp. 109–127, 2015.
DOI: 10.1007/978-3-662-48288-9_7

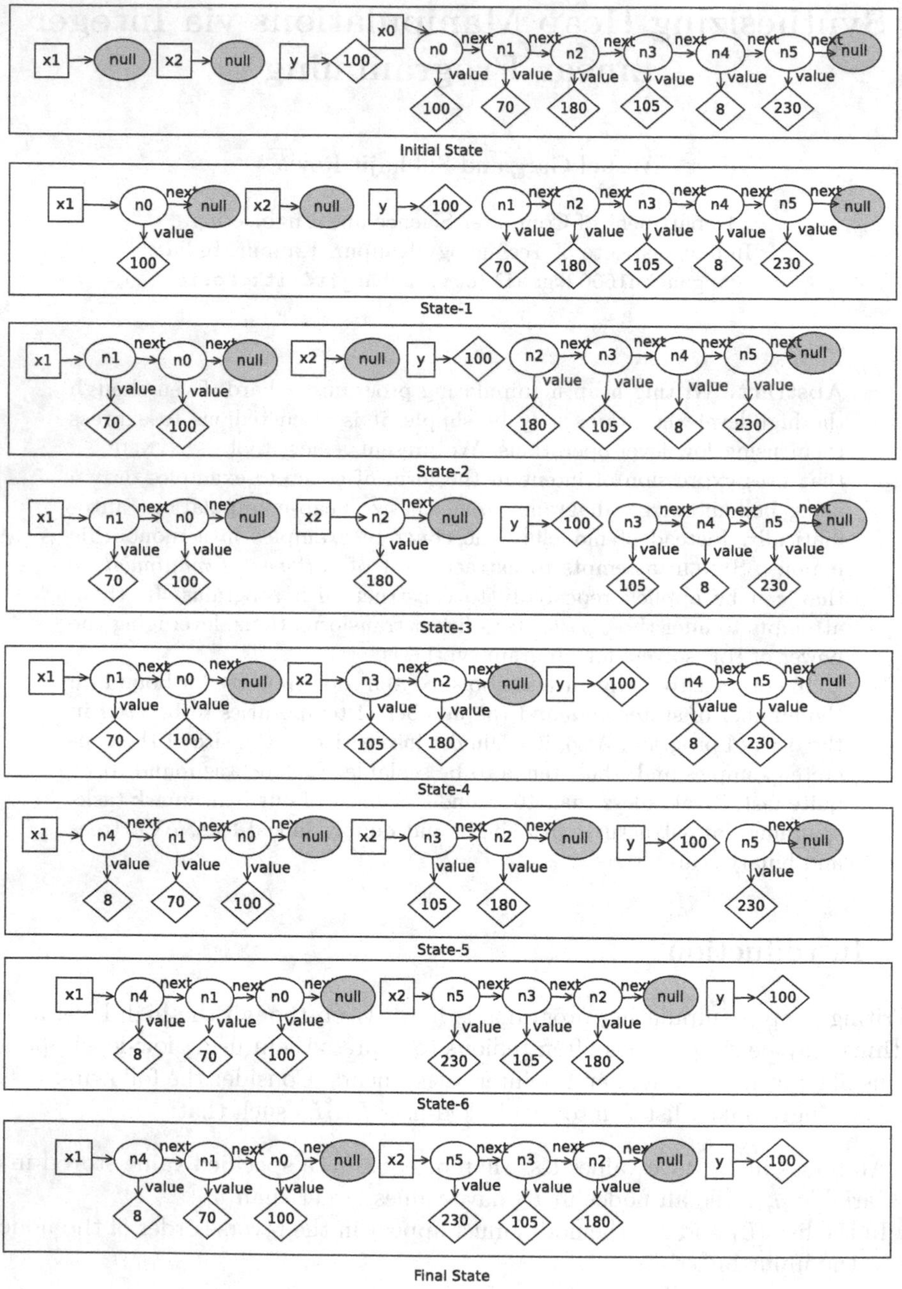

Fig. 1. Box-and-arrow diagrams for segregating nodes by the value in a given variable

example of six nodes. The round entities represent heap nodes, diamonds denote integer nodes and squares imply a program variable. The new lists L_1, L_2 are to be pointed to by program variables x_1, x_2 (respectively). The first diagram shows the initial state while the subsequent diagrams show the state of the heap and variables after each iteration of the program. For the first node n_0, its value field $n_0.value$ is equal to y, so node n_0 is added to the list pointed to by x_1. For the second node, $n_1.value$ is less than y, so it is also added to the same list. Note that n_1 is made to point to n_0 so that in L_1 the nodes appear in the reverse order of that in L (in accordance to the problem statement). Next, $n_2.value$ is greater than y, so n_2 is added to the list pointed to by x_2. It can be seen that the program would need six iterations to get to the desired output, thereby producing an output state as shown in the final diagram.

Now consider implementing the same solution using low-level pointer manipulations — not a task, it is an *ordeal*! Previous work [6] has attempted to build a tool, SYNBAD, that uses such expressions of intent in the form of concrete examples drawn using box-and-arrow diagrams to synthesize heap-manipulations automatically. However, the work had certain limitations:

- firstly, it required that the programmer provides a bound on the number of instructions in the program; such hints, in general, are difficult to provide. The time to synthesis was highly correlated with the looseness of this bound.
- secondly, it also required that the programmer provides a bound on the number of temporary variables used in the program. Again, providing tight bounds for the same is often a non-trivial effort.
- finally, as the whole example was modeled monolithically by SYNBAD to synthesize a correct program, the time to synthesis was quite sensitive to the size of the concrete examples (number of nodes in a concrete example).

Our current work attempts to circumvent the above limitations. Our system automatically infers the number of statements required by the solution program, thereby relieving the programmer of having to estimate the size of the desired program. Moreover, instead of modeling the whole example monolithically, we attempt to identify a set of *patterns of manipulation*, synthesize each such *pattern* independently, and finally combine these *patterns* into a final solution.

```
t1=null
t0=x0

while(t0!=null) {
    temp0=t0.next
    t0.next=t1
    if(t0.value <= y)  then
        x1=t0
    if(t0.value > y) then
        x2=t0
    t0=temp0
    if(temp0!=null &&
        y<=temp0.value) then
        t1=x2
    else
        t1=x1
}
```

Fig. 2. Generated program from SYNLIP for the task in Fig. 1

We have built a tool — SYNLIP *(Program SYNthesizer via Linear Integer Programming)* — that synthesizes programs as a set of linear transformations. To the best of our knowledge, this is the first attempt at powering synthesis from concrete examples via integer linear programming (ILP). SYNLIP consumes specification of intent expressed using box-and-arrow diagrams of concrete examples, attempts to identify repeated patterns that can describe the program, and then, synthesizes each pattern as a Linear Transformation. This makes SYNLIP almost insensitive to the size of the concrete examples but only to the complexity of the task. Also, SYNLIP tends to be more scalable as the size of the patterns is much smaller than the size of the overall program.

For instance, for the task of *reversing a linked-list* on a concrete example with five nodes, SYNBAD takes **6.2 seconds** when the *best* bound on the number of statements (seven statements) is provided. However, the synthesis time increases to **32.1 seconds when a looser bound of 10 statements** is provided [6]. In contrast, with the *same specification*, SYNLIP **does not require any bound on the number of statements** and takes a mere **1.16 s** (on an older machine configuration). Moreover, when the size of the example is doubled, the time just increases to **1.26 s** (i.e. by 0.1 s).

We have used SYNLIP to synthesize programs for many heap manipulating tasks involving linked-lists, doubly linked-lists, AVL trees and binary search trees. SYNLIP takes less than 10 seconds on most of our benchmarks. SYNLIP is also available as an Eclipse IDE plugin that provides a visual editor to specify examples and synthesizes Java code that appears on the programming editor. However, we skip details of the plugin in this current article for brevity.

Figure 2 shows the output program that SYNLIP synthesizes for our example (Fig. 1) of splitting a list on a specified value. As can be seen, in addition to the provided program variables $\{x_1, x_2, y\}$, new temporary variables $\{temp_0, t_0, t_1\}$ have also been generated — automatically synthesized by SYNLIP.

Following are our primary contributions in this work:

- We recognize that programs in many domains can be synthesized by combining operations that are easily expressible as linear transformations. This allows us to apply the power of fast ILP solvers to program synthesis. To the best of our knowledge, this is the first attempt at powering synthesis from concrete examples using Integer Linear Programming.
- We design an algorithm to recognize these operations or *patterns of manipulations*, and combine them efficiently into a program for the domain of heap manipulations. This allows us to relieve the programmer from having to specify the approximate number of statements and temporaries to use.
- We apply the above ideas in building a tool, SYNLIP, that is capable of synthesizing heap manipulating programs from concrete examples expressed as box-and-arrow diagrams. The tool is available as an eclipse plugin that emits Java code snippets for the synthesis tasks.
- We evaluate SYNLIP by synthesizing a few heap manipulating programs: we found SYNLIP to be quite fast at generating programs for our benchmark tasks, taking less than 10 seconds on most of our benchmarks.

2 Preliminaries

2.1 Notations

We use the notation Δ_i to denote the state of the program at a point i in an execution: the program state is described via *points-to* relations ($\rightarrow$) in terms of values assigned to a set of variables λ_V, heap nodes λ_H (we treat the value `null`

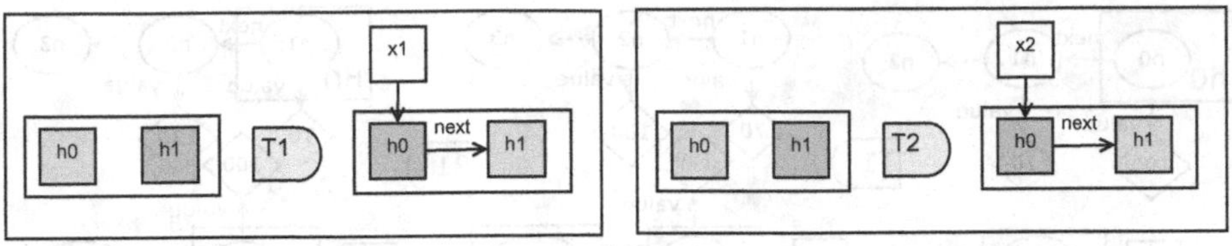

Fig. 3. Template transformers

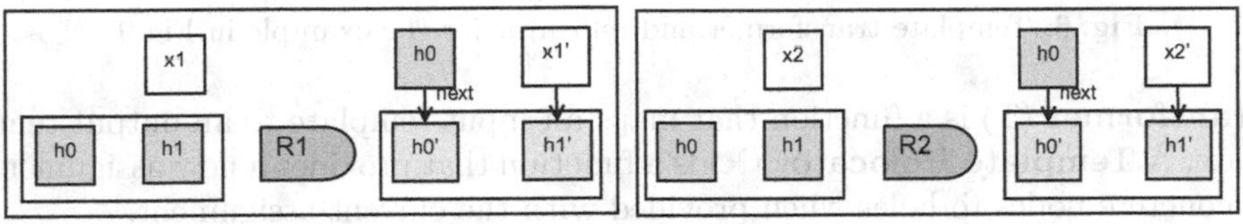

Fig. 4. Template relocators

as a special heap node with no fields), and fields λ_F of these heap nodes. $\mathbb{C}$ refers to a set of integer constants mined from the concrete examples; note that the points-to relation allows variables and fields of heap-nodes to "point-to" integer constants (which implies that these variables and fields contain the respective integer values). To summarize, we describe the state Δ of a program as: $\Delta : V \cup H$ where $V : \lambda_V \rightarrow (\lambda_H \cup \mathbb{C})$, and $H : (\lambda_H \times \lambda_F) \rightarrow (\lambda_H \cup \mathbb{C})$

For the example shown in Fig. 1, the initial program state Δ_0 is as follows: $\Delta_0 : V_0 \cup H_0$ where $V_0 : \{x_0 \rightarrow n_0, x_1 \rightarrow null, x_2 \rightarrow null, y \rightarrow 100\}$, and, $H_0 : \{(n_0, next) \rightarrow n_1, (n_1, next) \rightarrow n_2, \ldots, (n_5, next) \rightarrow null, (n_0, value) \rightarrow 100, \ldots, (n_5, value) \rightarrow 230\}$

We also define the *difference* operator ($-$) which allows us to compute the change from one state to the other. For example, in Fig.1, $\Delta_1 - \Delta_0 = (V_1 \setminus V_0) \cup (H_1 \setminus H_0)$ where $V_1 \setminus V_0 = \{x_1 \rightarrow n_0\}$ and $H_1 \setminus H_0 = \{(n_0, next) \rightarrow null\}$.

We use primed versions of variable to refer to the state of the variable in the next step. For example, {`x' = y`} means that the *new* state of variable `x` is same as the *old* state of the variable `y`.

2.2 Intuition

Our method is based on identifying operations on *templates*. We define an **(abstract) template** (Θ) as a set of representatives for heap nodes — that we refer to as **holes** — along with a set of points-to relations that must hold amongst these holes. A template can be *concretized* by "filling" the holes with heap nodes from a concrete example to form a **frame**. The relations on the holes specified in the template form a precondition: a frame can fill a template if and only if the set of concrete nodes satisfy the relations specified on the holes. A template Θ instantiated on frame f is denoted as $\Theta[f]$. A **Template**

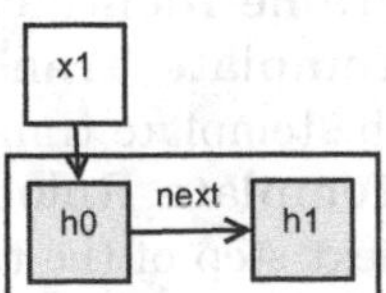

Fig. 5. Template

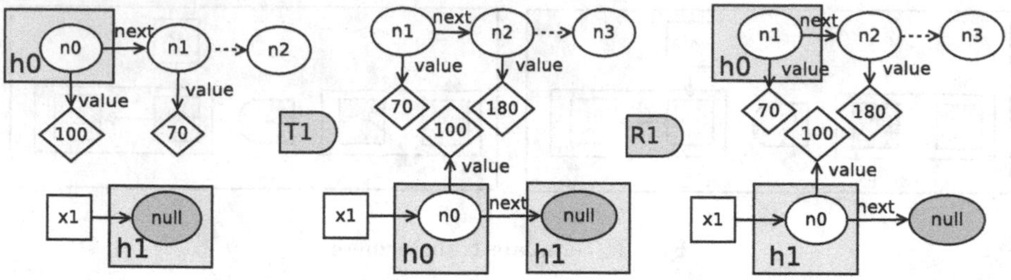

Fig. 6. Template transformer and relocator for the example in Fig. 1

Transformer ($\mathbb{T}$) is a function that maps an input template to an output template. A **Template Relocator** ($\mathbb{R}$) is a function that provides a new assignment of concrete nodes to holes when provided with the current assignment.

Figure 5 shows a template: the boxes h_0 and h_1 denote the holes and the arrow `next` denotes the precondition, i.e. the holes h_0 and h_1 can be filled by heap nodes n_0 and n_1 only if n_0 points to n_1 via the field `next`. Figure 3 shows two template transformers ($\mathbb{T}_1$ and $\mathbb{T}_2$): the transformer $\mathbb{T}_1$ takes a template (with precondition `true` as it imposes no relations on the holes), and transforms it to an output template by adding the relations $\{h_0.next \rightarrow h_1, x_1 \rightarrow h_0\}$, i.e. assigning $h_0.next$ to h_1 via field `next`, and making x_1 point to h_0. As shown in Fig. 6, for our motivating example (Fig. 1), the transformer $\mathbb{T}_1$ mutates the input state, having h_0 as n_0, and h_1 as *null*, to an output state in which $n_0.next$ points to *null* and x_1 points to n_0. Figure 4 shows two template relocators ($\mathbb{R}_1$ and $\mathbb{R}_2$): the relocator $\mathbb{R}_1$ takes the holes for the current state $\{h_0, h_1\}$ and provides their relocation in the next state (denoted as $\{h'_0, h'_1\}$): h_0 is relocated to the node pointed to by its `next` pointer ($h_0.next$) in its *current* state; h_1 is moved to whatever node x_1 points-to in the *next* state (i.e. after $\mathbb{T}_1$ is applied). Figure 6 shows an application of the template relocator $\mathbb{R}_1$ on our example (Fig. 1): the relocator accepts an input frame, where the holes h_0 and h_1 contain n_0 and *null* respectively, to return a new frame where the holes h'_0 and h'_1 contain n_1 (as $n_0.next$ points-to n_1 in the current state) and n_0 (as x_1 points-to n_0 in the next state) respectively.

The core idea driving our proposal is that most heap manipulation tasks can be described via the following steps:

- **Frame Identification:** Identify a (small) set of nodes for mutation;
- **Template Transformation:** Mutate the selected set of nodes (frame) via the template transformer;
- **Template Relocation:** Move the template to capture a new frame for the next step of the task;
- **Repeat:** Repeat the application of the template transformations and the template relocations till the task is accomplished.

Consider the task of reversing a linked-list (Fig. 7): the template transformation for this task corresponds to changing the link from the second node in the template to point to the first; the template relocation corresponds to "moving" the holes via their `next` pointers. For the first frame, we select the first two nodes, i.e. n_0 and n_1; the template transformation manipulates the template by adding a relation ($n_1.next \rightarrow n_0$), i.e. assigning $n_1.next$ to n_0; the template relocation *moves* the holes, thereby selecting the nodes n_1 and n_2 for the next frame. It is easily seen that this strategy, if continued till a `null` is encountered, will reverse the list.

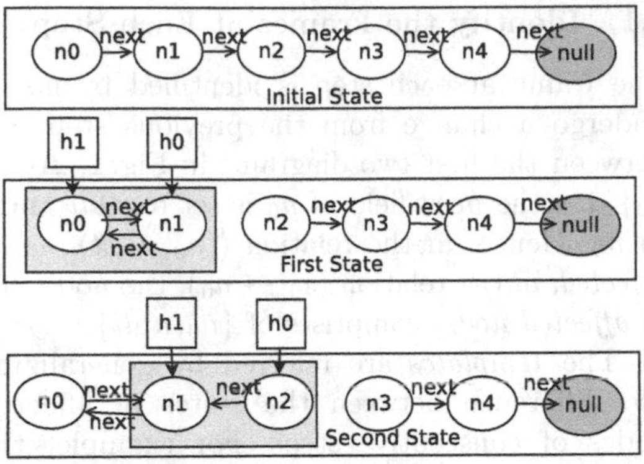

Fig. 7. Linked list reversal (few initial steps)

Our algorithm is based to two hypotheses:

- **Heap Manipulations Have Small Descriptions:** For most heap manipulation tasks, we can capture the essence of the task by a finite (and reasonably small) set of Template Transformers and Template Relocators. The task makes progress by applying one of these Transformer and Relocator functions at each step; this process is repeated till the task is accomplished. A selection logic dictates the selection of an appropriate Transformer and Relocator at each step. This assumption of an existence of a finite number of Transformers and Relocators should not be a surprise as such programs manipulate an unbounded number of heap objects, but with only a finite number of program variables and statements at their disposal.
- **Heap Manipulations are Linear Transformations:** In many domains (including heap manipulations expressed as concrete examples), the Transformers and Relocators can be expressed as linear transformations. This allows us to leverage the power of ILP solvers to synthesize these functions and, thus, programs in these domains.

Our synthesis strategy attempts to generate a program that is divided into three parts: loop prologue (head statements), loop body (loop statements) and loop epilogue (tail statements). Note that it is possible to extend our algorithm for other control-flow structures; however, our current implementation as well as the algorithms discussed in this paper are restricted to a single loop.

3 The Algorithm

In this section, we provide an overview of our synthesis algorithm; the detailed ILP formulations are provided in Sect. 4.

3.1 Identify the Frames at Each Step

The frame at each step is identified by noting the heap nodes whose states undergo a change from the previous step to the current step. For example, between the first two diagrams in Fig. 1, $\Delta_1 - \Delta_0 = \{(n_0, next) \rightarrow null, x_1 \rightarrow n_0\}$, i.e. the *next* field of n_0 is set to *null* and the variable x_1 is made to point to n_0. Hence, in the relation $((n_0, next) \rightarrow null)$, the nodes n_0 and *null* are *affected*; in the relation $(x_1 \rightarrow n_0)$, the node n_0 is *affected*. Thus, overall, the set of *affected nodes* comprises of $\{n_0, null\}$.

The *templates* are inferred by generalizing the difference between the states of affected nodes of consecutive steps. For example, the template for $\Delta_1 - \Delta_0 = \{(n_0, next) \rightarrow null, x_1 \rightarrow n_0\}$ can be obtained by abstracting n_0 and *null* by holes h_0 and h_1 (respectively), to obtain the abstract template $\{(h_0, next) \rightarrow h_1, x_1 \rightarrow h_0\}$ (see Fig. 5). Table 1 shows the concrete nodes that *fill* this template at each step.

Table 1. Affected Nodes

Holes	1	2	3	4	5	6
h_0	n_0	n_1	n_2	n_3	n_4	n_5
h_1	$null$	n_0	$null$	n_2	n_1	n_3

3.2 Infer the Transformation Function

We set up the problem of inferring a set of statements that transforms an input state (expressed as an input vector $\boldsymbol{S_1}$) to an output state (as another vector $\boldsymbol{S_2}$) as a linear algebraic problem of inferring a *linear transformation* $\mathbb{T}$ such that:

$$\mathbb{T}\ \boldsymbol{S_1} = \boldsymbol{S_2}$$

For example, the set of assignments {`x'=x.next; (x.next)'=x;`} can represented in the following manner:

$$\begin{bmatrix} 0 & 1 \\ 1 & 0 \end{bmatrix} \begin{bmatrix} x \\ x.next \end{bmatrix} = \begin{bmatrix} x' \\ (x.next)' \end{bmatrix}$$

Hence, the transformer $\mathbb{T}$ can be seen as a 0–1 matrix that assigns values amongst fields of heap nodes. Intuitively, one can view the scalar multiplication operation as *selection* (i.e. if multiplied by 1, a value is selected else it is not) and scalar addition as *set union*. In abstract domains, the final state of an entity in $\boldsymbol{S_2}$ can be represented as a union over multiple input values in $\boldsymbol{S_1}$. However, on concrete examples the set of all possible values that is assigned to the final state must be a singleton set; hence, all the rows in $\mathbb{T}$ must sum exactly to 1.

The template transformer $\mathbb{T}$ is inferred as a generalization that *explains* the frame transformations at each step. To begin with, we extract the frames from each diagram. Going by our hypothesis that these transformations are linear, we set up the problem of inferring the template transformer as the following linear algebraic problem: infer a linear transformer $\mathbb{T}$ such that all the input templates are transformed to the respective output templates. That is, infer $\mathbb{T}$ such that $\mathbb{T}\ \zeta_i = \zeta_{i+1}$ (using the notation $\zeta_i = \Theta[f_i]$) holds for all (relevant) i, where ζ_i is a column vector comprising the state of the nodes in the frame in the ith step. This is same as setting it up as inferring $\mathbb{T}$ such that:

$$\mathbb{T}\ \left[\boldsymbol{\zeta_1} | \boldsymbol{\zeta_2} | \cdots | \boldsymbol{\zeta_{k\text{-}1}}\right] = \left[\boldsymbol{\zeta_2} | \boldsymbol{\zeta_3} | \cdots | \boldsymbol{\zeta_k}\right] \qquad (1)$$

Here, $\mathbb{T}$ is constrained to be a 0-1 matrix where each row vector sums to 1. Note that $\mathbb{T}$ models a set of assignments that can transform the input template to the output template. New **temporary variables** are used to point to the holes in the template. All pointer variables and all fields of the affected nodes appear in both the input and output states while computing $\mathbb{T}$.

For example, consider the task of reversing a linked-list (Fig. 7): we allocate **new temporary variables** t_0 and t_1 that always point to the nodes that fill the holes h_0 and h_1 (respectively) in each frame. We set this problem up as inferring $\mathbb{T}$ such that:

$$[\mathbb{T}] \begin{array}{c} \\ t_0.next \\ t_1.next \\ t_0 \\ t_1 \end{array} \begin{array}{c} \begin{array}{ccccc} \varsigma_1 & \varsigma_2 & \varsigma_3 & \varsigma_4 & \varsigma_5 \end{array} \\ \begin{pmatrix} n_1 & n_2 & n_3 & n_4 & null \\ undef & null & n_0 & n_1 & n_2 \\ n_0 & n_1 & n_2 & n_3 & n_4 \\ null & n_0 & n_1 & n_2 & n_3 \end{pmatrix} \end{array} = \begin{array}{c} \\ t_0.next \\ t_1.next \end{array} \begin{array}{c} \begin{array}{ccccc} \varsigma_2 & \varsigma_3 & \varsigma_4 & \varsigma_5 & \varsigma_6 \end{array} \\ \begin{pmatrix} null & n_0 & n_1 & n_2 & n_3 \\ undef & null & n_0 & n_1 & n_2 \end{pmatrix} \end{array}$$

On solving the same (on an ILP solver), we get the following solution for $\mathbb{T}$:

$$\mathbb{T} = \begin{array}{c} \\ (t_0.next)' \\ (t_1.next)' \end{array} \begin{array}{c} \begin{array}{cccc} t_0.next & t_1.next & t_0 & t_1 \end{array} \\ \begin{pmatrix} 0 & 0 & 0 & 1 \\ 0 & 1 & 0 & 0 \end{pmatrix} \end{array}$$

The above transformer *explains* that the required state transformations can be reached by the following assignments: {**(t0.next)'=t1**, **(t1.next)'=t1.next**}.

However, in general, a single transformation function is often not capable of explaining each step in the task. For example, in Fig. 1, we need two transformation functions to explain the task: $\mathbb{T}_1$, that explains the transformation corresponding to the case when the value at a node is higher than the value in y, in which case the node is added to the list pointed to by x_1; the transformation $\mathbb{T}_2$ handles the other case when the node is added to the list pointed to by x_2.

In such cases, we attempt to infer a *minimal* set of transformation functions $\{\mathbb{T}_1, \mathbb{T}_2, \ldots, \mathbb{T}_n\}$, such that, at least one of them is capable of explaining the transformation at each step. Our algorithm applies a greedy strategy where we employ an objective function that strives to satisfy the maximum number of the yet-to-be-satisfied rows of the output matrix. For example, in Fig. 1, on the states {0,1,4}, the assignment to x_1 is inferred as {`x1' = t0`}, while on the states {2,3,5}, the same is inferred as {`x1' = x1`}. We use a *selection operator* (denoted by $\otimes$) that selects the *right* transformation at each step. So, in general,

$$\mathbb{T}\ S_{in} = \left[\mathbb{T}_1 \otimes \mathbb{T}_2 \otimes \cdots \otimes \mathbb{T}_n\right] S_{in} = S_{out} \tag{2}$$

3.3 Infer the Relocation Function

The relocation function *moves* each temporary variable t_i, that points to the node that fills the hole h_i in the current state, so as to point to the node that fills the same hole in the template in the next step.

Our algorithm for inferring the relocation function is very similar to inferring the transformation function. However, in this case, in addition to all the temporary variables t_i (corresponding to the holes h_i), all program variables, and all the fields of each affected node, we also provide the output states of all pointer variables computed by applying the transformation function on the input state. The reason behind it is that often the relocation depends both on the current and the next state (an example for the same was discussed in Sect. 2.2). Also, as relocation does not make sense for the final iteration of the loop, the state matrices S_{in} and S_{out} have one less column than the state matrices used while computing the transformation function.

For the example in Fig. 1, we need two relocation matrices ($\mathbb{R}_1, \mathbb{R}_2$) to capture the cases corresponding to the value at a node being greater-than-or-equal or less than the value contained in y; the selection operator $\otimes$ selects the right relocation function at each step:

$$[\mathbb{R}_1 \otimes \mathbb{R}_2] S_{in} = S_{out}$$

$$S_{in} = \begin{array}{c} t_0.n \\ t_1.n \\ t_0.v \\ t_1.v \\ y \\ x_0 \\ x_1 \\ x_2 \\ (x_0)' \\ (x_1)' \\ (x_2)' \\ t_0 \\ t_1 \end{array} \begin{pmatrix} n_1 & n_2 & n_3 & n_4 & n_5 \\ undef & null & undef & null & n_0 \\ 100 & 70 & 180 & 105 & 7 \\ undef & 100 & undef & 180 & 70 \\ 100 & 100 & 100 & 100 & 100 \\ n_0 & n_0 & n_0 & n_0 & n_0 \\ null & n_0 & n_1 & n_1 & n_1 \\ null & null & null & n_2 & n_3 \\ n_0 & n_0 & n_0 & n_0 & n_0 \\ n_0 & n_1 & n_1 & n_1 & n_4 \\ null & null & n_2 & n_3 & n_3 \\ n_0 & n_1 & n_2 & n_3 & n_4 \\ null & n_0 & null & n_2 & n_1 \end{pmatrix}$$

In the state matrices (S_{in} and S_{out}) shown, the primed variables are the values of these variables in the next state (i.e. after application of the transformation function $\mathbb{T}$ on the input state). We abbreviate the fields `next` and `value` to n and v.

$$S_{out} = \begin{array}{c} t_0 \\ t_1 \end{array} \begin{pmatrix} n_1 & n_2 & n_3 & n_4 & n_5 \\ n_0 & null & n_2 & n_1 & n_3 \end{pmatrix}$$

On solving with the required constraints, the ILP solver returns matrices for $\mathbb{R}_1$ and $\mathbb{R}_2$ as shown below:

$$\mathbb{R}_1 = \begin{array}{c} \\ t_0' \\ t_1' \end{array} \begin{array}{c} \begin{array}{ccccccccccccc} t_0.n & t_1.n & t_0.v & t_1.v & y & x_0 & x_1 & x_2 & (x_0)' & (x_1)' & (x_2)' & t_0 & t_1 \end{array} \\ \begin{pmatrix} 1 & 0 & 0 & 0 & 0 & 0 & 0 & 0 & 0 & 0 & 0 & 0 & 0 \\ 0 & 0 & 0 & 0 & 0 & 0 & 0 & 0 & 0 & 1 & 0 & 0 & 0 \end{pmatrix} \end{array};$$

$$\mathbb{R}_2 = \begin{array}{c} \\ t_0' \\ t_1' \end{array} \begin{array}{c} \begin{array}{ccccccccccccc} t_0.n & t_1.n & t_0.v & t_1.v & y & x_0 & x_1 & x_2 & (x_0)' & (x_1)' & (x_2)' & t_0 & t_1 \end{array} \\ \begin{pmatrix} 1 & 0 & 0 & 0 & 0 & 0 & 0 & 0 & 0 & 0 & 0 & 0 & 0 \\ 0 & 0 & 0 & 0 & 0 & 0 & 0 & 0 & 0 & 0 & 1 & 0 & 0 \end{pmatrix} \end{array}$$

3.4 Infer Selection Logic

The selection logic (denoted by the operator $\otimes$) dictates the selection of a transformation and relocation function at each step (i.e. loop iteration). The first step in inferring the selection logic is to construct a selection vector associated with each transformer $\mathbb{T}_i$ that records the loop iterations at which this transformer needs to be applied. Continuing with our running example (Fig. 1), the transformer $\mathbb{T}_1$ needs to be applied for the iterations {0,1,4}; we can represent the same as a 0–1 *selection* vector $\boldsymbol{V_1}$ = [1 1 0 0 1 0], where 1 at a position i implies that $\mathbb{T}_1$ needs to be applied for step i.

Corresponding to each relational operator $op \in \{=, \neq, \leq, \geq, <, >\}$, we construct a vector $\boldsymbol{P_{op}}$ according to the selection vector $\boldsymbol{V_k}$ for the respective transformer $\mathbb{T}_k$. On our example in Fig. 1: for the selection vector [1 1 0 0 1 0] and the operator $\leq$, the vector $\boldsymbol{P_{\leq}}$ is formed as:

$$\boldsymbol{P_{\leq}} = (\exists \alpha \leq 0, \beta > 0 : [\alpha\ \alpha\ \beta\ \beta\ \alpha\ \beta])$$

The intuition behind constructing the vector $\boldsymbol{P_{op}}$ is as follows: with a and b as the candidate operands, and $\leq$ as the relational operator, at the positions {0,1,4} the variables a and b must satisfy (a <= b); that is, $(a - b \leq 0)$ must hold. At the same time, at the other positions, $(a - b > 0)$ must hold to prevent the application of the respective transformer at these steps.

The conditional is synthesized via a search for candidate *row vectors* $\boldsymbol{b_i}$ and $\boldsymbol{b_j}$ from the matrix $\mathbb{B} = [\ \zeta_1\ |\zeta_1\ | \ldots |\ \zeta_n\ ]$, where ζ_k contains the states of all variables, temporaries and fields of the affected nodes (in terms of the variables pointing to them) for the frame in the kth loop-iteration. To construct the conditional, we set up the following search:

$$\textbf{FIND}(i, j, op) \textit{ such that } [\boldsymbol{b_i} - \boldsymbol{b_j}] \textit{ satisfies } \boldsymbol{P_{op}}$$

where $\boldsymbol{b_i}, \boldsymbol{b_j} \in$ *row-vectors of* $\mathbb{B}$ and $\boldsymbol{P_{op}} \in \{[\boldsymbol{P_>}], [\boldsymbol{P_<}], [\boldsymbol{P_=}], [\boldsymbol{P_{\neq}}], [\boldsymbol{P_{\leq}}], [\boldsymbol{P_{\geq}}]\}$.

For our running example (Fig. 1), with the selection vector [1 1 0 0 1 0], the above search yields the solution (2,5,$\leq$) implying that $\boldsymbol{b_2} - \boldsymbol{b_5}$ satisfies $\boldsymbol{P_{\leq}}$. The rows 2 and 5 correspond to $t_0.value$ and y (respectively), thus generating the condition (t0.value <= y).

However, as the search over each pair of row vectors is combinatorially expensive, we offload the search to the ILP solver by the following reformulation:

$$\textbf{FIND}(\sigma_0, \sigma_1, ..., \sigma_{n-2}, op) \textit{ such that } \sum_{i=0}^{n-2} \sigma_i [\boldsymbol{b_i} - \boldsymbol{b_{i+1}}] \textit{ satisfies } \boldsymbol{P_{op}}$$

where σ_i are scalars in {0, 1} and n is the number of rows in $\boldsymbol{B}$. The scalars σ_i are selected in a manner that only one stretch of *consecutive* σ_i can be 1.

Hence, any solution (i,j,op) is essentially of the form: $[\boldsymbol{b_i} - \boldsymbol{b_j}]$ *satisfies* $\boldsymbol{P_{op}}$.

The search over P_{op} is done exhaustively. SYNLIP is capable of constructing a conjunction of predicates as the condition by performing a bounded depth-first search (see Sect. 4.3).

The loop condition is synthesized in a similar manner as branch conditions. However, as the loop condition is **true** for all invocations except the last, the selection vector has a size one more than the number of loop iterations, where all except the last entry is 1. This is to enforce that the conditional should evaluate to **true** for all loop iterations except the last, for which it evaluates to **false** and exits the loop. For the same reason, the state matrix for inferring the loop condition also has an additional column that corresponds to the state at the end of the last iteration of the loop (i.e. just before exiting the loop); this state is constructed by simulating the execution of the synthesized loop statements on the concrete example. As there are six steps in our example (Fig. 1), the selection vector will be [1 1 1 1 1 1 0] and the loop condition is synthesized as $(t_0 \neq null)$; the fully synthesized loop is shown in Fig. 8.

```
while(t0!=null){
1:  (t0.next)'=t1
2:  (t1.next)'=t1.next
3:  (t0.value)'=t0.value
4:  (t1.value)'=t1.value
5:  y'=y
6:  x0'=x0
7:  if(t0.value <= y) then
8:      (x1)' = t0
9:  else
10:     (x1)' = x1
11: if(t0.value > y) then
12:     (x2)' = t0
13: else
14:     (x2)' = x2
15: t0'=t0.next
16: if(y<=t0.next.value
        && t0.next!=null) then
17:     t1'=x2'
18: else
19:     t1'=x1'
}
```

Fig 8. Loop statements inferred from $\mathbb{T}$ and $\mathbb{R}$ (the primed/unprimed variables refer to the current/next state).

3.5   Sequentialization and Dead-Code Elimination

The transformation matrices $\mathbb{T}$ and $\mathbb{R}$ attempt to transform a non-mutable input state to an output state. However, as imperative languages have mutable states, we need to arrange the set of inferred statements in a valid order. SYNLIP essentially performs a topological sort over the dependence graph of the statements to arrive at a sequential list of statements. In the process, new temporaries may be introduced to break cycles in the dependency graph (notice the introduction of temp0 in Fig. 2). We, then, perform dead-code elimination to remove statements that do not affect the program states.

3.6   Constructing the Prologue and Epilogue for the Loop

The loop prologue is inferred as the required change in program state from the initial state to the state at the beginning of the first iteration. Similarly, the epilogue is synthesized as the required state change from the end of the last iteration to the final state of the program (see Fig. 2).

4 The Integer Linear Programming (ILP) Formulation

4.1 Inferring Transformation and Relocation Functions

As discussed in Sect. 3.2, the formulation for the case when a single transformation function suffices is as follows:

$$\mathbb{T}\ [\zeta_1|\zeta_2|\cdots|\zeta_{k\text{-}1}] = [\zeta_2|\zeta_3|\cdots|\zeta_k] \tag{3}$$

To solve it with an ILP solver, we rewrite it: $\zeta_{in}^{\mathsf{T}}[\boldsymbol{W}_1|\boldsymbol{W}_2|\ldots|\boldsymbol{W}_n] = \zeta_{out}^{\mathsf{T}}$, where,
$\zeta_{in} = [\zeta_1|\zeta_2|\cdots|\zeta_{k\text{-}1}]$, $\zeta_{out} = [\zeta_2|\zeta_3|\cdots|\zeta_k]$, and, $[\boldsymbol{W}_1|\boldsymbol{W}_2|\ldots|\boldsymbol{W}_n] = \mathbb{T}^{\mathsf{T}}$

Note that each vector $\boldsymbol{W}_i$ corresponds to a single instruction (pointer assignment, get-field or put-field). So as to represent a valid set of instructions, the constraints on $\boldsymbol{W}_i$ are: for all $w_j \in W_i, \sum_j w_j = 1$.

In case the above set of equations have no solution, the synthesis algorithm proceeds to infer multiple transformations. In that case, to infer each vector $\boldsymbol{W}_i$, we apply the ILP formulation as shown.

$$\text{Minimize } \Psi = \sum_{j=1}^{m} p_j \in \boldsymbol{P} \tag{4a}$$

Subject To

$$\zeta_{in}^{\mathsf{T}}\, \boldsymbol{W}_i \leq \zeta_{out}^{\mathsf{T}(i)} + (\infty \boldsymbol{P}) \tag{4b}$$

$$\zeta_{in}^{\mathsf{T}}\, \boldsymbol{W}_i \geq \zeta_{out}^{\mathsf{T}(i)}.(\mathit{1} - \boldsymbol{P}) \tag{4c}$$

$$\sum_{j=1}^{n} w_j = 1 \tag{4d}$$

Here n, m denote the number of rows and columns (respectively) in the input matrix. $\mathit{1}$ is an m sized vector of all-1s. The notation $\boldsymbol{X}(i)$ fetches the ith column vector of matrix $\boldsymbol{X}$ and ∞ denotes a very large scalar.

$\boldsymbol{P}$ is an m-sized vector of 0–1 variables p_j, and is used to control the number of concrete examples that are explained by the vector $\boldsymbol{W}_i$. The dot product $\zeta_{out}^{\mathsf{T}(i)}.(\mathit{1} - \boldsymbol{P})$ allows the system of equations to *relax* by allowing some of the concrete examples to violate the transformation dictated by $\boldsymbol{W}_i$. We attempt to minimize the number of 1s (the examples it fails to explain) as a *greedy* attempt at explaining the maximum number of concrete examples, and hence, minimizing on the branching in the program.

After a solution is obtained, the examples that are explained by $\boldsymbol{W}_i$ are set to *don't-care*, and the solver is invoked with the modified equations till all examples are satisfied for some $\{W_i^0, W_i^1, \ldots\} \in W_i$. The inference of the relocation functions is also set up in a similar manner; we skip details for want of space.

4.2 Synthesizing Branch and Loop Conditions

Synthesizing a conditional entails a search for two operands for comparison and a suitable relational operator. As explained in Sect. 3.4, we search for predicates participating in a conditional expression by solving for:

$$\textbf{FIND}(\sigma_0, \sigma_1, ..., \sigma_{n-2}, op)\ \textit{such that} \sum_{i=0}^{n-2} \sigma_i[\boldsymbol{b}_i - \boldsymbol{b}_{i+1}]\ \textit{satisfies}\ \boldsymbol{P}_{op}$$

where $\boldsymbol{b_i}, \boldsymbol{b_j} \in$ *row-vectors of* $\mathbb{B}$ and $\boldsymbol{P_{op}} \in \{[\boldsymbol{P_>}], [\boldsymbol{P_<}], [\boldsymbol{P_=}], [\boldsymbol{P_{\neq}}], [\boldsymbol{P_{\leq}}], [\boldsymbol{P_{\geq}}]\}$. The vectors $\boldsymbol{P_{op}}$ are constructed by considering the high level idea that the generated condition (ζ_f *op* $\zeta_s = v_i$) can also be written as ($\zeta_f - \zeta_s$ *op* 0) if $v_i = 1$, otherwise $\neg(\zeta_f - \zeta_s$ *op* $0)$; here ζ_f denotes the first selected row vector, ζ_s denotes the second selected row vector and *op* denotes the relational operator.

The entities $\sigma_i \in \{0, 1\}$ are scalar variables and n is the number of rows in $\mathbb{B}$. We allow for only one stretch of *consecutive* σ_i to be `1`. Hence, any solution `(i,j,op)` is essentially of the form: $[\boldsymbol{b}_i - \boldsymbol{b}_j]^\intercal$ *satisfies* $\boldsymbol{P_{op}}$.

We model the above constraint by introducing `r` fresh variables $\gamma_i \in \{0, 1\}$, $\sum_{j=0}^{r-1} \gamma_j = 1$, such that each γ_i corresponds to such a valid sequence that has a single stream of contiguous `1`. For example, if there are three rows in $\mathbb{B}$, the possible valid sequences are `100`, `010`, `001`, `110`, `011`, and `111`. The kth sequence that has exactly `q` contiguous `1`s from position `i` to `(i+q-1)` is constrained as:

$$(\textstyle\sum_{j=i}^{i+q-1} \sigma_j) \geq q\gamma_k, \qquad \text{and} \qquad (\sum_{j=0}^{n-1} \sigma_j) - (\sum_{j=i}^{i+q-1} \sigma_j) \leq (1 - \gamma_k)\infty$$

Required type safety constraints also need to be imposed:

- **Type Safety for Operands:** Only variables of the same types can be compared; for instance, we cannot compare an integer with a pointer.
- **Type Safety for Operator:** The set of relational operators allowed for a condition depends on the type of the operands; for example, the operator $\geq$ cannot be allowed with pointer variables.

The above constraints make some of the patterns of σ_i invalid; this is handled by forcing the respective γ_i to 0. Finally, a search over all possible relational operators is unleashed by constructing an appropriate vector $\boldsymbol{P_{op}}$ in each case.

4.3 Synthesizing a Conjunction of Conditions

Consider the following task on a linked-list: print the `value` field of a node if it lies between the values stored in variables x_1 and x_2. Let us assume that the concrete example dictates that this `print` operation is *enabled* in loop iterations 0, 1 and 4; so our selection vector in this case would be $\boldsymbol{v} = 110010$ (i.e. $\boldsymbol{v} =$ `[1 1 0 0 1 0]`). However, as this condition requires a conjunction of multiple predicates, the formulation in Sect. 4.2 will provide no solution.

In this case, we **relax** our ILP formulation on each conditional for the case when $v_i = 0$, thereby allowing it to *miss* the constraint for some of the iterations. Consider the case of the relational operator $\leq$ for the loop iteration `i`: instead of requiring $p_i \geq 1$ (where p_i is the ith element in the vector $\boldsymbol{P_{op}}$), we allow it to violate this constraint by introducing variables $\delta_i \in \{0, 1\}$ by changing the constraint $p_i > 0$ to $p_i + \delta_i\infty > 0$ (if $\delta_i = 1$, the condition $p_i \geq 1$ may be violated). However, we enforce our greedy strategy of attempting to satisfy as many cases as possible by minimizing on the objective function $\sum_{j=0}^{n-1} \delta_j$. This attempts to select the *best* pair of operand vectors for this operator.

For this relational operator $\leq$, the best operand vectors correspond to `t0.value` and `x2`. The decisions (i.e. when to apply the `print` operation) dictated by this single conditional is described by the *decision vector* $\boldsymbol{d}$=`111010`: this corresponds to the boolean values evaluated by the conditional ($t_0.value \leq x_2$). This leaves the residual conditions to be satisfied, i.e. the *target decision vector* $\boldsymbol{t}$=`110?1?`. Here, the ? refer to *don't care* conditions.

The *target decision vector* $\boldsymbol{t}$ is constructed according to the following cases (let t_i denote the ith element of vector $\boldsymbol{t}$):

1. If $\{d_i = 1, v_i = 0\}$: In this case, d_i needs to be strengthened to 0. So, the target decision vector $t_i = 0$ for the next conditional.
2. If $\{d_i = 0, v_i = 1\}$: Note that this case should not be allowed, as no strengthening can restore d_i to 1.
3. If $\{d_i = 1, v_i = 1\}$: In this case, d_i needs to be retained at 1. So, the target decision vector $t_i = 1$ for the next conditional.
4. If $\{d_i = 0, v_i = 0\}$: In this case, no more strengthening is required, and so, the states of the subsequent conditionals does not matter. Hence, we set the target decision vector t_i =? (*don't care*) for the next conditional.

For case 1, we would like the strengthening to happen with the very next predicate, but we may allow to pend the strengthening to subsequent predicates. Due to conditions imposed by cases 2 and 3, we do not allow any relaxation of our constraints from Sect. 4.2 when $v_i = 1$. For case 4, we simply omit generating any constraints as the required strengthening has already been achieved.

We perform a bounded depth-first search on the operators to select the next conditional in the conjunction (see Fig. 9). For the example outlined above, selecting a relational operator == for the second operator is not able to satisfy the target vector; hence, we backtrack. Selecting the relational operator $\geq$ for the second conditional is able to infer operand vectors such that the target decision vector $\boldsymbol{t}$ is satisfied. This produces the final condition, $((t_0.value \leq x_2) \wedge (t_0.value \geq x_1))$, that would dictate the application of `print` in this example.

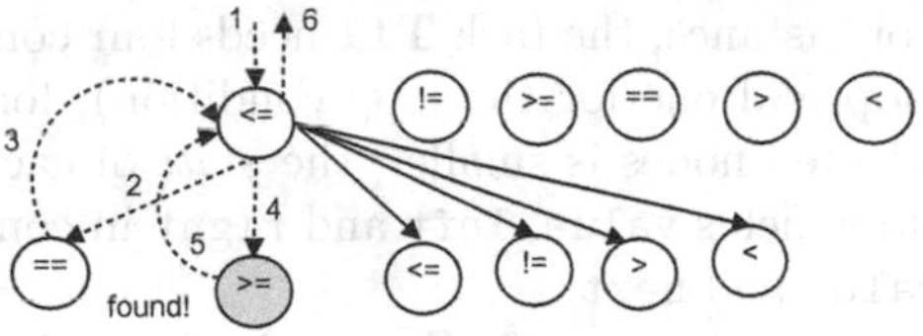

Fig 9. Conditionals with conjunctions

In case this bounded depth-first search does not yield a solution, we attempt again after extending the vectors ζ_i to also contain the values of longer deferences on the pointer fields of the temporaries (like `t0.next.next`).

5 Experimental Results

We have implemented SYNLIP in Java and used GNU Octave [1] for solving the ILP formulations. We have used SYNLIP to synthesize a variety of iterative programs. We report our timing statistics on a laptop of moderate configuration (as we target its use by common users in an IDE environment), running on Intel Core 2 Duo 2.20 GHz with 2 GB RAM. Table 2 describes each task and time taken by SYNLIP to synthesize each of the program.

- Column **Tasks** describes the heap manipulation task.
- Column **S** represents the size of the specification in terms of the number of loop iterations needed to accomplish the task for this concrete example.
- Column **C** shows the number of conditionals in the synthesized program.
- Column **A** shows the number of holes in the template.
- Column **Time** shows the total time (in seconds) taken by SYNLIP for each task. T_{inst} is the time taken in constructing program statements inside the loop, T_{cond} is the time taken in generating conditions and T_{total} is total time taken in synthesizing the complete program.
- Column **Time 2*S** shows the total time (in seconds) taken by SYNLIP to synthesize the complete program when the size of the specification is doubled.

SYNLIP is quite fast, taking less than 10 seconds on most of our benchmarks. On benchmarks where SYNLIP is slow, most of the time is spent in searching for the right conditionals. We have certain plans of improving these timings in the future by offloading the searching to an SMT solver.

As synthesizing conditions is the more expensive phase, the benchmarks with more conditions are seen to stretch SYNLIP on time. It can be observed that the tasks requiring no conditionals are synthesized in a couple of second, the tasks having only the loop condition take very few seconds, while for the tasks such as **T11** and **T12** the time increases due to a large number of branch conditions. For instance, the task **T11** needs four conditions to be inferred (three inside the loop and one for the loop condition); for the task **T12** though the number of affected nodes is smaller, the *state* of each node is larger as each node contains three fields `value`, `left` and `right` in contrast to **T11** which has only two fields `value` and `next`.

In contrast to [6], SYNLIP is almost insensitive to the size of the specification as can be seen by the difference in the columns T_{Total} and Time (2*S).

6 Related Work

The storyboard tool (SPT) [10] allows data-structure manipulations to be synthesized from *abstract* examples provided in 3-valued logic [7]. As abstract examples can correspond to multiple (possibly an unbounded number of) concrete examples, the users were supposed to provide *fold* and *unfold* operations to describe the possible concrete examples that an abstract example represents. SPT does not work well when only concrete examples are provided (as remarked in Sect. 6 of the article).

SYNBAD [6] allows the programmer to describe her intention simply using concrete examples. SYNBAD would appeal to frenzied programmers on their IDE who would shy away from structuring a formal abstract description that would have been required by SPT. Unlike SPT, SYNBAD rides on off-the-shelf SMT

Table 2. Experimental results

Tasks	S	C	A	Time(in secs)			Time
				T_{inst}	T_{cond}	T_{total}	2*S
(T1) Reversing a linked-list	4	1	2	0.763	0.403	1.166	1.267
(T2) Reversing a doubly linked-list	5	1	3	0.909	1.314	2.223	2.594
(T3) Change pointer of linked-list nodes s.t. nodes are made to point to specially marked red and black nodes alternately	5	2	2	1.273	0.545	1.818	2.055
(T4) Change value fields of all nodes of a linked-list to a specified value y	5	1	1	0.697	0.352	1.049	1.118
(T5) Print all nodes of a linked-list	7	1	1	1.273	0.389	1.076	1.212
(T6) Print all nodes of a linked-list which have value greater than a specified value	6	2	1	0.838	0.835	1.673	1.941
(T7) AVL-Tree Single Rotation (Left-Left)	1	0	3	0.752	0	0.752	NA
(T8) AVL-Tree Single Rotation (Right-Right)	1	0	4	0.908	0.005	0.913	NA
(T9) AVL-Tree Double Rotation (Left-Right)	1	0	3	0.968	0.007	0.975	NA
(T10) AVL-Tree Double Rotation (Right-Left)	1	0	3	0.752	0	0.752	NA
(T11) Segregating nodes according to a specified value in a linked-list (Fig. 1)	6	4	2	0.942	17.371	18.313	18.916
(T12) Search for an item in a Binary Search Tree	5	3	1	0.695	22.069	22.764	23.298
(T13) Print all nodes of a linked-list which have value greater than a specified value x and less than a specified value y	6	2	1	0.705	7.379	8.084	8.292
(T14) Change pointers of linked-list nodes s.t. if node value is greater then a specified value y then it points to (specially marked) red node o.w. (specially marked) black node	6	2	2	0.895	28.243	29.138	30.436
(T15) Insert a node in a sorted linked-list	5	5	3	4.317	4.871	9.188	9.711

solvers to efficiently synthesize programs from concrete examples expressed as box-and-arrow diagrams. SYNBAD achieves impressive run-times on similar synthesis tasks over SPT. However, such comparisons on the run-times is not fair as the difference in the format of the specifications causes SPT to explore a much larger search space. SYNBAD also provided a user-interaction model by exploiting techniques from automated test-case generation to help the users refine their specification, thereby, assisting them converge to their desired program. However, SYNBAD had a few weaknesses as described in our introduction section (which SYNLIP overcomes). SYNLIP adopts a new strategy for synthesis by leveraging ILP solvers rather than SMT solvers. However, we feel that integration of ILP- and SMT-based strategies (especially while synthesizing conditionals for branches and loops) can yield a more effective synthesis algorithm. We are keen to investigate this direction in the near future.

Use of linear algebra in programming languages has also seen many proposals. Coln et al. [2] exploit Farkas's Lemma to propose a method of inferring program invariants. Sharma et al. [9] reduce the problem of mining candidate invariants from concrete executions to computing the basis of the null space of a matrix. Ganapathy et al. [3] modeled C string manipulations as a linear program to detect vulnerabilities in programs. Markus Muller-Olm et al. [5] applied linear algebra for precise inter-procedural flow analysis. In the domain of synthesis, Kuncak et al. [4] essentially apply Fourier-Motzkin [8] style elimination techniques to synthesize program fragments from complete functional specifications in the domain of linear arithmetic. To the best of our knowledge, SYNLIP is the first attempt at using linear algebraic techniques to synthesize programs from concrete examples.

7 Conclusions

In this paper, we attempt to assert that, in many domains, programs can be efficiently synthesized as a set of linear transformations. This allows us to bring the power of the state-of-the-art advances in solvers for integer linear programming to solving synthesis tasks. Our tool, SYNLIP, exploits these ideas en route to synthesizing heap manipulating programs efficiently from concrete box and arrow diagrams. We envision the utility of such tools in Integrated Development Environments and thus, also build an Eclipse IDE plugin for our tool. In the future, we are interested in investigating on the possibility of applying a synergy of multiple solvers (primarily ILP and SMT solvers) to program synthesis.

References

1. GNU Octave. https://www.gnu.org/software/octave/
2. Colón, M.A., Sankaranarayanan, S., Sipma, H.B.: Linear invariant generation using non-linear constraint solving. In: Hunt Jr., W.A., Somenzi, F. (eds.) CAV 2003. LNCS, vol. 2725, pp. 420–432. Springer, Heidelberg (2003)
3. Ganapathy, V., Jha, S., Chandler, D., Melski, D., Vitek, D.: Buffer overrun detection using linear programming and static analysis. In: CCS 2003, pp. 345–354 (2003)
4. Kuncak, V., Mayer, M., Piskac, R., Suter, P.: Functional synthesis for linear arithmetic and sets. Int. J. Softw. Tools Technol. Transf. **15**, 455–474 (2013)
5. Müller-Olm, M., Seidl, H.: Precise interprocedural analysis through linear algebra. In: POPL 2004, pp. 330–341 (2004)

6. Roy, S.: From concrete examples to heap manipulating programs. In: Logozzo, F., Fähndrich, M. (eds.) Static Analysis. LNCS, vol. 7935, pp. 126–149. Springer, Heidelberg (2013)
7. Sagiv, M., Reps, T., Wilhelm, R.: Parametric shape analysis via 3-valued logic. In: POPL 1999 (1999)
8. Schrijver, A.: Theory of Linear and Integer Programming. Wiley, New York (1986)
9. Sharma, R., Gupta, S., Hariharan, B., Aiken, A., Liang, P., Nori, A.V.: A data driven approach for algebraic loop invariants. In: Felleisen, M., Gardner, P. (eds.) ESOP 2013. LNCS, vol. 7792, pp. 574–592. Springer, Heidelberg (2013)
10. Singh, R., Solar-Lezama, A.: Synthesizing data structure manipulations from storyboards. In: ESEC/FSE 2011, pp. 289–299 (2011)

Explaining the Effectiveness of Small Refinement Heuristics in Program Verification with CEGAR

Tachio Terauchi(✉)

JAIST, Nomi, Japan
terauchi@jaist.ac.jp

Abstract. Safety property (i.e., reachability) verification is undecidable for Turing-complete programming languages. Nonetheless, recent progress has lead to heuristic verification methods, such as the ones based on predicate abstraction with counterexample-guided refinement (CEGAR), that work surprisingly well in practice. In this paper, we investigate the effectiveness of the *small refinement heuristic* which, for abstraction refinement in CEGAR, uses (the predicates in) a small proof of the given counterexample's spuriousness [3,12,17,22]. Such a method has shown to be quite effective in practice but thus far lacked a theoretical backing. Our core result is that the heuristic guarantees certain bounds on the number of CEGAR iterations, relative to the size of a proof for the input program.

1 Introduction

The safety property (i.e., reachability) verification problem asks, given a program, if an error state (e.g., given as a line number in the program text) is unreachable for every execution of the program. The problem is undecidable for Turing-complete programming languages (and intractably hard for many natural decidable fragments – e.g., PSPACE-complete for Boolean programs). Despite the staggering complexity, recent research has lead to heuristic verification methods that work surprisingly well in practice. They have been used to verify non-trivial real-world programs such as operating system device drivers [4,11], and the yearly held software verification competition [1] shows an ever increasing variety of programs efficiently verified by the state-of-the-art automated software verifiers. By contrast, there has been comparatively less progress on explaining why such heuristics work. As a step toward bridging the gap, we present a theoretical explanation for the effectiveness of a heuristic used in predicate abstraction with counterexample-guided refinement (CEGAR).

CEGAR is a verification method that iteratively updates a finite set of predicates from some first-order logic (FOL) theory, called the *candidate predicate set*, until the candidate set forms sufficient proof of the given program's safety (i.e., an inductive invariant). In each iteration, a process called *abstraction* checks if the current candidate set is sufficient, and if not, a counterexample is generated. A process called *refinement* infers a proof of the counterexample's safety

S. Blazy and T. Jensen (Eds.): SAS 2015, LNCS 9291, pp. 128–144, 2015.
DOI: 10.1007/978-3-662-48288-9_8

(i.e., spuriousness) whereby the predicates in the proof are added as new candidates, and the iteration repeats.

In general, there is more than one proof that refutes the same counterexample, and which proof is inferred by the refinement process can significantly affect the performance of the overall verification process (cf. Sect. 2.2 for an example). A heuristic often used in practice is to infer a *small* proof (e.g., measured by the sum of the syntactic size of the predicates), and researchers have proposed methods for inferring a small proof of the given counterexample's spuriousness [3,12,17,22].[1] This paper analyzes the effect such a *small refinement heuristic* has on the overall verification performance.

As safety property verification is undecidable, we cannot establish any (finitary) complexity result without some assumption on the input problem instances. In general, we will state our results relative to the size of a proof of safety for the input program, and we will try to show that the verification converges quickly assuming that the input program has a small proof (e.g., polynomial in the size of the program). The assumption captures the conventional wisdom that correct programs are often correct for simple reasons, per Occam's razor.

Overview of the Main Results. We formalize the small refinement heuristic to be a refinement process that infers a proof of size at most polynomial in that of the smallest proof for the given counterexample. Let $\textsc{CegVerif}_{\textsc{SR}}$ be a CEGAR verification with such a refinement process. Let *mpfsize*(P) be the size of the smallest proof of safety for a program P. Our first main result is the following.

Theorem 1. $\textsc{CegVerif}_{\textsc{SR}}$ *converges in at most exp(mpfsize(P)) many CEGAR iterations given a program P.*

Theorem 1 implies that $\textsc{CegVerif}_{\textsc{SR}}$ is able to verify a program in an exponential number of iterations under the promise that the program has a polynomial size proof of safety. We prove Theorem 1 under a rather general setting.

Next, we consider a more concrete setting where a program is represented by a control flow graph (CFG) such that the program's proof is a Floyd-style nodewise inductive invariant [9], the abstraction process uses the Cartesian predicate abstraction, and the size of a proof is measured by the sum of the syntactic size of the predicates. We also assume that counterexamples are generated by unfolding each loop an arbitrary but the same number of times (copies of nested subloops are also unfolded the same number of times) which we show to be sufficient for the setting (cf. Theorem 9). Under such a setting, we show that $\textsc{CegVerif}_{\textsc{SR}}$ converges in at most $\mathit{poly}(\mathit{mpfsize}(P))^{\mathit{maxhds}(P)}$ many iterations where $\mathit{maxhds}(P)$ is the maximum number of loop entries per loop of the CFG (e.g., $\mathit{maxhds}(P) \leq 1$ for reducible CFGs) (Theorem 10). The result implies that, under such a setting, $\textsc{CegVerif}_{\textsc{SR}}$ is able to verify a program with a constant number of loop entries per loop in a polynomial number of iterations under the promise that the program has a polynomial size proof of safety.

[1] In this paper, a "proof" is a set of predicates. Note that this differs from the notion of proofs and proof sizes used in proof complexity [6].

The rest of the paper is organized as follows. We discuss related work next. Section 2 gives preliminary definitions pertaining to generic CEGAR verification and proves the first main result (Theorem 1). Section 3 gives additional preliminary definitions pertaining to CFG programs and proves the main result on CFG programs (Theorem 10). We discuss some limitations of our results in Sect. 4, and conclude the paper in Sect. 5. The extended report [20] contains the omitted proofs and extra materials.

Related Work. Previous works on the small refinement heuristic [3,12,17,22] have presented empirical evidences of the heuristic's effectiveness in the form of experiments. To our knowledge, this paper is the first work on a theoretical explanation for the heuristic's effectiveness.

A related but somewhat different heuristic proposed for CEGAR is the *stratified refinement* approach [13,15,21] where the proofs inferred in each refinement step is restricted to some finite set of proofs that is enlarged when the refinement fails to find a proof in the current set. The proof set is enlarged in such a way to ensure that the growing strata of proof sets eventually cover the underlying (possibly infinite) space of possible proofs. The stratified approach ensures an eventual convergence of CEGAR iterations under the promise that a proof of the program's safety exists in the underlying proof space, but the previous works give no results on the iteration bound.

2 Iteration Bound Under a Generic Setting

2.1 Preliminaries

Formulas and Predicates. We write finite sequences in boldface (e.g., $\boldsymbol{x}$ for $x_1, \ldots, x_n$). Let $\mathcal{T}$ be a FOL theory. A *term* a and *formula* ϕ in the signature of $\mathcal{T}$ is defined as follows.

$$\begin{array}{rcl} \textit{term}\ a & ::= & x \mid f(\boldsymbol{a}) \\ \textit{formula}\ \phi & ::= & p(\boldsymbol{a}) \mid \neg\phi \mid \phi \wedge \phi' \mid \phi \vee \phi' \mid \phi \Rightarrow \phi' \mid \exists x.\phi \mid \forall x.\phi \end{array}$$

Here, x is a variable, f is an arity $|\boldsymbol{a}|$ function symbol, and p is an arity $|\boldsymbol{a}|$ predicate symbol of $\mathcal{T}$. As usual, $\Rightarrow$ binds weaker than $\wedge$ or $\vee$. For a formula ϕ, we write $\mathit{fv}(\phi)$ for the set of free variables in ϕ. A *predicate* in $\mathcal{T}$ is of the form $\lambda\boldsymbol{x}.\phi$ where ϕ is a formula such that $\{\boldsymbol{x}\} = \mathit{fv}(\phi)$. We often omit the explicit λ abstraction and treat a formula ϕ as the predicate $\lambda\boldsymbol{x}.\phi$ where $\{\boldsymbol{x}\} = \mathit{fv}(\phi)$. We overload $\mathcal{T}$ for the set of predicates in $\mathcal{T}$, and write $\mathcal{T}(\boldsymbol{x})$ for the set of $\mathcal{T}$-predicates of arity $|\boldsymbol{x}|$. We write $\models_{\mathcal{T}} \phi$ if ϕ is valid in $\mathcal{T}$. We write $\top$ for tautology and $\bot$ for contradiction. (Note that the term "predicate" is not limited to just atomic predicates as sometimes is in the literature on CEGAR.)

Generic CEGAR. To state Theorem 1 for a general setting, following the style of [21], we give a definition of CEGAR in terms of generic properties that

```
1: procedure CegVerif(P)
2:     Cands := ∅;
4:     repeat
3:         match Abs(P, Cands) with
4:             safe → return safe
5:             | π → match Ref(π) with
6:                         unsafe → return unsafe
7:                         | F → Cands := Cands ∪ F
8:     end repeat
```

Fig. 1. CegVerif

abstraction and refinement processes are assumed to satisfy, but without specifying exactly when predicates form a proof of a program or how counterexamples are generated and refuted (we concretize such notions for CFG programs in Sect. 3.1).

In general, a *counterexample* is an "unwound" slice of the given program and is itself considered a program (typically, without loops or recursion). Let γ range over programs and counterexamples. For a finite set of predicates $F \subseteq \mathcal{T}$, we write $F \vdash \gamma$ to mean that F is a proof of safety of γ. We often simply say that F is a *proof of* γ when $F \vdash \gamma$ (i.e., omitting "of safety"), and if γ is a counterexample in addition, we sometimes say that F *refutes* γ, or F is a proof of *spuriousness* of γ. We require the proof relation $\vdash$ to be monotonic on the predicate set, that is, if $F \vdash \gamma$ and $F \subseteq F'$, then $F' \vdash \gamma$ (i.e., having more predicates can only increase the ability to prove). We use F, F', F_1, etc. to range over finite sets of predicates.

Figure 1 shows the overview of the verification process. CegVerif takes as input the program P be verified, and initializes the candidate predicate set *Cands* to $\emptyset$ (line 2). Then, it repeats the abstract-and-refine loop (lines 4–8) until convergence. Abs is the abstraction process which takes as input a program and a finite set of $\mathcal{T}$-predicates. For a program P and a finite $F \subseteq \mathcal{T}$, $\mathsf{Abs}(P, F)$ either returns safe, indicating that P has been proved safe using the predicates from F, or returns a counterexample. In the former case, the verification process halts, returning safe. Ref is the refinement process, which, given a counterexample π, either returns a proof of π's safety, or detects that π is irrefutable and returns unsafe. In the former case, the proof is added to the candidates, and in latter case, the verification halts by returning unsafe. For a run of CegVerif, the *number of CEGAR iterations* is defined to be the number of times the abstract-and-refine loop (lines 4–8) iterated.

We state the required assumptions on the abstraction and refinement processes. We require that if $F \vdash \gamma$ then $\mathsf{Abs}(\gamma, F) = \mathsf{safe}$, and that if $\mathsf{Abs}(P, F)$ returns a counterexample π then $\mathsf{Abs}(\pi, F) \neq \mathsf{safe}$ (i.e., Abs proves the safety of the program given a sufficient set of predicates, and otherwise returns a counterexample that it cannot prove safe with the given predicates). We also require that if $F \vdash P$ and $\mathsf{Abs}(P, F')$ returns π, then $F \vdash \pi$ (i.e., a proof for a program is also a proof for any counterexample of the program). We require that Abs is *sound* in that it only proves safe programs safe, that is, $\mathsf{Abs}(\gamma, F') = \mathsf{safe}$ only if

$\exists F \subseteq \mathcal{T}.F \vdash \gamma$. For the refinement process Ref, we require that Ref(π) returns F only if $F \vdash \pi$ (i.e., the returned proof is actually a proof for the counterexample), and that Ref(π) returns unsafe only if $\forall F \subseteq \mathcal{T}.F \nvdash \pi$ (i.e., only irrefutable counterexamples are detected irrefutable). Finally, we require Abs and Ref to halt on all inputs. We note that these assumptions are quite weak and satisfied by virtually any CEGAR verifiers.[2]

It is easy to see that CEGVERIF is sound in that it only proves safe programs safe.

Theorem 2 (Soundness). CEGVERIF(P) *returns* safe *only if* $\exists F \subseteq \mathcal{T}.F \vdash P$.

Note that Theorem 2 says nothing about how fast (or whether) CEGVERIF converges. The main results of the paper (Theorems 1 and 10) show that, when Ref is made to return a small proof of the given counterexample, CEGVERIF is guaranteed to converge in a number of iterations bounded by the size of a proof for the given program.

It is also easy to see that CEGVERIF is "complete" in the sense that it only detects unprovable programs unprovable.

Theorem 3 (Completeness). CEGVERIF(P) *returns* unsafe *only if* $\forall F \subseteq \mathcal{T}.F \nvdash P$.

Since the paper is only concerned with analyzing the behavior of CEGAR when given a provably safe program, in what follows, we disregard the situation where the given program is unprovable with the predicates from the background theory.

2.2 Main Result

To demonstrate the usefulness of the small refinement heuristic, we start with an example on which CEGVERIF (without the heuristic) may fail to converge despite the program having a small proof of safety (taken from [21]). Figure 2 shows the program P_{ex}. Here, `ndet()` returns a non-deterministic integer. The goal is to verify that the assertion failure is unreachable, that is, $a = b \Rightarrow y = x$ whenever line 9 is reached. We define a proof of the program to be the set of predicates that can be used as loop invariants at each of the loop heads (lines 3 and 6) and are sufficient to prove the unreachability (i.e., "safe" inductive invariant). For example, a possible proof is the singleton set $F_{inv} = \{a = b \Rightarrow y = x + z\}$.

```
1: int a = ndet(); int b = ndet();
2: int x = a; int y = b; int z = 0;
3: while (ndet()) {
4:   y++;z++;
5: }
6: while (z != 0) {
7:   y--;z--;
8: }
9: assert (a!=b || y=x);
```

Fig. 2. P_{ex}

[2] We do not impose $F \vdash P \Leftrightarrow \mathsf{Abs}(P, F) = \mathsf{safe}$ to allow modeling verifiers whose abstraction process can prove more from the same predicates than the refinement process (cf. Sect. 3.1).

```
1: int a=ndet(); int b=ndet();
2: int x=a; int y=b; int z=0;
3: if (ndet()) {
4:   y++;z++;
5: }
6: if (z!=0) {
7:   y--;z--;
8: }
9: assert (a!=b||y=x);
```

π_1

```
1: int a=ndet(); int b=ndet();
2: int x=a; int y=b; int z=0;
3: if (ndet()) {
4:   y++;z++;
5: }
6: if (ndet()) {
7:   y++;z++;
8: }
9: if (z!=0) {
10:   y--;z--;
11: }
12: if (z!=0) {
13:   y--;z--;
14: }
15: assert (a!=b||y=x);
```

π_2

Fig. 3. Counterexamples of P_{ex}

Running CEGVERIF on the program, Abs may return the counterexample π_1 shown in Fig. 3 in the first iteration, obtained by unfolding each loop once. Viewing the unfolded `if` statements at lines 3 and 6 as one-iteration loops, it can be seen that F_{inv} is a proof of π_1's safety. Thus, Ref(π_1) may return F_{inv}, which is also a proof for P_{ex} and would allow CEGVERIF to converge in the next iteration.

Unfortunately, the refinement process is not guaranteed to return F_{inv} but may choose any set of predicates that forms a proof of π_1's safety. For example, another possibility is $F_1 = \{\phi_0, \phi_1, \phi_0 \vee \phi_1\}$ where

$$\phi_0 \equiv x = a \wedge y = b \wedge z = 0$$
$$\phi_1 \equiv x = a \wedge y = b + 1 \wedge z = 1$$

Adding F_1 to the candidates is sufficient for proving the safety of π_1 but not that of P_{ex}, and so the abstraction process in the subsequent iteration would return yet another counterexample. For example, it may return π_2 shown in Fig. 3 obtained by unfolding each loop twice. Then, Ref may choose the proof $F_2 = \{\bigvee F \mid F \subseteq \{\phi_0, \phi_1, \phi_2\}\}$ where $\phi_2 \equiv x = a \wedge y = b + 2 \wedge z = 2$ to prove the spuriousness of this new counterexample, which is still insufficient for proving P_{ex}. The abstract-and-refine loop may repeat indefinitely in this manner, adding to the candidates the predicates $F_k = \{\bigvee F \mid F \subseteq \{\phi_i \mid 0 \leq i \leq k\}\}$ where $\phi_i \equiv x = a \wedge y = b + i \wedge z = i$ in each k-th run of the refinement process.

Here, a key observation is that F_{inv} is a proof of safety for *every* counterexample π_1, π_2, ... of P_{ex}. Because the size of F_{inv} is "small" (under a suitable proof size metric – made more precise below), when using the small refinement heuristic, the refinement process would have to infer F_{inv} (or other small proof of P_{ex}) before producing a large number of incorrect proofs (such as F_1, F_2, ...).

Our first main result, Theorem 1, states that the above observation holds in general. The result can be proved for a rather generic notion of *proof size*.

We assumed that $size(\cdot)$ satisfies the following: there is a constant $c > 1$ such that for all $n \geq 0$, $|\{F \subseteq \mathcal{T} \mid size(F) \leq n\}| \leq c^n$ (i.e., there are at most c^n proofs of size less than or equal to n). We call such a proof size metric *generic*. The size of the smallest proof for γ, $mpfsize(\gamma)$, is defined to be $\min_{F \in \{F \subseteq \mathcal{T} | F \vdash \gamma\}} size(F)$.

Definition 1 (Small Refinement Heuristic). We define CEGVERIF$_{\text{SR}}$ to be CEGVERIF with the refinement process Ref satisfying the following property: there is a polynomial f such that for all π and F, if $\mathsf{Ref}(\pi)$ returns F then $size(F) \leq f(mpfsize(\pi))$ (i.e., the refinement process returns proofs of size polynomially bounded in that of the smallest proof for the given counterexample).

We are now ready to prove Theorem 1.

Theorem 1. *Let the proof size metric be generic. Then,* CEGVERIF$_{\text{SR}}$ *converges in at most* $exp(mpfsize(P))$ *many CEGAR iterations given a program* P.

We informally describe the intuition behind the proof of the result. First, as remarked above, a proof of a program is also a proof of any of its counterexamples. Therefore, under the small refinement heuristic, the inferred proof in each refinement step is at most polynomially larger than the smallest proof of the program. Then, the result follows from the definition of the generic proof size metric and the fact that the proofs inferred in the refinement process runs must be distinct.

3 Iteration Bound for CFG-Represented Programs

The exponential bound shown in Theorem 1 still seems to have a gap from the performance observed with using the small refinement heuristic in practice. The observation is the motivation for studying a more concrete setting such as CFG-represented programs.

3.1 Preliminaries

Graphs. A finite directed graph $G = (V, E)$ consists of a finite set of nodes V and edges $E \subseteq V \times V$. We write $v(G)$ for V and $e(G)$ for E. For an edge $e = (v, v')$, we write $sc(e)$ for v (the *source* of e) and $tg(e)$ for v' (the *target* of e). Since we only work with finite directed graphs, in what follows, we omit the adjectives and simply write *graphs*.

We write $G \setminus E$ for $(v(G), e(G) \setminus E)$, and $G \setminus V$ for $(V', e(G) \cap V' \times V')$ where $V' = v(G) \setminus V$. For $E \subseteq v(G) \times v(G)$, we write $G \cup E$ for $(v(G), e(G) \cup E)$. A *path* of G is a finite sequence nodes $\varpi = v_1 v_2 \ldots v_n$ such that $(v_i, v_{i+1}) \in e(G)$ for each $i \in \{1, \ldots, n-1\}$. We write $|\varpi|$ for the length of ϖ and $\varpi(i)$ for the i-th node visited (i.e., $\varpi = \varpi(1)\varpi(2)\ldots\varpi(|\varpi|)$).

CFG Programs. We consider programs represented by control flow graphs (also known as *control flow automata* [5]). Formally, a *control flow graph* (CFG) is a tuple (G, T, v_{ini}, v_{err}) where G is a graph, $v_{ini} \in v(G)$ is the *initial node*, $v_{err} \in v(G)$ is the *error node*, and $T : e(G) \to \mathcal{T}(\boldsymbol{x}, \boldsymbol{x}')$ is the *transition relation* where $|\boldsymbol{x}| = |\boldsymbol{x}'|$. Roughly, each $v \in v(G)$ represents a program location (e.g., a basic block), and for $e \in E$, $T(e)(\boldsymbol{x}, \boldsymbol{x}')$ expresses the state transition from the location $sc(e)$ to $tg(e)$ where $\boldsymbol{x}$ (resp. $\boldsymbol{x}'$) represents the values of the program variables before (resp. after) the transition. A *path* of the CFG is a path of G. Without loss of generality, we assume that v_{ini} has no incoming edges, v_{err} has no outgoing edges, and all nodes are reachable from v_{ini}. Let Vals be the set of values. The set of states of the program is $\mathsf{States} = \mathsf{Vals}^{|\boldsymbol{x}|}$. The set of states reached from $S \subseteq \mathsf{States}$ by taking an edge $e \in e(G)$ is defined to be $Post_T[e](S) = \{s' \in \mathsf{States} \mid s \in S \wedge \models_{\mathcal{T}} T(e)(s, s')\}$. The set of states reached from $S \subseteq \mathsf{States}$ by taking a path ϖ, $Post_T^*[\varpi](S)$, is defined inductively as $Post_T^*[v_1 v_2 \varpi](S) = Post_T^*[v_2 \varpi](Post_T[(v_1, v_2)](S))$ and $Post_T^*[v](S) = Post_T^*[\varepsilon](S) = S$.

We say that a program $P = (G, T, v_{ini}, v_{err})$ is *safe* if for all paths ϖ of P such that $\varpi(1) = v_{ini}$ and $\varpi(|\varpi|) = v_{err}$, $Post_T^*[\varpi](\mathsf{States}) = \emptyset$. In what follows, we often implicitly assume that $|\boldsymbol{x}, \boldsymbol{x}'|$ is the arity of the predicates in the range of the transition relation of the CFG being discussed where $\boldsymbol{x}$ and $\boldsymbol{x}'$ are distinct variables such that $|\boldsymbol{x}| = |\boldsymbol{x}'|$.

We note that the class of CFG programs is already Turing complete when $\mathcal{T}$ is the set of quantifier-free predicates in the theory of linear rational arithmetic (QFLRA – *quantifier-free theory of linear rational arithmetic*) (and is equivalent to Boolean programs when $\mathcal{T}$ is propositional), taking the reachable states from States as the computation result. Checking the safety of CFG programs when $\mathcal{T} = \mathsf{QFLRA}$ is undecidable.

Loops. We review the notion of loops in a CFG [2]. A *loop decomposition* of G is a set $\{L_0, \ldots, L_n\}$ with each $L_i = (G_i, hds_i)$ satisfying 1.) $G_0 = G$, 2.) each G_i, G_j are either disjoint or one is a subgraph of the other, 3.) each hds_i, hds_j for $i \neq j$ are disjoint, and 4.) each L_i satisfies the following:

- G_i is a non-empty subgraph of G;
- $G_i \setminus (\{e \in e(G_i) \mid tg(e) \in hds_i\} \cup \bigcup_{j \in Sub(i)} e(G_j)) \cup \bigcup_{j \in Sub(i)} \mathit{flatten}(G_i, G_j)$ is acyclic;
- $hds_i = \{v \in v(G_i) \mid v' \notin v(G_i) \wedge (v', v) \in e(G)\}$; and
- G_i is strongly connected except for G_0

where $\mathit{flatten}(G_i, G_j) = \{(sc(e_1), tg(e_2)) \mid e_1 \in e(G_i) \wedge e_2 \in e(G_i) \wedge tg(e_1) \in v(G_j) \wedge tg(e_2) \in v(G_j)\}$ (i.e., the edges formed by "flattening" G_j in G_i) and $Sub(i) = \{j \mid G_j \text{ is a proper subgraph of } G_i\}$.

Roughly, each loop L_i is a subgraph of G comprising the "back edges" $B_i = \{e \in e(G_i) \mid tg(e) \in hds_i\}$ that take the control flow back to one of the loop entries, and the "loop body" $G_i \setminus B_i$ that is acyclic when the nested subloops are flattened. Note that the loop entries hds_i are the nodes in G_i with incoming edges from nodes outside of the loop. A loop decomposition forms a tree with L_0 as the root and nested subloops as children.[3]

A graph is *rooted* if there is a node with no incoming edges and from which every node in the graph is reachable. Clearly, the graph underlying a CFG is rooted. The following is a folk theorem (cf. the extended report [20] for a proof).

Theorem 4. *A rooted graph has a loop decomposition.*

We define a loop decomposition of a CFG (G, T, v_{ini}, v_{err}) to be a loop decomposition of G. In the following, we assume that each CFG P is associated with its loop decomposition $loops(P)$ (e.g., constructed by the algorithm given in the extended report [20]). We write $maxhds(P)$ for $\max_{(\_,hds)\in loops(P)} |hds|$. We remark that $maxhds(P) \leq 1$ if P is reducible [2].

Proofs and Counterexamples for CFG Programs. Informally, a counterexample of a CFG is an acyclic CFG obtained by *unfolding* the loops of the CFG. To formalize loop unfolding, we introduce a simple graph grammar below.

$$\begin{aligned} instr &::= v_0 \mapsto (\phi_1 : v_1, \phi_2 : v_2, \ldots, \phi_n : v_n) \\ t &::= \emptyset \mid \{instr\} \mid t_1 \cup t_2 \mid loop\ (h_1, \ldots, h_m)\ t \end{aligned}$$

Here, in each *instruction* $v_0 \mapsto (\phi_1 : v_1, \ldots, \phi_n : v_n)$, $v_1, \ldots, v_n$ are distinct and $\phi_i \in \mathcal{T}(\boldsymbol{x}, \boldsymbol{x}')$ for each $i \in \{1, \ldots, n\}$. We call v_0 the *source* and $v_1, \ldots, v_n$ the *targets* of the instruction. Roughly, $v_0 \mapsto (\phi_1 : v_1, \ldots, \phi_n : v_n)$ expresses the set of edges $\{(v_0, v_1), \ldots, (v_0, v_n)\}$ such that the transition relation of (v_0, v_i) is ϕ_i. A *term* t expresses the CFG comprising the edges represented by the instructions occurring in t. The *loop* annotations mark subparts of the CFG that correspond to loops, so that $loop\ (\boldsymbol{h})\ t$ expresses a loop with $\boldsymbol{h}$ being the entry nodes and t representing the union of the loop body, the back edges, and the edges from the loop body to the outer loops. We require the sources of the instructions occurring in a term to be distinct. We refer to the extended report [20] for the formal correspondence between CFGs and graph grammar terms. In what follows, we equate a CFG with the corresponding graph grammar term.

We overload t for the set of instructions occurring in t. We let $sc(v_0 \mapsto (\phi_1 : v_1, \ldots, \phi_n : v_n)) = \{v_0\}$, and $tg(v_0 \mapsto (\phi_1 : v_1, \ldots, \phi_n : v_n)) = \{v_1, \ldots, v_n\}$. We let $sc(t) = \bigcup_{instr \in t} sc(instr)$, and $tg(t) = \bigcup_{instr \in t} tg(instr)$. We let $v(t) = sc(t) \cup tg(t)$. For sets of nodes V_1 and V_2, we write $t\langle V_1, V_2\rangle$ for t with each source occurrence of $v \in V_1$ replaced by $`v$ and each target occurrence of $v \in V_2$ replaced by $`v$. For instance, for $t = \{v_0 \mapsto (\top : v_1, \top : v_2), v_1 \mapsto (\top : v_0, \top : v_3)\}$, $t\langle \{v_0\}, \{v_1, v_3\}\rangle = \{`v_0 \mapsto (\top : `v_1, \top : v_2), v_1 \mapsto (\top : v_0, \top : `v_3)\}$. We write $t \backslash V$ for t with each instruction $v_0 \mapsto (v_1 : \phi_1, \ldots, v_n : \phi_n)$ replaced by $v_0 \mapsto (v_{i1} : \phi_{i1}, \ldots, v_{im} : \phi_{im})$ where $\{v_{i1}, \ldots, v_{im}\} = \{v_1, \ldots, v_n\} \backslash V$, treating an instruction with empty targets as $\emptyset$. For $\boldsymbol{h} = h_1, \ldots, h_n$, we write $`\boldsymbol{h}$ for $`h_1, \ldots, `h_n$.

3 In the literature, L_0 is typically not treated as a loop, and a loop decomposition forms a forest.

Let rewriting contexts be defined as follows.

$$C ::= [\,] \mid C \cup t \mid loop\ (h_1, \ldots, h_m)\ C$$

Loop unfolding is defined by the following rewriting rules.

$$C[loop\ (\boldsymbol{h})\ t] \dashrightarrow C[t\langle v(t)\backslash\{\boldsymbol{h}\}, sc(t)\rangle \cup loop\ (\text{`}\boldsymbol{h})\ t\langle\{\boldsymbol{h}\},\{\boldsymbol{h}\}\rangle]$$
$$C[loop\ (\boldsymbol{h})\ t] \dashrightarrow C[t\backslash\{\boldsymbol{h}\}]$$

The first rule unfolds the loop once, whereas the second rule "closes" the loop by removing the back edges. We formalize the *counterexamples* of a CFG P, $\mathsf{cex}(P)$, to be the acyclic CFGs obtained by applying the above rewriting an arbitrary number of times, that is, $\mathsf{cex}(P) = \{\pi \mid P \dashrightarrow^* \pi \wedge \pi \text{ is acyclic}\}$.

A proof of a CFG program or counterexample is a set of predicates that forms a Floyd-style node-wise inductive invariant [9]. More formally, we say that $\sigma : v(G) \to \mathcal{T}(\boldsymbol{x})$ is a *node-wise inductive invariant* of $\gamma = (G, T, v_{ini}, v_{err})$, written $\sigma \vdash_{cfg} \gamma$, if 1.) $\sigma(v_{ini}) = \top$, 2.) $\sigma(v_{err}) = \bot$, and 3.) for each $e \in e(G)$, $\models_{\mathcal{T}} \sigma(sc(e))(\boldsymbol{x}) \wedge T(e)(\boldsymbol{x}, \boldsymbol{x}') \Rightarrow \sigma(tg(e))(\boldsymbol{x}')$. We say that F is a *proof* of γ, written $F \vdash_{cfg} \gamma$, if there exists $\sigma : v(G) \to F \cup \{\bot, \top\}$ such that $\sigma \vdash_{cfg} \gamma$. The following are immediate from the definition of $\vdash_{cfg}$.

Theorem 5 (Soundness of $\vdash_{cfg}$). *If $F \vdash_{cfg} \gamma$ then γ is safe.*

Theorem 6 (Monotonicity of $\vdash_{cfg}$). *If $F \vdash_{cfg} \gamma$ and $F \subseteq F'$, then $F' \vdash_{cfg} \gamma$.*

Theorem 7. *Suppose $F \vdash_{cfg} P$. Then, for any $\pi \in \mathsf{cex}(P)$, $F \vdash_{cfg} \pi$.*

Theorems 5, 6 and 7 justify us to use $\vdash_{cfg}$ for the proof relation $\vdash$ of CEGVERIF (cf. Sect. 2.1).

Next, we concretize the abstraction process and counterexample generation for CFGs. We present the Cartesian predicate abstraction, a form of predicate abstraction used in CEGAR, as the abstraction process. Then, we present a counterexample set that is *sound* for the abstraction process to generate and refute (made precise below). We note that, because our result is shown for the Cartesian predicate abstraction, it also holds for stronger abstraction processes such as the Boolean predicate abstraction.

We write $F^{\wedge}$ for the $\wedge$-closure of F (i.e., $\{\bigwedge F' \mid F' \subseteq F\}$) and $F^{\wedge\vee}$ for the $\wedge\vee$-closure of F (i.e., $\{\bigvee F' \mid F' \subseteq F^{\wedge}\}$). We write $F_{\bot}$ for $F \cup \{\bot\}$. For $\gamma = (G, T, v_{ini}, v_{err})$, $\sigma : v(G) \to \mathcal{T}$, and $F \subseteq \mathcal{T}$, we say that σ is a *F-Cartesian predicate abstraction node-wise inductive invariant* of γ, written $\sigma \vdash^{F}_{crt} \gamma$, if 1.) $\sigma(v_{ini}) = \top$, 2.) $\sigma(v_{err}) = \bot$, and 3.) for each $e \in e(G)$, we have $\sigma(sc(e)) = \bigvee F_1$, $\sigma(tg(e)) = \bigvee F_2$ for some $F_1 \subseteq {F_{\bot}}^{\wedge}$ and $F_2 \subseteq {F_{\bot}}^{\wedge}$ such that for each $\phi \in F_1$, there is $\psi \in F_2$ where $\models_{\mathcal{T}} \phi(\boldsymbol{x}) \wedge T(e)(\boldsymbol{x}, \boldsymbol{x}') \Rightarrow \psi(\boldsymbol{x}')$. We write $F \vdash_{crt} \gamma$ if there exists σ such that $\sigma \vdash^{F}_{crt} \gamma$. Clearly, $F \vdash_{cfg} \gamma$ implies $F \vdash_{crt} \gamma$, and $F \vdash_{crt} \gamma$ implies $F^{\wedge\vee} \vdash_{cfg} \gamma$.

The *Cartesian predicate abstraction* abstraction process $\mathsf{Abs}^{crt}(\cdot, F)$ is an abstract interpretation [7] over the finite lattice $(F^{\wedge\vee}, \models_{\mathcal{T}} \cdot \Rightarrow \cdot)$ with the abstract state transformer $\alpha^F(Post)$ that computes the strongest cube over $F_\bot$ implied in the next state (from the initial abstract state $\top$):

$$\alpha^F(Post)_T[e](\phi) = \bigwedge\{\psi \in F_\bot \mid \models_T \phi(\boldsymbol{x}) \wedge T(e)(\boldsymbol{x}, \boldsymbol{x}') \Rightarrow \psi(\boldsymbol{x}')\}$$

The abstraction process guarantees 1.) $F \vdash_{crt} \gamma$ if and only if $\mathsf{Abs}^{crt}(\gamma, F)$ returns safe, and 2.) if $\mathsf{Abs}^{crt}(P, F)$ returns a counterexample π, then $F \not\vdash_{crt} \pi$.

We show that Abs^{crt} satisfies the requirements of the abstraction process given in Sect. 2.1.

Theorem 8. Abs^{crt} *satisfies the requirements for* Abs. *That is,*

- *If* $F \vdash_{cfg} \gamma$ *then* $\mathsf{Abs}^{crt}(\gamma, F) = \mathsf{safe}$;
- *If* $\mathsf{Abs}^{crt}(\gamma, F)$ *returns* π *then* $\mathsf{Abs}^{crt}(\pi, F) \neq \mathsf{safe}$;
- *If* $F \vdash_{cfg} P$ *and* $\mathsf{Abs}^{crt}(P, F')$ *returns* π *then* $F \vdash_{cfg} \pi$; *and*
- *If* $\mathsf{Abs}^{crt}(\gamma, F) = \mathsf{safe}$ *then* $\exists F' \subseteq \mathcal{T}.F' \vdash_{cfg} \gamma$.

We say that the set of counterexamples $\mathcal{X}(P) \subseteq \mathsf{cex}(P)$ is *sound* for Abs if $\mathsf{Abs}(P, F) \neq \mathsf{safe}$ implies that there exists $\pi \in \mathcal{X}(P)$ such that $F \not\vdash_{cfg} \pi$ (i.e., generating and refuting only the counterexamples from $\mathcal{X}(P)$ is sufficient for verifying P). We say $\mathcal{X}$ is sound for Abs if $\mathcal{X}(P)$ is sound for Abs for each P. Let $\mathsf{cex}^{syn}(P) \subseteq \mathsf{cex}(P)$ be the set of counterexamples obtained by unfolding the loops $loops(P)$ an arbitrary but the same number of times for each loop (copies of nested subloops are also unfolded the same number of times – cf. the extended report [20] for the formal definition). We show that cex^{syn} is sound for Abs^{crt}.

Theorem 9. cex^{syn} *is sound for* Abs^{crt}.

Theorems 8 and 9 justify us to use Abs^{crt} with cex^{syn} as the counterexample generator for the abstraction process of CEGVERIF (cf. Sect. 2.1).

We note that, in the setting described above, a counterexample can be a general dag-shaped CFG. While early CEGAR verifiers often restricted the counterexamples to paths [4,11], more recent verifiers also use dag counterexamples, and researchers have proposed methods for inferring small refinements from such counterexamples [8,10,16,19,22]. Also, we note that, when $\mathcal{T}$ is QFLRA, checking the provability for a dag CFG γ (i.e., checking if $\exists F \subseteq \mathcal{T}.F \vdash_{cfg} \gamma$) is decidable, whereas it is undecidable for an arbitrary (i.e., cyclic) CFG [14].[4]

3.2 Main Result

We define the *syntactic size* of F to be the sum of the syntactic sizes of the predicates, that is, $size(F) = \sum_{\phi \in F} |\phi|$ where $|\phi|$ is the number of (logical and non-logical) symbols in ϕ. We state the main result.

Theorem 10. *Let the proof size metric be syntactic,* $\vdash_{cfg}$ *be the proof relation, and* Abs^{crt} *be the abstraction process with* cex^{syn} *as the counterexample generator. Then,* CEGVERIF$_{\mathrm{SR}}$ *converges in* $poly(mpfsize(P))^{maxhds(P)}$ *many CEGAR iterations given a CFG program* P.

[4] The decidability holds for any theory with effective interpolation (cf. the extended report [20]).

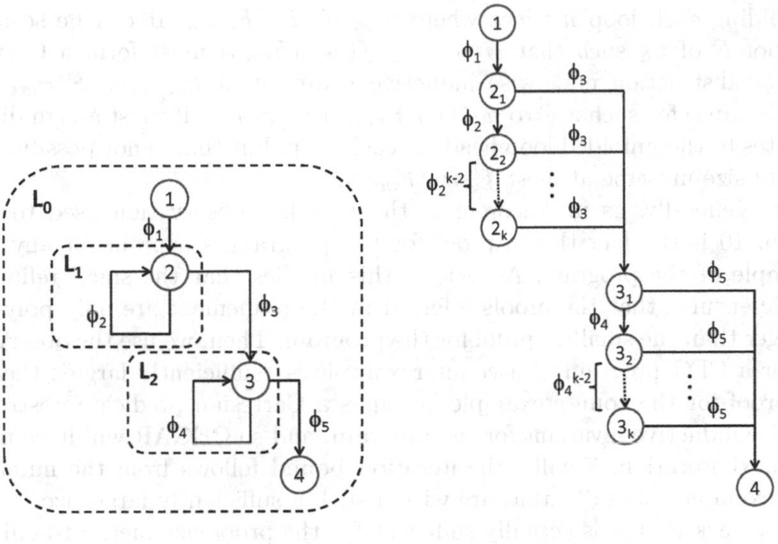

(a) (b)

Fig. 4. (a) CFG representation of P_{ex} and (b) CFG representation of $\mathsf{cex}^{syn}(P_{ex})$

We informally describe the intuition behind the proof of the result by analyzing the behavior of $\text{CEGVERIF}_{\text{SR}}$ on the program P_{ex} from Fig. 2, treated as a CFG program. Figure 4 (a) shows the CFG representation of the program. Here, node 1 is the initial node, node 4 is the error node, and the transition relation is as follows.

$$\begin{aligned}
&\phi_1(\boldsymbol{x},\boldsymbol{x}') \equiv x' = a' \wedge y' = b' \wedge z' = 0\\
&\phi_2(\boldsymbol{x},\boldsymbol{x}') \equiv z' = z+1 \wedge y' = y+1 \wedge x' = x \wedge a' = a \wedge b' = b\\
&\phi_3(\boldsymbol{x},\boldsymbol{x}') \equiv x' = x \wedge y' = y \wedge z' = z \wedge a' = a \wedge b' = b\\
&\phi_4(\boldsymbol{x},\boldsymbol{x}') \equiv z \neq 0 \wedge z' = z-1 \wedge y' = y-1 \wedge x' = x \wedge a' = a \wedge b' = b\\
&\phi_5(\boldsymbol{x},\boldsymbol{x}') \equiv z = 0 \wedge a = b \wedge x \neq y
\end{aligned}$$

where $\boldsymbol{x} = x, y, z, a, b$ and $\boldsymbol{x}' = x', y', z', a', b'$. P_{ex} has two non-root loops L_1 and L_2 such that L_1 corresponds to the first loop (lines 3–5) and L_2 corresponds to the second loop (lines 6–8) of Fig. 2. An element of $\mathsf{cex}^{syn}(P_{ex})$ is a CFG of the form shown in Fig. 4 (b) where each loop is unfolded k times for some $k > 0$. Nodes $2_1, \ldots, 2_k$ (resp. $3_1, \ldots, 3_k$) are the copies of the entry node of L_1 (resp. L_2) created by the unfolding.

Recall that the small refinement heuristic returns a proof of polynomially bounded in the size of the smallest proof of the given counterexample. Let f be the polynomial factor (i.e., Ref returns proofs of size at most $f(\mathit{mpfsize}(\pi))$ given a counterexample π). Then, because F_{inv} is a proof of any counterexample of P_{ex}, a proof returned by Ref in a run of $\text{CEGVERIF}_{\text{SR}}(P_{ex})$ would be of size at most $f(\mathit{size}(F_{inv}))$. Consider the counterexample $\pi_n \in \mathsf{cex}^{syn}(P_{ex})$ obtained by unfolding each loop n times where $n > f(\mathit{size}(F_{inv}))$. It can be seen that *any* proof F of π_n such that $\mathit{size}(F) \leq f(\mathit{size}(F_{inv}))$ must form a Cartesian predicate abstraction node-wise inductive invariant of P_{ex} (i.e., $F \vdash_{crt} P_{ex}$). This is because for such a F to *not* be a $\vdash_{crt}$-proof of P_{ex}, it must assign distinct predicates to the unfolded loop heads of each loop, but that is not possible when the proof size must be at most $f(\mathit{size}(F_{inv}))$.

More generally, as in Theorem 1, the first key observation used to prove Theorem 10 is the fact that a proof for the program is a proof for any counterexample of the program. As before, this implies that the small refinement heuristic ensures that the proofs inferred in the refinement are only polynomially larger than the smallest proof for the program. Then, we use the observation that, for a CFG program, if a counterexample is "sufficiently large", then *any* small proof for the counterexample becomes a Cartesian predicate abstraction node-wise inductive invariant for the program, and so CEGAR will have to halt in the next iteration. Finally, the iteration bound follows from the number of counterexamples in cex^{syn} that are within such a sufficiently large size.

We remark that it is actually sufficient for the proof size metric to only satisfy $\mathit{size}(F) \geq |F|$ for Theorem 10 to hold (i.e., at least the number of predicates in F). Also, as remarked before, the result also holds for stronger abstraction processes such as the Boolean predicate abstraction. Meanwhile, as we shall further discuss in Sect. 4, a limitation of the result is that it only considers counterexamples where all loops are unfolded the same number of times. This implies that the abstraction process may generate large counterexamples in relatively early stages of the verification, especially when the program contains nested loops (cf. the extended report [20]).

We end the section by showing that the proof size metric is crucial to the result. That is, under the generic proof size metric (cf. Sect. 2.2), we can only guarantee an exponential bound (which is ensured by the generic result of Theorem 1), even when the rest of the setting is left unchanged from Theorem 10.

Theorem 11. *Let the proof size metric be generic, $\vdash_{cfg}$ be the proof relation, and Abs^{crt} be the abstraction process with cex^{syn} as the counterexample generator. Then, there exists a CFG program P with a proof $F \vdash_{cfg} P$ on which* CEGVERIF$_{\mathrm{SR}}$ *may take $\mathit{exp}(\mathit{size}(F))$ many CEGAR iterations to converge.*

4 Limitations

While we believe that the paper's results are a step toward understanding the effectiveness of the small refinement heuristic, we still have ways to go to get the whole picture. Below, we discuss some limitations of our work.

First, we do not account for the cost of the abstraction process and the refinement process (i.e., we only show bounds on the number of CEGAR iterations). For instance, the running time of the abstraction process typically grows as the number of candidate predicates grows. Also, previous work has suggested that inferring a small proof of a counterexample may be computationally expensive (cf. Appendix F of [21]), and while there has been much progress on efficient algorithms for inferring a small proof of a counterexample [3,12,17,22], explaining why such algorithms work well in practice seems to be no easier than explaining the efficiency of the overall verification process.[5]

Secondly, in our setting of CFG programs, the counterexample form is rather restricted. That is, we only consider counterexamples obtained by unfolding the program's loops, and unfolding only the same number of times for every (copy of) loops (i.e., cex^{syn}). By contrast, an actual CEGAR verifier is often more liberal about the counterexample forms, and for example, may allow arbitrary unfoldings or paths as counterexamples.[6]

5 Conclusion

We have presented a theoretical explanation for the effectiveness of the small refinement heuristic used in program verification with CEGAR, which, to our knowledge, is the first of its kind. Specifically, we have formalized the small refinement heuristic to be a refinement process that returns a proof whose size is polynomially bounded in that of the smallest proof for the given counterexample, and shown that CEGAR with such a refinement is guaranteed to converge in a number of iterations bounded by the size of a proof of the given program. We have presented the results under a rather generic setting of CEGAR, and under a more concrete setting for CFG-represented programs.

Acknowledgements. We thank the anonymous reviewers for useful comments. This work was supported by MEXT Kakenhi 26330082 and 25280023, and JSPS Core-to-Core Program, A.Advanced Research Networks.

A Proofs of the Main Results

A.1 Proof of Theorem 1

The following lemma states that each run of the refinement process returns a new proof.

Lemma 1 (Progress). *Suppose* $\mathsf{Abs}(P, F)$ *returns* π *and* $\mathsf{Ref}(\pi)$ *returns* F'*. Then,* $F' \not\subseteq F$*.*

---

[5] In a sense, this paper poses and studies the question "assuming we have such algorithms for inferring small refinements, what can be said about the overall verification efficiency?". Note that a possible outcome of the study can be a negative result; for example, showing that inferring small refinements is hard because otherwise it would give an efficient algorithm to some provably hard verification problem.

[6] It is easy to reduce any CFG program to an equivalent one whose unfoldings/paths would coincide with cex^{syn} (e.g., by encoding program locations in transition relation – cf. the extended report [20]). But, such a reduction is likely to affect the cost of the abstraction process and the refinement process.

Proof. Because $\mathsf{Ref}(\pi)$ returns F', we have $F' \vdash \pi$. Also, because $\mathsf{Abs}(P, F)$ returns π, we have $\mathsf{Abs}(\pi, F) \neq \mathsf{safe}$, and so $F \not\vdash \pi$. Therefore, $F \neq F'$, and by the monotonicity of $\vdash$, it follows that $F' \not\subseteq F$. □

Theorem 1. *Let the proof size metric be generic. Then,* CEGVERIF$_{\text{SR}}$ *converges in at most exp(mpfsize(P)) many CEGAR iterations given a program P.*

Proof. Let F_P be a proof of P such that $mpfsize(P) = size(F_P)$. Then, for any counterexample π of P (i.e., $\mathsf{Abs}(P, F')$ returns π for some F'), $F_P \vdash \pi$, and therefore $mpfsize(\pi) \leq size(F_P)$. There are at most $c^{f(mpfsize(P))}$ proofs of size at most $f(size(F_P))$. Therefore, by Lemma 1, CEGVERIF$_{\text{SR}}$ converges in at most $exp(mpfsize(P))$ many CEGAR iterations. □

A.2 Proof of Theorem 10

Theorem 10. *Let the proof size metric be syntactic,* $\vdash_{cfg}$ *be the proof relation, and* Abs^{crt} *be the abstraction process with* cex^{syn} *as the counterexample generator. Then,* CEGVERIF$_{\text{SR}}$ *converges in* $poly(mpfsize(P))^{maxhds(P)}$ *many CEGAR iterations given a CFG program P.*

Proof. Let F_P be a proof of $P = (G, T, v_{ini}, v_{err})$ such that $mpfsize(P) = size(F_P)$. Then, for any counterexample π of P (i.e., $\mathsf{Abs}^{crt}(P, F)$ returns π for some F), $F_P \vdash \pi$, and so $mpfsize(\pi) \leq size(F_P)$. Let $lim = (f(size(F_P)) + 2)^{maxhds(P)} + 1$ ("+2" accounts for $\{\bot, \top\}$). Let π_{lim} be a counterexample in $\mathsf{cex}^{syn}(P)$ obtained by unfolding the loops at least lim many times. We show that for any F such that $F \vdash_{cfg} \pi_{lim}$ and $size(F) \leq f(size(F_P))$, $F \vdash_{crt} P$. (We call such a counterexample π_{lim} *sufficiently large.*) Then, the result follows from the fact that there are only lim many counterexamples in $\mathsf{cex}^{syn}(P)$ that are obtained by unfolding the loops at most lim many times, and the fact that no counterexample is returned more than once by the refinement process in a run of CEGVERIF$_{\text{SR}}$.

Let $\pi_{lim} = (G_{lim}, T_{lim}, v_{ini}, v_{err})$. Let $\sigma_{lim} : v(G_{lim}) \to F \cup \{\bot, \top\}$ be such that $size(F) \leq f(size(F_P))$ and $\sigma_{lim} \vdash_{cfg} \pi_{lim}$. Let $k \geq lim$ be the number of times the loops are unfolded in π_{lim}. We construct $\sigma : v(G) \to F^{\wedge\vee}$ such that $\sigma \vdash^F_{crt} P$ by "folding" the unfolded loops in a bottom up manner. We initialize $\sigma = \sigma_{lim}$, and $\gamma = \pi_{lim}$. We iteratively fold γ from leaf loops, while maintaining the property that $\sigma \vdash^F_{crt} \gamma$. Then, the result follows from the fact that γ becomes P at the root of the folding process.

Let γ and σ be the current CFG and its Cartesian predicate abstraction node-wise inductive invariant (i.e., $\sigma \vdash^F_{crt} \gamma$). Let $\gamma = C[t'_1 \cup t'_2 \cup \ldots t'_k \cup t_k \setminus \{\boldsymbol{h}_k\})]$ where $\boldsymbol{h}_0 = \boldsymbol{h}$, $t_0 = t$, $\boldsymbol{h}_{i+1} = `(\boldsymbol{h}_i)$, $t_i' = t_i\langle v(t_i) \setminus \{\boldsymbol{h}_i\}, sc(t_i)\rangle$, and $t_{i+1} = t_i\langle \boldsymbol{h}_i, \boldsymbol{h}_i \rangle$ for each $i \in \{0, \ldots, k-1\}$. Let $\gamma' = C[loop\ (\boldsymbol{h})\ t]$. That is, γ' is obtained by folding the unfolded loop of γ. We construct $\sigma' : v(\gamma') \to F^{\wedge\vee}$ such that $\sigma' \vdash^F_{crt} \gamma'$ as follows. Because $ran(\sigma_{lim}) = F \cup \{\bot, \top\}$, for some $1 \leq i_1 < i_2 \leq (f(size(F_P)) + 2)^{|\boldsymbol{h}|} + 1 \leq k$, $\sigma_{lim}(h^{i_1}) = \sigma_{lim}(h^{i_2})$ for each $h \in \{\boldsymbol{h}\}$. By construction, $\sigma_{lim}(h^i) = \sigma(h^i)$ for each $i \in \{1, \ldots, k\}$ and $h \in \{\boldsymbol{h}\}$. We set $\sigma'(v) = \bigvee_{i=1}^{i_2} \sigma(v^i)$ for each $v \in sc(t)$, and $\sigma'(v) = \sigma(v)$ for each $v \in v(\gamma) \setminus sc(t)$. Then, it can be seen that $\sigma' \vdash^F_{crt} \gamma'$. □

A.3 Proof of Theorem 11

Theorem 11. *Let the proof size metric be generic, $\vdash_{cfg}$ be the proof relation, and* Abs^{crt} *be the abstraction process with* cex^{syn} *as the counterexample generator. Then, there exists a CFG program P with a proof $F \vdash_{cfg} P$ on which* CEGVERIF$_{\text{SR}}$ *may take exp(size(F)) many CEGAR iterations to converge.*

Proof. We show that P_{ex} from Fig. 4 is such a program. As remarked before, we have $F_{inv} \vdash_{cfg} P_{ex}$ where $F_{inv} = \{a = b \Rightarrow y = x + z\}$. For each $k > 0$, let $\pi_k \in \mathsf{cex}^{syn}(P_{ex})$ be the counterexample obtained by unfolding each loop k times, and let $F_k = \{\bigvee F \mid F \subseteq \{\phi_i \mid 0 \leq i \leq k\}\}$ where $\phi_i = x = a \wedge y = b + i \wedge z = i$. Then, $F_k \vdash_{cfg} \pi_k$ for each $k > 0$, and $\bigcup_{i=1}^{j} F_i \not\vdash_{crt} \pi_k$ for each $k > j > 0$.

Let $\ell > 0$. Define *size* as follows: $size(F_{inv}) = \ell$, $size(F_k) = \lfloor \log k \rfloor$ for $k \in \{1, \ldots, 2^\ell - 1\}$, and $size(F') = \ell + syntactic(F')$ for $F' \in \mathcal{P}(\mathcal{T}) \setminus (\{F_{inv}\} \cup \{F_k \mid 1 \leq k \leq 2^\ell - 1\})$ where $syntactic(F')$ is the syntactic size of F'. Note that *size* is a generic proof size metric. Then, CEGVERIF$_{\text{SR}}$ takes $2^{size(F_{inv})}$ iterations to converge when Abs^{crt} returns the counterexamples $\pi_1, ...\pi_{2^\ell - 1}$ in the first $2^\ell - 1$ iterations and Ref returns the proofs $F_1, \ldots, F_{2^\ell - 1}$ before returning F_{inv}. □

References

1. International competition on software verification (SV-COMP). http://sv-comp.sosy-lab.org/
2. Aho, A.V., Sethi, R., Ullman, J.D.: Compilers: Principles, Techniques, and Tools. Addison-Wesley Longman Publishing Co., Inc., Boston (1986)
3. Albarghouthi, A., McMillan, K.L.: Beautiful interpolants. In: Sharygina and Veith [18], pp. 313–329
4. Ball, T., Rajamani, S.K.: The SLAM project: debugging system software via static analysis. In: Launchbury, J., Mitchell, J.C. (eds.) POPL, pp. 1–3. ACM (2002)
5. Beyer, D., Cimatti, A., Griggio, A., Keremoglu, M.E., Sebastiani, R.: Software model checking via large-block encoding. In: FMCAD, pp. 25–32. IEEE (2009)
6. Cook, S.A.: The complexity of theorem-proving procedures. In: Harrison, M.A., Banerji, R.B., Ullman, J.D. (eds.) STOC, pp. 151–158. ACM (1971)
7. Cousot, P., Cousot, R.: Abstract interpretation: a unified lattice model for static analysis of programs by construction or approximation of fixpoints. In: Graham, R.M., Harrison, M.A., Sethi, R. (eds.), POPL, pp. 238–252. ACM (1977)
8. Esparza, J., Kiefer, S., Schwoon, S.: Abstraction refinement with Craig interpolation and symbolic pushdown systems. JSAT **5**(1–4), 27–56 (2008)
9. Floyd, R.W.: Assigning meanings to programs. In: Symposia in Applied Mathematics, vol.19, pp. 19–32 (1967)
10. Gulavani, B.S., Chakraborty, S., Nori, A.V., Rajamani, S.K.: Refining abstract interpretations. Inf. Process. Lett. **110**(16), 666–671 (2010)
11. Henzinger, T.A., Jhala, R., Majumdar, R., McMillan, K.L.: Abstractions from proofs. In: Jones, N.D., Leroy, X. (eds.) POPL, pp. 232–244. ACM (2004)
12. Hoder, K., Kovács, L., Voronkov, A.: Playing in the grey area of proofs. In: Field, J., Hicks, M. (eds.) POPL, pp. 259–272. ACM (2012)
13. Jhala, R., McMillan, K.L.: A practical and complete approach to predicate refinement. In: Hermanns, H., Palsberg, J. (eds.) TACAS 2006. LNCS, vol. 3920, pp. 459–473. Springer, Heidelberg (2006)

14. N. Kobayashi. Personal communication, 30 Aug (2012)
15. McMillan, K.L.: Quantified invariant generation using an interpolating saturation prover. In: Ramakrishnan, C.R., Rehof, J. (eds.) TACAS 2008. LNCS, vol. 4963, pp. 413–427. Springer, Heidelberg (2008)
16. Rümmer, P., Hojjat, H., Kuncak, V.: Disjunctive interpolants for Horn-clause verification. In: Sharygina and Veith [18], pp. 347–363
17. Scholl, C., Pigorsch, F., Disch, S., Althaus, E.: Simple interpolants for linear arithmetic. In: DATE, pp. 1–6. IEEE (2014)
18. Sharygina, N., Veith, H. (eds.): CAV 2013. LNCS, vol. 8044. Springer, Heidelberg (2013)
19. Terauchi, T.: Dependent types from counterexamples. In: Hermenegildo, M.V., Palsberg, J. (eds.) POPL, pp. 119–130. ACM (2010)
20. Terauchi, T.: Explaining the effectiveness of small refinement heuristics in program verification with CEGAR (2015). http://www.jaist.ac.jp/terauchi
21. Terauchi, T., Unno, H.: Relaxed stratification: a new approach to practical complete predicate refinement. In: Vitek, J. (ed.) ESOP 2015. LNCS, vol. 9032, pp. 610–633. Springer, Heidelberg (2015)
22. Unno, H., Terauchi, T.: Inferring simple solutions to recursion-free horn clauses via sampling. In: Baier, C., Tinelli, C. (eds.) TACAS 2015. LNCS, vol. 9035, pp. 149–163. Springer, Heidelberg (2015)

Safety Verification and Refutation by *k*-Invariants and *k*-Induction

Martin Brain, Saurabh Joshi, Daniel Kroening, and Peter Schrammel(✉)

University of Oxford, Oxford, UK
{martin.brain,saurabh.joshi,daniel.kroening,
peter.schrammel}@cs.ox.ac.uk

Abstract. Most software verification tools can be classified into one of a number of established families, each of which has their own focus and strengths. For example, concrete counterexample generation in model checking, invariant inference in abstract interpretation and completeness via annotation for deductive verification. This creates a significant and fundamental usability problem as users may have to learn and use one technique to find potential problems but then need an entirely different one to show that they have been fixed. This paper presents a single, unified algorithm *k*I*k*I, which strictly generalises abstract interpretation, bounded model checking and *k*-induction. This not only combines the strengths of these techniques but allows them to interact and reinforce each other, giving a 'single-tool' approach to verification.

1 Introduction

The software verification literature contains a wide range of techniques which can be used to prove or disprove safety properties. These include:

Bounded Model Checking. Given sufficient time and resource, BMC will give counterexamples for all false properties, which are often of significant value for understanding the fault. However only a small proportion of true properties can be proven by BMC.

***k*-Induction.** Generalising Hoare logic's ideas of loop invariants, *k*-induction can prove true properties, and, in some cases provide counterexamples to false ones. However it requires inductive invariants, which can be expensive (in terms of user time, expertise and maintenance).

Abstract Interpretation. The use of over-approximations makes it easy to compute invariants which allow many true propositions to be proven. However false properties and true-but-not-provable properties may be indistinguishable. Tools may have limited support for a more complete analysis.

This research was supported by the ARTEMIS Joint Undertaking under grant agreement number 295311 (VeTeSS), the Toyota Motor Corporation and ERC project 280053 (CPROVER).

S. Blazy and T. Jensen (Eds.): SAS 2015, LNCS 9291, pp. 145–161, 2015.
DOI: 10.1007/978-3-662-48288-9_9

The range and variety of tools and techniques available is a sign of a healthy and vibrant research community but presents challenges for non-expert users. *The choice of which tools to use and where to expend effort depends on whether the properties are true or not – which is exactly what they want to find out.*

To build a robust and usable software verification system it is necessary to combine a variety of techniques. One option would be to run a series of independent tools, in parallel (as a portfolio, for example) or in some sequential order. However this limits the information that can be exchanged between the algorithms – what is needed is a genuine compound rather than a simple mixture. Another option would be to use monolithic algorithms such as CEGAR [5], IMPACT [20] or IC3/PDR [2,17] which combine some of the *ideas* of simpler systems. These are difficult to implement well as their components interact in complex and subtle ways. Also they require advanced solver features such as interpolant generation that are not widely available for all theories (bit-vectors, arrays, floating-point, etc.). In this paper, we argue for a compound with simple components and well-understood interaction.

This paper draws together a range of well-known techniques and combines them in a novel way so that they strengthen and reinforce each other. k-induction [26] uses syntactically restricted or simple invariants (such as those generated by abstract interpretation) to prove safety. Bounded model checking [1] allows us to test k-induction failures to see if they are real counter-examples or, if not, to build up a set of assumptions about system behaviour. Template-based abstract interpretation is used for invariant inference [15,23,24] with unrolling producing progressively stronger invariants. Using a solver and templates to generate invariants allows the assumptions to be used without the need for backwards propagators and 'closes the loop' allowing the techniques to strengthen each other. Specifically, the paper makes the following contributions:

1. A new, unified, simple and elegant algorithm, kIkI, for integrated invariant inference and counterexample generation is presented in Sect. 2. Incremental bounded model checking, k-induction and classical over-approximating abstract interpretation are shown to be restrictions of kIkI.
2. The techniques required to efficiently implement kIkI are given in Sect. 3 and an implementation, 2LS, is described in Sect. 4.
3. A series of experiments are given in Sect. 5. We show that kIkI *verified more programs and is faster* than a portfolio approach using incremental BMC, k-induction and abstract interpretation, showing genuine synergy between components.

2 Algorithm Concepts

This section reviews the key concepts behind kIkI. Basic familiarity with transition systems and first and second order logic will be assumed. As we intend to use kIkI to verify software using bit-vectors, we will focus on finite state systems.

2.1 Program Verification as Second Order Logic

To ease formalisation we view programs as symbolic transition systems. The state of a program is described by a logical interpretation with logical variables corresponding to each program variable, including the program counter. Formulae can be used to describe sets of states – the states in the set are the models of the formulae. Given $\boldsymbol{x}$, a vector of variables, $Start(\boldsymbol{x})$ is the predicate describing the start states. A *transition relation*, $Trans(\boldsymbol{x}, \boldsymbol{x}')$ is formula describing a relation between pairs of such interpretations which describes the (potentially non-deterministic) progression relations between states. From these we can derive the set of reachable states as the least fixed-point of the transition relation starting from the states described by $Start(\boldsymbol{x})$. Although this set is easily defined, computing a predicate that describes it (from *Start* and *Trans*) is often difficult and we will focus on the case when it is not practical. Instead *inductive invariant* are used; *Inv* is an inductive invariant if it has the following property:

$$\forall \boldsymbol{x}_0, \boldsymbol{x}_1 \,.\, (Inv(\boldsymbol{x}_0) \wedge Trans(\boldsymbol{x}_0, \boldsymbol{x}_1) \Rightarrow Inv(\boldsymbol{x}_1)) \tag{1}$$

Each inductive invariant is a description of *a* fixed-point of the transition relation but is not necessarily guaranteed to be *the least* one, nor is it guaranteed to include $Start(\boldsymbol{x})$ although many of the inductive invariants we use will do. For example, the predicate *true* is an inductive invariant for all systems as it describes the complete state space. From an inductive invariant we can find loop invariants and function and thread summaries by projecting on to a subset of variables $\boldsymbol{x}$.

Many verification tasks can be reduced to showing that the reachable states do not intersect with a set of error states, denoted by the predicate $Err(\boldsymbol{x})$. Techniques for proving systems safe can be seen as computing an inductive invariant that is disjoint from the error set. Using existential second order quantification (denoted $\exists_2$) we can formalise this as:

$$\begin{aligned} \exists_2 Inv \,.\, \forall \boldsymbol{x}_0, \boldsymbol{x}_1 \,.\, & (Start(\boldsymbol{x}_0) \Rightarrow Inv(\boldsymbol{x}_0)) \wedge \\ & (Inv(\boldsymbol{x}_0) \wedge Trans(\boldsymbol{x}_0, \boldsymbol{x}_1) \Rightarrow Inv(\boldsymbol{x}_1)) \wedge \\ & (Inv(\boldsymbol{x}_0) \Rightarrow \neg Err(\boldsymbol{x}_0)) \end{aligned} \tag{2}$$

Alternatively, if the system is not safe, then there is a reachable error state. One way of showing this is to find a concrete, n-step counterexample[1]:

$$\exists \boldsymbol{x}_0, \ldots, \boldsymbol{x}_n \,.\, Start(\boldsymbol{x}_0) \wedge \bigwedge_{i \in [0, n-1]} Trans(\boldsymbol{x}_i, \boldsymbol{x}_{i+1}) \wedge Err(\boldsymbol{x}_n) \tag{3}$$

2.2 Existing Techniques

Viewing program verification as existential second-order logic allows a range of existing tools to be characterised in a common framework and thus compared

[1] If the state space is finite and the system is not safe there is necessarily a finite, concrete counterexample. For infinite state spaces there are additional issues such as errors only reachable via infinite counterexamples and which fixed-points can be described by a finite formulae.

and contrasted. This section reviews some of the more widely used approaches. The following abbreviations, corresponding to k steps of the transition system and the first k states being error free, will be used:

$$T[k] = \bigwedge_{i \in [0,k-1]} \mathit{Trans}(\boldsymbol{x}_i, \boldsymbol{x}_{i+1}) \qquad P[k] = \bigwedge_{i \in [0,k-1]} \neg \mathit{Err}(\boldsymbol{x}_i)$$

Bounded Model Checking (BMC). [1] focuses on refutation by picking a *unwinding limit* k and solving:

$$\exists \boldsymbol{x}_0, \ldots, \boldsymbol{x}_k \,.\, \mathit{Start}(\boldsymbol{x}_0) \wedge T[k] \wedge \neg P[k+1] \tag{4}$$

Models of this formula correspond to concrete counterexamples of some length $n \leqslant k$. The unwinding limit gives an *under-approximation* of the set of reachable states and thus can fail to find counterexamples that take a large number of transition steps. In practice BMC works well as the formula is existentially quantified and thus is in a fragment handled well by SAT and SMT solvers. There are also various simplifications that can reduce the number of variables (see Sect. 3.1).

Incremental BMC (IBMC) (e.g. [9]) uses repeated BMC (often optimised by using the solver incrementally) checks with increasing bounds to avoid the need for a fixed bound. If the bound starts at 0 (i.e. checking $\exists x_0 \,.\, \mathit{Start}(\boldsymbol{x}_0) \wedge \mathit{Err}(\boldsymbol{x}_0)$) and is increased linearly (this is the common use-case), then it can be assumed that there are no errors at previous states, giving a simpler test:

$$\exists \boldsymbol{x}_0, \ldots, \boldsymbol{x}_k \,.\, \mathit{Start}(\boldsymbol{x}_0) \wedge T[k] \wedge P[k] \wedge \mathit{Err}(\boldsymbol{x}_k) \tag{5}$$

K-Induction [26] can be viewed as an extension of IBMC that can show system safety as well as produce counterexamples. It makes use of *k-inductive invariants*, which are predicates that have the following property:

$$\forall \boldsymbol{x}_0 \ldots \boldsymbol{x}_k \,.\, I[k] \wedge T[k] \Rightarrow \mathit{KInv}(\boldsymbol{x}_k) \tag{6}$$

where

$$I[k] = \bigwedge_{i \in [0,k-1]} \mathit{KInv}(\boldsymbol{x}_i)$$

k-inductive invariants have the following useful properties:

- Any inductive invariant is a 1-inductive invariant and vice versa.
- Any k-inductive invariant is a $(k+1)$-inductive invariant.
- A (finite) system is safe if and only if there is a k-inductive invariant *KInv* which satisfies:

$$\begin{aligned} \forall \boldsymbol{x}_0 \ldots \boldsymbol{x}_k \,.\, & (\mathit{Start}(\boldsymbol{x}_0) \wedge T[k] \Rightarrow I[k]) \wedge \\ & (I[k] \wedge T[k] \Rightarrow \mathit{KInv}(\boldsymbol{x}_k)) \wedge \\ & (\mathit{KInv}(\boldsymbol{x}_k) \Rightarrow \neg \mathit{Err}(\boldsymbol{x}_k)) \end{aligned} \tag{7}$$

Showing that a k-inductive invariant exists is sufficient to show that an inductive invariant exists *but it does not imply that the k-inductive invariant is an inductive invariant.* Often the corresponding inductive invariant is significantly more complex. Thus k-induction can be seen as a trade-off between invariant *generation* and *checking* as it is a means to benefit as much as possible from simpler invariants by using a more complex property check.

Finding a candidate k-inductive invariant is hard so implementations often use $\neg Err(\boldsymbol{x})$. Similarly to IBMC, linearly increasing k can be used to simplify the expression by assuming there are no errors at previous states:

$$\begin{aligned}\exists \boldsymbol{x}_0, \ldots, \boldsymbol{x}_k .\ & (Start(\boldsymbol{x}_0) \wedge T[k] \wedge P[k] \wedge Err(\boldsymbol{x}_k)) \vee \\ & (T[k] \wedge P[k] \wedge Err(\boldsymbol{x}_k))\end{aligned} \tag{8}$$

A model of the first part of the disjunct is a concrete counterexample (k-induction subsumes IBMC) and if the whole formula has no models, then $\neg Err(\boldsymbol{x})$ is a k-inductive invariant and the system is safe.

Abstract Interpretation. [6] While BMC and IBMC compute under-approximations of the set of reachable states, the classical use of abstract interpretation is to compute inductive invariants that include $Start(\boldsymbol{x})$ and thus are over-approximations of the set of reachable states. Elements of an abstract domain can be understood as sets or conjuncts of formulae [8], so abstract interpretation can be seen as:

$$\begin{aligned}\exists_2 AInv \in \mathscr{A} .\ \forall \boldsymbol{x}, \boldsymbol{x}_1 .\ & (Start(\boldsymbol{x}) \Rightarrow AInv(\boldsymbol{x})) \wedge \\ & (AInv(\boldsymbol{x}) \wedge Trans(\boldsymbol{x}, \boldsymbol{x}_1) \Rightarrow AInv(\boldsymbol{x}_1))\end{aligned} \tag{9}$$

where $\mathscr{A}$ is the set of formulae described by the chosen abstract domain. As a second step then one checks:

$$\forall \boldsymbol{x} .\ AInv(\boldsymbol{x}) \Rightarrow \neg Err(\boldsymbol{x}) \tag{10}$$

If this has no models then the system is safe, otherwise the safety cannot be determined without finding a more restrictive $AInv$ or increasing the set $\mathscr{A}$, i.e. choosing a more expressive abstract domain.

2.3 Our Algorithm: *k*I*k*I

The phases of the kIkI algorithm are presented as a flow chart in Fig. 1 with black arrows denoting transitions. Initially, $k = 1$ and $\mathscr{T}$ is a set of predicates that can be used as invariant with $\top \in \mathscr{T}$ (see Sect. 3 for details of how this is implemented).

After an initial test to see if any start states are errors[2], kIkI computes a k-inductive invariant that covers the initial state and includes the assumption

[2] If the transition system is derived from software and the errors are generated from assertions this will be impossible and the check can be skipped.

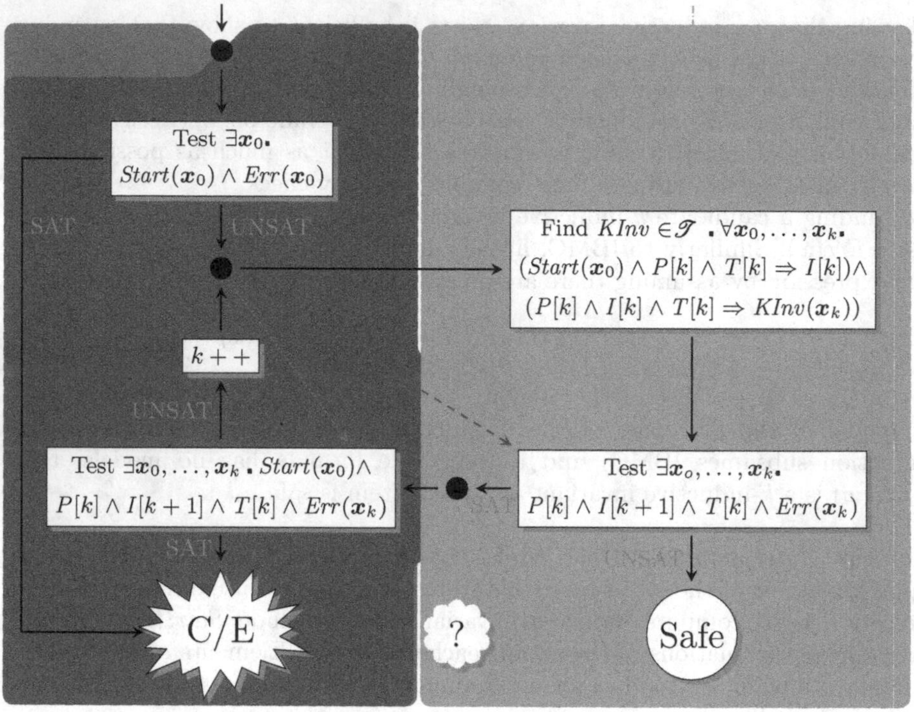

Fig. 1. The kIkI algorithm (colours in online version)

that there are no errors in earlier states. The invariant is then checked to see whether it is sufficient to show safety. If there are possible reachable error states then a second check is needed to see if the error is reachable in k steps (a genuine counterexample) or whether it is a potential artefact of a too weak invariant. In the latter case, k is incremented so that a stronger (k-)invariant can be found and the algorithm loops.

Also displayed in Fig. 1 are the steps of incremental BMC, k-induction and classical over-approximating abstract interpretation, given, respectively by the red dotted, blue dashed and green dashed/dotted boxes and arrows. kIkI can simulate k-induction by having $\mathscr{T} = \{\top\}$ and incremental BMC by over-approximating the first SAT check. Classical over-approximate abstract interpretation can be simulated by having $\mathscr{T} = \mathscr{A}$ and terminating with the result "unknown" if the first SAT check finds a model. These simulations give an intuition for the proof of the following results:

Theorem 1.

- *When kIkI terminates it gives either a k-inductive invariant sufficient to show safety or a length k counterexample.*

```
void main()
{
  unsigned x = 0;

  while (x<10)
  {
    ++x;
  }

  assert(x==10);
}
```

(a) The program

```
guard#0 == TRUE
x#0 == 0u

guard#1 == guard#0
x#phi1 == (guard#ls0 ? x#lb1 : x#0)
guard#2 == (x#phi1 < 10) && guard#1
x#2 == 1u + x#phi1

guard#3 == !(x#phi1 < 10) && guard#1
x#phi1 == 10u || !guard#3
```

(b) The annotated SSA

Fig. 2. Conversation from program to SSA

- *If IBMC or k-induction terminate with a length k counterexample, then kIkI will terminate with a length k counterexample.*
- *If k-induction terminates with a k-inductive invariant sufficient to show safety, then kIkI will terminate with a k-inductive invariant sufficient to show safety.*
- *If an (over-approximating) abstract interpreter returns an inductive invariant AInv that is sufficient to show safety and $\mathscr{A} \subseteq \mathscr{T}$, then kIkI will terminate with $k = 1$ and an inductive invariant sufficient to show safety.*

Hence *k*I*k*I strictly generalises its components by exploiting the following synergies between them: unrolling k times helps abstract interpretation to generate stronger invariants, namely k-invariants, which are further strengthened by the additional facts known from not having found a counterexample for $k-1$ iterations; stronger invariants help k-induction to successfully prove properties more often; and constraining the state space by invariants ultimately accelerates the countermodel search in BMC. We will observe these synergies also experimentally in Sect. 5.

3 Algorithm Details

Section 2 introduced *k*I*k*I but omitted a number of details which are important for implementing the algorithm efficiently. Key amongst these are the encoding from program to transition system and the generation of k-inductive invariants.

3.1 SSA Encoding

The presentation of *k*I*k*I used transition systems and it is possible to implement this directly. However the symbolic transition systems generated by software have structural properties that can be exploited. In most states the value of the program counter uniquely identifies its next value (i.e. most instructions do not branch) and most transitions update a single variable. Thus states in

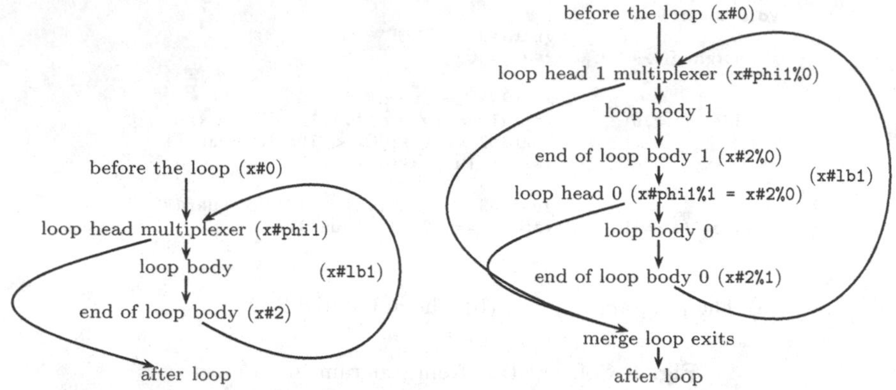

(a) The SSA form of a loop. (b) The SSA loop unwinding

Fig. 3. Illustrations of various SSA encodings

the transition can be merged by substituting in the symbolic values of updated variables, so reducing the size of the formulae generated.

Rather than building the transition system and then reducing it, it is equivalent and more efficient to convert the program to *single static assignment form* (SSA). For acyclic code, the SSA is a formula that exactly represents the strongest post condition of running the code and generation of this is a standard technique found in most software BMC and Symbolic Execution tools. We extend this with an over-approximate conversion of loops so that the SSA allows us to reason about abstractions of a program with a solver.

Figure 2 gives an example of the conversion. The SSA has been made acyclic by cutting loops at the end of the loop body: the variable[3] `x#2` at the end of the loop body ("poststate") corresponds to `x#lb1`, which is fed back into the loop head ("prestate"). A non-deterministic choice (using the free Boolean variable `guard#ls0`) is introduced at the loop head in order to join the values coming from before the loop and from the end of the loop body. Figure 3a illustrates how the SSA statements express control flow.

It is easy to see that this representation "havocs" loops because `x#lb1` is a free variable – this is why its models are an over-approximation of actual program traces. Precision can be improved by constraining the feedback variable `x#lb1` by means of a *loop invariant* which we are going to infer. Any property that holds at loop entry (`x#0`) and at the end of the body (`x#2`) can then be assumed to hold on the feedback variable `x#lb1`.

Loop unwinding is performed in the usual fashion; the conversion to SSA simply repeats the conversion of the body of the loop. Figure 3b illustrates an example of this. The top-most loop head multiplexer is kept and its feedback variable is constrained with the bottom-most loop unwinding. The only subtlety

[3] Variable name suffixes are use to denote the multiple *logical* variables that correspond to a single *program* variable at different points in the execution.

is that the value of variables from different loop exits must be merged. This can be achieved by use of the `guard` variables which track the reachability of various program points for a given set of values. The unwinding that we perform is incremental, in the sense that the construction of the formula is monotonic. Assumptions have to be used to deal with the end of loop merges as there always has to be a case for "value is merged from an unwinding that has not been added yet" and this has to be assumed false.

A more significant example is given in the extended version [3].

3.2 Invariant Inference via Templates

A key phase of kIkI is the generation of *KInv*, a k-inductive invariant. Perhaps the most obvious approach is to use an off-the-shelf abstract interpreter. This works but will fail to exploit the real power of kIkI. Each iteration, kIkI unrolls loops one more step (which can improve the invariant given by an abstract interpreter) and adds assumptions that previous unwindings do not give errors. Without backwards propagation it is difficult for an abstract interpreter to make significant use of these assumptions. For example, an abstract interpretation with intervals would need backwards propagation to make use of `assume(x + y < 10)`. Thus we use a solver-based approach to computing *KInv* as it can elegantly exploit the assumptions that are added without needing to (directly) implement transformers.

Directly using a solver we would need to handle (the existential fragment of) second-order logic. As these are not currently available, we reduce to a problem that can be solved by iterative application of a first-order solver. We restrict ourselves to finding invariants *KInv* of the form $\mathcal{T}(\boldsymbol{x},\boldsymbol{\delta})$ where $\mathcal{T}$ is a fixed expression, a so-called *template*, over program variables $\boldsymbol{x}$ and template parameters $\boldsymbol{\delta}$ (see Sect. 3.3). This restriction is analogous to choosing an abstract domain in an abstract interpreter and has similar effect - $\mathscr{T}$ only contains a the formulae that can be described by the template. Fixing a template reduces the second-order search for an invariant to the first-order search for template *parameters*:

$$\exists \boldsymbol{\delta}.\, \forall \boldsymbol{x}_0 \ldots \boldsymbol{x}_k.\, (Start(\boldsymbol{x}_0) \wedge T[k] \Rightarrow \mathcal{T}[k](\boldsymbol{\delta})) \wedge \\ (\mathcal{T}[k](\boldsymbol{\delta}) \wedge T[k] \Rightarrow \mathcal{T}(\boldsymbol{x_k},\boldsymbol{\delta})) \tag{11}$$

with $\mathcal{T}[k](\boldsymbol{\delta}) = \bigwedge_{i\in[0,k-1]} \mathcal{T}(\boldsymbol{x_i},\boldsymbol{\delta})$. Although the problem is now expressible in first-order logic, it contains quantifier alternation which poses a problem for current SMT solvers. However, we can solve this problem by iteratively checking the negated formula (to turn $\forall$ into $\exists$) for different choices of constants $\boldsymbol{d}$ for the parameters $\boldsymbol{\delta}$; as for the second conjunct in (11):

$$\exists \boldsymbol{x}_0 \ldots \boldsymbol{x}_k\,.\, \neg(\mathcal{T}[k](\boldsymbol{d}) \wedge T[k] \Rightarrow \mathcal{T}(\boldsymbol{x_k},\boldsymbol{d})) \tag{12}$$

The resulting formula can be expressed in quantifier-free logics and efficiently solved by SMT solvers. Using this as a building block, one can solve this $\exists\forall$ problem (see Sect. 3.4).

3.3 Guarded Template Domains

As discussed in the previous section, we use templates and repeated calls (with quantifier-free formulae) to a first-order solver to compute k-inductive invariants.

An abstract value $\boldsymbol{d}$ represents, i.e. *concretises* to, the set of all $\boldsymbol{x}$ that satisfy the formula $\mathcal{T}(\boldsymbol{x}, \boldsymbol{d})$. We require an abstract value $\bot$ denoting the empty set $\mathcal{T}(\boldsymbol{x}, \bot) \equiv \mathit{false}$, and $\top$ for the whole domain of $\boldsymbol{x}$: $\mathcal{T}(\boldsymbol{x}, \top) \equiv \mathit{true}$.

Template Polyhedra. We use template polyhedra [24], a class of templates for numerical variables which have the form $\mathcal{T} = (\mathbf{A}\boldsymbol{x} \leq \boldsymbol{\delta})$ where $\mathbf{A}$ is a matrix with fixed coefficients. Subclasses of such templates include *Intervals*, which require constraints $\begin{pmatrix} 1 \\ -1 \end{pmatrix} x_i \leq \begin{pmatrix} \delta_{i1} \\ \delta_{i2} \end{pmatrix}$ for each variable x_i, *Zones* (differences), and *Octagons* [21]. The rth *row* of the template are the constraint generated by the rth row of matrix $\mathbf{A}$.

In our template expressions, variables $\boldsymbol{x}$ are *bit-vectors* representing signed or unsigned integers. These variables can be mixed in template constraints. Type promotion rules are applied such that the bit-width of the types of the expressions are extended in order to avoid arithmetic under- and overflows in the template expressions. $\top$ corresponds to the respective maximum values in the promoted type, whereas $\bot$ must be encoded as a special symbol.

Guarded Templates. Since we use SSA form rather than control flow graphs, we cannot use numerical templates directly. Instead we use *guarded templates*. In a guarded template each row r is of the form $G_r \Rightarrow \widehat{\mathcal{T}}_r$ for the rth row $\widehat{\mathcal{T}}_r$ of the base template domain (e.g. template polyhedra). G_r is the conjunction of the SSA guards g_i associated with the definition of variables x_i occurring in $\widehat{\mathcal{T}}_r$. G_r denotes the guard associated to variables $\boldsymbol{x}$ appearing at the loop head, and G'_r the guard associated to the variables $\boldsymbol{x}'$ at the end of the respective loop body. Hence, template rows for different loops have different guards.

A guarded template in terms of the variables at the loop head is hence of the form $\mathcal{T}(\boldsymbol{x}_0, \boldsymbol{\delta}) = \bigwedge_r G_r(\boldsymbol{x}_0) \Rightarrow \widehat{\mathcal{T}}_r(\boldsymbol{x}_0, \boldsymbol{\delta})$. Replacing parameters $\boldsymbol{\delta}$ by the values $\boldsymbol{d}$ we get the invariants $\mathcal{T}(\boldsymbol{x}, \boldsymbol{d})$ at the loop heads.

For the example program in Sect. 3.1, we have the following guarded interval template:

$$\mathcal{T}(\texttt{x\#lb1}, (\delta_1, \delta_2)) = \begin{cases} \texttt{guard\#1} \wedge \texttt{guard\#ls0} \Rightarrow \texttt{x\#lb1} \leq \delta_1 \\ \texttt{guard\#1} \wedge \texttt{guard\#ls0} \Rightarrow -\texttt{x\#lb1} \leq \delta_2 \end{cases}$$

We denote $\mathcal{T}'(\boldsymbol{x}_1, \boldsymbol{\delta}) = \bigwedge_r G'_r(\boldsymbol{x}_1) \Rightarrow \widehat{\mathcal{T}}_r(\boldsymbol{x}_1, \boldsymbol{\delta})$ the guarded template expressed in terms of the variables at the end of the loop body. Here, we have to express the join of the initial value at the loop head (like `x#0`) and the values that are fed back into the loop head (like `x#2`). For the example above, the corresponding guarded template is as follows:

$$\mathcal{T}'(\texttt{x\#2}, (\delta_1, \delta_2)) = \begin{cases} (pg \Leftrightarrow \texttt{guard\#2}) \ \wedge \ (ig \Leftrightarrow \texttt{guard\#1} \wedge \neg\texttt{guard\#ls0}) \wedge \\ ((ig \Rightarrow x' = \texttt{x\#0}) \wedge (pg \wedge \neg ig \Rightarrow x' = \texttt{x\#2})) \wedge \\ (pg \vee ig \Rightarrow x' \leq \delta_1) \wedge (pg \vee ig \Rightarrow -x' \leq \delta_2) \end{cases}$$

3.4 Accelerated Solving of the ∃∀ Problem

As discussed in Sect. 3.2, it is necessary to solve an ∃∀ problem to find values for template parameters $\boldsymbol{\delta}$ to infer invariants.

Model Enumeration. The well-known method [4,23] for solving this problem in formula (12) using SMT solvers repeatedly checks satisfiability of the formula for an abstract value $\boldsymbol{d}$ (starting with $\boldsymbol{d} = \bot$):

$$\mathcal{T}[k](\boldsymbol{d}) \wedge T[k] \wedge \neg\mathcal{T}'(\boldsymbol{x_k}, \boldsymbol{d}) \tag{13}$$

If it is unsatisfiable, then we have found an invariant; otherwise we join the model returned by the solver with the previous abstract value $\boldsymbol{d}$.

However, this method corresponds to performing a classical Kleene iteration on the abstract lattice up to convergence. Convergence is guaranteed because our abstract domains are finite. Though, the height of the lattice is enormous and even for a one loop program incrementing an unconstrained 64-bit integer variable the naïve algorithm will not terminate within human life time. Hence, we are not going to use this method.

Optimisation. What we need is a convergence acceleration that makes the computational effort *independent* from the number of states and loop iterations. To this end, we use a technique that is inspired by an encoding used by max-*strategy iteration* methods [11,12,22]. These methods state the invariant inference problem over template polyhedra as a disjunctive linear optimisation problem, which is solved iteratively by an upward iteration in the lattice of template polyhedra: using SMT solving, a conjunctive subsystem ("strategy") whose solution extends the current invariant candidate is selected. This subsystem is then solved by an LP solver; the procedure terminates as soon as an inductive invariant is found.

This method can only be used if the domain is convex and the parameter values are ordered and monotonic w.r.t. concretisation, which holds true, for example, for template polyhedra $\mathbf{A}\boldsymbol{x} \le \boldsymbol{d}$ where $\boldsymbol{d}$ is a parameter, but not for those where $\mathbf{A}$ is a parameter. If the operations in the transition relation satisfy certain properties such as monotonicity of condition predicates, then the obtained result is the least fixed point, i.e. the *same* result as the one returned by the naïve model enumeration above, but much faster on average.

Our Algorithm. We adapt this method to our setting with bit-vector variables and guarded templates. Since we deal with finite domains (bit-vectors) we can use *binary search* as optimisation method instead of an LP solver.

The algorithm proceeds as follows: We start by checking whether the current abstract value $\boldsymbol{d}$ (starting from $\boldsymbol{d} = \bot$) is inductive (Eq. (13)). If so, we have found an invariant; otherwise there are template rows R whose values are not inductive yet. We construct the system

$$\bigwedge_{i\in[0,k-1]} \left\{ \begin{array}{l} \bigwedge_{r\notin R} G_r(\boldsymbol{x}_i) \Rightarrow (e_r(\boldsymbol{x}_i) \le d_r) \\ \wedge \bigwedge_{r\in R} G_r(\boldsymbol{x}_i) \Rightarrow (e_r(\boldsymbol{x}_i) \le \delta_r) \end{array} \right\} \wedge T[k] \wedge \bigwedge_{r\in R} G'_r(\boldsymbol{x}_k) \wedge (\delta_r \le e_r(\boldsymbol{x}_k)) \tag{14}$$

where e_r is the left-hand side of the inequality corresponding to the rth row of the template. Then we start the binary search for the optimal value of $\sum_{r\in R}\delta_r$ over this system. The initial bounds for $\sum_{r\in R}\delta_r$ are as follows:

- The lower bound ℓ is $\sum_{r\in R} d'_r$ where d'_r is the value of $e_r(\boldsymbol{x}_k)$ in the model of the inductivity check (13) above;
- The upper bound u is $\sum_{r\in R} max\_value(r)$ where max_value returns the maximum value that $e_r(\boldsymbol{x}_k)$ may have (dependent on variable type).

The binary search is performed by iteratively checking (14) for satisfiability under the assumption $\sum_{r\in R}\delta_r \geq m$ where $m = median(\ell, u)$. If satisfiable, set $\ell := m$, otherwise set $u := m$ and repeat until $\ell = u$. The values of δ_r in the last satisfiable query are assigned to d_r to obtain the new abstract value. The procedure is then repeated by testing whether $\boldsymbol{d}$ is inductive (13). Note that this algorithm uses a similar encoding for bound optimisation as strategy iteration, but potentially requires a higher number of iterations than strategy iteration. This choice has been made deliberately in order to keep the size of the generated SMT formulas small, at the cost of a potentially increased number of iterations.

A worked example is given in the extended version [3].

4 Implementation

We implemented *kIk*I in 2LS,[4] a verification tool built on the CPROVER framework, using MiniSAT-2.2.0 as a back-end solver (although other SAT and SMT solvers with incremental solving support can also be used). 2LS currently inlines all functions when running *kIk*I. The techniques described in Sect. 3 enable a single solver instance to be used where constraints and unwindings are added incrementally. This is essential because *kIk*I makes thousands of solver calls for invariant inference and property checks.

Our implementation is generic w.r.t. matrix $\mathbf{A}$ of the template polyhedral domain. In our experiments, we observed that very simple matrices $\mathbf{A}$ generating interval invariants are sufficient to compete with other state-of-the-art tools.

The tool can handle unrestricted sequential C programs (with the exception of programs with irreducible control flow). However, currently, invariants are not inferred over array contents or dynamically allocated data structures.

5 Experiments

We performed a number of experiments to demonstrate the utility and applicability of *kIk*I. All experiments were performed on an Intel Xeon X5667 at 3 GHz running Fedora 20 with 64-bit binaries. Each individual run was limited to 13 GB

[4] Version 0.2. The source code of the tool and instructions for its usage can be found on http://www.cprover.org/wiki/doku.php?id=2ls_for_program_analysis. In the experiments we ran it with the option `--competition-mode`.

of memory and 900 seconds of CPU time, enforced by the operating system kernel. We took the *loops* meta-category (143 benchmarks) from the SV-COMP'15 benchmark set.[5]

5.1 kIkI Verifies More Programs Than the Algorithms It Simulates

Table 1 gives a comparison between 2LS running kIkI (column 6) and *the same system* running as an incremental bounded model checker (IBMC) (column 2), incremental k-induction (i.e. without invariant inference, column 3) and as an abstract interpreter (AI) (column 4). kIkI is more complete than each of the restricted modes. This is not self-evident since it could be much less efficient and, thus, fail to solve the problems within the given time or memory limits. k-induction can solve 60.8 % of the benchmarks, 13 more than IBMC. 32 % of the benchmarks can be solved by abstract interpretation (bugs are only exposed if they are reachable with 0 loop unwindings). kIkI solves 62.9 % of the benchmarks, proving 3 more properties than k-induction.

Table 1. Comparison between kIkI, the algorithms it subsumes, the portfolio, and CPAchecker. The rows false alarms and false proofs indicate soundness bugs of the tool implementations.

	IBMC	k-induction	AI	portfolio	kIkI	CPAchecker	ESBMC
Counterexamples	**38**	**38**	17	**38**	**38**	36	35
Proofs	36	49	30	51	52	59	**91**
False proofs	0	0	0	0	0	2	12
False alarms	2	2	0	2	2	2	0
Inconclusive	0	0	93	0	0	4	2
Timeout	65	53	3	50	51	38	2
Memory out	2	1	0	2	0	2	1
Total runtime	17.1 h	13.8 h	0.89 h	13.3 h	13.2 h	10.9 h	0.54 h

5.2 kIkI Is at Least as Good as Their Naïve Portfolio

To show that kIkI is more than a mixture of three techniques and that they strengthen each other, consider column 5 of Table 1. This gives the results of an ideal portfolio in which the three restricted techniques are run in parallel on and the portfolio terminates when the first returns a conclusive result. Thus the CPU time taken is three times the time taken by the fastest technique for each benchmark (in practice these could be run in parallel, giving a lower *wall clock* time). In our setup, kIkI had a disadvantage as each component of virtual portfolio had the same memory restriction as kIkI, thus effectively giving the portfolio three times as much memory.

[5] http://sv-comp.sosy-lab.org/2015/benchmarks.php.

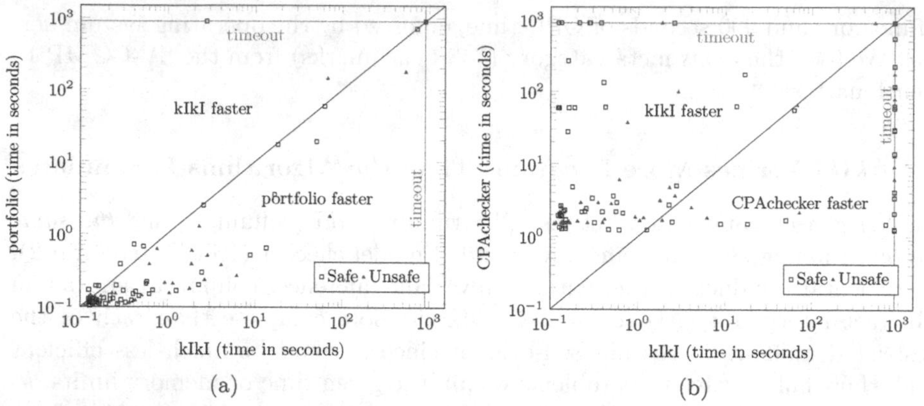

Fig. 4. Runtime comparison

Still, *kIk*I is slightly faster and more accurate than the portfolio as can be seen in Table 1. The scatter plot in Fig. 4a shows the results for each benchmark: one can observe that *kIk*I is up to one order of magnitude slower on many unsafe benchmarks, which is obviously due to the additional work of invariant inference that *kIk*I has to perform in contrast to IBMC. However, note that *kIk*I is faster than the portfolio on some safe and even one unsafe benchmarks. This suggests that *kIk*I is more than the sum of its parts.

5.3 *kIk*I Is Comparable with State-of-the-Art Approaches

We compared our implementation of *kIk*I with CPAchecker[6], and ESBMC[7], which uses *k*-induction. The results are shown in the last three columns in Table 1 and in the scatter plot in Fig. 4b. Additional results are given in the extended version [3]. In comparison to CPAchecker, the winner of SVCOMP'15, our prototype of *kIk*I is overall a bit slower and proves fewer properties (due to more timeouts), but as Fig. 4b shows, it significantly outperforms CPAchecker on most benchmarks. ESBMC exposes fewer bugs, but proves many more properties and is significantly faster. However, it has 6 times more soundness bugs than our implementation.[8] These results show that our prototype implementation of *kIk*I can keep up with state-of-the-art verification tools.

6 Related Work

Our work elucidates the connection between three well-studied techniques. Hence we can only give a brief overview of the vast amount of relevant literature.

[6] SVCOMP'15 version, http://cpachecker.sosy-lab.org/.
[7] SVCOMP'15 version, http://www.esbmc.org/.
[8] The two false alarms in our current implementation are due to limited support for dynamic memory allocation.

Since it was observed [26] that *k-induction* for finite state systems (e.g. hardware circuits) can be done by using an (incremental) SAT solver [9], it has become more and more popular also in the software community as a tool for safety proofs. Using SMT solvers, it has been applied to Lustre models [16] (monolithic transition relations) and C programs [7] (multiple and nested loops).

The idea of synthesising abstractions with the help of solvers can be traced back to predicate abstraction [13]; Reps et al. [23] proposed a method for symbolically computing best abstract transformers; these techniques were later refined [4, 18, 27] for application to various template domains. Using binary search for optimisation in this context was proposed by Gulwani et al. [15]. Similar techniques using LP solving for optimisation originate from strategy iteration [12]. Recently, SMT modulo optimisation [19, 25] techniques were proposed that foster application to invariant generation by optimisation.

k-induction often requires additional invariants to succeed, which can be obtained by abstract interpretation. For example, Garoche et al. [10] use SMT solving to infer intermediate invariants over templates for the use in k-induction of Lustre models. As most of these approaches (except [4]), they consider (linear) arithmetic over rational numbers only, whereas our target are C programs with bit-vectors (representing machine integers, floating-point numbers, etc.). Moreover, they do not exploit the full power of the approach because they compute only 1-invariants instead of k-invariants. Another distinguishing feature of our algorithm is that it operates on a single logical representation and hence enables maximum information reuse by incremental SAT solving using a single solver.

Formalising program analysis problems such as invariant inference in second order logic and suggesting to solve these formulae with generic solvers has been considered by [14]. In this paper we provide an implementation that solves the second order formula describing the invariant inference problem by reduction to quantifier elimination of a first order formula. Our approach can also solve other problems stated in [14], e.g., termination, by considering different abstract domains, e.g., for ranking functions.

7 Conclusions

This paper presents kIkI and shows that it can simulate incremental BMC, k-induction and classical, over-approximating abstract interpretation. Experiments performed with an implementation, 2LS, show that it is not only "more" complete than each individual technique – but it also suggests that it is stronger than their naïve combination. In other words, the components of the algorithm synergistically interact and enhance each other. Moreover, our combination enables a clean, homogeneous, tightly integrated implementation rather than a loose, heterogeneous combination of isolated building blocks or a pipeline of techniques where each only strengthens the next.

There are many possible future directions for this work. Enhancing 2LS to support additional kinds of templates, possibly including disjunctive template and improving the optimisation techniques used for quantifier elimination is one area of interest. In another direction, *kIkI* could be enhance to support function modular, intraprocedural, thread modular and possibly multi-threaded analysis. Automatic refinement of the template domains is another tantalising possibility.

References

1. Biere, A., Cimatti, A., Clarke, E., Zhu, Y.: Symbolic model checking without BDDs. In: Cleaveland, W.R. (ed.) TACAS 1999. LNCS, vol. 1579, p. 193. Springer, Heidelberg (1999)
2. Bradley, A.R., Manna, Z.: Checking safety by inductive generalization of counterexamples to induction. In: Formal Methods in Computer-Aided Design, pp. 173–180. IEEE Computer Society (2007)
3. Brain, M., Joshi, S., Kroening, D., Schrammel, P.: Safety verification and refutation by k-invariants and k-induction (extended version). Technical report (2015). arxiv.org/abs/1506.05671
4. Brauer, J., King, A., Kriener, J.: Existential quantification as incremental SAT. In: Gopalakrishnan, G., Qadeer, S. (eds.) CAV 2011. LNCS, vol. 6806, pp. 191–207. Springer, Heidelberg (2011)
5. Clarke, E.M., Grumberg, O., Jha, S., Lu, Y., Veith, H.: Counterexample-guided abstraction refinement. In: Emerson, E.A., Sistla, A.P. (eds.) CAV 2000. LNCS, vol. 1855. Springer, Heidelberg (2000)
6. Cousot, P., Cousot, R.: Abstract interpretation: a unified lattice model for static analysis of programs by construction or approximation of fixpoints. In: POPL, pp. 238–252 (1977)
7. Donaldson, A.F., Haller, L., Kroening, D., Rümmer, P.: Software verification using *k*-induction. In: Yahav, E. (ed.) SAS. LNCS, vol. 6887, pp. 351–368. Springer, Heidelberg (2011)
8. D'Silva, V., Kroening, D.: Abstraction of syntax. In: Giacobazzi, R., Berdine, J., Mastroeni, I. (eds.) VMCAI 2013. LNCS, vol. 7737, pp. 396–413. Springer, Heidelberg (2013)
9. Eén, N., Sörensson, N.: Temporal induction by incremental SAT solving. ENTCS **89**(4), 543–560 (2003)
10. Garoche, P.-L., Kahsai, T., Tinelli, C.: Incremental invariant generation using logic-based automatic abstract transformers. In: Brat, G., Rungta, N., Venet, A. (eds.) NFM 2013. LNCS, vol. 7871, pp. 139–154. Springer, Heidelberg (2013)
11. Gawlitza, T.M., Monniaux, D.: Improving strategies via SMT solving. In: Barthe, G. (ed.) ESOP 2011. LNCS, vol. 6602, pp. 236–255. Springer, Heidelberg (2011)
12. Gawlitza, T., Seidl, H.: Precise relational invariants through strategy iteration. In: Duparc, J., Henzinger, T.A. (eds.) CSL 2007. LNCS, vol. 4646, pp. 23–40. Springer, Heidelberg (2007)
13. Graf, S., Saïdi, H.: Construction of abstract state graphs with PVS. In: Grumberg, O. (ed.) CAV 1997. LNCS, vol. 1254. Springer, Heidelberg (1997)
14. Grebenshchikov, S., Lopes, N.P., Popeea, C., Rybalchenko, A.: Synthesizing software verifiers from proof rules. In: PLDI, pp. 405–416. ACM (2012)
15. Gulwani, S., Srivastava, S., Venkatesan, R.: Program analysis as constraint solving. In: PLDI, pp. 281–292. ACM (2008)
16. Hagen, G., Tinelli, C.: Scaling up the formal verification of lustre programs with SMT-based techniques. In: FMCAD, pp. 1–9. IEEE Computer Society (2008)

17. Hoder, K., Bjørner, N.: Generalized property directed reachability. In: Cimatti, A., Sebastiani, R. (eds.) SAT 2012. LNCS, vol. 7317, pp. 157–171. Springer, Heidelberg (2012)
18. Kahsai, T., Ge, Y., Tinelli, C.: Instantiation-based invariant discovery. In: Bobaru, M., Havelund, K., Holzmann, G.J., Joshi, R. (eds.) NFM 2011. LNCS, vol. 6617, pp. 192–206. Springer, Heidelberg (2011)
19. Li, Y., Albarghouthi, A., Kincaid, Z., Gurfinkel, A., Chechik, M.: Symbolic optimization with SMT solvers. In: POPL, pp. 607–618. ACM (2014)
20. McMillan, K.L.: Lazy abstraction with interpolants. In: Ball, T., Jones, R.B. (eds.) CAV 2006. LNCS, vol. 4144, pp. 123–136. Springer, Heidelberg (2006)
21. Miné, A.: The octagon abstract domain. In: Working Conference on Reverse Engineering, pp. 310–319. IEEE Computer Society (2001)
22. Monniaux, D., Schrammel, P.: Speeding up logico-numerical strategy iteration. In: Müller-Olm, M., Seidl, H. (eds.) SAS. LNCS, vol. 8723, pp. 253–267. Springer, Heidelberg (2014)
23. Reps, T., Sagiv, M., Yorsh, G.: Symbolic implementation of the best transformer. In: Steffen, B., Levi, G. (eds.) VMCAI 2004. LNCS, vol. 2937, pp. 252–266. Springer, Heidelberg (2004)
24. Sankaranarayanan, S., Sipma, H.B., Manna, Z.: Scalable analysis of linear systems using mathematical programming. In: Cousot, R. (ed.) VMCAI 2005. LNCS, vol. 3385, pp. 25–41. Springer, Heidelberg (2005)
25. Sebastiani, R., Tomasi, S.: Optimization in SMT with $\mathcal{LA}(\mathbb{Q})$ cost functions. In: Gramlich, B., Miller, D., Sattler, U. (eds.) IJCAR 2012. LNCS, vol. 7364, pp. 484–498. Springer, Heidelberg (2012)
26. Sheeran, M., Singh, S., Stålmarck, G.: Checking safety properties using induction and a SAT-solver. In: Johnson, S.D., Hunt Jr, W.A. (eds.) FMCAD 2000. LNCS, vol. 1954, pp. 108–125. Springer, Heidelberg (2000)
27. Thakur, A., Reps, T.: A method for symbolic computation of abstract operations. In: Madhusudan, P., Seshia, S.A. (eds.) CAV 2012. LNCS, vol. 7358, pp. 174–192. Springer, Heidelberg (2012)

Effective Soundness-Guided Reflection Analysis

Yue Li(✉), Tian Tan, and Jingling Xue

Programming Languages and Compilers Group,
School of Computer Science and Engineering, UNSW, Sydney, Australia
{yueli,tiantan,jingling}@cse.unsw.edu.au

Abstract. We introduce SOLAR, the first reflection analysis that allows its soundness to be reasoned about when some assumptions are met and produces significantly improved under-approximations otherwise. In both settings, SOLAR has three novel aspects: (1) lazy heap modeling for reflective allocation sites, (2) collective inference for improving the inferences on related reflective calls, and (3) automatic identification of "problematic" reflective calls that may threaten its soundness, precision and scalability, thereby enabling their improvement via lightweight annotations. We evaluate SOLAR against two state-of-the-art solutions, DOOP and ELF, with the three treated as under-approximate reflection analyses, using 11 large Java benchmarks and applications. SOLAR is significantly more sound while achieving nearly the same precision and running only several-fold more slowly, subject to only 7 annotations in 3 programs.

1 Introduction

Reflection is increasingly used in a range of software and framework architectures, allowing a software system to choose and change implementations of services at run-time, but posing significant challenges to static program analysis. In the case of Java programs, reflection has always been an obstacle for pointer analysis [1–10], a fundamental static analysis on which virtually all others [11–16] are built. All pointer analysis tools for Java [2,17–19] either ignore reflection or handle it partially since their underlying best-effort reflection analyses [5,17,18,20–22] provide only under-approximated handling of reflection heuristically.

However, such unsoundness can render much of the codebase invisible for analysis. There is a recent community initiative [23] calling for the development of soundy analysis to handle "hard" language features (such as reflection). A *soundy* analysis is one that is as sound as possible without excessively compromising precision and/or scalability. Thus, improving or even achieving soundness in reflection analysis will provide significant benefits to many clients, such as program verifiers, optimizing compilers, bug detectors and security analyzers.

In this paper, we make the following contributions:

- We introduce SOLAR, the first reflection analysis that allows its soundness to be reasoned about when some reasonable assumptions are met and yields significantly improved under-approximations otherwise (Sect. 2). We have developed SOLAR by adopting three novel aspects in its design: (N1) lazy heap

S. Blazy and T. Jensen (Eds.): SAS 2015, LNCS 9291, pp. 162–180, 2015.
DOI: 10.1007/978-3-662-48288-9_10

modeling for reflective allocation sites, (N2) collective inference for related reflective calls, and (N3) automatic identification of "problematic" reflective calls that may threaten its soundness, precision and scalability.

- We formalize SOLAR as part of a pointer analysis for Java (including a small core of its reflection API) and reason about its soundness under a set of assumptions (Sect. 3). We have produced an open source implementation on top of DOOP [18], which is a modern pointer analysis tool for Java.
- We evaluate SOLAR against two state-of-the-art reflection analyses, DOOP [5] and ELF [21], with 11 large Java benchmarks/applications (Sect. 4), where all the three are treated as under-approximate analyses (due to, e.g., native code). By instrumenting these programs under their associated inputs (when available), SOLAR is the only one to achieve total recall (for all reflective targets accessed), with 371 % (148 %) more target methods resolved than DOOP (ELF) in total, which translates into 49700 (40570) more true caller-callee relations statically calculated w.r.t. these inputs alone. SOLAR has done so by maintaining nearly the same precision as and running only several-fold more slowly than ELF and DOOP, subject to only 7 annotations in 3 programs.

2 Methodology

Figure 1 illustrates an example of reflection usage abstracted in real code. In line 2, a `Class` metaobject `c1` is created by calling `Class.forName(cName)` to represent the class named `cName`, where `cName`, i.e., `cName1` in line 10 is an input string to be read from a command line or a configuration file. In line 3, an object o is reflectively created as an instance of `c1` by calling `c1.newInstance()` and then assigned to `v` with the declared type as `Java.lang.Object` in line 10. Subsequently, o is used in two common scenarios. In the `if` branch, o is downcast to a specific type, `A`, and then used appropriately. The `else` branch is more interesting. In line 14, a `Method` metaobject `m` is created by calling `getMethod()` indirectly in line 7, with its class name, method name and formal parameters specified by `cName2`, `mName2` and "`...`" (elided) in line 7, respectively. In line 15, this method is called reflectively on the receiver object o (pointed to by `v`) with the actual argument being passed in an array, `new Object[] {x, y}`.

```
1 Object createObj(String cName) {
2   Class c1 = Class.forName(cName);
3   return c1.newInstance();
4 }

5 Method getMtd(String cName, String mName) {
6   Class c2 = Class.forName(cName);
7   return c2.getMethod(mName, ... );
8 }
```

```
9  void foo(X x, Y y, ... ) {
10   Object v = createObj(cName1); //cName1 is an input string
11   if ( ... ) {
12     A a = (A) v;
       ...
13   } else {
       ...
14     Method m = getMtd(cName2, mName2);
15     m.invoke(v, new Object[] {x, y});
16   }
17 }
```

Fig. 1. An example of reflection usage abstracted from `JDK 1.6.0_45`.

A reflection analysis infers, i.e., resolves statically the reflective targets accessed at reflective call sites. As usual, soundnesss demands over-approximation. Reflection introduces many challenges for static analysis. First, a modern reflection API is large and complex. Second, reflection is typically used as a means of supporting dynamic adaptation of object-oriented software. As such, metaobjects are often created reflectively as shown in Fig. 1 from input strings. Thus, reflective object creation via `newInstance()` is hard to model statically. Finally, picking judicious approximations to balance soundness, precision and scalability is non-trivial. A simple-minded sound modeling of a reflective call (e.g., by assuming arbitrary behaviour) would destroy precision. Imprecision, in turn, often destroys scalability because too many spurious results would be computed.

SOLAR automates reflection analysis for Java by working with a pointer analysis. We first define some assumptions (Sect. 2.1). We then look at the three limitations of the prior work (Sect. 2.2). Finally, we introduce SOLAR to address these limitations by adopting three novel aspects in its design (Sect. 2.3).

2.1 Assumptions

The first three are made previously on reflection analysis for Java [20,21]. The last one is introduced to allow reflective allocation sites to be modeled lazily.

Assumption 1 (Closed-World). *Only the classes reachable from the class path at analysis time can be used during program execution.*

This assumption is reasonable since we cannot expect static analysis to handle all classes that a program may conceivably download from the net and load at runtime. In addition, Java native methods are excluded as well.

Assumption 2 (Well-Behaved Class Loaders). *The name of the class returned by a call to `Class.forName(cName)` equals `cName`.*

Assumption 3 (Correct Casts). *Type cast operations applied to the results of reflective calls are correct, without throwing a ClassCastException.*

Assumption 4 (Object Reachability). *Every object `o` created reflectively in a call to `newInstance()` flows into (i.e., is used in) either (1) a type cast operation `... = (T) v` or (2) a call to `invoke(v, ...)`, `get(v)` or `set(v, ...)`, where `v` points to `o`, along every execution path in the program.*

As discussed in Sect. 4.2, Assumption 4 is found to hold for most reflective allocation sites in real code (as illustrated in Fig. 1). Here, (1) and (2) represent two kinds of usage points at which the class types of object o will be inferred lazily. This makes it possible to handle reflective allocation sites more accurately than before and to reason about the soundness of SOLAR for the first time.

2.2 Past Work: Best-Effort Reflection Resolution

All the existing solutions [5,17,18,20–22] adopt a best-effort approach to reflection analysis, and consequently, suffer from the following three limitations:

L1. Eager Heap Modeling. An abstract object o created at a call to, e.g., `c.newInstance()` is modeled eagerly if its type `c` can be inferred from a string constant or intraprocedural post-dominant cast, and ignored otherwise. Specifically, if `c` represents a known class name, e.g., "`A`", then o's type is "`A`". Otherwise, an intraprocedurally post-dominating cast operation `(T)` operating on the result of the `newInstance()` call will allow `c` to be over-approximated as `T` or any of its subtypes. This eager approach often fails in real code shown in Fig. 1, where `cName1` is an input string and the cast is not post-dominating. Thus, its `newInstance()` call is ignored. Recently, in Doop (r5459247-beta) [18], the objects created in line 10 (or line 3) are assumed to be of type `A` by taking advantage of the non-post-dominating cast `(A)` in line 12 to analyze more code. However, the objects with other types created along both the `if` and `else` branches are ignored. In prior work, such under-approximate handling of `newInstance()` is a significant source of unsoundness, as a large part of the program called on the thus ignored objects has been rendered invisible for analysis.

L2. Isolated Inferences. Many reflective calls (e.g., those in Fig. 1) are related but analysed mostly in isolation, resulting in under-approximated behaviours. In [21], we presented a *self-inferencing* reflection analysis, called Elf, that can infer more targets at a reflective call site than before [5,17,18,20,22], by exploiting more information available (e.g., from its arguments and return type). However, due to eager heap modeling, Elf will still ignore the `invoke()` call in line 15 as `v` points to objects of unknown types as discussed above.

L3. Design-Time Soundness, Precision and Scalability. When analysing a program heuristically, a best-effort approach does not know which reflective calls may potentially affect its soundness, precision and scalability. As a result, a developer is out of luck with a program if such best-effort analysis is either unscalable or scalable but with undesired soundness or precision or both.

2.3 Solar: Soundness-Guided Reflection Resolution

Figure 2 illustrates the Solar design, with its three novel aspects marked by N1 – N3, where Ni is introduced to overcome the afore-mentioned limitation Li.

N1. Lazy Heap Modeling (LHM). Solar handles reflective object creation lazily by delaying the creation of objects at their usage points where their types may be inferred, achieving significantly improved soundness and precision.

Let us describe the basic idea behind using the example in Fig. 1. As `cName` at `c1 = Class.forName(cName)` in line 2 is unknown, Solar will create a `Class` metaobject $\texttt{c1}^u$ that represents this unknown class and assign it to `c1`. As `c1` points to $\texttt{c1}^u$ at the allocation site `v = c1.newInstance()` in line 3, Solar will create an abstract object o_3^u of an unknown type for the site to mark it as being

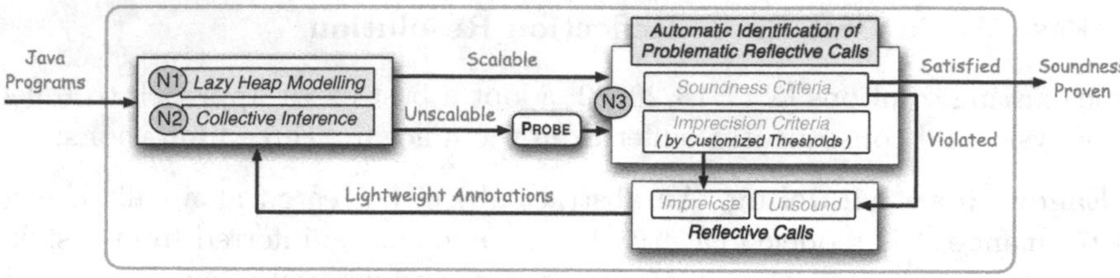

Fig. 2. SOLAR: A soundness-guided analysis with three novel aspects, N1 – N3.

unresolved yet. Subsequently, o_3^u will flow into two usage points: Case (I) a type cast operation in line 12 and Case (II) a reflective method call site in line 15.

In Case (I), where o_3^u is downcast to `A`, its type u is inferred to be `A` or any of its subtypes. Let $t_1, \ldots, t_n$ be all the inferred types. Then o_3^u is split into n distinct objects $o_3^{t_1}, \ldots, o_3^{t_n}$ to be assigned to `a` in line 12. In Case (II), SOLAR will infer u by performing a collective inference as described below, based on the information available in line 15. Let $t'_1, \ldots, t'_m$ be all the inferred types. Then o_3^u is split into m distinct objects $o_3^{t'_1}, \ldots, o_3^{t'_m}$ to be assigned to `v` in line 15.

According to Assumption 4 that states a key observation validated later, a reflectively created object like o_3^u is typically used in either Case (I) or Case (II) along every program path. The only but rare exception is that o_3^u is created but never used later. Then the corresponding constructor must be annotated to be analyzed statically unless ignoring it will not affect the points-to information.

N2. Collective Inference. SOLAR builds on the prior work [5,17,18,20–22] by relying on collective inference emphasized for the first time in reflection analysis. Let us return to the `invoke()` call, which cannot be analyzed previously. As `v` points to o_3^u, SOLAR can infer u based on the information available at the call site. This happens when Case (1) `cName2` is known or Case (2) `cName2` is unknown but `mName2` is known. In SOLAR, inference is performed "collectively", whereby inferences on related reflective calls (lines 3, 6 and 15 for Case (1) and lines 3, 7 and 15 for Case (2)) can mutually reinforce each other. We will examine the second case, i.e., the more complex of the two, in Sect. 3.4.3. This paper is the first to do so by exploiting the connection between `newInstance()` (via LHM) and reflective calls for manipulating methods and fields.

N3. Automatic Identification of "Problematic" Reflective Calls. Due to this capability, SOLAR is the first that can reason about its soundness. When such reasoning is not possible due to, e.g., native code, SOLAR reduces to an effective under-approximate analysis due to its soundness-guided design, allowing a disciplined tradeoff to be made among soundness, precision and scalability.

If SOLAR is scalable for a program, SOLAR can automatically identify "problematic" reflective calls (as opposed to reporting input strings as in [20]) that may threaten its soundness and precision to enable both to be improved with lightweight annotations. If SOLAR is unscalable for a program, a simplified version of SOLAR, denoted PROBE in Fig. 2, is called for next. With some "problematic" reflective calls to be annotated, SOLAR will re-analyze the program, scalably after one or more iterations of this "probing" process. We envisage providing a range of PROBE variants with different tradeoffs among soundness, precision and scalability, so that the scalability of PROBE is always guaranteed.

Consider Fig. 1 again. If both `cName2` and `mName2` are unknown (given that the type of o_3^u is unknown), then SOLAR will flag the `invoke()` call in line 15 as being potentially unsoundly resolved, detected automatically by verifying Condition (3) in Sect. 3.5. In addition, SOLAR will also automatically highlight reflective calls that may be potentially imprecisely resolved. Their lightweight annotations will allow SOLAR to yield improved soundness and precision.

Discussion. Under Assumptions 1 – 4, we can establish the soundness of SOLAR by verifying a soundness criterion (given in Sect. 3.5). Otherwise, our soundness-guided approach has made SOLAR demonstrably more effective than existing under-approximate reflection analyses [5,17,20,21] as validated later.

3 Formalism

We formalise SOLAR, illustrated in Fig. 2, for REFJAVA, which is Java restricted to a small core of its reflection API. SOLAR is flow-insensitive but context-sensitive. However, our formalisation is context-insensitive.

3.1 The REFJAVA Language

REFJAVA consists of all Java programs (under Assumptions 1 – 4) except that the Java reflection API is restricted to the four methods in Fig. 1: `Class.forName()`, `newInstance()`, `getMethod()` and `invoke()`. Our formalism is designed to allow its straightforward generalization to the entire API. For example, reflective field accesses via `getField()`, `get()` and `set()` can be handled similarly. As is standard, a Java program is represented only by five kinds of statements in the SSA form, as shown in Fig. 5. For simplicity, we assume that all the methods of a class accessed reflectively are its instance members, i.e., $\texttt{v} \neq \texttt{null}$ in `invoke(v,...)` in Fig. 1. We will discuss how to handle static members in Sect. 3.9.

3.2 Road Map

As depicted in Fig. 3, SOLAR's inference system, which consists of five components, works together with a pointer analysis. The arrow $\longleftrightarrow$ between a component and the pointer analysis indicates that each is both a producer and consumer of the other.

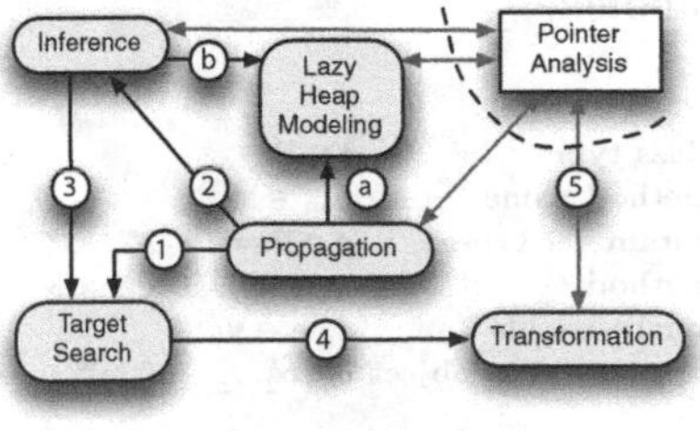

Fig. 3. SOLAR's inference system.

Let us see how SOLAR resolves the `invoke()` call in Fig. 1. If `cName2` and `mName2` are string constants, *Propagation* will create a `Method` metaobject (pointed to by m) carrying its known class and method information and pass it to *Target Search* (①). If `cName2` or `mName2` is not a constant, a `Method` metaobject marked as such is created and passed to *Inference* (②), which will infer the missing information and pass a freshly generated `Method` metaobject enriched with the missing information to *Target Search* (③). Then *Target Search* maps a `Method` metaobject to its reflective target *mtd* in its declaring class (④). Finally, *Transformation* turns the reflective call in line 15 into a regular call v.*mtd*(...) and pass it to the pointer analysis (⑤). *Lazy Heap Modeling* handles `newInstance()` in Fig. 1 to resolve the dynamic type of v based on the information discovered by *Propagation* (ⓐ) or *Inference* (ⓑ).

3.3 Notations

We will use the notations in Fig. 4. A method signature consists of the method name and descriptor (i.e., return type and parameter types) and, a method is specified by its method signature and the class where it is declared or inherited. $\mathbb{CO}$ and $\mathbb{MO}$ represent the set of `Class` and `Method` metaobjects, respectively. In particular, $\mathtt{c}^t$ denotes a `Class` metaobject of a known class t and $\mathtt{c}^u$ a `Class` metaobject of an unknown class u. As illustrated earlier with Fig. 1, we write o_i^t to represent an abstract object created at an allocation site i if it is an instance of a known class t and o_i^u of (an unknown class type) otherwise. For a `Method` metaobject, we write $\mathtt{m}_s^t$ if it is a member in a known class t and $\mathtt{m}_s^u$ otherwise, with its signature being s. In particular, we write $\mathtt{m}_u^-$ as a shorthand for $\mathtt{m}_s^-$ when s is unknown (with the return type $s.t_r$ being ignored), i.e., when $s.n_m = s.p = u$.

3.4 The Solar's Inference System

We present the inference rules used by all the components in Fig. 3, starting with the pointer analysis and moving to the five components of Solar.

3.4.1 Pointer Analysis. Fig. 5 gives a standard formulation of a flow-insensitive Andersen's pointer analysis for RefJava. *pt(x)* represents the *points-to set* of a pointer x. An array object is analyzed with its elements collapsed to a single field, denoted *arr*. For example, `x[i] = y` can be seen as x.*arr* = y. In [A-New], o_i^t uniquely identifies the abstract object created as an instance of t at this allocation site, labeled by i. In [A-Ld] and [A-St], the field accesses are handled.

class type	$t \in \mathbb{T}$	`Class` metaobject	$\mathtt{c}^t, \mathtt{c}^u \in \mathbb{CO}$
method name	$n_m \in \mathbb{N}$	`Method` metaobject*	$\mathtt{m}_s^t, \mathtt{m}_u^t, \mathtt{m}_s^u, \mathtt{m}_u^u \in \mathbb{MO} = \widehat{\mathbb{T}} \times \mathbb{S}_m$
parameter types	$p \in \mathbb{P} = \mathbb{T}^0 \cup \mathbb{T}^1 \cup \mathbb{T}^2 \ldots$	method signature*	$s \in \mathbb{S}_m = \widehat{\mathbb{T}} \times \widehat{\mathbb{N}} \times \widehat{\mathbb{P}}$
method	$m \in \mathbb{M} = \mathbb{T} \times \mathbb{T} \times \mathbb{N} \times \mathbb{P}$	return type*	$s.t_r \in \widehat{\mathbb{T}}$
local variable	$\mathtt{c}, \mathtt{m} \in \mathbb{V}$	method name*	$s.n_m \in \widehat{\mathbb{N}}$
abstract heap object	$o_1^t, o_2^t, \ldots, o_1^u, o_2^u, \cdots \in \mathbb{H}$	parameter types*	$s.p \in \widehat{\mathbb{P}}$

Fig. 4. Notations ($\widehat{X} = X \cup \{u\}$, where u is an unknown class type or an unknown method signature). A superscript '*' marks a domain that contains u.

$$\frac{i:\ \mathrm{x} = new\ t()}{\{o_i^t\} \in pt(\mathrm{x})}[\text{A-New}] \quad \frac{\mathrm{x} = \mathrm{y}}{pt(\mathrm{y}) \subseteq pt(\mathrm{x})}[\text{A-Cpy}] \quad \frac{\mathrm{x} = \mathrm{y.f}\ \ o_i^t \in pt(\mathrm{y})}{pt(o_i^t.\mathrm{f}) \subseteq pt(\mathrm{x})}[\text{A-Ld}] \quad \frac{\mathrm{x.f} = \mathrm{y}\ \ o_i^t \in pt(\mathrm{x})}{pt(\mathrm{y}) \subseteq pt(o_i^t.\mathrm{f})}[\text{A-St}]$$

$$\frac{\mathrm{x} = \mathrm{y}.m(\mathrm{arg}_1, \ldots, \mathrm{arg}_n) \quad o_i^- \in pt(\mathrm{y}) \quad m' = dispatch(o_i^-, m)}{\{o_i^-\} \subseteq pt(m'_{this}) \quad pt(m'_{ret}) \subseteq pt(\mathrm{x}) \quad \forall\, 1 \leqslant k \leqslant n : pt(\mathrm{arg}_k) \subseteq pt(m'_{pk})}[\text{A-Call}]$$

Fig. 5. Rules for *Pointer Analysis.*

$$\frac{Class\ \ \mathrm{c} = Class.forName(\mathrm{cName}) \quad o_i^{\mathtt{String}} \in pt(\mathrm{cName})}{pt(\mathrm{c}) \supseteq \begin{cases} \{\mathrm{c}^t\} & \text{if } o_i^{\mathtt{String}} \in \mathbb{SC} \\ \{\mathrm{c}^u\} & \text{otherwise} \end{cases} \quad \mathrm{c}^t = toClass(val(o_i^{\mathtt{String}}))}[\text{P-ForName}]$$

$$\frac{Method\ \ \mathrm{m} = \mathrm{c}'.getMethod(\mathrm{mName}, \ldots) \quad o_i^{\mathtt{String}} \in pt(\mathrm{mName}) \quad \mathrm{c}^- \in pt(\mathrm{c}')}{pt(\mathrm{m}) \supseteq \begin{cases} \{\mathtt{m}_s^t\} \text{ if } \mathrm{c}^- = \mathrm{c}^t \wedge o_i^{\mathtt{String}} \in \mathbb{SC} \\ \{\mathtt{m}_u^t\} \text{ if } \mathrm{c}^- = \mathrm{c}^t \wedge o_i^{\mathtt{String}} \notin \mathbb{SC} \\ \{\mathtt{m}_s^u\} \text{ if } \mathrm{c}^- = \mathrm{c}^u \wedge o_i^{\mathtt{String}} \in \mathbb{SC} \\ \{\mathtt{m}_u^u\} \text{ if } \mathrm{c}^- = \mathrm{c}^u \wedge o_i^{\mathtt{String}} \notin \mathbb{SC} \end{cases} \quad \begin{array}{c} s.t_r = u \\ s.n_m = val(o_i^{\mathtt{String}}) \\ s.p = u \end{array}}[\text{P-GetMtd}]$$

Fig. 6. Rules for *Propagation.*

In [A-Call] (for non-reflective calls), the function $dispatch(o_i^-, m)$ is used to resolve the virtual dispatch of method m on the receiver object o_i^- to be m' (when m is invokable on o_i^-). Following [24], we assume that m' has a formal parameter m'_{this} for the receiver object and $m'_{p1}, \ldots, m'_{pn}$ for the remaining parameters, and a pseudo-variable m'_{ret} is used to hold the return value of m'.

3.4.2 Propagation. Figure 6 gives the rules for `forName()` and `getMethod()` calls. Depending on whether their arguments are string constants or not, different kinds of `Class` and `Method` metaobjects are created. $\mathbb{SC}$ is a set of string constants and *toClass* returns a `Class` metaobject c^t, where t is the class specified by the string value returned by $val(o_i)$ (with $val : \mathbb{H} \to$ `java.lang.String`).

By design, $\mathtt{c}^t$ and $\mathtt{m}_s^t$ will flow to *Target Search* but all the others, i.e., $\mathtt{c}^u$, $\mathtt{m}_-^u$ and $\mathtt{m}_u^-$ will flow to *Inference*, where the missing information is inferred. During *Propagation*, only the name of a method signature s (i.e., $s.n_m$) can be discovered but its other parts are unknown: $s.t_r = s.p = u$.

3.4.3 Inference. Figure 7 gives three rules to infer the reflective target methods for `x = (A) m.invoke(y,args)`, where `A` indicates a post-dominating cast on its result. If `A = Object`, then no such cast exists. In [I-InvTp], we use the types of the objects pointed to by `y` to infer the class types of the target methods called. Note that $\mathtt{m}_-^t$ represents a freshly generated `Method` metaobject. In [I-InvSig], we use the information available at a call site (excluding `y`) to infer the descriptor in the signature of a target method. In [I-InvS2T], we use the signature of a method to infer the class types of the method.

As is standard, $t <: t'$ holds when t is t' or a subtype of t'. In [I-InvSig] and [I-InvS2T], $\ll:$ is used to take advantage of the post-dominating cast (`A`) during inference when `A` is not `Object`. By definition, $u \ll:$ `Object` holds. If t' is not `Object`, then $t \ll: t'$ holds if and only if $t <: t'$ or $t' <: t$ holds. The information on `args` is also exploited, where `args` is an array of type `Object[]`, only when

$$\frac{\text{m}.invoke(\text{y, args}) \quad \mathtt{m}^{u}_{-} \in pt(\text{m})}{pt(\text{m}) \supseteq \{\, \mathtt{m}^{t}_{-} \mid o^{t}_{i} \in pt(\text{y})\}}\text{[I-InvTp]} \quad \frac{\text{x} = (\mathsf{A})\ \text{m}.invoke(\text{y, args}) \quad \mathtt{m}^{-}_{u} \in pt(\text{m})}{pt(\text{m}) \supseteq \{\, \mathtt{m}^{-}_{s} \mid s.p \in Ptp(\text{args}), s.t_r \ll: \mathsf{A}, s.n_m = u\}}\text{[I-InvSig]}$$

$$\frac{\text{x} = (\mathsf{A})\ \text{m}.invoke(\text{y, args}) \quad \mathtt{m}^{u}_{s} \in pt(\text{m}) \quad o^{u}_{i} \in pt(\text{y}) \quad s.t_r \ll: \mathsf{A} \quad s.n_m \neq u \quad s.p \in Ptp(\text{args})}{pt(\text{m}) \supseteq \{\mathtt{m}^{t}_{s} \mid t \in \mathcal{M}(s.t_r, s.n_m, s.p)\}}\text{[I-InvS2T]}$$

Fig. 7. Rules for *Inference.*

it can be analyzed exactly element-wise by an intraprocedural analysis. In this case, suppose that **args** is an array of n elements. Let A_i be the set of types of the objects pointed to by its i-th element, `args[i]`. Let $P_i = \{t' \mid t \in A_i, t <: t'\}$. Then $Ptp(\texttt{args}) = P_0 \times \cdots \times P_{n-1}$. Otherwise, $Ptp(\texttt{args}) = \varnothing$, implying that **args** is ignored as it cannot be exploited effectively during inference.

To maintain precision in [I-InvS2T], we use a method signature to infer its classes when both its name and descriptor are known. In this rule, the function $\mathcal{M}(s_{t_r}, s.n_m, s.p)$ returns the set of class types where the method with the specified signature s is declared if $s.n_m \neq u$ and $s.p \neq u$, and $\varnothing$ otherwise. The return type of the matching method is ignored if $s.t_r = u$.

Let us illustrate some of our rules by considering our example in Fig. 1.

Example 1. Note that `cName1` is an input string. Suppose that `cName2` is also an input string but `mName2` is a string constant. By applying [P-ForName], [P-GetMtd] and [L-UkwTp] (in Fig. 9) to the calls to `forName()` in lines 2 and 6, `getMethod()` and `newInstance()`, respectively, we obtain $\texttt{c1}^u \in pt(\texttt{c1})$, $\texttt{c2}^u \in pt(\texttt{c2})$, $\mathtt{m}^u_s \in pt(\texttt{m})$ and $o^u_i \in pt(\texttt{v})$, where s is a signature with a known method name in `mName2`. Given `args = new Object[] {x,y}`, *Ptp(args)* is built as described earlier. Solar can infer the classes t where this method is declared by [I-InvS2T]. Finally, Solar will add all inferred `Method` objects $\mathtt{m}^t_s$ to $pt(\texttt{m})$ at the call site. □

3.4.4 Target Search. For a `Method` object $\mathtt{m}^t_s$ in a known class t (with s being possibly u), we define $MTD : \mathbb{MO} \to \mathcal{P}(\mathbb{M})$ to find all target methods matched:

$$MTD(\mathtt{m}^t_s) = \bigcup_{t <: t'} mtdLookUp(t', s.t_r, s.n_m, s.p) \tag{1}$$

where *mtdLookUp* is the standard lookup function for finding the methods according to a declaring class t' and a signature s except that (1) the return type $s.t_r$ is also considered and (2) any u that appears in s is treated as a wild card.

3.4.5 Transformation. Figure 8 gives the rules used for transforming a reflective call into a regular statement, which will be analyzed by the pointer analysis.

Let us examine [T-Inv] in more detail. The second argument **args** points to a 1-D array of type `Object[]`, with its elements collapsed to a single field *arr* during the pointer analysis, unless **args** can be analyzed exactly intraprocedurally in our current implementation. Let $\texttt{arg}_1, \ldots, \texttt{arg}_n$ be the n freshly created arguments to be passed to each potential target method m' found by *Target Search.* Let $m'_{p1}, \ldots, m'_{pn}$ be the n parameters (excluding *this*) of m', such that

$$\frac{\mathtt{x} = \mathtt{m}.\mathit{invoke}(\mathtt{y}, \mathtt{args}) \quad \mathtt{m}^t_- \in pt(\mathtt{m}) \quad m' \in MTD(\mathtt{m}^t_-) \quad o_i^- \in pt(\mathtt{args}) \quad o_j^{t'} \in pt(o_i^-.arr) \quad t'' \text{ is declaring type of } m'_{pk} \quad k \in [1,n] \quad t' <: t''}{\{o_j^{t'}\} \subseteq pt(\mathtt{arg}_k) \quad \mathtt{x} = \mathtt{y}.m'(\mathtt{arg}_1, ..., \mathtt{arg}_n)} \text{[T-Inv]}$$

Fig. 8. Rules for *Transformation.*

$$\frac{i : \mathtt{v} = \mathtt{c}'.newInstance() \quad \mathtt{c}^t \in pt(\mathtt{c}')}{\{o_i^t\} \subseteq pt(\mathtt{v})} \text{[L-KwTp]} \qquad \frac{i : \mathtt{v} = \mathtt{c}'.newInstance() \quad \mathtt{c}^u \in pt(\mathtt{c}')}{\{o_i^u\} \subseteq pt(\mathtt{v})} \text{[L-UkwTp]}$$

$$\frac{\mathsf{A}\ a = (\mathsf{A})\,\mathtt{x} \quad o_i^u \in pt(\mathtt{x}) \quad t <: \mathsf{A}}{\{o_i^t\} \subseteq pt(a)} \text{[L-Cast]} \qquad \frac{\mathtt{x} = \mathtt{m}.invoke(\mathtt{y}, ...) \quad o_i^u \in pt(\mathtt{y}) \quad \mathtt{m}^t_- \in pt(\mathtt{m}) \quad t' \ll: t}{\{o_i^{t'}\} \subseteq pt(\mathtt{y})} \text{[L-Inv]}$$

Fig. 9. Rules for *Lazy Heap Modeling.*

the declaring type of m'_{pk} is t''. We include $o_j^{t'}$ to $pt(\mathtt{arg}_k)$ only when $t' <: t''$ holds in order to filter out the objects that cannot be assigned to m'_{pk}. Finally, the regular call obtained can be analyzed by [A-Call] in Fig. 5.

3.4.6 Lazy Heap Modeling. Figure 9 gives the rules for resolving `newInstance()` lazily. In [L-KwTp], for each `Class` object $\mathtt{c}^t$ pointed to by $\mathtt{c}'$, an object, o_i^t, is created as an instance of this known type at allocation site i straightaway. In [L-UkwTp], as illustrated with Fig. 1, o_i^u is created to enable LHM if $\mathtt{c}'$ points to a $\mathtt{c}^u$ instead. Then its lazy object creation happens at a type cast by applying [L-Cast] (with o_i^u blocked from flowing from `x` to `a`) and an `invoke()` call site by applying [L-Inv]. Note that `A` is assumed not to be `Object` in [L-Cast].

3.5 Soundness Criterion

RefJava consists of the four methods from the Java reflection API as shown in Fig. 1. Solar is sound if their calls are resolved soundly under Assumptions 1 – 4. By construction, calls to `Class.forName()` and `getMethod()` are always soundly resolved (with the metaobjects created being modelled appropriately). Due to Assumption 4, there is no need to consider `newInstance()` calls since they are soundly resolved if all `invoke()` calls are. For convenience, we define:

$$AllKwn(v) = \nexists\, o_i^u \in pt(v) \tag{2}$$

which means that the dynamic type of every object pointed to by v is known.

Consider Fig. 7. For the `Method` metaobjects $\mathtt{m}_s^t$ with known classes t, these targets can be soundly resolved by *Target Search*, except that the signatures s can be further refined by applying [I-InvSig]. For the `Method` objects $\mathtt{m}_s^u$ with unknown class types u, the targets accessed are inferred by [I-InvTp] and [I-InvS2T]. Let us consider a call to `(A) m.invoke(y, args)`. Solar attempts to infer the missing classes of its `Method` metaobjects in two ways, by applying [I-InvTp] and [I-InvS2T]. Such a call is soundly resolved if the following condition holds:

$$SC(\mathtt{m.invoke(y,args)}) = AllKwn(\mathtt{y}) \lor \ \forall\, \mathtt{m}_s^u \in pt(\mathtt{m}) : s.n_m \neq u \land Ptp(\mathtt{args}) \neq \varnothing \tag{3}$$

If the first disjunct holds, applying [I-InvTp] to `invoke()` can over-approximate its target methods from the types of all objects pointed to by `y`. Thus, every `Method` metaobject $\mathtt{m}^u_- \in pt(m)$ is refined into a new one $\mathtt{m}^t_-$ for every $o^t_i \in pt(\mathtt{y})$.

If the second disjunct holds, then [I-InvS2T] comes into play. Its targets are over-approximated based on the known method names $s.n_m$ and the types of the objects pointed to by `args`. Thus, every `Method` metaobject $\mathtt{m}^u_s \in pt(m)$ is refined into a new one $\mathtt{m}^t_s$, where $s.t_r \ll: A$ and $s.p \in Ptp(\mathtt{args}) \neq \varnothing$. Note that $s.t_r$ is leveraged only when it is not u. The post-dominating cast `(A)` is considered not to exist if `A = Object`. In this case, $u \ll:$ `Object` holds (only for u).

Theorem 1. Solar is sound for RefJava if $SC(c)$ holds at every reflective call c of the form "`(A) m.invoke(y, args)`" under Assumptions 1 – 4.

3.6 Identifying *Unsoundly* Resolved Reflective Calls

Solar flags a call c to `invoke()` as resolved unsoundly if $SC(c)$ is false. This can be conservative as some points-to information at c can be over-approximate. However, our evaluation shows that Solar can analyze 7 out of the 10 large programs considered scalably with full automation, implying that its inference system is powerful and precise. In addition, all 13 unsound calls reported by Solar in the remaining three programs are truly unsound, as discussed in Sect. 4.4, validating Solar's effectiveness in identifying unsoundness.

3.7 Identifying *Imprecisely* Resolved Reflective Calls

Presently, Solar performs this task depicted in Fig. 2, by simply ranking the reflective call sites according to the number of reflective targets inferred. This simple metric often gives a good indication about the sources of imprecision.

3.8 Probe

For evaluation purposes, we instantiate Probe, as shown in Fig. 2, from Solar as follows. We refrain from performing Solar's LHM (by retaining [L-UkwTp] but ignoring [L-Cast] and [L-Inv]) and abandon some of Solar's sophisticated inference rules (by disabling [I-InvS2T]). In *Target Search*, Probe will restrict itself to only `Method` metaobjects $\mathtt{m}^t_s$, where the signature s is at least partially known.

3.9 Static Class Members

To handle static class members, our rules can be modified. In Fig. 7, `y = null`. [I-InvTp] is not needed (by assuming $pt(\mathtt{null}) = \varnothing$). In (3), the first disjunct is removed. [I-InvS2T] is modified with $o^u_i \in pt(\mathtt{y})$ replaced by $\mathtt{y} = \mathtt{null}$. The rules in Fig. 8 are modified to deal with static members. In Fig. 9, [L-Inv] is no longer relevant. The static initializers for the classes in the closed world are analyzed. This can happen at, say, loads/stores for static fields as is the standard but also when some classes are discovered in [P-ForName], [L-Cast] and [L-Inv].

4 Evaluation

We have implemented SOLAR on top of DOOP [18], a modern pointer analysis tool for Java. We compare SOLAR with two state-of-the-art under-approximate reflection analyses, ELF [21] and the reflection analysis provided in DOOP (also referred to as DOOP). In some programs, Assumptions 1 – 4 may not hold. Thus, SOLAR is also treated as being under-approximate. Due to its soundness-guided design, however, SOLAR can yield significantly better under-approximations than DOOP and ELF. Like DOOP and ELF, SOLAR is also implemented in the Datalog language. As far as we know, SOLAR is more comprehensive in handling the Java reflection API than the prior reflection analyses [2,5,17,18,20,21].

In particular, our evaluation addresses the following research questions (RQs):

- **RQ1.** How well does SOLAR achieve full automation without using PROBE?
- **RQ2.** How does SOLAR identify automatically "problematic" reflective calls affecting its soundness, precision and scalability, thereby facilitating their improvement by means of some lightweight annotations?
- **RQ3.** How significantly does SOLAR improve recall compared to DOOP [18] and ELF [21], while maintaining nearly the same precision?
- **RQ4.** How does SOLAR scale in analysing large reflection-rich applications?

4.1 Experimental Setup

The three reflection analyses are compared by running each together with the same DOOP pointer analysis framework (using its stable version r160113) [18]. For the DOOP framework, we did not use its beta release (r5459247). The beta release handles a larger part of the Java reflection API but discovers fewer reflective targets in our recall experiment, since it ignores reflective targets whose class types are in the libraries (for efficiency reasons). All the three reflection analyses operate on the SSA form of a program emitted by SOOT [19], context-sensitively under selective-2-type-sensitive+heap provided by DOOP.

We use the LogicBlox Datalog engine (v3.9.0) on a Xeon E5-2650 2 GHz machine with 64 GB of RAM. We consider 7 large DaCapo benchmarks (2006-10-MR2) and 4 real-world applications, `avrora`-1.7.115 (a simulator), `checkstyle`-4.4 (a checker), `freecs`-1.3.20111225 (a server) and `findbugs`-1.2.1 (a bug detector), under a large reflection-rich Java library, `JDK 1.6.0_45`.

4.2 Assumptions

When analysing real code under-approximately, we accommodate Assumptions 1 – 4 as follows. For Assumption 1, we rely on DOOP's pointer analysis to simulate the behaviors of Java native methods. Dynamic class loading is assumed to be resolved separately [25]. To simulate its effect, we create a closed world for a program, by locating the classes referenced with DOOP's fact generator and adding additional ones found through program runs under TAMIFLEX [22].

For the DaCapo benchmarks, `avrora` and `checkstyle`, their associated inputs are used. For `findbugs`, one Java program is developed as its input. For `freecs`, a server requiring user interactions, we only initialize it as the input in order to ensure repeatability. Assumptions 2 and 3 are taken for granted.

As for Assumption 4, we validate it for all reflective allocation sites where o_i^u is created in the application code of the 10 programs that can be analyzed scalably. This assumption is found to hold at 75 % of these sites automatically by performing a simple intraprocedural analysis. We have inspected the remaining 25 % interprocedurally and found only two violating sites (in `eclipse` and `checkstyle`), where o_i^u is never used. In the other sites inspected, o_i^u flows through only local variables with all the call-chain lengths being at most 2.

4.3 RQ1: Full Automation

Figure 10 compares SOLAR and existing reflection analyses [5,17,18, 20–22] denoted by "Others" by the degree of automation achieved. For an analysis, this is measured by the number of annotations required in order to improve the soundness of the reflective calls identified to be potentially unsoundly resolved.

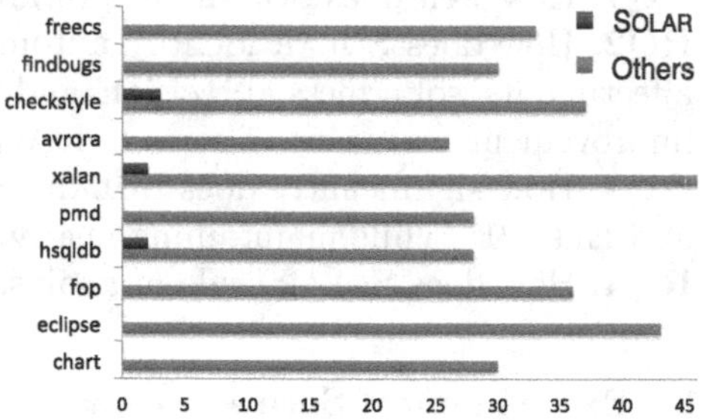

Fig. 10. The number of annotations required for improving the soundness of unsoundly resolved reflective calls.

SOLAR analyzes 7 out of the 11 programs scalably with full automation. For `hsqldb`, `xalan` and `checkstyle`, SOLAR is unscalable (under 3 hours). With PROBE, 13 reflective calls are flagged as being potentially unsoundly resolved. After 7 annotations, 2 in `hsqldb`, 2 in `xalan` and 3 in `checkstyle`, SOLAR is scalable, as discussed in Sect. 4.4. However, SOLAR, like DOOP and ELF, is unscalable (under 3 hours) for `jython`, an interpreter for Python in which the Java libraries and application code are invoked reflectively from the Python code.

"Others" cannot identify which reflective calls may be unsoundly resolved. However, they may improve soundness by requiring users to annotate the string arguments of calls to, e.g., `Class.forName()` and `getMethod()`, as suggested in [20]. As shown in Fig. 10, "Others" will require 338 annotations initially and possibly more in the subsequent iterations (when more code is discovered). As discussed in Sect. 2.3, SOLAR's annotation approach is also iterative. However, for these programs, SOLAR requires only 7 annotations in one iteration.

SOLAR outperforms "Others" due to its powerful inference system for performing reflection resolution and effective mechanism in identifying unsoundness.

4.4 RQ2: Automatically Identifying "Problematic" Reflective Calls

SOLAR is unscalable for `hsqldb`, `xalan` and `checkstyle` (under 3 hours). PROBE is then run to identify their "problematic" reflective calls, reporting 13 potentially unsound calls: 1 in `hsqldb`, 12 in `xalan` and 0 in `checkstyle`. Their handling is all unsound by code inspection, highlighting the effectiveness of SOLAR in pinpointing a small number of right parts of the program to improve unsoundness.

In addition, we presently adopt a simple approach to alerting users for potentially imprecisely resolved reflective calls. PROBE sorts all the `newInstance()` call sites according to the number of objects lazily created at the cast operations operating on the result of a `newInstance()` call (by [L-CAST]) in non-increasing order. In addition, PROBE ranks the remaining reflective call sites according to the number of reflective targets resolved, also in non-increasing order.

By focusing on unsoundly and imprecisely resolved reflective calls (as opposed to input strings), only lightweight annotations are needed as shown in Fig. 10, with 2 in `hsqldb`, 2 in `xalan` and 3 in `checkstyle`, as explained below. For the concepts of entry, member-introspecting and side-effect methods mentioned in Figs. 11 and 12, we refer to [21].

4.4.1 `hsqldb`. Figure 11 shows the unsound and imprecise lists automatically generated by PROBE, together with the suggested annotation points (found by tracing value flow). All the call sites to the same method are numbered from 0.

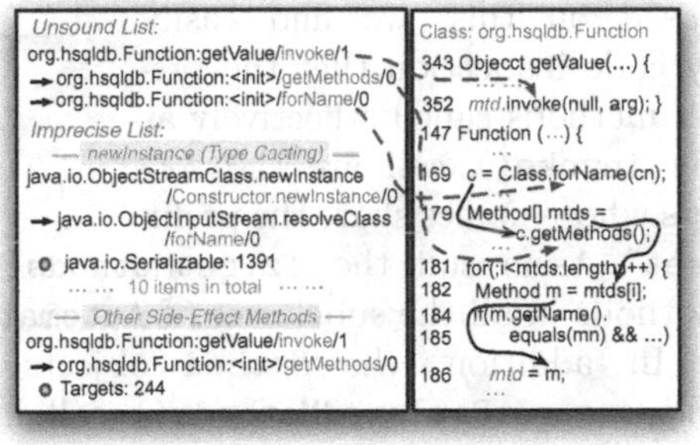

Fig. 11. Probing `hsqldb`.

The unsound list contains one `invoke()`, with its relevant code contained in class `org.hsqldb.Function` as shown. After PROBE has finished, `mtd` in line 352 points to a `Method` metaobject m_u^u that is initially created in line 179 and later flows into line 182, indicating that the class type of m_u^u is unknown since `cn` in line 169 is unknown. By inspecting the code, we find that `cn` can only be `java.lang.Math` or `org.hsqldb.Library`, read from some hash maps or obtained by string manipulations. So it has been annotated this way afterwards. The imprecise list for `hsqldb` is divided into two sections. In "newInstance (Type Casting)", there are 10 listed cast operations (T) reached by an o_i^u object such that the number of types inferred from T is larger than 10. The top cast `java.io.Serializable` has 1391 subtypes and is marked to be reached by a `newInstance()` call site in `java.io.ObjectStreamClass`. However, this is a false positive for the harness used due to imprecision in pointer analysis. Thus, we have annotated its corresponding `forName()` call site in method `resolveClass` of class `java.io.ObjectInputStream` to return nothing. With the two annotations, SOLAR terminates in 45 min with its unsound list being empty.

4.4.2 `xalan`. Probe reports 12 unsoundly resolved `invoke()` calls. All `Method` objects flowing into these call sites are created at two `getMethods()` call sites in class `extensions.MethodResolver`. By inspecting the code, we find that the string arguments for the two `getMethods()` calls and their corresponding entry methods are all read from a file with its name hard-wired as `xmlspec.xsl` in this benchmark. For this particular input file provided by DaCapo, these two calls are never executed and thus annotated to be disregarded. With these two annotations, Solar terminates in 28 min with its unsound list being empty.

4.4.3 `checkstyle`. Probe reports no unsoundly resolved call. To see why Solar is unscalable, we examine one `invoke()` call in line 1773 of Fig. 12 found automatically by Probe that stands out as being possibly imprecisely resolved.

There are 962 target methods inferred at this call site. Probe highlights its corresponding member-introspecting method `clz.getMethods()` (in line 1294) and its entry methods (with one of these being shown in line 926). Based on this, we find easily by code inspection that the target methods called reflectively at the `invoke()` call are the setters whose names share the prefix "`set`". As a result, the `clz.getMethods()` call is annotated to return 158 "`setX`" methods in all the subclasses of `AutomaticBean`.

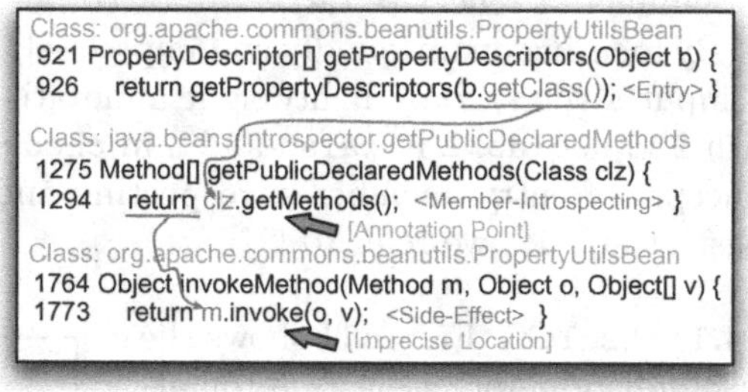

Fig. 12. Probing `checkstyle`.

In addition, the `Method` objects created at one `getMethods()` call and one `getDeclaredMethods()` call in class `*.beanutils.MappedProperty Descriptor$1` flow into the `invoke()` call in line 1773 as false positives due to imprecision in the pointer analysis. These `Method` objects have been annotated away.

After the three annotations, Solar is scalable, terminating in 38 minutes.

Given the same annotations, existing reflection analyses [5,17,20,21] still cannot handle the `invoke()` call in line 1773 soundly, because its argument `o` points to the objects that are initially created at a `newInstance()` call and then flow into a non-post-dominating cast operation (like the one in line 12 Fig. 1). However, Solar has handled this `invoke()` call soundly by using LHM, highlighting once again the importance of collective inference in reflection analysis.

4.5 RQ3: Recall and Precision

To compare the effectiveness of Doop, Elf and Solar as under-approximate reflection analyses, it is the most relevant to compare their *recall*, measured by the number of true reflective targets discovered at reflective call sites that are dynamically executed under certain inputs. In addition, we also compare their (static) analysis precision with two clients, but the results must be looked at with one caveat. Existing reflection analyses can happen to be "precise" due to their highly under-approximated handling of reflection. Therefore, our precision results are presented to show that SOLAR exhibits nearly the same precision as prior work despite its significantly improved recall achieved for real code.

Unlike DOOP and ELF, SOLAR can automatically identify "problematic" reflective calls for lightweight annotations. To ensure a fair comparison, the three annotated programs shown in Fig. 10 are used by all the three analyses.

4.5.1 Recall. We use TAMIFLEX [22] to find the targets accessed at reflective calls in our programs under the inputs described in Sect. 4.2. SOLAR is the only one to achieve total recall for all reflective targets accessed.

Here, we demonstrate one significant benefit of achieving higher recall, in practice. Figure 13 compares DOOP, ELF and SOLAR in terms of true caller-callee relations statically calculated and obtained by an instrumental tool written in terms of JAVASSIST [26]. SOLAR recalls a total of 371 % (148 %) more targets than DOOP (ELF) at the calls to `newInstance()` and `invoke()`, translating into 49700 (40570) more true caller-callee relations found for the 10 programs. These numbers are expected to improve when more inputs are used. Note that all targets recalled by DOOP are recalled by ELF and all targets recalled by ELF are recalled by SOLAR. These results demonstrate the effectiveness of our LHM and collective inference.

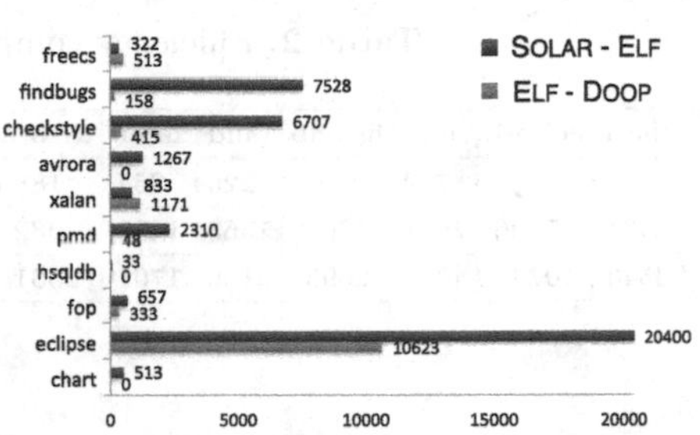

Fig. 13. More true caller-callee relations found in recall by SOLAR than ELF (SOLAR – ELF) and by ELF than DOOP (ELF – DOOP).

4.5.2 Precision. Table 1 compares the precision of DOOP, ELF and SOLAR with two popular clients. Note that DOOP is unscalable for `chart` and `hsqldb` (under 3 hours) in our setting. Despite achieving better recall (Fig. 13), SOLAR maintains nearly the same precision as DOOP and ELF, which tend to be more

Table 1. Precision comparison. There are two clients: DevirCall denotes the percentage of the virtual calls whose targets can be disambiguated and SafeCast denotes the percentage of the casts that can be statically shown to be safe.

		chart	eclipse	fop	hsqldb	pmd	xalan	avrora	checkstyle	findbugs	freecs	**Average**
Devir	DOOP	–	94.94	93.04	–	92.65	93.49	94.79	93.16	92.32	95.46	93.72
Call	ELF	93.53	88.07	92.34	94.80	92.87	92.70	94.50	93.19	92.53	94.94	92.93
(%)	SOLAR	93.51	87.69	92.26	94.51	92.39	92.65	92.43	93.39	92.37	95.26	92.63
Safe	DOOP	–	59.34	53.68	–	45.40	57.97	56.12	50.19	45.78	59.71	53.24
Cast	ELF	49.80	40.71	55.40	53.65	48.24	59.24	57.27	51.79	48.54	59.14	52.07
(%)	SOLAR	49.53	38.04	54.21	53.11	44.53	59.11	52.56	49.40	43.60	57.96	49.79

under-approximate than SOLAR. This suggests that SOLAR's soundness-guided design is effective in balancing soundness, precision and scalability.

4.6 RQ4: Efficiency

Table 2 compares the analysis times of DOOP, ELF and SOLAR. Despite producing significantly better under-approximations than DOOP and ELF, SOLAR is only several-fold slower. When analysing `hsqldb`, `xalan` and `checkstyle`, SOLAR requires some lightweight annotations. Their analysis times are the ones consumed by SOLAR on analysing the annotated programs. Note that these annotated programs are also used by DOOP and ELF (as discussed earlier).

Table 2. Efficiency comparison (secs).

	chart	eclipse	fop	hsqldb	pmd	xalan	avrora	checkstyle	findbugs	freecs	**Average**
DOOP	–	321	779	–	226	254	188	256	718	422	–
ELF	3434	5496	2821	1765	1363	1432	932	1463	2281	1259	1930
SOLAR	4543	10743	4303	2695	2156	1701	3551	2256	8489	2880	3638

5 Related Work

In addition to the prior work already discussed in Sect. 2.2, we highlight below a few open-source static reflection analysis tools available. BDDBDDB [2] represents a partial implementation of the reflection analysis introduced in [20].

DOOP [5,18] is a pointer analysis framework for Java programs written in Datalog. Its reflection handling was similar to the reflection analysis in [20] except that it is done context-sensitively. DOOP can now accept the analysis results of TAMIFLEX [22] on a program while analyzing the placeholder library generated by Averroes [27], which presently models only `newInstance()` and `invoke()`.

ELF [21] represents a recent reflection analysis, implemented in DOOP, for Java, by leveraging a so-called self-inferencing property inherent in a program. However, ELF opts to trade soundness for precision by inferring a target at a reflective call if and only if both its signature and declaring class can be inferred. Building on this, SOLAR advocates collective inference to improve and even achieve soundness under Assumptions 1 – 4, facilitated by lazy heap modeling for reflective object creation. SOLAR benefits greatly from the open-source code of ELF and DOOP. However, to the best of our knowledge, SOLAR is the most comprehensive analysis in handling the Java reflection API.

Wala [17] provides static analysis capabilities for Java and other languages like JavaScript. Its reflection handling is similar to [20] (by resolving values of string arguments of reflective calls) but does not handle `Field`-related methods.

6 Conclusion

Achieving soundness in reflection analysis can improve the effectiveness of many clients such as program verifiers, compilers, bug detectors and security analyzers. However, reflection is very challenging to analyze effectively, particularly for reflection-heavy applications. In this paper, we make one significant step forward by introducing a new reflection analysis that can reason about its soundness when certain assumptions are met and produce significantly improved under-approximations than prior art otherwise. We hope that our framework (www.cse.unsw.edu.au/~corg/solar) will be useful in future research.

Acknowledgements. The authors wish to thank the POPL 2015 and SAS 2015 reviewers for their comments, the Doop team for making Doop available, and LogicBlox Inc. for providing us its Datalog engine. This work is supported by ARC grants, DP130101970 and DP150102109.

References

1. Lhoták, O., Hendren, L.: Scaling java points-to analysis using SPARK. In: Hedin, G. (ed.) CC 2003. LNCS, vol. 2622, pp. 153–169. Springer, Heidelberg (2003)
2. Whaley, J., Lam, M.S.: Cloning-based context-sensitive pointer alias analysis using binary decision diagrams. PLDI **39**(6), 131–144 (2004)
3. Milanova, A., Rountev, A., Ryder, B.G.: Parameterized object sensitivity for points-to analysis for Java. ACM Trans. Softw. Eng. Methodol. **14**(1), 1–41 (2005)
4. Sridharan, M., Bodík, R.: Refinement-based context-sensitive points-to analysis for Java. PLDI **41**(6), 387–400 (2006)
5. Bravenboer, M., Smaragdakis, Y.: Strictly declarative specification of sophisticated points-to analyses. OOPSLA **44**(10), 243–262 (2009)
6. Shang, L., Xie, X., Xue, J.: On-demand dynamic summary-based points-to analysis. In: CGO (2012)
7. Lu, Y., Shang, L., Xie, X., Xue, J.: An incremental points-to analysis with CFL-reachability. In: Jhala, R., De Bosschere, K. (eds.) CC 2013. LNCS, vol. 7791, pp. 61–81. Springer, Heidelberg (2013)
8. Smaragdakis, Y., Bravenboer, M., Lhoták, O.: Pick your contexts well: understanding object-sensitivity. POPL **46**(1), 17–30 (2011)
9. Kastrinis, G., Smaragdakis, Y.: Hybrid context-sensitivity for points-to analysis. PLDI **48**(6), 423–434 (2013)
10. Smaragdakis, Y., Kastrinis, G., Balatsouras, G.: Introspective analysis: context-sensitivity, across the board. PLDI **49**(6), 485–495 (2014)
11. Hirzel, M., Dincklage, D.V., Diwan, A., Hind, M.: Fast online pointer analysis. ACM Trans. Program. Lang. Syst. **29**(2) (2007)
12. Sridharan, M., Artzi, S., Pistoia, M., Guarnieri, S., Tripp, O., Berg, R.: F4F: taint analysis of framework-based web applications. OOPSLA **46**(10), 1053–1068 (2011)
13. Zhang, X., Mangal, R., Grigore, R., Naik, M., Yang, H.: On abstraction refinement for program analyses in datalog. PLDI **49**(6), 239–248 (2014)
14. Arzt, S., Rasthofer, S., Fritz, C., Bodden, E., Bartel, A., Klein, J., Le Traon, Y., Octeau, D., McDaniel, P.: Flowdroid: precise context, flow, field, object-sensitive and lifecycle-aware taint analysis for android apps. PLDI **49**(6), 259–269 (2014)

15. Nguyen, P.H., Xue, J.: Interprocedural side-effect analysis and optimisation in the presence of dynamic class loading. In: ACSC (2005)
16. Xue, J., Nguyen, P.H.: Completeness analysis for incomplete object-oriented programs. In: Bodik, R. (ed.) CC 2005. LNCS, vol. 3443, pp. 271–286. Springer, Heidelberg (2005)
17. WALA.: T.J. Watson libraries for analysis. http://wala.sf.net
18. DOOP. http://doop.program-analysis.org
19. Vallée-Rai, R., Co, P., Gagnon, E., Hendren, L., Lam, P., Sundaresan, V.: Soot - a Java bytecode optimization framework. In: CASCON (1999)
20. Livshits, B., Whaley, J., Lam, M.S.: Reflection analysis for Java. In: Yi, K. (ed.) APLAS 2005. LNCS, vol. 3780, pp. 139–160. Springer, Heidelberg (2005)
21. Li, Y., Tan, T., Sui, Y., Xue, J.: Self-inferencing reflection resolution for Java. In: Jones, R. (ed.) ECOOP 2014. LNCS, vol. 8586, pp. 27–53. Springer, Heidelberg (2014)
22. Bodden, E., Sewe, A., Sinschek, J., Oueslati, H., Mezini, M.: Taming reflection: aiding static analysis in the presence of reflection and custom class loaders. In: ICSE (2011)
23. Livshits, B., Sridharan, M., Smaragdakis, Y., Lhotk, O., Amaral, J.N., Chang, B.-Y.E., Guyer, S.Z., Khedker, U.P., Mller, A., Vardoulakis, D.: In defense of soundiness: a manifesto. Commun. ACM **58**(2), 44–46 (2015)
24. Sridharan, M., Chandra, S., Dolby, J., Fink, S.J., Yahav, E.: Alias analysis for object-oriented programs. In: Clarke, D., Noble, J., Wrigstad, T. (eds.) Aliasing in Object-Oriented Programming. LNCS, vol. 7850, pp. 196–232. Springer, Heidelberg (2013)
25. Sawin, J., Rountev, A.: Improving static resolution of dynamic class loading in java using dynamically gathered environment information. Autom. Softw. Eng. **16**(2), 357–381 (2009)
26. Javassist.: A Java bytecode manipulation framework. http://www.javassist.org
27. Ali, K., Lhoták, O.: Averroes: whole-program analysis without the whole program. In: Castagna, G. (ed.) ECOOP 2013. LNCS, vol. 7920, pp. 378–400. Springer, Heidelberg (2013)

SJS: A Type System for JavaScript with Fixed Object Layout

Wontae Choi[1(✉)], Satish Chandra[2], George Necula[1], and Koushik Sen[1]

[1] University of California, Berkeley, USA
{wtchoi,necula,ksen}@cs.berkeley.edu
[2] Samsung Research America, Mountain View, USA
schandra@acm.org

Abstract. We propose a static type system for a significant subset of JavaScript, dubbed SJS, with the goal of ensuring that objects have a statically known layout at the allocation time, which in turn can enable an ahead-of-time (AOT) compiler to generate efficient code.The main technical challenge we address is to ensure fixed object layout, while supporting popular language features such as objects with prototype inheritance, structural subtyping, and method updates, with the additional constraint that SJS programs can run on any available standard JavaScript engine, with no deviation from JavaScript's standard operational semantics. The core difficulty arises from the way standard JavaScript semantics implements object attribute update with prototype-based inheritance. To our knowledge, combining a fixed object layout property with prototype inheritance and subtyping has not been achieved previously.

1 Introduction

JavaScript is the most popular programming language for writing client-side web applications. Over the last decade it has become the programming language for the web, and it has been used to write large-scale complex web applications including Gmail, Google docs, Facebook.com, Cloud9 IDE. The popularity of JavaScript is due in part to the fact that JavaScript can run on any platform that supports a modern web browser, and that applications written in JavaScript do not require to go through an installation process.

Given the breadth of applications written nowadays in JavaScript, significant effort has been put into improving JavaScript execution performance. Modern JavaScript engines implement just-in-time (JIT) compilation techniques combined with inline caching, which rely, among other things, on the fact that the layouts of most JavaScript objects do not change often. These optimization heuristics are ineffective when new fields and method are added to an object [16].

A promising alternative to JIT optimization is to use an ahead-of-time (AOT) compiler backed by a static type system. `asm.js` [2] pioneered this direction in the domain of JavaScript. `asm.js` is a statically-typed albeit low-level subset of JavaScript designed to be used as a compiler target, not by a human programmer. One of the lessons learned from `asm.js` is that a promising strategy for

S. Blazy and T. Jensen (Eds.): SAS 2015, LNCS 9291, pp. 181–198, 2015.
DOI: 10.1007/978-3-662-48288-9_11

improving JavaScript is to design a *subset* of JavaScript that has strong type-safety guarantees, so that it can be compiled into efficient code if a compiler is available, and yet, in the absence of a compiler, can also be run *with the same semantics* on any standard JavaScript engine.

Recently, we started to design a new subset of JavaScript [12], dubbed SJS, that can be compiled efficiently by AOT compilers. Unlike `asm.js`, our design includes popular high-level features of JavaScript, such as objects with prototype-based inheritance, structural subtyping, closures, and functions as first-class objects. Like `asm.js`, an important goal is to enable an AOT compiler to translate attribute accesses into direct memory accesses, which requires that objects have statically known layouts.

The first major technical challenge that we face is how to ensure fixed object layout, in the presence of a rich set of high-level language features, while also retaining the operational semantics as given by standard JavaScript engines. The challenge is due in large part to the way standard JavaScript semantics implements object attribute update. JavaScript allows writing to attributes that are unknown at object creation; a new attribute can be inserted into an object simply by writing to it, thereby altering the object's layout. Even if we addressed this issue, e.g. by having a type system disallow writes to unknown attributes, the problem does not go away, due to JavaScript's treatment of prototype inheritance. For read operations, an attribute that cannot be found in the object itself is looked-up recursively in the object's prototype chain. However, when updating an attribute, a new attribute is created in the inheritor object itself, even if the attribute is present in the prototype chain. Essentially, attribute updates do not follow the prototype chain. *This can lead to objects changing their layout even for programs that update attributes that seemingly are already available for reading.* We elaborate in Sect. 2 how this particular semantics interacts with high-level features such as structural subtyping and method updates.

Contributions. In this paper, we propose the underlying type system of SJS, with the following main contributions:

- The type system of SJS supports many attractive and convenient high-level features, such as prototype-based inheritance, closures, structural subtyping, and functions as first-class objects, and ensures that all objects have a statically known attribute layout once initialized. This makes SJS a good candidate for AOT compilation and optimization. As far as we know, this is the first type system ensuring fixed object layout for JavaScript programs with this combination of features.
- The type system of SJS is described as a composition of a standard base type system for records, along with *qualifiers* on object types designed to ensure the fixed object layout. This presentation of the type system highlights the design of the type qualifiers for fixed object layout, which is a novel contribution of this type system.

In this paper we focus on the design of the type system and the type checking algorithm. The paper also includes a brief summary of implementation and evaluation results. We refer to the companion technical report [12] for the other interesting aspects of the SJS language, such as type inference, typing declarations, type-directed compilation. The full details of the preliminary performance evaluation results and how the top-level language (SJS) integrates the proposed type system into JavaScript are also available in the technical report.

Comparison with Related Designs. A number of efforts are underway to design statically-typed languages for the web where programs could be type-checked statically and maintained easily. TypeScript [4,21] is a typed *super*set of JavaScript designed to simplify development and maintenance. Unlike SJS's type system, TypeScript's type system does not guarantee the fixed object layout property. Therefore, TypeScript programs cannot be compiled into efficient code ahead of time in the way SJS programs can.

As mentioned earlier, `asm.js` [2] is a statically-typed subset of JavaScript aimed at AOT compilation. If a program is written in `asm.js`, it can run efficiently in the Firefox browser with performance comparable with equivalent C programs. A key advantage of `asm.js`, is that being a strict subset of JavaScript, it can run on *any* JavaScript engine, even if the enginc is not tuned for `asm.js`, albeit at a regular JavaScript speed. However, since `asm.js` only supports primitive types and operations, the language is not suitable for regular object-oriented programming. SJS intends to offer the same kind of performance advantage, while mostly retaining the expressivity of JavaScript.

RPython [6] is a typed subset of Python designed for AOT compilation to efficient low-level code. Like SJS, RPython fixes object layouts statically in order to enable optimization. However, RPython's type system does not face the same challenges that we address in SJS, because Python does not use prototype-based inheritance. For a language not using a delegation-based prototype inheritance, a traditional notion of object type is sufficient to ensure the fixed object layout property.

2 Design Rationale for the SJS Type System

To illustrate the issues with dynamic object layout in JavaScript as well as our proposed type system, we consider the example program shown in Fig. 1.

```
1: var o1 = { a : 1, f : function (x) { this.a = 2 } }
2: var o2 = { b : 1, __proto__ : o1 }
3: o1.a = 3          //OK
4: o2.a = 2          //BAD
5: o2.f()            //BAD
```

Fig. 1. Example JavaScript program to demonstrate dynamic object layout.

In this example, in line 1 we create an object `o1` with a field `a` and a method `f`. In line 2 we create another object with a field `b` and with the prototype `o1`[1].

[1] Good programming practices of JavaScript discourage the use of non-standard `__proto__` field; however, we use this field to keep our examples concise.

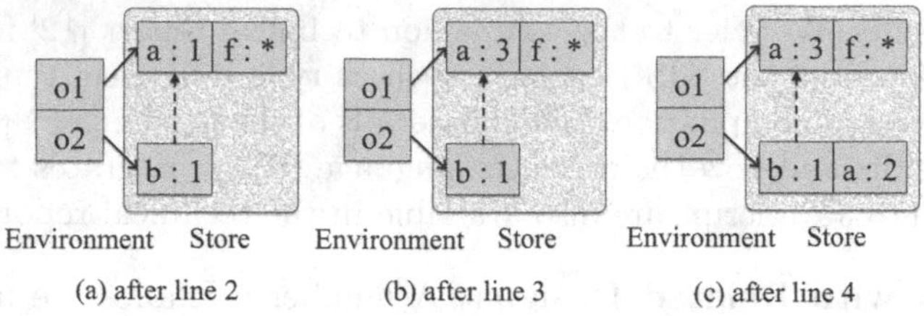

Fig. 2. Program state diagrams for Fig. 1. The dotted line is the prototype reference. The asterisk (*) is a function value

According to JavaScript semantics, the object `o2` will include a reference to the prototype object `o1`, as shown in Fig. 2(a). The value of `o2.a` in this state would be 1, which is found by searching for the nearest definition of the field `a` in the prototype chain for `o2`. Furthermore, since the value of the field `a` is aliased between `o1` and `o2`, the update to `o1.a` from line 3 results in the state shown in Fig. 2(b), and is immediately visible to `o2.a`.

The interesting behavior in this program is in line 4. According to JavaScript semantics, when an inherited field is updated in an object, the field is added to the object itself, and the update happens in the newly added field, resulting in the state shown in Fig. 2(c).

Note that the same effect of object changing its layout would happen at line 5 with the method call `o2.f()`. This method call would first resolve the method `o2.f` to the method `f` inherited from the prototype `o1`, and would then invoke the method with the implicit parameter `this` set to `o2`. We say that `o2` is the *receiver* object for this method invocation.

This example illustrates that in general we cannot assign fixed offsets relative to the location of the object in memory where to find attributes (e.g. `o2.a` refers to different locations at different times.) This poses challenges to efficient execution of JavaScript. A naive implementation would use potentially multiple memory accesses to retrieve the intended attribute value. Modern JavaScript JIT-compilers attempt to optimize attribute lookup computation by caching lookup computation for frequently appearing object layouts at each object operation.[2] Without statically known offset, an AOT compiler would have to either generate inefficient code for attribute lookup, or encode a JIT-compiler-like strategy at runtime.

2.1 Type System for Enforcing Static Object Layout

We propose a type system for a subset of JavaScript to ensure that well-typed programs have the following properties (hereon, we use the term *attribute* to refer to either a field or a method. In standard JavaScript, the term *property* is used instead of the term attribute.):

[2] This representation is called hidden class representation and the caching technique is called inline caching [11]. As noted before, this optimization can fail to apply under certain conditions [16].

- **Prop. 1.** All accesses must be to attributes that have been previously defined (in self or in a prototype.)
- **Prop. 2.** The layout of objects does not change after allocation, both in terms of the set of attributes, and in terms of their types.
- **Prop. 3.** Allow prototype inheritance as a language feature, as implemented in standard JavaScript runtime systems.
- **Prop. 4.** Allow subtyping in assignments, so a subtype instance can be used in contexts in which a base type instance can be used.

In addition, primitive operations do not result in runtime type errors. We believe that these properties are important for program maintainability, as well as for performance on modern JavaScript runtimes. At the same time we believe that it is important to enforce these properties without changes to JavaScript interpreters and just-in-time compilers, so we designed SJS as a subset of JavaScript that preserves standard behavior.

The safety of accessing an attribute (**Prop. 1**) can be enforced with standard static typing techniques that assign fixed static types to variables and attributes. The type of an object must mention the attributes inherited from the prototype chain to allow access to them. However, such a type system would be too forgiving: it would accept the program shown in Fig. 1, violating the fixed layout requirement (**Prop. 2**).

To support fixed layout (**Prop. 2**) and prototype inheritance (**Prop. 3**), while using the standard JavaScript execution model, we need to ensure that: *for any field update statement,* `e1.a = ...`, *the object denoted by* `e1` *must define the field* `a`. We say that an object *owns* the attributes that are defined in the object itself, as opposed to those that are inherited from a prototype. To enforce this property, the types of objects will include the list of attributes guaranteed to be owned by the object, in addition to the list of all attributes guaranteed to be accessible in the object.

Returning to the example from Fig. 1, the type of `o1` will mention that the field `a` and `f` are owned, while the type of `o2` will mention only `b` as owned. Based on these types, the assignment `o2.a = 2` from line 4 will be ill-typed, as we intended.

However, this is not enough to ensure static object layout. Consider replacing line 4 with the method invocation `o2.f()`. This would also attempt to set the field `a` for object `o2`, and should be disallowed. The problem is, however, that the body of the method `f` is type checked in the context of the receiver object `o1`, where it is defined, and in that context the assignment `this.a` is allowed.

There are several options here. One is to require that an object must own all attributes owned by its prototype, such that a function inherited from the prototype can assume that all attributes it may want to update are owned. In the context of our example, this would force us to redefine the fields `a` and `f` in `o2`. This is not a good option because it essentially disables completely the prototype inheritance mechanism and the flexibility it gives.

We therefore decided to allow the set of owned attributes to be different for an object and its prototype. The option that we propose is based on the observation that only a subset of the owned attributes are updated in methods using the receiver syntax, i.e., `this.a`. These are the only attributes that must be owned by all inheriting objects. We therefore propose to maintain a second set of attribute names for an object type: the subset of the owned attributes that must be owned also by its inheritors. We call these attributes *inheritor-owned* attributes. For the example in Fig. 1, the attribute `a` of `o1` is updated using receiver syntax, i.e., `this.a`, which means that `a` should be an inheritor-owned attribute of `o1`. This means that `a` should be an owned attribute for inheritors, e.g., `o2`. This, in turn, means that we should disallow the definition of `o2` in line 2.

We can summarize the requirements of our type system as follows. Object types are annotated with a set of owned attributes and a set of inheritor-owned attributes, with the following rules:

- **Rule 1**: Owned attributes are defined directly in an object.
- **Rule 2**: Only owned attributes of an object can be updated.
- **Rule 3**: Methods can only update inheritor-owned attributes of their receiver object (using `this.a` notation).
- **Rule 4**: Inheritor-owned attributes are among the owned attributes.
- **Rule 5**: The inheritor-owned attributes of an object include all the inheritor-owned attributes of the prototype object.

Applying these ideas to our example program, we assign the following type to variable `o1`:

$$\texttt{o1} : \{\texttt{a} : \mathit{Int}, \texttt{f} : \mathit{Int} \Rightarrow \mathit{Int}\}^{\mathbf{P}(\{\texttt{a},\texttt{f}\},\{\texttt{a}\})}$$

This type is composed of the base record type and the object-type qualifier written as superscript. The base record type says that the attributes `a` and `f` are all the accessible attributes. The double arrow in the type $\mathit{Int} \Rightarrow \mathit{Int}$ marks that this is the type of a method (i.e., a function that takes an implicit receiver object parameter), and distinguishes the type from $\mathit{Int} \rightarrow \mathit{Int}$, which we reserve for function values; we do not make the receiver type a part of the method type.[3] The object-type qualifier part of `o1` says that the object is precisely typed (marked as **P**, explained later), is guaranteed to own the attributes `a` and `f`, and all of its inheritors must own at least attribute `a`.

In our type system line 2 is ill-typed because it constructs an object that owns only the attribute `b`, yet it inherits from object `o1` that has an inheritor-owned attribute `a` (**Rule 5**). This is reasonable, because if we allow the definition of `o2`, say with type $\{a : \mathit{Int}, b : \mathit{Int}, f : \mathit{Int} \Rightarrow \mathit{Int}\}^{\mathbf{P}(\{b\},\{\})}$, then it would be legal to invoke `o2.f()`, which we know should be illegal because it causes the layout of `o2` to change. To fix this type error we need to ensure that `o2` also owns `a`. Note that the assignment in line 3 (`o1.a = 3`) is well-typed, as it should, because `a` is among the owned fields mentioned in the static type of `o1`.

2.2 Subtyping

Consider again the example in Fig. 1 with the object layouts as shown in Fig. 2(a). The assignment `o1.a = 3` from line 3 is valid, but the assignment `o2.a = 2` from line 4 is not, even though `o2` inherits from its prototype `o1`. This shows

[3] This is to allow comparison of method attribute types in subtyping.

```
6 : var o3 = { a : 11, c : 12,  f : function (x) { this.c = 13 } }
7 : o1 = o3;     //BAD

8 : var o4 = { a : 14, __proto__ : o1 }
9 : o4.f ();     //BAD

10: var o5 = { a : 1, b : 2, f : function (x) { this.a = 2 } }
11: var o6 = { a : 1, b : 3, f : function (x) { this.b = 3 } }
12: o6.f = function (x) { this.b = 4 }  // OK
13: var o7 = if ... then o5 else o6
14: o7.f = function (x) { this.b = 4 }  // BAD
15: console.log(o7.a);                  // OK

16: var o8 = if ... then o1 else o3  // OK
17: o8.f(3);                         // OK
18: o8.c = 2;                        // OK
19: var o9 = { a: 14, __proto__: o8} // BAD
```

Fig. 3. Example JavaScript program (continued from Fig. 1).

that inheritance does not automatically create a subtype relationship when fixed object layout is a concern.

In the spirit of a dynamic language like JavaScript, we propose to use a structural subtyping relationship between types, generated by the structure of the types and not by their prototype relationships.

Consider, for example, a new object `o3` such that the assignment `o1 = o3` is safe. The object `o3` would have to contain the attributes `a` and `f`. Furthermore, `o3` must own all the attributes owned by `o1`, so that it can be used in all the attribute-update operations where `o1` can be used. An example is available in line 6–7 of Fig. 3. The type of `o3` is

$$\mathtt{o3} : \{\mathtt{a} : \mathit{Int}, \mathtt{c} : \mathit{Int}, \mathtt{f} : \mathit{Int} \Rightarrow \mathit{Int}\}^{\mathbf{P}(\{\mathtt{a},\mathtt{c},\mathtt{f}\},\{\mathtt{c}\})}$$

To support subtyping (**Prop. 4**), the general rule is that an object type A is a subtype of B, if and only if (a) A contains all the attributes of B with the same type (as in the usual width subtyping), and (b) the owned attributes of A include all the owned attributes of B. However, this is still not enough to support fixed layout (**Prop. 2**), in presence of prototype inheritance as implemented in JavaScript (**Prop. 3**), and subtyping (**Prop. 4**).

Challenge: Subtyping and Prototype Inheritance. In our example, after the assignment `o1 = o3` the static type of `o1` suggests that the set of inheritor-owned attributes is {`a`}, while the true inheritor-owned attributes of the runtime object are {`c`}. This suggests that it would be unsafe to use the object `o1` as a prototype in a new object creation, as in the continuation of our example in line 8–9 of Fig. 3. If the object creation in line 8 is well typed, with the type:

$$\mathtt{o4} : \{\mathtt{a} : \mathit{Int}, \mathtt{f} : \mathit{Int} \Rightarrow \mathit{Int}\}^{\mathbf{P}(\{\mathtt{a}\},\{\mathtt{a}\})}$$

then, when executing line 9 the field `c` would be added to the receiver object `o4`.

One way to get out of this impasse is to restrict the subtype relationship to pay attention also to the inheritor-modified attributes. In particular, to allow the assignment `o1 = o3` followed by a use of `o1` as a prototype, we must ensure that the static type of o1 includes all the inheritor-owned attributes from the type of o3. This would mean that the inheritor-owned attributes in a supertype must be a superset of the inheritor-owned attributes in the subtype.

However, we show next that this is not enough if we want to allow method updates.

Challenge: Subtyping and Method Update. It is common in JavaScript to change the implementation of a method, especially on prototype objects, e.g., in order to change the behavior of a library. This technique is sometimes called monkey patching.Consider the code fragment in line 10–15 of Fig. 3. In our type system, the types of o5 and o6 can be:

$$\mathtt{o5} : \{\mathtt{a} : \mathit{Int}, \mathtt{b} : \mathit{Int}, \mathtt{f} : \mathit{Int} \Rightarrow \mathit{Int}\}^{\mathrm{P}(\{\mathtt{a},\mathtt{b},\mathtt{f}\},\{\mathtt{a}\})}$$
$$\mathtt{o6} : \{\mathtt{a} : \mathit{Int}, \mathtt{b} : \mathit{Int}, \mathtt{f} : \mathit{Int} \Rightarrow \mathit{Int}\}^{\mathrm{P}(\{\mathtt{a},\mathtt{b},\mathtt{f}\},\{\mathtt{b}\})}$$

The method update in line 12 is safe because it updates the method f of o6, with a method that modifies the same set of receiver fields, which are owned by o6 and all objects that may be inheriting from it. This can be verified statically by comparing the receiver attributes that may be changed by the new method (b) with the list of inheritor-owned fields listed in the type of o6.

In this example, subtyping arises in line 13. Notice that the type of o7 must be a supertype of the type of both o5 and o6. The access in line 15 is safe. However, the assignment in line 14 is unsafe, because it may associate with object o5 a method that changes the field b of the receiver object. This is unsafe since b is not listed as inheritor-owned, so the updated method is not safe for inheritance.

This example suggests that one way to ensure soundness of the assignment of o5 to o7 is to ensure that the inheritor-owned attributes in a supertype (e.g., type of o7, which is used for checking statically the safety of method update) must be a subset of the inheritor-owned attributes in the subtype, e.g., type of o5. In this particular case, the inheritor-owned attributes of the static type of o7 must be empty, i.e. a strict subset of that of the static types of o5 and o6. This is exactly opposite of the inclusion direction between the inheritor-owned attributes in a subtype relation proposed in the previous section to handle subtyping and prototype inheritance.

Solution: Subtyping with Approximate Types. We saw that a type system that supports fixed layout (**Prop. 2**) and prototype inheritance (**Prop. 3**) must reject the use of subtyping in line 13. We feel that this would be extremely restrictive, and not fulfill subtyping (**Prop. 4**). Moreover, prototype inheritance, method update, and the inheritor-owned fields, are about inheriting and sharing implementations, while subtyping is about interface compatibility. There are many more occurrences in practice of subtyping in assignments and method calls than there are prototype assignments and method updates.

Therefore, we propose to relax the subtyping relation to make it more flexible and more generally usable, but restrict the contexts where it can be used. In particular, for prototype definition or method update, we only allow the use of objects for which we know statically the dynamic type.

To implement this strategy, we use two kinds of object types. The *precise* object type that we used so far (marked as **P**), which includes a set of all attributes and their types, along with a set of owned attributes, and a set of inheritor-owned attributes. A precise object type means that the static type of the object is the same as the dynamic type, i.e., no subtyping has been used since the object construction. Expressions of precise type can appear in any context where an object is expected.

We also introduce an *approximate* object type, written as $\{Attr\}^{\mathbf{A}(\{Own\})}$, also including a set of attributes and their types, and a set of owned attribute names, but no inheritor-owned attributes. Approximate types allow subtyping, and are only an approximate description of the actual dynamic type of the object. These objects can be used for read/write attribute access and for method invocation, but cannot be used as prototypes or for method updates. Therefore, we do not need to track the inheritor-owned attributes for approximate types.

We can summarize the additional rules in our type system for dealing with subtyping

- **Rule 6**: There is no subtyping relation on precise object types.
- **Rule 7**: An approximate object type is a supertype of the precise object type with the same attributes and the same owned attributes.
- **Rule 8**: An approximate object type A is a subtype of another approximate object type B as long as the subtype A has a superset of the attributes and a superset of the owned attributes of the supertype B (as in standard width subtyping).
- **Rule 9:** Only objects with precise type can be used as prototypes.
- **Rule 10:** Method update can only be performed on objects of precise type, and only when the method writes only inheritor-owned attributes of the object (extension of **Rule 3**).

Returning to our motivating example, both `o1` and `o3` have precise distinct types, which do not allow subtyping, so the assignment `o1 = o3` from line 6 is ill-typed. However, the assignment at line 16 of Fig. 3 will be legal if the static type of `o8` is the following approximate type:

$$\texttt{o8} : \{\texttt{a} : Int, \texttt{c} : Int, \texttt{f} : Int \Rightarrow Int\}^{\mathbf{A}(\{\texttt{a},\texttt{c},\texttt{f}\})}$$

Moreover, we can perform attribute lookup and method invocation via `o8` as shown in line 17–18 of Fig. 3, because these operations are allowed on approximate types. However, it would be illegal to use `o8` as prototype, as in line 19 of Fig. 3. This is because an object with approximate type cannot be used as a prototype.

With approximate types, the subtyping assignment at line 13 can be well-typed: by giving the static type of `o7` the approximate type

$$\texttt{o7} : \{\texttt{a} : Int, \texttt{b} : Int, \texttt{f} : Int \Rightarrow Int\}^{\mathbf{A}(\{\texttt{a},\texttt{b},\texttt{f}\})}$$

The method update from line 14 will still be ill-typed because method update cannot be applied to an object with approximate type. This shows how the introduction of approximate types supports subtyping in certain contexts, while avoiding the unsoundness that can arise due to interaction of subtyping and prototype inheritance.

We have shown informally a type system that fulfills all of access safety (**Prop. 1**), fixed layout (**Prop. 2**), prototype inheritance (**Prop. 3**), and subtyping (**Prop. 4**), while placing few restrictions. We discuss this type system formally in Sect. 3.

3 A Formal Account of the Type System

This section provides a formal definition of the type system of SJS and a proof of the fixed object layout property. Throughout this section, we use a simplified core language that is designed to capture the essence of the prototype-based object-oriented programming in JavaScript. The language supports mutable objects, prototype inheritance, dynamic method updates, higher-order functions, and local variable bindings. To simplify the presentation, we do not include in the language: functions as objects, constructor functions, accessing undefined variables, and lookup of fields by dynamic names (e.g., `obj[''key'']`). Furthermore, we postpone the introduction of a number of other features to the companion technical report [12]: first-class method functions, recursive data types, and accessing `this` in a non-method function.

3.1 Expression

The syntax definition of the core language expressions is shown in Fig. 4. We are going to use the metavariables e for an expression, n for an integer number, x for a variable identifier, and a for an attribute identifier. A few expression types have type annotations in order to simplify type checking. The expression $\{a_1 : e_1, \ldots, a_n : e_n\}_T$ defines a new object with attributes $a_1, \ldots, a_n$ initialized with expressions $e_1, \ldots, e_n$, respectively. T is the type of the resulting object. The expression $e_1.a{=}e_2$ updates attribute a of the object e_1 with the value of e_2. The expression $e_1.a(e_2)$ invokes method a of object e_1 with argument e_2. The expression `this` accesses the receiver object. The expression $\{a_1 : e_1, \ldots\}_T$ `prototype` e_p creates a new object with prototype e_p. T is the expected type of the resulting object.[4]

3.2 Types and Qualifiers

Figure 4 also defines the types. The novel elements in this type system are the object-type qualifiers (q). If we erase the object-type qualifiers we are left with a standard object type system [5] with few modifications. Object-type qualifiers track the layout information required to constrain object operations in order to guarantee the fixed layout property in the presence of the JavaScript operational semantics.

[4] Please note that deviating from JavaScript (`prototype` expression) is for the clear presentation. The SJS language itself supports the usual prototyping mechanism of JavaScript, which is based on a prototype attribute of constructors. We refer to the companion technical report [12] for more details.

Expressions

$$e ::= n \mid x \mid x = e_1 \mid \texttt{var}\ x : T\texttt{=}e_1\ \texttt{in}\ e_2 \mid \{a_1 : e_1\ \ldots\ a_n : e_n\}_T \mid e.a \mid e_1.a\texttt{=}e_2$$
$$\mid \texttt{function}(x : T)\{e\} \mid e_1(e_2) \mid e_1.a(e_2) \mid \texttt{this} \mid \{a_1 : e_1\ \ldots\ a_n : e_n\}_T\ \texttt{prototype}\ e_p$$

Type

Type	$T ::= Int \mid O \mid T \to T \mid T \Rightarrow T \mid \top$	*ObjQual*	q	$::= \mathbf{P}(\texttt{own}, \texttt{iown}) \mid \mathbf{A}(\texttt{own})$
ObjTy	$O ::= \rho^{q}$	*OwnSet*	own	$\subseteq$ *Attr*
ObjBase	$\rho ::= \{\ldots a_i : T_i \ldots\}$	*ModSet*	iown	$\subseteq$ *Attr*
RcvTy	$R ::= \top \mid O$	*Attr*		set of atributes (a,b ...)
TyEnv	$\Gamma \in\ Var \rightharpoonup Type$	*Var*		set of variables (x,y ...)

Fig. 4. Syntax: expressions and types. The highlighted items are specific to our object-type qualifiers.

Well-formed Types

$$[\texttt{TW-EObj}]\ \frac{\forall a \in dom(\rho) \vdash \rho(a) \qquad \texttt{iown} \subseteq \texttt{own} \qquad \texttt{own} \subseteq dom(\rho)}{\vdash \rho^{\mathbf{P}(\texttt{own}, \texttt{iown})}} \qquad [\texttt{TW-Fun}]\ \frac{\vdash T_1 \quad \vdash T_2}{\vdash T_1 \to T_2}$$

$$[\texttt{TW-AObj}]\ \frac{\forall a \in dom(\rho) \vdash \rho(a) \qquad \texttt{own} \subseteq dom(\rho)}{\vdash \rho^{\mathbf{A}(\texttt{own})}} \qquad [\texttt{TW-Method}]\ \frac{\vdash T_1 \quad \vdash T_2}{\vdash T_1 \Rightarrow T_2} \qquad [\texttt{TW-Top}]\ \frac{}{\vdash \top}$$

Subtyping

$$[\texttt{ObjPA}_{<:}]\ \frac{\forall dom(\rho_2).\rho_1(a) \equiv \rho_2(a) \qquad dom(\rho_1) = dom(\rho_2) \qquad \texttt{own}_1 = \texttt{own}_2}{\rho_1^{\mathbf{P}(\texttt{own}_1, \texttt{iown}_1)} <: \rho_2^{\mathbf{A}(\texttt{own}_2)}}$$

$$[\texttt{ObjAA}_{<:}]\ \frac{\forall a \in dom(\rho_2).\rho_1(a) \equiv \rho_2(a) \qquad dom(\rho_2) \subseteq dom(\rho_1) \qquad \texttt{own}_2 \subseteq \texttt{own}_1}{\rho_1^{\mathbf{A}(\texttt{own}_1)} <: \rho_2^{\mathbf{A}(\texttt{own}_2)}}$$

$$[\texttt{Trans}_{<:}]\ \frac{T_1 <: T_2 \quad T_2 <: T3}{T_1 <: T_3} \qquad [\texttt{Refl}_{<:}]\ \frac{}{T <: T} \qquad [\texttt{Fun}_{<:}]\ \frac{T_3 <: T_1 \quad T_2 <: T_4}{T_1 \to T_2 <: T_3 \to T_4} \qquad [\texttt{Top}_{<:}]\ \frac{}{T <: \top}$$

Fig. 5. Well-formed types and subtyping. The highlighted items are specific to our object-type qualifiers.

Types (T) include the integer type (Int), object types (O), function types ($T \to T$), method types ($T \Rightarrow T$), and the top type ($\top$). A receiver type (R) is either the top type, when typing a non-method function, or an object type, when typing a method function. A type environment (Γ) is a map from variables to types. Object types are composed of a base object type (ρ) and an object-type qualifier (q). Object types can have either a precise qualifier ($\mathbf{P}(\texttt{own}, \texttt{iown})$) or an approximate qualifier ($\mathbf{A}(\texttt{own})$). Owned attribute sets (own), and inheritor-owned attribute sets (iown) are subsets of corresponding objects' attributes.

Operations on Object Types. $dom(\rho)$ denotes all attributes of the base object type ρ. We write $\texttt{own}(q)$ to denote the owned attribute set of the qualifier q We similarly define $\texttt{iown}(q)$ to denote the inheritor-owned attribute set of the qualifier q when q is precise. We are also going to use $\rho(a)$ to denote the type of attribute a in ρ.

Well-Formed Types. Figure 5 defines the rules to check well-formedness of a type, especially for object types. An object type with a precise qualifier is well-formed if all the inheritor-owned attributes are among the owned attributes, all owned attributes are among the attributes, and all attributes have well-formed types. The well-formedness check for an object type with an approximate qualifier is similarly defined without the check for inheritor-owned attributes.

Subtyping and Type Equality. Figure 5 also defines the subtyping relation. There is no subtyping between precise objects. However, precise objects can be relaxed to an approximate object having the same base object type and owned set ([ObjPA$_{<:}$]). This ensures that any read and write operation that is allowed by a precise type is still available after relaxed to an approximate type. Subtyping between approximate objects ([ObjAA$_{<:}$]) is defined as a traditional width-subtyping extended with an additional inclusion check between `own` sets: a subtype should own strictly more than a supertype. This ensures that any read and write operation allowed by a supertype can be safely performed on an object with a subtype.[5] We also have transitivity ([Trans$_{<:}$]), function ([Fun$_{<:}$]). We do not need subtyping among method types because that method types only appears as an attribute type (we will see this in the type system section), and only the equivalence of attributes are checked. Type equivalence ($\equiv$) is a syntactic equivalence check.

3.3 Typing Rules

The static typing rules are defined in Fig. 6. The type system is composed of two kinds of rules: *expression typing judgment* and *attribute-update typing judgment.*

Expression Typing. The expression typing judgment $R, \Gamma \vdash e : T$ means that expression e under receiver type R and type environment Γ has type T.

Variables and Functions. Rules [T-Var], [T-VarUpd], and [T-LetVar] handle variable lookup, variable update, and local binding. [T-This] applies to the `this` expression when the current receiver type is an object type. `this` cannot be used when the current receiver type is $\top$.

Functions. [T-Fun] extends the traditional typed lambda calculus with a receiver type in the context. Since functions, unlike methods, are invoked without a receiver object, the function body is type checked with the receiver type set to the top type ($\top$). As a consequence, accessing the `this` variable within a function is not allowed.

Objects. [T-Obj] types an object literal without inheritance. The created object has a well-formed type ρ^q as annotated in the expression. Each attribute of ρ^q should be an owned attribute and should appear in the object literal expression. The safety of initialization expressions and initialization operations are delegated

[5] Allowing depth-subtyping between mutable objects will make the type system unsound. We refer to Abadi and Cardell's work [5] for more details.

Expression Typing

$$\texttt{[T-Var]}\ \frac{\Gamma(x) = T}{R, \Gamma \vdash x : T} \qquad \texttt{[T-VarUpd]}\ \frac{\Gamma(x) = T_1 \quad R, \Gamma \vdash e : T_2 \quad T_2 <: T_1}{R, \Gamma \vdash x = e : T_1}$$

$$\texttt{[T-LetVar]}\ \frac{R, \Gamma \vdash e_1 : T_1 \quad \vdash T \quad T_1 <: T \qquad R, \Gamma[x \mapsto T] \vdash e_2 : T_2}{R, \Gamma \vdash \texttt{var}\ x{:}T\texttt{=}e_1\ \texttt{in}\ e_2 : T_2} \qquad \texttt{[T-FCall]}\ \frac{R, \Gamma \vdash e_1 : T_1 \to T_2 \qquad R, \Gamma \vdash e_2 : T_3 \quad T_3 <: T_1}{R, \Gamma, \vdash e_1(e_2) : T_2}$$

$$\texttt{[T-Fun]}\ \frac{\top, \Gamma[x \mapsto T_1] \vdash e : T_2 \qquad \vdash T_1}{R, \Gamma \vdash \texttt{function}(x : T_1)\{e\} : T_1 \to T_2} \qquad \texttt{[T-This]}\ \frac{}{\rho^q, \Gamma \vdash \texttt{this} : \rho^q}$$

$$\texttt{[T-Attr]}\ \frac{\rho = \{\ldots a : T \ldots\} \qquad R, \Gamma \vdash e : \rho^q \quad T \neq T_1 \Rightarrow T_2}{R, \Gamma \vdash e.a : T} \qquad \texttt{[T-AttrUpd]}\ \frac{R, \Gamma \vdash_{AU} \rho^q.a\texttt{=}e_2 \qquad \boxed{a \in \texttt{own}(q)} \quad R, \Gamma \vdash e_1 : \rho^q}{R, \Gamma \vdash e_1.a\texttt{=}e_2 : \top}$$

$$\texttt{[T-MCall]}\ \frac{R, \Gamma \vdash e_1 : \rho^q \qquad \rho = \{\ldots a : T_1 \Rightarrow T_2 \ldots\} \qquad R, \Gamma \vdash e_2 : T_3 \qquad T_3 <: T_1}{R, \Gamma \vdash e_1.a(e_2) : T_2}$$

$$\texttt{[T-Obj]}\ \frac{\vdash \rho^q \quad dom(\rho) = \{a_1 \ldots a_n\} \quad \forall i \in [1, n]. R, \Gamma \vdash_{AU} \rho^q.a_i\texttt{=}e_i \quad \boxed{q = \mathbf{P}(\texttt{own}, \texttt{iown})}}{R, \Gamma \vdash \{a_1 : e_1 \ldots a_n : e_n\}_{\rho^q} : \rho^q}$$

$$\texttt{[T-Proto]}\ \frac{\begin{array}{c}\vdash \rho^q \quad R, \Gamma \vdash e_p : {\rho_p}^{q_p} \quad dom(\rho) = dom(\rho_p) \cup \{a_1, \ldots, a_n\} \\ \forall i \in [1, n]. R, \Gamma \vdash_{AU} \rho^q.a_i\texttt{=}e_i \quad \forall a \in dom(\rho_p). \rho(a) \equiv \rho_p(a) \quad \boxed{\texttt{iown}_p \subseteq \texttt{iown}} \\ \boxed{q = \mathbf{P}(\texttt{own}, \texttt{iown})} \quad \boxed{q_p = \mathbf{P}(\texttt{own}_p, \texttt{iown}_p)} \quad \boxed{\texttt{own} = \{a_1, \ldots, a_n\}}\end{array}}{R, \Gamma \vdash \{a_1 : e_1 \ldots a_n : e_n\}_{\rho^q}\ \texttt{prototype}\ e_p : \rho^q}$$

Attribute-Update Typing

$$\texttt{[T-AttrUpdV]}\ \frac{\rho = \{\ldots a : T \ldots\} \qquad T \neq T_1 \Rightarrow T_2 \qquad R, \Gamma \vdash e : T' \qquad T' <: T}{R, \Gamma \vdash_{AU} \rho^q.a\texttt{=}e}$$

$$\texttt{[T-AttrUpdM]}\ \frac{\begin{array}{c} O = \rho^q \qquad \rho = \{\ldots a : T_1 \Rightarrow T_2 \ldots\} \qquad \rho^{q'}, \Gamma[x \mapsto T_1] \vdash e : T_2 \\ \boxed{q = \mathbf{P}(\texttt{own}, \texttt{iown})} \quad \boxed{q' = \mathbf{A}(\texttt{own}')} \quad \boxed{\texttt{own}' = \texttt{iown}}\end{array}}{R, \Gamma \vdash_{AU} O.a\texttt{=function}(x : T_1)\{e\}}$$

Fig. 6. Type system. The highlighted items are specific to object-type qualifiers.

to the *attribute-update typing judgments*, [T-AttrUpdV] and [T-AttrUpdM] described in the next section. [T-Attr] types an attribute read access. The rule restricts the reading of a method attribute. It is well-known that subtyping along with escaping methods can break the soundness of a type system [5]. [T-MCall] handles method calls. The rule checks only the parameter type and the return type since the safety of passing the receiver object is already discharged when the method is attached. [T-AttrUpd] types an attribute update. The rule requires the target attribute to be owned by the base object type. The determination of the type and type safety of the attribute-update operation is delegated to the attribute-update typing judgments. Note that the attribute-update typing judgment does not provide a type for the assignment result to prevent methods from escaping an object.

Inheritance. [T-Proto] types an object literal with inheritance. The rule is basically an extension of [T-Obj], with the following new checks: (1) attributes should be either owned fields of ρ^q or fields inherited from $\rho_p^{q_p}$, (2) the type of an attribute defined in prototype should remain the same in the newly defined object, and (3) inheritor-owned attributes of the newly defined object should include all the inheritor-owned attributes of the prototype object. The rule also requires $\rho_p^{q_p}$ to be a precise object type. Like in [T-Obj], the type safety of initialization expressions and initialization operations are delegated to the attribute-update typing rules.

Attribute-Update Typing. Attribute updates are handled by a different set of judgment rules. The attribute-update typing judgment $R, \Gamma \vdash_{AU} O.a{=}e$ means that "expression e is well typed under receiver type R (for the current method or function body) and type environment Γ, and the value of e can be safely assigned to attribute a of an object of type O. The judgment has two rules.

Field Update. If a non-method attribute is updated ([T-AttrUpdV]), the rule just typechecks the expression e.

Method Update. The method-update rule ([T-AttrUpdM]) requires the right-hand side expression to be a function literal[6] and the base object type to be a precise object type (we can only perform method update on objects whose type is known precisely, and in particular whose inheritor-owned set is known). This rule addresses the situations when the method is inherited and the receiver object is some subtype of the receiver type O. The method body is checked with an approximate version of the receiver type O whose owned attributes set is restricted to the inheritor-owned attributes of O. This ensures that the function body can only update the iown attributes of the receiver object.

3.4 Properties of the Type System

Theorem *(Fixed Object Layout). A well-typed program never modifies object layouts after object construction.*

Proof. (Sketch) To show this property, we first define an operational semantics of the core language such that any attempt to modify an object layout will result in the execution getting stuck. Then we show the usual type soundness property, i.e., a well-typed program never gets stuck. The fixed object layout property is a corollary of the soundness theorem. The full version of the proof and necessary definitions, such as operational semantics and value typing, are available in the companion technical report [12] (Section B).

4 Summary of Implementation and Evaluation

We have implemented a proof-of-concept type checker and compiler for SJS to evaluate the language. The SJS prototype supports the core type system described in this paper, along with typed arrays, hash tables, integer and floating point numbers, first-class methods, and recursively-defined object types.

[6] This syntactic restriction is posed to keep the presentation simple. The companion technical report [12] (Section A.2) extends the type system to remove this restriction.

We evaluate the usability of the language and the feasibility of type-based compilation. This section provides a short summary of the evaluation. The full details are in the companion technical report [12]. The programs used in this section can be found at http://goo.gl/nBtgXj.

Usability. We considered two programs from the *octane* benchmark suite [3] and two webapps from *01.org* [1] to evaluate the usability of the type system. Programs are moderate-sized (about 500 to 2000 lines of code) and use objects extensively. We managed to typecheck all four programs, after commenting out small portions of code handling Ajax communication, because we do not have enough contextual information to decide the types for this part.

SJS requires programmers to provide type annotations to infer the base type (type qualifiers are inferred without any user interaction). For the benchmarks, one type annotation is required per 8.34 lines of code. The majority of the annotations (86.5 %) are for function parameters, since SJS requires every function parameter to be annotated. The rest of the annotations are for local variables, **this** variables, attributes, returns, and some assignments when there is an ambiguity that the type inference engine cannot handle. Overall, we found that only 2.8 % of expressions and local variables need annotations.

Performance. We wrote a prototype ahead-of-time compiler to translate SJS to C. The compiler uses a flat object representation, which ensures at most two indirections when accessing an object attribute. Then it invokes an off-the-shelf C compiler to produce an executable binary. Besides the flat object representation, and the standard optimizations performed by the C compiler, the SJS compiler does not perform any high-level optimizations.

In our experiment, we used eight programs to evaluate the potential performance benefits of statically-known object layout. We compared the execution time of the output of our compiler with the execution time when using the just-in-time compiler from `node.js` version 0.10.29. On programs using prototype-based inheritance and subtpying, the executables produced by the SJS compiler showed notably better performance (1.5–2.5x). For programs using objects without inheritance, the binaries generated by the SJS compiler showed some improvement (1.02–1.25x). Finally, SJS showed poorer performance (0.65–0.87x) than `node.js` on programs with mostly numeric and array operations. We refer to the companion technical report [12] for more details on the evaluation. Considering the fact that the prototype SJS compiler does not perform any high-level optimizations, we believe that the results show that knowing statically the layout of objects can allow an ahead-of-time compiler to generate faster code for programs that use objects extensively.

5 Related Work

Inheritance Mechanism and Object Layout. There is a strong connection between the inheritance mechanism a language uses and the way a language ensures a fixed object layout property, which enables static compilation. Common inheritance mechanisms include class-based inheritance (e.g., SmallTalk, C++, Java, and Python), cloning-based prototype inheritance (Cecil [10])[7], and delegation-based prototype inheritance (e.g., Self [11], JavaScript, and Cecil).

Plain object types can be used to ensure fixed object layout property for a language using either class-based inheritance or cloning/sharing-based prototype inheritance. In both cases, it is impossible to change the offset of an attribute of an object once it is computed. Therefore, the type system only needs to ensure the following two requirements: (i) all objects generated using the same constructor should have the same layout, and (ii) an attribute cannot be added or removed once an object is created. Indeed, statically-typed languages in this category exactly implements these restrictions through their type system. Even static type systems proposed to enable static compilation of dynamic languages, such as StrongTalk [9] and RPython [6], impose these requirements.

However, these requirements are not enough for a language using a delegation-based inheritance mechanism, as we discussed in Sect. 2. Cecil solves this problem by making delegation explicit. When inheritance happens, attributes to be delegated to the prototype are marked with the keyword `share`. Then, updating a delegated attribute of an inheritor object changes the original owner of the attribute, rather than adding the attribute to the inheritor object.

Object Calculus. Our base type system borrows several ideas from the *typed imperative object calculus* of Abadi and Cardelli [5], especially subtyping of object types and how to handle method detachment in the existence of subtyping. Unfortunately, we could not use the type system as is because it uses cloning-based inheritance rather than prototype-based inheritance. Our notion of method type is also different from theirs in that ours exclude a receiver type from attached method types to have a simple formalism at the cost of not supporting recursive data types. We refer to the companion technical report [12] (Section A.1) for an extension of SJS to support recursive data types.

The type system proposed by Bono and Fisher [8], based on Fisher et al.'s earlier work [14], separates objects into *prototype objects* and *proper objects* similar to precise objects and approximate objects in SJS. Prototype/proper objects are similar to precise/approximate objects except in the context of subtyping. Despite the similarity, the two systems achieve opposite goals: Bono and Fisher's calculus is designed to support extensible (i.e., flexible) objects, while our type system tries to ensure that objects have a fixed layout. Moreover, their notion of prototyping is not based on delegation. Thus, the calculus is not suitable for JavaScript programs.

[7] A cloning-based inheritance approach populates inherited attributes to an inheritor object when extending the inheritor object with a prototype. After that, all read and write operations are performed local to the inheritor object, without consulting the prototype object. This approach has an effect of fixing object layout at the object creation time.

Type Systems for Dynamically Typed Language. Several static type systems for dynamically typed languages have been proposed [6,9,15,24,25] as well as for JavaScript [2,4,7,13,17–23]. However, only `asm.js` [2] and RPython [6], which we already discussed in Sect. 1, have the same goals as SJS: to define a typed subset of the base language, which can be compiled efficiently. Other type systems are designed to provide type safety and often to retrofit an existing code base. Therefore, it is difficult to compare them directly with SJS type system.

Acknowledgments. The work of the first author is supported in part by a research internship at Samsung Research America. The work of the last author is supported in part by Samsung Research America. This research is partially supported by NSF grants CCF-1018730, CCF-1017810, CCF-1409872, and CCF-1423645. The authors thank Colin S. Gordon, Frank Tip, Manu Sridharan, and the anonymous reviewers for their comments and suggestions.

References

1. 01.org. https://01.org/html5webapps/webapps/
2. asm.js. http://asmjs.org/
3. Octane Benchmarks. https://developers.google.com/octane/
4. TypeScript. http://www.typescriptlang.org
5. Abadi, M., Cardelli, L.: A Theory of Objects, 1st edn. Springer, New York (1996)
6. Ancona, D., Ancona, M., Cuni, A., Matsakis, N.D.: RPython: a step towards reconciling dynamically and statically typed oo languages. In: DSL 2007 (2007)
7. Anderson, C., Giannini, P., Drossopoulou, S.: Towards type inference for javascript. In: Gao, X.-X. (ed.) ECOOP 2005. LNCS, vol. 3586, pp. 428–452. Springer, Heidelberg (2005)
8. Bono, V., Fisher, K.: An imperative, first-order calculus with object extension. In: Jul, E. (ed.) ECOOP 1998. LNCS, vol. 1445, pp. 462–497. Springer, Heidelberg (1998)
9. Bracha, G., Griswold, D.: Strongtalk: typechecking smalltalk in a production environment. In: OOPSLA 1993 (1993)
10. Chambers, C., Group, T.C.: The Cecil language - specification and rationale (2004)
11. Chambers, C., Ungar, D.: Customization: optimizing compiler technology for SELF, a dynamically-typed object-oriented programming language. In: PLDI 1989 (1989)
12. Choi, P.W., Chandra, S., Necula, G., Sen, K.: SJS: a typed subset of JavaScript with fixed object layout. Technical report UCB/EECS-2015-13, EECS Department, University of California, Berkeley, April 2015
13. Chugh, R., Herman, D., Jhala, R.: Dependent types for JavaScript. In: OOPSLA 2012 (2012)
14. Fisher, K., Honsell, F., Mitchell, J.C.: A lambda calculus of objects and method specialization. Nord. J. Comput. **1**(1), 3–37 (1994)
15. Furr, M., An, J.H.D., Foster, J.S., Hicks, M.: Static type inference for ruby. In: SAC 2009 (2009)
16. Gong, L., Pradel, M., Sen, K.: JITProf: pinpointing JIT-unfriendly JavaScript code. In: ESEC/FSE 2015 (2015)

17. Heidegger, P., Thiemann, P.: Recency types for analyzing scripting languages. In: D'Hondt, T. (ed.) ECOOP 2010. LNCS, vol. 6183, pp. 200–224. Springer, Heidelberg (2010)
18. Lerner, B.S., Politz, J.G., Guha, A., Krishnamurthi, S.: TeJaS: retrofitting type systems for JavaScript. In: DLS 2013 (2013)
19. Politz, J.G., Guha, A., Krishnamurthi, S.: Semantics and types for objects with first-class member names. In: FOOL 2012 (2012)
20. Rastogi, A., Chaudhuri, A., Hosmer, B.: The ins and outs of gradual type inference. In: POPL 2012 (2012)
21. Rastogi, A., Swamy, N., Fournet, C., Bierman, G., Vekris, P.: Safe and efficient gradual typing for TypeScript. Technical report MSR-TR-2014-99, July 2014
22. Swamy, N., Fournet, C., Rastogi, A., Bhargavan, K., Chen, J., Strub, P.Y., Bierman, G.: Gradual typing embedded securely in JavaScript. In: POPL 2014 (2014)
23. Thiemann, P.: Towards a type system for analyzing JavaScript programs. In: Sagiv, M. (ed.) ESOP 2005. LNCS, vol. 3444, pp. 408–422. Springer, Heidelberg (2005)
24. Tobin-Hochstadt, S., Felleisen, M.: The design and implementation of typed Scheme. In: POPL 2008 (2008)
25. Tobin-Hochstadt, S., Felleisen, M.: Logical types for untyped languages. In: ICFP 2010 (2010)

Refinement Type Inference via Horn Constraint Optimization

Kodai Hashimoto(✉) and Hiroshi Unno

University of Tsukuba, Tsukuba, Japan
{kodai,uhiro}@logic.cs.tsukuba.ac.jp

Abstract. We propose a novel method for inferring refinement types of higher-order functional programs. The main advantage of the proposed method is that it can infer maximally preferred (i.e., Pareto optimal) refinement types with respect to a user-specified preference order. The flexible optimization of refinement types enabled by the proposed method paves the way for interesting applications, such as inferring most-general characterization of inputs for which a given program satisfies (or violates) a given safety (or termination) property. Our method reduces such a type optimization problem to a Horn constraint optimization problem by using a new refinement type system that can flexibly reason about non-determinism in programs. Our method then solves the constraint optimization problem by repeatedly improving a current solution until convergence via template-based invariant generation. We have implemented a prototype inference system based on our method, and obtained promising results in preliminary experiments.

1 Introduction

Refinement types [5,20] have been applied to safety verification of higher-order functional programs. Some existing tools [9,10,16–19] enable fully automated verification by refinement type inference based on invariant generation techniques such as abstract interpretation, predicate abstraction, and CEGAR. The goal of these tools is to infer refinement types precise enough to verify a given safety specification. Therefore, types inferred by these tools are often too specific to the particular specification, and hence have limited applications.

To remedy the limitation, we propose a novel refinement type inference method that can infer maximally preferred (i.e., Pareto optimal) refinement types with respect to a user-specified preference order. For example, let us consider the following summation function (in OCaml syntax)

```
let rec sum x = if x = 0 then 0 else x + sum (x - 1)
```

A refinement type of sum is of the form $(x : \{x : \mathtt{int} \mid P(x)\}) \to \{y : \mathtt{int} \mid Q(x, y)\}$. Here, $P(x)$ and $Q(x, y)$ respectively represent pre and post conditions of sum. Note that the postcondition $Q(x, y)$ can refer to the argument x as well

This work was supported by Kakenhi 25730035, 23220001, 15H05706, and 25280020.

S. Blazy and T. Jensen (Eds.): SAS 2015, LNCS 9291, pp. 199–216, 2015.
DOI: 10.1007/978-3-662-48288-9_12

as the return value y. Suppose that we want to infer a maximally-weak predicate for P and maximally-strong predicate for Q within a given underlying theory. Our method allows us to specify such preferences as type optimization constraints:

$$\mathit{maximize}(P), \qquad \mathit{minimize}(Q).$$

Here, $\mathit{maximize}(P)$ (resp. $\mathit{minimize}(Q)$) means that the set of the models of $P(x)$ (resp. $Q(x, y)$) should be maximized (resp. minimized). Our method then infers a Pareto optimal refinement type with respect to the given preferences.

In general, however, this kind of multi-objective optimization involves a trade-off among the optimization constraints. In the above example, P may not be weakened without also weakening Q. Hence, there often exist multiple optima. Actually, all the following are Pareto optimal refinement types of `sum`.[1]

$$(x : \{x : \mathtt{int} \mid x = 0\}) \rightarrow \{y : \mathtt{int} \mid y = x\} \tag{1}$$

$$(x : \{x : \mathtt{int} \mid \mathtt{true}\}) \rightarrow \{y : \mathtt{int} \mid y \geq 0\} \tag{2}$$

$$(x : \{x : \mathtt{int} \mid x < 0\}) \rightarrow \{y : \mathtt{int} \mid \mathtt{false}\} \tag{3}$$

Our method further allows us to specify a priority order on the predicate variables P and Q. If P is given a higher priority over Q (we write $P \sqsubset Q$), our method infers the type (2), whereas we obtain the type (3) if $Q \sqsubset P$. Interestingly, (3) expresses that `sum` is non-terminating for any input $x < 0$.

The flexible optimization of refinement types enabled by our method paves the way for interesting applications, such as inferring most-general characterization of inputs for which a given program satisfies (or violates) a given safety (or termination) property. Furthermore, our method can infer an upper bound of the number of recursive calls if the program is terminating, and can find a minimal-length counterexample path if the program violates a safety property.

Internally, our method reduces such a refinement type optimization problem to a constraint optimization problem where the constraints are expressed as existentially quantified Horn clauses over predicate variables [1,11,19]. The constraint generation here is based on a new refinement type system that can reason about (angelic and demonic) non-determinism in programs. Our method then solves the constraint optimization problem by repeatedly improving a current solution until convergence. The constraint optimization here is based on an extension of template-based invariant generation [3,7] to existentially quantified Horn clause constraints and prioritized multi-objective optimization.

The rest of the paper is organized as follows. Sections 2 and 3 respectively formalize our target language and its refinement type system. The applications of refinement type optimization are explained in Sect. 4. Section 5 formalizes Horn constraint optimization problems and the reduction from type optimization problems. Section 6 proposes our Horn constraint optimization method. Section 7 reports on a prototype implementation of our method and the results of preliminary experiments. We compare our method with related work in Sect. 8 and conclude the paper in Sect. 9. An extended version of the paper with proofs is available online [8].

[1] Here, we use quantifier-free linear arithmetic as the underlying theory and consider only atomic predicates for P and Q.

$$E[op(\widetilde{n})] \longrightarrow_D E[[\![op]\!](\widetilde{n})] \quad \text{(E-Op)} \qquad E[\texttt{let}\ x = v\ \texttt{in}\ e] \longrightarrow_D E[[v/x]e] \quad \text{(E-Let)}$$

$$\frac{D(f) = \lambda\widetilde{x}.e \qquad |\widetilde{x}| = |\widetilde{v}|}{E[f\ \widetilde{v}] \longrightarrow_D E[[\widetilde{v}/\widetilde{x}]e]} \text{(E-App)} \qquad E[\texttt{let}\ x = *_\forall\ \texttt{in}\ e] \longrightarrow_D E[[n/x]e] \quad \text{(E-Rand}\exists)$$

$$\frac{\text{if } n = 0 \text{ then } i = 1 \text{ else } i = 2}{E[\texttt{ifz}\ n\ \texttt{then}\ e_1\ \texttt{else}\ e_2] \longrightarrow_D E[e_i]} \text{(E-If)} \qquad E[\texttt{let}\ x = *_\exists\ \texttt{in}\ e] \longrightarrow_D E[[n/x]e] \quad \text{(E-Rand}\forall)$$

Fig. 1. The operational semantics of our language L

2 Target Language L

This section introduces a higher-order call-by-value functional language L, which is the target of our refinement type optimization. The syntax is defined as follows.

$$\begin{aligned}
\text{(programs)}\ D &::= \{f_i \mapsto \lambda\widetilde{x}_i.e_i\}_{i=1}^m \\
\text{(expressions)}\ e &::= x \mid e_1\ e_2 \mid n \mid op(e_1,\ldots,e_{ar(op)}) \mid \texttt{ifz}\ e_1\ \texttt{then}\ e_2\ \texttt{else}\ e_3 \\
&\quad\ \mid \texttt{let}\ x = e_1\ \texttt{in}\ e_2 \mid \texttt{let}\ x = *_\forall\ \texttt{in}\ e \mid \texttt{let}\ x = *_\exists\ \texttt{in}\ e \\
\text{(values)}\ v &::= n \mid f\ \widetilde{v} \\
\text{(eval. contexts)}\ E &::= [\,] \mid E\ v \mid \texttt{let}\ x\ =\ E\ \texttt{in}\ e
\end{aligned}$$

Here, x and f are meta-variables ranging over variables. n and op respectively represent integer constants and operations such as $+$ and $\geq$. $ar(op)$ expresses the arity of op. We write $\widetilde{x}$ (resp. $\widetilde{v}$) for a sequence of variables x_i (resp. values v_i) and $|\widetilde{x}|$ for the length of $\widetilde{x}$. For simplicity of the presentation, the language L has integers as the only data type. We encode Boolean values `true` and `false` respectively as non-zero integers and 0. A program $D = \{f_i \mapsto \lambda\widetilde{x}_i.e_i\}_{i=1}^m$ is a mapping from variables f_i to expressions $\lambda\widetilde{x}_i.e_i$, where $\lambda\widetilde{x}.e$ is an abbreviation of $\lambda x_1.\ldots\lambda x_{|\widetilde{x}|}.e$. We define $\mathrm{dom}(D) = \{f_1,\ldots,f_m\}$ and $ar(f_i) = |\widetilde{x}_i|$. A value $f\ \widetilde{v}$ is required to satisfy $1 \leq |\widetilde{v}| < ar(f)$.

The call-by-value operational semantics of L is given in Fig. 1. Here, $[\![op]\!]$ represents the integer function denoted by op. Both expressions $\texttt{let}\ x = *_\forall\ \texttt{in}\ e$ and $\texttt{let}\ x = *_\exists\ \texttt{in}\ e$ generate a random integer n, bind x to it, and evaluate e. They are, however, interpreted differently in our refinement type system (see Sect. 3). We support these expressions to model various non-deterministic behaviors caused by, for example, user inputs, inputs from communication channels, interrupts, and thread schedulers. We write $\longrightarrow_D^*$ to denote the reflexive and transitive closure of $\longrightarrow_D$.

3 Refinement Type System for L

In this section, we introduce a refinement type system for L that can reason about non-determinism in programs. We then formalize refinement type optimization problems (in Sect. 3.1), which generalize ordinary type inference problems.

The syntax of our refinement type system is defined as follows.

$$\begin{aligned}
\text{(refinement types)}\ & \tau ::= \{x \mid \phi\} \mid (x : \tau_1) \to \tau_2 \\
\text{(type environments)}\ & \Gamma ::= \emptyset \mid \Gamma, x : \tau \mid \Gamma, \phi \\
\text{(formulas)}\ & \phi ::= t_1 \leq t_2 \mid \top \mid \bot \mid \neg\phi \mid \phi_1 \wedge \phi_2 \mid \phi_1 \vee \phi_2 \mid \phi_1 \Rightarrow \phi_2 \\
\text{(terms)}\ & t ::= n \mid x \mid t_1 + t_2 \mid n \cdot t \\
\text{(predicates)}\ & p ::= \lambda\widetilde{x}.\phi
\end{aligned}$$

An integer refinement type $\{x \mid \phi\}$ equipped with a formula ϕ for type refinement represents the type of integers x that satisfy ϕ. The scope of x is within ϕ. We often abbreviate $\{x \mid \top\}$ as $\mathtt{int}$. A function refinement type $(x : \tau_1) \to \tau_2$ represents the type of functions that take an argument x of the type τ_1 and return a value of the type τ_2. Here, τ_2 may depend on the argument x and the scope of x is within τ_2. For example, $(x : \mathtt{int}) \to \{y \mid y > x\}$ is the type of functions whose return value y is always greater than the argument x. We often write $\mathit{fvs}(\tau)$ to denote the set of free variables occurring in τ. We define $\mathrm{dom}(\Gamma) = \{x \mid x : \tau \in \Gamma\}$ and write $\Gamma(x) = \tau$ if $x : \tau \in \Gamma$.

In this paper, we adopt formulas ϕ of the quantifier-free theory of linear integer arithmetic (QFLIA) for type refinement. We write $\models \phi$ if a formula ϕ is valid in QFLIA. Formulas $\top$ and $\bot$ respectively represent the tautology and the contradiction. Note that atomic formulas $t_1 < t_2$ (resp. $t_1 = t_2$) can be encoded as $t_1 + 1 \leq t_2$ (resp. $t_1 \leq t_2 \wedge t_2 \leq t_1$) in QFLIA.

The inference rules of our refinement type system are shown in Fig. 2. Here, a type judgment $\vdash D : \Gamma$ means that a program D is well-typed under a refinement type environment Γ. A type judgment $\Gamma \vdash e : \tau$ indicates that an expression e has a refinement type τ under Γ. A subtype judgment $\Gamma \vdash \tau_1 <: \tau_2$ states that τ_1 is a subtype of τ_2 under Γ. $[\![\Gamma]\!]$ occurring in the rules ISub and Rand$\exists$ is defined by $[\![\emptyset]\!] = \top$, $[\![\Gamma, x : \{\nu \mid \phi\}]\!] = [\![\Gamma]\!] \wedge [x/\nu]\phi$, $[\![\Gamma, x : (\nu : \tau_1) \to \tau_2]\!] = [\![\Gamma]\!]$, and $[\![\Gamma, \phi]\!] = [\![\Gamma]\!] \wedge \phi$. In the rule Op, $[\![op]\!]^{\mathrm{Ty}}$ represents a refinement type of op that soundly abstracts the behavior of the function $[\![op]\!]$. For example, $[\![+]\!]^{\mathrm{Ty}} = (x : \mathtt{int}) \to (y : \mathtt{int}) \to \{z \mid z = x + y\}$.

All the rules except Rand$\forall$ and Rand$\exists$ for random integer generation are essentially the same as the previous ones [18]. The rule Rand$\forall$ requires e to have τ for *any* randomly generated integer x. Therefore, e is type-checked against τ under a type environment that assigns $\mathtt{int}$ to x. By contrast, the rule Rand$\exists$ requires e to have τ for *some* randomly generated integer x. Hence, e is type-checked against τ under a type environment that assigns a type $\{x \mid \phi\}$ to x for some ϕ such that $\mathit{fvs}(\phi) \subseteq \mathrm{dom}(\Gamma) \cup \{x\}$ and $\models [\![\Gamma]\!] \Rightarrow \exists x.\phi$. For example, $x : \mathtt{int} \vdash \mathtt{let}\ y = *_\exists\ \mathtt{in}\ x + y : \{r \mid r = 0\}$ is derivable because we can derive $x : \mathtt{int}, y : \{y \mid y = -x\} \vdash x + y : \{r \mid r = 0\}$. Thus, our new type system allows us to reason about both angelic $*_\exists$ and demonic $*_\forall$ non-determinism in higher-order functional programs.

We now discuss properties of our new refinement type system. We can prove the following progress theorem in a standard manner.

Theorem 1 (Progress). *Suppose that we have* $\vdash D : \Gamma$, $\mathrm{dom}(\Gamma) = \mathrm{dom}(D)$, *and* $\Gamma \vdash e : \tau$. *Then, either* e *is a value or* $e \longrightarrow_D e'$ *for some* e'.

$$\frac{\Gamma \vdash D(f) : \Gamma(f) \quad \text{(for each } f \in \mathrm{dom}(D))}{\vdash D : \Gamma} \ (\textsc{Prog})$$

$$\frac{\Gamma \vdash e_1 : \tau_1 \quad \Gamma, x : \tau_1 \vdash e_2 : \tau_2 \quad x \notin \mathit{fvs}(\tau_2)}{\Gamma \vdash \mathtt{let}\ x = e_1\ \mathtt{in}\ e_2 : \tau_2} \ (\textsc{Let})$$

$$\frac{\Gamma(x) = \{\nu \mid \phi\}}{\Gamma \vdash x : \{\nu \mid \nu = x\}} \ (\textsc{IVar})$$

$$\frac{\Gamma, x : \mathtt{int} \vdash e : \tau \quad x \notin \mathit{fvs}(\tau)}{\Gamma \vdash \mathtt{let}\ x = *_\forall\ \mathtt{in}\ e : \tau} \ (\textsc{Rand}\forall)$$

$$\frac{\Gamma(x) = (\nu : \tau_1) \to \tau_2}{\Gamma \vdash x : (\nu : \tau_1) \to \tau_2} \ (\textsc{FVar})$$

$$\frac{\mathit{fvs}(\phi) \subseteq \mathrm{dom}(\Gamma) \cup \{x\} \quad \models [\![\Gamma]\!] \Rightarrow \exists x.\phi \quad \Gamma, x : \{x \mid \phi\} \vdash e : \tau \quad x \notin \mathit{fvs}(\tau)}{\Gamma \vdash \mathtt{let}\ x = *_\exists\ \mathtt{in}\ e : \tau} \ (\textsc{Rand}\exists)$$

$$\frac{\Gamma, x : \tau_1 \vdash e : \tau_2}{\Gamma \vdash \lambda x.e : (x : \tau_1) \to \tau_2} \ (\textsc{Abs})$$

$$\frac{\Gamma \vdash e_1 : (x : \tau_1) \to \tau_2 \quad \Gamma \vdash e_2 : \tau_1}{\Gamma \vdash e_1\ e_2 : \tau_2} \ (\textsc{App})$$

$$\frac{\Gamma \vdash e_1 : \{\nu \mid \phi\} \quad \Gamma, \phi \wedge \nu = 0 \vdash e_2 : \tau \quad \Gamma, \phi \wedge \nu \neq 0 \vdash e_3 : \tau}{\Gamma \vdash \mathtt{ifz}\ e_1\ \mathtt{then}\ e_2\ \mathtt{else}\ e_3 : \tau} \ (\textsc{If})$$

$$\Gamma \vdash n : \{\nu \mid \nu = n\} \ (\textsc{Int})$$

$$\frac{\Gamma \vdash [\![op]\!]^{\mathrm{Ty}} <: (x_1 : \tau_1) \to \ldots \to (x_m : \tau_m) \to \tau \quad \Gamma \vdash e_i : \tau_i \ \text{(for each } i \in \{1, \ldots, m\})}{\Gamma \vdash op(e_1, \ldots, e_m) : \tau} \ (\textsc{Op})$$

$$\frac{\Gamma \vdash e : \tau' \quad \Gamma \vdash \tau' <: \tau}{\Gamma \vdash e : \tau} \ (\textsc{Sub})$$

$$\frac{\models [\![\Gamma]\!] \wedge \phi_1 \Rightarrow \phi_2}{\Gamma \vdash \{\nu \mid \phi_1\} <: \{\nu \mid \phi_2\}} \ (\textsc{ISub})$$

$$\frac{\Gamma \vdash \tau_1' <: \tau_1 \quad \Gamma, \nu : \tau_1' \vdash \tau_2 <: \tau_2'}{\Gamma \vdash (\nu : \tau_1) \to \tau_2 <: (\nu : \tau_1') \to \tau_2'} \ (\textsc{FSub})$$

Fig. 2. The inference rules of our refinement type system

We can also show the type preservation theorem in a similar manner to [18].

Theorem 2 (Preservation). *Suppose that we have* $\vdash D : \Gamma$ *and* $\Gamma \vdash e : \tau$*. If* e *is of the form* $\mathtt{let}\ x = *_\exists\ \mathtt{in}\ e_0$*, then we get* $\Gamma \vdash e' : \tau$ *for* some e' *such that* $e \longrightarrow_D e'$*. Otherwise, we get* $\Gamma \vdash e' : \tau$ *for* any e' *such that* $e \longrightarrow_D e'$.

3.1 Refinement Type Optimization Problems

We now define refinement type optimization problems, which generalize refinement type inference problems addressed by previous work [9,10,15–19].

We first introduce the notion of *refinement type templates.* A refinement type template of a function f is the refinement type obtained from the ordinary ML-style type of f by replacing each base type `int` with an integer refinement type $\{\nu \mid P(\widetilde{x}, \nu)\}$ for some fresh predicate variable P that represents an unknown predicate to be inferred, and each function type $T_1 \to T_2$ with a (dependent) function refinement type $(x : \tau_1) \to \tau_2$. For example, from an ML-style type $(\mathtt{int} \to \mathtt{int}) \to \mathtt{int} \to \mathtt{int}$, we obtain the following template.

$$(f : (x_1 : \{x_1 \mid P_1(x_1)\}) \to \{x_2 \mid P_2(x_1, x_2)\}) \to$$
$$(x_3 : \{x_3 \mid P_3(x_3)\}) \to \{x_4 \mid P_4(x_3, x_4)\}$$

Note here that the first argument f is not passed as an argument to P_3 and P_4 because f is of a function type and never occurs in QFLIA formulas for type refinement. A refinement type template of a program D with $\mathrm{dom}(D) = \{f_1, \dots, f_m\}$ is the refinement type environment $\Gamma_D = f_1 : \tau_1, \dots, f_m : \tau_m$, where each τ_i is the refinement type template of f_i. We write $pvs(\Gamma_D)$ for the set of predicate variables that occur in Γ_D. A *predicate substitution* θ for Γ_D is a map from each $P \in pvs(\Gamma_D)$ to a closed predicate $\lambda x_1, \dots, x_{ar(P)}.\phi$, where $ar(P)$ represents the arity of P. We write $\theta\Gamma_D$ to denote the application of a substitution θ to Γ_D. We also write $\mathrm{dom}(\theta)$ to represent the domain of θ.

We can define ordinary refinement type inference problems as follows.

Definition 1 (Refinement Type Inference). *A* refinement type inference problem *of a program D is a problem to find a predicate substitution θ such that $\vdash D : \theta\Gamma_D$.*

We now generalize refinement type inference problems to optimization problems.

Definition 2 (Refinement Type Optimization). *Let D be a program, $\prec$ be a strict partial order on predicate substitutions, and $\Theta = \{\theta \mid \vdash D : \theta\Gamma_D\}$. A predicate substitution $\theta \in \Theta$ is called* Pareto optimal with respect to $\prec$ *if there is no $\theta' \in \Theta$ such that $\theta' \prec \theta$. A refinement type optimization problem $(D, \prec)$ is a problem to find a Pareto optimal substitution $\theta \in \Theta$ with respect to $\prec$.*

In the remainder of the paper, we will often consider type optimization problems extended with user-specified constraints and/or templates for some predicate variables (see Sect. 4 for examples and Sect. 5 for formal definitions).

The above definition of type optimization problems is abstract in the sense that $\prec$ is only required to be a strict partial order on predicate substitutions. We below introduce an example concrete order, which is already explained informally in Sect. 1 and adopted in our prototype implementation described in Sect. 7. The order is defined by two kinds of optimization constraints: the optimization direction (i.e. minimize/maximize) and the priority order on predicate variables.

Definition 3. *Suppose that*

- *$\mathcal{P} = \{P_1, \dots, P_m\}$ is a subset of $pvs(\Gamma_D)$,*
- *ρ is a map from each predicate variable in $\mathcal{P}$ to an optimization direction d that is either $\uparrow$ (for maximization) or $\downarrow$ (for minimization), and*
- *$\sqsubset$ is a strict total order on $\mathcal{P}$ that expresses the priority.*[2] *We below assume that $P_1 \sqsubset \cdots \sqsubset P_m$.*

We define a strict partial order $\prec_{(\rho,\sqsubset)}$ on predicate substitutions that respects ρ and $\sqsubset$ as the following lexicographic order:

$$\theta_1 \prec_{(\rho,\sqsubset)} \theta_2 \iff \exists i \in \{1, \dots, m\}.\ \theta_1(P_i) \prec_{\rho(P_i)} \theta_2(P_i) \land \forall j < i.\ \theta_1(P_j) \equiv_{\rho(P_j)} \theta_2(P_j)$$

Here, a strict partial order $\prec_d$ and an equivalence relation $\equiv_d$ on predicates are defined as follows.

[2] If $\sqsubset$ were partial, the relation $\prec_{(\rho,\sqsubset)}$ defined shortly would not be a strict partial order. Our implementation described in Sect. 7 uses topological sort to obtain a strict total order $\sqsubset$ from a user-specified partial one.

- $p_1 \prec_d p_2 \iff p_1 \preceq_d p_2 \wedge p_2 \not\preceq_d p_1$,
- $p_1 \equiv_d p_2 \iff p_1 \preceq_d p_2 \wedge p_2 \preceq_d p_1$,
- $\lambda\widetilde{x}.\phi_1 \preceq_\uparrow \lambda\widetilde{x}.\phi_2 \iff \models \phi_2 \Rightarrow \phi_1$, *and* $\lambda\widetilde{x}.\phi_1 \preceq_\downarrow \lambda\widetilde{x}.\phi_2 \iff \models \phi_1 \Rightarrow \phi_2$.

Example 1. Recall the function **sum** and its type template with the predicate variables P, Q in Sect. 1. Let us consider optimization constraints $\rho(P) = \uparrow$, $\rho(Q) = \downarrow$, and $P \sqsubset Q$, and predicate substitutions

- $\theta_1 = \{P \mapsto \lambda x.\, x = 0,\ Q \mapsto \lambda x, y.\, y = x\}$,
- $\theta_2 = \{P \mapsto \lambda x.\, \top,\ Q \mapsto \lambda x, y.\, y \geq 0\}$, and
- $\theta_3 = \{P \mapsto \lambda x.\, x < 0,\ Q \mapsto \lambda x, y.\, \bot\}$.

We then have $\theta_2 \prec_{(\rho,\sqsubset)} \theta_1$ and $\theta_2 \prec_{(\rho,\sqsubset)} \theta_3$, because $(\lambda x.\, \top) \prec_\uparrow (\lambda x.\, x = 0)$ and $(\lambda x.\, \top) \prec_\uparrow (\lambda x.\, x < 0)$. □

4 Applications of Refinement Type Optimization

In this section, we present applications of refinement type optimization to the problems of proving safety (in Sect. 4.1) and termination (in Sect. 4.3), and disproving safety (in Sect. 4.4) and termination (in Sect. 4.2) of programs in the language L. In particular, we discuss precondition inference, namely, inference of most-general characterization of inputs for which a given program satisfies (or violates) a given safety (or termination) property.

4.1 Proving Safety

We explain how to formalize, as a type optimization problem, a problem of inferring maximally-weak precondition under which a given program satisfies a given postcondition. For example, let us consider the following terminating version of **sum**.

```
let rec sum' x = if x <= 0 then 0 else x + sum' (x-1)
```

In our framework, a problem to infer a maximally-weak precondition on the argument x for a postcondition $x = \mathtt{sum}'\ x$ is expressed as a type optimization problem to infer **sum'**'s refinement type of the form $(x : \{x \mid P(x)\}) \to \{y \mid x = y\}$ under an optimization constraint *maximize*(P). Our type optimization method described in Sects. 5.2 and 6 infers the following type.

$$(x : \{x \mid 0 \leq x \leq 1\}) \to \{y \mid x = y\}$$

This type says that the postcondition holds if the actual argument x is 0 or 1.

Example 2 (Higher-Order Function). For an example of a higher-order function, consider the following.

```
let rec repeat f n e = if n<=0 then e else repeat f (n-1) (f e)
```

By inferring `repeat`'s refinement type of the form

$$(f\!:\!(x\!:\!\{x \mid P_1(x)\}) \!\rightarrow\! \{y \mid P_2(x,y)\}) \!\rightarrow\! (n\!:\!\texttt{int}) \!\rightarrow\! (e\!:\!\{e \mid P_3(n,e)\}) \!\rightarrow\! \{r \mid r \geq 0\}$$

under optimization constraints $\rho(P_1) = \downarrow$, $\rho(P_2) = \rho(P_3) = \uparrow$, and $P_3 \sqsubset P_2 \sqsubset P_1$, our type optimization method obtains

$$(f : (x : \{x \mid x \geq 0\}) \rightarrow \{y \mid y \geq 0\}) \rightarrow (n : \texttt{int}) \rightarrow (e : \{e \mid e \geq 0\}) \rightarrow \{r \mid r \geq 0\}$$

Thus, our type optimization method can infer maximally-weak refinement types for the function arguments of a given higher-order function that are sufficient for it to satisfy a given postcondition. □

4.2 Disproving Termination

In a similar manner to Sect. 4.1, we can apply type optimization to the problems of inferring maximally-weak precondition for a given program to violate the termination property. For example, consider the function `sum` in Sect. 1. For disproving termination of `sum`, we infer `sum`'s refinement type of the form $(x : \{x \mid P(x)\}) \rightarrow \{y \mid \bot\}$ under an optimization constraint *maximize*(P). Our type optimization method infers the following type.

$$(x : \{x \mid x < 0\}) \rightarrow \{y \mid \bot\}$$

The type expresses that `sum` returns no value (i.e., `sum` is non-terminating) if called with an argument x that satisfies $x < 0$.

Example 3 (Non-Deterministic Function). For an example of non-deterministic function, let us consider a problem of disproving termination of the following.

```
let rec f x = let n = read_int () in if n<0 then x else f x
```

Here, `read_int ()` is a function to get an integer value from the user and is modeled as $*_\exists$ in our language L. Note that the termination of `f` does not depend on the argument x but user inputs n. Our type optimization method successfully disproves termination of `f` by inferring a refinement type $(x : \texttt{int}) \rightarrow \{y \mid \bot\}$ for `f` and $\{n \mid n \geq 0\}$ for the user inputs n. These types mean that `f` never terminates if the user always inputs some non-negative integer. □

4.3 Proving Termination

Refinement type optimization can also be applied to bounds analysis for inferring upper bounds of the number of recursive calls. Our bounds analysis for functional programs is inspired by a program transformation approach to bounds analysis for imperative programs [6,7]. Let us consider `sum` in Sect. 1. By inserting additional parameters i and c to the definition of `sum`, we obtain

```
let rec sum_t x i c = if x=0 then 0 else x + sum_t (x-1) i (c+1)
```

Here, i and c respectively represent the initial value of the argument x and the number of recursive calls so far. For proving termination of `sum`, we infer `sum_t`'s refinement type of the form

$$(x : \{x \mid P(x)\}) \to (i : \texttt{int}) \to (c : \{c \mid \mathit{Inv}(x, i, c)\}) \to \texttt{int}$$

under optimization constraints $\mathit{maximize}(P)$, $\mathit{minimize}(\mathit{Bnd})$, $P \sqsubset \mathit{Bnd}$, and additional constraints on the predicate variables $P, \mathit{Bnd}, \mathit{Inv}$

$$\forall x, i, c.\ (\mathit{Inv}(x, i, c) \Leftarrow c = 0 \land i = x) \tag{4}$$

$$\forall x, i, c.\ (\mathit{Bnd}(i, c) \Leftarrow P(x) \land \mathit{Inv}(x, i, c)) \tag{5}$$

Here, $\mathit{Bnd}(i, c)$ is intended to represent the bounds of the number c of recursive calls of `sum` with respect to the initial value i of the argument x. We therefore assume that $\mathit{Bnd}(i, c)$ is of the form $0 \le c \le k_0 + k_1 \cdot i$, where k_0, k_1 represent unknown coefficients to be inferred. The constraint (4) is necessary to express the meaning of the inserted parameters i and c. The constraint (5) is also necessary to ensure that the bounds $\mathit{Bnd}(i, c)$ is implied by a precondition $P(x)$ and an invariant $\mathit{Inv}(x, i, c)$ of `sum`. Our type optimization method then infers

$$(x : \{x \mid x \ge 0\}) \to (i : \texttt{int}) \to (c : \{c \mid x \le i \land i = x + c\}) \to \texttt{int}$$

and $\mathit{Bnd}(i, c) \equiv 0 \le c \le i$. Thus, we can conclude that `sum` is terminating for any input $x \ge 0$ because the number c of recursive calls is bounded from above by the initial value i of the argument x.

Interestingly, we can infer a precondition for minimizing the number of recursive calls of `sum` by replacing the priority constraint $P \sqsubset \mathit{Bnd}$ with $\mathit{Bnd} \sqsubset P$, assuming that $\mathit{Bnd}(i, c)$ is of the form $0 \le c \le k_0$ for some unknown constant k_0, and adding an additional constraint $\exists x. P(x)$ (to avoid a meaningless solution $P(x) \equiv \bot$). In fact, our type optimization method obtains

$$(x : \{x \mid x = 0\}) \to (i : \texttt{int}) \to (c : \{c \mid c = 0\}) \to \texttt{int}$$

and $\mathit{Bnd}(i, c) \equiv c = 0$. Therefore, we can conclude that the minimum number of recursive calls is 0 when the actual argument x is 0.

We expect that our bounds analysis for functional programs can further be extended to infer non-linear upper bounds by adopting ideas from an elaborate transformation for bounds analysis of imperative programs [6].

4.4 Disproving Safety

We can use the same technique in Sect. 4.3 to infer maximally-weak precondition for a given program to violate a given postcondition. For example, let us consider again the function `sum`. A problem to infer a maximally-weak precondition on the argument x for violating a postcondition `sum` $x \ge 2$ can be reduced to a problem to infer `sum_t`'s refinement type of the form

$$(x : \{x \mid P(x)\}) \to (i : \texttt{int}) \to (c : \{c \mid \mathit{Inv}(x, i, c)\}) \to \{y \mid \neg(y \ge 2)\}$$

under the same constraints for bounds analysis in Sect. 4.3. The refinement type optimization method then obtains

$$(x : \{x \mid 0 \leq x \leq 1\}) \to (i : \mathtt{int}) \to (c : \{c \mid 0 \leq x \land i = x + c\}) \to \{y \mid \neg(y \geq 2)\}$$

and $Bnd(i, c) \equiv 0 \leq c \leq i$. This result says that if the actual argument x is 0 or 1, then `sum` terminates and returns some integer y that violates $y \geq 2$. In other words, $x = 0, 1$ are counterexamples to the postcondition `sum` $x \geq 2$.

We can instead find a minimal-length counterexample path[3] violating the postcondition `sum` $x \geq 2$ by replacing the priority constraint $P \sqsubset Bnd$ with $Bnd \sqsubset P$, assuming that $Bnd(i, c)$ is of the form $0 \leq c \leq k_0$ for some unknown constant k_0, and adding an additional constraint $\exists x.P(x)$. Our type optimization method then infers

$$(x : \{x \mid x = 0\}) \to (i : \mathtt{int}) \to (c : \{c \mid 0 \leq x \land i = x + c\}) \to \{y \mid \neg(y \geq 2)\}$$

and $Bnd(i, c) \equiv c = 0$. From the result, we can conclude that a minimal-length counterexample path is obtained when the actual argument x is 0.

5 Horn Constraint Optimization and Reduction from Refinement Type Optimization

We reduce refinement type optimization problems into constraint optimization problems subject to existentially-quantified Horn clauses [1,11,19]. We first formalize Horn constraint optimization problems (in Sect. 5.1) and then explain the reduction (in Sect. 5.2).

5.1 Horn Constraint Optimization Problems

Existentially-Quantified Horn Clause Constraint Sets (∃HCCSs) over QFLIA are defined as follows.

$$\begin{array}{rl}
(\exists\text{HCCSs}) & \mathcal{H} ::= \{hc_1, \ldots, hc_m\} \\
(\text{Horn clauses}) & hc ::= h \Leftarrow b \\
(\text{heads}) & h ::= P(\tilde{t}) \mid \phi \mid \exists \tilde{x}.(P(\tilde{t}) \land \phi) \\
(\text{bodies}) & b ::= P_1(\tilde{t}_1) \land \ldots \land P_m(\tilde{t}_m) \land \phi
\end{array}$$

We write $pvs(\mathcal{H})$ for the set of predicate variables that occur in $\mathcal{H}$.

A *predicate substitution* θ for an ∃HCCS $\mathcal{H}$ is a map from each $P \in pvs(\mathcal{H})$ to a closed predicate $\lambda x_1, \ldots, x_{ar(P)}.\phi$. We write $\Theta_{\mathcal{H}}$ for the set of predicate substitutions for $\mathcal{H}$. We call a substitution θ is a *solution* of $\mathcal{H}$ if for each $hc \in \mathcal{H}$, $\models \theta hc$. For a subset $\Theta \subseteq \Theta_{\mathcal{H}}$, we call a substitution $\theta \in \Theta$ is a *Θ-restricted solution* if θ is a solution of $\mathcal{H}$. Our constraint optimization method described in Sect. 6 is designed to find a Θ-restricted solution for some Θ consisting of

[3] Here, minimality is with respect to the number of recursive calls within the path.

substitutions that map each predicate variable to a predicate with a bounded number of conjunctions and disjunctions. In particular, we often use

$$\Theta_{atom} = \left\{ P \mapsto \lambda x_1, \ldots, x_{ar(P)}.n_0 + \Sigma_{i=1}^{ar(P)} n_i \cdot x_i \geq 0 \mid P \in pvs(\mathcal{H}) \right\}$$

consisting of atomic predicate substitutions.

Example 4. Recall the function sum and the predicate substitutions $\theta_1, \theta_2, \theta_3$ in Example 1. Our method reduces a type optimization problem for sum into a constraint optimization problem for the following HCCS $\mathcal{H}_{\mathtt{sum}}$ (the explanation of the reduction is deferred to Sect. 5.2).

$$\left\{ \begin{array}{l} Q(x, 0) \Leftarrow P(x) \wedge x = 0, \;\; P(x-1) \Leftarrow P(x) \wedge x \neq 0, \\ Q(x, x+y) \Leftarrow P(x) \wedge Q(x-1, y) \wedge x \neq 0 \end{array} \right\}$$

Here, θ_1 is a solution of $\mathcal{H}_{\mathtt{sum}}$, and θ_2 and θ_3 are Θ_{atom}-restricted solutions of $\mathcal{H}_{\mathtt{sum}}$. If we fix $Q(x, y) \equiv \bot$ (i.e., infer sum's type of the form $(x : \{x \mid P(x)\}) \to \{y \mid \bot\}$) for disproving termination of sum as in Sect. 4.2, we obtain the following HCCS $\mathcal{H}_{\mathtt{sum}}^{\bot}$.

$$\{\bot \Leftarrow P(x) \wedge x = 0, \;\; P(x-1) \Leftarrow P(x) \wedge x \neq 0\}$$

$\mathcal{H}_{\mathtt{sum}}^{\bot}$ has, for example, Θ_{atom}-restricted solutions $\{P \mapsto \lambda x.x < 0\}$ and $\{P \mapsto \lambda x.x < -100\}$. □

We now define Horn constraint optimization problems for ∃HCCSs.

Definition 4. *Let $\mathcal{H}$ be an ∃HCCS and $\prec$ be a strict partial order on predicate substitutions. A solution θ of $\mathcal{H}$ is called* Pareto optimal with respect to $\prec$ *if there is no solution θ' of $\mathcal{H}$ such that $\theta' \prec \theta$. A* Horn constraint optimization problem $(\mathcal{H}, \prec)$ *is a problem to find a Pareto optimal solution θ with respect to $\prec$. A* Θ-restricted Horn constraint optimization problem *is a Horn constraint optimization problem with the notion of solutions replaced by Θ-restricted solutions.*

Example 5. Recall $\mathcal{H}_{\mathtt{sum}}$ and its solutions θ_1, θ_2, θ_3 in Example 1. Let us consider a Horn constraint optimization problem $(\mathcal{H}_{\mathtt{sum}}, \prec_{(\rho,\sqsubset)})$ where $\rho(P) = \uparrow$, $\rho(Q) = \downarrow$, and $Q \sqsubset P$. We have $\theta_3 \prec_{(\rho,\sqsubset)} \theta_1$ and $\theta_3 \prec_{(\rho,\sqsubset)} \theta_2$. In fact, θ_3 is a Pareto optimal solution of $\mathcal{H}_{\mathtt{sum}}$ with respect to $\prec_{(\rho,\sqsubset)}$. □

In general, an ∃HCCS $\mathcal{H}$ may not have a Pareto optimal solution with respect to $\prec_{(\rho,\sqsubset)}$ even though $\mathcal{H}$ has a solution. For example, consider a Horn constraint optimization problem $(\mathcal{H}_{\mathtt{sum}}, \prec_{(\rho,\sqsubset)})$ where $\rho(P) = \uparrow$, $\rho(Q) = \downarrow$, and $P \sqsubset Q$. Because the semantically optimal solution $Q(x, y) \equiv y = \frac{x(x+1)}{2}$ is not expressible in QFLIA, it must be approximated, for example, as $Q(x, y) \equiv y \geq 0 \wedge y \geq x \wedge y \geq 2x - 1$. The approximated solution, however, is not Pareto optimal because we can always get a better approximation like $Q(x, y) \equiv y \geq 0 \wedge y \geq x \wedge y \geq 2x - 1 \wedge y \geq 3x - 3$ if we use more conjunctions.

We can, however, show that an ∃HCCS has a Θ_{atom}-restricted Pareto optimal solution with respect to $\prec_{(\rho,\sqsubset)}$ if it has any Θ_{atom}-restricted solution. Interested readers are referred to the extended version [8]. For the above example, θ_2 in Example 1 is a Θ_{atom}-restricted Pareto optimal solution.

```
1: procedure Optimize(H, ≺)
2:     match Solve(H) with
3:         Unknown → return Unknown
4:       | NoSol → return NoSol
5:       | Sol(θ_0) →
6:         θ := θ_0;
7:         while true do
8:             let H' = Improve_≺(θ, H) in
9:             match Solve(H') with
10:                Unknown → return Sol(θ)
11:              | NoSol → return OptSol(θ)
12:              | Sol(θ') → θ := θ'
13:        end
```

Fig. 3. Pseudo-code of the constraint optimization method for ∃HCCSs

5.2 Reduction from Refinement Type Optimization

Our method reduces a refinement type optimization problem into an Horn constraint optimization problem in a similar manner to the previous refinement type inference method [18]. Given a program D, our method first prepares a refinement type template Γ_D of D as well as, for each expression of the form `let` $x = *_\exists$ `in` e, a refinement type template $\{x \mid P(\widetilde{y}, x)\}$ of x, where P is a fresh predicate variable and $\widetilde{y}$ is the sequence of all the integer variables in the scope. Our method then generates an ∃HCCS by type-checking D against Γ_D and collecting the proof obligations of the forms $[\![\Gamma]\!] \wedge \phi_1 \Rightarrow \phi_2$ and $[\![\Gamma]\!] \Rightarrow \exists \nu.\phi$ respectively from each application of the rules ISub and Rand∃. We write $Gen(D, \Gamma_D)$ to denote the ∃HCCS thus generated from D and Γ_D.

We can show the soundness of our reduction in the same way as in [18].

Theorem 3 (Soundness of Reduction). *Let $(D, \prec)$ be a refinement type optimization problem and Γ_D be a refinement type template of D. If θ is a Pareto optimal solution of $Gen(D, \Gamma_D)$, then θ is a solution of $(D, \prec)$.*

6 Horn Constraint Optimization Method

In this section, we describe our Horn constraint optimization method for ∃HCCSs. The method repeatedly improves a current solution until convergence. The pseudo-code of the method is shown in Fig. 3. The procedure Optimize for Horn constraint optimization takes a (Θ-restricted) ∃HCCS optimization problem $(\mathcal{H}, \prec)$ and returns any of the following: *Unknown* (which means the existence of a solution is unknown), *NoSol* (which means no solution exists), *Sol*(θ) (which means θ is a possibly non-Pareto optimal solution), or *OptSol*(θ) (which means θ is a Pareto optimal solution). The sub-procedure Solve for Horn constraint solving takes an ∃HCCS $\mathcal{H}$ and returns any of *Unknown*, *NoSol*, or *Sol*(θ). The detailed description of Solve is deferred to Sect. 6.1.

Optimize first calls Solve to find an initial solution θ_0 of $\mathcal{H}$ (line 2). Optimize returns *Unknown* if Solve returns *Unknown* (line 3) and *NoSol* if Solve returns *NoSol* (line 4). Otherwise (line 5), OPTIMIZE repeatedly improves a current solution θ starting from θ_0 until convergence (lines 6 – 13). To improve θ, we call a sub-procedure $\text{IMPROVE}_{\prec}(\theta, \mathcal{H})$ that generates an $\exists$HCCS $\mathcal{H}'$ from $\mathcal{H}$ by adding constraints that require any solution θ' of $\mathcal{H}'$ satisfies $\theta' \prec \theta$ (line 8). OPTIMIZE then calls SOLVE to find a solution of $\mathcal{H}'$. If SOLVE returns *Unknown*, OPTIMIZE returns $Sol(\theta)$ as a (possibly non-Pareto optimal) solution (line 10). If SOLVE returns *NoSol*, it is the case that no improvement is possible, and hence the current solution θ is Pareto optimal. Thus, OPTIMIZE returns $OptSol(\theta)$ (line 11). Otherwise, we obtain an improved solution $\theta' \prec \theta$ (line 12). OPTIMIZE then updates the current solution θ with θ' and repeats the improvement process.

Example 6. Recall $\mathcal{H}^{\perp}_{\mathsf{sum}}$ in Example 4 and consider an optimization problem $(\mathcal{H}^{\perp}_{\mathsf{sum}}, \prec_{(\sqsubset,\rho)})$ where $\rho(P) = \uparrow$. We below explain how $\text{OPTIMIZE}(\mathcal{H}^{\perp}_{\mathsf{sum}}, \prec_{(\sqsubset,\rho)})$ proceeds. First, OPTIMIZE calls SOLVE and obtains an initial solution, e.g., $\theta_0 = \{P \mapsto \lambda x.\bot\}$ of $\mathcal{H}^{\perp}_{\mathsf{sum}}$. OPTIMIZE then calls $\text{IMPROVE}_{\prec_{(\sqsubset,\rho)}}(\theta_0, \mathcal{H}^{\perp}_{\mathsf{sum}})$ and obtains an $\exists$HCCS $\mathcal{H}' = \mathcal{H}^{\perp}_{\mathsf{sum}} \cup \{P(x) \Leftarrow \bot,\ \exists x.\neg(P(x) \Rightarrow \bot)\}$ that requires any solution θ of $\mathcal{H}'$ satisfies $\theta(P) \prec_{\rho(P)} \theta_0(P) = \lambda x.\bot$. OPTIMIZE then calls $\text{SOLVE}(\mathcal{H}')$ and obtains an improved solution, e.g., $\theta_1 = \{P \mapsto \lambda x.x < 0\}$. In the next iteration, OPTIMIZE returns θ_1 as a Pareto optimal solution because $\text{IMPROVE}_{\prec}(\theta_1, \mathcal{H}^{\perp}_{\mathsf{sum}})$ has no solution. □

We now discuss properties of the procedure OPTIMIZE under the assumption of the correctness of the sub-procedure SOLVE (i.e., θ is a Θ-restricted solution of $\mathcal{H}$ if $\text{SOLVE}(\mathcal{H})$ returns $Sol(\theta)$, and $\mathcal{H}$ has no Θ-restricted solution if $\text{SOLVE}(\mathcal{H})$ returns *NoSol*). The following theorem states the correctness of OPTIMIZE.

Theorem 4 (Correctness of the Procedure Optimize). *Let $(\mathcal{H}, \prec)$ be a Θ-restricted Horn constraint optimization problem. If $\text{OPTIMIZE}(\mathcal{H}, \prec)$ returns $OptSol(\theta)$ (resp. $Sol(\theta)$), θ is a Pareto optimal (resp. possibly non-Pareto optimal) Θ-restricted solution of $\mathcal{H}$ with respect to $\prec$.*

The following theorem states the termination of OPTIMIZE for Θ_{atom}-restricted Horn constraint optimization problems.

Theorem 5 (Termination of the Procedure Optimize). *Let $(\mathcal{H}, \prec_{(\sqsubset,\rho)})$ be a Θ_{atom}-restricted Horn constraint optimization problem. Suppose that*

(a) for any P such that $\rho(P) = \downarrow$, P is not existentially quantified in $\mathcal{H}$ and
(b) if SOLVE returns θ, for any P, θ^P defined as $\theta\{P \mapsto \lambda\tilde{x}.\phi\}$ (where $\phi \equiv \top$ if $\rho(P) = \uparrow$ and $\phi \equiv \bot$ if $\rho(P) = \downarrow$) is either not a solution or $\theta^P \not\prec_{(\sqsubset,\rho)} \theta$.

It then follows that $\text{OPTIMIZE}(\mathcal{H}, \prec_{(\sqsubset,\rho)})$ always terminates.

6.1 Sub-Procedure Solve for Solving ∃HCCSs

The pseudo-code of the sub-procedure SOLVE for solving $\exists$HCCSs is presented in Fig. 4. Here, SOLVE uses existing template-based invariant generation techniques

1: **procedure** SOLVE($\mathcal{H}$)
2: **let** $\theta = \left\{ P \mapsto \lambda\widetilde{x}.c_0 + \Sigma_{i=1}^{ar(P)} c_i \cdot x_i \geq 0 \mid P \in pvs(\mathcal{H}) \right\}$ **in**
3: **let** $\exists\widetilde{c}.\forall\widetilde{x}.\exists\widetilde{y}.\phi = \exists\widetilde{c}. \bigwedge_{hc \in \mathcal{H}} \forall fvs(hc).\theta(hc)$ **in**
4: **let** $\exists\widetilde{c},\widetilde{z}.\forall\widetilde{x}.\phi'$ = **apply Skolemization to** $\exists\widetilde{c}.\forall\widetilde{x}.\exists\widetilde{y}.\phi$ **in**
5: **let** $\exists\widetilde{c},\widetilde{z},\widetilde{w}.\phi''$ = **apply Farkas' lemma to** $\exists\widetilde{c},\widetilde{z}.\forall\widetilde{x}.\phi'$ **in**
6: **match** SMT(ϕ'') **with**
7:   $Sat(\sigma) \rightarrow$ **return** $Sol(\sigma(\theta))$
8: | *Unknown*
9: | $Unsat \rightarrow$ **match** SMT($\forall\widetilde{x}.\exists\widetilde{y}.\phi$) **with**
10:     $Unsat \rightarrow$ **return** *NoSol*
11:    | $Unknown \rightarrow$ **return** *Unknown*
12:    | $Sat(\sigma) \rightarrow$ **return** $Sol(\sigma(\theta))$

Fig. 4. Pseudo-code of the constraint solving method for ∃HCCSs based on template-based invariant generation

based on Farkas' lemma [3,7] and ∃HCCS solving techniques based on Skolemization [1,11,19]. SOLVE first generates a template substitution θ that maps each predicate variable in $pvs(\mathcal{H})$ to a template atomic predicate with unknown coefficients $c_0, \ldots, c_{ar(P)}$ (line 2).[4] SOLVE then applies θ to $\mathcal{H}$ and obtains a verification condition of the form $\exists\widetilde{c}.\forall\widetilde{x}.\exists\widetilde{y}.\phi$ without predicate variables (line 3). SOLVE applies Skolemization [1,11,19] to the condition and obtains a simplified condition of the form $\exists\widetilde{c},\widetilde{z}.\forall\widetilde{x}.\phi'$ (line 4). SOLVE further applies Farkas' lemma [3,7] to eliminate the universal quantifiers and obtains a condition of the form $\exists\widetilde{c},\widetilde{z},\widetilde{w}.\phi''$ (line 5). SOLVE then uses an SMT solver that supports the quantifier-free theory of non-linear integer arithmetic (QFNIA) to find a satisfying assignment to ϕ'' (line 6). If such an assignment σ is found, SOLVE returns $\sigma(\theta)$ as a solution (line 7). Otherwise (no assignment is found),[5] SOLVE uses an SMT solver that supports the quantified theory of non-linear integer arithmetic (NIA) to check the absence of a Θ_{atom}-restricted solution by checking the unsatisfiability of $\forall\widetilde{x}.\exists\widetilde{y}.\phi$ (line 9). SOLVE returns *NoSol* if *Unsat* is returned (line 10) and *Unknown* if *Unknown* is returned (line 11). Otherwise (a satisfying assignment σ is found), SOLVE returns $\sigma(\theta)$ as a solution (line 12).

Example 7. We explain how SOLVE proceeds for $\mathcal{H}'$ in Example 6. SOLVE first generates a template substitution $\theta = \{P \mapsto \lambda x.c_0 + c_1 \cdot x \geq 0\}$ with unknown

[4] The presented code here is thus specialized to solve Θ_{atom}-restricted Horn constraint optimization problems. To solve Θ-restricted optimization problems for other Θ, we need here to generate templates that conform to the shape of substitutions in Θ instead. Our implementation in Sect. 7 iteratively increases the template size.

[5] Note here that even though no assignment is found, $\mathcal{H}$ may have a Θ_{atom}-restricted solution because Farkas' lemma is not complete for QFLIA formulas [3,7] and Skolemization of $\exists\widetilde{c}.\forall\widetilde{x}.\exists\widetilde{y}.\phi$ into $\exists\widetilde{c},\widetilde{z}.\forall\widetilde{x}.\phi'$ here assumes that $\widetilde{y}$ are expressed as linear expressions over $\widetilde{x}$ [1,11,19].

coefficients c_0, c_1 and applies θ to $\mathcal{H}'$. As a result, we get a verification condition

$$\exists c_0, c_1. \left(\begin{array}{l} \forall x. \left(\begin{array}{l} (\bot \Leftarrow c_0 + c_1 \cdot x \geq 0 \land x = 0) \land \\ (c_0 + c_1 \cdot (x-1) \geq 0 \Leftarrow c_0 + c_1 \cdot x \geq 0 \land x \neq 0) \end{array} \right) \land \\ \exists x.\ c_0 + c_1 \cdot x \geq 0 \end{array} \right)$$

By applying Farkas' lemma, we obtain

$$\exists c_0, c_1. \left(\begin{array}{l} \exists w_1, w_2, w_3 \geq 0.\ (c_0 \cdot w_1 \leq -1 \land c_1 \cdot w_1 + w_2 - w_3 = 0) \land \\ \exists w_4, w_5, w_6 \geq 0. \left(\begin{array}{l} (-1 - c_0 + c_1) \cdot w_4 + c_0 \cdot w_5 - w_6 \leq -1 \land \\ c_1 \cdot (-w_4 + w_5) + w_6 = 0 \end{array} \right) \land \\ \exists w_7, w_8, w_9 \geq 0. \left(\begin{array}{l} (-1 - c_0 + c_1) \cdot w_7 + c_0 \cdot w_8 - w_9 \leq -1 \land \\ c_1 \cdot (-w_7 + w_8) - w_9 = 0 \end{array} \right) \land \\ \exists x.\ c_0 + c_1 \cdot x \geq 0 \end{array} \right)$$

By using an SMT solver, we obtain, for example, a satisfying assignment σ such that $\sigma(c_0) = \sigma(c_1) = -1$, $\sigma(w_1) = \sigma(w_2) = \sigma(w_5) = \sigma(w_6) = \sigma(w_7) = \sigma(w_9) = 1$, and $\sigma(w_3) = \sigma(w_4) = \sigma(w_8) = 0$. Thus, SOLVE returns $\sigma(\theta) = \{P \mapsto \lambda x. -1 - x \geq 0\} \equiv \theta_1$ in Example 6. □

The following theorem states the correctness of the sub-procedure SOLVE.

Lemma 1 (Correctness of the Sub-Procedure Solve). *Let $\mathcal{H}$ be an $\exists$HCCS. θ is a Θ_{atom}-restricted solution of $\mathcal{H}$ if* SOLVE($\mathcal{H}$) *returns Sol(θ), and $\mathcal{H}$ has no Θ_{atom}-restricted solution if* SOLVE($\mathcal{H}$) *returns NoSol.*

7 Implementation and Experiments

We have implemented a prototype refinement type optimization tool for OCaml based on the method presented in this paper. Our tool uses Z3 (https://z3.codeplex.com/) as its underlying SMT solver. We conducted preliminary experiments on a machine with Intel Core i7-3770 3.40GHz, 16GB of RAM.

Table 1. The results of a non-termination verification benchmark set used in [2,11,13].

	Verified	TimeOut	Other
Our tool	41	27	13
CPPINV [13]	70	6	5
T2-TACAS [2]	51	0	30
MoCHi [11]	48	26	7
TNT [4]	19	3	59

The experimental results are summarized in Tables 1 and 2. Table 1 shows the results of an existing first-order non-termination verification benchmark set used in [2,11,13]. Because the original benchmark set was written in the input language of T2 (http://mmjb.github.io/T2/), we used an OCaml translation of the benchmark set provided by [11]. The results for CPPINV, T2-TACAS, and TNT are according to Larraz et al. [13]. The result for MoCHi is according to [11]. Our tool was able to successfully disprove termination of 41 programs (out of 81) in the time limit of 100 seconds. Our prototype tool was not the best but performed reasonably well compared to the state-of-the-art tools dedicated to non-termination verification.

Table 2. The results of maximally-weak precondition inference.

Program	App.	#I	Time	Op.	Program	App.	#I	Time	Op.
fixpoint [11]	D/T	1	0.300	✓	append [12]	P/T	10	10.664	✓*
fib_CPS [11]	D/T	1	7.083	✓*	zip [12]	P/T	3	12.236	
indirect_e [11]	D/T	1	0.344	✓	repeat (Sec.4.1)	P/S	4	0.948	✓*
indirectHO_e [11]	D/T	1	0.312	✓	sum′ (Sec.4.1)	P/S	2	0.036	✓
loopHO [11]	D/T	1	16.094	✓*	sum (Sec.4.2)	D/T	1	0.174	✓
foldr [11]	D/T	3	8.048	✓	sum_t (Sec.4.3)	P/T($P \sqsubset Bnd$)	5	12.028	✓*
sum_geq3	P/S	4	2.654	✓*	sum_t (Sec.4.3)	P/T($Bnd \sqsubset P$)	2	15.504	✓*
append	P/S	5	3.608	✓*	sum_t (Sec.4.4)	D/S($P \sqsubset Bnd$)	4	12.020	✓*
fib	D/T	1	0.039	✓	sum_t (Sec.4.4)	D/S($Bnd \sqsubset P$)	1	20.780	✓*

Table 2 shows the results of maximally-weak precondition inference for proving safety (P/S) and termination (P/T), and disproving safety (D/S) and termination (D/T). We used non-termination (resp. termination) verification benchmarks for higher-order functional programs from [11] (resp. [12]). The column "#I" shows the number of optimization iterations, and the column "Time" shows the running time in seconds. The column "Op." shows whether Pareto optimal refinement types are inferred: ✓(resp. ✓*) indicates that the Pareto optimality of inferred types is checked automatically by our tool (resp. manually by us). The results show that our prototype tool is reasonably efficient for proving safety (P/S) and disproving termination (D/T) of higher-order functions. Further engineering work, however, is required to make the tool more efficient for proving termination (P/T) and disproving safety (D/S).

8 Related Work

Type inference problems for refinement type systems [5,20] have been intensively studied [9,10,15–19]. To our knowledge, this paper is the first to address type optimization problems, which generalize ordinary type inference problems. As we saw in Sects. 4 and 7, this generalization enables significantly wider applications in the verification of higher-order functional programs.

For imperative programs, Gulwani et al. have proposed a template-based method to infer maximally-weak pre and maximally-strong post conditions [7]. Their method, however, cannot directly handle higher-order functional programs, (angelic and demonic) non-determinism in programs, and prioritized multi-objective optimization, which are all handled by our new method.

Internally, our method reduces a type optimization problem to a constraint optimization problem subject to an existentially quantified Horn clause constraint set (∃HCCS). Constraint *solving* problems for ∃HCCSs have been studied by recent work [1,11,19]. They, however, do not address constraint *optimization* problems. The goal of our constraint optimization is to maximize/minimize the set of the models for each predicate variable occurring in the given ∃HCCS. Thus, our constraint optimization problems are different from Max-SMT [14] problems whose goal is to minimize the sum of the penalty of unsatisfied clauses.

9 Conclusion

We have generalized refinement type inference problems to type optimization problems, and presented interesting applications enabled by type optimization to inferring most-general characterization of inputs for which a given functional program satisfies (or violates) a given safety (or termination) property. We have also proposed a refinement type optimization method based on template-based invariant generation. We have implemented our method and confirmed by experiments that the proposed method is promising for the applications.

References

1. Beyene, T.A., Popeea, C., Rybalchenko, A.: Solving existentially quantified horn clauses. In: Sharygina, N., Veith, H. (eds.) CAV 2013. LNCS, vol. 8044, pp. 869–882. Springer, Heidelberg (2013)
2. Chen, H.-Y., Cook, B., Fuhs, C., Nimkar, K., O'Hearn, P.: Proving nontermination via safety. In: Ábrahám, E., Havelund, K. (eds.) TACAS 2014 (ETAPS). LNCS, vol. 8413, pp. 156–171. Springer, Heidelberg (2014)
3. Colón, M.A., Sankaranarayanan, S., Sipma, H.B.: Linear invariant generation using non-linear constraint solving. In: Hunt Jr, W.A., Somenzi, F. (eds.) CAV 2003. LNCS, vol. 2725, pp. 420–432. Springer, Heidelberg (2003)
4. Emmes, F., Enger, T., Giesl, J.: Proving non-looping non-termination automatically. In: Gramlich, B., Miller, D., Sattler, U. (eds.) IJCAR 2012. LNCS, vol. 7364, pp. 225–240. Springer, Heidelberg (2012)
5. Freeman, T., Pfenning, F.: Refinement types for ML. In: PLDI 1991, pp. 268–277. ACM (1991)
6. Gulwani, S., Mehra, K.K., Chilimbi, T.: SPEED: Precise and efficient static estimation of program computational complexity. In: POPL 2009, pp. 127–139. ACM (2009)
7. Gulwani, S., Srivastava,S., Venkatesan, R.: Program analysis as constraint solving. In: PLDI 2008, pp. 281–292. ACM (2008)
8. Hashimoto, K. Unno, H.: Refinement type inference via horn constraint optimization. An extended version (2015). http://www.cs.tsukuba.ac.jp/~uhiro/
9. Jhala, R., Majumdar, R., Rybalchenko, A.: HMC: verifying functional programs using abstract interpreters. In: Gopalakrishnan, G., Qadeer, S. (eds.) CAV 2011. LNCS, vol. 6806, pp. 470–485. Springer, Heidelberg (2011)
10. Kobayashi, N., Sato, R., Unno, H.: Predicate abstraction and CEGAR for higher-order model checking. In: PLDI 2011, pp. 222–233. ACM (2011)
11. Kuwahara, T., Sato, R., Unno, H., Kobayashi, N.: Predicate abstraction and CEGAR for disproving termination of higher-order functional programs. In: Kroening, D., Păsăreanu, C.S. (eds.) CAV 2015. LNCS, vol. 9207, pp. 287–303. Springer, Heidelberg (2015)
12. Kuwahara, T., Terauchi, T., Unno, H., Kobayashi, N.: Automatic termination verification for higher-order functional programs. In: Shao, Z. (ed.) ESOP 2014 (ETAPS). LNCS, vol. 8410, pp. 392–411. Springer, Heidelberg (2014)
13. Larraz, D., Nimkar, K., Oliveras, A., Rodríguez-Carbonell, E., Rubio, A.: Proving non-termination using max-SMT. In: Biere, A., Bloem, R. (eds.) CAV 2014. LNCS, vol. 8559, pp. 779–796. Springer, Heidelberg (2014)

14. Nieuwenhuis, R., Oliveras, A.: On SAT modulo theories and optimization problems. In: Biere, A., Gomes, C.P. (eds.) SAT 2006. LNCS, vol. 4121, pp. 156–169. Springer, Heidelberg (2006)
15. Rondon, P., Kawaguchi, M., Jhala, R.: Liquid types. In: PLDI 2008, pp. 159–169. ACM (2008)
16. Terauchi, T.: Dependent types from counterexamples. In: POPL 2010, pp. 119–130. ACM (2010)
17. Unno, H., Kobayashi, N.: On-demand refinement of dependent types. In: Garrigue, J., Hermenegildo, M.V. (eds.) FLOPS 2008. LNCS, vol. 4989, pp. 81–96. Springer, Heidelberg (2008)
18. Unno, H., Kobayashi, N.: Dependent type inference with interpolants. In: PPDP 2009, pp. 277–288. ACM (2009)
19. Unno, H., Terauchi,T., Kobayashi, N.: Automating relatively complete verification of higher-order functional programs. In: POPL 2013, pp. 75–86. ACM (2013)
20. Xi, H., Pfenning, F.: Dependent types in practical programming. In: POPL 1999, pp. 214–227. ACM (1999)

A Simple Abstraction of Arrays and Maps by Program Translation

David Monniaux[1,2] and Francesco Alberti[3(✉)]

[1] Université Grenoble Alpes, VERIMAG, 38000 Grenoble, France
[2] CNRS, VERIMAG, 38000 Grenoble, France
[3] Fondazione Centro San Raffaele, Milan, Italy
Francesco.Albe@gmail.com

Abstract. We present an approach for the static analysis of programs handling arrays, with a Galois connection between the semantics of the array program and semantics of purely scalar operations. The simplest way to implement it is by automatic, syntactic transformation of the array program into a scalar program followed analysis of the scalar program with any static analysis technique (abstract interpretation, acceleration, predicate abstraction,...). The scalars invariants thus obtained are translated back onto the original program as universally quantified array invariants. We illustrate our approach on a variety of examples, leading to the "Dutch flag" algorithm.

1 Introduction

Static analysis aims at automatically discovering program properties. Traditionally, it has focused on dataflow properties (e.g. "can this pointer be null?"), then on numerical properties (e.g. "$2x+y \leq 45$ at every iteration of this loop"). When it comes to programs operating over *arrays*, special challenges arise. For instance, the ASTRÉE static analyzer,[1] based on abstract interpretation and commercially used in the avionics, automotive and other industries, supports arrays simplistically: it either "smashes" all cells in a single array into a single abstract value, or expands an array of n cells into n variables; in many cases it is necessary to fully unroll loops operating over an array in order to prove the desired property[2].

D. Monniaux—The research leading to these results has received funding from the European Research Council under the European Union's Seventh Framework Programme (FP/2007–2013) / ERC Grant Agreement nr. 306595 "STATOR"
F. Alberti—This work has been carried out while the author was affiliated to the Università della Svizzera Italiana and supported by the Swiss National Science Foundation under grant no. P1TIP2_152261.

[1] [7,8,15] http://www.astree.ens.fr, http://absint.de/astree/.
[2] Possible since ASTRÉE targets safety-critical embedded systems where array sizes are typically fixed at system design and dynamic memory allocation is prohibited.

S. Blazy and T. Jensen (Eds.): SAS 2015, LNCS 9291, pp. 217–234, 2015.
DOI: 10.1007/978-3-662-48288-9_13

In general, however, analyzing arrays programs entails exhibiting inductive loop invariants with universal quantification over array indices. Neither smashing nor expansion can prove, in general, that a simple initialization loop truly does work:

Listing 1.1. Simple array initialization

```
int t[n]; for(int i=0; i<n; i++) t[i] = 0;
```

To derive the postcondition $\forall k.0 \leq k < n \rightarrow t[k] = 0$, one uses the loop invariant (in the Floyd-Hoare sense) $0 \leq i \leq n \wedge \forall k.0 \leq k < i \rightarrow t[k] = 0$. The $0 \leq i \leq n$ part (or generalizations, e.g., filling the upper triangular part of a matrix) can be automatically inferred by many existing numeric analysis techniques. In contrast, the $\forall k.0 \leq k < i \rightarrow t[k] = 0$ part is trickier and is the focus of this article.

Contribution. We propose a generic method for analyzing array programs, which can be implemented (i) as a normal abstract domain (ii) or by translating the program with arrays into a scalar program (a program without arrays), analyzing this program by any method producing invariants (back-end), and then recovering the array properties. Its precision depends on the back-end analysis. Our method has tunable precision and is formalized by Galois connections [12] and, contrary to most others, is not guided by a target property (here $\forall k.0 \leq k < n \rightarrow t[k] = 0$), though it can take advantage of it. It can therefore be used to supply information to the end-user "what does this program do?" as opposed to be useful only for proving properties. We demonstrate the flexibility of our approach on examples, using the acceleration procedure FLATA, the abstract interpreter CONCURINTERPROC and CPACHECKER as back-ends.

We also show a form of *completeness*: for any loop-free program, the precision of the analysis can be chosen so that it is exact with respect to universally quantified array properties (Sect. 4.3).

Our approach also applies to general maps *keys* $\rightarrow$ *values*, though certain optimizations apply only to totally ordered index types.

Contents. Section 2 introduces our approach on one example. Section 3 discusses the Galois connections, and Sect. 4 gives the formal definition of our transformation algorithm and associated correctness and partial completeness proofs. Section 5 discusses the use of various backends on more examples. We discuss the relevant related work in Sect. 6 and conclude in Sect. 7.

2 Example: The Sentinel

Our program transformation consists in (i) a replacement of reads and writes parameterized by a number of distinguished indices, formalized in Sect. 4 (ii) optionally, some "focusing" on a subset of index values (iii) for certain backends (CONCURINTERPROC), the addition of observer variables implementing a form of partitioning.

Listing 1.2. A "sentinel value" marks the penultimate array cell

```
const int N=1000; int i = 0, t[N];
initialize(N, t); t[N-2] = -1;
while (t[i]>=0) i++;
```

Obviously to us humans, this program cannot crash with an array access out of bounds, and the final value of i is, at most, 998 (its value depends on how the " initialize " procedure works). How can we obtain this result automatically?

Let x be a symbolic constant in $\{0, \ldots, N-1\}$. We abstract array t by the single cell t[x], represented by variable tx: reads and writes at position x in t translates to reads and writes to variable tx and reads and writes at other positions are ignored. Program 1.2 is thus abstracted as:[3]

```
const int N=1000, x = random(); assume(x >= 0 && x < N);
int i = 0, tx = random(); if (N-2 == x) tx=-1;
while(1) { int read = random(); if (i == x) { read = tx; }
           if (read < 0) { break; } i = i+1;                 }
```

FLATA [10,27] can compute an exact input/output relation of this program (to demonstrate generality, we left N unfixed and replaced N−2 by a parameter p; we thus use a precondition $0 \leq x < N \land 0 \leq p < N$):

$$\begin{aligned}
&(p = x \land i \leq x-1 \land i \geq 0 \land N \geq x+1) \lor (i = x \land i \geq 0 \land N \geq p+1 \land i \leq p-1) \lor \\
&(x \geq p+1 \land i \leq x-1 \land i \geq 0 \land N \geq x+1 \land p \geq 0) \lor (i = x \land i \leq N-1 \land i \geq p+1 \land p \geq 0) \lor \\
&(i \geq x+1 \land N \geq p+1 \land i \leq N-1 \land x \leq p-1 \land x \geq 0) \lor \qquad\qquad (F) \\
&(i \leq x-1 \land i \geq 0 \land N \geq p+1 \land x \leq p-1) \lor \\
&(i = x \land i = p \land i \geq 0 \land i \leq N-1) \lor (x \geq p+1 \land i \geq x+1 \land i \leq N-1 \land p \geq 0)
\end{aligned}$$

Note that our abstraction is valid *whatever the value of* x. This means that (i, p, N) should be a solution of $N > 0 \land \forall x\,(0 \leq x < N \Rightarrow F)$. One can check that this quantified formula entails $i \leq p$.

Arguably, we have done too much work: the only cell in the array whose content matters much is at index p (N−2 in the original program). Running FLATA with $x = p$ yields a postcondition implying $i \leq p$. Again, this is sound, because *any* choice of x yields a valid postcondition on (i, p).

3 Galois Connections

We shall now see that, for any choice of indices, there is a Galois connection $\underset{\alpha}{\overset{\gamma}{\leftrightarrows}}$ [12] between the concrete (the set of possible values of the vector of variables of the original program) and the abstract set of states (the set of possible values of the vector of variables in the transformed program). In general, this Galois connection is not onto: there are abstract elements $x^\natural$ that include "spurious" states, and which may be reduced to a strictly smaller $\alpha \circ \gamma(x^\natural)$.

[3] We have left out, for the sake of brevity, tests for array accesses out of bounds.

If A and B are sets, $A \to B$ denotes the set of total functions from A to B, and $\mathcal{P}(A)$ the set of parts of A. If A is finite, $A \to B$ denotes the set of *arrays* indexed by A; specifically, if A is $\{1,\ldots,l_1\} \times \cdots \times \{1,\ldots,l_d\}$ then $A \to B$ denotes the d-dimensional arrays of size $(l_1,\ldots,l_d)$. $f[x]$ denotes the application $f(x)$ where f is a program array or map.

Our constructions easily generalize to arbitrary combinations of numbers of arrays and numbers of indices; let us see a few common cases.

3.1 Single Index

Applied with a single index, our map abstraction is classical [14, Sect. 2.1].

Definition. Let $f \in A \to B$, we abstract it by its graph $\alpha_1(f) = \{(a, f[a]) \mid a \in A\}$; e.g., a constant array $\{1,\ldots,n\} \to \mathbb{Z}$ with value 42 is abstracted as $\{(i,42) \mid 1 \leq i \leq n\}$.

We lift α_1 (while keeping the same notation) to a function from $\mathcal{P}(A \to B)$ to $\mathcal{P}(A \times B)$: for $F^\flat \subseteq A \to B$, $\alpha_1(F^\flat) = \bigcup_{f \in F} \alpha_1(f)$, otherwise said

$$\alpha_1(F^\flat) = \left\{(a, f[a]) \mid a \in A, f \in F^\flat\right\} \tag{1}$$

Let $F^\natural \subseteq A \times B$. Then we define its concretization $\gamma_1(F^\natural)$:

$$\gamma_1(F^\natural) = \{f \in A \to B \mid \forall a \in A\ (a, f[a]) \in F^\natural\} \tag{2}$$

It is easy to see that $(\mathcal{P}(A \to B), \subseteq) \underset{\alpha_1}{\overset{\gamma_1}{\leftrightarrows}} \mathcal{P}(A \times B)$ is a Galois connection.

Non-surjectivity and Reduction. Remark that α_1 is not onto (if $|A| > 1$ and $|B| > 0$): there exist multiple $F^\natural$ such that $\gamma_1(F^\natural) = \emptyset$, namely all those such that $\exists a \in A \forall b \in B\ (a,b) \notin F^\natural$. For instance, if considering arrays of two integer elements ($A = \{0,1\}$, $B = \mathbb{Z}$), then $F^\natural = \{(1,0)\}$ yields $\gamma_1(F^\natural) = \emptyset$: there is no way to fill the array at index 0.

Let us now see the practical implication. Assume that the program has a single array in $A \to B$ and a vector of scalar variables ranging in S, then the memory state is an element of $X^\flat \triangleq S \times (A \to B)$. The scalar variables are combined into our abstraction as follows:

$$\mathcal{P}(S \times (A \to B)) \cong S \to \mathcal{P}(A \to B) \underset{\alpha_1^S}{\overset{\gamma_1^S}{\leftrightarrows}} S \to \mathcal{P}(A \times B) \cong \mathcal{P}(S \times A \times B) \triangleq X^\natural, \tag{3}$$

where α_1^S and γ_1^S lift α_1 and γ_1 pointwise. Let $s \in S$. While the absence of any $(s,a,b) \in x^\natural$ ($x^\natural \in X^\natural$) indicates that there is no $(s,f) \in \gamma_1^S(x^\natural)$, that is, scalar state s is unreachable, the converse is *not* true. Consider a single integer scalar variable s and an array a of length 2, and $x^\natural = \{(0,0,1),(1,0,0),(1,1,2)\}$, representing the triples $(s,i,a[i])$. It would seem that $s = 0$ is reachable, but it is not, because there is no way to fill the array at position 1: there is no element in $x^\natural$ of the form $(0,1,b)$.

A *reduction* is a function $\rho : X^\natural \to X^\natural$ such that $\gamma \circ \rho = \gamma$ and $\rho(x^\natural) \subseteq x^\natural$ for all $x^\natural$. The strongest reduction ρ_{opt} (the minimum for the pointwise ordering induced by $\subseteq$) is $\alpha \circ \gamma$. In the above, $\rho_{\text{opt}}(x^\natural) = \{(1,0,0),(1,1,2)\}$; intuitively, the strongest reduction discards all superfluous elements from the abstract value.

Class of Formulas. Assume now that the vector of scalar variables $s_1, \ldots, s_m$ lies within $S = \mathbb{Z}^m$, the index a lies in $\{1,\ldots,l_1\} \times \cdots \times \{1,\ldots,l_D\}$, and the values $f[a]$ also lie in $\mathbb{Z}$. Consider a formula ψ of the form

$$\forall a_1, \ldots, a_d \; \phi(s_1, \ldots, s_m, a_1, \ldots, a_d, f[a_1, \ldots, a_d]) \tag{4}$$

where ϕ is a first-order arithmetic formula (say, Presburger).

Then, $f \models \psi$ if and only if $\alpha_1^S(f) \subseteq \{((s_1, \ldots, s_m), (a_1, \ldots, a_d), b) \mid \phi(s_1,, \ldots,, s_m, a_1,, \ldots,, a_d, b)\}$. The sets of program states expressible by formulas of form 4 thus map through the Galois connection to a sub-lattice of $\mathcal{P}\left(\mathbb{Z}^m \times \mathbb{Z}^d \times \mathbb{Z}\right)$. This construction may be generalized to any theory or combination of theories over the sorts used for scalar variables, array indices, and array contents.

Checking that an invariant $\gamma_1^S(G)$ entails ψ, when the set G is defined by a formula Γ, just amounts to checking that $\Gamma \wedge \neg\psi$ is unsatisfiable.

3.2 Several Indices, One Per Array

The above settings can be extended to several arrays. Let $f, g \in A \to B$, we abstract them by the product of their graphs $\alpha_1(f,g) = \{(a, f[a], a', g[a']) \mid a, a' \in A\}$, $\gamma_1(x^\natural) = \{(f,g) \in (A \to B)^2 \mid \forall a, a' \in A \; (a, f[a], a', g[a']) \in x^\natural\}$. This abstraction can express properties of the form

$$\forall a_1, \ldots, a_d, a_1', \ldots, a_d' \; \phi(s_1, \ldots, s_m, a_1, \ldots, a_d, f[a_1, \ldots, a_d], a_1', \ldots, a_d', g[a_1', \ldots, a_d'])$$

As an example, the property that up to index k, monodimensional array f of length n has been copied into array g can be expressed as $\forall a, a' \in \{1, \ldots, n\} \; a < k \wedge a = a' \Rightarrow f[a] = g[a']$ within that class.

3.3 Dual Indices, Same Array

Definition. Let $f \in A \to B$, pose $\alpha_2(f) = \{(a, f[a], a', f[a']) \mid a, a' \in A\}$ and lift it to a function from $\mathcal{P}(A \to B)$ to $\mathcal{P}\left((A \times B)^2\right)$. Let $F^\natural \subseteq (A \times B)^2$. Then we define its concretization $\gamma_2(F^\natural)$:

$$\gamma_2(F^\natural) = \{f \in A \to B \mid \forall a, a' \in A \; (a, f[a], a', f[a']) \in F^\natural\} \tag{5}$$

It is easy to see that $(\mathcal{P}(A \to B), \subseteq) \underset{\alpha_2}{\overset{\gamma_2}{\leftrightarrows}} \mathcal{P}(A \times B)$ is a Galois connection.

If A is totally ordered, it seems a waste to include both $(a, f[a], a', f[a'])$ and $(a', f[a'], a, f[a])$ in the abstraction for $a < a'$. We thus define $\alpha_{2<}(f) = \{(a, f[a], a', f[a']) \mid a < a' \in A\}$ and $\gamma_{2<}(x^\natural) = \{f \in A \to B \mid \forall a, a' \in A \,, a < a' \Rightarrow (a, f[a], a', f[a']) \in x^\natural\}$.

Non-surjectivity. Remark, again, that α_2 is not onto. Consider an array of integers of length 3, that is, a function $f : \{1,2,3\} \to \mathbb{Z}$. An analysis computes its abstraction as $x^\natural = \{(1,0,2,0),(1,0,3,0),(2,0,3,0),(1,0,3,1)\}$; recall that each element of that set purports to denote $(a, f[a], a', f[a'])$ for $a < a'$. At first sight, it seems that $f(3) = 1$ is possible, as witnessed by the last element. Yet, there is then no way to fill $a[2]$: there is no x such that $(2, x, 3, 1) \in x^\natural$. This last element is therefore superfluous, and we can conclude that $\forall x\ f[x] = 0$. (See Sect. 5.5 for a real-life example.)

If $x^\natural$ is defined by a first-order formula ($x^\natural = \{(a, b, a', b') \mid \phi(a, b, a', b')\}$), then this reduction (removing all a', b' such that for some $a < a'$ there is no way to fill $f[a]$) is obtained as: $\forall a \exists b\ a < a' \Rightarrow \phi(a, b, a', b')$.

Class of Formulas. Assume now that the vector of scalar variables $s_1, \ldots, s_m$ lies within $S = \mathbb{Z}^m$, the indices $a < a'$ lie in $\{1, \ldots, n\}$, and the values $f[a], f[a']$ also lie in $\mathbb{Z}$. Consider a formula ψ of the form $\forall a, a'\ a < a' \Rightarrow \phi(s_1, \ldots, s_m, a, f[a], a', f[a'])$ where ϕ is a first-order arithmetic formula (say, Presburger). For instance, one may express *sortedness*: $\forall a, a'\ a < a' \Rightarrow f[a] \leq f[a']$.

Then, $f \models \psi$ if and only if $\alpha^S_{2<}(f) \in \{((s_1, \ldots, s_m), a, b, a', b') \mid \phi(s_1, \ldots, s_m, a, b, a', b')\}$. The sets of program states expressible by formulas of the form $\forall a, a'\ a < a' \Rightarrow \phi(s_1, \ldots, s_m, a, f[a], a', f[a'])$ thus map through the Galois connection to a sub-lattice of $\mathcal{P}\left(\mathbb{Z}^m \times (\mathbb{Z} \times \mathbb{Z})^2\right)$.

4 Abstraction of Program Semantics

Our analysis may be implemented by a syntactic transformation of array operations into purely scalar operations. In this section, for each operation (read, write) we describe the transformed operation and demonstrate the correctness of the transformation. We then discuss precision.

Without loss of generality, we consider only elementary reads and writes (r= f[i]; and f[i]=r; with i a variable). More complex constructs, e.g. f[e]=r; with e an expression, can always be decomposed into a sequence of scalar operations and elementary read and writes, using temporary variables.

4.1 Transformation and Correctness

Reading from the Array. Consider a program state composed of (s, r, i, f) where $r \in B$, $i \in A$ are scalars, $s \in S$ is the rest of the state, and $f \in A \to B$. Consider the instruction r=f[i];, its semantics is:

$$(s, r, i, f) \xrightarrow{\texttt{r=f[i];}} (s, f(i), i, f) \tag{6}$$

We wish to abstract it by the program fragment:

Listing 1.3. Read from array

```
r = random(); if (i==a) { r=b; }
```

Lemma 1. *The forward and backward semantics of Program 1.3 abstract the forward and backwards semantics of r=f[i]; by the* (α_1^S, γ_1^S) *Galois connection.*

More generally, a read with several indexes $a_1, a_2, \ldots$ is abstracted by

```
r=random();if (i==a1) assume(r==b1); if (i==a2) assume(r==b2); ...
```

The same lemma and proof carry to that setting.

Writing to the Array. Consider the instruction f[i]=r;, its semantics is:

$$(s, r, i, f) \xrightarrow{\texttt{f[i]=r;}} (s, r, i, f[i \mapsto r]) \tag{7}$$

We wish to abstract it by the program fragment:

Listing 1.4. Write to array

```
if (i==a) { b=r; }
```

Lemma 2. *The forward and backward semantics of Program 1.4 abstract the forward and backwards semantics of f[i]=r; by the* (α_1^S, γ_1^S) *Galois connection.*

The same carries over to writing to an array with several indices, abstracted as:

Listing 1.5. Write to array, multiple indexes

```
if (i==a1) { b1=r; }  if (i==a2) { b2=r; } ...
```

Operations on Scalars. Consider a program state composed of (s, f) where $f \in A \to B$ is an array and $s \in S$ is the rest of the state. Consider a scalar instruction $s \xrightarrow{P} s'$ and thus $(s, f) \xrightarrow{P^\flat} (s', f)$. We abstract P as: $(s, a, b) \xrightarrow{P^\natural} (s', a, b)$ if $s \to Ps'$. Essentially, operations on scalars are abstracted by themselves. The following result generalizes immediately to (α_2, γ_2) etc.

Lemma 3. *The forward and backward semantics of* $\xrightarrow{P^\natural}$ *abstract those of* $\xrightarrow{P^\flat}$ *by the* (α_1^S, γ_1^S) *Galois connection.*

4.2 Precision Loss

"Forgetting" the value of a scalar variable v corresponds to $(s, v, f) \to (s, f)$. This scalar operation may be correctly abstracted, as in Lemma 3, by $(s, v, a, b) \to (s, a, b)$. Surprisingly, applying this operation not only forgets the value of v, it may also enlarge the set of represented f.

Example: $x^\natural = \{(0, v, a, v) \mid a \in A \land v \in B\}$ abstracts by (α_1^S, γ_1^S) the set of triples $(0, v, f)$ where f is a constant function of value v. Forgetting v yields the set of pairs $(0, f)$ where f is a constant function. Applying $(s, v, a, b) \to (s, a, b)$ to $x^\natural$ yields $y^\natural = \{(0, a, v) \mid A \in A \land v \in B\}$, which concretizes to the set $\{(0, f) \mid f \in A \to B\}$. We have completely lost the "constantness" property.

4.3 Relative Completeness

We now consider the problem of *completeness* of this abstraction, assuming that the back-end analysis is perfectly precise (thus *relative completeness*).

Our analysis is incomplete in general. Consider the following program:

Listing 1.6. Fill with zero, test zero

```
int t[N];   for(int i=0; i<N; i++) t[i]=0;
for(int i=0; i<N; i++) if (t[i]!=0) break;
```

In the second loop, the **break** statement is never reached and thus at the end of the loop, $i = N$. Yet, if we distinguish $n < N$ different indices $i_1, \dots, i_n$, we cannot prove that this statement is never reached: for there will exist $i \in \{0, \dots, N-1\} \setminus \{i_1, \dots, i_n\}$ such that t[i] returns, in the abstracted program, an arbitrary value and thus the **break** statement is considered possibly reachable.

In contrast, when the program is loop-free, the abstraction is exact with respect to the scalar variables, provided the number of indices used for the abstraction is at least the number of array accesses:

Theorem 1. *Consider a loop-free array program P with arrays $a_1, \dots, a_d$ such that the number of accesses to these arrays are respectively $\alpha_1, \dots, \alpha_d$. By abstracting these arrays with, respectively, $n_1, \dots, n_d$ indices such that $n_i \geq \alpha_i$ for all i, we obtain a Galois connection $\underset{\alpha}{\overset{\gamma}{\leftrightarrows}}$ such that $\pi_S \circ \gamma \circ P^\natural \circ \alpha = \pi_S \circ P^\flat$ where π_S is the projection of the state to the scalar variables.*

This completeness results extends to universally quantified array properties $\forall i_1, \dots\ P(i_1, \dots) \rightarrow Q(a_1[i_1], \dots)$: one appends to the original program (assuming $i_1, \dots, i_n$ are fresh, nondeterministically initialized):

```
assume((P(i1,...)); assert(Q(i1,...));
```

5 More Examples

5.1 Matrix Initialization

Listing 1.7. Initialization of $m \times n$ matrix a with value v

```
void array_init_2d(int m, int n, int a[m][n], int v) {
  for(int i = 0; i < m; i++) {
    for(int j = 0; j < n; j++) a[i][j] = v;                } }
```

Again, we consider cell $a[x, y]$, where $0 \leq x < m$ and $0 \leq y < n$, and disregard all other cells. One should not convert this procedure into a single control-flow graph, because the resulting numerical transition system does not have the "flat" structure expected by FLATA [11]. Instead, one must encode the inner loop as a separate procedure:

```
void array_init_2d(int m, int n, int a, int v, int x, int y) {
  assume(x >= 0 && x < m);
  assume(y >= 0 && y < n);
  for(int i=0; i<m; i++)  innerloop(n, a, v, x, y, i);       }
void inner_loop(int n, int a, int v, int x, int y, int i) {
  for(int j=0; j<n; j++)  if (x==i && y==j) a = v;       }
```

FLATA then computes the exact input-output relation of inner_loop, and finally the exact input-output relation of array_init_2d:

$$(x = 0 \wedge m = 1 \wedge a' = v \wedge y \geq 0 \wedge n \geq y + 1) \vee (a' = v \wedge x \geq 1 \wedge y \geq 0 \wedge m \geq x + 1 \wedge n \geq y + 1) \vee$$
$$(n = 1 \wedge x = 0 \wedge y = 0 \wedge a' = v \wedge m \geq 2) \vee (x = 0 \wedge a' = v \wedge y \geq 0 \wedge m \geq 2 \wedge n \geq 2 \wedge n \geq y + 1)$$

Each disjunct implies $a' = v$, i.e., the final value of $a[x, y]$ is v. Again, because (x, y) are symbolic constants with no assumption except that they are valid indices for a, this proves that all cells contain v. Assuming $0 \leq x < m \wedge 0 \leq y < n$ this formula may indeed be simplified automatically into $a' = v$.[4]

5.2 Slice Initialization

Listing 1.8. Initialize $a[low \ldots high - 1]$ to v

```
void slice_init(int n, int a[n], int low, int high, int v) {
  for(int i=low; i<high; i++) a[i] = v;                     }
```

Again, we transform the program using a single index:

```
for(int i=low; i<high; i++) if (x == i) a = v;
```

FLATA produces as postcondition (assuming $0 \leq x < n \wedge 0 \leq low \leq high \leq n$):

$$\begin{aligned}(high = low \wedge a' = a \wedge high \geq 0 \wedge n \geq high \wedge n \geq x + 1 \wedge x \geq 0) \vee \\ (a' = v \wedge low \leq x \wedge n \geq high \wedge high \geq x + 1 \wedge low \geq 0) \vee \\ (a' = a \wedge n \geq high \wedge high \geq low + 1 \wedge low \geq x + 1 \wedge x \geq 0) \vee \\ (a' = a \wedge high \leq x \wedge n \geq x + 1 \wedge high \geq low + 1 \wedge low \geq 0) \quad (8)\end{aligned}$$

Again, under the assumptions $0 \leq x < n$ and $0 \leq low \leq high \leq n$, this formula is equivalent to: $((low \leq x < high) \rightarrow a' = v) \wedge (\neg(low \leq x < high) \rightarrow a' = a)$. Thus by quantification, the expected outcome:

$$(\forall x \in [low, high)\ a'[x] = v) \wedge (\forall x \notin [low, high) \rightarrow a'[x] = a[x]) \quad (9)$$

5.3 Array Copy

Listing 1.9. Copy array a into array b

```
void array_copy(int n, int a[n], int b[n]) {
  for(int i=0; i<n; i++) b[i] = a[i];       }
```

[4] We implemented a simplification algorithm for quantifier-free Presburger arithmetic inspired by [37] so as to understand the output of FLATA and CONCURINTERPROC.

Take a single cell $a[x]$ in a and a single cell $b[y]$ in b; after transformation:

```
int n, a, b, x, y, tmp;
assume(0 <= x && x < n && 0 <= y && y < n);
for(int i=0; i<n; i++) { if (x==i) tmp=a; if (y==i) b=tmp; }
```

Flata. FLATA yields: $(y \geq x+1 \wedge n \geq y+2 \wedge x \geq 0) \vee (n = y+1 \wedge y \geq x+1 \wedge x \geq 0) \vee (n = x+1 \wedge y \geq 0 \wedge y \leq x-1) \vee (y \geq 0 \wedge y \leq x-1 \wedge n \geq x+2) \vee (y = x \wedge b' = a \wedge n \geq x+2 \wedge x \geq 0) \vee (y = x \wedge b' = a \wedge n = x+1 \wedge x \geq 0)$. Assuming $0 \leq x < n \wedge 0 \leq y < n$, this is equivalent to $x = y \rightarrow a = b$. Thus by quantification, $\forall x, y. x = y \rightarrow a[x] = b[y]$, simplifiable into $\boldsymbol{\forall x. a[x] = b[x]}$.

Software Model Checking. Many software model checkers, including CPACHECKER[5], do not handle universally quantified array properties; yet we can use them as back-end analyses! We translate the target property (here $\forall x. 0 \leq x < n \rightarrow a[x] = b[x]$) into a precondition $x = y$ and an assertion on the postcondition $a = b$. CPACHECKER then proves the property.[6]

```
int main() {
  int n, a, b, x, y;
  if (0 <= x && x < n && 0 <= y && y < n && x==y) {
    for(int i=0; i<n; i++) {
      int tmp; if (x==i) tmp=a; if (y==i) b=tmp; }
    assert(a==b);                                        } }
```

5.4 In-Place Array Reversal

Listing 1.10. Array reversal

```
void array_reverse_inplace(int n, contents t[n]) {
  int i=0, j=n-1;
  while(i < j) {
    contents tmp1 = t[i], tmp2 = t[j];
    t[i] = tmp2; t[j] = tmp1;      i++; j--;     } }
```

For this program, we need to distinguish the initial values in the array from the values during the computation (which finally yield the final values). We use three indices $0 \leq x < n$, $0 \leq y \leq z < n$: a is the initial value of $t[x]$, b the current value of $t[y]$, c the current value of $t[z]$.

For each read, we check if the index of the read is equal to y (respectively, z) and return b (respectively, c) if this is the case. If the index is equal to both y and z, it is sound to return either b or c; we chose to return b. For each write, we test if the index is equal to y, in which case we write to b, and equal to z, in which case we write to c. If it is equal to both y and z, we write to both b and c.

[5] http://cpachecker.sosy-lab.org/.

[6] `scripts/cpa.sh -predicateAnalysis` after preprocessing with `assert.h`.

Listing 1.11. Array reversal, transformed

```
contents a, b, c;
int x, y, z, i=0, j=n-1;
if (y == x) b = a;  if (z == x) c = a;
while(i < j) { contents tmp1, tmp2;
  if (i == y) tmp1 = b;  else if (i == z) tmp1 = c;
  if (j == y) tmp2 = b;  else if (j == z) tmp2 = c;
  if (i == y) b = tmp2;  if (i == z) c = tmp2;
  if (j == y) b = tmp1;  if (j == z) c = tmp1;        i++; j--; }
```

Flata. FLATA takes 480 s[7] to process this program, and outputs an input-output relation ϕ in disjunctive normal form with 292 disjuncts (not reprinted). The output formula is very complicated, with explicit enumeration of many particular cases; the reason for the slowness and the size of the output formula seems to be that FLATA explicitly enumerates many cases up to saturation, with no attempt at intermediate simplifications. We shall now explain what this formula entails.

Let U be $0 \le x, y, z < n \wedge y + z = n - 1$. Let $U_<$ be $U \wedge y < z \wedge z = x \wedge y + z = n - 1$, then $\phi \wedge U_<$ is equivalent to $a = b \wedge U_<$. This means that under the precondition $U_<$, Prog. 1.11 has exact postcondition $a = b$. By universal quantification, this means that $\forall x, y, z. U_< \rightarrow t[x] = t'[y]$, where t is the input array to Prog. 1.10 and t' the output. This formula may be simplified into $\forall x. 0 \le x \wedge 2x \le n - 2 \rightarrow t[x] = t'[n - 1 - x]$; We can obtain similar formulas for the cases $y > z$ and $y = z$. The three cases can can be summarized into

$$\forall \boldsymbol{x}. \mathbf{0} \le \boldsymbol{x} < \boldsymbol{n} \rightarrow \boldsymbol{t}[\boldsymbol{x}] = \boldsymbol{t}'[\boldsymbol{n} - \mathbf{1} - \boldsymbol{x}] \tag{10}$$

Flata, Focused. The above execution time and the complexity of the resulting formula seem excessive, if all that matters is when $(x = y \vee x = z) \wedge y + z = n - 1$. Indeed, some easy static analysis (by FLATA or another tool) shows that the array accesses within the loop are done at indices i and j that satisfy $0 \le i \le j < n$ and $i + j = n - 1$. Such a pre-analysis suggests to target the main analysis to two positions $t[y]$ and $t[z]$ in the current array, satisfying $0 \le y \le z < n$ and $y + z = n - 1$. The only positions $a[x]$ that matter in the original array are those that can be read precisely, that is, $x = y$ and $x = z$.

We therefore re-run the analysis with precondition U: $(0 \le y \le z < n \wedge y + z = n - 1 \wedge x = y)$. FLATA runs for 6 s and outputs a formula with 8 disjuncts, with $a = c$ in all disjuncts. We thus have proved that $\forall x, y, z. U \rightarrow t[x] = t'[z]$, which can be simplified into $\forall \boldsymbol{z}. \mathbf{2}\boldsymbol{z} \ge \boldsymbol{n} - \mathbf{1} \wedge \boldsymbol{z} < \boldsymbol{n} \rightarrow \boldsymbol{t}'[\boldsymbol{z}] = \boldsymbol{t}[\boldsymbol{n} - \mathbf{1} - \boldsymbol{z}]$.

We may also run with the precondition, $(0 \le y \le z < n \wedge y + z = n - 1 \wedge x = z)$ and get the remainder of the cases to conclude as in Formula 10.

To summarize, when the exact analysis of the transformed program (that is, an exact analysis in the back-end) is too costly, one may choose to *focus* the analysis by restricting the range of the indices $(x, y, z, \dots)$ to some area U considered to be "meaningful", for instance obtained by pre-analysis of the relationships between the indices of the array accesses in the program. This is sound,

[7] All timings using one core of a 2.4 GHz Intel ® Core™ i3 running 32-bit Linux.

since the quantification in the resulting formula is over the indices satisfying U. Thus, a bad choice for U may only result in a sound, but uninteresting invariant (the worst case is to take an unsatisfiable U: we then obtain a formula talking about an empty set of positions in the arrays, thus a tautology).

ConcurInterproc, Focused. INTERPROC[8] applies classical abstract interpretation (Kleene iteration accelerated with widenings, with possible narrowing iterations) over a variety of numerical abstract domains provided by the APRON [29] library[9] (intervals, "octagons" [36], convex polyhedra [13,22]...).

CONCURINTERPROC[10] extends it to concurrency (which we will not use here) and partitioning of the state space according to enumerated types, including Booleans. In a nutshell, while INTERPROC assigns a single abstract element (product of intervals, octagon, polyhedron) to each program location, CONCURINTERPROC attaches 2^n abstract elements, where n is the number of Booleans (or,more generally, one per concrete instantiation of the enumerated variables). In order to achieve this at reasonable cost, the BDDAPRON library uses a compact representation, where identical abstract elements are shared and the associated set of concrete instantiations is represented by a binary decision diagram.

Program 1.11 contains no Boolean variable (or of any other enumerated type), thus directly applying CONCURINTERPROC over it will yield one convex polyhedron at the end; yet we need to express a disjunction of such polyhedra (e.g. there is the case where $x = y$, and the case where $x \neq y$, which may be subdivided into $x < y$ and $y < z$). Furthermore, inside the loop one would have to distinguish $i < y$, $i = y$, $i > y$. This is where, in other analysis of array properties by abstract interpretation [16,21,23,38,39] one introduces "slices" or "segments" of programs, often according to syntactic criteria. In our case, we wish to distinguish certain locations in the array (or combinations of several locations, as here with three indices x, y, z) according to more semantic criteria.

Our solution is to introduce *observer* variables, which are written to but never read and whose final value is discarded, but which will guide the analysis and the partitioning performed. Here, we choose to have one flag variable per access, initially set to "false", and set to "true" when the access has taken place. As previously, we use a precondition $y + z = n - 1 \wedge x = z$.

Listing 1.12. Array reversal, transformed and instrumented

```
contents a, b, c;
int x, y, z;
bool y0,z0,y1,z1,y2,z2,y3,z3,y4,z4;
x0=y0=y1=z1=y2=z2=y3=z3=y4=z4=false;
int i=0, j=n-1;
assume(y+z == n-1); assume(x==z);
if (y == x) { b = a; y0 = true; } if (z == x) { c = a; z0 = true; }
while(i < j) {
  contents tmp1, tmp2;
  if (i == y) {tmp1 = b; y1 = true;} else if (i == z) {tmp1 = c; z1 = true;}
  if (j == y) {tmp2 = b; y2 = true;} else if (j == z) {tmp2 = c; z2 = true;}
```

[8] http://pop-art.inrialpes.fr/people/bjeannet/bjeannet-forge/interproc/.
[9] http://apron.cri.ensmp.fr/library/.
[10] http://pop-art.inrialpes.fr/interproc/concurinterprocweb.cgi.

```
if (i == y) {b = tmp2; y3 = true;} if (i == z) {c = tmp2; z3 = true;}
if (j == y) {b = tmp1; y4 = true;} if (j == z) {c = tmp1; z4 = true;}
i++; j--;                                                              }
```

ConcurInterproc, within 0.16 s, concludes that $a = b$.

5.5 Dutch National Flag

Quicksort is a divide-and-conquer sorting algorithm: pick a *pivot*, swap array cells until the array is divided into two areas: elements less than the pivot, and elements greater than or equal to it; then recurse in both areas. An improvement, in case many elements may be identical, is to swap the array into three areas: elements less than the pivot, equal to it, and greater than it, and recurse in the "less" and "greater" areas. This three-way partition is equivalent to the "Dutch national flag problem" [18, ch. 14], of swapping pebbles of colors red, white and blue (corresponding to "less", "equal" and "greater") into three segments.

Listing 1.13. Dutch flag(Courtesy of Wikipedia.)

```
void threeWayPartition(int data[], int size, int low, int high){
 int p = -1, q = size;
 for (int i = 0; i < q;) {
  if(data[i] < low) {swap(&data[i], &data[++p]); ++i;}
  else if(data[i]>=high) {swap(&data[i], &data[--q]);} else ++i;
}}
```

We transform this program with two indices $0 \leq x < y < n$ (remark that this is valid only if $n \geq 2$) with associated values *datax* and *datay*, and instrument it with Boolean observer variables: for each read or write access to an index i, we keep a Boolean recording the value of predicate $x \leq i$ and one for $x \geq i$ (respectively for y). The values in the array are encoded as pebble colors LOW, MIDDLE, HIGH.

ConcurInterproc computes a postcondition within 1 min. The resulting formula ϕ has 52 cases; we will not print it here. We check that $\phi \wedge x \leq p \rightarrow \mathit{datax} = \text{BLUE}$, meaning that finally, $\boldsymbol{\forall x. 0 \leq x \leq p \rightarrow t[x] = \text{BLUE}}$. Similarly, $\phi \wedge y \geq q \rightarrow \mathit{datay} = \text{RED}$, thus $\boldsymbol{\forall y. q \leq y < n \rightarrow t[y] = \text{RED}}$. We would expect as well that $\forall x. p < x < q \rightarrow t[x] = \text{WHITE}$. Yet, this does not immediately follow from ϕ: $\phi \wedge p < y < q \wedge \mathit{datay} = \text{RED}$ is satisfiable! Could there be red cells in the supposedly white area?

Note that ϕ, for fixed values of n, p, q, encodes quadruples $(x, \mathit{datax}, y, \mathit{datay})$, which encompass all possible values of $(x, t[x], y, t[y])$ for $x < y$. In particular, for $t[y] = \text{RED}$ to be possible for given n, p, q, one must have suitable $t[x]$ for all $x < y$, such that $(x, t[x], y, \text{RED})$ satisfies ϕ for the same n, p, q. In other words, to have a cell $t[y] = \text{RED}$ one must be able to find values $t[x]$ for all cells to the left of it. We check that, indeed, $p < y < q \wedge \mathit{datay} \neq \text{WHITE} \wedge (\forall x. 0 \leq x < y \rightarrow \phi)$ is unsatisfiable,[11] meaning that $\forall y. (p < y < q \wedge y > 0) \rightarrow t[y] = \text{WHITE}$. Furthermore, $\phi \wedge x = 0 \wedge x < q \wedge \mathit{datax} \neq \text{WHITE}$ has no solution. We can thus conclude $\boldsymbol{\forall y. p < y < q \rightarrow t[y] = \text{WHITE}}$.

[11] From Presburger arithmetic, a decidable theory.

Thus, we encountered a case of "spurious" solutions in the abstract element, due to the fact that the abstraction is not onto and that certain abstract elements can be reduced to a smaller element with the same concretization; which was achieved through quantification (see Subsect. 3.3). This reduction can thus be performed through some form of *quantifier elimination.*

6 Related Work

Acceleration. For certain classes of loops, it is possible to compute exactly the transitive closure τ^+ of the relation τ encoding the semantics of the loop, within a decidable class. Acceleration for arrays has been studied by Bozga et al. [9], who obtain the transitive closure in the form of a *counter automaton.* The translation from counter automaton to array properties expressed in first-order logic then requires an abstraction step, resulting in a loss of precision. Alberti et al. [1,3] proposed a template-based solution. Certain classes of τ's admit a definable acceleration in Presburger arithmetic augmented with free function symbols, at the price of nested quantifiers. The $\exists^*\forall^*$ fragment of this theory is undecidable [24]; thus again abstraction is needed to apply this technique in practice. Yet, there are cases where exact acceleration is possible [4]. Contrary to these approaches, (i) ours does not put restrictions on the shape of the loop (and the program in general) (ii) we perform the tunable abstraction first, with the rest of the analysis being delegated to a back-end (which can possibly use exact acceleration on scalar programs [10]).

Abstract Interpretation. Various array abstractions [16,21,23,38,39] distinguish *slices* or *segments*, whose contents is then abstracted by another abstract domain. Depending on the approach, relationships between several slices may or may not be expressed, and the partitioning may be syntactic or based on some pre-analysis. To our best knowledge, none of these approaches work on multidimensional arrays or on maps, contrary to ours. One major difference between these approaches and ours is that ours separates the analysis, both in theory and implementation, into an abstraction that maps array programs to scalar programs and an analysis for the scalar programs, while theirs are more "monolithic". Even though they are parametric in abstract domains for values and possibly indexes, they must be used inside an abstract interpreter based on Kleene iterations with widening. In contrast, ours can use any back-end analysis for scalar programs, including exact acceleration, abstract interpretation with Kleene iterations, policy iteration, and even, if a target property is supplied, predicate abstraction (see CEGAR below).

Cox et al. [17] do not target array programs per se, but programs in highly dynamic object-oriented languages such as Javascript, where an object is a map from fields to values and the set of possible field names is not fixed. Dillig et al. [19] overcome the dichotomy of strong vs weak updates with *liquid updates.* Their approach is monolithic and cannot express properties such as sortedness.

Predicate Abstraction and CEGAR. Predicate abstraction starts from the control structure of a program and incrementally refines it by splitting control states according to predicates chosen by the user [20] or, commonly, obtained by counterexample/guided abstraction refinement (CEGAR). From an abstract counterexample trace not corresponding to a concrete counterexample, they refine the model using local predicates constituting a step-by-step proof that this abstract trace does not match any concrete trace. The hope is that this proof generalizes to more counterexample traces and that the predicates eventually converge to define an inductive invariant. The predicates are obtained from *Craig interpolants* [32,34,35] extracted from the proof of unsatisfiability produced by a *satisfiability modulo theory* (SMT) solver. The difficulty here is to generate Craig interpolants that tend to generalize to inductive invariants, on *quantified* formulas involving arrays [33]. We are interested in predicates such as $\forall 0 \leq k < i,\ t[k] = 0$, which generalizes to an inductive invariant on Program 1.1, as opposed to, say, $t[0] = 0 \wedge t[1] = 0$, which is equivalent for $i = 2$ but does not generalize to arbitrary i. In order to achieve practical scalability, some work restrict themselves to the inference of array predicates to certain forms, e.g. *range predicates* [30]. Others tune the interpolating procedure towards the generation of better interpolants [2,5]. A major difference between our approach and those based on CEGAR is that we do not require a "target" property to prove, which is necessary for having counterexamples, though we can use one if needed. If such a property is provided, our approach can use as a back-end a CEGAR system limited to scalar variables.

Theorem Proving and SMT-Based Approaches. The generation of invariants for programs with arrays has been also studied using automated theorem proving [25,26]; this approach is generally limited by the fact that theory reasoning (e.g. arithmetic) and superposition-based deductive reasoning (on which the Vampire first-order theorem prover is based [31]) are not yet efficiently integrated. As opposed to [6], we do not rely on quantifier-instantiation procedures.

Quantification. Flanagan et al. [20] also use Skolem constants that they quantify universally after analysis steps. As opposed to us, they require the user to specify the predicates on which the program will be abstracted.

Abstraction of Sets of Maps. Our approach generalizes a classical abstraction of sets of maps [14, Sect. 2.1]. Jeannet et al. [28] considered the problem of abstracting sets of functions of signature $D_1 \rightarrow D_2$, assuming a *finite* abstract domain A_1 of cardinality n abstracting subsets of D_1 and an abstract domain A_2 abstracting subsets of D_2^n. In contrast, we do not make any cardinality assumption.

Partitioning. Rival et al. [40] introduced partitioning according to an abstraction of the history of the computation. Our approach using observer variables for using ConcurInterproc (Subsect. 5.4) is akin to considering a finite abstraction of the trace of read/writes into a given array.

7 Conclusion and Future Work

We have shown that a number of properties of array programs can be proved by abstracting the array a using a few symbolic cells $a[x], a[y], \ldots$ by automatically translating the program into a scalar program, running a static analyzer over the scalar program and translating back the invariant for the original program. In some cases, a form of quantifier elimination is used over the resulting formulas.

Our approach is not specific to arrays, and can be applied to any map structure $X \to Y$ (e.g. hash tables and other container classes). A possible future extension is multiset properties, a multiset being map $X \to \mathbb{N}$.

The main weakness of our approach is the need for a rather precise back-end analysis (for the scalar program obtained by translation). Our experiments highlighted some inefficiencies in e.g. FLATA and CONCURINTERPROC: in the former, many paths can be enumerated and complicated formulas generated even though a much simpler equivalent form exists; in the latter, polyhedra that are only slightly different (say, one constraint is different) are handled wholly separately. This gives immediate directions for research for improving exact acceleration, as in FLATA, or disjunctions of polyhedra, as in CONCURINTERPROC. Another difficulty, if using CONCURINTERPROC or other tools focusing on convex sets of integer vectors, is the need to use observer variables and/or an auxiliary pre-analysis to "focus" the main analysis.

We stress again that we obtained our results using unmodified versions of very different back-end analyzers (CONCURINTERPROC, FLATA, CPACHECKER), which testifies to the flexibility of our approach. Performance and precision improvements can be expected by modifying the back-end analyzers (e.g. precision could be improved by performing reduction steps during the analysis, rather than after the computation of the invariants).

References

1. Alberti, F., Ghilardi, S., Sharygina, N.: Decision procedures for flat array properties. In: Ábrahám, E., Havelund, K. (eds.) TACAS 2014 (ETAPS). LNCS, vol. 8413, pp. 15–30. Springer, Heidelberg (2014)
2. Alberti, F., et al.: An extension of lazy abstraction with interpolation for programs with arrays. Form. Methods Syst. Des. **45**(1), 63–109 (2014)
3. Alberti, F., Ghilardi, S., Sharygina, N.: Definability of accelerated relations in a theory of arrays and its applications. In: Fontaine, P., Ringeissen, C., Schmidt, R.A. (eds.) FroCoS 2013. LNCS, vol. 8152, pp. 23–39. Springer, Heidelberg (2013)
4. Alberti, F., Ghilardi, S., Sharygina, N.: Decision procedures for flat array properties. J. Autom. Reasoning **54**(4), 327–352 (2015)
5. Alberti, F., Monniaux, D.: Polyhedra to the rescue of array interpolants. In: Symposium on applied computing (Software Verification & Testing). ACM (2015)
6. Bjørner, N., McMillan, K., Rybalchenko, A.: On solving universally quantified horn clauses. In: Logozzo, F., Fähndrich, M. (eds.) Static Analysis. LNCS, vol. 7935, pp. 105–125. Springer, Heidelberg (2013)
7. Blanchet, et al.: A static analyzer for large safety-critical software. In: PLDI, pp. 196–207. ACM (2003)

8. Blanchet, B., Cousot, P., Cousot, R., Feret, J., Mauborgne, L., Miné, A., Monniaux, D., Rival, X.: Design and implementation of a special-purpose static program analyzer for safety-critical real-time embedded software. In: Mogensen, T.Æ., Schmidt, D.A., Sudborough, I.H. (eds.) The Essence of Computation. LNCS, vol. 2566, pp. 85–108. Springer, Heidelberg (2002)
9. Bozga, M., Habermehl, P., Iosif, R., Konečný, F., Vojnar, T.: Automatic verification of integer array programs. In: Bouajjani, A., Maler, O. (eds.) CAV 2009. LNCS, vol. 5643, pp. 157–172. Springer, Heidelberg (2009)
10. Bozga, M., Iosif, R., Konečný, F.: Fast acceleration of ultimately periodic relations. In: Touili, T., Cook, B., Jackson, P. (eds.) CAV 2010. LNCS, vol. 6174, pp. 227–242. Springer, Heidelberg (2010)
11. Bozga, M., Iosif, R., Lakhnech, Y.: Flat parametric counter automata. Fundamenta Informaticae **91**, 275–303 (2009)
12. Cousot, P., Cousot, R.: Abstract interpretation frameworks. J. Log. Comput. **2**(4), 511–547 (1992)
13. Cousot, P., Halbwachs, N.: Automatic discovery of linear restraints among variables of a program. In: POPL, pp. 84–96 (1978)
14. Cousot, P., Cousot, R.: Invited talk: Higher order abstract interpretation. In: IEEE International Conference on Computer Languages, pp. 95–112. IEEE Computer Society (1994)
15. Cousot, P., Cousot, R., Feret, J., Mauborgne, L., Miné, A., Rival, X.: Why does Astrée scale up? Form. Methods Syst. Des. **35**(3), 229–264 (2009)
16. Cousot, P., Cousot, R., Logozzo, F.: A parametric segmentation functor for fully automatic and scalable array content analysis. In: POPL, pp. 105–118. ACM (2011)
17. Cox, A., Chang, B.-Y.E., Rival, X.: Automatic analysis of open objects in dynamic language programs. In: Müller-Olm, M., Seidl, H. (eds.) Static Analysis. LNCS, vol. 8723, pp. 134–150. Springer, Heidelberg (2014)
18. Dijkstra, E.W.: A discipline of programming. Prentice-Hall, Upper Saddle River (1976)
19. Dillig, I., Dillig, T., Aiken, A.: Fluid updates: beyond strong vs. weak updates. In: Gordon, A.D. (ed.) ESOP 2010. LNCS, vol. 6012, pp. 246–266. Springer, Heidelberg (2010)
20. Flanagan, C., Qadeer, S.: Predicate abstraction for software verification. In: POPL, pp. 191–202 (2002)
21. Gopan, D., Reps, T., Sagiv, S.: A framework for numeric analysis of array operations. In: POPL, pp. 338–350 (2005)
22. Halbwachs, N.: Détermination automatique de relations linéaires vérifiées par les variables d'un programme. Ph.D. thesis, Univ. Grenoble (Mar 1979). https://tel.archives-ouvertes.fr/tel-00288805
23. Halbwachs, N., Péron, M.: Discovering properties about arrays in simple programs. In: PLDI, pp. 339–348. ACM (2008)
24. Halpern, J.: Presburger arithmetic with unary predicates is Π_1^1 complete. J. Symbolic Log. **56**(2), 637–642 (1991)
25. Hoder, K., Kovács, L., Voronkov, A.: Invariant generation in vampire. In: Abdulla, P.A., Leino, K.R.M. (eds.) TACAS 2011. LNCS, vol. 6605, pp. 60–64. Springer, Heidelberg (2011)
26. Hoder, K., Kovács, L., Voronkov, A.: Interpolation and symbol elimination in vampire. In: Giesl, J., Hähnle, R. (eds.) IJCAR 2010. LNCS, vol. 6173, pp. 188–195. Springer, Heidelberg (2010)

27. Hojjat, H., Konečný, F., Garnier, F., Iosif, R., Kuncak, V., Rümmer, P.: A verification toolkit for numerical transition systems. In: Giannakopoulou, D., Méry, D. (eds.) FM 2012. LNCS, vol. 7436, pp. 247–251. Springer, Heidelberg (2012)
28. Jeannet, B., Gopan, D., Reps, T.: A relational abstraction for functions. In: Hankin, C., Siveroni, I. (eds.) SAS 2005. LNCS, vol. 3672, pp. 186–202. Springer, Heidelberg (2005)
29. Jeannet, B., Miné, A.: APRON: a library of numerical abstract domains for static analysis. In: Bouajjani, A., Maler, O. (eds.) CAV 2009. LNCS, vol. 5643, pp. 661–667. Springer, Heidelberg (2009)
30. Jhala, R., McMillan, K.L.: Array abstractions from proofs. In: Damm, W., Hermanns, H. (eds.) CAV 2007. LNCS, vol. 4590, pp. 193–206. Springer, Heidelberg (2007)
31. Kovács, L., Voronkov, A.: First-order theorem proving and VAMPIRE. In: Sharygina, N., Veith, H. (eds.) CAV 2013. LNCS, vol. 8044, pp. 1–35. Springer, Heidelberg (2013)
32. McMillan, K.L.: Applications of craig interpolation to model checking. In: Ciardo, G., Darondeau, P. (eds.) ICATPN 2005. LNCS, vol. 3536, pp. 15–16. Springer, Heidelberg (2005)
33. McMillan, K.L.: Quantified invariant generation using an interpolating saturation prover. In: Ramakrishnan, C.R., Rehof, J. (eds.) TACAS 2008. LNCS, vol. 4963, pp. 413–427. Springer, Heidelberg (2008)
34. McMillan, K.L.: Lazy abstraction with interpolants. In: Ball, T., Jones, R.B. (eds.) CAV 2006. LNCS, vol. 4144, pp. 123–136. Springer, Heidelberg (2006)
35. McMillan, K.: Interpolants from Z3 proofs. In: FMCAD, pp. 19–27 (2011)
36. Miné, A.: The octagon abstract domain. High. Order Symbolic Comput. **19**(1), 31–100 (2006)
37. Monniaux, D.: A quantifier elimination algorithm for linear real arithmetic. In: Cervesato, I., Veith, H., Voronkov, A. (eds.) LPAR 2008. LNCS (LNAI), vol. 5330, pp. 243–257. Springer, Heidelberg (2008)
38. Péron, M.: Contributions to the Static Analysis of Programs Handling Arrays. Theses, Université de Grenoble (September 2010). https://tel.archives-ouvertes.fr/tel-00623697
39. Perrelle, V.: Analyse statique de programmes manipulant des tableaux. Theses, Université de Grenoble (February 2013). https://tel.archives-ouvertes.fr/tel-00973892
40. Rival, X., Mauborgne, L.: The trace partitioning abstract domain. ACM Trans. Program Lang. Syst. **29**(5), 26 (2007)

Property-based Polynomial Invariant Generation Using Sums-of-Squares Optimization

Assalé Adjé[1], Pierre-Loïc Garoche[1(✉)], and Victor Magron[2]

[1] Onera, The French Aerospace laboratory,
Université de Toulouse, 31400 Toulouse, France
{Assale.Adje,Pierre-Loic.Garoche}@onera.fr

[2] Circuits and Systems Group, Department of Electrical and Electronic Engineering,
Imperial College London, South Kensington Campus, London SW7 2AZ, UK
v.magron@imperial.ac.uk

Abstract. While abstract interpretation is not theoretically restricted to specific kinds of properties, it is, in practice, mainly developed to compute linear over-approximations of reachable sets, aka. the collecting semantics of the program. The verification of user-provided properties is not easily compatible with the usual forward fixpoint computation using numerical abstract domains.

We propose here to rely on sums-of-squares programming to characterize a property-driven polynomial invariant. This invariant generation can be guided by either boundedness, or in contrary, a given zone of the state space to avoid.

While the target property is not necessarily inductive with respect to the program semantics, our method identifies a stronger inductive polynomial invariant using numerical optimization. Our method applies to a wide set of programs: a main while loop composed of a disjunction (if-then-else) of polynomial updates e.g. piecewise polynomial controllers. It has been evaluated on various programs.

1 Introduction

With the increased need for confidence in software, it becomes more than ever important to provide means to support the verification of specification of software. Among the various formal verification methods to support these analysis, a first line of approaches, such as deductive methods or SMT-based model checking, provide rich languages to support the expression of the specification and then try to discharge the associate proof obligation using automatic solvers. The current state of the art of these solvers is able to manipulate satisfiability problems over linear arithmetics or restricted fragments of non linear arithmetics. Another line of approaches, such as static analysis also known as abstract interpretation,

A. Adjé and P.-L. Garoche—is supported by the RTRA /STAE Project BRIEFCASE and the ANR ASTRID VORACE Project.

V. Magron—is supported by EPSRC (EP/I020457/1) Challenging Engineering Grant.

S. Blazy and T. Jensen (Eds.): SAS 2015, LNCS 9291, pp. 235–251, 2015.
DOI: 10.1007/978-3-662-48288-9_14

restricts, a priori, the kind of properties considered during the computation: these methods typically perform interval arithmetic analysis or rely on convex polyhedra computations. In practice this second line of work seems more capable of manipulating and generating numerical invariants through the computation of inductive invariants, while the first line of approaches hardly synthesize these required invariants through satisfiability checks.

However, when it comes to more than linear properties, the state of the art is not well developed. In the early 2000s, ellipsoid analyses [11], similar to restricted cases of Lyapunov functions, were designed to support the study of a family of Airbus controllers. This exciting result was used to provide the analysis of absence of runtime errors but could hardly be adapted to handle more general user provided specifications for polynomial programs.

However proving polynomial inequalities is NP-hard and boils down to show that the infimum of a given polynomial is nonnegative. Still, one can obtain lower bounds of such infima by decomposing certain nonnegative polynomials into sums-of-squares (SOS). This actually leads to solve hierarchies of semidefinite relaxations, introduced by Lasserre in [12]. Recent advances in semidefinite programming allowed to extensively apply these relaxations to various fields, including parametric polynomial optimization, optimal control, combinatorial optimization, *etc.* (see e.g. [13,17] for more details).

While these approaches were mentioned a decade ago in [8] and mainly applied to termination analysis, they hardly made their way through the software verification community to address more general properties.

Contributions. Our contribution allows to analyze high level properties defined as a sublevel set of polynomials functions, i.e. basic semialgebraic sets. This class of properties is rather large: it ranges from boundedness properties to the definition of a bad region of the state space to avoid. While these properties, when they hold, are meant to be invariant, i.e. they hold in each reachable state, they are not necessarily inductive. Our approach rely on the computation of a stronger inductive property using SOS programming. This stronger property is proved inductive on the complete system and, by construction, implies the target property specified by the user. We develop our analysis on discrete-time piecewise polynomial systems, capturing a wide class of critical programs, as typically found in current embedded systems such as aircrafts.

Organization of the paper. The paper is organized as follows. In Sect. 2, we present the programs that we want to analyze and their representation as piecewise polynomial discrete-time systems. Next, we recall in Sect. 3 the collecting semantics that we use and introduce the polynomial optimization problem providing inductive invariants based on target polynomial properties. Section 4 contains the main contribution of the paper, namely how to compute effectively such invariants with SOS programming. Practical computation examples are provided in Sect. 5. Finally, we explain in Sect. 6 how to derive template bases from generated invariants.

2 Polynomial Programs and Piecewise Polynomial Discrete-Time Systems

In this section, we describe the programs which are considered in this paper and we explain how to analyze them through their representation as piecewise polynomial discrete-time dynamical systems.

We focus on programs composed of a single loop with a possibly complicated switch-case type loop body. Moreover we suppose without loss of generality that the analyzed programs are written in Static Single Assignment (SSA) form, that is each variable is initialized at most once.

Definitions. We recall that a function f from $\mathbb{R}^d$ to $\mathbb{R}$ is a polynomial if and only if there exists $k \in \mathbb{N}$, a family $\{c_\alpha \mid \alpha = (\alpha_1, \ldots, \alpha_d) \in \mathbb{N}^d,\ |\alpha| = \alpha_1 + \ldots + \alpha_d \leq k\}$ such that for all $x \in \mathbb{R}^d$, $f(x) = \sum_{|\alpha| \leq k} c_\alpha x_1^{\alpha_1} \ldots x_d^{\alpha_d}$. By extension a function $f : \mathbb{R}^d \mapsto \mathbb{R}^d$ is a polynomial if and only if all its coordinate functions are polynomials. Let $\mathbb{R}[x]$ stands for the set of d-variate polynomials.

In this paper, we consider assignments of variables using only *parallel polynomial assignments* $(x_1, \ldots, x_d) = T(x_1, \ldots, x_d)$ where $(x_1, \ldots, x_d)$ is the vector of the program variables. Tests are either weak polynomial inequalities $r(x_1, \ldots, x_d) \leq 0$ or strict polynomial inequalities $r(x_1, \ldots, x_d) < 0$. We assume that assignments are polynomials from $\mathbb{R}^d$ to $\mathbb{R}^d$ and test functions are polynomials from $\mathbb{R}^d$ to $\mathbb{R}$. In the program syntax, the notation $\ll$ will be either <= or <. The form of the analyzed program is described in Fig. 1.

```
x ∈ X^in;
while (r_1^0(x)≪0 and ... and r_{n_0}^0(x)≪0){
  case (r_1^1(x)≪0 and ... and r_{n_1}^1(x)≪0): x = T^1(x);
  case ...
  case (r_i^1(x)≪0 and ... and r_{n_i}^1(x)≪0): x = T^i(x);
}
```

Fig. 1. One-loop programs with nested conditional branches

A set $C \subseteq \mathbb{R}^d$ is said to be a *basic semialgebraic set* if there exist $g_1, \ldots, g_m \in \mathbb{R}[x]$ such that $C = \{x \in \mathbb{R}^d \mid g_j(x) \ll 0, \forall j = 1, \ldots, m\}$, where $\ll$ is used to encode either a strict or a weak inequality.

As depicted in Fig. 1, an update $T^i : \mathbb{R}^d \to \mathbb{R}^d$ of the i-th condition branch is executed if and only if the conjunction of tests $r_j^i(x) \ll 0$ holds. In other words, the variable x is updated by $T^i(x)$ if the current value of x belongs to the basic semialgebraic set

$$X^i := \{x \in \mathbb{R}^d \mid \forall j = 1, \ldots, n_i,\ r_j^i(x) \ll 0\}. \tag{1}$$

Piecewise Polynomial Systems. Consequently, we interpret programs as *constrained piecewise polynomial discrete-time dynamical systems* (PPS for short). The term *piecewise* means that there exists a partition $\{X^i, i \in \mathcal{I}\}$ of $\mathbb{R}^d$ such that for all $i \in \mathcal{I}$, the dynamics of the system is represented by the following relation, for $k \in \mathbb{N}$:

$$\text{if } x_k \in X^i \cap X^0,\ x_{k+1} = T^i(x_k)\,. \tag{2}$$

We assume that $\mathcal{I}$ is finite and that the initial condition x_0 belongs to some compact basic semialgebraic set X^{in}. For the program, X^{in} is the set where the variables are supposed to be initialized in. Since the test entry for the loop condition can be nontrivial, we add the term *constrained* and X^0 denotes the set representing the conjunctions of tests for the loop condition. The iterates of the PPS are constrained to live in X^0: if for some step $k \in \mathbb{N}$, $x_k \notin X^0$ then the PPS is stopped at this iterate with the terminal value x_k.

We define a partition as a family of nonempty sets such that:

$$\bigcup_{i\in\mathcal{I}} X^i = \mathbb{R}^d,\ \forall\, i,j \in \mathcal{I},\ i \neq j, X^i \cap X^j \neq \emptyset\,. \tag{3}$$

From Eq. (3), for all $k \in \mathbb{N}^*$ there exists a unique $i \in \mathcal{I}$ such that $x_k \in X^i$. A set X^i can contain both strict and weak polynomial inequalities and characterizes the set of the n_i conjunctions of tests polynomials r^i_j. Let $r^i = (r^i_1, \ldots, r^i_{n_i})$ stands for the vector of tests functions associated to the set X^i. We suppose that the basic semialgebraic sets X^{in} and X^0 also admits the representation given by Eq. (1) and we denote by r^0 the vector of tests polynomials $(r^0_1, \ldots, r^0_{n_0})$ and by r^{in} the vector of test polynomials $(r^{\text{in}}_1, \ldots, r^{\text{in}}_{n_{\text{in}}})$. To sum up, we give a formal definition of PPS.

Definition 1 (PPS). *A constrained polynomial piecewise discrete-time dynamical system (PPS) is the quadruple* $(X^{\text{in}}, X^0, \mathcal{X}, \mathcal{L})$ *with:*

- $X^{\text{in}} \subseteq \mathbb{R}^d$ *is the compact basic semialgebraic set of the possible initial conditions;*
- $X^0 \subseteq \mathbb{R}^d$ *is the basic semialgebraic set where the state variable lives;*
- $\mathcal{X} := \{X^i, i \in \mathcal{I}\}$ *is a partition as defined in Eq. (3);*
- $\mathcal{L} := \{T^i, i \in \mathcal{I}\}$ *is the family of the polynomials from* $\mathbb{R}^d$ *to* $\mathbb{R}^d$*, w.r.t. the partition* $\mathcal{X}$ *satisfying Eq. (2).*

From now on, we associate a PPS representation to each program of the form described at Fig. 1. Since a program admits several PPS representations, we choose one of them, but this arbitrary choice does not change the results provided in this paper. In the sequel, we will often refer to the running example described in Example 1.

Example 1 (Running example). The program below involves four variables and contains an infinite loop with a conditional branch in the loop body. The update of each branch is polynomial. The parameters c_{ij} (resp. d_{ij}) are given parameters. During the analysis, we only keep the variables x_1 and x_2 since $oldx_1$ and $oldx_2$ are just memories.

```
x1, x2 ∈ [a1, a2] × [b1, b2];
oldx1 = x1;
oldx2 = x2;
while (-1 <= 0){
  oldx1 = x1;
  oldx2 = x2;
  case : oldx1^2 + oldx2^2 <= 1 :
      x1 = c11 * oldx1^2 + c11 * oldx2^3;
      x2 = c21 * oldx1^3 + c22 * oldx2^2;
  case :  -oldx1^2 - oldx2^2 < -1
      x1 = d11 * oldx1^3 + d12 * oldx2^2;
      x2 = d21 * oldx1^2 + d22 * oldx2^2;
  }
}
```

The associated PPS corresponds to the quadruple $(X^{\text{in}}, X^0, \{X^1, X^2\}, \{T^1, T^2\})$, where the set of initial conditions is:

$$X^{\text{in}} = [a_1, a_2] \times [b_1, b_2],$$

the system is not globally constrained, i.e. the set X^0 in which the variable $x = (x_1, x_2)$ lies is:

$$X^0 = \mathbb{R}^d,$$

the partition verifying Eq. (3) is:

$$X^1 = \{x \in \mathbb{R}^2 \mid x_1^2 + x_2^2 \leq 1\}, \quad X^2 = \{x \in \mathbb{R}^2 \mid -x_1^2 - x_2^2 < -1\},$$

and the polynomials relative to the partition $\{X^1, X^2\}$ are:

$$T^1(x) = \begin{pmatrix} c_{11}x_1^2 + c_{12}x_2^3 \\ c_{21}x_1^3 + c_{22}x_2^2 \end{pmatrix} \text{ and } T^2(x) = \begin{pmatrix} d_{11}x_1^3 + d_{12}x_2^2 \\ d_{21}x_1^2 + d_{22}x_2^2 \end{pmatrix}.$$

3 Program Invariants as Sublevel Sets

The main goal of the paper is to decide automatically if a given property holds for the analyzed program, i.e. for all its reachable states. We are interested in numerical properties and more precisely in properties on the values taken by the d-uplet of the variables of the program. Hence, in our point-of-view, a property is just the membership of some set $P \subseteq \mathbb{R}^d$. In particular, we study properties which are valid after an arbitrary number of loop iterates. Such properties are called *loop invariants* of the program. Formally, we use the PPS representation of a given program and we say that P is a loop invariant of this program if:

$$\forall k \in \mathbb{N},\ x_k \in P\,,$$

where x_k is defined at Eq. (2) as the state variable at step $k \in \mathbb{N}$ of the PPS representation of the program. Our approach addresses any property expressible as a polynomial level set property. This section defines formally these notions and develop our approach: synthesize a property-driven inductive invariant.

3.1 Collecting Semantics as Postfixpoint Characterization

Now, let us consider a program of the form described in Fig. 1 and let us denote by $\mathcal{S}$ the PPS representation of this program. The set $\mathfrak{R}$ of *reachable values* is the set of all possible values taken by the state variable along the running of $\mathcal{S}$. We define $\mathfrak{R}$ as follows:

$$\mathfrak{R} = \bigcup_{k\in\mathbb{N}} T_{|_{X^0}}^k (X^{\text{in}}) \tag{4}$$

where $T_{|_{X^0}}$ is the restriction of T on X^0 and $T_{|_{X^0}}$ is not defined outside X^0. To prove that a set P is a loop invariant of the program is equivalent to prove that $\mathfrak{R} \subseteq P$. We can rewrite $\mathfrak{R}$ inductively:

$$\mathfrak{R} = X^{\text{in}} \cup \bigcup_{i\in\mathcal{I}} T^i \left(\mathfrak{R} \cap X^i \cap X^0\right). \tag{5}$$

Let us denote by $\wp(\mathbb{R}^d)$ the set of subsets of $\mathbb{R}^d$ and introduce the map F : $\wp(\mathbb{R}^d) \to \wp(\mathbb{R}^d)$ defined by:

$$F(C) = X^{\text{in}} \cup \bigcup_{i\in\mathcal{I}} T^i \left(C \cap X^i \cap X^0\right) \tag{6}$$

We equip $\wp(\mathbb{R}^d)$ with the partial order of inclusion. The infimum is understood in this sense i.e. as the greatest lower bound with respect to this order. The smallest fixed point problem is:

$$\inf \left\{C \in \wp(\mathbb{R}^d) \mid C = F(C)\right\}.$$

It is well-known from Tarski's theorem that the solution of this problem exists, is unique and in this case, it corresponds to $\mathfrak{R}$. Tarski's theorem also states that $\mathfrak{R}$ is the smallest solution of the following Problem:

$$\inf \left\{C \in \wp(\mathbb{R}^d) \mid F(C) \subseteq C\right\}.$$

Note also that the map F corresponds to a standard transfer function (or collecting semantics functional) applied to the PPS representation of a program. We refer the reader to [9] for a seminal presentation of this approach.

To prove that a subset P is a loop invariant, it suffices to show that P satisfies $F(P) \subseteq P$. In this case, such P is called *inductive invariant.*

3.2 Considered Properties: Sublevel Properties $\mathcal{P}_{\kappa,\alpha}$

In this paper, we consider special properties: those that are encoded with sublevel sets of a given polynomial function.

Definition 2 (Sublevel Property). *Given a polynomial function $\kappa \in \mathbb{R}[x]$ and $\alpha \in \mathbb{R} \cup \{+\infty\}$, we define the sublevel property $\mathcal{P}_{\kappa,\alpha}$ as follows:*

$$\mathcal{P}_{\kappa,\alpha} := \{x \in \mathbb{R}^d \mid \kappa(x) \ll \alpha\}.$$

where $\ll$ denotes $\leq$ when $\alpha \in \mathbb{R}$ and denotes $<$ for $+\infty$. The expression $\kappa(x) < +\infty$ expresses the boundedness of $\kappa(x)$ without providing a specific bound α.

Example 2 Sublevel property examples.

Boundedness. When one wants to bound the reachable values of a system, we can try to bound the l_2-norm of the system: $\mathcal{P}_{\|\cdot\|_2^2,\infty}$ with $\kappa(x) = \|x\|_2^2$. The use of $\alpha = \infty$ does not impose any bound on $\kappa(x)$.

Safe set. Similarly, it is possible to check whether a specific bound is matched. Either globally using the l_2-norm and a specific α: $\mathcal{P}_{\|\cdot\|_2^2,\alpha}$, or bounding the reachable values of each variable: $\mathcal{P}_{\kappa_i,\alpha_i}$ with $\kappa_i : x \mapsto x_i$ and $\alpha_i \in \mathbb{R}$.

Avoiding bad regions. If the bad region can be encoded as a sublevel property $k(x) \leq 0$ then its negation $-k(x) \leq 0$ characterize the avoidance of that bad zone. Eg. if one wants to prove that the square norm of the program variables is always greater than 1, then we can consider the property $\mathcal{P}_{\kappa,\alpha}$ with $\kappa(x) = 1 - \|x\|_2^2$ and $\alpha = 0$.

A sublevel property is called *sublevel invariant* when this property is a loop invariant. This turns out to be difficult to prove loop invariant properties while considering directly $\mathfrak{R}$, thus we propose to find a more tractable over-approximation of $\mathfrak{R}$ for which such properties hold.

3.3 Approach: Compute a $\mathcal{P}_{\kappa,\alpha}$-Driven Inductive Invariant P

In this subsection, we explain how to compute a d-variate polynomial $p \in \mathbb{R}[x]$ and a bound $w \in \mathbb{R}$, such that the polynomial sublevel sets $P := \{x \in \mathbb{R}^d \mid p(x) \leq 0\}$ and $\mathcal{P}_{\kappa,w}$ satisfy:

$$\mathfrak{R} \subseteq P \subseteq \mathcal{P}_{\kappa,w} \subseteq \mathcal{P}_{\kappa,\alpha} \,. \tag{7}$$

The first (from the left) inclusion forces P to be valid for the whole reachable values set. The second inclusion constraints all elements of P to satisfy the given sublevel property for a certain bound w. The last inclusion requires that the bound w is smaller than the desired level α. When $\alpha = \infty$, any bound w ensures the sublevel property.

Now, we derive sufficient conditions on p and w to satisfy Eq. (7). We decompose the problem in two parts. To satisfy the first inclusion, i.e. ensure that P is a loop invariant, it suffices to guarantee that $F(P) \subseteq P$, namely that P is an inductive invariant. Using Eq. (5), P is an inductive invariant if and only if:

$$X^{\text{in}} \cup \bigcup_{i \in \mathcal{I}} T^i \left(P \cap X^i \cap X^0\right) \subseteq P \,,$$

or equivalently:

$$\begin{cases} X^{\text{in}} \subseteq P \,, \\ \forall i \in \mathcal{I}, \; T^i \left(P \cap X^i \cap X^0\right) \subseteq P \,. \end{cases} \tag{8}$$

Thus, we obtain:

$$\begin{cases} p(x) \leq 0 \,, & \forall x \in X^{\text{in}} \,, \\ \forall i \in \mathcal{I} \,, p(T^i(x)) \leq 0 \,, & \forall x \in P \cap X^i \cap X^0 \,. \end{cases} \tag{9}$$

Now, we are interested in the second and third inclusions at Eq. (7) that is the sublevel property satisfaction. The condition $P \subseteq \mathcal{P}_{\kappa,w} \subseteq \mathcal{P}_{\kappa,\alpha}$ can be formulated as follows:

$$\kappa(x) \leq w \leq \alpha\,, \quad \forall x \in P\,. \tag{10}$$

We recall that we have supposed that P is written as $\{x \in \mathbb{R}^d \mid p(x) \leq 0\}$ where $p \in \mathbb{R}[x]$. Finally, we provide sufficient conditions to satisfy both (9) and (10), gathered in (11), so one can find a polynomial p ensuring the constraint involving κ:

$$\begin{cases} \inf_{p \in \mathbb{R}[x], w \in \mathbb{R}} & w\,, \\ \quad\text{s.t.} & p(x) \leq 0\,, & \forall x \in X^{\text{in}}\,, \\ & \forall\, i \in \mathcal{I}\,, p\left(T^i(x)\right) \leq p(x)\,, & \forall x \in X^i \cap X^0\,, \\ & \kappa(x) \leq w + p(x)\,, & \forall x \in \mathbb{R}^d\,. \end{cases} \tag{11}$$

We remark that α is not present in Problem (11). Indeed, since we minimize w, either there exists a feasible w such that $w \leq \alpha$ and we can exploit this solution or such w is not available and we cannot conclude. However, from Problem (11), we can extract (p, w) and in the case where the optimal bound w is greater than α, we could use this solution with another method such as policy iteration [2].

Lemma 1. *Let* (p, w) *be any feasible solution of Problem* (11) *with* $w \leq \alpha$ *or* $w < \infty$ *in the case of* $\alpha = \infty$. *Then* (p, w) *satisfies both* (9) *and* (10) *with* $P := \{x \in \mathbb{R}^d \mid p(x) \leq 0\}$. *Finally,* P *and* $\mathcal{P}_{\kappa,w}$ *satisfy Eq.* (7).

In practice, we rely on sum-of-squares programming to solve a strengthened version of Problem (11).

4 SOS Programming for Invariant Generation

We first recall some basic background about sums-of-squares certificates for polynomial optimization. Let $\mathbb{R}[x]_{2m}$ stands for the set of polynomials of degree at most $2m$ and $\Sigma[x] \subset \mathbb{R}[x]$ be the cone of sums-of-squares (SOS) polynomials, that is $\Sigma[x] := \{\sum_i q_i^2,\ \text{with } q_i \in \mathbb{R}[x]\}$. Our work will use the simple fact that for all $p \in \Sigma[x]$, then $p(x) \geq 0$ for all $x \in \mathbb{R}^d$ i.e. $\Sigma[x]$ is a restriction of the set of the nonnegative polynomials. For $q \in \mathbb{R}[x]_{2m}$, finding a SOS decomposition $q = \sum_i q_i^2$ valid over $\mathbb{R}^d$ is equivalent to solve the following matrix linear feasibility problem:

$$q(x) = b_m(x)^T\, Q\, b_m(x)\,, \quad \forall x \in \mathbb{R}^d, \tag{12}$$

where $b_m(x) := (1, x_1, \ldots, x_d, x_1^2, x_1 x_2, \ldots, x_d^m)$ (the vector of all monomials in x up to degree m) and Q being a *semidefinite positive* matrix (i.e. all the eigenvalues of Q are nonnegative). The size of Q (as well as the length of b_m) is $\binom{d+m}{d}$.

Example 3. consider the bi-variate polynomial $q(x) := 1+x_1^2-2x_1x_2+x_2^2$. With $b_1(x) = (1, x_1, x_2)$, one looks for a semidefinite positive matrix Q such that the polynomial equality $q(x) = b_1(x)^T Q\, b_1(x)$ holds for all $x \in \mathbb{R}^2$. The matrix

$$Q = \begin{pmatrix} 1 & 0 & 0 \\ 0 & 1 & -1 \\ 0 & -1 & 1 \end{pmatrix}$$

satisfies this equality and has three nonnegative eigenvalues, which are 0, 1, and 2, respectively associated to the three eigenvectors $e_0 := (0, 1/\sqrt{2}, 1/\sqrt{2})^\intercal$, $e_1 := (1, 0, 0)^\intercal$ and $e_2 := (0, 1/\sqrt{2}, -1/\sqrt{2})^\intercal$. Defining the matrices $L := (e_1\, e_2\, e_0) = \begin{pmatrix} 1 & 0 & 0 \\ 0 & \frac{1}{\sqrt{2}} & \frac{1}{\sqrt{2}} \\ 0 & -\frac{1}{\sqrt{2}} & \frac{1}{\sqrt{2}} \end{pmatrix}$ and $D = \begin{pmatrix} 1\,0\,0 \\ 0\,2\,0 \\ 0\,0\,0 \end{pmatrix}$, one obtains the decomposition $Q = L^\intercal D\, L$ and the equality $q(x) = (L\, b_1(x))^T D\, (L\, b_1(x)) = \sigma(x) = 1 + (x_1 - x_2)^2$, for all $x \in \mathbb{R}^2$. The polynomial σ is called a *SOS certificate* and guarantees that q is nonnegative.

In practice, one can solve the general problem (12) by using semidefinite programming (SDP) solvers (e.g. MOSEK [5], SDPA [26]). For more details about SDP, we refer the interested reader to [24].

Problem (11) is infinite dimensional, thus difficult to handle in practice. We solve a more tractable problem (13), obtained by strengthening the constraints of (11). One way to strengthen the three nonnegativity constraints of Problem (11) is to consider the following *hierarchy* of SOS programs, parametrized by the integer m representing the half of the degree of p:

$$\left\{ \begin{array}{ll} \inf\limits_{p \in \mathbb{R}[x]_{2m}, w \in \mathbb{R}} & w \,, \\ \text{s.t.} & -p = \sigma_0 - \sum\limits_{j=1}^{n_{\text{in}}} \sigma_j r_j^{\text{in}} \,, \\ & \forall i \in \mathcal{I},\ p - p \circ T^i = \sigma^i - \sum\limits_{j=1}^{n_i} \mu_j^i r_j^i - \sum\limits_{j=1}^{n_0} \gamma_j^i r_j^0 \,, \\ & w + p - \kappa = \psi \,, \\ & \\ & \forall j = 1, \ldots, n_{\text{in}} \,,\ \sigma_j \in \Sigma[x] \,,\ \deg(\sigma_j r_j^{\text{in}}) \leq 2m \,, \\ & \sigma_0 \in \Sigma[x] \,,\ \deg(\sigma_0) \leq 2m \,, \\ & \forall i \in \mathcal{I} \,,\ \sigma^i \in \Sigma[x] \,,\ \deg(\sigma^i) \leq 2m \deg T^i \,, \\ & \forall i \in \mathcal{I} \,,\ \forall j = 1, \ldots, n_i \,,\ \mu_j^i \in \Sigma[x] \,,\ \deg(\mu_j^i r_j^i) \leq 2m \deg T^i, \\ & \forall i \in \mathcal{I} \,,\ \forall j = 1, \ldots, n_0 \,,\ \gamma^i \in \Sigma[x] \,,\ \deg(\gamma_j^i r_j^0) \leq 2m \deg T^i, \\ & \psi \in \Sigma[x] \,,\ \deg(\psi) \leq 2m. \end{array} \right. \tag{13}$$

The variables of Problem (13) are w, the coefficients of p and of the SOS polynomials $\sigma_j, \mu_j^i, \gamma_j^i, \psi$, whose degrees are fixed to yield finite dimensional problems.

Proposition 1. *For a given $m \in \mathbb{N}$, let (p_m, w_m) be any feasible solution of Problem (13). Then (p_m, w_m) is also a feasible solution of Problem (11). Moreover, if $w_m \leq \alpha$ then both $P_m := \{x \in \mathbb{R}^d \mid p_m(x) \leq 0\}$ and $\mathcal{P}_{\kappa,w_m}$ satisfy Eq. (7).*

Proof. The feasible solution (p_m, w_m) is associated with SOS certificates ensuring that the three equality constraints of Problem (13) hold: $\{\sigma_0, \sigma_j\}$ is associated to the first one, $\{\sigma^i, \mu_j^i, \gamma_j^i\}$ is associated to the second one and ψ is associated to the third one. We recall that the set X^{in} admits a representation similar to the one given by Eq. (1): $X^{\text{in}} := \{x \in \mathbb{R}^d \mid \forall j = 1, \dots, n_{\text{in}}, r_j^{\text{in}}(x) \leq 0\}$. The first equality constraint, namely

$$-p_m(x) = \sigma_0(x) - \sum_{j=1}^{n_{\text{in}}} \sigma_j(x) r_j^{\text{in}}(x) , \quad \forall x \in \mathbb{R}^d ,$$

implies that $\forall x \in X^{\text{in}}, p_m(x) \leq 0$. Similarly, recalling the definition $X^i := \{x \in \mathbb{R}^d \mid \forall j = 1, \dots, n_i, \ r_j^i(x) \leq 0\}$, one has $\forall i \in \mathcal{I}, \forall x \in X^i \cap X^0, p_m(T^i(x)) \leq p_m(x)$ and $\forall x \in \mathbb{R}^d, \kappa(x) \leq w_m + p_m(x)$. Then (p_m, w_m) is a feasible solution of Problem (11). The second statement comes directly from Lemma 1.

While increasing $2m$, we obtain a sequence of abstractions, called a hierarchy of SOS problems in optimization (see [12]). Polynomials p_m and bounds w_m are related through their dependencies to the PPS input data.

Computational considerations. Define $t := \max\{\deg T^i, i \in \mathcal{I}\}$. At step m of this hierarchy, the number of SDP variables is proportional to $\binom{d+2mt}{d}$ and the number of SDP constraints is proportional to $\binom{d+mt}{d}$. Thus, one expects tractable approximations when the number d of variables (resp. the degree $2m$ of the template p) is small. However, one can handle bigger instances of Problem (13) by taking into account the system properties. For instance one could exploit sparsity as in [25] by considering the variable sparsity correlation pattern of the polynomials $\{T^i, i \in \mathcal{I}\}, \{r_j^i, i \in \mathcal{I}, j = 1, \dots, n_i\}, \{r_j^0, j = 1, \dots, n_0\}, \{r_j^{\text{in}}, j = 1, \dots, n_{\text{in}}\}$ and κ.

5 Benchmarks

Here, we perform some numerical experiments while solving Problem (13) (given in Sect. 4) on several examples. Different properties yield different instances of Problem (13). In Sect. 5.1, we verify that the program of Example 1 satisfies some boundedness property. We also provide examples involving higher dimensional cases. Then, Sect. 5.2 focuses on other properties, such as checking that the set of variable values avoids an unsafe region. Numerical experiments are performed on an Intel Core i5 CPU (2.40 GHz) with YALMIP being interfaced with the SDP solver MOSEK.

5.1 Checking Boundedness of the Set of Variables Values

Example 4. Following Example 1, we consider the constrained piecewise discrete-time dynamical system $\mathcal{S} = (X^{\text{in}}, X^0, \{X^1, X^2\}, \{T^1, T^2\})$ with $X^{\text{in}} = [0.9, 1.1] \times [0, 0.2]$, $X^0 = \{x \in \mathbb{R}^2 \mid r^0(x) \le 0\}$ with $r^0 : x \mapsto -1$, $X^1 = \{x \in \mathbb{R}^2 \mid r^1(x) \le 0\}$ with $r^1 : x \mapsto \|x\|^2 - 1$, $X^2 = \{x \in \mathbb{R}^2 \mid r^2(x) < 0\}$ with $r^2 = -r^1$ and $T^1 : (x_1, x_2) \mapsto (c_{11}x_1^2 + c_{12}x_2^3, c_{21}x_1^3 + c_{22}x_2^2)$, $T^2 : (x_1, x_2) \mapsto (d_{11}x_1^3 + d_{12}x_2^2, d_{21}x_1^2 + d_{22}x_2^2)$. We are interested in showing that the boundedness property $\mathcal{P}_{\|\cdot\|_2^2, \alpha}$ holds for some positive α.

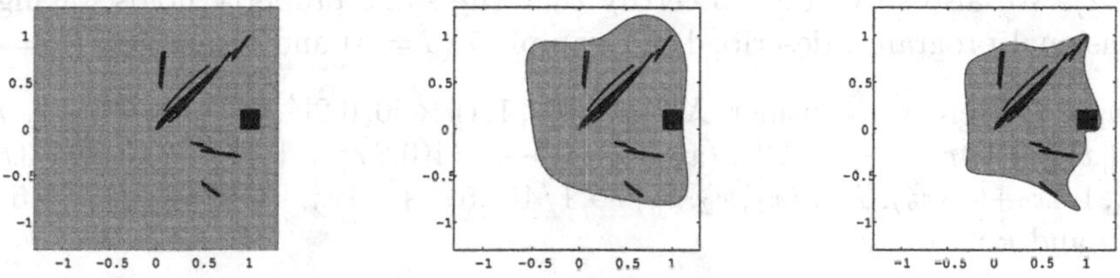

(a) $m = 3$ (b) $m = 4$ (c) $m = 5$

Fig. 2. A hierarchy of sublevel sets P_m for Example 4

Here we illustrate the method by instantiating the program of Example 1 with the following input: $a_1 = 0.9$, $a_2 = 1.1$, $b_1 = 0$, $b_2 = 0.2$, $c_{11} = c_{12} = c_{21} = c_{22} = 1$, $d_{11} = 0.5$, $d_{12} = 0.4$, $d_{21} = -0.6$ and $d_{22} = 0.3$. We represent the possible initial values taken by the program variables (x_1, x_2) by picking uniformly N points $(x_1^{(i)}, x_2^{(i)})$ $(i = 1, \ldots, N)$ inside the box $X^{\text{in}} = [0.9, 1.1] \times [0, 0.2]$ (see the corresponding square of dots on Fig. 2). The other dots are obtained after successive updates of each point $(x_1^{(i)}, x_2^{(i)})$ by the program of Example 1. The sets of dots in Fig. 2 are obtained with $N = 100$ and six successive iterations.

At step $m = 3$, Program (13) yields a solution[1] $(p_3, w_3) \in \mathbb{R}[x]_6 \times \mathbb{R}$ together with SOS certificates, which guarantee the boundedness property, that is $x \in \mathfrak{R} \implies x \in P_3 := \{p_3(x) \le 0\} \subseteq \mathcal{P}_{\|\cdot\|_2^2, w_3} \implies \|x\|_2^2 \le w_3$. The corresponding instance of Problem (13) is

$$\begin{cases} \inf & w, \\ \text{s.t.} & -p(x_1, x_2) = \sigma_0(x_1, x_2) - \sigma_1(x_1, x_2)(1.1 - x_1)(0.9 - x_1) - \sigma_2(x_1, x_2)(x_2 - 0.2)x_2 \ , \\ & p(x_1, x_2) - p(x_1^2 + x_2^3, x_1^3 + x_2^2) = \sigma^1 - \mu^1(\|x\|^2 - 1) \ , \\ & p(x_1, x_2) - p(0.5x_1^2 + 0.4x_2^3, -0.6x_1^3 + 0.3x_2^2) = \sigma^2 - \mu^2(1 - \|x\|^2) \ , \\ & w + p(x) - \|x\|^2 = \psi(x) \ , \\ & w \in \mathbb{R}, \ p \in \mathbb{R}[x]_6 \ , \ \sigma_0, \sigma^1, \sigma^2, \psi \in \Sigma[x]_6 \ , \ \sigma_1, \sigma_2, \mu^1, \mu^2 \in \Sigma[x]_4 \ . \end{cases}$$

[1] Note that most existing SDP solvers are implemented based on inexact computation. In practice, we perform post-processing verification (YALMIP command "checkset"), ensuring that computed polynomials are SOS.

One has $p_3(x) := -2.510902467 - 0.0050x_1 - 0.0148x_2 + 3.0998x_1^2 - 0.8037x_2^3 - 3.0297x_1^3 + 2.5924x_2^2 + 1.5266x_1x_2 - 1.9133x_1^2x_2 - 1.8122x_1x_2^2 + 1.6042x_1^4 + 0.0512x_1^3x_2 - 4.4430x_1^2x_2^2 - 1.8926x_1x_2^3 + 0.5464x_2^4 - 0.2084x_1^5 + 0.5866x_1^4x_2 + 2.2410x_1^3x_2^2 + 1.5714x_1^2x_2^3 - 0.0890x_1x_2^4 - 0.9656x_2^5 + 0.0098x_1^6 - 0.0320x_1^5x_2 - 0.0232x_1^4x_2^2 + 0.2660x_1^3x_2^3 + 0.7746x_1^2x_2^4 + 0.9200x_1x_2^5 + 0.6411x_2^6$ (for the sake of conciseness, we do not display p_4 and p_5). Figure 2 displays in light gray outer approximations of the set of possible values X_1 taken by the program of Example 4 as follows: (a) the degree six sublevel set P_3, (b) the degree eight sublevel set P_4 and (c) the degree ten sublevel set P_5. The outer approximation P_3 is coarse as it contains the box $[-1.5, 1.5]^2$. However, solving Problem (13) at higher steps yields tighter outer approximations of $\mathfrak{R}$ together with more precise bounds w_4 and w_5 (see the corresponding row in Table 2). We also succeeded to certify that the same property holds for higher dimensional programs, described in Example 5 ($d = 3$) and Example 6 ($d = 4$).

Example 5. Here we consider $X^{\text{in}} = [0.9, 1.1] \times [0, 0.2]^2$, $r^0 : x \mapsto -1$, $r^1 : x \mapsto \|x\|_2^2 - 1$, $r^2 = -r^1$, $T^1 : (x_1, x_2, x_3) \mapsto 1/4(0.8x_1^2 + 1.4x_2 - 0.5x_3^2, 1.3x_1 + 0.5x_3^2, 1.4x_2 + 0.8x_3^2)$, $T^2 : (x_1, x_2, x_3) \mapsto 1/4(0.5x_1 + 0.4x_2^2, -0.6x_2^2 + 0.3x_3^2, 0.5x_3 + 0.4x_1^2)$ and $\kappa : x \mapsto \|x\|_2^2$.

Example 6. Here we consider $X^{\text{in}} = [0.9, 1.1] \times [0, 0.2]^3$, $r^0 : x \mapsto -1$, $r^1 : x \mapsto \|x\|_2^2 - 1$, $r^2 = -r^1$, $T^1 : (x_1, x_2, x_3, x_4) \mapsto 0.25(0.8x_1^2 + 1.4x_2 - 0.5x_3^2, 1.3x_1 + 0.5, x_2^2 - 0.8x_4^2, 0.8x_3^2 + 1.4x_4, 1.3x_3 + 0.5x_4^2)$, $T^2 : (x_1, x_2, x_3, x_4) \mapsto 0.25(0.5x_1 + 0.4x_2^2, -0.6x_1^2 + 0.3x_2^2, 0.5x_3 + 0.4x_4^2, -0.6x_3 + 0.3x_4^2)$ and $\kappa : x \mapsto \|x\|_2^2$.

Table 1 reports several data obtained while solving Problem (13) at step m, ($2 \leq m \leq 5$), either for Examples 4, 5 or 6. Each instance of Problem (13) is recast as a SDP program, involving a total number of "Nb. vars" SDP variables, with a SDP matrix of size "Mat. size". We indicate the CPU time required to compute the optimal solution of each SDP program with Mosek.

The symbol "–" means that the corresponding SOS program could not be solved within one day of computation. These benchmarks illustrate the computational considerations mentioned in Sect. 4 as it takes more CPU time to analyze higher dimensional programs. Note that it is not possible to solve Problem (13) at step 5 for Example 6. A possible workaround to limit this computational blow-up would be to exploit the sparsity of the system.

5.2 Other Properties

Here we consider the program given in Example 7. One is interested in showing that the set X_1 of possible values taken by the variables of this program does not meet the ball B of center $(-0.5, -0.5)$ and radius 0.5.

Example 7. Let consider the PPS $\mathcal{S} = (X^{\text{in}}, X^0, \{X^1, X^2\}, \{T^1, T^2\})$ with $X^{\text{in}} = [0.5, 0.7] \times [0.5, 0.7]$, $X^0 = \{x \in \mathbb{R}^2 \mid r^0(x) \leq 0\}$ with $r^0 : x \mapsto -1$, $X^1 = \{x \in \mathbb{R}^2 \mid r^1(x) \leq 0\}$ with $r^1 : x \mapsto \|x\|_2^2 - 1$, $X^2 = \{x \in \mathbb{R}^2 \mid r^2(x) \leq 0\}$ with $r^2 = -r^1$ and $T^1 : (x_1, x_2) \mapsto (x_1^2 + x_2^3, x_1^3 + x_2^2)$, $T^2 : (x, y) \mapsto (0.5x_1^3 + 0.4x_2^2, -0.6x_1^2 + 0.3x_2^2)$. With $\kappa : (x_1, x_2) \mapsto 0.25 - (x_1 + 0.5)^2 - (x_2 + 0.5)^2$,

Table 1. Comparison of timing results for Examples 4, 5 and 6

Degree $2m$		4	6	8	10
Example 4	Nb. vars	1513	5740	15705	35212
	Mat. size	368	802	1404	2174
$(d = 2)$	Time	$0.82\,s$	$1.35\,s$	$4.00\,s$	$9.86\,s$
Example 5	Nb. vars	2115	11950	46461	141612
	Mat. size	628	1860	4132	7764
$(d = 3)$	Time	$0.84\,s$	$2.98\,s$	$21.4\,s$	$109\,s$
Example 6	Nb. vars	7202	65306	18480	–
	Mat. size	1670	6622	373057	–
$(d = 4)$	Time	$2.85\,s$	$57.3\,s$	$1534\,s$	–

Table 2. Hierarchies of bounds obtained for various properties

Benchmark	κ	w_2	w_3	w_4	w_5
Example 4	$\\| \cdot \\|_2^2$	639	17.4	2.44	2.02
Example 7	$x \mapsto 0.25 - \\|x + 0.5\\|_2^2$	0.25	0.249	0.0993	-0.0777
Example 8	$\\| \cdot \\|_2^2$	10.2	2.84	2.84	2.84
	$x \mapsto \\|T^1(x) - T^2(x)\\|_2^2$	5.66	2.81	2.78	2.78

one has $B := \{x \in \mathbb{R}^2 \mid 0 \leq \kappa(x)\}$. Here, one shall prove $x \in \mathfrak{R} \implies \kappa(x) < 0$ while computing some negative α such that $\mathfrak{R} \subseteq \mathcal{P}_{\kappa,\alpha}$. Note that κ is not a norm, by contrast with the previous examples.

At step $m = 3$ (resp. $m = 4$), Program (13) yields a nonnegative solution w_3 (resp. w_4). Hence, it does not allow to certify that $\mathfrak{R} \cap B$ is empty. This is illustrated in both Fig. 3 (a) and (b), where the light grey region does not avoid the ball B. However, solving Program (13) at step $m = 5$ yields a negative bound w_5 together with a certificate that $\mathfrak{R}$ avoids the ball B (see Fig. 3 (c)). The corresponding values of w_m ($m = 3, 4, 5$) are given in Table 2.

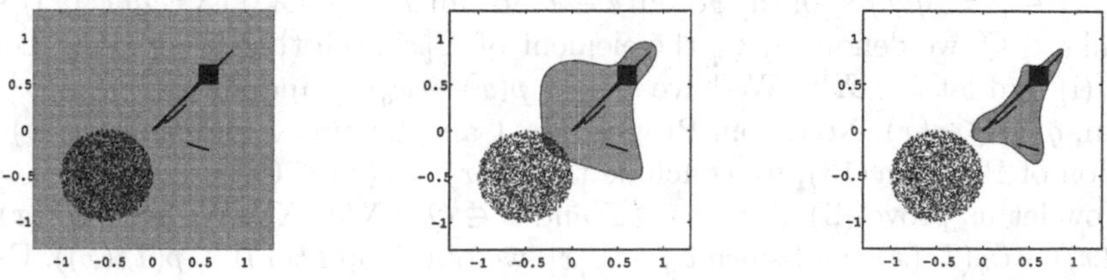

(a) $m = 3$ (b) $m = 4$ (c) $m = 5$

Fig. 3. A hierarchy of sublevel sets P_m for Example 7

Finally, one analyzes the program given in Example 8.

Example 8. (adapted from Example 3 in [4])

Let $\mathcal{S}$ be the PPS $(X^{\text{in}}, X^0, \{X^1, X^2\}, \{T^1, T^2\})$ with $X^{\text{in}} = [-1,1] \times [-1,1]$, $X^0 = \{x \in \mathbb{R}^2 \mid r^0(x) \leq 0\}$ with $r^0 : x \mapsto -1$, $X^1 = \{x \in \mathbb{R}^2 \mid r^1(x) \leq 0\}$ with $r^1 : x \mapsto x_2 - x_1$, $X^2 = \{x \in \mathbb{R}^2 \mid r^2(x) \leq 0\}$ with $r^2 = -r^1$ and $T^1 : (x_1, x_2) \mapsto (0.687x_1 + 0.558x_2 - 0.0001 * x_1x_2, -0.292x_1 + 0.773x_2)$, $T^2 : (x, y) \mapsto (0.369x_1 + 0.532x_2 - 0.0001x_1^2, -1.27x_1 + 0.12x_2 - 0.0001x_1x_2)$. We consider the boundedness property $\kappa_1 := \| \cdot \|_2^2$ as well as $\kappa_2(x) := \|T^1(x) - T^2(x)\|_2^2$. The function κ_2 can be viewed as the absolute error made by updating the variable x after a possibly "wrong" branching. Such behaviors could occur while computing wrong values for the conditionals (e.g. r^1) using floating-point arithmetics. Table 2 indicates the hierarchy of bounds obtained after solving Problem (13) with $m = 3, 4, 5$, for both properties. The bound $w_5 = 2.84$ (for κ_1) implies that the set of reachable values may not be included in the initial set X^{in}. A valid upper bound of the error function κ_2 is given by $w_5 = 2.78$.

6 Templates Bases

We finally present further use of the set P defined at Eq. (7). This sublevel set can be viewed as a template abstraction, following from the definition in [3], with a fixed template basis p and an associated 0 bound. This representation allows to develop a policy iteration algorithm [2] to obtain more precise inductive invariants.

We now give some simple method to complete this template basis to improve the precision of the bound w found with Problem (13).

Proposition 2 (Template Basis Completions). *Let (p, w) be a solution of Problem (13) and $\mathcal{Q}$ be a finite subset of $\mathbb{R}[x]$ such that for all $q \in \mathcal{Q}$, $p - q \in \Sigma[x]$. Then $\mathfrak{R} \subseteq \{x \in \mathbb{R}^d \mid p(x) \leq 0,\ q(x) \leq 0,\ \forall q \in \mathcal{Q}\} \subseteq \mathcal{P}_{\kappa,w} \subseteq \mathcal{P}_{\kappa,\alpha}$ and $\{x \in \mathbb{R}^d \mid p(x) \leq 0,\ q(x) \leq 0,\ \forall q \in \mathcal{Q}\}$ is an inductive invariant.*

Proof Let Q be the set $\{x \in \mathbb{R}^d \mid p(x) \leq 0,\ q(x) \leq 0,\ \forall q \in \mathcal{Q}\}$. It is obvious that $Q \subseteq P = \{x \in \mathbb{R}^d \mid p(x) \leq 0\}$ and hence $Q \subseteq \mathcal{P}_{\kappa,w}$. Now let us prove that Q is an inductive invariant. We have to prove that Q satisfies Eq. (8) that is: (i) For all $x \in X^{\text{in}}$, $q(x) \leq 0$; (ii) For all $i \in \mathcal{I}$, for all $x \in Q \cap X^i \cap X^0$, $q(T^i(x)) \leq 0$. For all $q \in \mathcal{Q}$, we denote by ψ_q the element of $\Sigma[x]$ such that $p - q = \psi_q$. Let us show (i) and let $x \in X^{\text{in}}$. We have $q(x) = p(x) - \psi_q(x)$ and since $\psi_q \in \Sigma[x]$, we obtain, $q(x) \leq p(x)$. Now from Proposition 1 and Lemma 1 and since (p, w) is a solution of Problem (13), we conclude that $q(x) \leq p(x) \leq 0$.

Now let us prove (ii) and let $i \in \mathcal{I}$ and $x \in Q \cap X^i \cap X^0$. We get $q(T^i(x)) = p(T^i(x)) - \psi_q(T^i(x))$ and since $\psi_q \in \Sigma[x]$, we obtain $q(T^i(x)) \leq p(T^i(x))$. Using the fact that (p, w) is a solution of Problem (13) and using Proposition 1 and Lemma 1, we obtain $q(T^i(x)) \leq p(T^i(x)) \leq p(x)$. Since $x \in Q \subseteq P = \{y \in \mathbb{R}^d \mid p(y) \leq 0\}$, we conclude that $q(T^i(x)) \leq 0$.

Actually, we can weaken the hypothesis of Proposition 2 to construct an inductive invariant. Indeed, after the computation of p following Problem (13), it suffices to take a polynomial q such that $p - q \geq 0$. Nevertheless, we cannot compute easily such a polynomial q. By using the hypothesis $p - q \in \Sigma[x]$, we can compute q by sum-of-squares. Proposition 2 allows to define a simple method to construct a basic semialgebraic inductive invariant set. Then the polynomials describing this basic semialgebraic set defines a new templates basis and this basic semialgebraic set can be used as initialisation of the policy iteration algorithm developed in [2]. Note that the link between the templates generation and the initialisation of policy iteration has been addressed in [1].

Example 9 Let us consider the property $\mathcal{P}_{\|\cdot\|_2^2,\infty}$ and let (p, w) be a solution of Problem (13). We have $\kappa(x) = \sum_{1\leq j\leq k} x_j^2$ and $w + p - \kappa = \psi$ where $\psi \in \Sigma[x]$. In [21], the templates basis used to compute bounds on the reachable values set consists in the square variables plus a Lyapunov function. Let us prove that, in our setting, $\mathcal{Q} = \{x_k^2 - w,\ k = 1, \ldots, d\}$ can complete $\{p\}$ in the sense of Proposition 2. Let $k \in \{1, \ldots, d\}$ and let $x \in \mathbb{R}^d$, $p(x) - (x_k^2 - w) = p(x) - \kappa(x) + w + \sum_{j\neq k} x_j^2 = \psi(x) + \sum_{j\neq k} x_j^2 \in \Sigma[x]$.

7 Related Works and Conclusion

Roux et al. [21] provide an automatic method to compute floating-point certified Lyapunov functions of perturbed affine loop body updates. They use Lyapunov functions with squares of coordinate functions as quadratic invariants in case of single loop programs written in affine arithmetic. In the context of hybrid systems, certified inductive invariants can be computed by using SOS approximations of parametric polynomial optimization problems [14]. In [18], the authors develop a SOS-based methodology to certify that the trajectories of hybrid systems avoid an unsafe region.

In the context of static analysis for semialgebraic programs, the approach developed in [8] focuses on inferring valid loop/conditional invariants for semialgebraic programs[2]. This approach relaxes an invariant generation problem into the resolution of nonlinear matrix inequalities, handled with semidefinite programming. Our method bears similarities with this approach but we generate a hierarchy of invariants (of increasing degree) with respect to target polynomial properties and restrict ourselves to linear matrix inequality formulations. In [6], invariants are given by polynomial inequalities (of bounded degree) but the method relies on a reduction to linear inequalities (the polyhedra domain). Template polyhedra domains allow to analyze reachability for polynomial systems: in [22], the authors propose a method that computes linear templates to improve the accuracy of reachable set approximations, whereas the procedure in [10] relies on Bernstein polynomials and linear programming, with linear templates being fixed in advance. Bernstein polynomials also appear in [20] as polynomial templates but they are not generated automatically. In [23],

[2] This approach also handles semialgebraic program termination.

the authors use SMT-based techniques to automatically generate templates which are defined as formulas built with arbitrary logical structures and predicate conjunctions. Other reductions to systems of polynomial *equalities* (by contrast with polynomial inequalities, as we consider here) were studied in [16,19] and more recently in [7].

In this paper, we give a formal framework to relate the invariant generation problem to the property to prove on analyzed program. We proposed a practical method to compute such invariants in the case of polynomial arithmetic using sums-of-squares programming. This method is able to handle non trivial examples, as illustrated through the numerical experiments. Topics of further investigation include refining the invariant bounds generated for a specific sublevel property, by applying the policy iteration algorithm. Such a refinement would be of particular interest if one can not decide whether the set of variable values avoids an unsafe region when the bound of the corresponding sums-of-squares program is not accurate enough. For the case of boundedness property, it would allow to decrease the value of the bounds on the variables. Finally, our method could be generalized to a larger class of programs, involving semialgebraic or transcendental assignments, while applying the same polynomial reduction techniques as in [15].

References

1. Adjé, A.: Policy iteration in finite templates domain. In: 7th International Workshop on Numerical Software Verification (NSV 2012), July 2014
2. Adjé, A., Garoche, P.-L., Magron. V.: A Sums-of-squares extension of policy iterations. Technial report (2015)
3. Adjé, A., Gaubert, S., Goubault, E.: Coupling policy iteration with semi-definite relaxation to compute accurate numerical invariants in static analysis. Log. Methods Comput. Sci. **8**(1), 1–32 (2011)
4. Ahmadi, A.A., Jungers, R.M.: Switched stability of nonlinear systems via sos-convex lyapunov functions and semidefinite programming. In: CDC 2013, pp. 727–732 (2013)
5. Andersen, E.D., Andersen, K.D.: The mosek interior point optimizer for linear programming: an implementation of the homogeneous algorithm. In: Frenk, H., Roos, K., Terlaky, T., Zhang, S. (eds.) High Performance Optimization. Applied Optimization, vol. 33, pp. 197–232. Springer, US (2000)
6. Bagnara, R., Rodríguez-Carbonell, E., Zaffanella, E.: Generation of basic semi-algebraic invariants using convex polyhedra. In: Hankin, C., Siveroni, I. (eds.) SAS 2005. LNCS, vol. 3672, pp. 19–34. Springer, Heidelberg (2005)
7. Cachera, D., Jensen, T., Jobin, A., Kirchner, F.: Inference of polynomial invariants for imperative programs: a farewell to gröbner bases. Sci. Comput. Program. **93**, 89–109 (2014)
8. Cousot, P.: Proving program invariance and termination by parametric abstraction, lagrangian relaxation and semidefinite programming. In: Cousot, R. (ed.) VMCAI 2005. LNCS, vol. 3385, pp. 1–24. Springer, Heidelberg (2005)

9. Cousot, P., Cousot, R.: Abstract interpretation: a unified lattice model for static analysis of programs by construction or approximation of fixpoints. In: Conference Record of the Fourth Annual ACM SIGPLAN-SIGACT Symposium on Principles of Programming Languages, pp. 238–252. ACM Press, Los Angeles, California, New York (1977)
10. Dang, T., Testylier, R.: Reachability analysis for polynomial dynamical systems using the bernstein expansion. Reliab. Comput. **17**(2), 128–152 (2012)
11. Feret, J.: Static analysis of digital filters. In: Schmidt, D. (ed.) ESOP 2004. LNCS, vol. 2986, pp. 33–48. Springer, Heidelberg (2004)
12. Lasserre, J.B.: Global optimization with polynomials and the problem of moments. SIAM J. Optim. **11**(3), 796–817 (2001)
13. Laurent, M.: Sums of squares, moment matrices and optimization over polynomials. In: Putinar, M., Sullivant, S. (eds.) Emerging Applications of AlgebraicGeometry. The IMA Volumes in Mathematics and its Applications, vol. 149, pp. 157–270. Springer, New York (2009)
14. Lin, W., Wu, M., Yang, Z., Zeng, Z.: Exact safety verification of hybrid systems using sums-of-squares representation. Sci. China Inf. Sci. **57**(5), 1–13 (2014)
15. Magron, V., Allamigeon, X., Gaubert, S., Werner, B.: Certification of real inequalities - templates and sums of squares. Math. Program. Ser. B **151**, 1–30 (2014). Volume on Polynomial Optimization
16. Müller-Olm, M., Seidl, H.: Computing polynomial program invariants. Inf. Process. Lett. **91**(5), 233–244 (2004)
17. Parrilo, P.A.: Semidefinite programming relaxations for semialgebraic problems. Math. Program. **96**(2), 293–320 (2003)
18. Prajna, S., Jadbabaie, A.: Safety verification of hybrid systems using barrier certificates. In: Alur, R., Pappas, G.J. (eds.) HSCC 2004. LNCS, vol. 2993, pp. 477–492. Springer, Heidelberg (2004)
19. Rodríguez-Carbonell, E., Kapur, D.: Automatic generation of polynomial invariants of bounded degree using abstract interpretation. Sci. Comput. Program. **64**(1), 54–75 (2007)
20. Roux, P., Garoche, P.-L.: A polynomial template abstract domain based on bernstein polynomials. In: Sixth International Workshop on Numerical Software Verification, NSV 2013 (2013)
21. Roux, P., Jobredeaux, R., Garoche, P.-L., Feron, E.: A generic ellipsoid abstract domain for linear time invariant systems. In: Dang, T., Mitchell, I.M. (eds.) HSCC, pp. 105–114. ACM (2012)
22. Ben Sassi, M.A., Testylier, R., Dang, T., Girard, A.: Reachability analysis of polynomial systems using linear programming relaxations. In: Chakraborty, S., Mukund, M. (eds.) ATVA 2012. LNCS, vol. 7561, pp. 137–151. Springer, Heidelberg (2012)
23. Srivastava, S., Gulwani, S.: Program verification using templates over predicate abstraction. SIGPLAN Not. **44**(6), 223–234 (2009)
24. Vandenberghe, L., Boyd, S.: Semidefinite programming. SIAM Rev. **38**(1), 49–95 (1994)
25. Waki, H., Kim, S., Kojima, M., Muramatsu, M.: Sums of squares and semidefinite programming relaxations for polynomial optimization problems with structured sparsity. SIAM J. Optim. **17**(1), 218–242 (2006)
26. Yamashita, M., Fujisawa, K., Nakata, K., Nakata, M., Fukuda, M., Kobayashi, K., Goto, K.: A high-performance software package for semidefinite programs : Sdpa7. Depatrment of Information Sciences, Tokyo Institute of Technology, Tokyo, Japan, Technical report (2010)

Modularity in Lattices: A Case Study on the Correspondence Between Top-Down and Bottom-Up Analysis

Ghila Castelnuovo[1], Mayur Naik[2], Noam Rinetzky[3](✉), Mooly Sagiv[1], and Hongseok Yang[3]

[1] Tel Aviv University, Tel Aviv, Israel
[2] Georgia Institute of Technology, Atlanta, GA, USA
[3] University of Oxford, Oxford, UK
maon@cs.tau.ac.il

Abstract. Interprocedural analyses are *compositional* when they compute over-approximations of procedures in a bottom-up fashion. These analyses are usually more scalable than top-down analyses, which compute a different procedure summary for every calling context. However, compositional analyses are rare in practice as it is difficult to develop them with enough precision.

We establish a connection between compositional analyses and *modular lattices*, which require certain associativity between the lattice join and meet operations, and use it to develop a compositional version of the connection analysis by Ghiya and Hendren. Our version is slightly more conservative than the original top-down analysis in order to meet our modularity requirement. When applied to real-world Java programs our analysis scaled much better than the original top-down version: The top-down analysis times out in the largest two of our five programs, while ours incurred only 2–5% of precision loss in the remaining programs.

1 Introduction

Scaling program analysis to large programs is an ongoing challenge for program verification. Typical programs include many relatively small procedures. Therefore, a promising direction for scalability is analyzing each procedure in isolation, using pre-computed summaries for called procedures and computing a summary for the analyzed procedure. Such analyses are called *bottom-up interprocedural analysis* or *compositional analysis*. Notice that the analysis of the procedure itself need not be compositional and can be costly. Indeed, bottom-up interprocedural analyses have been found to scale well [3,5,11,20,32].

The theory of compositional analysis has been studied in [6,10,15,16,18]. However, designing and implementing such an analysis is challenging, for several reasons: it requires accounting for all potential calling contexts of a procedure in a sound and precise way; the summary of the procedures can be quite large leading to infeasible analyzers; and it may be costly to instantiate procedure

S. Blazy and T. Jensen (Eds.): SAS 2015, LNCS 9291, pp. 252–274, 2015.
DOI: 10.1007/978-3-662-48288-9_15

summaries. An example of these challenges is the unsound original formulation of the compositional pointer analysis algorithm in [32]. A modified version of the algorithm was subsequently proposed in [29] and, more recently, proven sound in [23] using abstract interpretation. In contrast, top-down interprocedural analysis [8,27,30] is much better understood and has been integrated into existing tools such as SLAM [1], Soot [2], WALA [12], and Chord [26].

Our goal is to contribute to a better understanding of bottom-up interprocedural analysis. Specifically, we aimed to characterize cases under which bottom-up and top-down interprocedural analysis yield the same results when both analyses use the same underlying abstract domains. We partially achieved our goal by formulating a sufficient condition on the effect of primitive commands on abstract states that guarantees bottom-up and top-down interprocedural analyses will yield the same results. The condition is based on lattice theory. Informally, the idea is that the abstract semantics of primitive commands can only use meet and join operations with constant elements, and that elements used in the meet must be *modular* in a lattice theoretical sense [19].

The description of the general framework and proofs of soundness and precision can be found in [4]. For space reasons, we do not provide the general theory here. Instead, we present our results by means of an application: We present a variant of *connection analysis* [14] which we developed using our approach. Connection analysis is a kind of pointer analysis that aims to prove that two references can never point to the same undirected heap component. It thus ignores the direction of pointers. This problem arose from the need to automatically parallelize sequential programs. Despite its conceptual simplicity, connection analysis is flow- and context-sensitive, and the effect of program statements is non-distributive. In fact, the top-down interprocedural connection analysis is exponential; indeed our experiments indicate that this analysis scales poorly.

More specifically, in this paper, we present a formulation of a variant of the connection analysis in a way that satisfies the requirements of our general framework. Intuitively, the main difference from the original analysis is that we had to over-approximate the treatment of variables that point to null in all program states that occur at a program point. We implemented two versions of the top-down interprocedural connection analysis for Java programs in order to measure the extra loss of precision of our over-approximation. We also implemented the bottom-up interprocedural analysis for Java programs. We report empirical results for five benchmarks of sizes 15 K–310 K bytecodes for a total of 800 K bytecodes. The original top-down analysis times out in over six hours on the largest two benchmarks. For the remaining three benchmarks, only 2–5% of precision was lost by our bottom-up analysis due to the modularity requirement.

2 Informal Overview and Running Example

In this section, we illustrate the use of *modular lattices* in the design of our compositional connection analysis, focusing on the use of *modular elements* to ensure precision.

Definition 1. *An element* d_p *in a lattice* $\mathcal{D}$ *is* (right) modular *if*

$$\forall d, d' \in \mathcal{D}.\ d' \sqsubseteq d_p \Rightarrow d_p \sqcap (d \sqcup d') = (d_p \sqcap d) \sqcup d' .$$

We call a lattice $\mathcal{D}$ modular *if all of its elements are modular.*

One way to understand the modularity condition in lattices is to think about it as a requirement of commutativity between two operators $(d_p \sqcap -)$ and $(- \sqcup d')$ [19]. A particular case in which this condition holds for every element d_p is if the lattice meet operation distributes over the join operation, e.g., as in the powerset lattice $(\mathcal{P}(S), \subseteq)$.

Consider a program in Fig. 1. It consists of procedures `main`() and $\mathtt{p_1}(), \ldots, \mathtt{p_n}()$. The `main`() procedure first allocates four objects and connects them into two disjoint pairs. Then, it invokes $\mathtt{p_1}()$ using either $\mathtt{a_0}$ or $\mathtt{b_0}$ as the actual parameter. This invocation triggers subsequent calls to $\mathtt{p_2}(), \ldots, \mathtt{p_n}()$, where all the invoked procedures behave almost the same as $\mathtt{p_1}$: procedure $\mathtt{p_i}()$ assigns its formal parameter $\mathtt{c_{i-1}}$ either to $\mathtt{a_i}$ or to $\mathtt{b_i}$, and then calls $\mathtt{p_{i+1}}$ using $\mathtt{c_{i-1}}$ as the actual parameter, unless $i = n$.

We say that two heap objects are *connected* in a state when it is possible to reach from one object to the other, following paths in the heap ignoring pointer direction. Two variables are *connected* when they point to connected heap objects. Connection analysis soundly estimates the connection relationships between variables. The abstract states d of the analysis are families $\{X_i\}_{i \in I}$ of disjoint sets of variables ordered by refinement: Two variables x, y are in the same set X_i, which we call a *connection set*, when x and y may be connected, and $d_1 \sqsubseteq d_2 \iff \forall X_1 \in d_1.\, \exists X_2 \in D_2.\, X_1 \subseteq X_2$.

Example 1. Figure 1 depicts the two possible concrete states, σ_1 and σ_2, that can occur at the entry to $\mathtt{p_1}()$, and their respective connection abstractions. In the concrete states, variables $\mathtt{a_1}, \ldots, \mathtt{b_1} \ldots$ point to `null`. Hence, they are represented by separate connection sets.

The abstract states $\alpha(\{\sigma_1\})$ and $\alpha(\{\sigma_2\})$ are incomparable. However, both are more precise than the abstraction of a state in which all the variables point to the same object and less precise than that of state where the values of all the variables is null.

A standard approach for an interprocedural analysis is to follow the execution flow of a program top-down (i.e., from callers to callees), and to re-analyze each procedure for every different calling context. This approach often suffers from the scalability issue. One reason is the explosion of different calling contexts. Indeed, note that in our example program, each procedure $\mathtt{p_i}()$ calls the procedure $\mathtt{p_{i+1}}()$ with two different calling contexts. As a result, a top-down connection analysis, e.g., [14], computes 2^i abstract states at the entry to procedure $\mathtt{p_i}()$.

Example 2. The abstract state d_t shown below arises at the entry to $\mathtt{p_n}()$ when the then-branch is always selected, while d_e arises when only $\mathtt{p_{n-1}}()$ selects the else-branch.

$$d_t = \{\{\mathtt{g_1}, \mathtt{a_0}, \mathtt{a_1}, \ldots, \mathtt{a_{n-2}}, \mathtt{a_{n-1}}, \mathtt{c_{n-1}}\}, \{\mathtt{g_2}, \mathtt{b_0}\}, \{\mathtt{a_n}\}, \{\mathtt{b_1}\}, \ldots, \{\mathtt{b_{n-1}}\}, \{\mathtt{b_n}\}\}$$
$$d_e = \{\{\mathtt{g_1}, \mathtt{a_0}, \mathtt{a_1}, \ldots, \mathtt{a_{n-2}}, \mathtt{b_{n-1}}, \mathtt{c_{n-1}}\}, \{\mathtt{g_2}, \mathtt{b_0}\}, \{\mathtt{a_{n-1}}\}, \{\mathtt{a_n}\}, \{\mathtt{b_1}\}, \ldots, \{\mathtt{b_{n-2}}\}, \{\mathtt{b_n}\}\}$$

```
static main() {
  g1=new h1; g2=new h2;
  a0=new h3; b0=new h4;
  a0.f=g1; b0.f=g2;
  if(*) p1(a0);
  else p1(b0);}
```

```
pi(ci-1) {
  if(*)
    ai=ci-1;
  else
    bi=ci-1;
  pi+1(ci-1);}
```

```
pn(cn-1) {
  if(*)
    an=cn-1;
  else
    bn=cn-1;}
```

σ_1

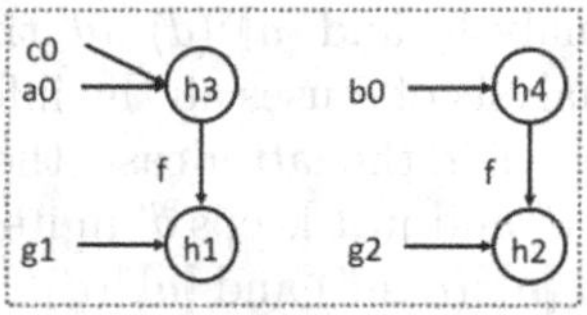

σ_2

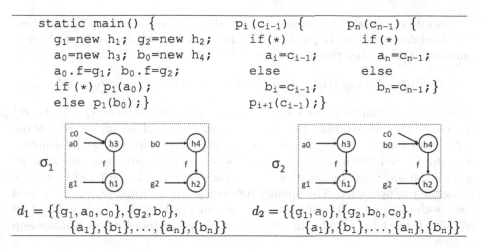

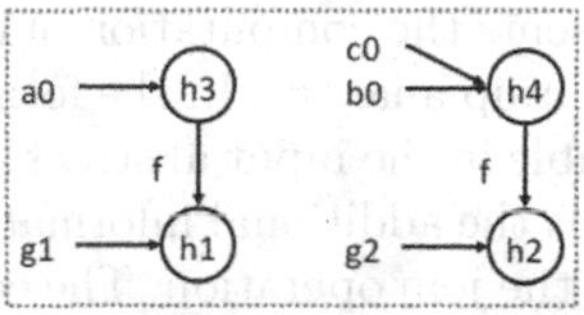

$d_1 = \{\{\mathtt{g}_1, \mathtt{a}_0, \mathtt{c}_0\}, \{\mathtt{g}_2, \mathtt{b}_0\}, \{\mathtt{a}_1\}, \{\mathtt{b}_1\}, \ldots, \{\mathtt{a}_n\}, \{\mathtt{b}_n\}\}$ $\quad d_2 = \{\{\mathtt{g}_1, \mathtt{a}_0\}, \{\mathtt{g}_2, \mathtt{b}_0, \mathtt{c}_0\}, \{\mathtt{a}_1\}, \{\mathtt{b}_1\}, \ldots, \{\mathtt{a}_n\}, \{\mathtt{b}_n\}\}$

Fig. 1. First row: example program. All of $\mathtt{g}_1, \mathtt{g}_2, \mathtt{a}_1, \ldots, \mathtt{b}_1 \ldots$ are global variables. Second row: the concrete states at the entry of $\mathtt{p}_1()$ and the corresponding connection abstractions.

The bottom-up (compositional) approach avoids the explosion of the calling contexts that occur in the top-down analysis. It does so by analyzing each procedure independently to compute a summary, which is then instantiated as a function of a calling context. Unfortunately, it is rather difficult to analyze a procedure independently of its calling contexts and at the same time compute a summary that is sound and precise enough. One of the reasons is that the abstract transformers may depend on the input abstract state, which is often unavailable for the compositional analysis.

We formulate a precise compositional connection analysis. The key feature of the analysis is that the abstract transformers of primitive commands a have the form

$$[\![a]\!]^\sharp = \lambda d.\, (d \sqcap d_p) \sqcup d_g \ ,$$

where d_p and d_g are some constant abstract states, independent of the input, and d_p is a modular element in the lattice of all abstract states. For example, the abstract transformer of the statement $\mathtt{x} = \mathtt{y}$ has the form above with $d_p = S_{x'}$ and $d_g = U_{x'y'}$, where $S_{x'}$ consists of two connection sets, $\{x'\}$ and the set of all the other variables, and $U_{x'y'}$ has the set $\{x', y'\}$ of x', y' and the singleton sets $\{z\}$ for all variables z other than x', y'. Intuitively, taking the meet with $S_{x'}$ separates out the variable x from its connection set in d, and joining the result with $U_{x'y'}$ adds x to the connection set of y.[1]

[1] The subscripts p and g are used as mnemonics: d_p is used to partition a connection set and d_g to group two connection sets together.

Note that the abstract domain is not distributive.[2] However it does contain modular elements. In particular, d_p in the abstract transfer for a above is modular. This implies that for all $d, d' \in \mathcal{D}$ such that $d' \sqsubseteq d_p$,

$$[\![a]\!]^\sharp(d \sqcup d') = d_p \sqcap (d \sqcup d') \sqcup d_g = (d_p \sqcap d) \sqcup d' \sqcup d_g = [\![a]\!]^\sharp(d) \sqcup d'$$

where the modularity is used in the second equality. Intuitively, $[\![a]\!]^\sharp(d \sqcup d')$ represents the computation of the top-down analysis, and $[\![a]\!]^\sharp(d) \sqcup d'$ that of the bottom-up analysis. In the former case, the analysis of a uses all the information available in the input abstract state $d \sqcup d'$, whereas in the latter case, the analysis ignores the additional information recorded in d' and just keeps d' in its outcome using the join operation. The equality between $[\![a]\!]^\sharp(d \sqcup d')$ and $[\![a]\!]^\sharp(d) \sqcup d'$ means that both approaches lead to the same outcome, as long as $d' \sqsubseteq d_p$ holds. This equality is the basis of our coincidence result between top-down and bottom-up analyses.

Concretely, consider the case that a is the assignment $\mathtt{a_i{=}c_{i\text{-}1}}$ in the body of the procedure $\mathtt{p_i}$. Let $\{d_k\}_k$ be all the abstract states at the entry of $\mathtt{p_i}$ encountered during the top-down analysis. Suppose that there exists d such that $\forall k : \exists d'_k \sqsubseteq S_{\mathtt{a_i}'} : d_k = d \sqcup d'_k$. Our compositional approach analyzes $\mathtt{a_i} = \mathtt{c_{i\text{-}1}}$ only once with the abstract state d, and computes $d' = [\![\mathtt{a_i} = \mathtt{c_{i\text{-}1}}]\!]^\sharp(d)$. Later when $\mathtt{p_i}$ gets called with d_k's, the analysis adapts d' by simply joining it with d'_k, and returns this outcome of this adaption as a result. This adaptation of the bottom-up approach gives the same result as the top-down approach, which applies $[\![\mathtt{a_i} = \mathtt{c_{i\text{-}1}}]\!]^\sharp$ on d_k directly:

$$\begin{aligned}[\![\mathtt{a_i{=}c_{i\text{-}1}}]\!]^\sharp(d_k) &= (d_k \sqcap S_{\mathtt{a_i}'}) \sqcup U_{\mathtt{a_i}'\mathtt{c_{i\text{-}1}}'} &&= ((d \sqcup d'_k) \sqcap S_{\mathtt{a_i}'}) \sqcup U_{\mathtt{a_i}'\mathtt{c_{i\text{-}1}}'} \\ &= (d \sqcap S_{\mathtt{a_i}'}) \sqcup d'_k \sqcup U_{\mathtt{a_i}'\mathtt{c_{i\text{-}1}}'} &&= [\![\mathtt{a_i{=}c_{i\text{-}1}}]\!]^\sharp(d) \sqcup d'_k \ .\end{aligned}$$

The third equality holds due to the modularity property.

3 Programming Language

We formalize our results for a simple imperative procedural programming language.

$$\begin{aligned} \textit{Primitive commands} \quad a &::= \mathtt{x} = \mathtt{null} \mid \mathtt{x} = \mathtt{new} \mid \mathtt{x.f} = \mathtt{y} \mid \mathtt{x} = \mathtt{y} \mid \mathtt{x} = \mathtt{y.f} \\ \textit{Commands} \quad C &::= \mathtt{skip} \mid a \mid C;C \mid C+C \mid C^* \mid p() \\ \textit{Declarations} \quad D &::= \mathsf{proc}\ p() = \{\mathsf{var}\ \boldsymbol{x}; C\} \\ \textit{Programs} \quad Pr &::= \mathsf{var}\ \boldsymbol{g}; C \mid D; Pr \end{aligned}$$

We denote by PComm, G, L, and PName the sets of primitive commands, global variables, local variables, and procedure names, respectively. We use the following symbols to range over these sets: $a \in \mathsf{PComm}$, $g \in \mathsf{G}$, $x, y, z \in \mathsf{G} \cup \mathsf{L}$, and $p \in \mathsf{PName}$. We assume that L and G are fixed arbitrary finite sets. Also, we consider only well-defined programs where all the called procedures are defined.

[2] For example, let $d_1 = \{\{x, z\}, \{y\}\}$, $d_2 = \{\{x, y\}, \{z\}\}$, and $d_3 = \{\{y, z\}, \{x\}\}$. Then $d_1 \sqcap (d_2 \sqcup d_3) = d_1 \sqcap \{\{x, y, z\}\} = d_1$, but $(d_1 \sqcap d_2) \sqcup (d_1 \sqcap d_3) = \{\{x\}, \{y\}, \{z\}\}$.

Syntax. A program Pr in our language is a sequence of procedure declarations, followed by a sequence of declarations of global variables and a main command. Commands contain primitive commands $a \in \mathsf{PComm}$, sequential composition $C; C'$, nondeterministic choice $C + C'$, iteration C^*, and procedure calls $p()$. We use $+$ and * instead of conditionals and while loops for theoretical simplicity: given appropriate primitive commands, conditionals and loops can be easily defined. We use the standard primitive commands for pointer programs.

Declarations D give the definitions of procedures. A procedure p is comprised of a sequence of local variables declarations $\boldsymbol{x}$ and a command, denoted by C_{body_p}, which we refer to as procedure p's *body*. Procedures do not take any parameters or return any values explicitly; values can instead be passed to and from procedures using global variables. To simplify presentation, we do not consider mutually recursive procedures in our language; direct recursion is allowed.

Operational Semantics. A state $\sigma = \langle s_g, s_l, h \rangle$ is a triplet comprised of a global environment s_g, a local environment s_l and an heap h mapping locations and field names to values. For simplicity, values are either locations in the heap or the special value `null`. We say that locations o_1 and o_2 are *connected* in heap h, denoted by $o_1 \leftrightsquigarrow_h o_2$, if there exists an *undirected* path of pointer fields between o_1 and o_2. We use a relational (input-output tracking) store-based large step operational semantics which manipulates pairs of states $\langle \bar{\sigma}, \sigma' \rangle$: $\bar{\sigma}$ records the state of the program at the entry to the active procedure and σ' records the current state. For further details see [4].

4 Intraprocedural Connection Analysis

We first show how the modular elements can help in *intra*procedural analysis. For simplicity, we use in this section a non-relational semantics, i.e., the semantics only tracks the current state. In Sect. 5, we adapt the analysis to abstract the relational semantics.

Partition Domains. We first define a general notion of *partition domains*, and then instantiate it to an abstract domain suitable for connection analysis of programs without procedures. (Sect. 5 defines the general setup.) We denote by $\mathsf{Equiv}(\Upsilon) \subseteq \mathcal{P}(\Upsilon)$ the set of equivalence relations over a set Υ, ranged over by metavariable d. We use $v_1 \cong_d v_2$ to denote that $\langle v_1, v_2 \rangle \in d$, and $[v]_d$ to denote the equivalence class of $v \in \Upsilon$ induced by d. We omit the d subscript when it is clear from context. $(d_1 \cup d_2)^+$ denotes the transitive closure of $d_1 \cup d_2$. By abuse of notation, we sometimes treat an equivalence relation d as the partitioning $\{[v]_d \mid v \in \Upsilon\}$ of Υ into equivalence classes it induces.

Definition 2. *The* partition lattice $\mathcal{D}_{\mathsf{part}}(\Upsilon)$ *over a set* Υ *is a 6-tuple*

$$\mathcal{D}_{\mathsf{part}}(\Upsilon) = \langle\, \mathsf{Equiv}(\Upsilon),\, \sqsubseteq,\, \bot_{\mathsf{part}} = \{\{a\} \mid a \in \Upsilon\},\, \top_{\mathsf{part}} = \{\Upsilon\},\, \sqcup = (- \cup -)^+,\, \sqcap = - \cap - \,\rangle$$
$$\text{where } d_1 \sqsubseteq d_2 \Leftrightarrow \forall v_1, v_2 \in \Upsilon, v_1 \cong_{d_1} v_2 \Rightarrow v_1 \cong_{d_2} v_2\,.$$

$$[\![x = \texttt{null}]\!]^\sharp(d) = d \sqcap S_{x'} \qquad [\![x = \texttt{new}]\!]^\sharp(d) = d \sqcap S_{x'} \qquad [\![x.f = y]\!]^\sharp(d) = d \sqcup U_{x'y'}$$
$$[\![x = y]\!]^\sharp(d) = (d \sqcap S_{x'}) \sqcup U_{x'y'} \qquad [\![x = y.f]\!]^\sharp(d) = (d \sqcap S_x) \sqcup U_{x'y'}$$
where $U_{x'y'} = \{\{x', y'\}\} \cup \{\{z'\} \mid z' \in \Upsilon \setminus \{x', y'\}\}$, $S_{x'} = \{\{x'\}\} \cup \{\{z' \mid z' \in \Upsilon \setminus \{x'\}\}\}$

Fig. 2. Abstract transfer functions for primitive commands in the connection analysis where $d \neq \bot$. For $d = \bot$, the transfer function of any primitive command $a \in \mathsf{PComm}$ is $[\![a]\!]^\sharp(d) = d$.

The connection abstract domain $\mathcal{D}(\Upsilon)$ *is an extension of the partition domain* $\mathsf{Equiv}(\Upsilon)$ *to include a bottom element* $\bot$ *in its carrier set, i.e.,* $\bot \sqsubset d$ *for every* $\bot \neq d \in \mathcal{D}(\Upsilon)$*, with the lattice operations extended in the obvious way. We refer to the equivalence class* $[x]_d$ *of* $x \in \Upsilon$ *as the* connection set *of* x *in* $\bot \neq d \in \mathcal{D}(\Upsilon)$.

The connection abstract domain $\mathcal{D}(\Upsilon)$ is parametrized by a set Υ pertaining to the set $\mathsf{G} \cup \mathsf{L}$ of pointer variables. For example, in the intraprocedural settings we use $\Upsilon = \{x' \mid x \in \mathsf{G} \cup \mathsf{L}\}$. Intuitively, x' and y' belong to different partitions in an abstract state $d \in \mathcal{D}(\Upsilon)$ that arises as at a program point *pt* during the analysis if the pointer variables x and y never point to connected heap objects when the execution of the program reaches *pt*. For instance, if there is a program state occurring at *pt* in which x.f and y point to the same heap object, then it must be that x' and y' belong to the same connection set in d. In the following, we omit Υ when it is clear from context. More formally, the abstraction map α is defined as follows: $\alpha(\emptyset) = \bot$ and $\alpha(S) = \{[x]_{d_S} \mid x \in \mathsf{G} \cup \mathsf{L}\}$ for any other set of states, where d_S is the reflective transitive closure of the relation $\bigcup_{\sigma \in S}\{(x, y) \mid \{x, y\} \subseteq \mathsf{G} \cup \mathsf{L}, \sigma = \langle s_g, s_l, h\rangle, \text{and } (s_g \cup s_l)x \leftrightsquigarrow_h (s_g \cup s_l)y\}$.

Abstract Semantics. The abstract semantics of primitive commands is defined in Fig. 2 using meet and join operations with constant elements to conform with the requirement of Definition 3. (Note that, as expected, the functions are strict, i.e., they map $\bot$ to $\bot$.)

Assigning `null` or a fresh object to a variable x separates x' from its connection set. Therefore, the analysis takes the meet of the current abstract state with $S_{x'}$ — the partition with two connection sets $\{x'\}$ and the rest of the variables. The concrete semantics of x.f = y redirects the f-field of the object pointed to by x to the object pointed to by y. The abstract semantics treats this statement quite conservatively, performing "weak updates": It merges the connection sets of x' and y' by computing the least upper bound of the current abstract state with $U_{x'y'}$ — a partition with $\{x', y'\}$ as a connection set and singleton connection sets for the other variables. The effect of the statement x = y is to separate the variable x' from its connection set and to add x' to the connection set of y'. This is realized by performing a meet of the current abstract state with $S_{x'}$, and then joining the result with $U_{x'y'}$. Following [14], the effect of the assignment x = y.f is handled in a very conservative manner, treating y and $y.f$ in the same connection set since the abstraction does not distinguish between the objects pointed to by y and y.f. Thus, the same abstract semantics is used for x = y.f and x = y.

The transformers defined in Fig. 2 are in fact the best transformers [9]: For every abstract state d, there exists a concrete state σ which has an object o_X for every partition X in d which is pointed to by all the variables in X and has a pointer field pointing to itself. It easy to verify that it holds that $\alpha(\sigma) = d$ and $\alpha(\llbracket a \rrbracket(\sigma)) = \llbracket a \rrbracket^\sharp(\alpha(\sigma))$, where $\llbracket a \rrbracket$ is the concrete operational semantics of command a. The abstract semantics of composite commands is standard, and omitted [4].

Conditionally Compositional Intraprocedural Analysis. In the following we show that under certain restrictions it is possible to utilize the modularity property to compute summaries of intraprocedural commands.

Definition 3. *A function* $f : \mathcal{D} \to \mathcal{D}$ *is* conditionally adaptable *if* $f(\bot) = \bot$ *and for every* $d \neq \bot$, $f(d) = (d \sqcap d_p) \sqcup d_g$ *for some* $d_p, d_g \in \mathcal{D}$ *and the element* d_p *is modular. We refer to* d_p *as* f*'s* meet element *and to* d_g *as* f*'s* join element.

Lemma 1. *All the abstract transfer functions of the primitive commands in the intraprocedural connection analysis (shown in Fig. 2) are conditionally adaptable.*

We denote the meet and join elements of the abstract transformer $\llbracket a \rrbracket^\sharp$ of a primitive command a by $P\llbracket a \rrbracket^\sharp$ and $G\llbracket a \rrbracket^\sharp$, respectively. For a command C, we denote by $P\llbracket C \rrbracket^\sharp$ the set of the meet elements of the primitive commands occurring in C.

Lemma 2. *Let C be a command composed of primitive commands whose transfer functions are conditionally adaptable and which does not contain procedure calls. For every* $d_1, d_2 \in \mathcal{D}$ *such that* $d_1 \neq \bot$, *if* $d_2 \sqsubseteq \bigsqcap P\llbracket C \rrbracket^\sharp$ *then*

$$\llbracket C \rrbracket^\sharp(d_1 \sqcup d_2) = \llbracket C \rrbracket^\sharp(d_1) \sqcup d_2.$$

Intraprocedural Summaries. Lemma 2 can justify the use of compositional summaries in intraprocedural analyses in certain conditions: Take a command C and an abstract value d_2 such that the conditions of the lemma hold. An analysis that needs to compute the abstract value $\llbracket C \rrbracket^\sharp(d_1 \sqcup d_2)$ can do so by computing $d = \llbracket C \rrbracket^\sharp(d_1)$, possibly caching (d_1, d) in a summary for C, and then adapting the result by joining d with d_2.

Lemmas 1 and 2 allow only for *conditional* intraprocedural summaries to be used in the connection analysis; a summary for a command C can be used only when $d_2 \sqsubseteq d_p$ for all $d_p \in P\llbracket C \rrbracket^\sharp$. In contrast, and perhaps counter-intuitively, the interprocedural analysis has non-conditional summaries, which do not have a proviso like $d_2 \sqsubseteq P\llbracket C \rrbracket^\sharp$. It achieves this by requiring certain properties of the abstract domain used to record procedures summaries, which we now describe.

5 Interprocedural Connection Analysis

In this section we define top-down and bottom-up interprocedural connection analyses, and prove that their results coincide. The main message of this section is that we can summarize the effects of procedures in a bottom-up manner, and use the modularity property to prove that the results of the bottom-up and top-down

```
main(){
```
[$d_{l_0} = \{\{u', \overline{u}\}, \{v', \overline{v}\}, \{w', \overline{w}\}, \{x', \overline{x}\}, \{y', \overline{y}\}, \{z', \overline{z}\}\}$]
```
  l0: x = new(); y = new(); z = new();
  l3: w = new(); u = new(); v = new();
```
[$d_{l_6} = \{\{u'\}, \{\overline{u}\}, \{v'\}, \{\overline{v}\}, \{w'\}, \{\overline{w}\}, \{x'\}, \{\overline{x}\}, \{y'\}, \{\overline{y}\}, \{z'\}, \{\overline{z}\}\}$]
```
  l6: z.f = w; u.f = v;
```
[$d_{l_8} = \{\{u', v'\}, \{\overline{u}\}, \{\overline{v}\}, \{w', z'\}, \{\overline{w}\}, \{x'\}, \{\overline{x}\}, \{y'\}, \{\overline{y}\}, \{\overline{z}\},$]
```
  l8: p();
```
[$d_{l_9} = \{\{u'\}, \{v', z'\}, \{\overline{u}\}, \{\overline{v}\}, \{w', x', y'\}, \{\overline{w}\}, \{\overline{x}\}, \{\overline{y}\}, \{\overline{z}\}\}$]
```
  l9: }
```

```
p(){
```
[$d_{l_{10}} = \{\{u', \overline{u}, v', \overline{v}\}, \{w', \overline{w}, z', \overline{z}\}, \{x', \overline{x}\}, \{y', \overline{y}\}\}$]
```
 l10: v = null; x.f = z; y.f = w;
```
[$d_{l_{13}} = \{\{u', \overline{u}, \overline{v}\}, \{v'\}, \{w', \overline{w}, x', \overline{x}, y', \overline{y}, z', \overline{z}\}\}$]
```
 l13: q()
```
[$d_{l_{14}} = \{\{u', \overline{u}, \overline{v}\}, \{v', z'\}, \{w', \overline{w}, x', \overline{x}, y', \overline{y}, \overline{z}\}\}$]
```
 l14: }
```

```
q(){
```
[$d_{l_{15}} = \{\{u', \overline{u}\}, \{v', \overline{v}\}, \{w', \overline{w}, x', \overline{x}, y', \overline{y}, z', \overline{z}\}\}$]
```
 l15: z = null;
```
[$d_{l_{16}} = \{\{u', \overline{u}\}, \{v', \overline{v}\}, \{w', \overline{w}, x', \overline{x}, y', \overline{y}, \overline{z}\}, \{z'\}\}$]
```
 l16: v.f = z;
```
[$d_{l_{17}} = \{\{u', \overline{u}\}, \{v', \overline{v}, z'\}, \{w', \overline{w}, x', \overline{x}, y', \overline{y}, \overline{z}\}\}$]
```
 l17: }
```

Fig. 3. Example program annotated with abstract states. Abstract state $d_{\mathtt{l_i}}$ is computed by the interprocedural *top-down* analysis at program point $\mathtt{l_i}$. All the variables are globals.

analyses coincide. This coincidence, together with the soundness of the top-down analysis (Lemma 3), ensures the soundness of the bottom-up analysis.[3]

5.1 Abstract Domain

The abstract domain $\mathcal{D}$ of the interprocedural connection analyses is obtained by lifting the one used for the *intra*procedural analysis to the *inter*procedural setting. Technically, it is an instantiation of the connection abstract domain $\mathcal{D}(\Upsilon)$ with $\Upsilon = \overline{\mathsf{G}} \cup \mathsf{G}' \cup \dot{\mathsf{G}} \cup \mathsf{L}'$, where $\mathsf{G}' = \{g' \mid g \in \mathsf{G}\}$, $\overline{\mathsf{G}} = \{\overline{g} \mid g \in \mathsf{G}\}$, $\dot{\mathsf{G}} = \{\dot{g} \mid g \in \mathsf{G}\}$, and $\mathsf{L}' = \{x' \mid x \in \mathsf{L}\}$.

The set Υ contains four kinds of elements. Intuitively, the analysis computes at every program point a relation between the objects pointed to by global variables at the entry to the procedure, represented by $\overline{\mathsf{G}}$, and the ones pointed to by global variables and local variables at the current state, represented by G' and L', respectively. As before, abstract states represent partitioning over variables. For technical reasons, described later, Υ also includes the set $\dot{\mathsf{G}}$. The latter is used to compute the effect of procedure calls.

5.2 Interprocedural Top-Down Connection Analysis

The abstract semantics of procedure calls in the top-down analysis is defined in Fig. 4, which we explain below. Intraprocedural commands are handled as described in Sect. 4.

[3] We analyze recursive procedures in a standard way using a fixpoint computation. As a result, a recursive procedure might be analyzed more than once. However, and unlike in top-down analyses, the procedure is analyzed only using a single input, namely ι_{entry}, defined in Sect. 5.2.

When a procedure is entered, local variables of the procedure and all the global variables $\overline{g}$ at the entry to the procedure are initialized to `null`. This is realized by applying the meet operation to d with $R_{\mathsf{G}'}$, effectively, refining the partitioning of d by placing every non-current variable in its own connection set. (We use $d|_S = d \sqcap R_S$ as a shorthand, and say that d is projected on S.) The result, $d|_{\mathsf{G}'}$, represents the connection relation in d between the objects pointed-to by global variables at the call-site. Then, $d|_{\mathsf{G}'}$ is joined with (the particular constant abstract state) ι_{entry}.

The ι_{entry} element abstracts the identity relation between input and output states. It is defined as a partition containing $\{\overline{g}, g'\}$ connection sets for all global variables g. Intuitively, the aforementioned join operation records the current value of variable g into $\overline{g}$. Recall that at the entry to a procedure, the "old" value of every global variable is the same as its current value.

$[\![\mathsf{return}]\!]^\sharp$ computes the return value at the caller after the callee returns. It takes two arguments: d_{call}, which represents the partition of variables into connections sets at the call-site, and d_{exit}, which represents the partition at the exit-site of the callee, projected on $\overline{\mathsf{G}} \cup \mathsf{G}'$. This projection emulates the nullification of local variables when exiting a procedure. $[\![\mathsf{return}]\!]^\sharp$ emulates the composition of the input-output relation of the call-site with that of the exit-site using a natural join. The latter is implemented using variables of the form $\dot{g}$: $f_{\mathsf{call}}(d_{\mathsf{call}})$ renames global variables from g' to $\dot{g}$ and $f_{\mathsf{exit}}(d_{\mathsf{exit}})$ renames global variables from $\overline{g}$ to $\dot{g}$. The renamed relations are then joined. Intuitively, the old values $\overline{g}$ of the callee at the exit-site are matched with the current values g' of the caller at the call-site. Finally, the temporary variables are projected away.

Example 3. In Fig. 3, $d_{1_{13}} = \{\{u', \overline{u}, \overline{v}\}, \{v'\}, \{w', \overline{w}, x', \overline{x}, y', \overline{y}, z', \overline{z}\}\}$ is the abstract state at $\mathtt{l}_{13}$, $\mathtt{q}()$'s call-site in $\mathtt{p}()$, and $d_{1_{14}}$ is the abstract state at $\mathtt{q}()$'s exit-site.

$$\begin{aligned}
&[\![q()]\!]^\sharp(d_{1_{13}}) = [\![\mathsf{return}]\!]^\sharp(([\![C_{\mathsf{body}_q}]\!]^\sharp \circ [\![\mathsf{entry}]\!]^\sharp)(d_{1_{13}}), d_{1_{13}})\\
&= [\![\mathsf{return}]\!]^\sharp([\![C_{\mathsf{body}_q}]\!]^\sharp(\{\{u', \overline{u}\}, \{v', \overline{v}\}, \{w', \overline{w}, x', \overline{x}, y', \overline{y}, z', \overline{z}\}\}), d_{1_{13}})\\
&\quad = [\![\mathsf{return}]\!]^\sharp(\{\{u', \overline{u}\}, \{v', \overline{v}, z'\}, \{w', \overline{w}, x', \overline{x}, y', \overline{y}, \overline{z}\}\}, \{\{u', \overline{u}, \overline{v}\}, \{v'\}, \{w', \overline{w}, x', \overline{x}, y', \overline{y}, z', \overline{z}\}\})\\
&\quad = (f_{\mathsf{exit}}(\{\{u', \overline{u}\}, \{v', \overline{v}, z'\}, \{w', \overline{w}, x', \overline{x}, y', \overline{y}, \overline{z}\}\}|_{\overline{\mathsf{G}} \cup \mathsf{G}'}) \sqcup\\
&\qquad\qquad\qquad f_{\mathsf{call}}(\{\{u', \overline{u}, \overline{v}\}, \{v'\}, \{w', \overline{w}, x', \overline{x}, y', \overline{y}, z', \overline{z}\}\}))|_{\overline{\mathsf{G}} \cup \mathsf{G}' \cup \mathsf{L}}\\
&\quad = (\{\{u', \dot{u}\}, \{v', \dot{v}, z'\}, \{w', \dot{w}, x', \dot{x}, y', \dot{y}, \dot{z}\}\} \sqcup \{\dot{u}, \overline{u}, \overline{v}\}, \{\dot{v}\}, \{\dot{w}, \overline{w}, \dot{x}, \overline{x}, \dot{y}, \overline{y}, \dot{z}, \overline{z}\}\})|_{\overline{\mathsf{G}} \cup \mathsf{G}' \cup \mathsf{L}}\\
&\quad = \{\{u', \dot{u}, \overline{u}, \overline{v}\}, \{v', \dot{v}, z'\}, \{w', \dot{w}, \overline{w}, x', \dot{x}, \overline{x}, y', \dot{y}, \overline{y}, \dot{z}, \overline{z}\}\}|_{\overline{\mathsf{G}} \cup \mathsf{G}' \cup \mathsf{L}}\\
&\quad = \{\{u', \overline{u}, \overline{v}\}, \{v', z'\}, \{w', \overline{w}, x', \overline{x}, y', \overline{y}, \overline{z}\}\} = d_{1_{14}}
\end{aligned}$$

$$\begin{aligned}
&[\![p()]\!]^\sharp(d) = [\![\mathsf{return}]\!]^\sharp(([\![C_{\mathsf{body}_p}]\!]^\sharp \circ [\![\mathsf{entry}]\!]^\sharp)(d), d)\ , \text{ where}\\
&\qquad [\![\mathsf{entry}]\!]^\sharp(d) = d|_{\mathsf{G}'} \sqcup \iota_{\mathsf{entry}}\\
&\qquad [\![\mathsf{return}]\!]^\sharp(d_{\mathsf{exit}}, d_{\mathsf{call}}) = (f_{\mathsf{call}}(d_{\mathsf{call}}) \sqcup f_{\mathsf{exit}}(d_{\mathsf{exit}}|_{\overline{\mathsf{G}} \cup \mathsf{G}'}))|_{\overline{\mathsf{G}} \cup \mathsf{G}' \cup \mathsf{L}}\\
&d|_S = d \sqcap R_S \qquad \iota_{\mathsf{entry}} = \textstyle\bigsqcup_{g \in \mathsf{G}} U_{g'\overline{g}} \qquad R_X = \{\{x \mid x \in X\}\} \cup \{\{x\} \mid x \in \Upsilon \setminus X\}\\
&f_{\mathsf{call}}(d) = \{\{\langle n2d(\alpha), n2d(\beta)\rangle \mid \langle \alpha, \beta\rangle \in P\} \mid P \in d\}, \text{ where } n2d(\alpha) = \dot{g} \text{ if } \alpha = g' \text{ and } \alpha \text{ otherwise}\\
&f_{\mathsf{exit}}(d) = \{\{\langle o2d(\alpha), o2d(\beta)\rangle \mid \langle \alpha, \beta\rangle \in P\} \mid P \in d\}, \text{ where } o2d(\alpha) = \dot{g} \text{ if } \alpha = \overline{g} \text{ and } \alpha \text{ otherwise}
\end{aligned}$$

Fig. 4. The abstract semantics of procedure calls in the top-down analysis. The constant elements $U_{g'\overline{g}}$ are defined in Fig. 2. Note that the renaming functions $f_{\mathsf{call}}(\text{-})$ and $f_{\mathsf{call}}(\text{-})$ are isomorphisms.

Lemma 3 (Soundness of the Top-Down Analysis). *The abstract semantics of the top-down interprocedural connection analysis is an over-approximation of the standard concrete semantics for heap manipulating programs* [4].

The crux of the proof is the observation that the abstract transfer of the return statements is sound because the "old" values of the global variables of a procedure are never modified and are the same as their "current" values when it was invoked.

5.3 Bottom Up Compositional Connection Analysis

The abstract semantics $[\![-]\!]^{\sharp}{}_{\mathsf{BU}}(-)$ of procedure calls in the bottom-up analysis is defined in Eq. 1. Again, intraprocedural commands are handled as described in Sect. 4.

$$[\![p()]\!]^{\sharp}{}_{\mathsf{BU}}(d) = [\![\mathsf{return}]\!]^{\sharp}([\![C_{\mathsf{body}_p}]\!]^{\sharp}(\iota_{\mathsf{entry}}), d) \quad (1)$$

$[\![p()]\!]^{\sharp}{}_{\mathsf{BU}}(d)$ and $[\![p()]\!]^{\sharp}(d)$, defined in Fig. 4, differ in the way in which the value of the first argument to $[\![\mathsf{return}]\!]^{\sharp}(\cdot, d)$ is computed: $[\![p()]\!]^{\sharp}{}_{\mathsf{BU}}(d)$ uses the abstract state resulting at the exit of p's body when it is analyzed with state ι_{entry}. Hence, it uses the same value at every call. In contrast, $[\![p()]\!]^{\sharp}(d)$ computes that argument by analyzing the call to p() with the particular *call state* d. Note that as a corollary of the theorem we get that the bottom-up interprocedural connection analysis is sound.

Theorem 1 (Coincidence). $\forall C \in \mathit{Commands}. \forall d \in \mathcal{D}. [\![C]\!]^{\sharp}{}_{\mathsf{BU}}(d) = [\![C]\!]^{\sharp}(d)$.

In the rest of the section, we sketch the main arguments in the proof of Theorem 1, in lieu of more formal mathematical arguments, which are shown in the proof of [4, Theorem 22]. We focus on the case where C is a procedure invocation, i.e., $C = p()$.

Notation. We denote by $\mathcal{D}_X$ the sublattice representing the closed interval $[\bot, R_X]$ for a set $\emptyset \neq X \subseteq \Upsilon$, which consists of all the elements between $\bot$ and R_X. For example, $\mathcal{D}_{\overline{\mathsf{G}}}$ includes only partitions where all the variables not in $\overline{\mathsf{G}}$ are in singleton sets. We define the sets $S_{\widehat{x}}$ and $U_{\widehat{x}\widehat{y}}$, where $\widehat{x}$ is either x', $\overline{x}$, or $\dot{x}$ in the same way as $S_{x'}$ and $U_{x'y'}$ are defined in Fig. 2. For example, $U_{\overline{x}y'} = \{\{\overline{x}, y'\}\} \cup \{\{\alpha\} \mid \alpha \in \Upsilon \setminus \{\overline{x}, y'\}\}$.

5.3.1 Uniform Representation of Entry Abstract States

The abstract states at the entry to procedures in the top-down analysis are *uniform*: for every global variable g, we have a connection set containing only $\overline{g}$ and g'. This is a result of the definition of function entry, which projects abstract call states on G' and then joins the result with the ι_{entry} element. The projection results in an abstract state where all connection sets containing more than a single element are comprised only of primed variables. Then, after joining $d|_{\mathsf{G}'}$ with ι_{entry}, each old variable $\overline{g}$ resides in the same partition as its corresponding current primed variable g'. For example, see $d_{1_{10}}$ in Fig. 3.

We point out that the uniformity of the entry states is due to the property of ι_{entry} that its connection sets are comprised of pairs of variables of the form $\{x', \overline{x}\}$. One important implication of this uniformity is that every entry abstract state d to any procedure has a dual representation. In one representation, d is the join of ι_{entry} with some elements $U_{x'y'} \in \mathcal{D}_{\mathsf{G}'}$. In the other representation, d is expressed as the join of ι_{entry} with some elements $U_{\overline{x}\overline{y}} \in \mathcal{D}_{\overline{\mathsf{G}}}$. In the following, we use the function o that replaces relationships among current variables by those among old ones: $o(U_{x'y'}) = U_{\overline{x}\overline{y}}$; and $o(d)$ is the least upper bounds of ι_{entry} and elements $U_{\overline{x}\overline{y}}$ for all x, y such that x' and y' are in the same connection set of d.

Example 4. $d_{1_{10}}$ is the abstract element at the entry point of procedure p of Fig. 3.
$$\begin{aligned}\iota_{\mathsf{entry}} \sqcup (U_{u'v'} \sqcup U_{w'z'}) &= o(\iota_{\mathsf{entry}} \sqcup (U_{u'v'} \sqcup U_{w'z'})) = \iota_{\mathsf{entry}} \sqcup o(U_{u'v'} \sqcup U_{w'z'}) \\ &= \iota_{\mathsf{entry}} \sqcup (U_{\overline{u}\overline{v}} \sqcup U_{\overline{w}\overline{z}}) = \{\{u', \overline{u}, v', \overline{v}\}, \{w', \overline{w}, z', \overline{z}\}, \{x', \overline{x}\}, \{y', \overline{y}\}\} = d_{1_{10}} .\end{aligned}$$

Delayed Evaluation of the Effect of Calling Contexts. Elements of the form $U_{\overline{x}\overline{y}}$, coming from $\mathcal{D}_{\overline{\mathsf{G}}}$, are smaller than or equal to the meet elements $S_{x'}$ of intraprocedural statements. This is because for any $x, y \in \mathsf{G}$ it holds that

$$S_{x'} = \{\{x'\}\} \cup \{\{z\} | z \in \Upsilon \setminus \{x'\}\}\} \sqsupseteq \{\{\overline{x}, \overline{y}\}\} \cup \{\{z\} | z \in \Upsilon \setminus \{\overline{x}, \overline{y}\}\} = U_{\overline{x}\overline{y}} .$$

In Lemma 1 of Sect. 4 we proved that the semantics of the connection analysis is conditionally adaptable. Thus, computing the composed effect of any sequence τ of intraprocedural transformers on an entry state of the form $d_0 \sqcup U_{\overline{x}_1\overline{y}_1} \ldots \sqcup U_{\overline{x}_n\overline{y}_n}$ results in an element of the form $d_0' \sqcup U_{\overline{x}_1\overline{y}_1} \ldots \sqcup U_{\overline{x}_n\overline{y}_n}$, where d_0' results from applying the transformers in τ on d_0. Using the observations made in Sect. 5.3.1, this means that for any abstract element d resulting at a call-site there exists an element $d_2 \in \mathcal{D}_{\overline{\mathsf{G}}}$ which is a join of elements of the form $U_{\overline{x}\overline{y}} \in \mathcal{D}_{\overline{\mathsf{G}}}$, such that $d = d_1 \sqcup d_2$, and $d_1 = [\![\tau]\!]^\sharp(\iota_{\mathsf{entry}})$.

$$d = d_1 \sqcup U_{\overline{x}_1\overline{y}_1} \ldots \sqcup U_{\overline{x}_n\overline{y}_n} . \tag{2}$$

Example 5. The abstract state at entry point of p is $d_{1_{10}} = \iota_{\mathsf{entry}} \sqcup (U_{\overline{u}\overline{v}} \sqcup U_{\overline{w}\overline{z}})$. (See Example 4.) The sequence of commands at 1_{10} is $C :=$ v = null; x.f = z; y.f = w. Thus, $d_{1_{13}} = [\![C]\!]^\sharp(d_{1_{10}})$. Note that $d_{1_{13}}$ can also be computed using the effect of C to ι_{entry}:

$$\begin{aligned}[\![C]\!]^\sharp(\iota_{\mathsf{entry}}) \sqcup (U_{\overline{w}\overline{z}} \sqcup U_{\overline{u}\overline{v}}) &= \{\{u', \overline{u}\}, \{v'\}, \{\overline{v}\}, \{w', \overline{w}, y', \overline{y}\}, \{x', \overline{x}, z', \overline{z}\}\} \sqcup (U_{\overline{u}\overline{v}} \sqcup U_{\overline{w}\overline{z}}) \\ &= \{\{u', \overline{u}, \overline{v}\}, \{v'\}, \{w', \overline{w}, x', \overline{x}, y', \overline{y}, z', \overline{z}\}\} = d_{1_{13}} \\ [\![C]\!]^\sharp(\iota_{\mathsf{entry}}) &= [\![\mathtt{v = null; x.f = z; y.f = w}]\!]^\sharp(\{\{u', \overline{u}\}, \{v', \overline{v}\}, \{w', \overline{w}\}, \{x', \overline{x}\}, \{y', \overline{y}\}, \{z', \overline{z}\}\}) \\ &= \{\{u', \overline{u}\}, \{v'\}, \{\overline{v}\}, \{w', \overline{w}, y', \overline{y}\}, \{x', \overline{x}, z', \overline{z}\}\}\end{aligned}$$

5.3.2 Counterpart Representation for Calling Contexts

The previous reasoning ensures that any abstract value at the call-site to a procedure $p()$ is of the form $d_1 \sqcup d_2$, where $d_2 \in \mathcal{D}_{\overline{\mathsf{G}}}$ and, thus, is a join of elements of form $U_{\overline{x}\overline{y}}$. Furthermore, the state resulting at the entry of $p()$ when the calling context is $d_1 \sqcup U_{\overline{x}\overline{y}}$ can be obtained either directly from d_1 or after merging two of d_1's connection sets. Note that the need to merge occurs only if there are variables w' and z' such that w' and $\overline{x}$ are in one of the connection sets and z' and $\overline{y}$ are in another. This means that the effect of $U_{\overline{x}\overline{y}}$ on the entry state can be expressed via primed variables: $d_1 \sqcup U_{\overline{x}\overline{y}} = d_1 \sqcup U_{w'z'}$. Thus, if the abstract state at the call-site is $d_1 \sqcup d_2$, then there is an element $d_2' \in \mathcal{D}_{\mathsf{G}'}$ such that

$$(d_1 \sqcup d_2)|_{\mathsf{G}'} = d_1|_{\mathsf{G}'} \sqcup d_2' \tag{3}$$

We refer to the element $d_2' \in \mathcal{D}_{\mathsf{G}'}$, which can be used to represent the effect of $d_2 \in \mathcal{D}_{\overline{\mathsf{G}}}$ at the call-site as d_2's *counterpart*, and denote it by $\widehat{d_2}$.

Example 6. Let $d_1 = \{\{u', \overline{u}\}, \{v'\}, \{\overline{v}\}, \{w', \overline{w}, y', \overline{y}\}, \{x', \overline{x}, z', \overline{z}\}\}$ and $d_2 = U_{\overline{w}\overline{z}}$. Joining d_1 with $U_{\overline{w}\overline{z}}$ causes connection sets $[\overline{w}]$ and $[\overline{z}]$ to be merged, and, consequently, $[y']$ and $[x']$ are merged, since $[y'] = [\overline{w}]$ and $[x'] = [\overline{z}]$. Therefore, for $\widehat{d_2} = U_{x'z'}$ it holds that $(d_1 \sqcup d_2)|_{\mathsf{G}'} = \{\{u', \overline{u}\}, \{v'\}, \{\overline{v}\}, \{w', \overline{w}, y', \overline{y}, x', \overline{x}, z', \overline{z}\}\}|_{\mathsf{G}'} = \{\{u'\}, \{v'\}, \{w', y', x', z'\}\}$. Similarly, $d_1|_{\mathsf{G}'} \sqcup \widehat{d_2} = \{\{u'\}, \{v'\}, \{w', y'\}, \{x', z'\}\} \sqcup U_{x'z'} = \{\{u'\}, \{v'\}, \{w', y', x', z'\}\}$.

Representing Entry States with Counterparts. The above facts imply that we can represent an abstract state d at the call-site as $d = d_1 \sqcup d_2$, where $d_2 = d_3 \sqcup d_4$ for some $d_3, d_4 \in \mathcal{D}_{\overline{\mathsf{G}}}$ such that: (i) d_3 is a join of the elements of the form $U_{\overline{x}\overline{y}}$ such that $\overline{x}$ and $\overline{y}$ reside in d_1 in different partitions, which also contain current (primed) variables, and thus possibly affect the entry state, and (ii) d_4 is a join of all the other elements $U_{\overline{x}\overline{y}} \in \mathcal{D}_{\overline{\mathsf{G}}}$, which are needed to represent d in this form, but either $\bar{x}$ or $\bar{y}$ resides in the same partition in d_1 or one of them is in a partition containing only old variables. Recall that there is an element $d_3' = \widehat{d_3}$ that joins elements of the form $U_{x'y'}$ such that $d_1 \sqcup d_3 = d_1 \sqcup d_3'$, and therefore

$$d = d_1 \sqcup d_3 \sqcup d_4 = d_1 \sqcup d_3' \sqcup d_4 \,. \tag{4}$$

Thus, after applying the entry's semantics, we get that abstract states at the entry point of procedure are always of the form

$$[\![\mathsf{entry}]\!]^\sharp(d) = (d_1 \sqcup d_3' \sqcup d_4)|_{\mathsf{G}'} \sqcup \iota_{\mathsf{entry}} = (d_1 \sqcup d_3')|_{\mathsf{G}'} \sqcup \iota_{\mathsf{entry}} = (d_1|_{\mathsf{G}'} \sqcup d_3') \sqcup \iota_{\mathsf{entry}}$$

where d_3' represents the effect of $d_3 \sqcup d_4$ on partitions containing current variables g' in d_1. The second equality holds because the *modularity of* $R_{G'}$: d_3' joins elements of form $U_{x'y'}$ and $U_{x'y'} \sqsubseteq R_{G'}$. This implies that every state d_0 at an entry point to a procedure is of the following form:

$$\begin{aligned} d_0 &= \iota_{\mathsf{entry}} \sqcup \overbrace{(U_{x'y'} \ldots \sqcup U_{x_l'y_l'})}^{d_1|_{\mathsf{G}'}} \sqcup \overbrace{(U_{x_{l+1}'y_{l+1}'} \ldots \sqcup U_{x_n'y_n'})}^{d_3'} \\ &= \iota_{\mathsf{entry}} \sqcup o(U_{x_1'y_1'} \ldots \sqcup U_{x_n'y_n'}) = \iota_{\mathsf{entry}} \sqcup U_{\overline{x}_1\overline{y}_1} \sqcup \ldots \sqcup U_{\overline{x}_n\overline{y}_n} \end{aligned} \tag{5}$$

The second equality is obtained using the dual representation of entry state (see Sect. 5.3.1) and the third one is justified because $o(\text{-})$ is an isomorphism.

Example 7. The abstract state at the call-site of procedure q() is $d_{1_{13}} = d_1 \sqcup d_2$ where $d_1 = \{\{u', \overline{u}\}, \{v'\}, \{\overline{v}\}, \{w', \overline{w}, y', \overline{y}\}, \{x', \overline{x}, z', \overline{z}\}\}$ and $d_2 = U_{\overline{uv}} \sqcup U_{\overline{wz}}$. (See the first equality in Example 5.) In Example 6 we showed that $U_{\overline{wz}}$ affects the relations in d_1 between current variables and that $\widehat{U_{\overline{wz}}} = U_{x'y'}$. In contrast, joining the result with $U_{\overline{uv}}$ has no effect on relations between current variables, because the connection set $[\overline{v}]$ does not contain any current variable. Indeed, $d_1 \sqcup U_{\overline{wz}} \sqcup U_{\overline{uv}} = d_1 \sqcup U_{x'y'} \sqcup U_{\overline{uv}}$. Following the reasoning above, consider the abstract state at the entry to procedure q()

$$\begin{aligned} d_{1_{15}} &= \{\{u', \overline{u}\}, \{v', \overline{v}\}, \{w', \overline{w}, x', \overline{x}, y', \overline{y}, z', \overline{z}\}\} \\ &= \iota_{\mathsf{entry}} \sqcup \{\{u'\}, \{\overline{u}\}, \{v'\}, \{\overline{v}\}, \{w', y'\}, \{\overline{w}\}, \{x', z'\}, \{\overline{x}\}, \{\overline{y}\}, \{\overline{z}\}\} \sqcup U_{\overline{wz}} \\ &= \iota_{\mathsf{entry}} \sqcup d_1|_{\mathsf{G}'} \sqcup U_{x'y'} \end{aligned}$$

Adapting the Result for Different Contexts. We now show that the interprocedural connection analysis can be done compositionally. Intuitively, we show that the effect of the caller's calling context can be carried over procedure invocations. Alternatively, the effect of the callee on the caller's context can be adapted unconditionally for different caller's calling contexts. The proof goes by induction on the structure of the program. We sketch the proof for the case where $C = p()$.

In Eq. 4 we showed that every abstract value that arises at the call-site is of the form $d_1 \sqcup d_3 \sqcup d_4$, where $d_3, d_4 \in \mathcal{D}_{\overline{\mathsf{G}}}$. Thus, we need to show for any $d_1 \neq \bot$ that

$$[\![p()]\!]^\sharp(d_1 \sqcup d_3 \sqcup d_4) = [\![p()]\!]^\sharp(d_1) \sqcup d_3 \sqcup d_4 . \tag{6}$$

According to the *top-down* abstract semantics the effect of invoking $p()$ is

$$[\![p()]\!]^\sharp(d) = [\![\mathsf{return}]\!]^\sharp(d_{\mathsf{exit}}, d) = [\![\mathsf{return}]\!]^\sharp\big(\big(([\![C_{\mathsf{body}_p}]\!]^\sharp \circ [\![\mathsf{entry}]\!]^\sharp)(d)\big), d\big) .$$

Because d is of the form $d_1 \sqcup d_3 \sqcup d_4$, we can write d_{exit} as below, where first equalities are mere substitutions based on observations we made before and the last one comes from the induction assumption.

$$\begin{aligned} d_{\mathsf{exit}} &= [\![C_{\mathsf{body}_p}]\!]^\sharp([\![\mathsf{entry}]\!]^\sharp(d_1 \sqcup d_3 \sqcup d_4)) = [\![C_{\mathsf{body}_p}]\!]^\sharp(((d_1 \sqcup d_3 \sqcup d_4)|_{\mathsf{G}'}) \sqcup \iota_{\mathsf{entry}}) \\ &= [\![C_{\mathsf{body}_p}]\!]^\sharp(((d_1 \sqcup d_3)|_{\mathsf{G}'}) \sqcup \iota_{\mathsf{entry}}) = [\![C_{\mathsf{body}_p}]\!]^\sharp(d_1|_{\mathsf{G}'} \sqcup d_3' \sqcup \iota_{\mathsf{entry}}) \\ &= [\![C_{\mathsf{body}_p}]\!]^\sharp(d_1|_{\mathsf{G}'} \sqcup o(d_3') \sqcup \iota_{\mathsf{entry}}) = [\![C_{\mathsf{body}_p}]\!]^\sharp(d_1|_{\mathsf{G}'} \sqcup \iota_{\mathsf{entry}}) \sqcup o(d_3') \end{aligned} \tag{7}$$

When applying the return semantics, we first compute the natural join and then remove the temporary variables. Therefore, we get

$$[\![p()]\!]^\sharp(d) = (f_{\mathsf{call}}(d_1 \sqcup d_3 \sqcup d_4) \sqcup f_{\mathsf{exit}}([\![C_{\mathsf{body}_p}]\!]^\sharp(d_1|_{\mathsf{G}'} \sqcup \iota_{\mathsf{entry}}) \sqcup o(d_3')))|_{\overline{\mathsf{G}} \cup \mathsf{G}' \cup \mathsf{L}} \cdot$$

Equation 8 shows the result of computing the inner parentheses. The first equality is by the definition of d_3' and the last equality is by the isomorphism of $f_{\mathsf{call}}(\text{-})$ and $f_{\mathsf{exit}}(\text{-})$.

$$\begin{aligned}
&f_{\mathsf{call}}(d_1 \sqcup d_3 \sqcup d_4) \sqcup f_{\mathsf{exit}}([\![C_{\mathsf{body}_p}]\!]^\sharp(d_1|_{\mathsf{G}'} \sqcup \iota_{\mathsf{entry}}) \sqcup o(d_3'))\\
&= f_{\mathsf{call}}(d_1 \sqcup d_3' \sqcup d_4) \sqcup f_{\mathsf{exit}}([\![C_{\mathsf{body}_p}]\!]^\sharp(d_1|_{\mathsf{G}'} \sqcup \iota_{\mathsf{entry}}) \sqcup o(d_3'))\\
&= f_{\mathsf{call}}(d_3') \sqcup f_{\mathsf{call}}(d_1 \sqcup d_4) \sqcup f_{\mathsf{exit}}(o(d_3')) \sqcup f_{\mathsf{exit}}([\![C_{\mathsf{body}_p}]\!]^\sharp(d_1|_{\mathsf{G}'} \sqcup \iota_{\mathsf{entry}})) \quad (8)
\end{aligned}$$

Note, among the join arguments, $f_{\mathsf{exit}}(o(d_3'))$ and $f_{\mathsf{call}}(d_3')$. Let's look at the first element. $o(d_3')$ replaces all the occurrences of $U_{x'y'}$ in d_3' with $U_{\overline{x}\overline{y}}$. f_{exit} replaces all the occurrences of $U_{\overline{x}\overline{y}}$ in $o(d_3')$ with $U_{\dot{x}\dot{y}}$. Thus, the first element is $U_{\dot{x}_1\dot{y}_1} \sqcup \ldots \sqcup U_{\dot{x}_n\dot{y}_n}$ which is the result of replacing in d_3' all the occurrences of $U_{x'y'}$ with $U_{\dot{x}\dot{y}}$. Let's look now at the second element. f_{call} replaces all occurrences of $U_{x'y'}$ in d_3' with $U_{\dot{x}\dot{y}}$. Thus, also the second element is $U_{\dot{x}_1\dot{y}_1} \sqcup \ldots \sqcup U_{\dot{x}_n\dot{y}_n}$, i.e., $f_{\mathsf{call}}(d_3') = f_{\mathsf{exit}}(o(d_3'))$, and we get

$$\begin{aligned}
(8) &= f_{\mathsf{call}}(d_3') \sqcup f_{\mathsf{call}}(d_1 \sqcup d_4) \sqcup f_{\mathsf{exit}}([\![C_{\mathsf{body}_p}]\!]^\sharp(d_1|_{\mathsf{G}'} \sqcup \iota_{\mathsf{entry}}))\\
&= f_{\mathsf{call}}(d_3 \sqcup d_1 \sqcup d_4) \sqcup f_{\mathsf{exit}}([\![C_{\mathsf{body}_p}]\!]^\sharp(d_1|_{\mathsf{G}'} \sqcup \iota_{\mathsf{entry}}))\\
&= f_{\mathsf{call}}(d_1) \sqcup f_{\mathsf{exit}}([\![C_{\mathsf{body}_p}]\!]^\sharp(d_1|_{\mathsf{G}'} \sqcup \iota_{\mathsf{entry}}) \sqcup (d_3 \sqcup d_4) = [\![p()]\!]^\sharp(d_1) \sqcup d_3 \sqcup d_4
\end{aligned}$$

The first equality is by the idempotence of $\sqcup$. The second equality is by the isomorphism of f_{call} and Eq. 4. To justify the third equality, recall (Eq. 2) that d_3 and d_4 are both of form $U_{\overline{x}_1\overline{y}_1} \sqcup \ldots \sqcup U_{\overline{x}_n\overline{y}_n}$ and that $f_{\mathsf{call}}(d)$ only replaces g' occurrences in d; and thus $f_{\mathsf{call}}(U_{\overline{x}_1\overline{y}_1} \sqcup \ldots \sqcup U_{\overline{x}_n\overline{y}_n}) = U_{\overline{x}_1\overline{y}_1} \sqcup \ldots \sqcup U_{\overline{x}_n\overline{y}_n}$.

Example 8. By Example 5, $d_{1_{13}} = \{\{u', \overline{u}\}, \{v'\}, \{\overline{v}\}, \{w', \overline{w}, y', \overline{y}\}, \{x', \overline{x}, z', \overline{z}\}\} \sqcup (U_{\overline{u}\overline{v}} \sqcup U_{\overline{w}\overline{z}})$. Let $d_1 = \{\{u', \overline{u}\}, \{v'\}, \{\overline{v}\}, \{w', \overline{w}, y', \overline{y}\}, \{x', \overline{x}, z', \overline{z}\}\}$ and $d_2 = U_{\overline{u}\overline{v}} \sqcup U_{\overline{w}\overline{z}}$. Thus, $d_{1_{13}} = d_1 \sqcup d_2$ and $d_2 \in \mathcal{D}_{\overline{\mathsf{G}}}$. Let's compute (i) $[\![q()]\!]^\sharp(d_1)$ and (ii) $[\![q()]\!]^\sharp(d_1) \sqcup d_2$.

$$\begin{aligned}
&[\![q()]\!]^\sharp(d_1) = [\![\mathsf{return}]\!]^\sharp(([\![C_{\mathsf{body}_q}]\!]^\sharp \circ [\![\mathsf{entry}]\!]^\sharp)(d_1), d_1)\\
&= [\![\mathsf{return}]\!]^\sharp(([\![C_{\mathsf{body}_q}]\!]^\sharp \circ [\![\mathsf{entry}]\!]^\sharp)(\{\{u', \overline{u}\}, \{v'\}, \{\overline{v}\}, \{w', \overline{w}, y', \overline{y}\}, \{x', \overline{x}, z', \overline{z}\}\}), d_1)\\
&= [\![\mathsf{return}]\!]^\sharp([\![C_{\mathsf{body}_q}]\!]^\sharp(\{\{u', \overline{u}\}, \{v', \overline{v}\}, \{w', \overline{w}, y', \overline{y}\}, \{x', \overline{x}, z', \overline{z}\}\}), d_1)\\
&= [\![\mathsf{return}]\!]^\sharp(\{\{u', \overline{u}\}, \{v', \overline{v}, z'\}, \{w', \overline{w}, y', \overline{y}\}, \{x', \overline{x}, \overline{z}\}\}, \{\{u', \overline{u}\}, \{v'\}, \{\overline{v}\},\\
&\quad \{w', \overline{w}, y', \overline{y}\}, \{x', \overline{x}, z', \overline{z}\}\})\\
&= (f_{\mathsf{exit}}(\{\{u', \overline{u}\}, \{v', \overline{v}, z'\}, \{w', \overline{w}, y', \overline{y}\}, \{x', \overline{x}, \overline{z}\}\}|_{\overline{\mathsf{G}} \cup \mathsf{G}'}) \sqcup\\
&\qquad\qquad f_{\mathsf{call}}(\{\{u', \overline{u}\}, \{v'\}, \{\overline{v}\}, \{w', \overline{w}, y', \overline{y}\}, \{x', \overline{x}, z', \overline{z}\}\}))|_{\overline{\mathsf{G}} \cup \mathsf{G}' \cup \mathsf{L}}\\
&= (\{\{u', \dot{u}\}, \{v', \dot{v}, z'\}, \{w', \dot{w}, y', \dot{y}\}, \{x', \dot{x}, \dot{z}\}\} \sqcup \{\{\dot{u}, \overline{u}\}, \{\dot{v}\}, \{\overline{v}\}, \{\dot{w}, \overline{w}, \dot{y}, \overline{y}\}, \{\dot{x}, \overline{x}, \dot{z}, \overline{z}\}\})_{\overline{\mathsf{G}} \cup \mathsf{G}' \cup \mathsf{L}}\\
&= (\{\{u', \dot{u}, \overline{u}\}, \{v', \dot{v}, z'\}, \{\overline{v}\}, \{w', \dot{w}, \overline{w}, y', \dot{y}, \overline{y}\}, \{x', \dot{x}, \overline{x}, \dot{z}, \overline{z}\}\})|_{\overline{\mathsf{G}} \cup \mathsf{G}' \cup \mathsf{L}}\\
&= \{\{u', \overline{u}\}, \{v', z'\}, \{\overline{v}\}, \{w', \overline{w}, y', \overline{y}\}, \{x', \overline{x}, \overline{z}\}\}
\end{aligned}$$

$$\begin{aligned}
[\![q()]\!]^\sharp(d_1) \sqcup d_2 &= \{\{u', \overline{u}\}, \{v', z'\}, \{\overline{v}\}\}, \{w', \overline{w}, y', \overline{y}\}, \{x', \overline{x}, \overline{z}\}\} \sqcup (U_{\overline{u}\overline{v}} \sqcup U_{\overline{w}\overline{z}})\\
&= \{\{u', \overline{u}, \overline{v}\}, \{z', v'\}, \{w', \overline{w}, x', \overline{x}, y', \overline{y}, \overline{z}\}\} d_{1_{14}} = [\![q()]\!]^\sharp(d_{1_{13}}) = [\![q()]\!]^\sharp(d_1 \sqcup d_2)
\end{aligned}$$

Precision Coincidence. We combine the observations we made to informally show the coincidence result between the top-down and the bottom-up semantics

(Theorem 1). By Eq. 4, every state d at a call-site can be represented as $d = d_1 \sqcup d_3 \sqcup d_4$, where $d_3, d_4 \in \mathcal{D}_{\overline{\mathsf{G}}}$. Furthermore, there exists $d_3' = \widehat{d_3} \in \mathcal{D}_{\mathsf{G}'}$ such that $d_1 \sqcup d_3 \sqcup d_4 = d_1 \sqcup d_3' \sqcup d_4$. We also showed that for every command C and every $d = d_1 \sqcup d_3 \sqcup d_4$, such that $d_3, d_4 \in \mathcal{D}_{\overline{\mathsf{G}}}$, it holds that $[\![C]\!]^\sharp(d_1 \sqcup d_3 \sqcup d_4) = [\![C]\!]^\sharp(d_1) \sqcup d_3 \sqcup d_4$. Finally,

$$\begin{aligned}
[\![p()]\!]^\sharp(d) &= [\![\mathsf{return}]\!]^\sharp([\![C_{\mathsf{body}_p}]\!]^\sharp([\![\mathsf{entry}]\!]^\sharp(d)), d) \\
&= [\![\mathsf{return}]\!]^\sharp([\![C_{\mathsf{body}_p}]\!]^\sharp(d_1|_{\mathsf{G}'} \sqcup \iota_{\mathsf{entry}} \sqcup d_3'), d) \\
&= [\![\mathsf{return}]\!]^\sharp([\![C_{\mathsf{body}_p}]\!]^\sharp(\iota_{\mathsf{entry}} \sqcup o(d_1|_{\mathsf{G}'}) \sqcup o(d_3')), d) \\
&= [\![\mathsf{return}]\!]^\sharp([\![C_{\mathsf{body}_p}]\!]^\sharp(\iota_{\mathsf{entry}}) \sqcup o(d_1|_{\mathsf{G}'}) \sqcup o(d_3'), d_1 \sqcup d_3 \sqcup d_4) \\
&= [\![\mathsf{return}]\!]^\sharp([\![C_{\mathsf{body}_p}]\!]^\sharp(\iota_{\mathsf{entry}}), d_1 \sqcup d_3 \sqcup d_4) = [\![p()]\!]^\sharp{}_{\mathsf{BU}}(d)\ .
\end{aligned}$$

The second equality is by Eq. 7. The third equality holds because $d_3', d_1|_{\mathsf{G}'} \in \mathcal{D}_{\mathsf{G}'}$ and by Eq. 5. The forth equality holds since $o(d_3'), o(d_1|_{\mathsf{G}'}) \in \mathcal{D}_{\overline{\mathsf{G}}}$ and by Eq. 8. The fifth equality holds because we can remove $o(d_3')$ as $f_{\mathsf{exit}}(o(d_3'))$ is redundant in the natural join. Using a similar reasoning, we can remove $f_{\mathsf{exit}}(o(d_1|_{\mathsf{G}'}))$, since f_{exit} is an isomorphism and $f_{\mathsf{exit}}(o(d_1|_{\mathsf{G}'})) = f_{\mathsf{call}}(d_1|_{\mathsf{G}'}) \sqsubseteq f_{\mathsf{call}}(d_1)$.

Example 9. Let's compute the result of applying p() to d_{1_8} using the bottom-up semantics, starting by computing $[\![C_{\mathsf{body}_p}]\!]^\sharp(\iota_{\mathsf{entry}})$ and then $[\![p()]\!]^\sharp{}_{\mathsf{BU}}(d_{1_8})$.

$$\begin{aligned}
&[\![C_{\mathsf{body}_p}]\!]^\sharp(\iota_{\mathsf{entry}}) = \{\{u', \overline{u}\}, \{\overline{v}\}, \{v', z'\}, \{w', \overline{w}, y', \overline{y}\}, \{x', \overline{x}, \overline{z}\}\} \\
&[\![p()]\!]^\sharp{}_{\mathsf{BU}}(d_{1_8}) = [\![\mathsf{return}]\!]^\sharp([\![C_{\mathsf{body}_p}]\!]^\sharp(\iota_{\mathsf{entry}}), d_{1_8}) \\
&= (f_{\mathsf{exit}}(\{\{u', \overline{u}\}, \{v', z'\}, \{\overline{v}\}, \{w', \overline{w}, y', \overline{y}\}, \{x', \overline{x}, \overline{z}\}\}) \\
&\qquad \sqcup f_{\mathsf{call}}(\{\{u', v'\}, \{\overline{u}\}, \{\overline{v}\}, \{\overline{w}\}, \{x'\}, \{\overline{x}\}, \{y'\}, \{\overline{y}\}, \{w', z'\}, \{\overline{z}\}\}|_{\overline{\mathsf{G}} \cup \mathsf{G}'}))|_{\overline{\mathsf{G}} \cup \mathsf{G}' \cup \mathsf{L}} \\
&= (\{\{u', \dot{u}\}, \{v', z'\}, \{\dot{v}\}, \{w', \dot{w}, y', \dot{y}\}, \{x', \dot{x}, \dot{z}\}\} \\
&\qquad \sqcup \{\{\dot{u}, \dot{v}\}, \{\overline{u}\}, \{\overline{v}\}, \{\overline{w}\}, \{\dot{x}\}, \{\overline{x}\}, \{\dot{y}\}, \{\overline{y}\}, \{\dot{w}, \dot{z}\}, \{\overline{z}\}\})|_{\overline{\mathsf{G}} \cup \mathsf{G}' \cup \mathsf{L}} \\
&= (\{\{u', \dot{u}, \dot{v}\}, \{v', z'\}, \{\overline{u}\}, \{\overline{v}\}, \{w', \dot{w}, x', \dot{x}, y', \dot{y}, \dot{z}\}, \{\overline{w}\}, \{\overline{x}\}, \{\overline{y}\}, \{\overline{z}\}\})|_{\overline{\mathsf{G}} \cup \mathsf{G}' \cup \mathsf{L}} \\
&= \{\{u'\}, \{v', z'\}, \{\overline{u}\}, \{\overline{v}\}, \{w', x', y'\}, \{\overline{w}\}, \{\overline{x}\}, \{\overline{y}\}, \{\overline{z}\}\} = d_{1_9} = [\![p()]\!]^\sharp(d_{1_8})
\end{aligned}$$

6 Implementation and Experimental Evaluation

We implemented three versions of the connection analysis: the original top-down version [14], our modified top-down version, and our modular bottom-up version that coincides in precision with the modified top-down version. We next describe these versions.

The abstract transformer of the destructive update statements $x.f = y$ in [14] does not satisfy the requirements described in Sect. 4; its effect depends on the abstract state. Specifically, the connection sets of x and y are not merged if x or y points to `null` in all the executions leading to this statement. We therefore conservatively modified the analysis to satisfy our requirements, by changing the abstract transformer to always merge x's and y's connection sets. Our bottom-up

Table 1. Benchmark characteristics for reachable code. (Reachable methods computed by a static 0-CFA call-graph analysis.) The "total" columns report numbers for *all* reachable code, whereas the "app only" columns report numbers for only application code (excluding JDK library code).

	Description	# of classes		# of methods		# of bytecodes	
		app only	total	app only	total	app only	total
grande2	Java Grande kernels	17	61	112	237	8,146	13,724
grande3	Java Grande large-scale applications	42	241	231	1,162	27,812	75,139
antlr	Parser and translator generator	116	358	1,167	2,400	128,684	186,377
weka	Machine-learning library for data-mining tasks	62	530	575	3,391	40,767	223,291
bloat	Java bytecode optimization and analysis tool	277	611	2,651	4,699	194,725	311,727

modular analysis that coincides with this modified top-down analysis operates in two phases. The first phase computes a summary for every procedure by analyzing it with an input state ι_{entry}. The summary over-approximates relations between all possible inputs of this procedure and each program point in the body of the procedure. The second phase is a chaotic iteration algorithm which propagates values from callers to callees using the precomputed summaries, and is similar to the second phase of the interprocedural functional algorithm of [28, Fig. 7].

We implemented the aforementioned versions of connection analysis using Chord [26] and applied them to the five Java benchmark programs listed in Table 1. (For space reasons, however, we do not discuss the modified top-down version of connection analysis.) They include two programs (grande2 and grande3) from the Java Grande benchmark suite and two (antlr and bloat) from the DaCapo benchmark suite. We excluded programs from these suites that use multi-threading, since our analyses assume sequential programs. Our larger three benchmark programs are commonly used in evaluating pointer analyses. All our experiments were performed using Oracle HotSpot JRE 1.6.0 on a Linux machine with Intel Xeon 2.13 GHz processors and 128 Gb RAM.

We omit the modified top-down version of connection analysis from further evaluation, as its performance is similar to the original top-down version and its precision is (provably, and experimentally confirmed) identical to our bottom-up version.

Precision. Following [14], we measure precision by the size of the connection sets of pointer variables at program points of interest. Each pair of variable and

Table 2. A comparison of the scalability of the original top-down and our compositional bottom-up version. The measurements in the "query" sub-columns include only query points. The "total" sub-columns account for all points. All three metrics show that the top-down analysis scales much more poorly than the bottom-up analysis.

	# of queries	Bottom-Up analysis						Top-Down analysis			
		summary computation		summary instantiation							
		time	memory	time	memory	# of abstract states		time	memory	# of abstract states	
						queries	total			queries	total
grande2	616	0.6 sec	78 Mb	0.9 sec	61 Mb	616	1,318	1 sec	37 Mb	616	3,959
grande3	4,236	43 sec	224 Mb	1:21 min	137 Mb	4,373	8,258	1:11 min	506 Mb	4,354	27,232
antlr	5,838	16 sec	339 Mb	30 sec	149 Mb	6,207	21,437	1:23 min	1.1 Gb	8,388	79,710
weka	2,205	46 sec	503 Mb	2:48 min	228 Mb	2,523	25,147	> 6 hrs	26 Gb	5,694	688,957
bloat	10,237	3:03 min	573 Mb	30 min	704 Mb	36,779	131,665	> 6 hrs	24 Gb	139,551	962,376

program point can be viewed as a separate *query* to the connection analysis. To obtain such queries, we chose the parallelism client proposed in the original work of [14], which demands the connection set of each dereferenced pointer variable in the program. In Java, this corresponds to variables of reference type that are dereferenced to access instance fields or array elements. More specifically, our queries constitute the base variable in each occurrence of a getfield, putfield, aload, or astore bytecode instruction in the program. The number of such queries for our five benchmarks are shown in the "# of queries" column of Table 2. To avoid counting the same set of queries across benchmarks, we only consider queries in application code, ignoring those in JDK library code. This number of queries ranges from around 0.6 K to over 10 K for our benchmarks.

Figure 5 provides a detailed comparison of precision, based on the above metric, of the original top-down and bottom-up versions of connection analysis when applied to the antlr benchmark. Each graph in columns (a) and (b) plots, for each distinct connection set size (on the X axis), the fraction of queries (on the Y axis) for which each analysis computed connection sets of equal or smaller size. The graph shows that the precision of our modular bottom-up analysis closely tracks that of the original top-down analysis: the points for the bottom-up and top-down analyses, denoted ▲ and ○, respectively, overlap almost perfectly in each of the six graphs. The ratio of the connection set size computed by the top-down analysis to that computed by the bottom-up analysis on average across all queries is 0.952 for antlr (and 0.977 for grande2 and 0.977 for grande3). We do not, however, measure the impact of this precision loss of 2–5% on a real client. Note that for the largest two benchmarks, the top-down analysis timed-out.

Scalability. Table 2 compares the scalability of the top-down and bottom-up analyses in terms of three different metrics: running time, memory consumption, and the total number of computed abstract states. As noted earlier, the bottom-up analysis runs in two phases: a summary computation phase followed by a summary instantiation phase. The above data for these phases is reported in separate columns of the table. On our largest benchmark (bloat), the bottom-up analysis takes around 50 min and 873 Mb memory, whereas the top-down analysis times out after six hours, not only on this benchmark but also on the second largest one (weka).

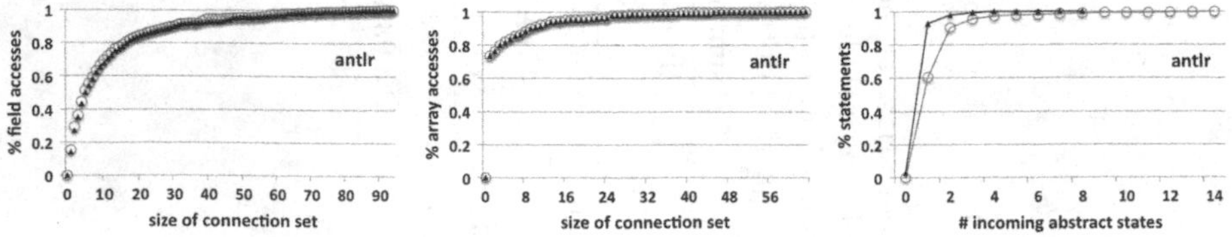

(a) Precision of field accesses. (b) Precision of array accesses. (c) Scalability.

Fig. 5. Comparison of the precision and scalability of the original top-down and our modular bottom-up versions of connection analysis for the antlr benchmark.

The "# of abstract states" columns provide the sum of the sizes of the computed abstractions in terms of the number of abstract states, including only incoming states at program points of queries (in the "queries" sub-column), and incoming states at all program points, including the JDK library (in the "total" sub-column). Column (c) of Fig. 5 provides more detailed measurements of the latter numbers. The graph shows, for each distinct number of incoming states computed at each program point (on the X axis), the fraction of program points (on the Y axis) with equal or smaller number of incoming states. The graphs clearly show the blow-up in the number of states computed by the top-down analysis over the bottom-up analysis.

7 Related Work, Discussion and Conclusions

The main technical observation in our work is that using right-modular abstract domains can help develop modular analyses. This observation is, in a way, similar to the frame rule in separation logic, in the sense that the join (resp. $*$) distributes over the transfer functions, and to the notion of *condensation* in logic programs [21].

The first compositional analysis framework was introduced in [6], and served as the basis for the concept of *abductive analysis* [15]. In [16], it has been shown that the semantic construction in [6] necessitates abstract domains which include functional objects and to a generalization of the reduced cardinal power domain [7] to arbitrary spaces of functions over a lattice. The latter was used to provide compositional semantics of logic programs [16]. These works paved the way to establishing the connection between modularity of analyses and *condensation* [17,18].

Condensation is an algebraic property of abstract unification that ensures that it is possible to approximate the behavior of a query and then unify it with a given context and the obtained results are as precise as the ones obtained by analyzing the query after instantiating it in that specific context. Abstract domain which have this property are called condensing. Intuitively, in condensing domains it is possible to derive context-independent interprocedural (bottom-up) analyses with the same precision as the corresponding context-dependent (top-down) analysis. Examples for such domains are Boolean functions [24], Herbrand abstractions [17], equality based domain [25], or combinations of thereof [31]. (See [17] for further discussion.)

A lattice theoretic characterization of condensing abstract domains was suggested in [18] and later generalized in [17]. Intuitively, let C be an abstract domain, $S : C \rightarrow C$ the abstract semantics used in the analysis, and $\otimes$ an associate commutative binary operator $\otimes$, e.g., unification. S is said to be condensing for $\otimes$ if $S(a \otimes b) = a \otimes S(b)$ for any a and b in C [17, Definition 4.1]. In fact, a weaker characterization of condensation is given in [18] which, by using the notion of *weak completeness* [18, Definition 3.8] requires the equality to hold only for ordered pairs, i.e., when either $a \sqsubseteq b$ or $b \sqsubseteq a$ [18, Theorem 4.7]. However, when the order of the lattice is induced by the binary operator, as it is in our case where $\otimes = \sqcup$, the equality has to hold for any pair of elements. Thus, our requirements are less restrictive than theirs, as shown by the following example: Let $d_1 = d_2 = \{\{\bar{x}, x'\}, \{\bar{y}, y'\}\}$, then $[\![x = \texttt{null}]\!]^\sharp(d_1 \sqcup d_2) = \{\{\bar{x}\}, \{x'\}, \{\bar{y}, y'\}\}$ but $[\![x = \texttt{null}]\!]^\sharp(d_1) \sqcup d_2 = (d_1 \sqcap S_{x'}) \sqcup d_2) = \{\{\bar{x}, x'\}, \{\bar{y}, y'\}\}$.

The above example points to, what is arguably, the most subtle part of our work. Note that $d_2 \not\sqsubseteq S_{x'}$. Hence, although $[\![x = \texttt{null}]\!]^\sharp$ is conditionally adaptable (see Defnition 3 and Lemma 1), we cannot take advantage of the modularity of $S_{x'}$. Surprisingly, we can benefit from the modularity of $S_{x'}$ when we adapt the result of the analysis of a procedure p (with ι_{entry} as input) to an arbitrary calling context. This is possible because the counterpart representation of calling contexts. Specifically, we can represent any calling context as a join between ι_{entry} and elements of the form $U_{\overline{xy}}$. Recall that $U_{\overline{xy}} = \{\{\bar{x}, \bar{y}\}\{x'\}\{y'\}$. Thus, it holds that $U_{\overline{xy}} \sqsubseteq S_{x'}$. In fact, for every x, y and z, it holds that $U_{\overline{xy}} \sqsubseteq S_{z'}$ (see Sect. 5.3.1).[4]

Conclusions. This paper shows that the notion of modularity from lattice theory can help for developing a precise bottom-up program analysis. In lieu of discussing the general framework [4], we illustrated the point by developing a compositional bottom-up connection analysis that has the same precision as the top-down counterpart, while enjoying the performance benefit of typically bottom-up analyses. Our analysis heavily uses modular elements in the abstract semantics of primitive commands, and their modularity property plays the key role in our proof that the precision of the compositional analysis coincides with that of the top-down counterpart. We also derived a new compositional analysis for a variant of the copy-constant propagation problem [13]. (See [4].) Our connection analysis can be used as a basis for a simple form of compositional taint analysis [22], essentially, by adding taint information to every partition. We hope that the connection we found between modularity in lattices and program analyses can help design precise and efficient compositional bottom-up analyses.

Acknowledgments. We thank the anonymous referees for their helpful comments. This work was supported by EU FP7 project ADVENT (308830), ERC grant agreement no. [321174-VSSC], Broadcom Foundation and Tel Aviv University Authentication Initiative, DARPA award #FA8750-12-2-0020 and NSF award #1253867.

[4] We note that if we only use elements in the analysis which are smaller than all the meet elements, then our analysis would become flow-insensitive. Let d, P_1, G_1, P_2, G_2 be abstract elements such that P_1 and P_2 are modular elements, $d \sqsubseteq P_1$, $((d \sqcap P_1) \sqcup G_1) \sqsubseteq P_2$, $((d \sqcap P_2) \sqcup G_2) \sqsubseteq P_1$. It holds that $G_1 \sqsubseteq P_2$, $G_2 \sqsubseteq P_1$, and thus $(((d \sqcap P_1) \sqcup G_1) \sqcap P_2) \sqcup G_2 = (((d \sqcap P_1) \sqcap P_2) \sqcup G_1) \sqcup G_2 = (d \sqcap P_2 \sqcap P_1) \sqcup G_2 \sqcup G_1 = ((d \sqcap P_2) \sqcup G_2) \sqcap P_1) \sqcup G_1$. (This is in fact the case if the meet elements are $\top$.) Note that this would imply that $[\![x = null]\!]^\sharp \circ [\![x = y]\!]^\sharp = [\![x = y]\!]^\sharp \circ [\![x = null]\!]^\sharp$, which is neither desired nor the case in our analysis.

References

1. Ball, T., Rajamani, S.: Bebop: a path-sensitive interprocedural dataflow engine. In: PASTE (2001)
2. Bodden, E.: Inter-procedural data-flow analysis with ifds/ide and soot. In: SOAP (2012)
3. Calcagno, C., Distefano, D., O'Hearn, P.W., Yang, H.: Compositional shape analysis by means of bi-abduction. J. ACM **58**(6), 26 (2011)
4. Castelnuovo, G.: Modular lattices for compositional interprocedural analysis. Master's thesis, School of Computer Science, Tel Aviv University (2012)
5. Chatterjee, R., Ryder, B.G., Landi, W.: Relevant context inference. In: POPL (1999)
6. Codish, M., Debray, S., Giacobazzi, R.: Compositional analysis of modular logic programs. In: POPL (1993)
7. Cousot, P., Cousot, R.: Abstract interpretation: A unified lattice model for static analysis of programs by construction of approximation of fixed points. In: POPL (1977)
8. Cousot, P., Cousot, R.: Static determination of dynamic properties of recursive procedures. In: Formal Descriptions of Programming Concepts (1978)
9. Cousot, P., Cousot, R.: Systematic design of program analysis frameworks. In: POPL (1979)
10. Cousot, P., Cousot, R.: Modular static program analysis. In: CC (2002)
11. Dillig, I., Dillig, T., Aiken, A., Sagiv, M.: Precise and compact modular procedure summaries for heap manipulating programs. In: PLDI (2011)
12. Dolby, J., Fink, S., Sridharan, M.: T. J. Watson Libraries for Analysis (2006)
13. Fischer, C.N., Cytron, R.K., LeBlanc, R.J.: Crafting A Compiler. Addison-Wesley, New York (2009)
14. Ghiya, R., Hendren, L.: Connection analysis: a practical interprocedural heap analysis for C. IJPP **24**(6), 547–578 (1996)
15. Giacobazzi, R.: Abductive analysis of modular logic programs. JLP **8**(4), 457–483 (1998)
16. Giacobazzi, R., Ranzato, F.: The reduced relative power operation on abstract domains. TCS **216**(1), 159–211 (1999)
17. Giacobazzi, R., Ranzato, F., Scozzari, F.: Making abstract domains condensing. TOCL **6**(1), 33–60 (2005)
18. Giacobazzi, R., Scozzari, F.: A logical model for relational abstract domains. TOPLAS **20**(5), 1067–1109 (1998)
19. Gratzer, G.: General Lattice Theory. Birkhauser Verlag, Berlin (1978)
20. Gulavani, B., Chakraborty, S., Ramalingam, G., Nori, A.: Bottom-up shape analysis using LISF. TOPLAS,33(5) (2011)
21. Jacobs, D., Langen, A.: Static analysis of logic programs for independent and parallelism. JLP **13**(2–3), 291–314 (1992)
22. Livshits, V.B., Lam, M.S.: Finding security vulnerabilities in java applications with static analysis. In: USENIX Security (2005)
23. Madhavan, R., Ramalingam, G., Vaswani, K.: Purity analysis: an abstract interpretation formulation. In: Yahav, E. (ed.) Static Analysis. LNCS, vol. 6887, pp. 7–24. Springer, Heidelberg (2011)
24. Marriott, K., Søndergaard, H.: Precise and efficient groundness analysis for logic programs. LOPLAS **2**(1–4), 181–196 (1993)

25. Müller-Olm, M., Seidl, H.: Precise interprocedural analysis through linear algebra. In: POPL (2004)
26. Naik, M.: Chord: A program analysis platform for Java (2006)
27. Reps, T., Horwitz, S., Sagiv, M.: Precise interprocedural dataflow analysis via graph reachability. In: POPL (1995)
28. Sagiv, M., Reps, T., Horwitz, S.: Precise interprocedural dataflow analysis with applications to constant propagation. TCS **167**(1), 131–170 (1996)
29. Sălcianu, A., Rinard, M.: Purity and side effect analysis for java programs. In: Cousot, R. (ed.) VMCAI 2005. LNCS, vol. 3385, pp. 199–215. Springer, Heidelberg (2005)
30. Sharir, M., Pnueli, A.: Two approaches to interprocedural data flow analysis. In: Program Flow Analysis: Theory and Applications (1981)
31. Simon, A.: Deriving a complete type inference for hindley-milner and vector sizes using expansion. In: PEPM (2013)
32. Whaley, J., Rinard, M.: Compositional pointer and escape analysis for java programs. In: OOPSLA (1999)

Parallel Cost Analysis of Distributed Systems

Elvira Albert[1], Jesús Correas[1], Einar Broch Johnsen[2],
and Guillermo Román-Díez[3](✉)

[1] DSIC, Complutense University of Madrid, Madrid, Spain
[2] Department of Informatics, University of Oslo, Oslo, Norway
[3] DLSIIS, Technical University of Madrid, Madrid, Spain
groman@fi.upm.es

Abstract. We present a novel static analysis to infer the *parallel cost* of distributed systems. Parallel cost differs from the standard notion of *serial cost* by exploiting the truly concurrent execution model of distributed processing to capture the cost of synchronized tasks executing in parallel.It is challenging to analyze parallel cost because one needs to soundly infer the parallelism between tasks while accounting for waiting and idle processor times at the different locations. Our analysis works in three phases: (1) It first performs a *block-level* analysis to estimate the serial costs of the blocks between synchronization points in the program; (2) Next, it constructs a *distributed flow graph* (DFG) to capture the parallelism, the waiting and idle times at the locations of the distributed system; Finally, (3) the parallel cost can be obtained as the path of maximal cost in the DFG. A prototype implementation demonstrates the accuracy and feasibility of the proposed analysis.

1 Introduction

Welcome to the age of distributed and multicore computing, in which software needs to cater for massively parallel execution. Looking beyond parallelism between independent tasks, *regular parallelism* involves tasks which are mutually dependent [17]: synchronization and communication are becoming major bottlenecks for the efficiency of distributed software. This paper is based on a model of computation which separates the asynchronous spawning of new tasks to different locations, from the synchronization between these tasks. The extent to which the software succeeds in exploiting the potential parallelism of the distributed locations depends on its synchronization patterns: synchronization points between dynamically generated parallel tasks restrict concurrency.

This paper introduces a novel static analysis to study the efficiency of computations in this setting, by approximating how synchronization between blocks of serial execution influences parallel cost. The analysis builds upon well-established static cost analyses for serial execution [2,8,21]. We assume that a serial cost

This work was funded partially by the EU project FP7-ICT-610582 ENVISAGE: Engineering Virtualized Services (http://www.envisage-project.eu), by the Spanish MINECO project TIN2012-38137, and by the CM project S2013/ICE-3006.

S. Blazy and T. Jensen (Eds.): SAS 2015, LNCS 9291, pp. 275–292, 2015.
DOI: 10.1007/978-3-662-48288-9_16

analysis returns a "cost" for the serial blocks which measures their efficiency. Traditionally, the metrics used in cost analysis [19] is based on counting the number of execution steps, because this cost model appears as the best abstraction of time for software. Our parallel cost analysis could also be used in combination with worst-case execution time (WCET) analysis [1] by assuming that the cost of the serial blocks is given by a WCET analysis.

Previous work on cost analysis of distributed systems [2] accumulates costs from different locations, but ignores the parallelism of the distributed execution model. This paper presents, to the best of our knowledge, the first static analysis to infer the parallel cost of distributed systems which takes into account the parallel execution of code across the locations of the distributed system, to infer more accurate bounds on the parallel cost. Our analysis works in the following steps, which are the main contributions of the paper:

1. *Block-level cost analysis of serial execution.* We extend an existing cost analysis framework for the serial execution of distributed programs in order to infer information at the granularity of synchronization points.
2. *Distributed flow graph (DFG).* We define the notion of DFG, which allows us to represent all possible (equivalence classes of) paths that the execution of the distributed program can take.
3. *Path Expressions.* The problem of finding the parallel cost of executing the program boils down to finding the path of maximal cost in the DFG. Paths in the DFG are computed by means of the single-source path expression problem [18], which finds regular expressions that represent all paths.
4. *Parallel cost with concurrent tasks.* We leverage the previous two steps to the concurrent setting by handling tasks whose execution might suspend and interleave with the execution of other tasks at the same location.

We demonstrate the accuracy and feasibility of the presented cost analysis by implementing a prototype analyzer of parallel cost within the SACO system, a static analyzer for distributed concurrent programs. Preliminary experiments on some typical applications for distributed programs achieve gains up to 29 % w.r.t. a serial cost analysis. The tool can be used online from a web interface available at http://costa.ls.fi.upm.es/web/parallel.

2 The Model of Distributed Programs

We consider a distributed programming model with explicit locations. Each location represents a processor with a procedure stack and an unordered buffer of pending tasks. Initially all processors are idle. When an idle processor's task buffer is non-empty, some task is selected for execution. Besides accessing its own processor's global storage, each task can post tasks to the buffer of any processor, including its own, and synchronize with the reception of tasks (synchronization will be presented later in Sect. 6). When a task completes, its processor becomes idle again, chooses the next pending task, and so on.

2.1 Syntax

The number of distributed locations need not be known a priori (e.g., locations may be virtual). Syntactically, a location will therefore be similar to an *object* and can be dynamically created using the instruction newLoc. The program consists of a set of methods of the form $M::=T\ m(\overline{T\ x})\{s\}$. Statements s take the form $s::=s;s \mid x{=}e \mid \text{if } e \text{ then } s \text{ else } s \mid \text{while } e \text{ do } s \mid \text{return } x \mid x{=}\text{newLoc} \mid x.m(\bar{z})$, where e is an expression, x, z are variables and m is a method name. The notation $\bar{z}$ is used as a shorthand for $z_1, \ldots, z_n$, and similarly for other names. The special location identifier *this* denotes the current location. For the sake of generality, the syntax of expressions e and types T is left open.

2.2 Semantics

A *program state* S has the form $loc_1 \| \ldots \| loc_n$, denoting the currently existing distributed locations. Each *location* is a term $loc(lid, tid, \mathcal{Q})$ where *lid* is the location identifier, *tid* the identifier of the *active task* which holds the location's lock or $\bot$ if the lock is free, and $\mathcal{Q}$ the set of tasks at the location. Only the task which holds the location's *lock* can be *active* (running) at this location. All other tasks are *pending*, waiting to be executed, or *finished*, if they have terminated and released the lock. A *task* is a term $tsk(tid, m, l, s)$ where *tid* is a unique task identifier, m the name of the method executing in the task, l a mapping from local variables to their values, and s the sequence of instructions to be executed or $s = \epsilon(v)$ if the task has terminated and the return value v is available.

The execution of a program starts from a method m, in an initial state with an initial location with identifier 0 executing task 0 of the form $S_0{=}loc(0, 0, \{tsk(0, \mathsf{m}, l, body(\mathsf{m}))\})$. Here, l maps parameters to their initial values and local references to null (standard initialization), and $body(\mathsf{m})$ refers to the sequence of instructions in the method m. The execution proceeds from S_0 by evaluating *in parallel* the distributed locations. The transition $\rightarrow$ denotes a parallel transition W in which we perform an evaluation step $\rightsquigarrow$ (as defined in Fig. 1) at every distributed location loc_i with $i{=}1, \ldots, n$, i.e., $W{\equiv}loc_1 \| \ldots \| loc_n \rightarrow loc'_1 \| \ldots \| loc'_m$.

$$(\textsc{newLoc})\ \frac{\text{fresh}(lid'),\ l' = l[x \rightarrow lid']}{\begin{array}{l} loc(lid, tid, \{tsk(tid, m, l, \langle x = \mathsf{newLoc}; s\rangle)\} \cup \mathcal{Q}) \rightsquigarrow \\ loc(lid, tid, \{tsk(tid, m, l', s)\} \cup \mathcal{Q}) \parallel loc(lid', \bot, \{\}) \end{array}}$$

$$(\textsc{async})\ \frac{l(x) = lid_1,\ \text{fresh}(tid_1),\ l_1 = buildLocals(\bar{z}, m_1)}{\begin{array}{c} loc(lid, tid, \{tsk(tid, m, l, \langle x.m_1(\bar{z}); s\rangle)\} \cup \mathcal{Q}) \rightsquigarrow \\ loc(lid, tid, \{tsk(tid, m, l, s)\} \cup \mathcal{Q}) \| loc(lid_1, \_, \{tsk(tid_1, m_1, l_1, body(m_1))\}) \end{array}}$$

$$(\textsc{select})\ \frac{\begin{array}{c} select(\mathcal{Q}) = tid, \\ t = tsk(tid, \_, \_, s) \in \mathcal{Q}, s \neq \epsilon(v) \end{array}}{loc(lid, \bot, \mathcal{Q}) \rightsquigarrow loc(lid, tid, \mathcal{Q})} \qquad (\textsc{return})\ \frac{v = l(x)}{\begin{array}{c} loc(lid, tid, \{tsk(tid, m, l, \langle \mathsf{return}\ x; \rangle)\} \cup \mathcal{Q}) \rightsquigarrow \\ loc(lid, \bot, \{tsk(tid, m, l, \epsilon(v))\} \cup \mathcal{Q}) \end{array}}$$

Fig. 1. Summarized semantics for distributed execution

If a location is idle and its queue is empty, the evaluation simply returns the same location state. Due to the dynamic creation of distributed locations, we have that $m \geq n$.

The transition relation $\rightsquigarrow$ in Fig. 1 defines the evaluation at each distributed location. The treatment of sequential instructions is standard and thus omitted. In NewLoc, an active task *tid* at location *lid* creates a location *lid'* with a free lock, which extends the program state. This explains that $m \geq n$. Async spawns a new task (the initial state is created by *buildLocals*) with a fresh task identifier tid_1 in a singleton queue for the location lid_1 (which may be *lid*). We here elide the technicalities of remote queue insertion in the parallel transition step, which basically merges locations with the same identifier by taking the union of the queues. Rule Select returns a task that is not finished, and it obtains the lock of the location. When Return is executed, the return value is stored in v. In addition, the lock is released and will never be taken again by that task. Consequently, that task is *finished* (marked by adding instruction $\epsilon(v)$).

3 Parallel Cost of Distributed Systems

The aim of this paper is to infer an *upper bound* which is an over-approximation of the *parallel cost* of executing a distributed system.Given a parallel transition $W \equiv loc_1 \| \ldots \| loc_n \rightarrow loc'_1 \| \ldots \| loc'_m$, we denote by $\mathcal{P}(W)$ the parallel cost of the transition W.If we are interested in counting the number of executed transitions, then $\mathcal{P}(W) = 1$. If we know the time taken by the transitions, $\mathcal{P}(W)$ refers to the time taken to evaluate all locations. Thus, if two instructions execute in parallel, the parallel cost only accumulates the largest of their times. For simplicity, we assume that all locations execute one instruction in one cost unit. Otherwise, it must be taken into account by the cost analysis of the serial cost (see Sect. 8). Given a trace $t \equiv S_o \rightarrow \ldots \rightarrow S_{n+1}$ of the parallel execution, we define $\mathcal{P}(t) = \sum_{i=0}^{n} \mathcal{P}(W_i)$, where $W_i \equiv S_i \rightarrow S_{i+1}$. Since execution is non-deterministic in the selection of tasks, given a program $P(x)$, multiple (possibly

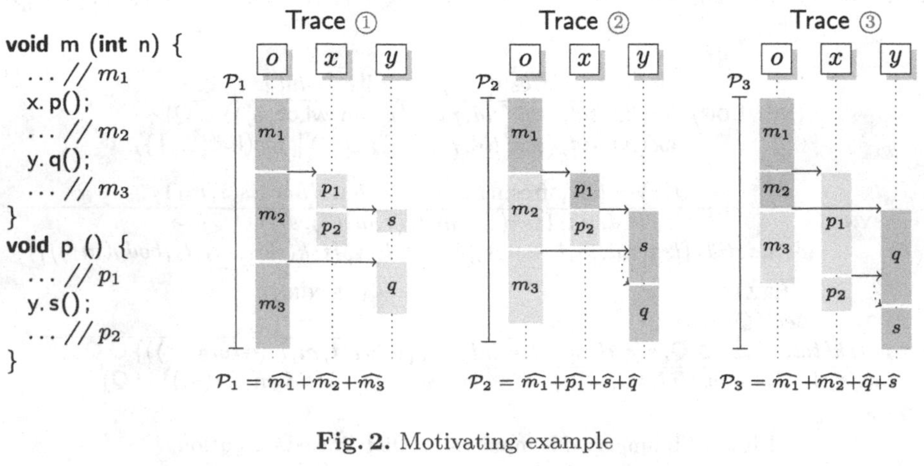

Fig. 2. Motivating example

infinite) traces may exist. We use $executions(P(\overline{x}))$ to denote the set of all possible traces for $P(\overline{x})$.

Definition 1 (Parallel Cost). *The parallel cost of a program P on input values $\overline{x}$, denoted $\mathcal{P}(P(\overline{x}))$, is defined as $max(\{\mathcal{P}(t) | t \in executions(P(\overline{x}))\})$.*

Example 1. Figure 2 (left) shows a simple method m that spawns two tasks by calling p and q at locations x and y, resp. In turn, p spawns a task by calling s at location y. This program only features distributed execution, concurrent behaviours within the locations are ignored for now. In the sequel we denote by $\widehat{m}$ the cost of block m. $\widehat{m_1}$, $\widehat{m_2}$ and $\widehat{m_3}$ denote, resp., the cost from the beginning of m to the call x.p(), the cost between x.p() and y.q(), and the remaining cost of m. $\widehat{p_1}$ and $\widehat{p_2}$ are analogous. Let us assume that the block m_1 contains a loop that performs n iterations (where n is equal to the value of input parameter n if it is positive and otherwise n is 0) and at each iteration it executes 10 instructions, thus $\widehat{m_1}$=$10 * n$. Let us assume that block m_2 contains a loop that divides the value of n by 2 and that it performs at most $log_2(n+1)$ iterations. Assume that at each iteration it executes 20 instructions, thus $\widehat{m_2}$=$20 * log_2(n + 1)$. These expressions can be obtained by cost analyzers of serial execution [2]. It is not crucial for the contents of this paper to know how these expressions are obtained, nor what the cost expressions are for the other blocks and methods. Thus, in the sequel, we simply refer to them in an abstract way as $\widehat{m_1}$, $\widehat{m_2}$, $\widehat{p_1}$, $\widehat{p_2}$ etc. ∎

The notion of parallel cost $\mathcal{P}$ corresponds to the cost consumed between the first instruction executed by the program at the initial location and the last instruction executed at any location by taking into account the parallel execution of instructions and idle times at the different locations.

Example 2. Figure 2 (right) shows three possible traces of the execution of this example (more traces are feasible). Below the traces, the expressions $\mathcal{P}_1$, $\mathcal{P}_2$ and $\mathcal{P}_3$ show the parallel cost for each trace. The main observation here is that the parallel cost varies depending on the duration of the tasks. It will be the worst (maximum) value of such expressions, that is, $\mathcal{P}$=$max(\mathcal{P}_1, \mathcal{P}_2, \mathcal{P}_3, \ldots)$. In ② p_1 is shorter than m_2, and s executes before q. In ③, q is scheduled before s, resulting in different parallel cost expressions. In ①, the processor of location y becomes idle after executing s and must wait for task q to arrive. ∎

In the general case, the inference of parallel cost is complicated because: (1) It is unknown if the processor is available when we spawn a task, as this depends on the duration of the tasks that were already in the queue; e.g., when task q is spawned we do not know if the processor is idle (trace ①) or if it is taken (trace ②). Thus, all scenarios must be considered; (2) Locations can be dynamically created, and tasks can be dynamically spawned among the different locations (e.g., from location o we spawn tasks at two other locations). Besides, tasks can be spawned in a circular way; e.g., task s could make a call back to location x; (3) Tasks can be spawned inside loops, we might even have non-terminating loops that create an unbounded number of tasks. The analysis must approximate (upper bounds on) the number of tasks that the locations might have in their queues. These points make the static inference of parallel cost a challenging problem that, to the best of our knowledge, has not been previously addressed. Existing frameworks for the cost analysis of distributed systems [2,3] rely on a *serial* notion of cost, i.e., the resulting cost accumulates the cost executed by all locations created by the program execution. Thus, we obtain a serial cost that simply adds the costs of all methods: $\widehat{m_1}+\widehat{m_2}+\widehat{m_3}+\widehat{p_1}+\widehat{p_2}+\widehat{q}+\widehat{s}$.

4 Block-Level Cost Analysis of Serial Execution

The first phase of our method is to perform a *block-level* cost analysis of *serial* execution. This is a simple extension of an existing analysis in order to provide costs at the level of the blocks in which the program is partitioned, between synchronization points. In previous work, other extensions have been performed that use costs at the level of specific program points [4] or at the level of complete tasks [3], but the partitioning required by our parallel cost analysis is different. Later, we need to be able to cancel out the cost associated to blocks whose execution occurs in parallel with other blocks that have larger cost. The key notion of the extension is *block-level cost centers*, as defined below.

Block Partitioning. The need to partition the code into blocks will be clear when presenting the second phase of the analysis. Essentially, the subsequent analysis needs to have cost information for the following sets of blocks: $\mathcal{B}_{\mathsf{init}}$, the set of entry blocks for the methods; $\mathcal{B}_{\mathsf{exit}}$, the set of exit blocks for the methods, and $\mathcal{B}_{\mathsf{call}}$, the set of blocks ending with an asynchronous call. Besides these blocks, the standard partitioning of methods into blocks used to build the control flow graph (CFG) for the method is performed (e.g., conditional statement and loops introduce blocks for evaluating the conditions, edges to the continuations, etc.). We use $\mathcal{B}$ to refer to all block identifiers in the program. Given a block identifier b, $pred(b)$ is the set of blocks from which there are outgoing edges to block b in the CFG. Function *pred* can also be applied to sets of blocks. We write $pp \in b$ (resp. $i \in b$) to denote that the program point pp (resp. instruction i) belongs to the block b.

Example 3. In Fig. 2, the traces show the partitioning in blocks for the methods m, p, q and s. Note that some of the blocks belong to multiple sets as defined above, namely $\mathcal{B}_{\mathsf{init}} = \{m_1, p_1, s, q\}$, $\mathcal{B}_{\mathsf{exit}}=\{m_3, p_2, s, q\}$, $\mathcal{B}_{\mathsf{call}}=\{m_1, m_2, p_1\}$. For instance, m_1 is both an entry and a call block, and s, as it is not partitioned, is both an entry and exit block. ■

Points-to Analysis. Since locations can be dynamically created, we need an analysis that abstracts them into a *finite* abstract representation, and that tells us which (abstract) location a reference variable is pointing-to. Points-to analysis [2,13,14] solves this problem. It infers the set of memory locations which a reference variable can *point-to*. Different abstractions can be used and our method is parametric on the chosen abstraction. Any points-to analysis that provides the following information with more or less accurate precision can be used (our implementation uses [2,13]): (1) $\mathcal{O}$, the set of abstract locations; (2) $\mathcal{M}$, the set of abstract tasks of the form $o.m$ where $o \in \mathcal{O}$ and m is a method name; (3) a function $pt(pp, v)$ which for a given program point pp and a variable v returns the set of abstract locations in $\mathcal{O}$ to which v may point to.

Example 4. In Fig. 2 we have three different locations, which are pointed to by variables o, x, y. For simplicity, we will use the variable name in italics to refer to the abstract location inferred by the points-to analysis. Thus, $\mathcal{O}=\{o, x, y\}$. The abstract tasks spawned in the program are $\mathcal{M}=\{o.m, x.p, y.s, y.q\}$. In this example, the points-to abstraction is very simple. However, in general, locations can be reassigned, passed in parameters, have multiple aliases, etc., and it is fundamental to keep track of points-to information in an accurate way. ■

Cost Centers. The notion of cost center is an artifact used to define the granularity of a cost analyzer. In [2], the proposal is to define a cost center for each distributed component; i.e., cost centers are of the form $c(o)$ where $o \in \mathcal{O}$ and $c(\_)$ is the artifact used in the cost expressions to attribute the cost to the different components. Every time the analyzer accounts for the cost of executing an instruction $inst$ at program point pp, it also checks at which location the instruction is executing. This information is provided by the points-to analysis as $O_{pp} = pt(pp, this)$. The cost of the instruction is accumulated in the cost centers of all elements in O_{pp} as $\sum c(o)*cost(inst), \forall o \in O_{pp}$, where $cost(inst)$ expresses in an abstract way the cost of executing the instruction. If we are counting steps, then $cost(inst) = 1$. If we measure time, $cost(inst)$ refers to the time to execute $inst$. Then, given a method $m(\bar{x})$, the cost analyzer will compute an upper bound for the serial cost of executing m of the form $\mathcal{S}_m(\bar{x}) = \sum_{i=1}^{n} c(o_i)*C_i$, where $o_i \in \mathcal{O}$ and C_i is a cost expression that bounds the cost of the computation carried out by location o_i when executing m. Thus, cost centers allow computing costs at the granularity level of the distributed components. If one is interested in studying the computation performed by one particular component o_j, we simply replace all $c(o_i)$ with $i \neq j$ by 0 and $c(o_j)$ by 1. The idea of using cost centers in an analysis is of general applicability and the different approaches to cost analysis (e.g., cost analysis based on recurrence equations [19], invariants [8], or type systems [9]) can trivially adopt this idea in order to extend their frameworks to a distributed setting. This is the only assumption that we make about the cost analyzer. Thus, we argue that our method can work in combination with any cost analysis for serial execution.

Example 5. For the code in Fig. 2, we have three cost centers for the three locations that accumulate the costs of the blocks they execute; i.e., we have $\mathcal{S}_m(n) = c(o)*\widehat{m_1} + c(o)*\widehat{m_2} + c(o)*\widehat{m_3} + c(x)*\widehat{p_1} + c(x)*\widehat{p_2} + c(y)*\widehat{s} + c(y)*\widehat{q}$. ■

Block-level Cost Centers. In this paper, we need *block-level* granularity in the analysis. This can be captured in terms of block-level cost centers $\overline{\mathcal{B}}$ which contain all blocks combined with all location names where they can be executed. Thus, $\overline{\mathcal{B}}$ is defined as the set $\{o{:}b \in \mathcal{O} \times \mathcal{B} \mid o \in pt(pp, this) \wedge pp \in b\}$. We define $\overline{\mathcal{B}}_{\mathsf{init}}$ and $\overline{\mathcal{B}}_{\mathsf{exit}}$ analogously. In the motivating example, $\overline{\mathcal{B}} = \{o{:}m_1, o{:}m_2, o{:}m_3, x{:}p_1, x{:}p_2, y{:}q, y{:}s\}$. Every time the analyzer accounts for the cost of executing an instruction *inst*, it checks at which location *inst* is executing (e.g., o) and to which block it belongs (e.g., b), and accumulates $c(o{:}b) * cost(inst)$. It is straightforward to modify an existing cost analyzer to include block-level cost centers. Given a method $m(\bar{x})$, the cost analyzer now computes a *block-level upper bound* for the cost of executing m. This upper bound is of the form $\mathcal{S}_m(\bar{x}) = \sum_{i=1}^{n} c(o_i{:}b_i) * C_i$, where $o_i{:}b_i \in \overline{\mathcal{B}}$, and C_i is a cost expression that bounds the cost of the computation carried out by location o_i while executing block b_i. Observe that b_i need not be a block of m because we can have transitive calls from m to other methods; the cost of executing these calls accumulates in $\mathcal{S}_m$. The notation $\mathcal{S}_m(\bar{x})|_{o:b}$ is used to express the cost associated to $c(o{:}b)$ within the cost expression $\mathcal{S}_m(\bar{x})$, i.e., the cost obtained by setting all $c(o'{:}b')$ to 0 (for $o' \neq o$ or $b' \neq b$) and setting $c(o{:}b)$ to 1. Given a set of cost centers $N = \{o_0{:}b_0, \ldots, o_k{:}b_k\}$, we let $\mathcal{S}_m(\bar{x})|_N$ refer to the cost obtained by setting to one the cost centers $c(o_i{:}b_i)$ such that $o_i{:}b_i \in N$. We omit m in $\mathcal{S}_m(\bar{x})|_N$ when it is clear from the context.

Example 6. The cost of the program using the blocks in $\mathcal{B}$ as cost centers, is $\mathcal{S}_m(n){=}c(o{:}m_1){*}\widehat{m_1}{+}c(o{:}m_2){*}\widehat{m_2}{+}c(o{:}m_3){*}\widehat{m_3}{+}c(x{:}p_1){*}\widehat{p_1}{+}c(x{:}p_2){*}\widehat{p_2}{+}c(y{:}s){*}\widehat{s}{+}$ $c(y{:}q){*}\widehat{q}$. We can obtain the cost for block $o{:}m_2$ as $\mathcal{S}_m(n)|_{o:m_2} = \widehat{m_2}$. With the serial cost assumed in Sect. 3, we have $\mathcal{S}_m(n)|_{o:m_2} = 20 * log_2(n+1)$. ■

5 Parallel Cost Analysis

This section presents our method to infer the cost of executing the distributed system by taking advantage of the fact that certain blocks of code must execute in parallel, thus we only need to account for the largest cost among them.

5.1 Distributed Flow Graph

The *distributed flow graph* (DFG), introduced below, aims at capturing the different flows of execution that the program can perform. According to the distributed model of Sect. 2, when the processor is released, any pending task of the same location could start executing. We use an existing *may-happen-in-parallel* (MHP) analysis [5,12] to approximate the tasks that could start their execution when the processor is released. This analysis infers pairs of program points (x, y) whose execution *might* happen in parallel. The soundness of the analysis guarantees that if (x, y) is not an MHP pair then there are no instances of the methods to which x or y belong whose program points x and y can run in parallel. The MHP analysis can rely on a points-to analysis in exactly the same way as our overall analysis does. Hence, we can assume that MHP pairs are of the form $(x{:}p_1, y{:}p_2)$ where x and y refer to the locations in which they execute. We use the notation $x{:}b_1 \parallel y{:}b_2$, where b_1 and b_2 are blocks, to denote that the program points of $x{:}b_1$ and $y{:}b_2$ might happen in parallel, and, $x{:}b_1 \nparallel y{:}b_2$ to indicate that they cannot happen in parallel.

Example 7. The MHP analysis of the example shown in Fig. 2 returns that $y{:}s \parallel y{:}q$, indicating that s and q might happen in parallel at location y. In addition, as we only have one instance of m and p, the MHP guarantees that $o{:}m_1 \nparallel o{:}m_3$ and $x{:}p_1 \nparallel x{:}p_2$. ■

The nodes in the DFG are the cost centers which the analysis in Sect. 4 has inferred. The edges represent the control flow in the sequential execution (drawn with normal arrows) and all possible orderings of tasks in the location's queues (drawn with dashed arrows). We use the MHP analysis results to eliminate the dashed arrows that correspond to unfeasible orderings of execution.

Definition 2 (Distributed Flow Graph). *Given a program P, its block-level cost centers $\overline{\mathcal{B}}$, and its points-to analysis results provided by function pt, we define its* distributed flow graph *as a directed graph $\mathcal{G} = \langle V, E\rangle$ with a set of vertices $V = \overline{\mathcal{B}}$ and a set of edges $E = E_1 \cup E_2 \cup E_3$ defined as follows:*

$$\begin{aligned}
E_1 =& \{o{:}b_1 \rightarrow o{:}b_2 \mid b_1 \rightarrow b_2 \text{ exists in } CFG\}\\
E_2 =& \{o_1{:}b_1 \rightarrow o_2{:}\mathsf{m}_{\mathsf{init}} \mid b_1 \in \mathcal{B}_{\mathsf{call}}, pp : \mathsf{x.m()} \in b_1, o_2 \in pt(pp, \mathsf{x})\}\\
E_3 =& \{o{:}b_1 \dashrightarrow o{:}b_2 \mid b_1 \in \mathcal{B}_{\mathsf{exit}}, b_2 \in \mathcal{B}_{\mathsf{init}}, o{:}b_1 \parallel o{:}b_2\}
\end{aligned}$$

Here, E_1 is the set of edges that exist in the CFG, but using the points-to information in $\overline{\mathcal{B}}$ in order to find out at which locations the blocks are executed. E_2 joins each block that contains a method invocation with the initial block $\mathsf{m}_{\mathsf{init}}$ of the invoked method. Again, points-to information is used to know all possible locations from which the calls originate (named o_1 above) and also the locations where the tasks are sent (named o_2 above). Arrows are drawn for all possible combinations. These arrows capture the parallelism in the execution and allow us to gain precision w.r.t. the serial execution. Intuitively, they allow us to consider the maximal cost of the path that continues the execution and the path that goes over the spawned tasks. Finally, dashed edges E_3 are required for expressing the different orderings of the execution of tasks within each abstract location. Without further knowledge, the exit blocks of methods must be joined with the entry blocks of others tasks that execute at the same location. With the MHP analysis we can avoid some dashed edges in the DFG in the following way: given two methods m, whose initial block is m_1, and p, whose final block is p_2, if we know that m_1 cannot happen in parallel with p_2, then we do not need to add a dashed edge between them. This is because the MHP guarantees that when the execution of p finishes there is no instance of method m in the queue of pending tasks. Thus, we do not consider this path in E_3 of the DFG.

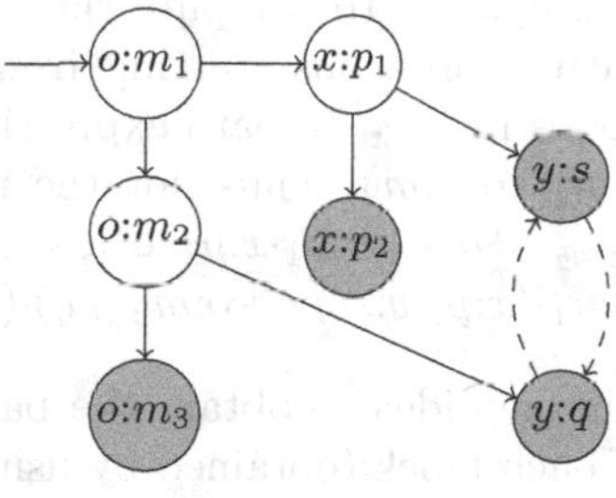

Fig. 3. DFG for Fig. 2

Example 8. Figure 3 shows the DFG for the program in Fig. 2. The nodes are the cost centers in Example 6. Nodes in gray are the nodes in $\overline{\mathcal{B}}_{\mathsf{exit}}$, and it implies that the execution can terminate executing $o{:}m_3$, $x{:}p_2$, $y{:}s$ or $y{:}q$. Solid edges include those existing in the CFG of the sequential program but combined with the location's identity (E_1) and those derived from calls (E_2). Since $y{:}s \parallel y{:}q$ (see Example 7), the execution order of s and q at location y is unknown (see Sect. 3). This is modelled by means of the dashed edges (E_3). In contrast, since $o{:}m_1 \nparallel o{:}m_3$ and $x{:}p_1 \nparallel x{:}p_2$, we neither add a dashed edge from $o{:}m_3$ to $o{:}m_1$ nor from $x{:}p_2$ to $x{:}p_1$. ■

5.2 Inference of Parallel Cost

The next phase in our analysis consists of obtaining the maximal parallel cost from all possible executions of the program, based on the DFG. The execution paths in the DFG start in the initial node that corresponds to the entry method of the program, and finish in any node in $\overline{\mathcal{B}}_{\mathsf{exit}}$. The first step for the inference is to compute the set of execution paths by solving the so-called *single-source path expression problem* [18], which finds a regular expression (named *path expression*) for each node $v \in \overline{\mathcal{B}}_{\mathsf{exit}}$ representing all paths from an initial node to v. Given a DFG $\mathcal{G}$, we denote by *pexpr*($\mathcal{G}$) the set of path expressions obtained from the initial node to all exit nodes in $\mathcal{G}$.

Example 9. To compute the set *pexpr* for the graph in Fig. 3, we compute the path expressions starting from $o{:}m_1$ and finishing in exit nodes, that is, the nodes in $\overline{\mathcal{B}}_{\mathsf{exit}}$. In path expressions, we use $o{:}m_1 {\cdot} o{:}m_2$ to represent the edge from $o{:}m_1$ to $o{:}m_2$. Thus, for the nodes in $\overline{\mathcal{B}}_{\mathsf{exit}}$ we have $\mathsf{e}_{o:m_3} = o{:}m_1{\cdot}o{:}m_2{\cdot}o{:}m_3$, $\mathsf{e}_{x:p_2} = o{:}m_1{\cdot}x{:}p_1{\cdot}x{:}p_2$, $\mathsf{e}_{y:s} = o{:}m_1{\cdot}(x{:}p_1{\cdot}y{:}s \mid o{:}m_2{\cdot}y{:}q{\cdot}y{:}s){\cdot}(y{:}q{\cdot}y{:}s)^*$ and $\mathsf{e}_{y:q} = o{:}m_1{\cdot}(x{:}p_1{\cdot}y{:}s{\cdot}y{:}q \mid o{:}m_2{\cdot}y{:}q){\cdot}(y{:}s{\cdot}y{:}q)^*$. ■

The key idea to obtain the parallel cost from path expressions is that the cost of each block (obtained by using the block-level cost analysis) contains not only the cost of the block itself but this cost is multiplied by the number of times the block is visited. Thus, we use sets instead of sequences since the multiplicity of the elements is already taken into account in the cost of the blocks. Given a path expression e, we define *sequences*(e) as the set of paths produced by e and *elements*(p) as the set of nodes in a given path p. We use the notions of *sequences* and *elements* to define the set $\mathcal{N}(\mathsf{e})$.

Definition 3. *Given a path expression* e, $\mathcal{N}(\mathsf{e})$ *is the following set of sets:*

$$\{s \mid p \in sequences(\mathsf{e}) \ \wedge \ s = elements(p)\}.$$

In practice, this set $\mathcal{N}(\mathsf{e})$ can be generated by splitting the disjunctions in e into different elements in the usual way, and adding the nodes within the repeatable subexpressions once. Thus, to obtain the parallel cost, it is sufficient to compute $\mathcal{N}^+(\mathsf{e})$, the set of *maximal* elements of $\mathcal{N}(\mathsf{e})$ with respect to set inclusion, i.e., those sets in $\mathcal{N}(\mathsf{e})$ which are not contained in any other set in $\mathcal{N}(\mathsf{e})$. Given a graph $\mathcal{G}$, we denote by $paths(\mathcal{G}) = \bigcup \mathcal{N}^+(\mathsf{e})$, $\mathsf{e} \in pexpr(\mathcal{G})$, i.e., the union of the sets of sets of elements obtained from each path expression.

Example 10. Given the path expressions in Example 9, we have the following sets:

$$\mathcal{N}^+(\mathsf{e}_{o:m_3}) = \{\underbrace{\{o{:}m_1, o{:}m_2, o{:}m_3\}}_{N_1}\}, \quad \mathcal{N}^+(\mathsf{e}_{x:p_2}) = \{\underbrace{\{o{:}m_1, x{:}p_1, x{:}p_2\}}_{N_2}\}$$

$$\mathcal{N}^+(\mathsf{e}_{y:s}) = \mathcal{N}^+(\mathsf{e}_{y:q}) = \{\underbrace{\{o{:}m_1, x{:}p_1, y{:}s, y{:}q\}}_{N_3}, \underbrace{\{o{:}m_1, o{:}m_2, y{:}s, y{:}q\}}_{N_4}\}$$

Observe that these sets represent traces of the program. The execution captured by N_1 corresponds to trace ① of Fig. 2. In this trace, the code executed at location o leads to the maximal cost. Similarly, the set N_3 corresponds to trace ② and N_4 corresponds to trace ③. The set N_2 corresponds to a trace where $x{:}p_2$ leads to the maximal cost (not shown in Fig. 2). Therefore, the set *paths* is $\{N_1, N_2, N_3, N_4\}$. ■

Given a set $N \in paths(\mathcal{G})$, we can compute the cost associated to N by using the block-level cost analysis, that is, $\mathcal{S}(\bar{x})|_N$. The parallel cost of the distributed system can be over-approximated by the maximum cost for the paths in $paths(\mathcal{G})$.

Definition 4 (Inferred Parallel Cost). *The* inferred parallel cost *of a program* $P(\overline{x})$ *with distributed flow graph* $\mathcal{G}$, *is defined as* $\widehat{\mathcal{P}}(P(\overline{x})) = \max_{N \in paths(\mathcal{G})} \mathcal{S}(\bar{x})|_N$.

Although we have obtained the parallel cost of the whole program, we can easily obtain the parallel cost associated to a location o of interest, denoted $\widehat{\mathcal{P}}(P(\bar{x}))|_o$, by considering only the paths that lead to the exit nodes of this location. In particular, given a location o, we consider the set of path expressions $pexpr(\mathcal{G}, o)$ which are the subset of $pexpr(\mathcal{G})$ that end in an exit node of o. The above definition simply uses $pexpr(\mathcal{G}, o)$ instead of $pexpr(\mathcal{G})$ in order to obtain $\widehat{\mathcal{P}}(P(\bar{x}))|_o$.

Example 11. The cost is obtained by using the block-level costs for all nodes that compose the sets in *paths*. With the sets computed in Example 10, the overall parallel cost is: $\widehat{\mathcal{P}}(\mathsf{m}(n)) = max(\mathcal{S}(n)|_{N_1}, \mathcal{S}(n)|_{N_2}, \mathcal{S}(n)|_{N_3}, \mathcal{S}(n)|_{N_4})$. Importantly, $\widehat{\mathcal{P}}$ is more precise than the serial cost because all paths have at least one missing node. For instance, N_1 does not contain the cost of $x{:}p_1, x{:}p_2, y{:}s, y{:}q$ and N_3 does not contain the cost of $o{:}m_2, o{:}m_3, x{:}p_2$. Additionally, as $o{:}m_3$ is the only final node for location o, we have that $\widehat{\mathcal{P}}(\mathsf{m}(n))|_o = \mathcal{S}(n)|_{N_1}$. Similarly, for location y we have two exit nodes, $y{:}s$ and $y{:}q$, thus $\widehat{\mathcal{P}}(\mathsf{m}(n))|_y = max(\mathcal{S}(n)|_{N_3}, \mathcal{S}(n)|_{N_4})$. ■

Recall that when there are several calls to a block $o{:}b$ the graph contains only one node $o{:}b$ but the serial cost $\mathcal{S}(\bar{x})|_{o:b}$ accumulates the cost of all calls. This is also the case for loops or recursion. The nodes within an iterative construct form a cycle in the DFG and by setting to one the corresponding cost center, the serial cost accumulates the cost of all executions of such nodes.

Example 12. The program to the right shows a modification of method m that adds a loop which includes the call y.q(). The DFG for this code contains a cycle caused by the loop, composed by the nodes $o{:}w$, $o{:}m_3$ and $o{:}m_4$, where $o{:}w$ represents the entry block to the while loop. The execution might traverse such nodes multiple times and consequently multiple instances of $y{:}q$ might be spawned.

A serial cost analyzer (e.g. [2]) infers that the loop is traversed at most n times and obtains a block-level serial cost of the form:

$$\mathcal{S}(n) = c(o{:}m_1)*\widehat{m_1} + c(o{:}m_2)*\widehat{m_2} + n*c(o{:}w)*\widehat{w} + n*c(o{:}m_3)*\widehat{m_3} + n*c(o{:}m_4)*\widehat{m_4} + c(o{:}m_5)*\widehat{m_5} + c(x{:}p_1)*\widehat{p_1} + c(x{:}p_2)*\widehat{p_2} + n*c(y{:}q)*\widehat{q} + c(y{:}s)*\widehat{s}$$

```
void m (int n) {
  ... // m1 instr
  x.p();
  ... //m2 instr
  while(n > 0) {
    n=n−1;
    ... //m3 instr
    y.q();
    ... //m4 instr
  }
  ... // m5 instr
}
```

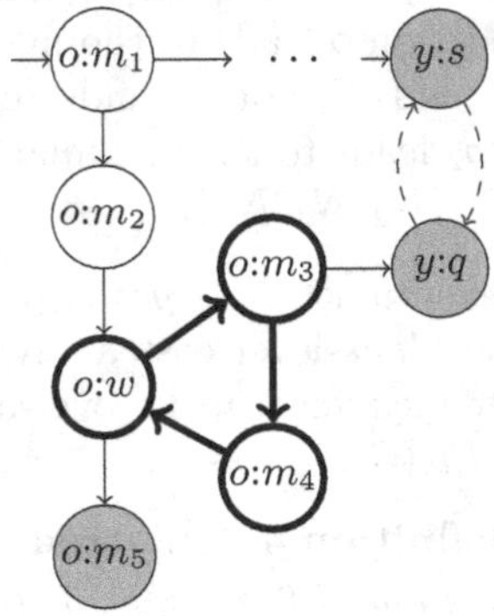

For the DFG we obtain some interesting sets that traverse the loop: $N_1 = \{o{:}m_1, o{:}m_2, o{:}w, o{:}m_3, o{:}m_4, o{:}m_5\}$ and $N_2 = \{o{:}m_1, o{:}m_2, o{:}w, o{:}m_3, o{:}m_4, y{:}q, y{:}s\}$. Observe that N_1 represents a trace that traverses the loop and finishes in $o{:}m_5$ and N_2 represents a trace that reaches $y{:}q$ by traversing the loop. The cost associated to N_1 is computed as $\mathcal{S}(n)|_{N_1} = \widehat{m_1}+\widehat{m_2}+n*\widehat{w}+n*\widehat{m_3}+n*\widehat{m_4}+\widehat{m_5}$. Note that $\mathcal{S}(n)|_{N_1}$ includes the cost of executing the nodes of the loop multiplied by n, capturing the iterations of the loop. Similarly, for N_2 we have $\mathcal{S}(n)|_{N_2}=\widehat{m_1}+\widehat{m_2}+n*\widehat{w}+n*\widehat{m_3}+n*\widehat{m_4}+n*\widehat{q}+\widehat{s}$, which captures that q might be executed n times. ■

Theorem 1. $\mathcal{P}(P(\bar{x})) \leq \widehat{\mathcal{P}}(P(\bar{x}))$.

6 Parallel Cost Analysis with Cooperative Concurrency

We now extend the language to allow cooperative concurrency between the tasks at each location, in the style of concurrent (or active) object systems such as ABS [11]. The language is extended with *future variables* which are used to check if the execution of an asynchronous task has finished. In particular, an asynchronous call is associated with a future variable f as follows f=x.p(). The instruction await f? allows synchronizing the execution of the current task with the task p to which the future variable f is pointing; f.get is used to retrieve the value returned by the completed task. The semantics for these instructions is given in Fig. 4. The semantics of ASYNC+FUT differs from ASYNC in Fig. 1 in that it stores the association of the future variable to the task in the local variable table l. In AWAIT1, the future variable we are awaiting points to a finished task and await can be completed. The finished task t_1 is looked up at all locations in

$$\text{(ASYNC+FUT)}\ \frac{l(x) = lid_1,\ \text{fresh}(tid_1),\ l' = l[f \to tid_1],\ l_1 = buildLocals(\bar{z}, m_1)}{\begin{array}{c} loc(lid, tid, \{tsk(tid, m, l, \langle f = x.m_1(\bar{z}); s\rangle\} \cup \mathcal{Q}) \leadsto \\ loc(lid, tid, \{tsk(tid, m, l', s)\} \cup \mathcal{Q}) \parallel loc(lid_1, \_, \{tsk(tid_1, m_1, l_1, body(m_1))\}) \end{array}}$$

$$\text{(AWAIT1)}\ \frac{l(f) = tid_1,\ loc(lid_1, \_, \mathcal{Q}_1) \in \texttt{Locs},\ tsk(tid_1, \_, \_, s_1) \in \mathcal{Q}_1,\ s_1 = \epsilon(v)}{loc(lid, tid, \{tsk(tid, m, l, \langle \mathsf{await}\ f?; s\rangle)\} \cup \mathcal{Q}) \leadsto loc(lid, tid, \{tsk(tid, m, l, s)\} \cup \mathcal{Q})}$$

$$\text{(AWAIT2)}\ \frac{l(f) = tid_1,\ loc(lid_1, \_, \mathcal{Q}_1) \in \texttt{Locs},\ tsk(tid_1, \_, \_, s_1) \in \mathcal{Q}_1,\ s_1 \neq \epsilon(v)}{loc(lid, tid, \{tsk(tid, m, l, \langle \mathsf{await}\ f?; s\rangle)\} \cup \mathcal{Q}) \leadsto loc(lid, \bot, \{tsk(tid, m, l, \langle \mathsf{await}\ f?; s\rangle)\} \cup \mathcal{Q})}$$

$$\text{(GET1)}\ \frac{l(f) = tid_1,\ tsk(tid_1, \_, \_, s_1) \in \texttt{Locs}, s_1 = \epsilon(v),\ l' = l[x \to v])}{loc(lid, tid, \{tsk(tid, m, l, \langle \mathsf{x}{=}f.\mathsf{get}; s\rangle)\} \cup \mathcal{Q}) \leadsto loc(lid, tid, \{tsk(tid, m, l', s)\} \cup \mathcal{Q})}$$

$$\text{(GET2)}\ \frac{l(f) = tid_1,\ tsk(tid_1, \_, \_, s_1) \in \texttt{Locs}, s_1 \neq \epsilon(v)}{\begin{array}{c} loc(lid, tid, \{tsk(tid, m, l, \langle \mathsf{x}{=}f.\mathsf{get}; s\rangle)\} \cup \mathcal{Q}) \\ \leadsto loc(lid, tid, \{tsk(tid, m, l, \langle \mathsf{x}{=}f.\mathsf{get}; s\rangle)\} \cup \mathcal{Q}) \end{array}}$$

Fig. 4. Summarized semantics of concurrent execution

the current state (denoted by Locs). Otherwise, AWAIT2 yields the lock so any other task at the same location can take it. In GET1 the return value is retrieved after the task has finished and in GET2 the location is blocked allowing time to pass until the task finishes and the return value can be retrieved.

Handling concurrency in the analysis is challenging because we need to model the fact that we can lose the processor at the await instructions and another pending task can interleave its execution with the current task. The first extension needed is to refine the block partitioning in Sect. 4 with the set of blocks: $\mathcal{B}_{\mathsf{get}}$, the set of blocks starting with a get; and $\mathcal{B}_{\mathsf{await}}$, the set of blocks starting with an await. Such blocks contain edges to the preceding and subsequent blocks as in the standard construction of the CFG (and we assume they are in the set of edges E_1 of Definition 2). Fortunately, task interleavings can be captured in the graph in a clean way by treating await blocks as initial blocks, and their predecessors as ending blocks. Let b be a block which contains a f.get or await f? instruction. Then $awaited(\mathsf{f}, pp)$ returns the (set of) exit blocks to which the future variable f can be linked at program point pp. We use the points-to analysis results to find the tasks a future variable is pointing to. Furthermore, the MHP analysis learns information from the await instructions, since after an await f? we know that the execution of the task to which f is linked is finished and thus it will not happen in parallel with the next tasks spawned at the same location.

Definition 5 (DFG with Cooperative Concurrency). *We extend Definition 2:*

$$E_4 = \{o_1{:}m_{exit} \to o_2{:}b_2 \mid \textit{either } pp{:}f.\mathsf{get} \textit{ or } pp{:}\mathsf{await}\ f? \in b_2, m_{exit} \in awaited(f, pp)\}$$
$$E_5 = \{o{:}b_1 \dashrightarrow o{:}b_2 \mid b_1 \in pred(\mathcal{B}_{await}), b_2 \in \mathcal{B}_{await} \cup \mathcal{B}_{init}, o{:}b_1 \parallel o{:}b_2\}$$
$$E_6 = \{o{:}b_1 \dashrightarrow o{:}b_2 \mid b_1 \in \mathcal{B}_{exit}, b_2 \in \mathcal{B}_{await}, o{:}b_1 \parallel o{:}b_2\}$$

Here, E_4 contains the edges that relate the last block of a method with the corresponding synchronization instruction in the caller method, indicating that the execution can take this path after the method has completed. E_5 and E_6 contain dashed edges that represent the orderings between parts of tasks split by await instructions and thus capture the possible interleavings. E_5 considers the predecessor as an ending block from which we can start to execute another interleaved task (including await blocks). E_6 treats await blocks as initial blocks which can start their execution after another task at the same location finishes. As before, the MHP analysis allows us to discard those edges between blocks that cannot be pending to execute when the processor is released. Theorem 1 also holds for DFG with cooperative concurrency.

Example 13. Figure 5 shows an example where the call to method p is synchronized by using either await or get. Method p then calls method q at location o. The synchronization creates a new edge (the thick one) from $x{:}p_2$ to the synchronization point in block $o{:}m_3$. This edge adds a new path to reach $o{:}m_3$ that represents a trace in which the execution of m waits until p is finished. For the graph in Fig. 5 we have that *paths* is $\{\{o{:}m_1, x{:}p_1, x{:}p_2, o{:}m_3, o{:}q\}, \{o{:}m_1, o{:}m_2, o{:}m_3, o{:}q\}\}$. Observe that the thick edge is crucial for creating the first set in *paths*. The difference between the use of await and get is visible in the edges labelled with ⊛, which are only added for await. They capture the traces in which the execution of m waits for the termination of p, and q starts its execution interleaved between $o{:}m_2$ and $o{:}m_3$, postponing the execution of $o{:}m_3$. In this example, the edges labelled with ⊛ do not produce new sets in *paths*. ■

Finally, let us remark that our work is parametric in the underlying points-to and cost analyses for serial execution. Hence, any accuracy improvement in these auxiliary analyses will have an impact on the accuracy of our analysis. In particular, a context-sensitive points-to analysis [15] can lead to big accuracy gains. Context-sensitive points-to analyses use the program point from which tasks are spawned as context information. This means that two different calls $o.m$, one from program point p_1 and another from p_2 (where $p_1 \neq p_2$) are distinguished in the analysis as $o{:}p_1{:}m$ and $o{:}p_2{:}m$. Therefore, instead of representing them by a single node in the graph, we will use two nodes. The advantage of this finer-grained information is that we can be more accurate when considering task parallelism. For instance, we can have one path in the graph which includes a single execution of $o{:}p_1{:}m$ (and none of $o{:}p_2{:}m$). However, if the nodes are merged into a single one, we have to consider either that both or none are executed.

```
void m () {
  ... // m1 instr
  f = x.p(this);
  ... //m2 instr
  await f? | f.get
  ... // m3 instr
}
void p (Node o) {
  ... // p1 instr
  o.q();
  ... // p2 instr
}
```

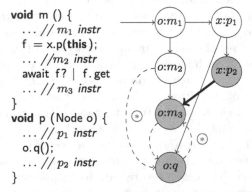

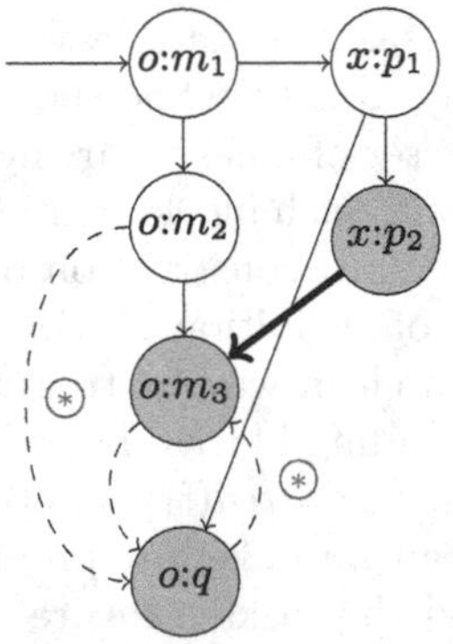

Fig. 5. DCG with synchronization

There are also techniques to gain precision in points-to analysis in the presence of loops [16] that could improve the precision of our analysis.

7 Experimental Evaluation

We have implemented our analysis in SACO and applied it to some distributed based systems: BBuffer, the typical bounded-buffer for communicating several producers and consumers; MailServer, which models a distributed mail server system with multiple clients; Chat, which models chat application; DistHT, which implements and uses a distributed hash table; BookShop, which models a web shop client-server application; and P2P, which represents a peer-to-peer network formed by a set of interconnected peers. Experiments have been performed on an Intel Core i7 at 2.0 GHz with 8 GB of RAM, running Ubuntu 14.04. Table 1 summarizes the results obtained for the benchmarks. Columns Benchmark and loc show, resp., the name and the number of program lines of the benchmark. Columns $\#_N$ and $\#_E$ show the number of nodes and edges of the DFG with concurrency (Definition 5). Columns $\#_F$ and $\#_P$ contain the number of terminal nodes in the DFG and the number of elements in the set *paths*. Columns $\mathbf{T}_{\mathcal{S}}$ and $\mathbf{T}_{\widehat{\mathcal{P}}}$ show, resp., the analysis times for the serial cost analysis and the additional time required by the parallel cost analysis (in milliseconds) to build the DFG graphs and obtain the cost from them. The latter includes a simplification of the DFG to reduce the strongly connected components (SCC) to one node. Such simplification significantly reduces the time in computing the path expressions and we can see that the overall overhead is reasonable.

Column $\%_{\widehat{\mathcal{P}}}$ aims at showing the gain of the parallel cost $\widehat{\mathcal{P}}$ w.r.t. the serial cost $\mathcal{S}$ by evaluating $\widehat{\mathcal{P}}(\bar{e})/\mathcal{S}(\bar{e}){*}100$ for different values of $\bar{e}$. Namely, $\%_{\widehat{\mathcal{P}}}$ is the average of the evaluation of the cost expressions $\widehat{\mathcal{P}}(\bar{e})$ and $\mathcal{S}(\bar{e})$ for different values of the input arguments $\bar{e}$ to the programs. The number of evaluations performed is shown in column $\#_I$. The accuracy gains range from 4.8 % in P2P to 28.9 % in BookShop. The gain of more than 20 % for DistHT, BookShop and BBuffer is explained by the fact that these examples take advantage of parallelism: the different distributed locations execute a similar number of instructions and besides their code mostly runs in parallel. MailServer, Chat and P2P achieve smaller gains

Table 1. Experimental results (times in ms)

Benchmark	loc	$\#_N$	$\#_E$	$\#_F$	$\#_P$	$\mathbf{T}_{\mathcal{S}}$	$\mathbf{T}_{\widehat{\mathcal{P}}}$	$\#_I$	$\%_m$	$\%_a$	$\%_{\widehat{\mathcal{P}}}$
BBuffer	105	37	50	7	50	256	26	1000	3.0	19.7	77.4
MailServer	115	28	35	6	36	846	12	1000	61.1	68.6	88.5
Chat	302	84	245	25	476	592	126	625	5.7	56.0	85.4
DistHT	353	38	47	6	124	950	49	625	3.7	25.5	76.3
BookShop	353	60	63	7	68	2183	214	2025	9.2	50.9	71.1
P2P	240	168	533	27	730	84058	1181	512	13.0	85.9	95.2

because the blocks that are not included in the path (those that are guaranteed to happen in parallel with longer blocks) are non-recursive. Thus, when the number of instructions is increased, the improvements are reduced proportionally. Moreover, Chat and P2P create very dense graphs, and the paths that lead to the maximum cost include almost all nodes of the graph. Column $\%_m$ shows the ratio obtained for the location that achieves the maximal gain w.r.t. the serial cost. In most examples, except in MailServer, such maximal gain is achieved in the location that executes the entry method. MailServer uses synchronization in the entry method that leads to a smaller gain. Column $\%_a$ shows the average of the gains achieved for all locations. The average gain ranges from 80.3 % to 31.4 %, except for P2P, which has a smaller gain 14.1 % due to the density of its graph as mentioned above.

8 Conclusions and Related Work

We have presented what is to the best of our knowledge the first static cost analysis for distributed systems which exploits the parallelism among distributed locations in order to infer a more precise estimation of the parallel cost. Our experimental results show that parallel cost analysis can be of great use to know if an application succeeds in exploiting the parallelism of the distributed locations. There is recent work on cost analysis for distributed systems which infers the peak of the *serial* cost [3], i.e., the maximal amount of resources that a distributed component might need along its execution. This notion is different to the parallel cost that we infer since it is still serial; i.e., it accumulates the resource consumption in each component and does not exploit the overall parallelism as we do. Thus, the techniques used to obtain it are also different: the peak cost is obtained by abstracting the information in the queues of the different locations using graphs and finding the cliques in such graphs [3]. The only common part with our analysis is that both rely on an underlying resource analysis for the serial execution that uses cost centers and on a MHP analysis, but the methods used to infer each notion of cost are fundamentally different. This work is improved in [4] to infer the peak for non-cumulative resources that increase and decrease along the execution (e.g., memory usage in the presence of garbage collection). In this sense, the notion of parallel cost makes sense only for cumulative resources since its whole purpose is to observe the efficiency gained by parallelizing the program in terms of resources used (and accumulated) in parallel by distributed components. Recent work has applied type-based amortized analysis for deriving bounds of parallel first-order functional programs [10]. This work differs from our approach in the concurrent programming model, as they do not allow explicit references to locations in the programs and there is no distinction between blocking and non-blocking synchronization. The cost measure is also quite different from the one used in our approach.

To simplify the presentation, we have assumed that the different locations execute one instruction in one cost unit. This is without loss of generality because if they execute at a different speed we can weight their block-level costs according to their relative speeds. We argue that our work is of wide applicability as it can be used in combination with any cost analysis for serial execution which provides us with cost information at the level of the required fragments of code (e.g., [8,9,21]). It can also be directly adopted to infer the cost of parallel programs which spawn several tasks to different processors and then use a join operator to synchronize with the termination of all of them (the latter would be simulated in our case by using a get instruction on all spawned tasks). As future work, we plan to incorporate in the analysis information about the scheduling policy used by the locations (observe that each location could use a different scheduler). In particular, we aim at inferring (partial) orderings among the tasks of each location by means of static analysis.

Analysis and verification techniques for concurrent programs seek finite representations of the program traces to avoid an exponential explosion in the number of traces (see [7] and its references). In this sense, our DFG's provide a finite representation of all traces that may arise in the distributed system. A multithread concurrency model entails an exponential explosion in the number of traces, because task scheduling is preemptive. In contrast, cooperative concurrency as studied in this paper limits is gaining attention both for distributed [11] and for multicore systems [6,20], because the amount of interleaving between tasks that must be considered in analyses is restricted to synchronization points which are explicit in the program.

References

1. WCET tools. http://www.rapitasystems.com/WCET-Tools (2012)
2. Albert, E., Arenas, P., Correas, J., Genaim, S., Gómez-Zamalloa, M., Puebla, G., Román-Díez, G.: Object-Sensitive Cost Analysis for Concurrent Objects. Softw. Test. Verification Reliab. **25**(3), 218–271 (2015)
3. Albert, E., Correas, J., Román-Díez, G.: Peak cost analysis of distributed systems. In: Müller-Olm, M., Seidl, H. (eds.) Static Analysis. LNCS, vol. 8723, pp. 18–33. Springer, Heidelberg (2014)
4. Albert, E., Fernández, J.C., Román-Díez, G.: Non-cumulative resource analysis. In: Baier, C., Tinelli, C. (eds.) TACAS 2015. LNCS, vol. 9035, pp. 85–100. Springer, Heidelberg (2015)
5. Albert, E., Flores-Montoya, A.E., Genaim, S.: Analysis of may-happen-in-parallel in concurrent objects. In: Giese, H., Rosu, G. (eds.) FORTE 2012 and FMOODS 2012. LNCS, vol. 7273, pp. 35–51. Springer, Heidelberg (2012)
6. Brandauer, S., Castegren, E., Clarke, D., Fernandez-Reyes, K., Johnsen, E.B., Pun, K.I., Tarifa, S.L.T., Wrigstad, T., Yang, A.M.: Parallel objects for multicores: a glimpse at the parallel language encore. Formal Methods for Multicore Programming. LNCS, vol. 9104, pp. 1–56. Springer, Heidelberg (2015)
7. Farzan, A., Kincaid, Z., Podelski, A.: Inductive data flow graphs. In: POPL, pp. 129–142. ACM (2013)
8. Gulwani, S., Mehra, K.K., Chilimbi, T.M.: Speed: precise and efficient static estimation of program computational complexity. In: Proceedings of POPL 2009, pp. 127–139. ACM (2009)
9. Hoffmann, J., Aehlig, K., Hofmann, M.: Multivariate amortized resource analysis. In: Proceedings of POPL 2011, pp. 357–370. ACM (2011)

10. Hoffmann, J., Shao, Z.: Automatic static cost analysis for parallel programs. In: Vitek, J. (ed.) ESOP 2015. LNCS, vol. 9032, pp. 132–157. Springer, Heidelberg (2015)
11. Johnsen, E.B., Hähnle, R., Schäfer, J., Schlatte, R., Steffen, M.: ABS: A core language for abstract behavioral specification. In: Aichernig, B.K., de Boer, F.S., Bonsangue, M.M. (eds.) Formal Methods for Components and Objects. LNCS, vol. 6957, pp. 142–164. Springer, Heidelberg (2011)
12. Lee, J.K., Palsberg, J., Majumdar, R.: Complexity results for may-happen-in-parallel analysis. Manuscript (2010)
13. Milanova, A., Rountev, A., Ryder, B.G.: Parameterized object sensitivity for points-to analysis for java. ACM Trans. Softw. Eng. Methodol. **14**, 1–41 (2005)
14. Shapiro, M., Horwitz, S.: Fast and accurate flow-insensitive points-to analysis. In: POPL 1997: 24th ACM SIGPLAN-SIGACT Symposium on Principles of Programming Languages, pp. 1–14. ACM, Paris, France, January 1997
15. Smaragdakis, Y., Bravenboer, M., Lhoták, O.: Pick your contexts well: understanding object-sensitivity. In: Proceedings of POPL 2011, pp. 17–30. ACM (2011)
16. Sridharan, M., Bodík, R.: Refinement-based context-sensitive points-to analysis for Java. In: PLDI, pp. 387–400 (2006)
17. Sutter, H., Larus, J.R.: Software and the concurrency revolution. ACM Queue **3**(7), 54–62 (2005)
18. Tarjan, R.E.: Fast algorithms for solving path problems. J. ACM **28**(3), 594–614 (1981)
19. Wegbreit, B.: Mechanical program analysis. Commun. ACM **18**(9), 528–539 (1975)
20. Yi, J., Sadowski, C., Freund, S.N., Flanagan, C.: Cooperative concurrency for a multicore world. In: Khurshid, S., Sen, K. (eds.) RV 2011. LNCS, vol. 7186, pp. 342–344. Springer, Heidelberg (2012)
21. Zuleger, F., Gulwani, S., Sinn, M., Veith, H.: Bound analysis of imperative programs with the size-change abstraction. In: Yahav, E. (ed.) Static Analysis. LNCS, vol. 6887, pp. 280–297. Springer, Heidelberg (2011)

A Forward Analysis for Recurrent Sets

Alexey Bakhirkin[1], Josh Berdine[2(✉)], and Nir Piterman[1]

[1] Department of Computer Science, University of Leicester, Leicester, UK
{ab643,nir.piterman}@le.ac.uk
[2] Microsoft Research, Cambridge, UK
jjb@microsoft.com

Abstract. Non-termination of structured imperative programs is primarily due to infinite loops. An important class of non-terminating loop behaviors can be characterized using the notion of recurrent sets. A recurrent set is a set of states from which execution of the loop cannot or might not escape. Existing analyses that infer recurrent sets to our knowledge rely on one of: the combination of forward and backward analyses, quantifier elimination, or SMT-solvers. We propose a purely forward abstract interpretation–based analysis that can be used together with a possibly complicated abstract domain where none of the above is readily available. The analysis searches for a recurrent set of every individual loop in a program by building a graph of abstract states and analyzing it in a novel way. The graph is searched for a witness of a recurrent set that takes the form of what we call a recurrent component which is somewhat similar to the notion of an end component in a Markov decision process.

1 Introduction

Termination is a fundamental property of software routines. The majority of code is required to terminate, e.g., dispatch routines of device drivers or other event-driven code, GPU programs – and the existence of non-terminating behaviors is a severe bug that might freeze a device, an entire system, or cause a multi-region cloud service disruption [1]. The problem of proving *termination* has seen much attention lately [15,16,27] but the techniques are sound and hence necessarily incomplete. That is, failure to prove termination does not imply the existence of non-terminating behaviors. Therefore, proving *non-termination* is an interesting complementary problem.

Several modern analyses [11,13,14] characterize non-terminating behaviors of programs or fragments of programs by a notion of *recurrent set*, i.e., a set of input states from which execution of the program or fragment cannot or might not escape (there are different flavors of recurrent sets). The analyses that can infer recurrent sets to our knowledge rely on one of: the combination of forward and backward analyses [13], quantifier elimination [11,14], or SMT-solvers [12]. We propose a purely forward abstract interpretation–based analysis that can be used with a potentially complicated abstract domain where none of the above is readily available. In our approach, we consider structured imperative programs

S. Blazy and T. Jensen (Eds.): SAS 2015, LNCS 9291, pp. 293–311, 2015.
DOI: 10.1007/978-3-662-48288-9_17

without recursion where loops are the only source of non-termination. Our analysis searches for what we call a *universal* recurrent set (that cannot be escaped) of every individual loop in a program by building and analyzing a graph of its abstract states. The main challenge of a forward approach is that while recurrent sets can be characterized by greatest fixed points of *backward transformers* (and this gives an intuition into the success of the approach [13] combining forward and backward analyses), we are not aware of a way to characterize them in terms of forward transformers. Instead, we produce a *condition* for a set of states to be recurrent and systematically explore the state space of a program searching for satisfying sets of abstract states. Our approach is similar to the one of Brockschmidt et al. [12], but the analysis of the state graph that we employ is novel. The graph is searched for a witness of a recurrent set that takes the form of what we call a *recurrent component* which is somewhat similar to the notion of an *end component* in a Markov decision process [8].

Note that finding a recurrent set is a *sub-problem* of proving non-termination. To prove non-termination, we would need to show that a recurrent set is reachable from the program entry. Also, some divergent behaviors do not fit the form discussed in this paper, and a non-terminating loop need not necessarily have a universal recurrent set.

2 Background

We define the analysis for a simple structured language without procedures. For a set of *atomic statements* A ranged over by a, statements C of the language are built as follows:

$C ::= a$	atomic statement
$\mid C_1 \; ; C_2$	sequential composition: executes C_1 and then C_2
$\mid C_1 + C_2$	branch: non-deterministically branches to either C_1 or C_2
$\mid C^*$	loop: iterated sequential composition of ≥ 0 copies of C

We assume that A contains the passive statement *skip* and an assumption statement $[\theta]$ for each state formula θ, and that the language of state formulas is closed under negation. Informally, assumption statements work by filtering out the violating executions. Standard conditionals `if(`θ`)` C_1 `else` C_2 can be expressed by $([\theta]; C_1) + ([\neg\theta]; C_2)$. Similarly, loops `while(`$\theta$`)` C can be expressed by $([\theta]; C)^* \; ; [\neg\theta]$.

2.1 Concrete Semantics

We use 1 and 0 to mean logical truth and falsity respectively. For a set S, we use Δ_S to mean the diagonal relation $\Delta_S = \{(s, s) \mid s \in S\}$. For a relation T, we use $T(s, s')$ to mean $(s, s') \in T$. We use $\circ$ for right composition of relations: $T_2 \circ T_1 = \{(s, s'') \mid \exists s'. \, (s, s') \in T_1 \wedge (s', s'') \in T_2\}$. For a function F, we use lfp F to mean its least fixed point. We use Kleene's 3-valued logic [21] to represent truth values of state formulas in abstract, and sets of concrete, states. It uses a set of three values $\mathcal{K} = \{1, 0, {}^1\!/_2\}$ meaning *true*, *false*, and *maybe* respectively. $\mathcal{K}$ is arranged in partial *information order* $\sqsubseteq_\mathcal{K}$, s.t. 1 and 0 are incomparable, $1 \sqsubseteq_\mathcal{K} {}^1\!/_2$, and $0 \sqsubseteq_\mathcal{K} {}^1\!/_2$. For $k_1, k_2 \in \mathcal{K}$ the least upper bound $\sqcup_\mathcal{K}$ is defined s.t. $k_1 \sqcup_\mathcal{K} k_2 = k_1$ if $k_1 = k_2$, and ${}^1\!/_2$ otherwise.

Let $\mathcal{U}$ be the set of all *memory* states. The concrete domain of the analysis is the powerset $\mathcal{P}(\mathcal{U})$ with least element $\varnothing$, greatest element $\mathcal{U}$, partial order $\subseteq$, and join $\cup$. This particular concrete domain is used for clarity of presentation, and another domain can be used if needed. A state formula θ denotes a set of states $[\![\theta]\!] \subseteq \mathcal{U}$. We say that a state s *satisfies* θ if $s \in [\![\theta]\!]$. For a state formula θ and a set of states S, the *value* of θ over S is defined by: $\mathit{eval}(\theta, S) = 1$ if $S \subseteq [\![\theta]\!]$; $\mathit{eval}(\theta, S) = 0$ if $S \cap [\![\theta]\!] = \varnothing$; $\mathit{eval}(\theta, S) = {}^1\!/_2$ otherwise. That is, a formula evaluates to 1 in a *set* of states, if all states in the set satisfy the formula, to 0 if none satisfy the formula, and to ${}^1\!/_2$ if some of the states satisfy the formula and some do not.

The semantics of a statement C is a relation $[\![C]\!] \subseteq \mathcal{U} \times \mathcal{U}$. For a state s, $[\![C]\!](s, s')$ holds for every state s' that it is possible to reach by executing C from s. For an atomic statement a, we assume that $[\![a]\!]$ is pre-defined. Then $[\![C]\!]$ is defined as follows:

$$
\begin{aligned}
[\![\mathit{skip}]\!] &= \Delta_\mathcal{U} & [\![C_1 \,;\, C_2]\!] &= [\![C_2]\!] \circ [\![C_1]\!] \\
[\![[\theta]]\!] &= \{(s, s) \mid s \in [\![\theta]\!]\} & [\![C_1 + C_2]\!] &= [\![C_1]\!] \cup [\![C_2]\!] \\
& & [\![C^*]\!] &= \mathrm{lfp}\,\lambda X.\, \Delta_\mathcal{U} \cup (X \circ [\![C]\!])
\end{aligned}
$$

If for a state s, there exists no state s' s.t. $[\![C]\!](s, s')$, we say that the execution of C *diverges* from s. For "normal" programs, this definition agrees with the common one based on a small-step semantics: all traces starting from s are infinite, and there exists at least one. That is, if assumption statements appear only at the start of a branch or at the entry or exit of a loop (they cannot be used as normal atomic statements):

$$C ::= a \mid C_1 \,;\, C_2 \mid ([\varphi] \,;\, C_1) + ([\psi] \,;\, C_2) \mid ([\psi] \,;\, C)^* \,;\, [\varphi]$$

and branch and loop guard assumptions are exhaustive: $\varphi \vee \psi = 1$, then the only way for an execution to diverge is to get stuck in an infinite loop.

As standard, we define a *state transformer*, *post*, that for a statement C and a set of states S, gives the states a program might reach after executing C from a state in S: $\mathit{post}(C, S) = \{s' \mid \exists s \in S.\, [\![C]\!](s, s')\}$.

In what follows, we focus on the loop statement:

$$C_\mathrm{loop} = ([\psi_\mathrm{ent}] \,;\, C_\mathrm{body})^* \,;\, [\varphi_\mathrm{exit}] \tag{1}$$

where C_body is the *loop body*; if ψ_ent holds the execution may enter the loop body; if φ_exit holds the execution may exit the loop; and $\psi_\mathrm{ent} \vee \varphi_\mathrm{exit} = 1$. What is important for us is that this form of loop has a single point serving as both the entry and the exit. As currently formulated, our analysis relies on this property, although we anticipate that more complicated control flow graphs can be analyzed in a similar way.

For a loop as in (1), a *universal recurrent set* is a set $R_\forall$, s.t.,

$$R_\forall \subseteq [\![\neg\varphi_{\text{exit}}]\!] \qquad \forall s \in R_\forall.\, (\forall s' \in \boldsymbol{\mathcal{U}}.\, [\![C_{\text{body}}]\!](s, s') \Rightarrow s' \in R_\forall)$$

These are states that *must* cause non-termination, i.e., must cause the computation to stay inside the loop forever. Chen et al. [13] call a similar notion *closed recurrence set.* There is also a related notion of an *existential, or open, recurrent set*, i.e., a set of states that *may* cause non-termination, but it is not discussed here. Thus, in what follows, by just *recurrent set* we mean universal recurrent set.

Lemma 1. *For a loop as in* (1), *the set* $R \subseteq \boldsymbol{\mathcal{U}}$ *is universally recurrent iff* $\mathit{eval}(\neg\varphi_{\text{exit}}, R) = 1$ *and* $\mathit{post}(C_{\text{body}}, R) \subseteq R$.

Proof. Follows from the definitions of *eval*, *post*, and universal recurrent set. □

2.2 Recurrent Sets in the Abstract

It is standard for forward program analyses to introduce an abstract domain $\mathcal{D}$ with least element $\bot_\mathcal{D}$, greatest element $\top_\mathcal{D}$, partial order $\sqsubseteq_\mathcal{D}$, and join $\sqcup_\mathcal{D}$. Every *element* of the abstract domain $d \in \mathcal{D}$ represents the set of concrete states $\gamma(d) \subseteq \boldsymbol{\mathcal{U}}$. Then, over-approximate versions of *post* and *eval*, are introduced, s.t. for a statement C, state formula θ and abstract element d,

$$\gamma(\mathit{post}^\mathcal{D}(C, d)) \supseteq \mathit{post}(C, \gamma(d)) \qquad \mathit{eval}^\mathcal{D}(\theta, d) \sqsupseteq_\mathcal{K} \mathit{eval}(\theta, \gamma(d))$$

We require that $\mathit{eval}^\mathcal{D}$ is homomorphic: for a formula θ and $d_1, d_2 \in \mathcal{D}$, $d_1 \sqsubseteq d_2 \Rightarrow \mathit{eval}^\mathcal{D}(\theta, d_1) \sqsubseteq_\mathcal{K} \mathit{eval}^\mathcal{D}(\theta, d_2)$. Normally, $\mathit{eval}^\mathcal{D}$ is given for atomic statements, and for arbitrary formulas it is defined by induction over the formula structure, using 3-valued logical operators, possibly over-approximate with respect to $\sqsubseteq_\mathcal{K}$.

Theorem 1. *For a loop as in* (1), *an abstract domain* $\mathcal{D}$, *and an element* $d \in \mathcal{D}$, *if* $\mathit{eval}^\mathcal{D}(\neg\varphi_{\text{exit}}, d) = 1$ *and* $\mathit{post}^\mathcal{D}(C_{\text{body}}, d) \sqsubseteq_\mathcal{D} d$, *then* $\gamma(d)$ *is universally recurrent.*

For proofs, please, see the companion technical report [9].

Note that in Theorem 1, the post-condition is taken with respect to the loop body *without* the preceding assumption statement.

3 Finding a Universal Recurrent Set

We define our analysis for a finite powerset domain $\mathcal{P}(\mathcal{L})$, where the underlying set $\mathcal{L}$ of abstract elements is partially ordered by $\sqsubseteq_\mathcal{L}$ with least element $\bot_\mathcal{L}$. For example, in a numeric analysis, $\mathcal{L}$ may be the domain of intervals or polyhedra [17]. We call the elements of $\mathcal{L}$ *abstract states.* We assume that $\mathcal{P}(\mathcal{L})$ uses the Hoare order, and that concretization is defined as shown below. For $L, L_1, L_2 \subseteq \mathcal{L}$,

$$\gamma(L) = \bigcup \{\gamma(l) \mid l \in L\} \qquad L_1 \sqsubseteq_{\mathcal{P}(\mathcal{L})} L_2 \text{ iff } \forall l_1 \in L_1.\, \exists l_2 \in L_2.\, l_1 \sqsubseteq_\mathcal{L} l_2$$

We assume that evaluation function $eval^{\mathcal{P}(\mathcal{L})}$ and forward transformers $post^{\mathcal{P}(\mathcal{L})}$ for all statements (e.g. C_{body} in (1)) are given. We assume that $\bot_{\mathcal{L}}$ represents unreachability, and is transformed and evaluated precisely: $\gamma(\bot_{\mathcal{L}}) = \varnothing$, $post^{\mathcal{P}(\mathcal{L})}(C, \{\bot_{\mathcal{L}}\}) = \varnothing$, and $eval^{\mathcal{P}(\mathcal{L})}(\theta, \{\bot_{\mathcal{L}}\}) = 1$. Then, we define *pointwise* transformers $eval^{\sharp}$ and $post^{\sharp}$ as follows. For $L \subseteq \mathcal{L}$, statement C, and state formula θ,

$$post^{\sharp}(C, L) = \bigcup_{l \in L} post^{\mathcal{P}(\mathcal{L})}(C, \{l\}) \qquad eval^{\sharp}(\theta, L) = \bigsqcup_{l \in L}{}_{\mathcal{K}}\, eval^{\mathcal{P}(\mathcal{L})}(\theta, \{l\})$$

Note that $post^{\sharp}$ and $eval^{\sharp}$ are sound over-approximations of concrete *post* and *eval*. Also, if $post^{\mathcal{P}(\mathcal{L})}$ and $eval^{\mathcal{P}(\mathcal{L})}$ distribute over set union, then $post^{\sharp} = post^{\mathcal{P}(\mathcal{L})}$ and $eval^{\sharp} = eval^{\mathcal{P}(\mathcal{L})}$. For a single state $l \in \mathcal{L}$, we overload $post^{\sharp}(C, l)$ to mean $post^{\sharp}(C, \{l\})$ and $eval^{\sharp}(\theta, l)$ to mean $eval^{\sharp}(\theta, \{l\})$. We use $[\theta, l]^{\sharp}$ and $[\theta, L]^{\sharp}$ to mean $post^{\sharp}([\theta], l)$ and $post^{\sharp}([\theta], L)$ respectively.

We use a powerset domain for the following reason. Only a subset of the loop invariant belongs to a recurrent set, so there needs to be a mechanism in the abstract domain to partition the "interesting" and "not interesting" states. Therefore, we search for a recurrent set in the form of a *set of* abstract elements. We use Theorem 1 to show soundness: $\mathcal{P}(\mathcal{L})$ is $\mathcal{D}$ for its purposes; $post^{\sharp}$ and $eval^{\sharp}$ are $post^{\mathcal{D}}$ and $eval^{\mathcal{D}}$.

3.1 Idea of the Algorithm

```
while x ≥ 1:
  if x = 60:  x ← 50
  x ← x + 1
  if x = 100:  x ← 0
```

Fig. 1. Program for Example 1.

For a loop as in (1), if we find $X \subseteq \mathcal{L}$, s.t. $eval^{\sharp}(\neg\varphi_{\text{exit}}, X) = 1$ and $post^{\sharp}(C_{\text{body}}, X) \sqsubseteq X$, then $\gamma(X)$ is *definitely* a recurrent set. The idea is to explore the state space of the program with forward analysis until such an X is found. We proceed as follows. Separately for every loop, we build a graph where vertices are abstract elements, or *states*, from $\mathcal{L}$, all representing sets of concrete states at the loop head. We initialize the graph with some set of states $I \subseteq \mathcal{L}$ and then repeatedly apply the transformer for the whole loop body, $post^{\sharp}(C_{\text{body}}, \cdot)$, to the vertices and add the elements of the resulting set to the graph as successors. Our experiments suggest that in many cases a subset X of vertices satisfying the conditions of Theorem 1 will emerge as a result. To be able to efficiently find such a subset, we remember which elements are related w.r.t. abstract order $\sqsubseteq$, as a second kind of edges in the graph. Note that in case of nested loops, we analyze inner and outer loops separately; when analyzing the outer one, the effect of the inner needs to be summarized in an over-approximating way.

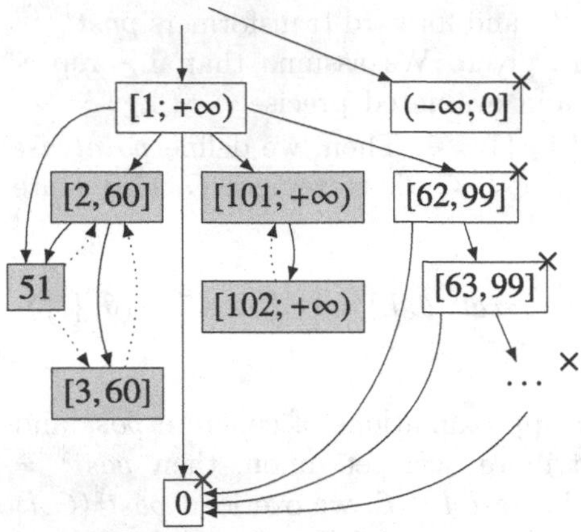

Fig. 2. Graph of the states of the program in Fig. 1.

We use a number of heuristics to help the analysis. First, we try to distinguish states that took different paths through the loop body. Currently, we take a simplistic approach: when possible, we prefer powerset domains where join is set union, s.t. states produced by different branches are not joined, and $post^\sharp(C_1 + C_2, l) = post^\sharp(C_1, l) \cup post^\sharp(C_2, l)$. If needed, a more involved trace partitioning [24] could be introduced instead. Second, with a similar intent, we compute the post-conditions with respect to a modified loop body $C_{\text{body}}{}' = C_{\text{body}}$; $([\psi_{\text{ent}}] + [\neg\psi_{\text{ent}}])$. This is sound since in the concrete case, for every set $S \subseteq \mathcal{U}$, $post(C_{\text{body}}{}', S) = post(C_{\text{body}}, S)$. Also, for a set of initial states I, we initialize the graph with a set $I' = [\psi_{\text{ent}}, I]^\sharp \cup [\neg\psi_{\text{ent}}, I]^\sharp$. This is helpful when (as is often the case) there is a specific path through the loop body that infinite traces take. The heuristics introduce control-flow distinctions and enable states taking such path to be partitioned from others. But these heuristics may not be helpful when additional distinguishing power is needed for the data in states, e.g., when certain kinds of non-determinism are present, when non-termination depends on the properties of mathematical functions that the program implements, or when the abstract domain is not expressive enough to capture the states that take the interesting control paths.

Example 1. Consider the loop shown in pseudocode in Fig. 1. The loop does not terminate for some inputs, and the maximal recurrent set is $(1 \leq x \leq 60) \vee (x \geq 100)$. Let us informally demonstrate how the algorithm that we propose works, assuming that x ranges over integers and using intervals to represent its values. Since we do not know the initial value of x, we start with a graph consisting of a pair of states: $\{(-\infty; 0], [1; +\infty)\}$ – one represents the loop condition and another represents its complement. We then start adding new states to the graph by computing $post^\sharp$ as described above, s.t. paths through the loop body are represented in a post-condition of a state by different disjuncts. For example, let us see what happens to $[1; +\infty)$ when it enters the loop. In line 2, we consider three cases. If $x < 60$, then the conditional body in line 2 is skipped, x is incremented at line 3, the conditional body in line 4 is skipped, and the output state is $[2, 60]$. If $x = 60$, the conditional body in line 2 sets x to 50, at line 3 x is incremented, the conditional body in line 4 is skipped, and the output state is 51. If $x > 60$, the conditional body at line 2 is skipped and at line 3 x is incremented to $[62; +\infty)$. Then, if $x < 100$, the conditional body at line 4 is skipped, and the output state is $[62, 99]$. If $x = 100$, the conditional body at line 4 sets x to 0, and the output state is 0. If $x > 100$, the conditional body at line 4 is skipped, and the output state is $[101; +\infty)$. Thus, $post^\sharp(C_{\text{body}}, [1; +\infty)) = \{[3, 60], 51, [62, 99], 0, [101; +\infty)\}$. We add these states to the graph and continue the exploration. Figure 2 shows a state graph that could be produced this way after a number of steps. In the graph, boxes represent states, and solid edges represent post-conditions. Note that in the graph, there exists a subset of states $X = \{[2, 60], [101; +\infty)\}$ has the desired property: $eval^\sharp(\neg\varphi_{\text{exit}}, X) = 1$ and $post^\sharp(C_{\text{body}}, X) \sqsubseteq X$, thus $\gamma(X)$ is a recurrent set. In what follows, we discuss how to efficiently find such subset of states if it exists. We revisit this example in Sect. 4.

For some domains (e.g., for shape analysis with 3-valued logic [26]), the analysis benefits from case splits that $post^\sharp$ naturally performs. For example, when a program traverses a potentially cyclic list, $post^\sharp$ would consider a definitely cyclic list as a separate case. If the abstraction is expressive enough, the cyclic list case will appear as a separate vertex and become part of a recurrent set.

Finally, the choice of the set of initial states I may matter. When the abstract domain is finite (and no widening is required) and the loop is not nested, we initialize the graph with the states that reach the loop via the rest of the program, i.e., produced by the standard forward analysis of the preceding part of the program. In this case, the analysis will explore all the states reachable at the head of the loop, and the success relies only on how refined the resulting graph is. When the abstract domain is infinite (e.g., for intervals or polyhedra) or for inner nested loops, we normally initialize the graph with a pre-fixpoint of $post^\sharp$. That is, we assume that initially, a standard forward analysis is run to produce a pre-fixpoint for every loop. Starting with a state below (w.r.t. $\sqsubseteq$) a pre-fixpoint makes it less likely that the analysis terminates, as our procedure does not include widening. Starting with a state above a pre-fixpoint is more likely to drive the search towards the states unreachable from the program entry. Note that it is *sound* to start with any set of states, and we sometimes use $\top$.

Our procedure is sound (by Theorems 1 and 2), but incomplete: if we do not find a recurrent set after a number of steps, we do not know the reason: whether the loop does not have a universal recurrent set; or the abstraction and $post^\sharp$ are not expressive enough; or we did not explore enough states. And for an infinite domain, the procedure might not terminate. So, we perform the exploration incrementally: we proceed breadth-first until some recurrent set is found. Then, we may decide to stop or to continue the search for a larger recurrent set.

3.2 Abstract State Graph

For a loop as in (1), an *abstract state graph* is a graph $G = \langle V, E_p, E_c \rangle$, s.t.,

- V is finite non-empty set of vertices which are abstract elements, or *states*: $V \subseteq \mathcal{L}$. All states belong to the loop entry location.
- There are two independent sets of edges: $E_c, E_p \subseteq V \times V$.
- E_p is a set of *post-edges*. For every state $l \in V$, *one* of the following holds:
  (i) there are no outgoing post-edges: $(\{l\} \times V) \cap E_p = \varnothing$; or

(ii) ψ_{ent} may hold in l, $eval^\sharp(\psi_{\text{ent}}, l) \neq 0$; post-condition of l with respect to the loop body is not empty, $post^\sharp(C_{\text{body}}, l) \neq \varnothing$; the whole post-condition is in the graph, $post^\sharp(C_{\text{body}}, l) \subseteq V$, and connected to l by post-edges, $(\{l\} \times V) \cap E_p = \{l\} \times post^\sharp(C_{\text{body}}, l)$; or

(iii) ψ_{ent} may hold in l, $eval^\sharp(\psi_{\text{ent}}, l) \neq 0$; post-condition of l is empty, $post^\sharp(C_{\text{body}}, l) = \varnothing$; l has $\bot_{\mathcal{L}}$ as the only post-successor, $\{l\} \times V \cap E_p = \{(l, \bot_{\mathcal{L}})\}$; and $\bot_{\mathcal{L}}$ has a post-self-loop $(\bot_{\mathcal{L}}, \bot_{\mathcal{L}}) \in E_p$.

– E_c is a set of *containment-edges*. For $l_1, l_2 \in V, (l_1, l_2) \in E_c \Leftrightarrow (l_1 \neq l_2 \wedge l_1 \sqsubseteq l_2)$.

This forbids self-loops. Due to properties of $\sqsubseteq$, G may not have containment cycles.

Note that this is similar to the notion of *termination graph* of [12]. For a loop as in (1), a state graph $G = \langle V, E_p, E_c \rangle$, a state $l \in V$, and a set of states $L \subseteq V$, let

$$post^G(l) = \{l' \in V \mid (l, l') \in E_p\} \qquad post^G(L) = \{l' \in V \mid \exists l \in L.\ (l, l') \in E_p\}$$

For a loop as in (1) and a graph $G = \langle V, E_p, E_c \rangle$, a *recurrent component* is a set of states $R \subseteq V$, s.t. for every state $l \in R$, l cannot exit the loop, $eval^\sharp(\neg\varphi_{\text{exit}}, l) = 1$, l has at least one outgoing edge, $\exists l' \in V.\ (l, l') \in E_p \cup E_c$, and *at least one* is true:

(i) l has a containment-edge into R, $\exists l' \in R.\ (l, l') \in E_c$; or
(ii) the outgoing post-edges of l lead exclusively into R, $post^G(l) \neq \varnothing \wedge post^G(l) \subseteq R$.

Lemma 2. *The union of two recurrent components is a recurrent component.*

Lemma 3. *In a state graph G, there exists a unique maximal (possibly, empty) recurrent component.*

Proof. Lemma 2 follows from the definition of recurrent component. Lemma 3 follows from Lemma 2 and finiteness of G. □

Theorem 2. *For a loop as in* (1) *and a state graph $G = \langle V, E_p, E_c \rangle$ we say $X \subseteq V$ is* fully closed *if $eval^\sharp(\neg\varphi_{\text{exit}}, X) = 1$, $\forall l \in X.\ post^G(l) \neq \varnothing$, and $post^\sharp(C_{\text{body}}, X) \sqsubseteq X$. Note that in this case, $\gamma(X)$ is a recurrent set. Then, for every state graph G:*

(i) For a recurrent component R, there exists a fully closed $X \subseteq R$ s.t. $\gamma(X) = \gamma(R)$.
(ii) For a fully closed X, there exists a recurrent component $R \supseteq X$, s.t. $\gamma(R) = \gamma(X)$.

3.3 The Algorithm

The algorithm, whose main body is shown in pseudocode in Fig. 3, is applied individually to every loop in a program. Initially, we call *FindFirst* giving it the set of elements $I \subseteq \mathcal{L}$ to start the search from (normally, a loop invariant). After performing initialization, *FindFirst* calls *FindNext* once. *FindNext* contains a loop in which we build the state graph $G = \langle V, E_p, E_c \rangle$. In every iteration, proceeding in breadth-first order, we pick from the worklist F a state without post-edges and add its successors to the graph, together with relevant post- and containment-edges. This happens in lines 12–17 of Fig. 3; new states and post-edges are created by *MakeStates* shown in Fig. 4. We choose not to explore the successors of a state belonging to a recurrent component (line 13) even though when $post^\sharp$ is non-monotonic, they might lie outside the recurrent component. Similarly, we do not explore the successors of a must-exiting state, even if ψ_{ent} may hold in it. If adding new states and edges could create a larger recurrent component, we call *FindRecComp* to search for it (lines 20–21). If a new recurrent component is found, we return 1, and *Rec* contains those states of the component found so far that have no outgoing containment-edges (lines 22–27). If we wish to find a larger recurrent component, we can call *FindNext* again to resume the search. If the search terminates and no new recurrent component can be found, the procedure returns 0.

For every abstract state $l \in V$, we maintain the *status* as follows.

The state $l \in V$ *must exit*, $mustE(l) = 1$, if all executions starting in it exit the loop, i.e., if it is definitely the case that for every concrete state $s \in \gamma(l)$ the loop eventually terminates. We mark l as must-exiting if

(i) $eval^\sharp(\psi_{\text{ent}}, l) = 0$; or if
(ii) All post-successors of l are already must-exiting; or if
(iii) There exists a larger (w.r.t. $\sqsubseteq$) state that is already must-exiting.

The state $l \in V$ *may exit*, $mayE(l) = 1$, if we know that it cannot be part of a recurrent component. We mark l as may-exiting if

(i) it is must-exiting or if $eval^\sharp(\neg\varphi_{\text{exit}}, l) \neq 1$; or if
(ii) $post^\sharp$ is monotonic and l has a post-successor that is already may-exiting; or if
(iii) $post^\sharp$ is monotonic, and there exists a smaller (w.r.t. $\sqsubseteq$) already may-exiting state.

The state $l \in V$ is *recurrent*, $rec(l) = 1$, if it is a part of a recurrent component. If $post^\sharp$ is monotonic, we also mark as recurrent all successors of a recurrent state. Note that here, the term *recurrent* is overloaded. For a recurrent *state* $l \in V$, $\gamma(l)$ is in general not a recurrent *set* itself, but is included in some recurrent set.

Otherwise, the state $l \in V$ is *unknown*, $unk(l) = 1$, i.e., $unk(l) \Rightarrow (\neg mayE(l) \wedge \neg rec(l))$. This is the case if $eval^\sharp(\neg\varphi_{\text{exit}}, l) = 1$, and the state may potentially be a part of a recurrent component, but is not part of the recurrent component found so far.

Lemma 4. *May-exiting states cannot be part of a recurrent component.*

When searching for a recurrent component, it is only necessary to consider unknown and recurrent states, therefore every step of the algorithm only creates new containment-edges between unknown states or from an unknown to a recurrent state.

```
 1 │ while   G = ⟨V, E_p, E_c⟩, F, Rec
 2 │
 3 │ proc FindFirst(I):
 4 │    for l ∈ L:
 5 │       mayE(l) ← mustE(l) ← rec(l) ← 0;  unk(l) ← 1
 6 │    MakeStates(I, nil)
 7 │    F ← {l ∈ V | ¬mustE(l) ∧ l ≠ ⊥_L}
 8 │    FindNext()
 9 │
10 │ proc FindNext():
11 │    while F ≠ ∅:
12 │       l ← first(F);  F ← F \ {l}
13 │       if mustE(l) ∨ rec(l): continue
14 │       newPost ← MakeStates(post^♯(C_body, l), l)
15 │       E_c^+ ←{(l', l'') ∈ V × V | unk(l') ∧ (unk(l'') ∨ rec(l'')) ∧ l' ⊑ l'' ∧
         │              (l'' ∈ newPost ∨ l' ∈ newPost)}
16 │       E_c ← E_c ∪ E_c^+
17 │       F ← F ∪ {l' ∈ newPost | ¬mustE(l') ∧ l' ≠ ⊥_L}
18 │       PropagateStatus()
19 │       R ← ∅
20 │       if (newPost = ∅ ∧ (∀l' ∈ post^G(l). unk(l') ∨ rec(l'))) ∨ E_c^+ ≠ ∅:
21 │          R ← FindRecComp()
22 │       if R ≠ ∅:
23 │          for l ∈ R: rec(l) ← 1;  unk(l) ← 0
24 │          PropagateStatus()
25 │          Rec' ← Rec
26 │          Rec ← {l' ∈ V | rec(l') ∧ ({(l', l'') | l'' ∈ V ∧ rec(l'')} ∩ E_c = ∅)}
27 │          if (Rec ≠ Rec'): return 1
28 │    return 0
```

Fig. 3. Main algorithm

Note that when new states or edges are added to the graph, or the status of an existing state changes, we make a call to *PropagateStatus*. For brevity, we do not show the pseudocode, and only informally describe its effect. *PropagateStatus* propagates the statuses through the edges of the graph according to the following rules. For a state l:

1. if $post^G(l) \neq \emptyset \wedge \forall l' \in post^G(l).\ mustE(l')$, then $mustE(l)$
2. if $mustE(l)$, then $\forall l'.\ (l', l) \in E_c \Rightarrow mustE(l')$
3. if $post^G(l) \neq \emptyset \wedge \forall l' \in post^G(l).\ rec(l')$, then $rec(l)$
4. if $rec(l)$, then $\forall l'.\ (l', l) \in E_c \Rightarrow rec(l')$

Additionally, if $post^♯$ is monotonic:

5. if $\exists l' \in post^G(l).\ mayE(l')$, then $mayE(l)$
6. if $mayE(l)$, then $\forall l'.\ (l, l') \in E_c \Rightarrow mayE(l')$
7. if $rec(l)$, then $\forall l' \in post^G(l).\ rec(l')$
8. if $mustE(l)$, then $\forall l' \in post^G(l).\ mustE(l')$

```
proc MakeStates(L,l_p):
  N ← ∅
  if L = ∅: L′ ← {⊥_ℒ}
  else: L′ ← [ψ_ent, L]♯ ∪ [¬ψ_ent, L]♯
  for l ∈ L′:
    if l_p ≠ nil: E_p ← E_p ∪ (l_p, l)
    if l ∉ V:
      if eval♯(ψ_ent, l) = 0:
        unk(l) ← 0
        mayE(l) ← mustE(l) ← 1
      elif eval♯(¬φ_exit, l) ≠ 1:
        unk(l) ← 0
        mayE(l) ← 1
      V ← V ∪ l
      N ← N ∪ l
      if l = ⊥_ℒ:
        E_p ← E_p ∪ {(l, l)}
  return N
```

Fig. 4. Adding new states. New states are unknown unless marked otherwise.

```
proc FindRecComp():
  C ← {l ∈ V | unk(l)}
  R ← {l ∈ V | rec(l)}
  While 1:
    C⁻ ← {l ∈ C |
          {(l, l′) | l′ ∈ C ∪ R} ∩ E_c = ∅ ∧
          (post^G(l) = ∅ ∨ post^G(l) ⊈ C ∪ R)}
    if C⁻ = ∅: break
    C ← C \ C⁻
  return C
```

Fig. 5. Finding a recurrent component

Rules 1 and 2 are derived from the definition of must-exiting state. Rules 3 and 4 mark as recurrent those states that would be included in a recurrent component next time *FindRecComp* is called. Rules 5 and 6 are derived from the definition of may-exiting states. Rule 7 is for the case when for some l, first its post-condition is computed, and later, l is marked as recurrent by rule 4. If $post^\sharp$ is monotonic, the successors of l would eventually become part of a recurrent component. Similarly, rule 8 is for the case when for some l, first its post-condition is computed, and later, l is marked as must-exiting by rule 2. If $post^\sharp$ is monotonic, the successors of l would eventually be marked as must-exiting. This is not necessary for the correctness: every state that *PropagateStatus* marks as may- or must-exiting, cannot be part of a recurrent component, and every state that it marks as recurrent would eventually become a part of a recurrent component. But this allows to eliminate unknown states earlier, create fewer containment-edges, and search for recurrent component in a smaller portion of the graph.

Figure 4 shows the procedure *MakeStates* that adds new states to the graph. Given a set of abstract elements $L \subseteq \mathcal{L}$ and a predecessor state $l_p \in V$, it adds abstract states corresponding to L to the graph and creates post-edges from l_p to them. Every $l \in L$ is split into a pair of states with $[\cdot]^\sharp$, then is possibly marked as may- or must- exiting depending on the values of φ_{exit} and ψ_{ent} and added to the graph together with a post-edge from l_p. The procedure returns the set N of new states produced from L that were not present in the graph before.

Figure 5 shows the procedure *FindRecComp* that finds a recurrent component among the unknown states. It is called from *FindNext* when a new containment-edge is created or a state is discovered such that all its outgoing post-edges lead to existing unknown or recurrent states (i.e., when a larger recurrent component could emerge). It starts the search with the whole set of unknowns as the candidate C and iteratively removes the states C^- that make the candidate violate the definition of recurrent component. Note that *FindRecComp* works incrementally: assuming that R is a set of states that are currently marked as recurrent (i.e., R is the recurrent component found so far), the procedure produces a set C, s.t. $C \cup R$ is a recurrent component. In general, C might not be a recurrent component by itself.

Theorem 3. *For an abstract state graph $G = \langle V, E_p, E_c \rangle$ and* some *recurrent component $R \subseteq V$, FindRecComp produces $C \subseteq V$ such that $C \cup R$ is the maximal recurrent component of G.*

4 Examples

In this section, we demonstrate how our analysis can be successfully applied to numeric and heap-manipulating programs. Examples 1 and 2 present **Numeric Programs**. Program variables range over integers, and we use intervals to represent their values.

Example 1 (Continued). Let us revisit Fig. 2. The figure displays a state graph of the program in Fig. 1 at a stage when the algorithm cannot find a larger recurrent component, and *FindNext* returns 0. The recurrent component is shown grayed, post-edges are solid, containment edges are dotted, and for clarity, containment-edges to and from may-exiting states are not displayed. The state $[1; +\infty)$ is may-exiting, and must-exiting states are marked with a cross. The resulting recurrent set is $\{[2, 60], [101; +\infty)\}$. Note that the states $x = 1$ and $x = 100$ are lost compared to the maximal recurrent set, and the discovered recurrent set is closed under application of the forward transformer, but not the backward transformer. This can be the case for some other tools based on forward semantics. For example, E-HSF [11] when presented with this example, may report the recurrent set to be $\{[4, 60], [100; +\infty)\}$. Also, note the set of must-exiting states (on the right in Fig. 2). While our algorithm often succeeds in proving that a recurrent set exists, it behaves badly when no recurrent set can be found. For example, in this case, it had to enumerate all states of the form $[62, 99]$, $[63, 99]$, $[64, 99]$, and so on. Finally, note that our procedure did terminate, although the domain is infinite and no measures were taken to guarantee termination.

Example 2. Figure 6 demonstrates a bug in the software of Zune players that on 31 Dec 2008 caused many devices to freeze [2]. The example is extracted from a procedure that was used to calculate the year based on the number of days passed since 1 Jan 1980. The loop repeatedly subtracts 365 or 366 from the number of days depending on whether the year is leap and increases the year by 1. Due to a logical error, if the year is leap and the number of days is 366, the variables are not updated, and the program goes into an infinite loop. We presented this program to our tool with the starting state being the loop invariant: $year \geq 1980 \wedge days \geq 0$. Every call to *FindNext* extends the recurrent set with a single state: $year = 1980 \wedge days = 366$, $year = 1984 \wedge days = 366$, $year = 1988 \wedge days = 366$, and so on. The abstract domain was not strong enough to infer that every leap year causes non-termination. Also, because the analysis is forward-only, it did not explore the predecessors of those states: e.g., from the state $year = 1983 \wedge days = 731$, the loop also diverges, but this was not discovered by the tool. Still, we count this result as success: our tool does expose the bug even if it does not find all inputs for which the bug manifests.

```
days ← a number ≥ 0
year ← 1980
while days > 365:
  if leap(year):
    if days > 366:
      days ← days − 366
      year ← year + 1
  else :
    days ← days − 365
    year ← year + 1
```

Fig. 6. A potentially non-terminating loop in Zune software (simplified).

Shape Analysis. Examples 3 and 4 present heap-manipulating programs. We use 3-valued logic [26] to represent heaps, and build the analysis on top of TVLA [3,23]. For more information on shape analysis with 3-valued logic, please refer to Sagiv et al. [26] and related papers [7,23,25]. In this framework, abstract heaps are represented by *3-valued structures*, i.e., models of 3-valued first-order logic with transitive closure. Every individual represents either a single heap cell or a set of heap cells that share some properties. Pointer variables are represented by unary predicates: the predicate is true for the cell where the variable points. Pointer fields are represented by binary predicates: the predicate is true for those pairs of cells where the corresponding field of one cell points to another. The analysis also maintains in the form of predicates additional information about the heap: whether the cells are reachable from each other, whether some condition is true of the cells, and so on. Three-valued structures can be displayed as *shape graphs*, and an example is shown in Fig. 7. The graph represents an acyclic singly-linked list with two or more elements and is read as follows. Left node represents a single cell which is the head of the list and is pointed to by pointer variables x and y. The text $c = {}^1/_2$ means that some condition c might or might not be true for the head – we do not know. The right node displayed with double border represents a finite non-empty set of cells that are the tail of the list. The dotted edge annotated by n between the head and the tail means that the pointer field n of the head points to some node of the tail, but not to all of them. The analysis is usually instructed that predicate n induces a function, but this is not reflected in the shape graph. The analysis also keeps track of reachability between cells with the predicate t_n. Solid t_n-edge between the head and the tail means that all cells of the tail are reachable from the head by traversing the n-pointers. Dotted n- and t_n-loops on the tail mean that there are pointers and reachability between some pairs of cells in the tail but not between all of them. Absence of n- and t_n edges from the tail to the head means that no cell in the tail points to or can reach head. In this case, the analysis is also instructed that there are no *shared* cells, i.e., every cell is pointed to by at most one cell. The above is sufficient for Fig. 7 to represent exactly the set of acyclic

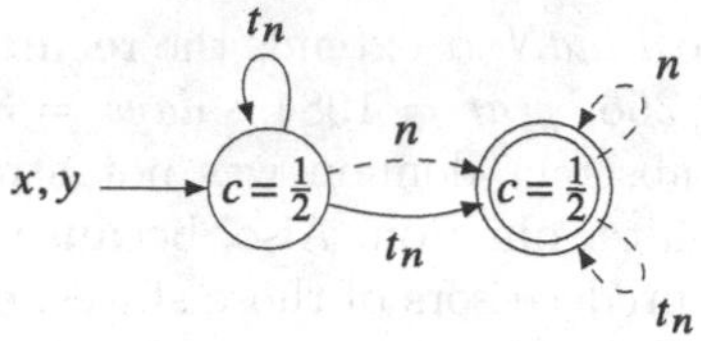

Fig. 7. Acyclic list with 2+ elements.

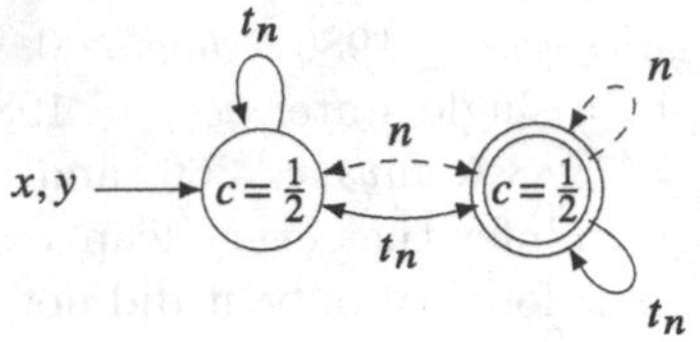

Fig. 8. Cyclic list with 2+ elements.

```
y ← x
while  y ≠ nil ∧ ¬c(y):
  y ← (y → n)
```

Fig. 9. Search in a list.

```
y ← x
while  y ≠ nil:
  y ← new struct
  if  y ≠ nil:
    (y → n) ← x
    x ← y
```

Fig. 10. Prepending to a non-empty list.

singly-linked lists with two or more elements. Similarly, Fig. 8 represents a set of cyclic lists with two or more elements.

Example 3. One source of non-termination in heap-manipulating programs is incorrect traversal of cyclic data structures. The companion technical report [9] discusses such non-termination bug in a device driver that was found by a termination prover [10]. Figure 9 shows a procedure that searches a list pointed to by x for an element y s.t. the condition $c(y)$ holds. The search terminates when such y is found or when the end of the list is reached, and it does not handle cyclic lists correctly. In this and the next example, the initial statement: $y \leftarrow x$ – is disregarded by the analysis and only emphasizes that when the loop is reached for the first time, both x and y point to the head of the list. Due to canonical abstraction [26], the set of 3-valued structures that we can explore is finite, and there is no need to perform pre-analysis for the loop invariant. Thus, we analyze the loop starting with the set of states containing cyclic and acyclic lists with both x and y pointing to the head and with unknown value of c for all the cells: the structures shown in Figs. 7 and 8, plus structures to represent single-element lists and an empty list. This way, our tool reports as the recurrent set all the heaps that cause non-termination of the loop, i.e., the cyclic lists where the condition c is false for all the elements. One of such lists (with three or more elements, y pointing into the list) is shown in Fig. 11.

Example 4. Another interesting class of bugs in heap-manipulating programs is related to heap allocation. Sometimes, models of programs do not take into account that heap allocation can fail. For example, in a real program, an infinite loop performing allocation would usually lead to an out-of-memory error and may consume much time and system resources. But in a model of the program

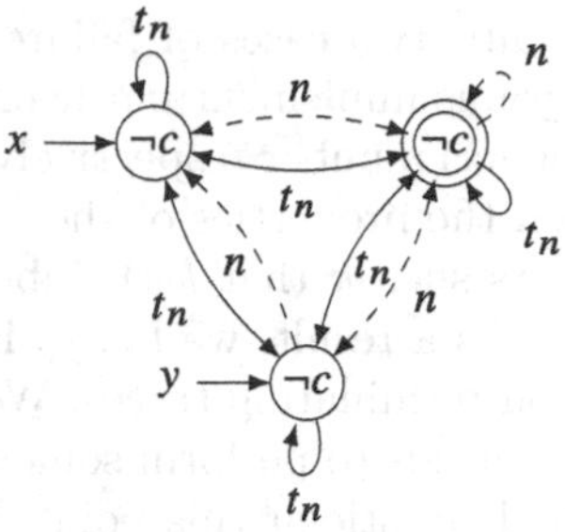

Fig. 11. Example of a cyclic list where c is false for all elements.

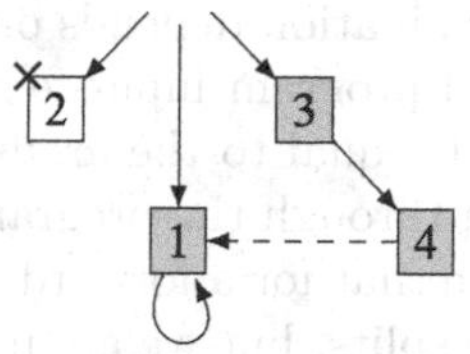

Fig. 12. State graph for the program in Fig. 10. State 1 is shown in Fig. 7. Grayed are recurrent states and must-exiting state is marked with a cross.

this may appear as potential non-termination. Figure 10 shows a program that repeatedly prepends a newly allocated element to a (non-empty) list. The loop is supposed to terminate if the allocation fails, but this is not possible in our TVLA model. The state space for the example is shown in Fig. 12. The initial states are: a list with two or more elements (state 1, as shown in Fig. 7), an empty heap (2), and a single-element list (3). The empty heap is must-exiting, and the states 1, 3, and 4 (list with exactly two elements) form the recurrent set. State 4 does not have an outgoing post-edge as the algorithm finishes before the post-condition of the state is computed. Note the post-loop on state 1. Because of canonical abstraction [26], the post-condition of a list with two or more elements is again a list with two or more elements, i.e., the analysis loses track of the length of the list.

5 Experiments

We implemented our technique in a prototype tool that supports numeric and 3-valued programs. The analysis of 3-valued programs is based on TVLA [23], and for numeric programs, we use interval domain with ad hoc support for *modulo* operation: we perform some artificial case splits when modulo operation is invoked. We applied our analysis to the test set [4] of Invel [28], and to the non-terminating programs from the Ultimate Büchi Automizer [20] test set [5]. *For detailed test results, please, see the companion technical report* [9]. Out of 52 non-terminating Invel programs, our tool was able to find recurrent sets in 39. For the remaining 13, the analysis either terminates without producing a result or diverges. We attribute 8 cases of failure to the lack of expressiveness in the abstract domain. In those programs, successful analysis would require relational reasoning, e.g., with polyhedra [17]. Another two cases of failure come from the limitations of our prototype tool that does not support nested loops (while the approach does). In one case, the program uses a `break` statement which is not currently supported by our technique. Finally, two cases of failure seem problematic for our general approach. Those programs implement mathematical functions (least common multiplier and k-th Fibonacci number respectively) and their termination depends on the relation between the properties of those functions and program input, e.g., whether there exists such k that k-th Fibonacci number is equal to the argument of the function. As a result, we fail to isolate the path through the program that is taken by non-terminating traces. We may speculate that for a forward analysis to succeed, it needs to perform some artificial case splits, but we are not aware of a possible heuristic at this point. While specialized numeric tools (e.g., AProVE with SMT backend [12]) handle more of the Invel test programs [6], they do not subsume our tool. We believe, our approach can complement existing numeric tools in cases when the underlying linear solvers struggle.

Out of 18 Automizer programs that we considered, our tool handles 10 successfully. Among the remaining 8 programs, five use unsupported features (arrays, `break` statements, recursion), one would require additional case splits that our tool does not perform, and two have non-terminating behaviors, but do not have universal recurrent sets (non-termination relies on making a specific series of non-deterministic choices in the loop body). The latter points to a limitation of universal recurrent sets. Though a non-termination bug may cause the program to have one, it may be hard to build an abstraction that preserves it and does not introduce spurious terminating traces from every interesting state.

In some of the test programs, the main loop was preceded by a loop-free stem that performed initialization of the variables. We observed that in all cases (where our tool was able to find a recurrent set) this initial state had non-empty intersection with the recurrent set produced by the tool. For example, the program 'GCD' from the Invel test set, has two integer valuables: a an b – and the stem sets up the initial state $a \geq b$. The recurrent set that our tool finds is of the form $(a \geq 1 \wedge b \leq -1) \vee (a \leq -1 \wedge b \geq 1)$. The fact that this recurrent set has non-empty intersection with the initial state can be checked using the operations of the polyhedral abstract domain. This result is specific to the tests programs and the choice of abstract domain. In general, it might not be possible to check the recurrent sets for concrete reachability using standard forward analysis techniques.

6 Related Work

The approach [12] implemented in AProVE [18] is similar to ours in that it builds and analyzes an abstract state graph (*termination graph*, in their terms). However, they are interested in proving the existence of at least one non-terminating trace (which is dual to the notion of universal recurrent set) and they analyze the graph differently. They relate cycles in the graph to loops in the program and either try to prove that some loop does not modify the variables affecting termination, or employ SMT-based analysis (available when non-termination relies on integer arithmetic) to show that for some loop, at least one path through it is always enabled. In contrast, we introduce a notion of recurrent component which witnesses a recurrent set and search the graph for those.

Cook et al. [14] analyze *linear* over-approximations of programs and use Farkas' lemma to find universal recurrent sets. Their soundness result is similar to ours and is more general: they state it for arbitrary transition systems and require a property of *upward termination* (for every concrete final state, the corresponding abstract state is also final) which for us implicitly holds. Note that linear abstractions have not yet demonstrated to be very effective for analyzing heap-manipulating programs.

The analysis of Chen et al. [13] combines a forward model checker and backwards analysis of single traces to modify the original program and turn it into a non-terminating one, by adding assumption statements. On the low level their approach is dual to ours, as they work with under-approximations of programs and try to prove the existence of at least one infinite trace.

The above analyses are predated by that of Gupta et al. [19] where existential recurrent sets are produced from lasso-shaped symbolic executions using Farkas' lemma.

Velroyen and Rümmer developed their analysis [28] independently of Gupta et al. [19]. They propose a template and a refinement scheme to infer invariants proving that terminating states of a program are unreachable.

Larraz et al. [22] use the notion of an edge-closed quasi-invariant (a set of states that, one reached, cannot be escaped) as a generalization of recurrent set. They encode the search for such set as a max-SMT problem.

We note that the above analyses focus on *proving non-termination*, while we consider a sub-problem of finding a recurrent set. To prove non-termination of a program we would need to show that a recurrent set is reachable from the program entry.

The analysis implemented in E-HSF [11] allows to specify the semantics of programs and express verified properties in the form of ∀∃ quantified Horn clauses extended with well-foundedness conditions. In particular, the input language allows to query for the existence of universal and existential recurrent sets. The *implementation* is to our knowledge targeted at linear programs and relies on Farkas' lemma.

7 Conclusion and Future Work

We have described a forward technique for finding recurrent sets in imperative programs where loops of a specific form are the source of non-termination. The recurrent sets that we produce are genuine, but may not be reachable from the program entry. We applied our analysis to numeric and heap-manipulating programs and were successful if (i) we were able to capture the paths through the program that infinite traces take, and (ii) we were able to perform enough case splits to isolate the recurrent set into a separate set of abstract states. The latter point can benefit from heuristics in some cases.

Our analysis only admits structured programs without `goto` statements and a restricted form of loops: `while`-loops without statements that affect control flow (`break`, `continue`, etc.). One direction for future work is to enable the analysis of a larger class of loops: either by introducing relevant program transformations and studying their effect on the outcome of the analysis or by extending the technique to handle more complicated control flow graphs. Another direction is to solidify the analysis: eliminate the need for a separate forward pre-analysis by weaving it into the main algorithm, introduce a proper trace partitioning, etc.

Acknowledgements. We thank Mooly Sagiv and Roman Manevich for the source code of TVLA. A. Bakhirkin is supported by a Microsoft Research PhD Scholarship.

References

1. http://azure.microsoft.com/blog/2014/11/19/update-on-azure-storage-service-interruption. Accessed March 2015
2. http://www.zuneboards.com/forums/showthread.php?t=38143. Accessed March 2015
3. http://www.cs.tau.ac.il/~tvla/. Accessed March 2015
4. http://www.key-project.org/nonTermination/. Accessed March 2015
5. http://cl2-informatik.uibk.ac.at/mercurial.cgi/TPDB/file/d085ae59ef47/C/Ultimate. Accessed March 2015
6. http://aprove.informatik.rwth-aachen.de/eval/JBC-Nonterm/. Accessed June 2015
7. Arnold, G., Manevich, R., Sagiv, M., Shaham, R.: Combining shape analyses by intersecting abstractions. In: Emerson, E.A., Namjoshi, K.S. (eds.) VMCAI 2006. LNCS, vol. 3855, pp. 33–48. Springer, Heidelberg (2006)
8. Baier, C., Katoen, J.: Principles of Model Checking. MIT Press, Cambridge (2008)
9. Bakhirkin, A., Berdine, J., Piterman, N.: A forward analysis for recurrent sets. Technical report CS-15-001, University of Leicester (2015)
10. Berdine, J., Cook, B., Distefano, D., O'Hearn, P.W.: Automatic termination proofs for programs with shape-shifting heaps. In: Ball, T., Jones, R.B. (eds.) CAV 2006. LNCS, vol. 4144, pp. 386–400. Springer, Heidelberg (2006)
11. Beyene, T.A., Popeea, C., Rybalchenko, A.: Solving existentially quantified horn clauses. In: Sharygina, N., Veith, H. (eds.) CAV 2013. LNCS, vol. 8044, pp. 869–882. Springer, Heidelberg (2013)
12. Brockschmidt, M., Ströder, T., Otto, C., Giesl, J.: Automated detection of non-termination and NullPointerExceptions for Java Bytecode. In: Beckert, B., Damiani, F., Gurov, D. (eds.) FoVeOOS 2011. LNCS, vol. 7421, pp. 123–141. Springer, Heidelberg (2012)
13. Chen, H.-Y., Cook, B., Fuhs, C., Nimkar, K., O'Hearn, P.: Proving nontermination via safety. In: Ábrahám, E., Havelund, K. (eds.) TACAS 2014 (ETAPS). LNCS, vol. 8413, pp. 156–171. Springer, Heidelberg (2014)
14. Cook, B., Fuhs, C., Nimkar, K., O'Hearn, P.W.: Disproving termination with overapproximation. In: FMCAD, pp. 67–74. IEEE (2014)
15. Cook, B., Podelski, A., Rybalchenko, A.: Proving program termination. Commun. ACM **54**(5), 88–98 (2011)

16. Cook, B., See, A., Zuleger, F.: Ramsey vs. Lexicographic termination proving. In: Piterman, N., Smolka, S.A. (eds.) TACAS 2013 (ETAPS 2013). LNCS, vol. 7795, pp. 47–61. Springer, Heidelberg (2013)
17. Cousot, P., Halbwachs, N.: Automatic discovery of linear restraints among variables of a program. In: Aho, A.V., Zilles, S.N., Szymanski, T.G. (eds.) POPL, pp. 84–96. ACM Press (1978)
18. Giesl, J., Brockschmidt, M., Emmes, F., Frohn, F., Fuhs, C., Otto, C., Plücker, M., Schneider-Kamp, P., Ströder, T., Swiderski, S., Thiemann, R.: Proving termination of programs automatically with AProVE. In: Demri, S., Kapur, D., Weidenbach, C. (eds.) IJCAR 2014. LNCS, vol. 8562, pp. 184–191. Springer, Heidelberg (2014)
19. Gupta, A., Henzinger, T.A., Majumdar, R., Rybalchenko, A., Xu, R.G.: Proving non-termination. In: Necula, G.C., Wadler, P. (eds.) POPL, pp. 147–158. ACM (2008)
20. Heizmann, M., Hoenicke, J., Leike, J., Podelski, A.: Linear ranking for linear lasso programs. In: Van Hung, D., Ogawa, M. (eds.) ATVA 2013. LNCS, vol. 8172, pp. 365–380. Springer, Heidelberg (2013)
21. Kleene, S.: Introduction to Metamathematics, 2nd edn. Literary Licensing, LLC, Amsterdam (1987)
22. Larraz, D., Nimkar, K., Oliveras, A., Rodríguez-Carbonell, E., Rubio, A.: Proving non-termination using Max-SMT. In: Biere, A., Bloem, R. (eds.) CAV 2014. LNCS, vol. 8559, pp. 779–796. Springer, Heidelberg (2014)
23. Lev-Ami, T., Manevich, R., Sagiv, S.: TVLA: a system for generating abstract interpreters. In: Jacquart, R. (ed.) IFIP 2004. IFIP, vol. 156, pp. 367–375. Springer, Heidelberg (2004)
24. Mauborgne, L., Rival, X.: Trace partitioning in abstract interpretation based static analyzers. In: Sagiv, M. (ed.) ESOP 2005. LNCS, vol. 3444, pp. 5–20. Springer, Heidelberg (2005)
25. Reps, T., Sagiv, M., Loginov, A.: Finite differencing of logical formulas for static analysis. In: Degano, P. (ed.) ESOP 2003. LNCS, vol. 2618, pp. 380–398. Springer, Heidelberg (2003)
26. Sagiv, S., Reps, T.W., Wilhelm, R.: Parametric shape analysis via 3-valued logic. ACM Trans. Program. Lang. Syst. **24**(3), 217–298 (2002)
27. Urban, C., Miné, A.: A decision tree abstract domain for proving conditional termination. In: Müller-Olm, M., Seidl, H. (eds.) Static Analysis. LNCS, vol. 8723, pp. 302–318. Springer, Heidelberg (2014)
28. Velroyen, H., Rümmer, P.: Non-termination checking for imperative programs. In: Beckert, B., Hähnle, R. (eds.) TAP 2008. LNCS, vol. 4966, pp. 154–170. Springer, Heidelberg (2008)

Unbounded-Time Analysis of Guarded LTI Systems with Inputs by Abstract Acceleration

Dario Cattaruzza, Alessandro Abate, Peter Schrammel(✉), and Daniel Kroening

Department of Computer Science, University of Oxford, Oxford, UK
{dario.cattaruzza,alessandro.abate,peter.schrammel, daniel.kroening}@cs.ox.ac.uk

Abstract. Linear Time Invariant (LTI) systems are ubiquitous in software systems and control applications. Unbounded-time reachability analysis that can cope with industrial-scale models with thousands of variables is needed. To tackle this general problem, we use *abstract acceleration*, a method for unbounded-time polyhedral reachability analysis for linear systems. Existing variants of the method are restricted to closed systems, i.e., dynamical models without inputs or non-determinism. In this paper, we present an extension of abstract acceleration to linear loops *with inputs*, which correspond to discrete-time LTI control systems, and further study the interaction with guard conditions. The new method relies on a relaxation of the solution of the linear dynamical equation that leads to a precise over-approximation of the set of reachable states, which are evaluated using support functions. In order to increase scalability, we use floating-point computations and ensure soundness by interval arithmetic. Our experiments show that performance increases by several orders of magnitude over alternative approaches in the literature. In turn, this tremendous speedup allows us to improve on precision by computing more expensive abstractions. We outperform state-of-the-art tools for unbounded-time analysis of LTI system with inputs in speed as well as in precision.

1 Introduction

Linear loops are an ubiquitous programming template. Linear loops iterate over continuous variables, which are updated with a linear transformation. Linear loops may be guarded, i.e., terminate if a given linear condition holds. Inputs from the environment can be modelled by means of non-deterministic choices within the loop. These features make linear loops expressive enough to capture the dynamics of many hybrid dynamical models. The prevalence of such models

This research was supported by Oxford Instruments PLC, by the ARTEMIS Joint Undertaking under grant agreement number 295311 (VeTeSS), by the ERC project 280053 (CPROVER), by the EC IAPP project 324432 (AMBI) and by the John Fell OUP Research Fund.

S. Blazy and T. Jensen (Eds.): SAS 2015, LNCS 9291, pp. 312–331, 2015.
DOI: 10.1007/978-3-662-48288-9_18

in safety-critical embedded systems makes linear loops a fundamental target for formal methods.

Many high-level requirements for embedded control systems can be modelled as safety properties: the problem is deciding reachability of certain "bad states", in which the system exhibits unsafe behaviour. In linear loops, bad states may be represented by guard assertions.

Reachability in linear programs, however, is a formidable challenge for automatic analysers: the problem is undecidable despite the restriction to linear transformations (i.e., linear dynamics) and linear guards. Broadly, there are two principal approaches to solving reachability problems.

The first approach is to surrender exhaustive analysis over the infinite time horizon, and to restrict the exploration to system dynamics up to some given finite time bound. Bounded-time reachability is decidable, and decision procedures for the resulting satisfiability problem have made much progress in the past decade. The precision related to the bounded analysis is offset by the price of uncertainty: behaviours beyond the given time bound are not considered, and may thus violate a safety requirement. Representatives are STRONG [11] and SpaceEx [16].

The second approach is to attempt to infer a *loop invariant*, i.e., an inductive set of states that includes all reachable states. If the computed invariant is disjoint from the set of bad states, this proves that the latter are unreachable and hence that the loop is safe. However, analysers frequently struggle to obtain an invariant that is precise enough with acceptable computational cost. The problem is evidently exacerbated by non-determinism in the loop, which corresponds to the case of open systems. Prominent representatives of this analysis approach include Passel [30], Sting [7], and abstract interpreters such as ASTRÉE [2] and InterProc [28].

The goal of this paper is to push the frontiers of unbounded-time reachability analysis: we aim at devising a method that is able to reason soundly about unbounded trajectories. We present a new approach for performing *abstract acceleration*. Abstract acceleration [21,22,29] captures the effect of an arbitrary number of loop iterations with a single, non-iterative transfer function that is applied to the entry state of the loop (i.e., to the set of initial conditions of the linear dynamics). The key contribution of this paper is to lift the restriction of [29] to closed systems, and thus to allow non-deterministic choice or inputs.

In summary, the contributions of this work are as follows:

1. We present a new technique to include inputs (non-determinism) in the abstract acceleration of general linear loops, thus overcoming its greatest limitation.
2. We introduce the use of support functions in complex spaces, in order to increase the precision of previous abstract acceleration methods.
3. By extending abstract acceleration and combining it with the use of support functions, we produce a time-unbounded reachability analysis that overcomes the main barrier of state-of-the-art techniques and tools for linear hybrid systems with inputs.

4. We employ floating-point computations associated to bounded error quantification, to significantly increase the speed and scalability of previous abstract acceleration techniques, while retaining soundness.

Related Work. We review contributions within the two main perspectives in reachability analysis of hybrid systems, dealing respectively with bounded- and unbounded-time problems.

The first approach deals with bounded-time horizons: set-based simulation methods generalise guaranteed integration [32] from enclosing intervals to relational domains. They use precise abstractions with low computational cost to over-approximate sets of reachable states up to a given time horizon. Early tools used polyhedral sets (HyTech [26] and PHAVer [15]), polyhedral flow-pipes [5], ellipsoids [3] and zonotopes [19]. A breakthrough has been achieved by [20,23], with the representation of convex sets using template polyhedra and support functions. This method is implemented in the tool SpaceEx [16], which can handle dynamical systems with hundreds of variables. It performs computations using floating-point numbers: this is a deliberate choice to boost performance, which, although quite reasonable, is implemented in a way that is unsound and that does not provide genuine formal guarantees. Other approaches use specialised constraint solvers (HySAT [14], iSAT [12]), or SMT encodings [6,24] for bounded model checking of hybrid automata.

The second approach, epitomised in static analysis methods [25], explores unbounded-time horizons. It employs conservative over-approximations to achieve completeness and decidability over infinite time horizons. Early work in this area has used implementations of abstract interpretation and widening [8], which are still the foundations of most modern tools. The work in [25] uses abstract interpretation with convex polyhedra over piecewise-constant differential inclusions. Dang and Gawlitza [10] employ optimisation-based (max-strategy iteration) with linear templates for hybrid systems with linear dynamics. Relational abstractions [33] use ad-hoc "loop summarisation" of flow relations, whilst abstract acceleration focuses on linear relations analysis [21,22], which is common in program analysis. Abstract acceleration has been extended from its original version to encompass inputs over reactive systems [35] but restricted to subclasses of linear loops, and later to general linear loops but without inputs [29]. This paper lifts these limitations by presenting abstract acceleration for *general* linear loops *with* inputs.

2 Preliminaries

Abstract acceleration [21,22] is a key technique for the verification of programs with loops. The state of the art for this technique has reached the level where we can perform abstract acceleration of general linear loops without inputs [29], and of some subclasses of linear loops with inputs [34,35], to an acceptable degree of precision. We develop an abstract acceleration technique for *general* linear loops *with bounded inputs*, whilst improving the precision and ease of computation, in order to overcome the negative effects on the precsion caused by non-determinism.

2.1 Model Syntax

We are interested in loops expressed in the following form:

$$\textit{while}(\boldsymbol{Gx} \leq \boldsymbol{h}) \;\; \boldsymbol{x} := \boldsymbol{Ax} + \boldsymbol{Bu},$$

where $\boldsymbol{x} \in \mathbb{R}^p$ are the state variables, $\psi := \boldsymbol{Gx} \leq \boldsymbol{h}$ is a linear constraint on the states (with $\boldsymbol{G} \in \mathbb{R}^{r \times p}$ and $\boldsymbol{h} \in \mathbb{R}^r$), $\boldsymbol{u} \in \mathbb{R}^q$ is a non-deterministic input, and $\boldsymbol{A} \in R^{p \times p}$ and $\boldsymbol{B} \in \mathbb{R}^{p \times q}$ are linear transformations characterising the dynamics of the system. In particular, the special instance where $\psi = \top$ (i.e., "while true") represents a time-unbounded loop with no guards, for which the discovery of a suitable invariant (when existing) is paramount. As evident at a semantical level (see next), this syntax can be interpreted as the dynamics of a discrete-time LTI model with inputs, under the presence of a guard set which, for ease of notation, we denote as $G = \{\boldsymbol{x} \mid \boldsymbol{Gx} \leq \boldsymbol{h}\}$.

2.2 Model Semantics

The traces of the model starting from an initial set $X_0 \subseteq \mathbb{R}^p$, with inputs restricted to $U \subseteq \mathbb{R}^q$, are sequences $\boldsymbol{x}_0 \xrightarrow{\boldsymbol{u}_0} \boldsymbol{x}_1 \xrightarrow{\boldsymbol{u}_1} \boldsymbol{x}_2 \xrightarrow{\boldsymbol{u}_2} \ldots$, where $\boldsymbol{x}_0 \in X_0$ and $\forall n \geq 0, \boldsymbol{x}_{n+1} = \tau(\boldsymbol{x}_n, \boldsymbol{u}_n)$, where

$$\tau(\boldsymbol{x}_n, \boldsymbol{u}_n) = \left(\boldsymbol{Ax}_n + \boldsymbol{Bu}_n \mid \boldsymbol{Gx}_n \leq \boldsymbol{h} \wedge \boldsymbol{u}_n \in U\right). \tag{1}$$

We extend the notation above to convex sets of initial conditions and inputs (X_0 and U), and write $\tau(X_0, U)$ to denote the set of states $\{\boldsymbol{x} \mid \boldsymbol{x}_0 \in X_0 \wedge \boldsymbol{u} \in U \wedge \boldsymbol{x} = \tau(\boldsymbol{x}_0, \boldsymbol{u})\}$ reached from X_0 by τ in one step. We furthermore write $\tau^n(X_0, U)$ to denote the set of states reached from X_0 via τ in n steps (*n-reach set*), i.e. for $n \geq 1$

$$\tau^n(X_0, U) = \{\boldsymbol{x}_n \mid \boldsymbol{x}_0 \in X_0 \wedge \forall k \in [0, n-1] : \boldsymbol{u}_k \in U \wedge \boldsymbol{x}_{k+1} = \tau(\boldsymbol{x}_k, \boldsymbol{u}_k)\}. \tag{2}$$

Since the transformations $\boldsymbol{A}$ and $\boldsymbol{B}$ are linear and vector sums preserve convexity, the sets $X_n = \tau^n(X_0, U)$ are also convex. We define the *n-reach tube* $\hat{X}_n = \hat{\tau}^n(X_0, U) = \bigcup_{k \in [0,n]} \tau^k(X_0, U)$ as the union of the reachable sets over n iterations. Moreover, $\hat{X} = \bigcup_{n \geq 0} \tau^n(X_0, U)$ extends the previous notion over an unbounded time horizon.

2.3 Abstract Acceleration

Abstract Acceleration [22] is a method to over-approximate the *reach tube* of linear systems over any given time interval, including the infinite time horizon. The work in [29] discusses this abstraction technique for systems without inputs, where an *abstract matrix* $\mathcal{A}^n$ is synthesised to encompass the combined dynamics generating all reach sets up to the nth iteration. The abstract matrix $\mathcal{A}^n$ over-approximates the set of matrices $\bigcup_{k\in[0,n]} \boldsymbol{A}^k$. The reach tube $\hat{\tau}^n(X_0)$ (tailoring the notation above to a system *without* inputs) can then be over-approximated via the *abstract matrix multiplication* $\mathcal{A}^n X_0$ [29]. We will employ the notation $\mathcal{A}$ (rather than $\mathcal{A}^\infty$) to represent this notion over an infinite time horizon.

In this paper we extend this approach to systems with inputs, so that

$$\hat{\tau}^n(X_0, U) \subseteq \mathcal{A}^n X_0 \oplus \mathcal{B}^n U \ , \tag{3}$$

where $A \oplus B$ represents the Minkowski sum of two sets, namely $\{a + b \mid a \in A \wedge b \in B\}$, whereas the abstract matrix $\mathcal{B}^n$ over-approximates the set of matrices $\bigcup_{k\in[0,n]} (\boldsymbol{I} - \boldsymbol{A}^k)(\boldsymbol{I} - \boldsymbol{A})^{-1}\boldsymbol{B}$, where $\boldsymbol{I}$ is a properly-sized identity matrix – this second approximation will be discussed in detail in Sect. 3.

2.4 Support Functions

There exist many over-approximating abstract domains for representing sets of states that are suitable for systems with linear dynamics, of which by far the most popular is that of *convex polyhedra* [9]. Rectangular abstractions are easy to process [36], but the over-approximations may be too coarse, a problem which is exacerbated by non-deterministic inputs.

Abstract acceleration requires two abstract domains: the first to abstract the model dynamics – the original approach for abstract acceleration [29] uses *logahedra* [27] – and the second to represent spatial sets (convex polyhedra in [29]). In [29] the estimation of the number of loop iterations (time steps) leverages abstractions of initial sets as hypercubes, which is a source of imprecision that our method will not exhibit.

In this work, we use support functions [18,31] for the abstract domains. Support functions have proven to be one of the most successful abstractions for the representation of reachability sets for dynamical and hybrid linear systems. A general assertion $\boldsymbol{C}\boldsymbol{x} \leq \boldsymbol{d}$ (of which the guard $\boldsymbol{G}\boldsymbol{x} \leq \boldsymbol{h}$ is just an example) entails a set of states that is a convex polyhedron, where each row in $\boldsymbol{C}$ is a direction orthogonal to a face in the polyhedron, and the corresponding value in $\boldsymbol{d}$ is the distance of that face to the origin.

Support functions represent a set by defining the distance of its convex hull with respect to a number of given directions. More specifically, the distance from the origin to the hyperplane that is orthogonal to the given direction and that touches its convex hull at its farthest. Finitely sampled support functions are template polyhedra in which the directions are not fixed, which helps avoiding wrapping effects [20]. The larger the number of directions provided, the more precisely represented the set will be. In more detail, given a direction $\boldsymbol{v} \in \mathbb{R}^p$, the support function of a non-empty set $X \subseteq \mathbb{R}^p$ in the direction of $\boldsymbol{v}$ is defined as

$$\rho_X : \mathbb{R}^p \to \mathbb{R}, \quad \rho_X(\boldsymbol{v}) = \sup\{< \boldsymbol{x}, \boldsymbol{v} >: \boldsymbol{x} \in X\} \ .$$

where $< \boldsymbol{x}, \boldsymbol{v} >$ is the dot product of the two vectors.

Support functions do not exclusively apply to convex polyhedra, but in fact to any set $X \subseteq \mathbb{R}^p$ represented by a general assertion $\theta(X)$. We will restrict ourselves to the use of convex polyhedra, in which case the support function definition translates to solving the linear program

$$\rho_X(\boldsymbol{v}) = \max\{< \boldsymbol{x}, \boldsymbol{v} >\mid \boldsymbol{C}\boldsymbol{x} \leq \boldsymbol{d}\}\ . \tag{4}$$

Several properties of support functions allow us to reduce operational complexity. The most significant are [18]:

$$\begin{array}{ll} \rho_{kX}(\boldsymbol{v}) = \rho_X(k\boldsymbol{v}) = k\rho_X(\boldsymbol{v}) : k \geq 0 & \rho_{AX}(\boldsymbol{v}) = \rho_X(A^T\boldsymbol{v}) : A \in \mathbb{R}^{p\times p} \\ \rho_{X_1 \oplus X_2}(\boldsymbol{v}) = \rho_{X_1}(\boldsymbol{v}) + \rho_{X_2}(\boldsymbol{v}) & \rho_X(\boldsymbol{v}_1 + \boldsymbol{v}_2) \leq \rho_X(\boldsymbol{v}_1) + \rho_X(\boldsymbol{v}_2) \\ \rho_{conv(X_1 \cup X_2)}(\boldsymbol{v}) = \max\{\rho_{X_1}(\boldsymbol{v}), \rho_{X_2}(\boldsymbol{v})\} & \rho_{X_1 \cap X_2}(\boldsymbol{v}) \leq \min\{\rho_{X_1}(\boldsymbol{v}), \rho_{X_2}(\boldsymbol{v})\} \end{array}$$

As can be seen by their structure, some of these properties reduce complexity to lower-order polynomial or even to constant time, by turning matrix-matrix multiplications ($\mathcal{O}(p^3)$) into matrix-vector ($\mathcal{O}(p^2)$), or into scalar multiplications.

3 Abstract Acceleration with Inputs

3.1 Overview of the Algorithm

Our algorithm takes as input the set of initial states X_0, the set of bounded inputs U and the dynamics of a linear loop characterised by $\boldsymbol{G}, \boldsymbol{h}, \boldsymbol{A}$, and $\boldsymbol{B}$. It returns as output an over-approximation $\hat{X}^\sharp$ of the reach tube $\hat{X}$ (or corresponding quantities for the bounded-horizon case). We over- and under-approximate the number of loop iterations n that are required to first intersect and completely go beyond the guard set G, respectively, by means of the reach sets computed with the model dynamics: we denote these two quantities by $\underline{n}$ and $\overline{n}$. In the following we employ the notations $\sqcap$ for intersection of polyhedra, and $\sqcup$ for the convex hull $conv(X_1 \cup X_2)$.

If $\underline{n}$ or $\overline{n}$ are unbounded, we compute the abstract matrices $\mathcal{A}$ and $\mathcal{B}$ (as defined shortly), and return the quantity

$$\hat{X}^\sharp = X_0 \sqcup (\mathcal{A}(X_0 \sqcap G) \oplus \mathcal{B}U) \sqcap G \tag{5}$$

as the resulting reach tube, where again $G = \{\boldsymbol{x} \mid \boldsymbol{G}\boldsymbol{x} \leq \boldsymbol{h}\}$. Otherwise, in the finite case, we compute the abstract matrices $\mathcal{A}^{\underline{n}}$ and $\mathcal{A}^{\overline{n}-\underline{n}}$ and set

$$\hat{X}^\sharp_n = X_0 \sqcup ((\mathcal{A}^{\underline{n}}(X_0 \sqcap G) \oplus \mathcal{B}^{\underline{n}}U) \sqcap G) \sqcup ((\mathcal{A}^{\overline{n}-\underline{n}}(X_{\underline{n}} \sqcap G) \oplus (\mathcal{B}^{\overline{n}-\underline{n}}U)) \sqcap G)\ . \tag{6}$$

In this formula, the abstract matrices $\mathcal{A}^n$ and $\mathcal{B}^n$ are obtained as an over-approximation of sets of matrices, as described in Sect. 3.3.

3.2 Abstract Acceleration Without Guards

With reference to (3), we now detail the abstract acceleration with inputs. Unfolding (2), we obtain

$$\boldsymbol{x}_n = \boldsymbol{A}^n \boldsymbol{x}_0 + \boldsymbol{A}^{n-1}\boldsymbol{B}\boldsymbol{u}_0 + \boldsymbol{A}^{n-2}\boldsymbol{B}\boldsymbol{u}_1 + \ldots + \boldsymbol{B}\boldsymbol{u}_{n-1} = \boldsymbol{A}^n \boldsymbol{x}_0 + \sum_{k\in[1,n]} \boldsymbol{A}^{n-k}\boldsymbol{B}\boldsymbol{u}_{k-1} \; .$$

Let us now consider the following over-approximation for τ on sets:

$$\tau^{\sharp}(X_0, U) = \boldsymbol{A}(X_0 \cap G) \oplus \boldsymbol{B}U \; . \tag{7}$$

Then the reach set (as said, we ignore the presence of the guard set G for the time being) can be computed as

$$X_n = \boldsymbol{A}^n X_0 \oplus \boldsymbol{A}^{n-1}\boldsymbol{B}U + \boldsymbol{A}^{n-2}\boldsymbol{B}U \oplus \ldots \oplus \boldsymbol{B}U = \boldsymbol{A}^n X_0 \oplus \textstyle\sum_{k\in[0,n-1]} \boldsymbol{A}^k \boldsymbol{B}U.$$

What is left to do is to further simplify the sum $\sum_{k\in[0,n-1]} \boldsymbol{A}^k\boldsymbol{B}U$. We can exploit the following simple results from linear algebra.

Lemma 1. *If $\boldsymbol{I}-\boldsymbol{A}$ is invertible, then $\sum_{k=0}^{n-1}\boldsymbol{A}^k = (\boldsymbol{I}-\boldsymbol{A}^n)(\boldsymbol{I}-\boldsymbol{A})^{-1}$. If furthermore $\lim_{n\to\infty}\boldsymbol{A}^n = 0$, then $\lim_{n\to\infty}\sum_{k=0}^{n}\boldsymbol{A}^k = (\boldsymbol{I}-\boldsymbol{A})^{-1}$.*

It is evident that there are some restrictions on the nature of matrix $\boldsymbol{A}$: since we need to calculate the inverse $(\boldsymbol{I}-\boldsymbol{A})^{-1}$, $\boldsymbol{A}$ must not include the eigenvalue 1, i.e. $1 \notin \sigma(\boldsymbol{A})$, where $\sigma(A)$ is the spectrum (the set of all the eigenvalues) of matrix $\boldsymbol{A}$. In order to overcome this problem, we introduce the eigen-decomposition of $\boldsymbol{A} = \boldsymbol{S}\boldsymbol{J}\boldsymbol{S}^{-1}$, and setting trivially $\boldsymbol{I} = \boldsymbol{S}\boldsymbol{I}\boldsymbol{S}^{-1}$, by the distributive and transitive property we obtain

$$(\boldsymbol{I}-\boldsymbol{A}^n)(\boldsymbol{I}-\boldsymbol{A})^{-1} = \boldsymbol{S}(\boldsymbol{I}-\boldsymbol{J}^n)(\boldsymbol{I}-\boldsymbol{J})^{-1}\boldsymbol{S}^{-1} \; .$$

While this does not directly eliminate the problem of the inverse for eigenvalues equal to 1, it allows us to set

$$\sum_{k=0}^{n-1}\lambda^k = \begin{cases} n & \lambda = 1 \\ \frac{1-\lambda^n}{1-\lambda} & \lambda \neq 1 \end{cases} \Rightarrow (\boldsymbol{I}-\boldsymbol{A}^n)(\boldsymbol{I}-\boldsymbol{A})^{-1} = \boldsymbol{S}\; diag\begin{pmatrix} n & \lambda_i = 1 \\ \frac{1-\lambda_i^n}{1-\lambda_i} & \lambda_i \neq 1 \end{pmatrix} \boldsymbol{S}^{-1} \; . \tag{8}$$

In the case of Jordan blocks of size > 1, the entries in the kth upper diagonal of the block are filled with the value: $\frac{-1^k}{k+1}\frac{1-\lambda^n}{(1-\lambda)^{k+1}} + \sum_{j=1}^{k}\frac{-1^{k-j}}{k-j}\binom{n}{j-1}\frac{\lambda^{n-j-1}}{(1-\lambda)^{k-j}}$.

This result can be only directly applied under restricted conditions, for instance whenever $\forall k > 0 : \boldsymbol{u}_k = \boldsymbol{u}_{k-1}$. In order to generalise it (in particular to non-constant inputs), we will over-approximate $\boldsymbol{B}U$ over the eigenspace by a spheral enclosure with centre $\boldsymbol{u}'_c$ and radius U'_b. To this end, we first rewrite

$$U'_J = \boldsymbol{S}^{-1}\boldsymbol{B}U = \{\boldsymbol{u}'_c\} \oplus U'_d \; , \text{ with } \boldsymbol{u}'_c[i] = \frac{1}{2}(\rho_{U'_J}(\boldsymbol{v}_i) + \rho_{U'_J}(-\boldsymbol{v}_i)), \boldsymbol{v}_i[j] = \begin{cases} 1 & j = i \\ 0 & j \neq i \end{cases}$$

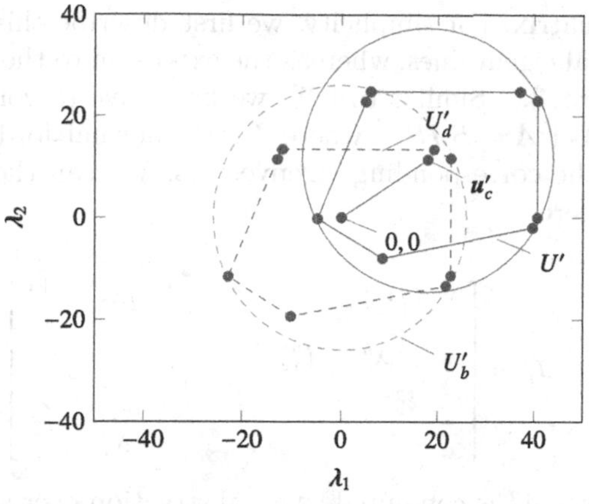

Fig. 1. Relaxation of an input set in a complex subspace making it invariant to matrix rotations. The dashed orange line is the red circle translated onto the origin (Color figure online).

We then over-approximate U'_d via U'_b, by the maximum radius in the directions of the complex eigenvalues and non-singular Jordan blocks, as illustrated in Fig. 1:

$$U'_b \supseteq U'_d \;:\; \forall i,j,\; \rho_{U'_b}(\boldsymbol{v}) = \begin{cases} max(\rho_{U'_d}(\boldsymbol{v}')) & \text{if } \lambda_i = \lambda_j^* \wedge |\boldsymbol{v}'| = |\boldsymbol{v}| \wedge (\boldsymbol{v}'[j] \neq 0 \vee \boldsymbol{v}'[i] \neq 0) \\ \rho_{U'_d}(\boldsymbol{v}) & \text{otherwise} \end{cases}$$

Since the description of U'_b is no longer polyhedral, we will also create an image $\boldsymbol{A}_b$ of $\boldsymbol{A}$ that describes non-polyhedral faces in the directions of the complex eigenvectors ($\lambda_{bi} = ||\boldsymbol{A}||$).

Returning to our original equation for the n-reach set, we obtain[1]

$$X_n \subseteq \boldsymbol{A}^n X_0 \oplus (\boldsymbol{I} - \boldsymbol{A}^n)(\boldsymbol{I} - \boldsymbol{A})^{-1}\boldsymbol{B}U_c \oplus (\boldsymbol{I} - \boldsymbol{A}_b^n)(\boldsymbol{I} - \boldsymbol{A}_b)^{-1}\boldsymbol{B}U_b, \quad (9)$$

with $U_c = \{\boldsymbol{u}_c\}$

Shifting the attention from reach sets to tubes, we can now over-approximate the *reach tube* by abstract acceleration of the three summands in (9), as follows.

Theorem 1. *The abstract acceleration* $\tau^{\sharp n}(X_0, U) =_{\text{def}} \mathcal{A}^n X_0 \oplus \mathcal{B}_c^n U_c \oplus \mathcal{B}_b^n U_b$ *is an over-approximation of the n-reach tube, namely* $\hat{X}_n \subseteq \tau^{\sharp n}(X_0, U)$.

We will discuss in the next section how to compute the abstract matrices $\mathcal{A}^n$, $\mathcal{B}_c^n$, and $\mathcal{B}_b^n$, with focus in particular on $\mathcal{A}^n$.

3.3 Computation of Abstract Matrices

We define the abstract matrix $\mathcal{A}^n$ as an over-approximation of the union of the powers of matrix $\boldsymbol{A}^k$: $\mathcal{A}^n \supseteq \bigcup_{k\in[0,n]} \boldsymbol{A}^k$. Next we explain how to compute

[1] Note that $\forall U'_b, U'_c, U'_d$; $\exists U_b, U_c, U_d$: $U'_b = \boldsymbol{S}^{-1}BU_b$ so that $U'_c = \boldsymbol{S}^{-1}BU_c$ and $U'_d = \boldsymbol{S}^{-1}BU_d$. Hence, this inclusion is also valid in the original state space.

such an abstract matrix. For simplicity, we first describe this computation for matrices $\boldsymbol{A}$ with real eigenvalues, whereas the extension to the complex case will be addressed in Sect. 3.5. Similar to [29], we first have to compute the Jordan normal form of $\boldsymbol{A}$. Let $\boldsymbol{A} = \boldsymbol{S}\boldsymbol{J}\boldsymbol{S}^{-1}$ where $\boldsymbol{J}$ is the normal Jordan form of $\boldsymbol{A}$, and $\boldsymbol{S}$ is made up by the corresponding eigenvectors. We can then easily compute $\boldsymbol{A}^n = \boldsymbol{S}\boldsymbol{J}^n\boldsymbol{S}^{-1}$, where

$$\boldsymbol{J}^n = \begin{bmatrix} \boldsymbol{J}_1^n & & \\ & \ddots & \\ & & \boldsymbol{J}_r^n \end{bmatrix}, \quad \boldsymbol{J}_s^n = \begin{bmatrix} \lambda_s^n & \binom{n}{1}\lambda_s^{n-1} & \cdots & \binom{n}{p_s-1}\lambda_s^{n-p_s+1} \\ & \lambda_s^n & \binom{n}{1}\lambda_s^{n-1} & \vdots \\ \vdots & & \ddots & \vdots \\ & & & \lambda_s^n \end{bmatrix} \quad \text{for } s \in [1, r]\,. \tag{10}$$

The abstract matrix $\mathcal{A}^n$ is computed as an abstraction over a vector $\boldsymbol{m}$ of non-constant entries of $\boldsymbol{J}^n$. The vector $\boldsymbol{m}$ is obtained by a transformation φ such that $\boldsymbol{J}^n = \varphi(\boldsymbol{m})$. If $\boldsymbol{J}^n$ is diagonal [29], then $\boldsymbol{m}$ equals the vector of powers of eigenvalues $(\lambda_0^n, \dots, \lambda_r^n)$. An interval abstraction can thus be simply obtained by computing the intervals $[\min\{\lambda_s^0, \lambda_s^n\}, \max\{\lambda_s^0, \lambda_s^n\}], s \in [1, r]$. We observe that the spectrum of the interval matrix $\sigma(\mathcal{A}^n)$ (defined as intuitively) is an over-approximation of $\bigcup_{k\in[0,n]} \sigma(\boldsymbol{A}^k)$.

In the case of the sth Jordan block $\boldsymbol{J}_s$ with geometric non-trivial multiplicity p_s $(\lambda_i = \lambda_{i-1} = \dots)$, observe that the first row of $\boldsymbol{J}_s^n$ contains all (possibly) distinct entries of $\boldsymbol{J}_s^n$. Hence, in general, the vector section $\boldsymbol{m}_s$ is the concatenation of the (transposed) first row vectors $\left(\lambda_s^n, \binom{n}{1}\lambda_s^{n-1}, \cdots, \binom{n}{p_s-1}\lambda_s^{n-p_s+1}\right)^T$ of $\boldsymbol{J}_s^n$.

Since the transformation φ transforms the vector $\boldsymbol{m}$ into the shape of (10) of $\boldsymbol{J}^n$, it is called a *matrix shape* [29]. We then define the abstract matrix as

$$\mathcal{A}^n = \{\boldsymbol{S}\ \varphi(\boldsymbol{m})\ \boldsymbol{S}^{-1} \mid \boldsymbol{\Phi}\boldsymbol{m} \le \boldsymbol{f}\}\,, \tag{11}$$

where the constraint $\boldsymbol{\Phi}\boldsymbol{m} \le \boldsymbol{f}$ is synthesised from intervals associated to the individual eigenvalues and to their combinations. More precisely, we compute polyhedral relations: for any pair of eigenvalues (or binomials) within $\boldsymbol{J}$, we find an over-approximation of the convex hull containing the points $\cup\{\boldsymbol{m}^k \mid 1{\le}k{\le}n\} \subseteq \{\boldsymbol{m} \mid \boldsymbol{\Phi}\boldsymbol{m}{\le}\boldsymbol{f}\}$ with component-wise exponentiation $\boldsymbol{m}^k$.

As an improvement over [29], the rows in $\boldsymbol{\Phi}$ and $\boldsymbol{f}$ are synthesised by discovering support functions in these sets. The freedom of directions provided by these support functions results in an improvement over the logahedral abstractions used in previous papers (see Fig. 2).

An additional drawback of [29] is that calculating the exact Jordan form of any matrix is computationally expensive and hard to achieve for large-dimensional matrices. We will instead use numerical algorithms in order to get an approximation of the Jordan normal form and account for numerical errors. In particular, if we examine the nature of (5)–(6), we find out that the numerical operations are not iterative, therefore the errors do not accumulate with time. We use properties of eigenvalues to relax $\boldsymbol{f}$ by finding the maximum error in the calculations that can be determined by computing the norm

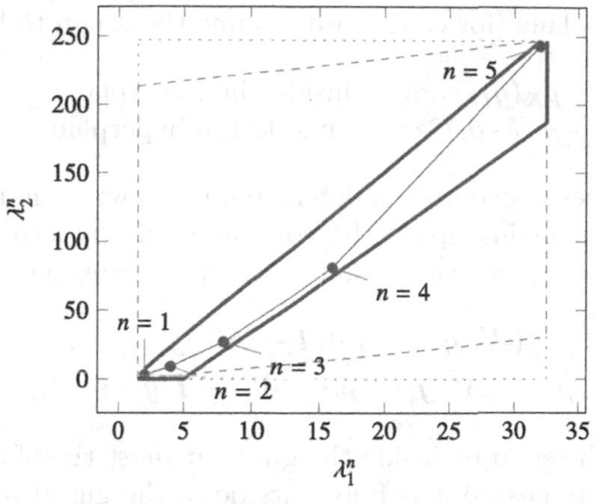

Fig. 2. Polyhedral faces from an $\mathbb{R}^2$ subspace, where $(\lambda_1^n, \lambda_2^n)$ so that $\lambda_1{=}2, \lambda_2{=}3, 1{\leq}n{\leq}5$. Bold purple lines represent supports found by this paper. The dotted grey and dashed red polytopes show logahedral approximations (box and octagon) used in [29]. Note the scales (sloped dashed lines are parallel to the x=y line, and dashed red polytope hides two small sides yielding an octagon) (Color figure online).

$\delta_{max} = |\boldsymbol{A} - \boldsymbol{S}\boldsymbol{J}_{est}\boldsymbol{S}^{-1}|$. The constraints $\boldsymbol{\Phi m} < \boldsymbol{f}$ are then computed by considering the ranges of eigenvalues $\lambda_s \pm \delta_{max}$ (represented in Fig. 2 as the diameter of the blue dots). The outward relaxation of the support functions ($\boldsymbol{f}$), which follows a principle similar to that introduced in [17], reduces the tightness of the over-approximation, but ensures the soundness of the abstract matrix $\mathcal{A}^n$ obtained. One can still use exact arithmetic with a noticeable improvement over previous work; however, for larger-scale systems the option of using floating-point arithmetic, while taking into account errors and meticulously setting rounding modes, provides a 100-fold plus improvement, which can make a difference towards rendering verification practically feasible.

The abstract matrices $\mathcal{B}_c^n$ and $\mathcal{B}_d^n$ (see Theorem 1), as well as $\mathcal{B}^n$, are defined similarly but using a similar assertion for the eigenvalues based on the transformations described in (8).

3.4 Abstract Acceleration with Guards: Estimation of the Number of Iterations

The most important task remaining is how to calculate the number of iterations dealing with the presence of the guard set G.

Given a convex polyhedral guard expressed as the assertion $\{\boldsymbol{x} \mid \boldsymbol{Gx} \leq \boldsymbol{h}\}$, we define G_i as the ith row of $\boldsymbol{G}$ and h_i as the corresponding element of $\boldsymbol{h}$. We denote the normal vector to the ith face of the guard as $\boldsymbol{g}_i = G_i^T$. The distance of the guard to the origin is thus $\gamma_i = \frac{h_i}{|\boldsymbol{g}_i|}$.

Given a convex set X, we may now describe its position with respect to each face of the guard through the use of its support function alongside the normal vector of the hyperplane (for clarity, we assume the origin to be inside set X):

$$\begin{aligned} \rho_X(\boldsymbol{g}_i) &\leq \gamma_i, \quad \text{inside the hyperplane,} \\ -\rho_X(-\boldsymbol{g}_i) &\geq \gamma_i, \quad \text{outside the hyperplane.} \end{aligned}$$

From the inequalities above we can determine up to which number of iterations $\underline{n_i}$ the reach tube remains inside the corresponding hyperplane, and starting from which iteration $\overline{n_i}$ the corresponding reach set goes beyond the guard:

$$\begin{aligned} \rho_{X_0}(\boldsymbol{A}^{\underline{n_i}}\boldsymbol{g}_i) + \rho_{U'}((\boldsymbol{I} - \boldsymbol{A}^{\underline{n_i}})\boldsymbol{g}_i) &\leq \gamma_i, \\ \rho_{X_0}(-\boldsymbol{A}^{\overline{n_i}}\boldsymbol{g}_i) + \rho_{U'}((\boldsymbol{A}^{\overline{n_i}} - \boldsymbol{I})\boldsymbol{g}_i) &\leq -\gamma_i. \end{aligned} \tag{12}$$

In order for a reach set to be inside the guard it must therefore be inside all of its faces, and we can ensure it is fully outside of the guard set when it is fully beyond any of them. Thus, we have $\underline{n} = \min\{\ \underline{n_i}\ \}$, and $\overline{n} = \min\{\ \overline{n_i}\ \}$.

Computing the maximum $\underline{n_i}$ such that (12) is satisfied is not easy, because the unknown $\underline{n_i}$ occurs in the exponent of the equation. However, if $\boldsymbol{g}_i$ was an eigenvector $\boldsymbol{v}_j$ of $\boldsymbol{A}$, we would have that $\boldsymbol{A}^{\underline{n_i}}\boldsymbol{v}_j = \lambda_j^{\underline{n_i}}\boldsymbol{v}_j$, which turns a p-dimensional problem into a 1-dimensional problem. However, since it is unlikely that the guards will be aligned to the eigenvectors, thus, we will use our support function properties to under- and over-approximate the number of iterations.

Let $\boldsymbol{g}_i = \sum_{j=1}^{p} a_{ij}\boldsymbol{v}_j$, where $\boldsymbol{v}_j$ are generalised eigenvectors of $\boldsymbol{A}$. For simplicity we assume that all $a_{ij}\boldsymbol{v}_j$ are positive, extending the procedure for the general case through the development of the complex case in the extended version [4]. Then $\boldsymbol{A}^n\boldsymbol{g}_i = \sum_{j=1}^{p} \lambda_j^n a_{ij}\boldsymbol{v}_j$ where λ_j is the corresponding eigenvalue of $\boldsymbol{v}_j$.

This way we can bound the first summand in (12) by $\rho_{X_0}(\boldsymbol{A}^n\boldsymbol{g}_i) \leq \sum_{j=1}^{p} \lambda_j^n a_{ij}\rho_{X_0}(\boldsymbol{v}_j)$. Using the support function properties detailed in Sect. 2.4, we obtain for (12):

$$\begin{aligned} \rho_{X_0}(A^n\boldsymbol{g}_i) + \rho_{U'}((I - A^n)\boldsymbol{g}_i) \leq \textstyle\sum_{j=1}^{p} \lambda_j^n a_{ij}\rho_{X_0}(\boldsymbol{v}_j) + (\lambda_j^n a_{ij} - 1)\rho_{U'}(-\boldsymbol{v}_j) \\ -\rho_{U'}(-\boldsymbol{res}(\boldsymbol{g}_i)) \leq \gamma_i \end{aligned}$$

In order to solve for n we transfer the constant terms to one side, taking into account that $\sum_{j=1}^{p} -\rho_{U'}(-\boldsymbol{v}_j) - \rho_{U'}(-\boldsymbol{res}(\boldsymbol{g}_i)) = -\rho_{U'}(-\boldsymbol{g}_i)$, as

$$\textstyle\sum_{j=1}^{p} \lambda_j^n a_{ij}(\rho_{X_0}(\boldsymbol{v}_j) + \rho_{U'}(-\boldsymbol{v}_j)) \leq \gamma_i + \rho_{U'}(-\boldsymbol{g}_i).$$

To separate the divergent element of the dynamics from the convergent one, let us define $b_{ij} = a_{ij}(\rho_{X_0}(\boldsymbol{v}_j) + \rho_{U'}(-\boldsymbol{v}_j))$ and $\lambda_m = max(\lambda_j)$ for all $j \in [1, p]$. Replacing, we obtain

$$\lambda_m^n \textstyle\sum_{j=1}^{p} b_{ij} \left(\frac{\lambda_j}{\lambda_m}\right)^n \leq \gamma_i + \rho_{U'}(-\boldsymbol{g}_i)\ ,$$

which allows to finally formulate an iteration scheme for approximating n.

Proposition 1. *An iterative under-approximation of the number of iterations n can be computed by starting with $\underline{n_i} = 0$ and iterating over*

$$\underline{n_i} \geq \log_{\lambda_m}(\gamma_i + \rho_{U'}(-\boldsymbol{g}_i)) - \log_{\lambda_m}\left(\sum_{j=1}^{p} b_{ij}\left(\frac{\lambda_j}{\lambda_m}\right)^{\underline{n_i}}\right),$$

substituting the value of n_i on the right-hand side and repeating a given number of times or up to convergence.

In the case of $\overline{n_i}$ we must invert the eigenvectors and approximate from above, starting at a sufficiently large number (e.g. $\overline{n_i} = 10^{15}$), thus

$$\overline{n_i} \leq \log_{\lambda_m}(\gamma_i - \rho_{U'}(\boldsymbol{g}_i)) - \log_{\lambda_m}\left(\sum_{j=1}^{p} c_{ij}\left(\frac{\lambda_j}{\lambda_m}\right)^{\overline{n_i}}\right).$$

where $c_{ij} = a_{ij}(\rho_{X_0}(-\boldsymbol{v}_j) - \rho_{U'}(\boldsymbol{v}_j))$. If the initial $\overline{n_i}$ is not large enough, we simply double the exponent until the left hand side yields a smaller number than the one chosen originally.

3.5 Abstract Matrices for Complex Eigenvalues

To deal with complex numbers in eigenvalues and eigenvectors, [29] employs the real Jordan form for conjugate eigenvalues $\lambda = re^{i\theta}$ and $\lambda^* = re^{-i\theta}$ ($\theta \in [0, \pi]$), so that

$$\begin{pmatrix} \lambda & 0 \\ 0 & \lambda^* \end{pmatrix} \quad \text{is replaced by} \quad r\begin{pmatrix} \cos\theta & -\sin\theta \\ \sin\theta & \cos\theta \end{pmatrix}.$$

Although this equivalence will be of use once we evaluate the progression of the system, calculating powers under this notations is often more difficult than handling directly the original matrices with complex values.

In Sect. 3.3, in the case of real eigenvalues we have abstracted the entries in the power matrix $\boldsymbol{J}_s^n$ by ranges of eigenvalues $[\min\{\lambda_s^0, \lambda_s^n\}, \max\{\lambda_s^0, \lambda_s^n\}]$. In the complex case we can do something similar by rewriting eigenvalues into polar form $\lambda_s = r_s e^{i\theta_s}$ and abstracting by $[\min\{r_s^0, r_s^n\}, \max\{r_s^0, r_s^n\}]e^{i[0, \min(\theta_s, 2\pi)]}$.

What is left to do is to evaluate the effect of complex numbers on support functions: to the best of the authors' knowledge, there is no definition in the literature for support functions on complex numbers. We will therefore extend the manipulations for the real case directly to the complex one. For lack of space, please refer to extended version of this paper [4].

4 Case Study

We have selected a known benchmark to illustrate the discussed procedure: the room temperature control problem [13]. The temperature (variable `temp`) of a room is controlled to a user-defined set point (`set`), which can be changed at any time through a heating (`heat`) element, and is affected by ambient temperature (`amb`) that is out of the control of the system.

We formalise the description of such a system both via a linear loop and via hybrid dynamics. Observe that since such a system may be software controlled, we assume that part of the system is coded, and further assume that it is possible to discretise the physical environment for simulation. A pseudo-code fragment for the temperature control problem follows:

```
temp=5+read(35);
heat=read(1);
while(temp<400 && heat<300)
{
    amb=5+read(35);
    set=read(300);
    temp=.97 temp + .02 amb + .1 heat;
    heat=heat + .05(set-temp);
}
```

We use the `read` function to represent non-deterministic values between 0 and the maximum given as argument. Alternatively, this loop corresponds to the following hybrid dynamical model:

$$\begin{bmatrix} temp \\ heat \end{bmatrix}_{k+1} = \begin{bmatrix} 0.97 & 0.1 \\ -0.05 & 1 \end{bmatrix} \begin{bmatrix} temp \\ heat \end{bmatrix}_k + \begin{bmatrix} 0.02 & 0 \\ 0 & 0.05 \end{bmatrix} \begin{bmatrix} amb \\ set \end{bmatrix}_k,$$

with initial condition $\begin{bmatrix} temp \\ heat \end{bmatrix}_0 \in \begin{bmatrix} [5 \;\; 40] \\ [0 \;\; 1] \end{bmatrix},$

non-deterministic inputs $\begin{bmatrix} amb \\ set \end{bmatrix}_k \in \begin{bmatrix} [5 \;\; 40] \\ [0 \;\; 300] \end{bmatrix},$

and guard set $G = \left\{ \begin{bmatrix} temp \\ heat \end{bmatrix} : \begin{bmatrix} 1 & 0 \\ 0 & 1 \end{bmatrix} \begin{bmatrix} temp \\ heat \end{bmatrix} < \begin{bmatrix} 400 \\ 300 \end{bmatrix} \right\}.$

In this model the variables are continuous and take values over the real line, whereas within the code they are represented as long double precision floating-point values, with precision of $\pm 10^{-19}$, moreover the error of the approximate Jordan form computation results in $\delta_{max} < 10^{-17}$. Henceforth we focus on the latter description, as in the main text of this work. The eigen-decomposition of the dynamics is (the values are rounded to three decimal places):

$$A = SJS^{-1} \subseteq \begin{bmatrix} 0.798 & 0.173 \\ 0 & 0.577 \end{bmatrix} \begin{bmatrix} 0.985 \pm 10^{-16} & 0.069 \pm 10^{-17} \\ -0.069 \pm 10^{-17} & 0.985 \pm 10^{-16} \end{bmatrix} \begin{bmatrix} 1.253 & -0.376 \\ 0 & 1.732 \end{bmatrix}.$$

The discussed over-approximations of the reach-sets indicate that the temperature variable intersects the guard at iteration $\underline{n} = 32$. Considering the pseudo-eigenvalue matrix (described in the extended version for the case of complex eigenvalues) along these iterations, we use Equation (11) to find that the corresponding complex pair remains within the following boundaries:

$$\mathcal{A}^{32} = \begin{bmatrix} r & i \\ -i & r \end{bmatrix} \begin{cases} 0.4144 < \quad r \quad < 0.985 \\ 0.0691 < \quad i \quad < 0.7651 \\ 0.1082 < r+i < 1.247 \\ 0.9159 < i-r < 0.9389 \end{cases} \quad \mathcal{B}^{32} = \begin{bmatrix} r & i \\ -i & r \end{bmatrix} \begin{cases} 1 < \quad r \quad < 13.41 \\ 0 < \quad i \quad < 17.98 \\ 1 < r+i < 29.44 \\ 6.145 < i-r < 6.514 \end{cases}$$

The reach tube is calculated by multiplying these abstract matrices with the initial sets of states and inputs, as described in Equation (3), by the following inequalities:

$$\hat{X}^{\#}_{32} = \mathcal{A}^{32} \left[\begin{bmatrix} 5 & 40 \\ 0 & 1 \end{bmatrix} \right] + \mathcal{B}^{32} \left[\begin{bmatrix} 5 & 40 \\ 0 & 300 \end{bmatrix} \right] = \begin{bmatrix} temp \\ heat \end{bmatrix} \begin{cases} -24.76 < \quad temp \quad < 394.5 \\ -30.21 < \quad heat \quad < 253 \\ -40.85 < temp + heat < 616.6 \\ -86.31 < temp - heat < 843.8 \end{cases}$$

The negative values represent the lack of restriction in the code on the lower side and correspond to system cooling (negative heating). The set is displayed in Fig. 3, where for the sake of clarity we display only 8 directions of the 16 constraints. This results in a rather tight over-approximation that is not much looser than the convex hull of all reach sets obtained by [16] using the given directions. In Fig. 3, we can see the initial set in black colour, the collection of reach sets in white, the convex hull of all reach sets in dark blue (as computed by [16]), and finally the abstractly accelerated set in light yellow (dashed lines). The outer lines represent the guards.

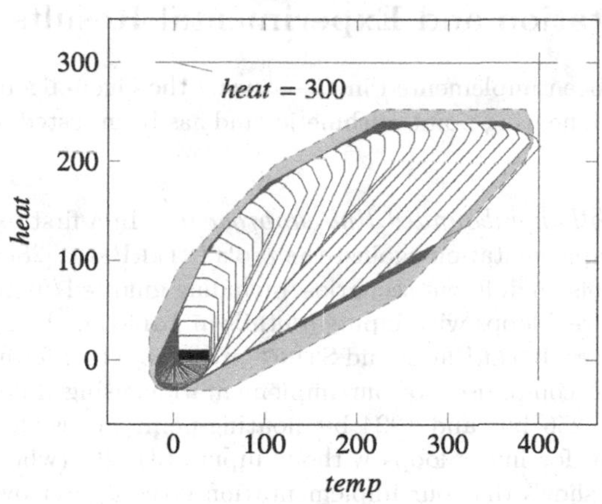

Fig. 3. The abstractly accelerated tube (yellow, dashed boundary), representing an over-approximation of the thermostat reach tube (dark blue). The set of initial conditions is shown in black, whereas successive reach sets are shown in white. The guards and the reach set that crosses them are close to the boundary in red (Color figure online).

Table 1. Experimental comparison of unbounded-time analysis tools with inputs

	Characteristics				Improved		Analysis time [sec]		
name	type	dim	inputs	bounds	IProc	Sti	IProc	Sti	J+I
parabola_i1	$\neg s$,$\neg c$,g	2	1	80	+25	+28	0.007	237	0.049
parabola_i2	$\neg s$,$\neg c$,g	2	1	80	+24	+35	0.008	289	0.072
cubic_i1	$\neg s$,$\neg c$,g	3	1	120	+44	+50	0.015	704	0.097
cubic_i2	$\neg s$,$\neg c$,g	3	1	120	+35	+55	0.018	699	0.124
oscillator_i0	s,c,$\neg g$	2	0	56	+24	+24	0.004	0.990	0.021
oscillator_i1	s,c,$\neg g$	2	0	56	+24	+24	0.004	1.060	0.024
inv_pendulum	s,c,$\neg g$	4	0	16	+8	+8	0.009	0.920	0.012
convoyCar2_i0	s,c,$\neg g$	3	2	12	+9	+9	0.007	0.160	0.043
convoyCar3_i0	s,c,$\neg g$	6	2	24	+15	+15	0.010	0.235	0.513
convoyCar3_i1	s,c,$\neg g$	6	2	24	+15	+15	0.024	0.237	0.901
convoyCar3_i2	s,c,$\neg g$	6	2	24	+15	+15	0.663	0.271	1.416
convoyCar3_i3	s,c,$\neg g$	6	2	24	+15	+15	0.122	0.283	2.103

type: s – stable loop, c – complex eigenvalues, g – loops with guard; **dim**: system dimension (variables); **bounds**: nb. of half-planes defining the polyhedral set; **IProc** is [28]; **Sti** is [7]; **J+I** is this work; **improved**: number of bounds newly detected by J+I over the existing tools (IProc, Sti)

5 Implementation and Experimental Results

The algorithm has been implemented in C++ using the eigen-algebra package (v3.2), with double precision floating-point arithmetic, and has been tested on a 1.6 GHz core 2 duo computer.

Comparison with other unbounded-time approaches. In a first experiment we have benchmarked our implementation against the tools InterProc [28] and Sting [7]. We have tested these tools on different scenarios, including guarded/unguarded, stable/unstable and complex/real loops with inputs (details in Table 1).[2] It is important to note that in many instances, InterProc and Sting are unable to infer finite bounds at all.

Table 2 gives the comparison of our implementation using different levels of precision (long double, 256 bit, and 1024 bit floating-point precision) with the original abstract acceleration for linear loops without inputs (J) [29] (where inputs are fixed to constants). This shows that our implementation gives tighter over-approximations on most benchmarks (column 'improved'). Whilst on a limited number of instances the current implementation is less precise (Fig. 2 gives a hint why this is happening), the overall increased precision is owed to lifting the limitation on directions caused by the use of logahedral abstractions.

At the same time, our implementation is faster – even when used with 1024 bit floating-point precision – than the original abstract acceleration (using rationals). The fact that many bounds have improved with the new approach, while speed has increased by several orders of magnitude, provides evidence of the advantages of the new approach.

[2] The tool and the benchmarks are available from http://www.cprover.org/LTI/.

Table 2. Experimental comparison with previous work

	characteristics			improved		analysis time (sec)			
name	type	dim	bounds	tighter	looser	J (jcf)	mpfr+(jcf)	mpfr	ld
parabola_i1	$\neg s,\neg c,g$	3	80	+4(5%)	0(0%)	2.51 (2.49)	0.16 (0.06)	0.097	0.007
parabola_i2	$\neg s,\neg c,g$	3	80	+4(5%)	0(0%)	2.51 (2.49)	0.26 (0.06)	0.101	0.008
cubic_i1	$\neg s,\neg c,g$	4	120	0(0%)	0(0%)	2.47 (2.39)	0.27 (0.20)	0.110	0.013
cubic_i2	$\neg s,\neg c,g$	4	120	0(0%)	0(0%)	2.49 (2.39)	0.32 (0.20)	0.124	0.014
oscillator_i0	$s,c,\neg g$	2	56	0(0%)	-1(2%)	2.53 (2.52)	0.12 (0.06)	0.063	0.007
oscillator_i1	$s,c,\neg g$	2	56	0(0%)	-1(2%)	2.53 (2.52)	0.12 (0.06)	0.078	0.008
inv_pendulum	$s,c,\neg g$	4	12	+8(50%)	0(0%)	65.78 (65.24)	0.24 (0.13)	0.103	0.012
convoyCar2_i0	$s,c,\neg g$	5	12	+9(45%)	0(0%)	5.46 (4.69)	3.58 (0.22)	0.258	0.005
convoyCar3_i0	$s,c,\neg g$	8	24	+10(31%)	-2(6%)	24.62 (11.98)	3.11 (1.01)	0.552	0.051
convoyCar3_i1	$s,c,\neg g$	8	24	+10(31%)	-2(6%)	23.92 (11.98)	4.94 (1.01)	0.890	0.121
convoyCar3_i2	$s,c,\neg g$	8	24	+10(31%)	-2(6%)	1717.00 (11.98)	6.81 (1.01)	1.190	0.234
convoyCar3_i3	$s,c,\neg g$	8	24	+10(31%)	-2(6%)	1569.00 (11.98)	8.67 (1.01)	1.520	0.377

type: s – stable loop, c – complex eigenvalues, g – loops with guard; **dim**: system dimension (including fixed inputs); **bounds**: nb. of half-planes defining the polyhedral set; **improved**: number of bounds (and percentage) that were tighter (better) or looser (worse) than [29]; J is [29]; **mpfr+** is this paper using 1024bit mantissas ($e < 10^{-152}$); **mpfr** uses a 256bit mantissa ($e < 10^{-44}$); **ld** uses a 64bit mantissa ($e < 10^{-11}$); here e is the accumulated error of the dynamical system; **jcf**: time taken to compute Jordan form

The speed-up is due to the faster Jordan form computation, which takes between 2 and 65 seconds for [29] (using the ATLAS package), whereas our implementation requires at most one second. For the last two benchmarks, the polyhedral computations blow up in [29], whereas our support function approach shows only moderately increasing runtimes. The increase of speed is owed to multiple factors, as detailed in Table 3. The difference of using long double precision floating-point vs. arbitrary precision arithmetic is negligible, as all results in the given examples match exactly to 9 decimal places. Note that, as explained above, soundness can be ensured by appropriate rounding in the floating-point computations.

Table 3. Performance improvements by feature

Optimization	Speed-up
Eigen vs. ATLAS (http://eigen.tuxfamily.org/index.php?title=Benchmark)	2–10
Support functions vs. generators for abstract matrix synthesis	2–40
long double vs. multiple precision arithmetic	5–200
Total	20–80000

Comparison with bounded-time approaches. In a third experiment, we compare our method with the LGG algorithm [23] used by SpaceEx [16]. In order to set up a fair comparison we have provided the implementation of the native algorithm in [23]. We have run both methods on the convoyCar example [29] with inputs, which presents an unguarded, scalable, stable loop with complex dynamics, and focused on octahedral abstractions. For convex reach sets, the approximations computed by abstract acceleration are quite tight in comparison to those computed by the LGG algorithm. However, storing finite disjunctions of convex polyhedra, the LGG algorithm is able to generate non-convex reach tubes, which are arguably more proper in case of oscillating or spiralling dynamics. Still, in many applications abstract acceleration can provide a tight over-approximation of the convex hull of those non-convex reach sets.

Table 4 gives the results of this comparison. For simplicity, we present only the projection of the bounds along the variables of interest. As expected, the LGG algorithm performs better in terms of tightness, but its runtime increases with the number of iterations. Our implementation of LGG using Convex Polyhedra with octagonal templates is slower than the abstractly accelerated version even for small time horizons (our implementation of LGG requires ~ 4 ms for each iteration on a 6-dimensional problem with octagonal abstraction). This can be improved by the use of zonotopes, or by careful selection of the directions along the eigenvectors, but this comes at a cost on precision. Even when finding combinations that outperform our approach, this will only allow the time horizon of the LGG approach to be slightly extended before matching the analysis time from abstract acceleration, and the reachable states will still remain unknown beyond the extended time horizon.

The evident advantage of abstract acceleration is its speed over finite horizons without much precision loss, and of course the ability to prove properties for unbounded-time horizons.

Table 4. Comparison on convoyCar2 benchmark, between this work and the LGG algorithm [23]

	This paper		LGG		
name	100 iterations	unbounded	100 iterations	200 iterations	300 iterations
run time	5 ms	5 ms	50 ms	140 ms	195 ms
car acceleration	[-0.895 1.34]	[-1.038 1.34]	[-0.802 1.31]	[-0.968 1.31]	[-0.968 1.31]
car speed	[-1.342 5.27]	[-4.059 5.27]	[-1.331 4.98]	[-3.651 4.98]	[-3.677 4.98]
car position	[42.66 83.8]	[42.66 90.3]	[43.32 95.5]	[43.32 95.5]	[43.32 95.6]

Scalability. Finally, in terms of scalability, we have an expected $\mathcal{O}(n^3)$ complexity worst-case bound (from the matrix multiplications in Eq. 3). We have parameterised the number of cars in the convoyCar example [29] (also seen in Table 2), and experimented with up to 33 cars (each car after the first requires 3 variables, so that for example $(33 - 1) \times 3 = 96$ variables), and have adjusted the initial states/inputs sets. We report an average of 10 runs for each configuration. These results demonstrate that our method scales to industrial-size problems.

# of variables	3	6	12	24	48	96
runtime	4 ms	31 ms	62 ms	477 ms	5.4 s	56 s

6 Conclusions and Future Work

We have presented an extension of the Abstract Acceleration paradigm to guarded LTI systems (linear loops) with inputs, overcoming the limitations of existing work that is restricted to closed systems. We have decisively shown the new approach to outperform state-of-the-art tools for unbounded-time reachability analysis in both precision and scalability. The new approach is capable of performing general unbounded-time safety analysis for large scale open systems with reasonable precision and fast computation times. Conditionals inside loops and nested loops are out of the scope of this paper.

Work to be done is extending the approach to non-linear dynamics, which we believe can be explored via hybridisation techniques [1], and to formalise the framework for general hybrid models with multiple guards and location-dependent dynamics, with the aim to accelerate transitions across guards rather than integrate individual accelerations on either side of the guards.

References

1. Asarin, E., Dang, T., Girard, A.: Hybridization methods for the analysis of non-linear systems. Acta Informatica **43**(7), 451–476 (2007)
2. Blanchet, B., Cousot, P., Cousot, R., Feret, J., Mauborgne, L., Miné, A., Monniaux, D., Rival, X.: A static analyzer for large safety-critical software. In: PLDI, pp. 196–207. ACM (2003)
3. Botchkarev, O., Tripakis, S.: Verification of hybrid systems with linear differential inclusions using ellipsoidal approximations. In: Lynch, N.A., Krogh, B.H. (eds.) HSCC 2000. LNCS, vol. 1790, pp. 73–88. Springer, Heidelberg (2000)
4. Cattaruzza, D., Abate, A., Schrammel, P., Kroening, D.: Unbounded-time analysis of guarded lti systems with inputs by abstract acceleration (extended version). Technical report, University of Oxford (2015). arxiv.org/abs/1506.05607
5. Chutinan, A., Krogh, B.H.: Computing polyhedral approximations to flow pipes for dynamic systems. In: CDC, pp. 2089–2094. IEEE Computer Society (1998)
6. Cimatti, A., Mover, S., Tonetta, S.: SMT-based verification of hybrid systems. In: AAAI Conference on Artificial Intelligence. AAAI Press (2012)
7. Colón, M.A., Sankaranarayanan, S., Sipma, H.B.: Linear invariant generation using non-linear constraint solving. In: Hunt Jr, W.A., Somenzi, F. (eds.) CAV 2003. LNCS, vol. 2725, pp. 420–432. Springer, Heidelberg (2003)
8. Cousot, P., Cousot, R.: Abstract interpretation: a unified lattice model for static analysis of programs by construction or approximation of fixpoints. In: POPL, pp. 238–252 (1977)
9. Cousot, P., Halbwachs, N.: Automatic discovery of linear restraints among variables of a program. In: POPL, pp. 84–97. ACM (1978)
10. Dang, T., Gawlitza, T.M.: Template-based unbounded time verification of affine hybrid automata. In: Yang, H. (ed.) APLAS 2011. LNCS, vol. 7078, pp. 34–49. Springer, Heidelberg (2011)
11. Deng, Y., Rajhans, A., Julius, A.A.: STRONG: A Trajectory-Based Verification Toolbox for Hybrid Systems. In: Joshi, K., Siegle, M., Stoelinga, M., D'Argenio, P.R. (eds.) QEST 2013. LNCS, vol. 8054, pp. 165–168. Springer, Heidelberg (2013)
12. Eggers, A., Fränzle, M., Herde, C.: SAT modulo ODE: a direct SAT approach to hybrid systems. In: Cha, S.S., Choi, J.-Y., Kim, M., Lee, I., Viswanathan, M. (eds.) ATVA 2008. LNCS, vol. 5311, pp. 171–185. Springer, Heidelberg (2008)
13. Fehnker, A., Ivančić, F.: Benchmarks for hybrid systems verification. In: Alur, R., Pappas, G.J. (eds.) HSCC 2004. LNCS, vol. 2993, pp. 326–341. Springer, Heidelberg (2004)

14. Fränzle, M., Herde, C.: HySAT: an efficient proof engine for bounded model checking of hybrid systems. Formal Methods in System Design **30**(3), 179–198 (2007)
15. Frehse, G.: PHAVer: algorithmic verification of hybrid systems past HyTech. In: Morari, M., Thiele, L. (eds.) HSCC 2005. LNCS, vol. 3414, pp. 258–273. Springer, Heidelberg (2005)
16. Frehse, G., Le Guernic, C., Donzé, A., Cotton, S., Ray, R., Lebeltel, O., Ripado, R., Girard, A., Dang, T., Maler, O.: SpaceEx: scalable verification of hybrid systems. In: Gopalakrishnan, G., Qadeer, S. (eds.) CAV 2011. LNCS, vol. 6806, pp. 379–395. Springer, Heidelberg (2011)
17. Clarke, E.M., Gao, S., Avigad, J.: δ-complete decision procedures for satisfiability over the reals. In: Gramlich, B., Miller, D., Sattler, U. (eds.) IJCAR 2012. LNCS, vol. 7364, pp. 286–300. Springer, Heidelberg (2012)
18. Ghosh, P.K., Kumar, K.V.: Support function representation of convex bodies, its application in geometric computing, and some related representations. Comput. Vis. Image Underst. **72**, 379–403 (1998)
19. Girard, A.: Reachability of uncertain linear systems using zonotopes. In: Morari, M., Thiele, L. (eds.) HSCC 2005. LNCS, vol. 3414, pp. 291–305. Springer, Heidelberg (2005)
20. Girard, A., Le Guernic, C., Maler, O.: Efficient computation of reachable sets of linear time-invariant systems with inputs. In: Hespanha, J.P., Tiwari, A. (eds.) HSCC 2006. LNCS, vol. 3927, pp. 257–271. Springer, Heidelberg (2006)
21. Gonnord, L., Halbwachs, N.: Combining widening and acceleration in linear relation analysis. In: Yi, K. (ed.) SAS 2006. LNCS, vol. 4134, pp. 144–160. Springer, Heidelberg (2006)
22. Gonnord, L., Schrammel, P.: Abstract acceleration in linear relation analysis. Sci. Comput. Program. **93**(Part B), 125–153 (2014)
23. Le Guernic, C., Girard, A.: Reachability analysis of hybrid systems using support functions. In: Bouajjani, A., Maler, O. (eds.) CAV 2009. LNCS, vol. 5643, pp. 540–554. Springer, Heidelberg (2009)
24. Gulwani, S., Tiwari, A.: Constraint-based approach for analysis of hybrid systems. In: Gupta, A., Malik, S. (eds.) CAV 2008. LNCS, vol. 5123, pp. 190–203. Springer, Heidelberg (2008)
25. Halbwachs, N., Raymond, P., Proy, Y.E.: Verification of linear hybrid systems by means of convex approximations. In: LeCharlier, B. (ed.) SAS 1994. LNCS, vol. 864, pp. 223–237. Springer, Heidelberg (1994)
26. Henzinger, T.A., Ho, P.H., Wong-Toi, H.: HyTech: A model checker for hybrid systems. J. Softw. Tools Technol. Transfer **1**(1–2), 110–122 (1997)
27. Howe, J.M., King, A.: Logahedra: a new weakly relational domain. In: Liu, Z., Ravn, A.P. (eds.) ATVA 2009. LNCS, vol. 5799, pp. 306–320. Springer, Heidelberg (2009)
28. Jeannet, B.: Interproc analyzer for recursive programs with numerical variables (2010). http://pop-art.inrialpes.fr/interproc/interprocweb.cgi
29. Jeannet, B., Schrammel, P., Sankaranarayanan, S.: Abstract acceleration of general linear loops. In: POPL, pp. 529–540. ACM (2014)
30. Johnson, T.T., Mitra, S.: Passel: A verification tool for parameterized networks of hybrid automata (2012). https://publish.illinois.edu/passel-tool/
31. Le Guernic, C.: Reachability analysis of hybrid systems with linear continuous dynamics. Univerité Joseph Fourier (2009)
32. Löhner, R.: Einschließung der Lösung gewöhnlicher Anfangs- und Randwertaufgaben und Anwendungen. Ph.D. thesis, Universität Karlsruhe (1988)

33. Sankaranarayanan, S., Tiwari, A.: Relational abstractions for continuous and hybrid systems. In: Gopalakrishnan, G., Qadeer, S. (eds.) CAV 2011. LNCS, vol. 6806, pp. 686–702. Springer, Heidelberg (2011)
34. Schrammel, P., Jeannet, B.: Extending abstract acceleration to data-flow programs with numerical inputs. In: Numerical and Symbolic Abstract Domains. ENTCS, vol. 267, pp. 101–114. Elsevier (2010)
35. Schrammel, P., Jeannet, B.: Applying abstract acceleration to (co-)reachability analysis of reactive programs. J. Symbolic Comput. **47**(12), 1512–1532 (2012)
36. Stursberg, O., Krogh, B.H.: Efficient representation and computation of reachable sets for hybrid systems. In: Maler, O., Pnueli, A. (eds.) HSCC 2003. LNCS, vol. 2623, pp. 482–497. Springer, Heidelberg (2003)

Author Index

Printed in the United States
By Bookmasters